ENCYCLOPEDIA OF THE
AFRICAN DIASPORA

ENCYCLOPEDIA OF THE

AFRICAN DIASPORA

Origins, Experiences, and Culture

Volume 3
N–Z

Carole Boyce Davies, Editor

A B C CLIO

Santa Barbara, California
Denver, Colorado
Oxford, England

Copyright © 2008 by ABC-CLIO, Inc.

Library of Congress Cataloging-in-Publication Data

Encyclopedia of the African diaspora : origins, experiences, and culture / Carole E. Boyce-Davies, editor.
     p.   cm.
  Includes bibliographical references and index.
  ISBN 978-1-85109-700-5 (acid-free paper)
  ISBN 978-1-85109-705-0 (ebook)
  1. African diaspora-Encyclopedias.   2. Africans-Migrations-Encyclopedias.   3. African Americans-Encyclopedias.   4. Blacks-Encyclopedias.   5. Africans-Encyclopedias. 6. Africa-Civilization-Encyclopedias.   I. Boyce Davies, Carole.

  DT16.5.E53 2008
  305.896003—dc22

               2008011880

12 11 10 09 08   1 2 3 4 5 6 7 8

Production Editor: Anna A. Moore
Production Manager: Don Schmidt
Media Editor: Ellen Rasmussen
Media Resources Manager: Caroline Price
File Management Coordinator: Paula Gerard

ABC-CLIO, Inc.
130 Cremona Drive, P.O. Box 1911
Santa Barbara, California 93116–1911

This book is also available on the World Wide Web as an ebook.
Visit www.abc-clio.com for details.

This book is printed on acid-free paper. ∞

Manufactured in the United States of America

Contents

Volume 2

Contributors

Keshia Abraham
Florida Memorial University

Lawrence Abraham
Florida International University, Miami

Tomi Adeaga
University of Siegen, Siegen, Germany

Opal Palmer Adisa
California College of the Arts, San Francisco
  and Oakland

Kwame K. Afoh
N'COBRA, Fort Lauderdale, Florida

Ivor Agyeman-Duah
Embassy of Ghana, Washington, DC

Funso Aiyejina
University of the West Indies, Saint Augustine,
  Trinidad and Tobago

Omofolabo Ajayi-Soyinka
University of Kansas, Lawrence

Chiji Akoma
Villanova University, Villanova, Pennsylvania

Folashade Alao
Emory University, Atlanta

Jessica M. Alarcón
Independent Scholar, Miami, Florida

Delores P. Aldridge
Emory University, Atlanta

Simone A. James Alexander
Seton Hall University, South Orange, New
  Jersey

Williams H. Alexander
Virginia State University, Petersburg

Omar H. Ali
Towson University, Towson, Maryland

Andrea Allen
Harvard University, Cambridge,
  Massachusetts

Michael Alleyne
George Washington University, Washington,
  DC

Patricia Alleyne-Dettmers
University of Hamburg, Hamburg, Germany

Jeannette Allsopp
University of the West Indies, Cave Hill
  Campus

Giselle Liza Anatol
University of Kansas, Lawrence

Juan Angola Maconde
FUNDAFRO, La Paz, Bolivia

Molefi Kete Asante
Temple University, Philadelphia

Kwaku Asare
Independent Scholar

Uche Azikiwe
University of Nigeria, Nigeria

Chukwuma Azuonye
University of Massachusetts, Boston

Mariam Bagayoko
University of Versailles Paris, France

Julius Bailey
University of Redlands, Redlands, California

Phyllis Baker
Miami Dade College, Miami

Sharada Balachandran-Orihuela
University of California—Davis, Davis,
    California

Ivan Banks
New Jersey City University, Jersey City, New
    Jersey

Sarah Barbour
Wake Forest University, Winston-Salem,
    North Carolina

LaShonda Katrice Barnett
Sarah Lawrence College, Bronxville, New York

Michael Barnett
University of the West Indies, Mona Campus,
    Jamaica

Kanika Batra
Janki Devi Memorial College and University
    of Delhi, Delhi, India

Pascal Becel
Florida International University, Miami

Dixie-Anne Belle
Florida International University, Miami

Jesse Benjamin
Kennesaw State University, Atlanta, Georgia

Brett A. Berliner
Morgan State University, Baltimore

Celeste-Marie Bernier
University of Nottingham, England

June Bert-Bobb
Queens College, Queens, New York

Dhoruba bin Wahad
Independent Scholar, Ghana

Yaba Amgborale Blay
Lehigh University, Philadelphia

Nemata Blyden
George Washington University, Washington,
    DC

Yvonne Bobb-Smith
Independent Scholar, Trinidad and Tobago

Rosabelle Boswell
Rhodes University, South Africa

John K. Brackett
University of Cincinnati, Ohio

Brian Brazeal
University of Chicago, Illinois

Pam Brooks
Oberlin College, Oberlin, Ohio

La Tasha A. Brown
University of Warwick, Coventry, United
    Kingdom

Linda Spears Bunton
Florida International University, Miami

Joan Hamby Burroughs
Florida A&M University, Tallahassee

Kim D. Butler
Rutgers University, New Brunswick, New
    Jersey

Leana Cabral
Spelman College, Atlanta

Horace Campbell
Syracuse University, Syracuse, New York

Kathy Campbell
East Tennessee State University, Johnson City

Ben Carrington
University of Texas at Austin

Joan Cartwright
FYIICOM, Ford Lauderdale, Florida

Jorge L. Chinea
Wayne State University, Detroit

Veve A. Clark (deceased)
University of California, Berkeley

George Elliott Clarke
York University, New Haven, Connecticut

Christine Cohn
American University, Washington, DC

Amanda Conrad
University of Kansas, Lawrence

Carolyn Cooper
University of the West Indies, Mona, Jamaica

Vincent O. Cooper
University of the Virgin Islands, St. Thomas,
    Virgin Islands

María de Jesús Cordero
Utah State University, Logan

Alexandra Cornelius-Diallo
Florida International University, Miami

Sandra Courtman
University of Sheffield, England

Julie Crooks
Independent Filmmaker, Toronto, Canada

Iréne Assiba d'Almeida
University of Arizona, Tucson

Yvonne Daniel
Smith College (emerita)

William A. Darity Jr.
Duke University, Durham, North Carolina

Carole Boyce Davies
Florida International University, Miami

Dalia Davies
Journalist, MTV & *Trace* Magazine

Jonelle A. Davies
Savannah College of Art and Design

Darrell Davis
Afro-in Books and Things

Paula de Almeida Silva

Alexis Brooks de Vita
Notre Dame University, Notre Dame, Indiana

Pietro Deandrea
Università degli Studi di Torino, Torino, Italy

Milagros Denis
Hunter College, New York, New York

Diarapha Diallo-Gibert
University of Virginia, Charlottesville

Gloria Harper Dickinson
The College of New Jersey, Ewing

Ronald Donk
Royal Netherlands Institute of South Eastern,
    Asian and Caribbean Studies, Leiden, The
    Netherlands

Joseph Dorsey
Purdue University, West Lafayette, Indiana

Jocelio dos Santos
Universidade Federal da Bahia (UFBA), Bahia,
    Brazil

Kate Dossett
University of Leeds, Leeds, England

Marcia Douglas
University of Colorado, Boulder

Dawn Duke
University of Tennessee

Quince Duncan
Costa Rica

Jessica Durand
Florida International University, Miami

Esma Durugönül
Akdeniz University, Antalya, Turkey

Erika Denise Edwards
Florida International University, Miami

Constance Ejuma
Actress, Silver Springs, Maryland

Jacob D. Elder (deceased)
Trinidad and Tobago

Jason Esters
Lincoln University, Pennsylvania

Michael Ezra
Sonoma State University, Rohnert Park,
California

Richard Fantina
University of Miami, Miami

Gérard Alphonse Férère
Retired Scholar, Boca Raton, Florida

Eve Ferguson
Florida International University, Miami

Odile Ferly
Clark University, Worcester, Massachusetts

Rev. Raul Fernandez Calienes
Saint Thomas University, Miami Gardens,
Florida

Giovanna Fiume
University of Palermo, Palermo, Italy

Nicola Foote
Florida Gulf Coast University, Fort Myers,
Florida

Camille F. Forbes
University of California, San Diego

Charles H. Ford
Virginia State University, Petersburg

Meredith Gadsby
Oberlin College, Oberlin, Ohio

Pramod B. Gai
Karnatak University, Dharwad, India

Jesus Chucho Garcia
Afro-Venezuelan Network, Caracas, Venezuela

Marybeth Gasman
University of Pennsylvania, Philadelphia

Janice Giles
Florida International University, Miami

Angela Gillam
Evergreen State University, Olympia,
Washington (emerita)

Delia C. Gillis
Central Missouri State University,
Warrensburg

Philippe R. Girard
McNeese State University, Lake Charles,
Louisiana

Chege Githiora
School of Oriental and African Studies,
London

David Gold
California State University, Los Angeles

Randi Gray Kristensen
George Washington University, Washington,
DC

Jeffrey Green
Independent Scholar, England

Jean-Germain Gros
University of Missouri, Saint Louis

Carla Guerron-Montero
University of Delaware, Newark

Beverly Guy-Sheftall
Spelman College, Atlanta

Miriam Gyimah
University of Maryland–Eastern Shore

Kathleen Gyssells
University of Antwerp, Antwerp, Belgium

Philipa Hall
University of Central Lancashire, Lancashire,
England

Veronique Helenon
Florida International University, Miami

Marco Polo Hernandez
North Carolina Central University

Gerise Herndon
Nebraska Wesleyan University, Lincoln

Nefertari Patricia Hilliard-Nunn
Makare Publishing, Gainesville, Florida

Jesse Hingson
Honorary Consul of Belize

Rita Honotorio
Nucleo Cultural Afro-Brasiliero, Salvador-
Bahia, Brazil

Rosalyn Howard
University of Central Florida, Orlando

Delridge Hunter
Medgar Evers College, Brooklyn, New York

Scot Ickes
University of South Florida

Joseph E. Inikori
University of Rochester, Rochester, New York

Siga Fatima Jagne
Pro-Poor Advocacy Group, Bakau, The
Gambia

Monica Jardine
State University of New York, Buffalo

Shihan De Silva Jayasuriya
King's College London, University of London

Régine Michelle Jean-Charles
Harvard University, Cambridge,
Massachusetts

Cheryl Jeffries
Florida International University, Miami

Earnestine Jenkins
University of Memphis, Tennessee

Lee M. Jenkins
University College, Cork, Ireland

Beverly John
Chicago State University

David J. Johns
Columbia University, New York

Anthony B. Johnson
Grambling University, Grambling, Louisiana

Nadia I. Johnson
University of Miami, Miami, Florida

Newtona (Tina) Johnson

Tarnue Johnson
East West University, Chicago, Illinois

Justin M. Johnston
Independent Scholar

Christina Violeta Jones
Howard University, Washington, DC

Kenneth Julien
University of Trinidad and Tobago

Safietou Kane
Florida International University, Miami

Annette I. Kashif
Associate Professor

Tricia Keaton
University of Minnesota

Sean Kheraj
York University, Toronto, Canada

Martin Klein
University of Toronto, Canada

Marie H. Koffi-Tessio
Princeton University, Princeton, New Jersey

Kwasi Konadu
Winston-Salem State University, Winston-
Salem, North Carolina

Perry Kyles
University of Tennessee, Knoxville

Renee Larrier
Rutgers University, New Brunswick, New
Jersey

Angela Michele Leonard
Loyola College, Baltimore, Maryland

Jeremy I. J. D. Levitt
Florida International University, College of
Law, Miami

Dominique Licops
Northwestern University, Evanston, Illinois

Hollis Urban Liverpool
University of the Virgin Islands, St. Thomas

Nia Love
Smith College, Northampton, Massachusetts

Antonia MacDonald-Smythe
St. George's University, Grenada, West Indies

Elizabeth MacGonagle
University of Kansas, Lawrence

Marcia Magnus
Florida International University, Miami

Tony Martin
Wellesley College, Wellesley, Massachusetts

Karen J. Matthew
Florida International University, Miami

Janis A. Mayes
Syracuse University, Syracuse, New York

Babacar M'bow
Broward County Libraries Division, Florida

Penda M'Bow
Universite Cheikh Anta Diop, Dakar, Senegal

Cher L. McAllister
Temple University, Philadelphia

Christopher McCauley
University of California, Santa Barbara

John H. McClendon III
Michigan State University

Pellom McDaniels III
Emory University, Atlanta

Erik S. McDuffie
University of Illinois, Urbana-Champaign

Brian Meeks
University of the West Indies, Mona, Jamaica

Khadijah O. Miller
Norfolk State University, Norfolk, Virginia

Shamika Ann Mitchell
Temple University, Pleasantville, Pennsylvania

Julie E. Moody-Freeman
DePaul University, Chicago

Paula Moreno-Zapata
University of Cambridge and Colombia

Jo-Ann Morgan
York University, Toronto, Canada

Sharon Morgan Beckford
Rochester Institute of Technology, Rochester,
New York

Anthony Ugalde Muhammad
Miami Dade County Public Schools, Miami

Sharron Muhammad
Howard University, Washington, DC

Michelle Murray
Florida International University, Miami

Claire A. Nelson
Inter American Development Bank,
Washington, DC

Caryn E. Neumann
The Ohio State University, Columbus, Ohio

Claire Newstead
University of Nottingham-Trent, United
Kingdom

Charles Muiru Ngugi
Truman State University, Kirksville, Missouri

Beatrice Nicolini
Catholic University of the Sacred Heart,
Milan, Italy

Mario Nisbett
University of California, Berkeley

Nkiru Nzegwu
Binghamton University, Binghamton, New
York

Marie-José N'Zengou-Tayo
University of the West Indies, Mona,
Jamaica

Khonsura G. K. Ofei (Aaron J. Wilson)
Independent Scholar

Aaron Ogletree
Florida International University,
Miami

Femi Ojo-Ade
Saint Mary's College, University of
Lagos, Nigeria

Fred Oladeinde
WHADN, Washington, DC

Amy Abugo Ongiri
University of Florida, Gainesville

Roberto Pacheco
Florida International University,
Miami

Melina Pappademos
University of Connecticut, Wood Hall

Prakash Patil
J/N Medical College, India

David W. H. Pellow
North Carolina Central University
(emeritus)

Sharon M. Peniston
Independent Scholar

Charles Peterson
College of Wooster, Wooster, Ohio

Francoise Pfaff
Howard University, Washington, DC

Esther Phillips
University College of Barbados,
Barbados

Tiffany D. Pogue
Florida International University,
Miami

Marc Prou
University of Massachusetts, Boston

Matthew Quest
Brown University, Providence, Rhode
Island

Diego Quiroga
Universidad San Francisco de Quito,
Quito, Ecuador

Carlos A. Rabasso
Rouen School of Management Groupe
Ecole Supérieure de Commerce de
Rouen, France

Fco. Javier Rabasso
Rouen School of Management Groupe
Ecole Supérieure de Commerce de
Rouen, France

Kara Rabbitt
William Paterson University, Wayne,
New Jersey

Chaman Lal Raina
Florida International University,
Miami

Louis D. Ramos
Independent Scholar

Paulette A. Ramsay

Runoko Rashidi
Independent Scholar

Thelma Ravell-Pinto
Hobart & William Smith Colleges,
Geneva, New York

Rhoda Reddock
University of the West Indies

Lorriane Rivera-Newberry
Independent Scholar

Nicole Roberts
University of the West Indies

Florence Bellande Robertson
Independent Scholar

Maria Soledad Rodriguez
University of Puerto Rico, Rio Piedras
Campus

Sybil Rosado
Benedict College, Columbia, South Carolina

Gregory Rutledge
University of Nebraska, Lincoln

Amon Saba Saakana
Karnak House, London

Alicia M. Sanabria
Independent Scholar, Brazil

Leslie Sanders
York University, Toronto, Canada

Meshak Sangini
Langston University, Langston, Oklahoma

Rick Santos
Nassau Community College, Garden City,
New York

Chris Saunders
University of Cape Town, Cape Town, South
Africa

Mark Q. Sawyer
Ralph J. Bunche Center for African American
Studies, University of California, Los
Angeles

Jason M. Schultz
Georgia State University Library, Atlanta

Ralph Schusler
Florida International University, Miami

Daryl Michael Scott
Howard University, Washington, DC

Hillary Scott
The University of California, Berkeley

Paula Marie Seniors
Virginia Tech, Blacksburg, Virginia

Macheo Shabaka
American Association of Professional Ringside
Physicians (AAPRP)

Martin S. Shanguhyia
West Virginia University, Morgantown

Malik Simba
California State University, Fresno

Kerry Sinanan
University of the West of England, Bristol,
United Kingdom

Walter Sistrunk
Michigan State University, East Lansing

Zipporah Slaughter
Broward Community College, Fort
Lauderdale, Florida

Fouzi Slisli
Saint Cloud State University, Saint Cloud,
Minnesota

Andre L. Smith
Florida International University College of
Law, Miami

Valerie Smith
Florida Gulf Coast University, Fort Myers

Yushau Sodiq
Texas Christian University, Fort Worth, Texas

Augusto Soledade
Florida International University, Miami

Maboula Soumahoro
Barnard College, New York City

Andrew Stafford
Independent Scholar

John H. Stanfield, II
Indiana University, Bloomington

Michelle Stephens
Mount Holyoke College, South Hadley,
Massachusetts

Andrea Stone
University of Toronto, Canada

Kaila Adia Story
University of Louisville Louisville, Kentucky

Ida Tafari
Florida International University, Miami

Clarence Taylor
Baruch College, City University of New York

Clyde Taylor
New York University, New York

Furukawa Tetsushi
Otani University, Kyoto, Japan

Noelle Theard
Florida International University, Miami

Rose C. Thevenin
Florida Memorial University, Miami

H. U. E. Thoden van Velzen
University of Amsterdam and Utrecht

Gregory Thomas
Syracuse University, Syracuse, New York

Valeria Thompson-Ramos
Independent Scholar, North Carolina

Antonio D. Tillis
Purdue University, West Lafayette, Indiana

Neila Todd
Ministry of Education, Trinidad and Tobago

Neri Torres
Ife Ile Dance Company, Miami

Charles Tshimanga
University of Nevada, Reno

Horen Tudu
Independent Scholar

Elizabeth Turnbull
Florida International University, Miami, Florida

Grace Turner
College of William and Mary, Williamsburg, Virginia

Ineke van Kessel
African Studies Centre, Leiden, The Netherlands

W. van Wetering
Free University, Amsterdam, The Netherlands

Nadege Veldwachter
University of California, Los Angeles

Lucie Viakinnou-Brinson
Kennesaw State University, Kennesaw, Georgia

Rinaldo Walcott
University of Toronto, Canada

Carlton Waterhouse
Florida International University, Miami

C. S'thembile West
Western Illinois University, Macomb

Alan West-Durán
Northeastern University, Boston

Derrick White
Florida Atlantic University, Boca Raton

Dessima Williams
Independent Scholar, Grenada

Ian Williams
Fitchburg College, Fitchburg, Massachusetts

Regennia N. Williams
Cleveland State University, Cleveland, Ohio

Deborah Willis
Tisch School of the Arts, New York University, New York

Ludger Wimmerlbucker
University of Hamburg, Germany

Graeme Wood
The American University in Cairo, Egypt

Gloria-yvonne
University of Illinois, Chicago

Mary Ziegler
University of Tennessee, Knoxville, Tennessee

Advisory Board

About the Editors

Carole Boyce Davies is professor of African–New World Studies and English at Florida International University and served as director of African–New World Studies for three terms between 1997and 2006. From Trinidad and Tobago, she has worked and studied in Africa, the Caribbean, Europe, Brazil and the United States. In 2000–2001, she was Herskovits Professor of African Studies and Comparative Literary Studies at Northwestern University. She is the author of *Migrations of the Subject. Black Women, Writing Identity* (1994) and *Left of Karl Marx. The Political Life of Black Communist Claudia Jones* (2008). She has coedited several critical collections on African Diaspora literatures, most recent, *The African Diaspora. African Origins and New World Identities* (1999) and *Decolonizing the Academy. African Diaspora Studies* (2003).

Managing Editor

Babacar M'Bow is originally from Senegal. He curates international art exhibitions and develops museum management policy with an emphasis on African Diaspora cultures, cultural institutions building, and community cultural patrimony. He also supervises international conferences and symposia for Broward County Libraries Division. A well-known curator of African and African diaspora art one of his recent works is as curator and editor of *Benin: A Kingdom in Bronze. The Royal Court Art* (2005).

Local Contributing Editors

Keshia Abraham was born in Pittsburgh, Pennsylvania, and is a world traveler who identifies as a diasporic African. She is a popular professor at Florida Memorial University, in Miami, Florida, and specializes in literatures of the African Diaspora. She is also an independent scholar and a cultural worker committed to international education and social change.

Veronique Helenon is from Martinique and studied in France. She is an assistant professor at Florida International University who specializes in African Diaspora history. A specialist on the African Diaspora in Europe, she has published essays on areas of African diaspora history and is completing a manuscript on colonial relationships between African and the Caribbean.

Linda Spears Bunton is an associate professor of education in the College of Education at Florida International University. Her areas of specialization are literature, language literacy, and the African American experience. Her new book is *A Literacy of Promise The African American Experience* (2008).

Rose C. Thevenin is originally from Haiti and is an associate professor of history and college historian at Florida Memorial University. Her areas of specialization are African American History and Black social movements. She is an executive member of Association of Black Women Historians and has published in works such as *Diasporic Africa: A Reader* (2006).

Acknowledgments

For a project of the magnitude of the *Encyclopedia of the African Diaspora,* gratitude is owed to a variety of people who assisted in various ways in its conceptualization, execution, and realization. I will identify these both chronologically and in order of importance to the history of this project. First of all, Babacar M'bow, a knowledgeable cultural programmer, coordinator of International Programs and Exhibits of Broward County Libraries, whom I met soon after being contacted by the publishers, was instinctively conscious of the importance and the need to pursue this project to its end. We worked together on the proposal to submit to ABC-CLIO, and he was an invaluable resource, because of his knowledge of the United Nations Educational, Scientific, Cultural Organization (UNESCO) *General History of Africa* project, having seen it grow from its inception under the leadership of Mahtar M'bow, then director general of UNESCO. Babacar M'Bow assisted in myriad ways in the development and execution of this project, serving as managing editor for the encyclopedia, contacting contributors and giving shape to its conceptual and technical aspects. In this regard, International Programs, Broward County Libraries, Fort Lauderdale, Florida is also acknowledged.

The encyclopedia's formidable research assistant, Karen Matthew, very competently took up the project at a critical time when it was stalling and worked meticulously, in a very professional, reliable and mature way, to reorganize the encyclopedia files, finalize entries, reestablish contacts with contributors, format and submit entries, and bring this project to completion. I am sure that we would not have been able to complete this encyclopedia successfully without her diligence and steady professionalism. A major debt of gratitude is owed to Ms. Matthew for her work in this regard.

The International Advisory Board is acknowledged for encouraging, advancing, and supporting the realization of this project by their experience and by their intellectual understanding that this was a doable project. The first major related event we had was a symposium that allowed us to create the international advisory board and a local advisory board. The idea of creating large subject essays on various African Diaspora topics came out of this April 2003 meeting, as well as a variety of fruitful discussions on how to proceed. From this point, we created a logo and literature with which to promote the project, and we attended major conferences to begin the process of disseminating materials.

Jonelle A. Davies is acknowledged for her work in designing the logo for the Encyclopedia's promotion. The staff of the Florida International University (FIU) Studio of Digital Arts (SODA) who created and managed the project's Web site, especially Rob Yunk, have been wonderfully responsive as we have moved the project through its various stages. SODA understood the importance of the project and the ways in which we could promote it on the World Wide Web.

Two graduate students in the African New World Studies program, Safietou Kane and Sabrina Collins, were tasked with promoting and disseminating information on the project and attended the African Studies Association conference in Boston in 2004. Sabrina Collins served as the first research assistant and began the process of receiving and organizing entries. La Tasha Amelia Brown worked during one summer on the encyclopedia assisting Sabrina Collins at a critical time.

A major international conference, "The African Diaspora Knowledge Exchange" was held at Florida Memorial University in 2005 at which many of the subject essays were presented. Safietou Kane was the primary student liaison on this conference and helped receive subject essays ahead of time. The format intended was to provide an opportunity for authors of subject essays to present their work for critical feedback. This proved to be a very successful approach as it allowed the audiences (including teachers from south Florida) to review the material presented and ask the kinds of questions to which those knowledgeable in the field were able to respond. The late Mr. Thirlee Smith, Jr., of Miami-Dade Public Schools and leading supporter of the Florida Statute on Teaching African American Studies (1994 Florida Legislature, Section 1003.43 [g]), ensured that his teachers had access to the content aspects of African Diaspora material at various conferences.

We encouraged all the graduate students at FIU, and in graduate programs around the country, to contribute entries on the African Diaspora. We acknowledge the significant contributions and support of Dr. Karl S. Wright, Dr. Sandra Thompson, faculty, staff and students of Florida Memorial University who hosted our various conferences and assisted with this project. We thank all the graduate students who contributed, especially Jessica Alarcon, who came into the program as a new student and immediately offered assistance. Then a pre-dissertation fellow in the African-New World Studies (ANWS) program (2006–2007), Yaba Blay of Temple University, also provided links to other graduate students who could contribute their research to the encyclopedia. Rosa Henriquez, the program coordinator of ANWS, also steered potential contributors, interested individuals, and others with questions to the appropriate individuals who could help or answer their questions.

In the process of executing this project, ANWS received a grant from the Ford Foundation, which led to the creation of the Florida Africana Studies Consortium (FLASC), which formed the kind of academic community in south Florida that supported intellectual and community work on the African Diaspora. All the conferences we organized in the succeeding period were done with the assistance and collaboration of FLASC. Many FLASC members served on the local advisory board of the *Encyclopedia of the African Diaspora*, and the encyclopedia became a place where these faculty could publish their work. FLASC then has to be recognized for its help in ensuring that this project was successfully realized. In this regard as well, the Ford Foundation is acknowledged for providing the financial support for the African Diaspora Knowledge Exchange Conference.

During my tenure as director of ANWS at FIU (1997–2000; 2001–2006), the ANWS program and the College of Arts and Sciences provided space for advancing African diaspora projects such as this one which began to have impact nationally. We acknowledge them for that support. We are pleased that this project came out of the south Florida community proving that there is an intellectual community that could produce an encyclopedia of this magnitude.

All the writers of entries are acknowledged for their understanding of the need for this encyclopedia, for contributing their work, but above all for patience and for responding promptly (at times) to requests for information, corrections, and updates. Several entries, at the end, could not be accommodated because of space allocation. We thank those contributors nevertheless. Angela Leonard of Loyola University in particular reached out to us at a critical stage in the project's history, offering support and contacts for entries, as she terminated a related project. Veronique Helenon, assistant professor of history in ANWS, is recognized as well for instinctively expecting a quality program and demonstrating this by her contributions to this project. And in particular, the south Florida community members who encouraged this work's completion. Out of this has come other related works on the African Diaspora.

Jesse Benjamin, on the international advisory board, is recognized for consistent support of this project, often going beyond normal expectations, pursuing leads diligently, finding contributors for some areas not often covered and finally assisting with responding to queries in the final editing stage, always in a professional and politically committed manner.

The *Encyclopedia of the African Diaspora* project was presented at three African Diaspora conferences (the Association of the World Wide African Diaspora [ASWAD] in Rio de Janeiro in 2005; The African Diaspora in Asia [TADIA] Conference in Goa, India, in January 2006; and the African Literature [ALA] Conference in Ghana in 2006). We thank the audiences of these presentations for feedback. Finally, all of the people who helped in various unrecognized ways, whether by informing colleagues, circulating flyers, offering verbal support, or dropping by to help at critical times, to make this project happen are also acknowledged. In particular, the scholars and activists from Ecuador are offered special recognition and thanks for responding rapidly to the need for an Afro-Ecuadorian entry. Thanks are due to Chucho Garcia, Diego Quiroga, Edson Leon, Catherine Walsh for finding ways to strategically fill this gap, knowing that a project like this is larger than individual/personal dramas and that what is most important is for these communities to be recognized. Above all, the staff at ABC-CLIO are acknowledged for their vision, patience, and understanding at the various turns in the completion of this encyclopedia.

Carole Boyce Davies,
General Editor

Introduction

The African Diaspora and the African World

To study the African Diaspora is, indeed, to study the world. This is the first realization to which any scholar of the African Diaspora comes very early in the process, for at least two reasons: (a) Africa is the birthplace of human civilization, and from there human beings migrated to various locations worldwide; and (b) African peoples in our contemporary understandings (continental Africans and African-descended peoples) exist globally, following a series of subsequent migrations. While all migrations do not necessarily create a diaspora, what is particular to diaspora creation includes, first of all, a migration, but second, some historical, emotive, political, economic, and cultural connections to that homeland and a consciousness of that interaction. The study of the African Diaspora has involved various generations of scholarship, various disciplinary approaches, various conceptual formulations, and various identifications and interrogations of what and/or who constitute/s the African Diaspora.

The Encyclopedia of the African Diaspora then attempts to account for as many of these peoples and communities as possible within its limited space and organizational abilities. All we claim to do at this point is to present as much of the available research as is possible, making connections as we exchange knowledge about who African Diaspora peoples are and where they live, and as we try to understand the kinds of cultural transformations they have engaged in; to document their leading ideas; to provide future researchers with information that can lead to further inquiry. By these means, we already recognize that each contribution, such as this three-volume one, merely adds to the developing knowledge about the African Diaspora. As we make additional connections, we prepare for a further expansion of the discourse.

As we recognized in the production of this work, a three-volume encyclopedia merely scratches the surface. This *Encyclopedia of the African Diaspora* engages the contemporary, covers the emergence of new levels and discourses of blackness, and deliberately extends to include areas such as the African Diaspora in the Indian

Ocean and other areas of the world, such as the Mediterranean, often not covered in African Diaspora projects. We recognize at the outset that an encyclopedia of this type at its best can offer only snapshots of the phenomenon, its people, and the processes it describes.

As we bring this project to a close for publication, we acknowledge that much has to be left out; much more needs to be included. The range and the staff, for example, of the more than 25 volumes of the *Encyclopedia Britannica,* Compton's *Encyclopedia,* or *World Book Encyclopedia* are perhaps closer to what is needed. The difference in access and coverage has already been identified in the institutional dominance of European studies and the general marginalization or subordination of Africana Studies in the various academic structures. *Decolonizing the Academy: African Diaspora Studies* (2003) is one of the places that discusses this issue. What is represented here must be seen as a selection that moves toward a more complete rendering at some later date, if that is ever an attainable goal. We say this knowing that no encyclopedia can ever claim complete coverage, as it will always have to be updated at a later time when more information is available.

Encyclopedias, like anthologies, are often seen as creating canons—as definitive, when in reality they contain only a selection of the available material based on access, time, resources, reach, and, of course, the force of scholarly knowledge production and the nature of publication arrangements. The range of other particular encyclopedias emphasizes the point about coverage, as each geographical region as well as several particularized groups, fields, and subject areas have produced, or require, their own encyclopedia. There are already several encyclopedias of U.S. African American history, biography, and major events, perhaps largely because African Americans in the United States have been at the forefront of making their voices heard, establishing their presence through the various media available; and clearly, U.S. capitalism has often marketed itself via media. *The African American Encyclopedia* (ed. Michael Williams), which appeared first as five volumes in 1993 and now appears as ten volumes, and the *Encyclopedia of African American Culture and History* (1996, supplement in 2001; ed. Jack Salzman, David Lionel Smith, and Cornel West) indicated the growing nature of the knowledge base and the trepidation at the thought of leaving out important information. All editors also indicate a number of other challenges, including space limitations, difficult choices, timelines, authors' schedules, changes in subjects' lives, and the sense that some people's favorite subjects may not be covered. The new edition of the *Encyclopedia of African American Culture and History: The Black Experience in the Americas* (2005, ed. Colin Palmer and Howard Dodson) is a six-volume set described as updating the 1996 edition. With Schomburg Library collaboration, it attempts to be more expansive and contemporary and moves away from a U.S.-centered approach to include more on the Americas in general. It moves the definition of *African American* outward, extending the coverage to the rest of the Americas. Still, as already indicated, the African American field has been fairly well covered by such early works as the *Ebony Black America: Pictorial History* (1973) and *The African American Almanac,* now in its ninth edition in 2003 (formerly *The Negro Almanac*). And there are particular works, such as the two-volume *Black Women in America: An Historical Encyclopedia* (1993, ed. Darlene Clark Hine with Rosalyn Terborg Penn and Elsa Barkley Brown) and The *Encyclopedia of Black Studies* (2005, ed. Molefi Asante and Ama Mazama).

More particular regional encyclopedias provide more detailed coverage than general field encyclopedias. The *Encyclopedia of Twentieth-Century African History* (2002, ed. Paul Zeleza) includes entries that provide important documentation of places, regions, countries, and language groups, as well as topical and thematic essays. But the editor chose not to include biographical entries. The *Encyclopedia of Africa South of the Sahara*, although it continues the error of dividing Africa into upper and lower Sahara, is four volumes, with John Middleton as editor in chief. The introduction by the then-leading African historian J. F. Ade Ajayi, who served as a primary local editor, indicates the difficulty in attempting such a project, some of which we share. The two-volume *Encyclopedia of Contemporary Latin American and Caribbean Cultures* (2002, ed. Daniel Balderson, Mike Gonzalez, and Anne M. Lopez) lists entries under various countries. And *Enciclopedia Brasileira da Diaspora Africana* (2004, ed. Nei Lopes) is a very important and useful reference guide that covers Afro-Brazilian culture but reaches into the rest of the African Diaspora as well, thereby demonstrating the magnitude of the field for the Brazilian audience, though entries are very short, sometimes only a few lines long. The ambitious *Encyclopedia of Diasporas: Immigrant and Refugee Cultures Around the World* (2004, ed. Melvin Ember, Carol R. Ember, and Ian Skoggard) is a two-volume compilation of essays divided into *Volume I: Diaspora Overviews and Topics* and *Volume II: Diaspora Communities,* attempting by these means to cover the larger communities of world peoples. *Africana: The Encyclopedia of the African and African-American Experience* (1999, ed. Henry Louis Gates and Anthony Appiah; CD version is Microsoft's *Encarta Encyclopedia Africana*) began as an attempt to complete the Du Bois encyclopedia project but ended up dealing more with the relations between Africa and the Americas. The updated version was extended to five volumes, signifying in its more expansive coverage the point I made earlier about size and relational work.

DEFINING AND CONCEPTUALIZING THE AFRICAN DIASPORA

The term *African Diaspora* refers to the dispersal of African peoples all over the world. The word *diaspora* comes from the Greek *diaspora* (*dia*, meaning "through," and *spora*, which refers to the process of sowing) (1). Thus, it refers to dispersal of seeds as well as the result of the dispersal. The implication of "through" in the first part of the word also gives a metaphorical sense of the movement aspects of diaspora, that is, "through different routes." In this reading, then, the Diaspora can be seen as a kind of harvest of peoples, cultures, and knowledge that comes initially out of Africa—a demographic globalization, and internationalization, of African peoples created through centuries of migration. Indeed, African Diaspora peoples have been the products or the recipients of this economic globalization, often the demographic/human resource engine through the expropriation of their labor for the advancement of current economic and communications structures now defined as globalization (2). As a result, it has a different intent and political identity than the globalization created for economic oppression. The dispersal that created the African diaspora occurred through (a) voluntary means (economic and pre-Columbian exploratory journeys); (b) trade, servitude, and military expeditions (early Indian Ocean trade journeys from the sixth century); (c) forced migrations (transatlantic slavery over at least four centuries in the modern period, from the 15th to the 19th centuries); and (d) induced migration, the more recent 20th- and 21st-century migrations of African peoples based on world economic imbalances. These have resulted, thereby, in the relocation and redefinition of African peoples in a range of now-international locations (3).

While one aspect of the definition of the African Diaspora is fairly constant in terms of its association with dispersal or scattering, there is a plurality of interpretations of the nature of the result of that dispersal, that is, what constitutes the African Diaspora. Some would argue that this plurality is in fact a good thing, as it allows for multiple perspectives, which engender further research and additional subjects of study. Others see forced exodus as the most important constitutive element in diaspora creation. As far as the Atlantic end of the Diaspora, in terms of numbers, in this encyclopedia Inikori has argued that the conservative Curtin statistics of 11 million people moved via transatlantic slavery, and the more generous 19 million people, are not a source for debate, as the numerical basis for the forced migration (which of course does not include the uncountable numbers lost in passage) is enough to make the arguments about demographic shifts as well as the transformation of the economic patterns on both sides of the Atlantic, but largely benefiting Europe and America (4).

A number of scholars over the years have provided definitions and the history of the use of the term *African Diaspora*. George Shepperson's (1993) "African Diaspora: Concept and Context" documents the usage of this particular combination and provides much of the language that is used still to define the African Diaspora, identifying the origin of the use of the term to refer to the Jewish Diaspora (5) and therefore also emphasizing the "homeland" element. The first usages of the term for African peoples he identifies as being linked to the rise of black political organizing during the immediate decolonization period beginning in the 1950s, particularly around the time of the First International Congress of Negro Writers and Artists in 1956 and the International Congress of African Historians held in Dar es Salaam in October 1965.

Clearly, the use of the term *African Diaspora* is linked to decolonization activity and therefore has political intent, and that is to account for the "status and prospects" of various peoples of African descent scattered around the world, who are often denied their humanity. Thus, one sees at least two broad tendencies in African Diaspora studies: (a) to account for dispersal mainly from a common source in Africa; and (b) to account for those communities that have migrated in various directions and thereby have reconfigured identities in those now-home locations. By these means, one often has a sense of studying (a) Africa and the Diaspora or the continent and the dispersal and/or (b) the African Diaspora itself as a unit that includes the continent and the various intra-African migrations and movements. We propose to bring these two tendencies together in this *Encyclopedia of the African Diaspora*.

Shepperson (1993) is careful to point out, however, that although usage of the expression *African Diaspora* began in the mid-20th century, the concept's usage is older than its 20th-century definition, extending all the way back to the Biblical reference that "Ethiopia shall soon stretch forth her hands" (Psalm 68:31). Shepperson credits Edward Wilmot Blyden with his 1880s "Ethiopia Stretching Out Her Hands unto God: or, Africa's Service to the World" as one of the first places to see the conceptualizing of the African Diaspora in an intellectual approach. For him, though, African Diaspora is a framework for comparative study; it must be approached through different languages. It cannot be a mere statistical rendering but must engage ideas, and it must not deal solely with dispersal outward, as it "loses much of its force if it is limited to dispersal in an outward direction only" (Shepperson 1993, 44). But even before Blyden, in the U.S. context, David Walker's 1829 *Appeal* was directed to the *Coloured Citizens of the World*, and thus already embodied a consciousness of political challenge of oppression that would be echoed later in Fanon but was definitely imbued with the sense of an African Diaspora in its conceptual framing.

Brent Hayes Edwards, *The Practice of Diaspora: Literature, Translation, and the Rise of Black Internationalism* (2003), then, is a very important intervention, as it addresses the particular ways in which Diaspora has been put to use for political, emotive, and cultural reasons. But one must also consider the disjunctures, as did Appadurai (2006), as well as the differences in terms of application. In this particular case, the political connections between the Anglophone and Francophone diaspora become importantly identified via the political organizing of George Padmore (Trinidad/United Kingdom/Ghana) and Garame Kouyate (Ivory Coast/Paris).

Thus, in terms of the first tendency, the concept of the African Diaspora is much older than its contemporary formulation. If we accept that, based on archaeological evidence, the birthplace of human beings is Africa, and that humankind from there began its dispersal around the world, then we can argue logically that the African Diaspora is the first constituted formulation of human migration. Therefore, some aspects of African cultures have touched all societies.

While this may seem too loose and floppy a category, too totalizing in a way, one still must consider the credible historical research in this area. Chancellor Williams (1976), in *The Destruction of Black Civilization*, for example, identifies the early migrations from the "Ethiopian empire which once extended from the Mediterranean to the north and southward to the source of the Nile" (44) in present-day Ethiopia, based on a series of human and natural disasters. Thus, there are particular historical movements, periods, and places that allow us to identify specific communities—cultural, social, economic, and political formulations in our contemporary realities. Nkiru Nzegwu's subject entry, "Art in the African Diaspora," seems to follow this logic as it identifies seven formulations of the African Diaspora and insists that the categories received from European scholarship have been arbitrary and indeed limit our fuller understandings of African Diaspora as it relates to creativity and the arts, at least. More expansive than the five phases of Colin Palmer, she identifies seven phases, as follows: the Paleolithic; the Egyptian Diaspora; the Kemetic; the Kushite phase; the Atlantic; the colonial and anticolonial phase; and the postcolonial phase. In this way, art-related creations for those earlier periods, she argues, also fall under African Diaspora. Importantly, then, in her formulation she would want to include the Egyptian or Ethiopian Diaspora.

The intellectual work of the premodern African Diaspora can be traced to the universities in Alexandria, Egypt; to the University of Timbuktu and Djenne in the actual republic of Mali; and to the various centers of learning of the West African kingdom of Ghana (University of Kumbi-sahel) that were burned by the Almoravids in the 14th century. The library of African/Diaspora studies, then, eventually must address this earlier information even as it extends into the contemporary. Thus, *temporally*, as the research has moved in two directions: backward to the early historical periods, as Afrocentrists do, and forward to embrace new formations of African Diaspora; *spatially*, it can address the range of existing communities worldwide; and *conceptually* it can examine the nature of epistemological contributions of the African Diaspora.

While we acknowledge the existence of a preslavery migration to the Americas, as Van Sertima (2003) asserted, the more contemporary African Diaspora, which constitutes our second tendency, can be more firmly identified in the period after European enslavement and forced migration of Africans to the New World. Following the work of the first Pan-Africanists, such as Edgar Wilmot Blyden (1886) in his famous speech in Liberia College, 20th-century studies of the African Diaspora have made major contributions toward the understanding of the dispersal of African peoples. Such early and mid-20th-century scholars as Anna Julia Cooper, W. E. B. DuBois, Melville Herskovits, Carter G. Woodson, and Katherine Dunham (United States); J. J. Thomas, George Padmore, Una Marson, and Fernando Ortiz (Caribbean); Casely Hayford, Funimalayo Ransome Kuti, and Cheikh Anta Diop (Africa); and Nina Rodrigues and Abdias do Nascimento (Brazil) have helped to provide frameworks of analysis as well as documented research and activism that advanced possibilities or studies of various aspects of the African Diaspora.

Ruth Simms Hamilton's (1995) "Conceptualizing the African Diaspora" works theoretically within the framework of world systems analysis. She defines the African Diaspora as a social formation that includes a "global aggregate of actors and subpopulations differentiated in social and geographical space, yet exhibiting a commonality based on shared historical experiences conditioned by and within the world ordering system" (Hamilton 1995, 394). She deploys three historical characteristics to identify the Diaspora as distinct from other groups:

a. Geosocial displacement and the circularity of a people (the historical dialectic between geographical mobility and the establishment of "roots")
b. Social oppression: relations of domination and subordination (conflict, discrimination, and inequality based primarily, although not exclusively, on race, color, and class)
c. Endurement, resistance, and struggle: cultural and political action (creative actions of people as subjects of their history; psychocultural and ideological transformations; social networks and dynamics).

Hamilton's work offers important categories for situating a range of African Diaspora movements, histories, and cultural transformations; above all, it includes the issues of dominance and subordination but also resistance. Her diaspora as a "field of action" predates "unit of analysis" formations and identifies a more dynamic praxis as it also includes a range of literary, cultural, and political movements.

The field of African Diaspora studies thus promises an engaging and rewarding study for scholars of the African Diaspora. In the contemporary moment in the academy, the study of the African Diaspora has continued with a surge in intensity as manifested in a series of texts, conferences, journal articles, and academic programs at the end of the 20th century and into the 21st century. And a range of post-1960s scholars in the academy have maintained a solid interest, which has led to this contemporary articulation. For example, "Interrogating the African Diaspora," which was the theme of a graduate seminar at Florida International University (2003–2006) will have an impact on the next generation of scholars. A 2006 conference entitled "Diaspora Hegemonies" at the University of Toronto tried to account for some of the complexity in the field in its recent incarnations, raising a number of questions about what and who is privileged in African Diaspora studies. And an issue of the journal *Radical History* has the special theme of contemporary reconceptualizations of the African Diaspora.

HISTORICAL BACKGROUND AND GEOGRAPHICAL RANGE OF THE CONTEMPORARY AFRICAN DIASPORA

The trans-Saharan passage and the opening up of the Arabian Peninsula, as well as the circum-Indian Ocean geography, located a range of African peoples in what is now called the African Diaspora in the Indian Ocean (6). Although the Atlantic Diaspora (the 14th through the 21st centuries) has been studied more extensively, scholars have begun to advance the study of this earlier migration to the Indian Ocean (from the fifth century onward), ensuring that this migration was driven not so much by enslavement but more often by sailors, merchants, and soldiers, some of whom became members of royalty and attained political and military leadership, as did Malik Ambar in India. Thus, earlier migrations across the Mediterranean Sea, the Eritrean (Red) Sea, and the Indian Ocean, as both free and enslaved people from approximately the sixth century, must now be a central understanding of the formation of the contemporary African Diaspora.

The long history of forced migration that displaced African peoples across Europe and the Americas via transatlantic slavery from the 15th century onward has been well addressed. Historians of the African Diaspora have continued to document the ways in which this transatlantic slave trade displaced and disrupted the lives of peoples of numerous already-intact African nations, locating them in the New World for the services of plantation systems (7). Subsequent industrial developments in the Americas (the 15th to the 19th centuries) were facilitated, with slavery abolished in the various New World locations only in a sliding 19th-century date arrangement based on decisions in the various colonizing centers of power (French, Spanish, English, American, Portuguese) from 1838 to 1888 (8).

The history of Euro-American imperialism's border transgression and its larger assumption of control of human and physical resources, unlimited space and movement, serves as one contextual background for the Atlantic African Diaspora. In the development of triangular trade routes through the "Middle Passage," the economics of slavery and colonialism facilitated the rise of European modernity. We can conclude, then, that contemporary notions of globalization have always been economic, and that globalization has used African peoples' labor in its processes. Preexisting frameworks of operation that ensured

European control of the world's resources were put in place with the rise of European modernity.

The result of all these processes of free and forced migration was the appearance of Africans in the Americas, in Europe, and in Asia, and the simultaneous re-creation of sociocultural practices in these various locations, making Africans essentially a global people. Africans moved from a range of political formations from the precolonial nations, empires, and other smaller ethnic political structures (often misnamed "tribes" by anthropologists) (9).

This relocation of African peoples to different geographical locations often meant subordination or dispossession. So, even though some, such as Gwyn Campbell (at the TADIA converence in Goa in 2006), would make hard distinctions between the nature of the Atlantic African Diaspora and the Indian Ocean Diaspora, suggesting that the latter is not a "victim Diaspora," today in India, African Indians—or Indo-Africans who describe themselves more particularly as Siddis or Habshis—still live visibly oppressed by the state and its elites, located as "backward tribes" and later "scheduled tribes" and accorded few benefits of citizenship (Caitlin-Jairazbhoy and Alpers 2004; Prasad 2005).

Still, there are other groups whose lives remained consistently debased in their new locations. The condition of African peoples in the Americas is an example. Following enslavement in the Americas, the most glaring of inequities continued as a period of colonialism in which Africans as colonial subjects were powerless, until formal political independence some 300 years later, to fully represent their rights both in Africa and the Americas. Postindependence nation-states have often been neocolonial systems, which were therefore not reliable protectors of rights, because within them were already imposed race- and class-based hierarchies that subordinated sometimes majority populations (10). In many countries, these peoples remained disenfranchised under various colonialisms (English, French, Spanish, Portuguese, Dutch, Arab, and Asian), without the means to return to their native lands and subject to horrendous conditions violating every tenet of human rights and with no other legitimate recourse but to fight for those rights. Throughout the Americas, the abuse of labor, the denial of rights, and beatings, maimings, and other forms of physical brutality accompanied the processes of colonialism that succeeded plantation slavery.

The work of historians of the African Diaspora has been fundamental in backgrounding and detailing the nature of these movements. Joseph Harris's lead in this area has been absolutely pivotal in the development of the field. From the late 1970s and through the Howard University conference that produced the landmark *Global Dimensions of the African Diaspora* (Harris 1982), Harris has maintained the African Diaspora as a subject of study and as its own unit of analysis, pushing as well for an expanded scope beyond the Atlantic Diaspora. This recent phase has also been advanced by work such as Colin Palmer's "Defining and Studying the Modern African Diaspora" (1998), which led into the 1999 American Historical Association conference, "Diasporas and Migrations in History," raised a number of questions about definition, and identified five major African diasporic streams: the first dispersal, which Palmer estimates occurred about 100,000 years ago and constituted the beginning dispersal of humankind; the second, taking place about 3000 BCE with the movement of Bantu-speaking peoples from the region around west Africa to other parts of the continent; the third, the trading Diaspora to parts of Europe, the Middle East, and Asia, which began around the fifth century; the fourth, the transatlantic migration of enslaved Africans, from the 15th century; the fifth, after the 19th century and continuing to the present day, the movement of Africans and peoples of African descent and their resettlement in various societies. For this reason, the framework that Tiffany Patterson and Robin D. G. Kelley (2000) used is "Unfinished Migrations: Reflections on the African Diaspora and the Making of the Modern World" (11), which provided a conceptual overview of the logic of the Diaspora as a process still in formation as it summarized the important literature and theoretical positions advanced in African Diaspora up to the end of the 20th century.

The work of a variety of other historians has been critical, such as Michael Gomez's *Exchanging Our Country Marks: The Transformation of African Identities in the Colonial and Antebellum South* (1998); *Reversing Sail: A History of the African Diaspora (New Approaches to African History)* (2004) (12); and *Black Crescent: The Experience and Legacy of African Muslims in the Americas* (2005). Earlier, Darlene Clark Hine and Jacqueline McLeod, from another conference, produced the book *Crossing Boundaries: Comparative History of Black People in the Diaspora* (1999), which provided useful additions to the library of African Diaspora Studies. And Gwendolyn Midlo Hall's "Making Invisible Africans Visible: Coasts, Ports, Regions and Ethnicities" in her *Slavery and African Ethnicities in the Americas: Restoring the Links* (2005) provides a good analysis of the various studies of the African Diaspora in the Americas and ends up identifying from her related databases the various movements of African Diaspora peoples and their ethnic origins.

POLITICAL MOVEMENTS AND PROJECTS: AFRICAN PEOPLES, DIASPORA, PAN-AFRICANISM

The African Diaspora is also understood as a political and cultural category. At the political level, its primary ideological formations have been expressed as Pan-Africanism, a political philosophy articulated through a variety of congresses and projects. For some scholars, such as Tony Martin, the rudiments of Pan-Africanism exist in the yearnings of Africans displaced via transatlantic slavery to return to their homelands. Thus, the flying back stories are seen as a kind of proto-Pan-Africanism, as are some of the myths, legends, songs, and spirituals, and also spiritual possessions and chants that talk about wings and homes and heaven and have continued to give African entities and practices presence in other diasporic locations. From the start, there has been a logic linking Diaspora to Pan-Africanism as St. Clair Drake (1993) identifies in his analyses of the relationships between these two discourses. Thus, Diaspora can be seen as condition, Pan-Africanism as political project.

The primary motivation of Pan-Africanism can be summarized as follows: Because a range of capitalist policies and projects have produced African peoples who live all over the world, how, then, can we represent their rights fully if the various nation-states in which they live do not always guarantee those rights? How can we produce a political system that coordinates these rights? What political projects need to be advanced in a coordinated way? How are African citizenship rights to be internationally understood alongside issues of nation-state sovereignty, jurisdiction, and the rights and duties of citizens who are located everywhere in nation-states to which they may have primary loyalty? One such formation (13) would create usable policies for transcendence of limitations of geographies, nation-state boundaries, and ethnic and linguistic differences for progressive social transformation of the lived realities of African peoples globally. Kwame Nkrumah's vision of Pan-Africanism on the continent, Malcolm X's vision of an Organization for Afro-American Unity (OAAU) as linked to, and expressed at, the Organization of African Unity (OAU) meeting in Cairo additionally attempted to make some of these connections (14). In similar ways, Kwame Toure's All-African Peoples Revolutionary Party describes itself in terms of the practice of Pan-Africanism already identified. But even before that, the work of Marcus Garvey and his "Africa for the Africans" and "Back to Africa" constructs critiqued the oppressed conditions of black peoples in the Diaspora as it articulated the possibility of a conceptual (if not a physical) return and began the process of instituting economic systems that could ensure that that possibility would become the reality that it is for many today. The problematic knot, though, is the extent to which African peoples can give primary or sole allegiance to the nation-states in which they live, particularly when those nation-states often do not identify or respect their human rights.

The "Constitutive Act of the African Union" (July 2001) begins its preamble with a direct assertion concerning African peoples, invoking generations of Pan-Africanists as follows:

> INSPIRED by the noble ideals that guided the founding fathers of our Continental Organization and generations of Pan-Africanists in their determination to promote unity, solidarity, cohesion and cooperation among the peoples of Africa and the African States (15).

All the research reveals that these Pan-Africanists were members of the worldwide leadership community of African Diaspora and African continental peoples with a commitment to working toward the liberation and advancement of the continent and its dispersed peoples (16).

The African Charter (written in Banjul, The Gambia) consistently refers to African peoples in the plural, thus leaving in the possibility of including a multiplicity of peoples across the continent of Africa. This definition of African peoples is an advance in the sense that it allows space for a definition of African peoples in a broad continental and Diaspora sense. And beyond that, the African Union's acceptance of the Diaspora as its sixth region (2005) has meant the possibility of some sort of political assertion for the African Diaspora. The full articulation of this structure has yet to be fully worked out; movement toward this goal has been deliberate and careful.

The African Union, replacing the OAU, in its Constitutive Act took into consideration The Lusaka Summit Decision on the "establishment of a strategic framework for a Policy of Migration in Africa" and gestures therefore toward the development of a definite future relationship with the African Diaspora (17).

Through the African Union Diaspora Conference in Washington, D.C., in December 2002, two objectives were established: the development of "capacity building projects by Diaspora Civil Society organization in the Western Hemisphere Diaspora," and the development of a "plan of ongoing collaboration with the African Union including a plan of action and a hemispheric steering committee" (18). One of the most important resolutions of this conference was the creation of a coordinating body for the African Union Western Hemisphere Diaspora, accepted unanimously by the meeting on December 19, 2002. This body had as one of its initiatives the proposal of an African Diaspora component of the African Union and its representative bodies, particularly the Pan-African Parliament (Article 17) and the Commission (Article 20) of the Constitutive Act of the African Union (19).

Since then, the African Union has taken significant steps toward operationalizing the African Diaspora within its framework. The Executive Council, in its third extraordinary session held in Sun City, South Africa, May 21–24, 2003, took several decisions, among which was convening a technical workshop held in Port-of-Spain, Trinidad, in June 2004 for the elaboration of a framework and recommendations on the relationship between the African Union and the Diaspora (20). The definition of Diaspora that came out of this workshop and was finally approved in 2005 reads as follows: "Peoples of African origin living outside the continent, irrespective of their citizenship and nationality and who are willing to contribute to the development of the continent and the building of the African Union. It includes communities created by the movements and cultures of persons from the continent of Africa and their descendants throughout the world — Asia, The Pacific, Europe and the Americas including United States and Canada, the Caribbean, South and Central America" (AU Web site, www.africanunion.com). The operational definition interestingly includes *willing* membership in the African Diaspora, as opposed to generic descent or other historical connections, and therefore becomes a kind of 21st-century political definition different from the initial usage of the term *African Diaspora*.

In this encyclopedia, African peoples are defined as those who have historical origins in Africa, irrespective of time period and current geographical location. In this way, descendants of those who were displaced from the continent forcibly and voluntarily in the Indian Ocean migrations, those moved forcibly during the period of transatlantic slavery, and those who have migrated more recently for economic, educational, social, and other reasons, also have claims to the status of African peoples or African-descended peoples as used in Latin America. African peoples in this understanding refer to peoples of African origin, comprising a variety of African ethnicities, on the continent of Africa and in the international African community termed African Diaspora.

A number of contemporary nation-states and regions have also begun to claim their own Diasporas. The Jamaican Diaspora and the Haitian Diaspora have already had a major impact on the politics and economics of their home communities, particularly in the areas of remittances, often more than the gross domestic product of these countries, and have increasing impact on the politics of their home countries, such as the right to vote and the choices for political leadership. And while the trade and circulation of people and commodities brings people, places, and things into contact, at times in diaspora that can be collaborative or conflictual, at other times they can lead to heightened articulations of particular nation-state diaspora. In a related manner, a number of larger nation-states (such as India) are recognizing their communities abroad as essential to the full access of all their human and material resources. And work is taking place on specific African nation-state Diaspora created by contemporary migration, such as the Somali Diaspora by Issa Farah, a young Somali scholar in Australia. His research, presented at La Trobe University, Australia seminar (March 2007) identifies at least 1 million Somalis in Diaspora with significant populations in North America (the United States, from as early as 1915 based on photographs taken in Chicago, and Canada), Europe (England, Scandinavia, Norway, Denmark, Sweden, and France), Middle East (United Arab Emirates, Saudi Arabia), Australia, and New Zealand.

Regional definitions are also being articulated as in the African Diaspora in the Andean region of South America and the Caribbean Diaspora. The Caribbean is already well recognized as a place for the practice of overlapping or intersecting Diaspora as say the Indian and African communities but also the African and native Carib, Arawak and Taino communities as well. In Canada as well, African Diaspora work on indigeneity (to a lesser degree in the United States, though work on the Black Seminoles in Florida in relation to maroon communities is increasing) means recognizing the importance of native peoples and the ways they have been dispossessed of their land even as Africans claim their diasporic existence in those same expropriated lands. This poignant articulation from Native Americans has to be consistently readdressed by African Diaspora peoples, also themselves exploited, so as to avoid the errors of settlers in the Americas and Australia who assumed appropriated land to be theirs. By these means, earlier collaborations between Native peoples and Africans can be maintained. While these competing claims to geographical location can make for conflict, they can also make for collaboration as oppressed groups struggle against these earlier and contemporary imperialist projects that have indeed driven and in some cases created these Diaspora. Andrea Smith, in *Conquest, Sexual Violence and North American Indian Genocide* (2005), describes well how these issues of imperialism are and were carried through sexual violence and often literally on the backs of women. Another work, Greg Thomas's *Sexual Demon of Colonial Power* (2007), indicates a similar set of arguments of the intersection of sexual constructions and indeed sexual exploitation in advancing colonial projects.

But resistance has also overlapped or intersected. The importance of Indian ahimsa or nonviolence, as advanced by Mahatma Gandhi, who gained his understandings of oppression in apartheid South Africa, had a significant impact on the Indian anticolonial struggle as it challenged offensive traditional practices, like child marriages. Gandhi, in turn, influenced Martin Luther King and his particular strategies to resist white racist dominance, as manifested in Jim Crowism and segregation in the United States. And a politicocultural movement like the Afro-bloco, *Filhos de Gandhy* in Salvador-Bahia, Brazil, also demonstrates the logic of diasporic collaborations in their appropriation of the meaning of Gandhi for carnival production. In making a political statement against Brazilian demonization of Afro-Brazilian cultural practices the Afro-bloco movement initially articulated itself as coming out in peace, and therefore used Gandhi paraphernalia and iconography, combined with the symbology of the Yoruba-derived Candomblé. And African and Indian cultures converge, even as political allegiances diverge. Thus, the *tassa,* an African drum is played by both Africans and Indians: both Trinidadians and Siddis (Afro-Indians). Food like roti and curry are now staples of the Eastern Caribbean and Guyanese (Afro-Caribbean) diet, and the exchanges continue based on close proximity as in the pejorative "douglarization." "Dougla," a word that is even worse than "mulatto" (which means "little mule") in various languages ranging from Persian to Hindi, means among other things according to Shalini Puri in a lecture at Florida International University (Interad, Summer 2006), "bastard," "stain," "blot," "polluted," "dirty," and other terms even more offensive. It is a formation that some still embrace to challenge logics of single belonging and interpret miscegenation in terms of what their dual heritages mean in this particular version of hybridity. Many who use "dougla" as definition are not fully aware of this historical meaning of the term and embrace it in a way similar to how some reappropriate other offensive terms used to describe black people. The existence of self-identified Indo-Africans or Siddis provides alternative political readings of this particular blend.

So in terms of political projects, as Michael Hanchard's experimental *Global Mappings Atlas* of the African Diaspora demonstrates (21), we can chart the influences and collaborations of political movements across the African world and understand more fully how these movements and their primary actors begin to have an impact on diverse geographical locations.

SOCIOCULTURAL PROJECTS: COMPLICATING THE AFRICAN DIASPORA STORY
The question of how best to identify African Diasporan peoples and their cultures continues to be a source of important scholarly debate. Zeleza, using Appadurai's framework of flows, identifies demographic, cultural, economic, political, ideological and imagistic flows. The hyphenated logic is one that has been followed by a number of communities as they attempt to account for these dual heritages, such as U.S. African Americans, African Caribbeans or Afro-Caribbeans, and Afro-Latin Americans, at the start of the 21st century. *Afro descendientes* (African descendants) is the agreed-upon descriptor. Some sort of connection to the African continent is assumed in terms of direct and discernable historical lines, physiognomy, and clearly recognized sociocultural practices.

Thus, in the field of anthropology, the early work of Herskovits and his contemporaries has been preeminent as it led to a variety of discussions about how to recognize and/or measure African cultural patterns and practices and how to name African communities worldwide. Though this early work of Herskovits has been criticized by subsequent generations of anthropologists for operating on the basis of some versions of African essentialism and/or for making too easy conclusions (J. D. Elder, personal communication, 2003) based on not enough research, the idea of identifying aspects of African culture in New World cultures has not died. For many in the Caribbean and Latin America, this kind of work was one of the only sources for claiming a history and human identity that was being erased or denied by dominant cultural formations.

The follow-up work by scholars like Yale University's Robert Farris Thompson provided a bridge into the contemporary period of cultural studies work and specificity to more general contemporary assertions. Thus, the study of Africanisms and/or African cultural retentions, raised through the group of anthropologists who worked on this throughout the early and mid 20th century, is not as important today in terms of proving one-to-one correspondences and equivalences that held sway in the early 20th-century period of African Diaspora research. Thus, questions of transformation or re-elaboration continue to be addressed substantially in the Americas.

In the contemporary early 21st century, the task of building one-to-one correspondences via the study of Africanisms has been replaced by discussions of representation and transformation. Tendencies in the field still demonstrate that the nature of these latter movements and the meaning of African-generated cultural practices are worth fighting for in many locations, particularly as a people's culture is the place from which they can begin to assert their freedom.

Indeed, current discussions about creolization, syncretism, and even hybridity assume some combination of African cultural forms with either European or indigenous/native American patterns. But as the work of Olendorp shows, as discussed in this encyclopedia, creating hybrid cultures was precisely the project of enslavers in the immediate postenslavement period. Hybridity and creolity have long antecedents in the range of created "blood" and proportional categories such as mulatto, creole, octoroon, and others by which the slaving class tried to literally "breed" ideal and complicit and interesting variations of Africans as they similarly did animals and grafted plants.

What connects the Diaspora continues to be a fundamental issue. For some it is related sociocultural formations; for others it is history, the human chain of slavery, and above all contemporary realities of subordination; and for others political practice. The definition of blackness is therefore an aspect, though not an equivalent, for these African diasporan definitions. A consciousness of racial identification and oppression generated from enslavement and other forms of subordination is one of these connecting points (Hanchard 1990, 1991) that have been present from all the early attempts to examine the status of African peoples. Though disparagingly called "victim Diaspora" by scholars like Robin Cohen in his *Global Diasporas: An Introduction* (1997) some of these points of connection generated for political effect have found their bases in prior or present situations of oppression and the need to effect some sort of political solidarity in order to challenge these. In his global Diaspora frame, Cohen also attempts some classification of Diaspora communities, not specifically African Diaspora communities, but ranging from Chinese to Sikhs and Zionists.

Works such as *The African Diaspora. African Origins and New World Identities* (1999, ed. Isidore Okpewho, Carole Boyce Davies, and Ali A. Mazrui) include contributions from a range of African Diaspora locations in the Americas and pursue such issues as theater, art, photography, music, and literature. In this regard, the cultural studies work of scholars like Stuart Hall (2006) and Paul Gilroy (2006) becomes important as they engage the idea of membership. Gilroy favors the "routes" model over the "roots," preferring to look at contemporary formations rather than some difficult-to-prove historical connections (Gilroy 1993). Stuart Hall wisely sees both the political strategy in the construct as well as its articulation possibilities and difficulties. But it is precisely in culture, as expressed in music, literature, and art, where some of these connections have been most visible.

The lyrics of Peter Tosh, "No matter where you come from/as long as you are a black man/you are an African," resonates with the logic of African Diaspora and Pan-Africanism. The wide-range exportation and dissemination of reggae music and the culture, lifestyle, and politics of Rastafarianism with Bob Marley as a leading exponent are also critical signs of the mobility of African diasporic cultural practice.

However, recent DNA work, as championed by Henry Louis Gates of Harvard University, has seemed to be able to make some direct connections using scientific evidence. By sampling continental African peoples, researchers have created a database for subsequent matches with people in the African Diaspora (as in *Oprah's Roots*, a television inquiry into the genealogy of the African American talk show host Oprah Winfrey, aired in January 2007). Pretty soon one may know with some scientific certainty, using some definite types that already exist in DNA databases collected on the continent, what has been relegated so far to speculation based on physiognomic appearance. This brings a bit more certainty to genealogical studies like the oral history work of Alex Haley in *Roots*. In this regard, new scientific work gives a kind of contemporary restatement of the kind of early scientific work undertaken by Cheikh Anta Diop in his carbon dating projects (described in *Civilization and Barbarism*) as far as the original human Diaspora in Africa is concerned

THE FIELD OF AFRICAN DIASPORA STUDIES

The field of African Diaspora studies can be seen through the generations of intellectual projects and their products. These have ranged from initial and individual or group scholarly research of people like Edward Blyden, J. J. Thomas, Melville Herskovits, and, more contemporaneously, Joseph Harris, Michael Gomez, Sheila Walker, Robert Farris Thompson, Darlene Clark Hine, and Colin Palmer in each generation. These individual projects have produced disciplinary studies of various communities that have then made some connections to the larger field of African Diaspora studies.

The second major way in which the field has advanced has been scholarly conferences of specific institutions or organizations, which have been able to produce their collections as already described. For example, at Florida International University, the conferences that produced the *African Presence in the Americas* (1995) and *Decolonizing the Academy. African Diaspora Studies* (2003) attempted to intervene in the production of knowledge, all challenging the Eurocentric assumptions of knowledge of U.S. and European institutions, but also those in the Caribbean, Africa, Latin America, Australia, Asia, all formed as auxiliaries for maintaining European hegemony. Each conference brings forward additional connections as for example did The African Diaspora in Asia (TADIA) Conference in Goa, India, in January, 2006 (22) with an earlier publication *The African Diaspora in the Indian Ocean* (2003) edited by Shihan de S. Jayasuriya, whose work also appears in this encyclopedia. The Conferences of Intellectuals of the African Diaspora (CIAD I and II, Senegal 2004 and Salvador Bahia 2006) have papers as well as declarations available online at the African Union Web site (www.africanunion.org). The ASWAD Conferences and formation of an association to do some of this work similarly advanced the field in innumerable ways. The first tangible product of ASWAD has been *Diasporic Africa. A Reader* (2006, ed. Michael Gomez).

AFRICAN DIASPORA LITERATURES AND CULTURES

While we have not presented a large subject essay on literature, we point here to some important references, this perhaps because literature has been one of the most popular ways by which African diaspora knowledge has been advanced. The best place to find the presentation and discussion of a range of African diaspora literatures is the journal *Callaloo: A Journal of African Diaspora Arts and Letters* (see "Calalu/Callaloo" entry) which for the last forty years, under the leadership of Charles Rowell, has indeed presented creative and critical work in literature from a wide range of African Diaspora communities. And for many years, *Presence Africaine* has served this function in francophone letters. The more recent creation of journals like *Diasporas*, though, has advanced the discussion of the larger field of Diaspora studies in general, specifically targeting the Diaspora as an area of study and the variety of overlapping or intersecting Diaspora that have an impact on these various world communities. In a similar way, *Wadabagei: A Journal of the Caribbean and Its Diaspora* has supported the development of a Caribbean Diaspora knowledge field. But a variety of particular journals, like *Caribbean Quarterly,* and the work of scholars like Maureen Warner-Lewis in her study of language and culture, have maintained an ongoing space for the discussion of a variety of diasporic subjects as they manifest themselves in the Caribbean.

A range of professional organizations like the African Literature Association, the Caribbean Studies Association, and the American Historical Association and their publications also provide a place for discussing aspects of the African Diaspora as they pertained to those fields. Encyclopedia production is another strand in this process, pulling together a range of scholars and their research but also creating that necessary library of materials that advance a field.

The Congress of Negro Artists marked the beginnings of this phase of African Diaspora intellectual and creative work in the middle of the 20th century, as already established. And formed in the late 1970s, the African Literature Association, through its conferences and publications, has been a place where African Diaspora literature has been consistently addressed. Thus, literature has been one of the foremost ways by which Diaspora identities have been articulated and a primary area in which this field of African Diaspora studies has taken shape. Some of the best pieces of literature have confronted this issue directly. The definition of "African Literatures" in the plural that comes out of journals like *Presence Africaine* and the African Literature Association refers to the range of genres and types of African literature one finds on the continent and other parts of the world. A vast field, with its specialized encyclopedias, bibliographies, yearbooks, journals, and numerous publications, has been documenting these literatures. While not including a large subject entry on African diaspora literatures, we have included salient writers, themes, concepts and texts in most categories. There are several dictionaries and encyclopedias of African-American and African literatures. Still, we can point to some classic African Diaspora texts that have engaged the themes of African Diaspora directly. *Equaiano's* Travels. *The Interesting Narrative* of the *Life of Olaudah Equiano or Gustavus Vassa, the African* (1789) as well as Mary Prince's *The History of Mary Prince, a West Indian Slave, Related by Herself* (1831) are among the first. Ayi Kwei Armah's *Two Thousand Seasons* (1973), Kamau Brathwaite's *The Arrivants* (1967), Ama Ata Aidoo's *Dilemma of a Ghost* (1965), and *Anowa* (1970), Earl Lovelace's *Salt* (1996), Grace Nichols's *I Is a Long Memoried Woman* (1983), Paule Marshall's *Praisesong for the Widow* (1983), Alice Walker's *The Color Purple* (1982), Toni Morrison's *Beloved* (1987), and Okepwho's *Call Me by My Rightful Name* (1994), Sandra Jackson-Opoku's *The River Where Blood Is Born* (1997), are some texts that have addressed African Diaspora themes. A helpful reference is Killam and Rowe, *The Companion to African Literatures* (2000), which offers larger coverage of major categories of African diaspora literatures, and Mark de Brito's *The Trickster's Tongue. An Anthology of Poetry in Translation from Africa and the African Diaspora* (2006), an ambitious collection of poetry.

A range of helpful and related concepts have come out of these literatures as we develop frameworks for doing relational work. Literary reimaginings have come through the work of writers like Ishmael Reed, Fred d'Aguiar, and Alice Walker. Aimé Césaire has talked about unboundedness in his no-fence island, expressed in his long poem, *Cahier,* and Edouard Glissant has developed the idea of *errance* or wandering. He has also advanced the discussions of creolization as conceptualized by Kamau Brathwaite, whose *tidalectics* is as fluid a construct as is Antonio Benítez-Rojo's *repeating island* imagery, both driven by water, by the sea. In this way, Gilroy's "Black Atlantic," a theoretical rearticulation of Farris Thompson's "Black Atlantic Civilizations," provides tremendous theoretical mileage (Gilroy 2006).

Discourses of migrations in history and literature continue to drive research on Diaspora. And rememory makes literature one of the central places where creative articulations take place. Aboriginal Australians have a theoretical and cultural category called "dreaming" that is worth invoking here as it has to do not only with the flow of the imagination in storytelling but also in art, history, and movement, in terms of life experience. Thus, for African Americans, concepts like polyrhythms and improvisation, as articulated in jazz or quilting, have had great utility in vernacular theory and signifying. Rinaldo Walcott's (2003) call for a Diaspora reading practice that allows for the "uncovering of the histories, memories, desires, free associations, disappointments, pleasures, and investments we bring to any given texts" (118) resonates with "diaspora literacy" (Clark) or "cultural fluency" (Mayes).

In the same way, as far as music in the African Diaspora is concerned, we have included a range of African Diaspora music forms—blues, jazz, hip-hop, highlife, salsa—though not a single entry on music. The vastness of the field forbids reduction and synthesis. A related project to which one can refer is *The African Diaspora: A Musical Perspective*, which includes a range of essays on different aspects of African Diaspora musical forms, genres, and styles. The field of ethnomusicology is a rich one, and through it much of the early African Diaspora work was carried out. Work done by Alan Lomax, J. D. Elder, Alan Waterman, and others documented a range of forms that demonstrated how African rhythmic patterns could be subjected to structural analysis. Recent DVD collections such as "*Songs of the Orisha Palais, Trinidad and Tobago*" (2005) could only be credibly mounted and sustained with that earlier sustaining work already in place. In this regard, Maureen Warner-Lewis's work in linguistics has also been amazingly solid. Her *Trinidad Yoruba* (1996) and earlier *Guinea's Other Suns* (1991) have been formidable in documenting African religions in the Caribbean at a time when African Diaspora work was not the popularly engaged in research field that it is today.

In this contemporary period, one can identify a range of academic programs and departments dedicated to the study of the African Diaspora, some of which have doctoral programs, like the University of California, Berkeley, one of the first programs to specifically offer an advanced degree in African Diaspora Studies. Approximately 25 programs (see the www.africandiasporastudies.com) have an Africana studies program or do Diaspora work in other departments. Courses like Spelman College's two-semester "African Diaspora and the World," attempt to give a general coverage of the African Diaspora akin to the Western civilizations courses that are staples of the major universities, in order to provide students with knowledge of the major historical, philosophical, artistic, and scientific developments of the African world. Therefore, work on African Diaspora communities within the larger construct of African Diaspora, can be advanced. Quite a number of scholars have engaged with or are engaging with Afro-Brazilian communities in various ways, and Afro-Brazilians themselves are beginning to be the major and best articulators of their own history and culture. Work on the Caribbean has also become a very dynamic field advanced by scholars and associations internationally. For example, the Australian Association of Caribbean Studies held a February 2007 conference in Melbourne, "Mo(ve)ments: Local, Regional, Global in Caribbean Popular Culture," that covered issues of migration and thereby of Diaspora. In this regard, the work of Linda Heywood, Maureen Warner-Lewis, and J. D. Elder has deliberately engaged Diaspora as a theoretical framework, and, as already indicated, the work on the Caribbean Diaspora (by Harry Goulbourne, Winston James, Stuart Hall, Beryl and Paul Gilroy, Alrick Cambridge, C. L. R. James, John La Rose, Claudia Jones, Amon Saba Saakana) as it relates to Caribbean communities in the United Kingdom has often offered theoretical leadership in articulating this construct, as have a range of scholars in the United States.

The broadening of the definition of Afro-America to include the north and the south brings back into focus the African Diaspora communities throughout South America. As already indicated, work on Asia and the Maghreb is also increasing, and work on Australia is another area that will likely soon be advanced. Besides the premodern migration that produced black Aboriginal inhabitants in Australia, from 1888 to 1901, black convicts are reported to have entered Australia—a group of 13 black convicts arrived with the first shipment. Often they were those convicted for minor crimes and a kind of debt peonage. And in the early 1900s there was reportedly a Sydney branch of Marcus Garvey's Universal Negro Improvement Association. Documents of letters of representatives sent overseas are available in the Garvey archives, and this is an area well worth a fuller exploration.

Overlapping or intersecting diaspora allows further relational work that looks at Indian, Jewish, Arab, Asian, Native American, Aboriginal, Latin American, and Caribbean Diasporas as these overlap or extend the boundaries of the African Diaspora. This is another area that is going to be very significant in the future. And a new African Diaspora, created by Africans migrating for economic reasons to various metropolises and other continents in the 20th century, is another key area for research. By some counts, more Africans have crossed the Atlantic in this period than in the earlier transatlantic slavery period. The products of some of these overlapping or intersecting Diaspora have been often named, misnamed, and claimed under douglarization, creolity, mulatto consciousness, hybridity, mestizaje, concepts that are also presented in this *Encyclopedia*.

WOMEN AND THE AFRICAN DIASPORA

The question of gendering the African Diaspora is one that is long in being fully articulated from the early work of conferences like the Michigan "Black Woman Writer in the African Diaspora" in 1985. Audre Lorde's work in building an international community for black women has articulated in Europe, Africa, the Caribbean, and the United States the kind of black women's Diaspora politics that parallels earlier work by Pan-Africanists to create a Zami community. Lorde's essay "Sisterhood and Survival," available in *Sister Outsider*, provides the impetus for a black woman's Diaspora. And as she stated in an interview with Pratibha Parmar and Jackie Kay, Lorde (1988) also believed some kind of international network of black women was absolutely essential.

Throughout the 1980s, the journal *Sage* had an African Diaspora orientation in terms of the kind of research it included from black women internationally. In this regard, Beverly Guy-Sheftall's essay "Feminism and Black Women and the African Diaspora," which is included in this encyclopedia, provides some important connections between women as political and intellectual organizers throughout the 20th century. A conference organized by Rosalyn Terborg-Penn at Howard University, out of which was produced *Women in Africa and the African Diaspora* (1989; ed. Rosalyn Terborg-Penn, Sharon Harley and Andrea Benton Rushing), has also been significant, recalling as it does the work of Filomena Steady in *The Black Woman Crossculturally* (1989). Both contexts have influenced at least two generations of scholars studying women and the African Diaspora. Describing itself as producing concepts, methodology, and projected guidelines for studies of women and the African Diaspora, *Women in Africa and the African Diaspora* included a nice range of scholarship on Latin American, Brazilian, African American, Caribbean, and African women and often used a quilting metaphor for the Diaspora. See also *In Praise of Black Women*, Volume 4: *Modern Women of the Diaspora* (2003). *Writings of Black Women of the Diaspora* by Lean' tin L. Bracks (1998) also used the quilting metaphor, but applies it specifically to literature. *Daughters of Africa. An International Anthology of Words and Writings by Women of African Descent from the Ancient Egyptian to the Present* (1992; ed. Margaret Busby) is an expansive and ambitious project. Earlier, Chinosole had spoken of "matrilineal Diaspora" and Grewal et al. had produced a collection of creative works titled *Charting the Journey*.

Similarly, *Black Women's Diasporas*, the second volume of *International Dimensions of Black Women's Writing* (1994; ed. Carole Boyce Davies), is perhaps one of the only places one can see the formation of black women's Diasporas in practice. Another would be Miriam DeCosta-Williams's edited collection *Daughters of the Diaspora: Afra-Hispanic Writers* (2003). In 2002, Judy Byfield organized a conference at Dartmouth College on the subject of "Gendering the African Diaspora: Gender, Culture and Historical Change in the Caribbean and Nigerian Hinterland." One of its general aims was to "encourage the production of scholarship that both extends and challenges our current writing of African and Caribbean women's history/cultures, and integrates gender analysis more systematically into our conceptualization of the African Diaspora." And the two Yari Yari Pamberi international black women's writing conferences at the turn of the century hosted by New York University brought together black women writers from all over the world.

Since then, not much has happened in an organized way on this topic, and this area of study requires further development. Individual works of a new generation of scholars, like Michelle Stephens (*Black Empire: The Masculine Global Imaginary of Caribbean Intellectuals in the United States, 1914–1962*, 2005) and Michelle Wright (*Becoming Black: Creating Identity in the African Diaspora*, 2004), have challenged the masculinist constructions of black internationalism as they have cleared the ground for the study of new African Diaspora identities that are appropriately gendered. Thus, Jane Ifekuwingwe's *Scattered Belongings. Cultural Paradoxes of "Race," Nation and Gender* (1999) and Meredith Gadsby's *Sucking Salt: Caribbean Women Writers, Migration, and Survival* (2006) advance the discourse on black women's identity in migration as earlier articulated by Carole Boyce Davies in *Black Women, Writing and Identity. Migrations of the Subject* (1994). Gadsby's own research into salt and the African Diaspora is included in this encyclopedia.

More recently, Katherine McKittrick's *Demonic Grounds. Black Women and the Cartographies of Struggle* (2006) uses Sylvia Wynter's formulation to advance the study of the geographies of women in the Diaspora. It is important to point out then, that although there have been a fair number of works on black women, the work has often dealt with individual/national or regional specifics like the United States or the Caribbean. Confronting the contributions of black women as a larger category not limited to specific national boundaries is what seems to be appearing in this new round of scholarship.

This *Encyclopedia of the African Diaspora*, although it does not specify a section on women in the African Diaspora, covers the issue of women in specific entries. It includes proportionately a large number of entries on and by women and includes subjects not often covered in general works on black women, like an entry on the 1950s black women's activist organization, Sojourners for Truth and Justice.

Early work on specific African Diaspora communities, particularly in the United States, has, for the most part, marked this discussion. Audre Lorde's "Zami" formation has already been mentioned as one model in which issues of black women's sexuality have migrated across the African Diaspora from Carricacou and the Eastern Caribbean, its places of origin, to the United States, Germany, the United Kingdom, and even South Africa in terms of Lorde's organizational schema. By these means, submerged discourses of black female sexuality that challenged heteronormatives began to be articulated. Gloria's Wekker's "Mati" work has also articulated another version, this time coming out of Suriname and the Dutch Caribbean; in many ways it is a sexual-cultural formation that is related to, although not identical to, black lesbian constructions in the United States. And though Ifi Amadiume resists the limitation of the meaning of her work to issues of sexuality in the European-American sense, her discussion of some aspects of African gender constructions in *Male Daughters, Female Husbands* (1987) has opened up issues of gender in the African context, with variations by Ronke Oyewumi *(The Invention of Women*, 1997) in her subsequent work.

A 2006 special issue of *Feminist Africa*, guest edited by Rhoda Reddock, was subtitled "Diaspora Voices" and included a range of essays from scholars in the African Diaspora. In her introductory essay, Reddock brings together for analysis the passing of the *African Protocol on Women* in relation to the passing of the African Union's African Diaspora definition, both in 2005, to underscore an African Union recommitted to gender equity and to solidifying its ongoing relationship between the continent and the Diaspora.

As far as black gay communities are concerned, work on the U.S. black gay experience has been advanced by the work of poet/activist Essex Hemphill and the filmic interventions of Marlon Riggs, such as "Black Is Black Ain't." Dwight McBride's work on James Baldwin and in advancing a more inclusive Africana Studies in general has done some of the kind of institutional work that allows the field to be cleared and that is required to advance this discourse. More substantial work has been produced for a special issue on GLBT literature and culture for the journal *Callaloo* (vol. 23, issue 1, 2000). An edited collection by Thomas Glave on literature of Caribbean/Antillean Gay communities, titled *Our Caribbean: A Gathering of Lesbian and Gay Writing from the Antilles,* is described as the first anthology of lesbian and gay writing from the Caribbean.

For scholars who discuss the question of essential identities, one has to always place the dialectics of Diaspora in the foreground. Although the idea of the home and exile is one formation raised by Elliott Skinner in the Harris book, *Global Dimensions of the African Diaspora*, some would argue that this borrows too much from the Jewish Diaspora. Although a consciousness of homeland is critical, often returning to a homeland, as in the case of Palestine, Liberia, and Sierra Leone, can be laden with conflict as it means dispossessing people who are already occupying that place and who have similar claims. Diaspora discourse can look relationally at a range of communities, even as it evokes some older historical realities. Thus, what does it include? What does it exclude? What are the erasures and disclosures? What are the loci of contradictory or contestatory understandings of Diaspora? These are still questions worth pursuing.

SCOPE OF THIS ENCYCLOPEDIA

Producing the *Encyclopedia of the African Diaspora* has been a daunting task. It was driven by the fact that many colleagues and community supporters were clear that this was a project that needed to be done and therefore they were supportive of its intent. We began with a meeting of consultants from a range of areas across the African Diaspora in order to develop a pool of intellectuals that we could engage, call on, and encourage to contribute subject essays in their specialization areas. That group decided on the pattern we have used, which covers *subject entries* of major aspects and disciplines of the African Diaspora; people, represented by *selected biographies* and coverage of ethnic groups that have contributed to the African Diaspora or had significant impact on the advancement of the discourse; *regional and country essays* on some critical areas of the African Diaspora; and topical essays on African Diaspora *concepts.* Entries were organized in terms of places (geography), people (personalities), movements (e.g., Pan-Africanism), theories (e.g., Négritude) in a straightforward A to Z order. Each entry also provides cross-references: at the end of each entry is a "See also" listing that provides researchers with a way of finding additional material on a topic.

We developed a Web site (www.africandiasporastudies.com) to update contributors on the project, solicited entries at major conferences, and created entry format models, which included original research and full coverage of the field in well-documented and concise entries, including recent discoveries and theories. A list of recommended readings for further research accompanies entries.

In terms of scope, the volumes are international in reach, covering the five continents with documented African Diaspora communities. We had excellent coverage from Latin American communities like Colombia, Bolivia, Brazil, and the Dominican Republic, Ecuador, calling on young scholars from those areas, like Paula Moreno-Zapata (Colombia), to contribute recent work, or Leana Cabral, the niece of Amilcar Cabral, also a young scholar-activist, to do an entry on Cape Verde. More experienced scholars like Marco Polo Hernandez Cuevas on Afro-Mexico or Quince Duncan on Costa Rica were contacted to contribute their research. Juan Angola Maconde of Bolivia entered this project after the ASWAD conference in Rio de Janeiro, Brazil, in 2005. And we have identified the important contribution on Afro-Ecuadorians. All of these scholars have provided knowledge of their research on their own communities. Many of these scholars have been working on their own communities in isolation and are pleased to have a location for collaborative research.

The Indian Ocean Diaspora was also well covered because of the advances in the knowledge of scholars like Shihan De Silva from that area and the TADIA (The African Diaspora in Asia) organization which hosted its first conference in Goa in January 2006. Subject essays from expert scholars in their fields, including Nkiru Nzegwu on art and the African Diaspora, Joseph Inikori on the political economy of the African Atlantic system, Monica Jardine on the Caribbean migration, and Brian Meeks on Caribbean black power have been important contributions. Many of these subject essays were presented at a conference held at Florida Memorial University in 2005. In this regard, we also encouraged and solicited entries from graduate students, allowing them by these means to have a publication profile and benefiting from the fact that they are usually the ones doing the freshest work in the field. Part of this has been advanced through the creation of FLASC—the Florida Africana Studies Consortium, which has been one of the umbrellas for this project as has African–New World Studies at Florida International University.

The purpose of this publication, as we have indicated, is to provide in one place a well-documented and readily accessible body of information about the most important historical, political, economic and cultural relations between people of African descent in the world community. What connects such a diverse group of people and wide-ranging locations across time and space? How they have affected and been affected by their environments? How have they created and re-created cultural forms and movements?

For hip-hop we decided to go with a general subject entry on hip-hop culture in the African Diaspora and then a second entry on hip-hop in Latin America. We also decided on a few exponents of the tradition, like Mos Def, rather than the proliferation of artists that one could end up having. Perhaps a future "Encyclopedia of Hip Hop Culture" will be planned at some later date.

We, the editors of this encyclopedia, envisage a library of African Diaspora materials as one similarly encounters materials on other area subjects. The audience includes students, journalists, policy makers, activists, scholars, libraries, international organizations, and all those with an interest in the African Diaspora. Our editors at ABC-CLIO have been helpful in this process, making sure that we had balance and distribution, and even providing a grid by which we could check off where each contribution came from, thereby ensuring a more even coverage. Biographies were the hardest entries to make decisions about, though the easiest submissions to receive. Though these entries tended to be shorter than most, we had to make selections carefully about what to include so the biographical entries did not go on ad infinitum. And of course everyone had his or her own list of people he or she thought should be included. At one time someone submitted his entire family for inclusion. For major contributors — scholars-activists-theoreticians like C. L. R. James—we allotted a bit more space, as they were often difficult to limit to a short 500-word entry without doing a disservice to what these people represented. The discipline that was enforced by our publisher limited entries to those who had a significant impact on the African Diaspora itself rather than on a single nation or community. The African Diaspora then and its subformations, like the "Black Atlantic" or the "Black Pacific," as units of analysis, have allowed the kind of academic inquiry that will also have impact on policy and on people's understandings of themselves in the world. This is therefore one area that does not remain as a singly academic enterprise, for in our increasingly globalized world, "Diaspora literacy," a term developed by Veve Clark and included in this volume, becomes an important way of reading the world.

Although we have attempted to obtain entries on a wide range of African Diaspora forms and manifestations that display cultural connections, we are conscious of the need to expand the knowledge base in a range of areas. We have included subject essays or shorter entries on health, sports, carnivals, hair, dance, music, and religion. For scholars in the field, a number of subject areas still remain underresearched. These include style and fashion in the African Diaspora, body, sound, food, architecture, "livity" or lived experience, and language. New work is being done on the relationships of Diaspora to transnationalism and on theories of Diaspora. Additional work on contemporary African Diasporas in places like

Australia and the South Pacific needs to be done. Some work on the Arabian Peninsula and the Mediterranean is being carried out. As we connect the nodal points of the African Diaspora via various knowledge exchanges and publications like this one, we advance understanding of world communities in that still unfinished process of reclaiming the epistemologies and thereby the humanity of African Diaspora peoples. Ideally, a web-based project that can be infinitely updated is perhaps the direction that one can pursue in the future (23).

Carole Boyce Davies
Editor

REFERENCES

Appadurai. 2006. "Disjuncture and Difference in the Global Cultural Economy." In *Theorizing Diaspora*, ed. Jana Evans Braziel and Anita Mannur, 26–48. Malden, MA: Blackwell.

Baptiste, Fitzroy A. 1998. "African Presence in India —I and II." *African Quarterly* 38 (1998): 76–90, 91–126.

Brah, A. 1996. *Cartographies of Diaspora. Contesting Identities.* London: Routledge.

Byfield, Judith. 2000. "Introduction: Rethinking the African Diaspora." Special issue on Diaspora. *African Studies Review* 43:1 (April):1–9.

Caitlin-Jairazbhoy, Amy, and Edward Alpers, eds. 2004. *Siddis and Scholars. Essays on African Indians.* Trenton, NJ: Red Sea Press.

Clifford, James. 1994. "Diasporas." *Cultural Anthropology* 9:3:302–338.

de Silva, Shihan Jayasuriya, and Richard Pankurst, eds. 2003. *The African Diaspora in the Indian Ocean.* Lawrenceville, N.J.: Africa World Press, 2003.

Diop, Cheikh Anta. 1991. *Civilization or Barbarism.* Brooklyn, New York: Lawrence Hill Books (Paris: Presence Africaine, 1981).

Drake, St. Clair. 1993. "Panafricanism and Diaspora." In *Global Dimensions of the African Diaspora*, 2nd ed., ed. Joseph E. Harris, 451–514. Washington, D.C.: Howard University Press.

Edwards, Brent Hayes. 2003. *The Practice of Diaspora: Literature, Translation, and the Rise of Black Internationalism.* Cambridge: Harvard University Press.

Gilroy, Paul. 2006. "The Black Atlantic as a Counterculture of Modernity." In *Theorizing Diaspora*, ed. Jana Evans Braziel and Anita Mannur, 49–80. Malden, MA: Blackwell.

Gomez, Michael A. 2005. *Reversing Sail. A History of the African Diaspora.* New York: Cambridge University Press.

Gomez, Michael, ed. 2006. *Diasporic Africa: A Reader.* New York: New York Univeristy Press.

Grewal, Shabnam, Jackie Kay, Liliane Landor, Gail Lewis and Pratibha Parmar. 1988. *Charting the Journey: Writing by Black and Third World Women.* London: Sheba Feminist Publishers.

Hall, Gwendolyn Midlo. 2005. *Slavery and African Ethnicities in the Americas. Restoring the Links.* Chapel Hill: University of North Carolina Press, 2005.

Hall, Stuart. "Epilogue: Through the Prism of an Intellectual Life." In Meeks (2007): 269–291.

Hall, Stuart. 2006. "Cultural Identity and Diaspora." In *Theorizing Diaspora*, ed. Jana Evans Braziel and Anita Mannur, 233–247. Malden, MA: Blackwell.

Hamilton, Ruth Simms. 1995. "Conceptualizing the African Diaspora." In *African Presence in the Americas*, ed. Carlos Moore, Taunya Saunders, and Shawna Moore, 393–410. Trenton, NJ: Africa World Press.

Hanchard, Michael. 1990. "Identity, Meaning and the African American." *Social Text* 24:31–42.

Hanchard, Michael. 1991. "Racial Consciousness and Afro-Diasporic Experiences. Antonio Gramsci Reconsidered." *Socialism and Democracy* 3 (Fall): 83–106.

Harris, Joseph E., ed. 1982. *Global Dimensions of the African Diaspora*. Washington, D.C.: Howard University Press.

Harris, Joseph. 2003. "Expanding the Scope of African Diaspora Studies: The Middle East and India, a Research Agenda." *Radical History Review* 87 (Fall): 157–68.

Hesse, Barnor, ed. 2000. *Un/settled Multiculturalisms: Diaspora, Entanglements, "Transruptions."* London: Zed Press.

Hine, Darlene Clark, and J. McLeod. 1999. *Crossing Boundaries. Comparative History of Black People in Diasporas*. Bloomington: Indiana University Press.

Hintzen, Percy C. 2007. "Diaspora, Globalization and the Politics of Identity." In Meeks, *Culture, Politics, Race and Diaspora. The Thought of Stuart Hall*, 248–268. Jamaica: Ian Randle.

Jalloh, Alusine, and Stephen E. Maizlish, eds. 1996. *The African Diasporas by Joseph Harris, Alusine Jalloh, Joseph Inikori, Colin A. Palmer, Douglas B. Chambers, Dale T. Graden*. Arlington, Texas: Texas A & M Press.

Killam, Douglas, and Ruth Rowe, eds. 2000. *The Companion to African Literatures*. Oxford: James Currey and Bloomington: Indiana University Press.

McKittrick, Katherine. 2007. "I Entered the Lists: Diaspora Catalogues." *XCP: Cross-Cultural Poetics* 17:7–29.

Meeks, Brian, ed. 2007. *Culture, Politics, Race and Diaspora. The Thought of Stuart Hall*. Kingston: Ian Randle.

Morehouse, Maggi M. 2007. "The African Diaspora: Using the Multivalent Theory to Understand Slave Autobiographies." *Diaspora, Indigenous, and Minority Education: An International Journal*. 1:3 (July-September): 199–216.

Palmer, Colin. 1998. "Defining and Studying the Modern African Diaspora." *American Historical Association Newsletter* 36 (6 September): 21–25.

Patterson, Tiffany, and Robin D. G. Kelley. 2000. "Unfinished Migrations: Reflections on the African Diaspora and the Making of the Modern World." *African Studies Review* 43 (1 April): 11–45.

Prasad, Kiran Kamal. 2005. *In Search of an Identity. An Ethnographic Study of the Siddis in Karnataka*. Bangalore, India: Jana Jagrati Prakashana.

Rashidi, Runoko, and Ivan van Sertima, eds. 1999. *African Presence in Early Asia*. New Brunswick: Transaction Publishers.

Shepperson, George. 1993. "African Diaspora: Concept and Context." In *Global Dimensions of the African Diaspora*, 2nd ed., ed. Joseph E. Harris, 41–49. Washington, D.C.: Howard University Press.

van Kessel, Ineke. 2006. "Conference Report: Goa Conference on the African Diaspora in Asia." *African Affairs (Oxford)* (June).

Van Sertima, Ivan. 2003. *They Came Before Columbus. The African Presence in Ancient America.* New York: Random House.

Walker, Sheila S., ed. 2001. *African Roots/American Cultures. Africa in the Creation of the Americas.* Lanham, Maryland: Rowman and Littlefield.

Williams, Chancellor. 1976. *Destruction of Black Civilization. Great Issues of a Race from 4500 B.C. to 2000 A.D.* Chicago: Third World Press.

Zimba, Benigna, Edward Alpers and Allen Isaacman, eds. 2005. *Slave Routes and Oral Tradition in Southeastern Africa.* Maputo, Mozambique: Filsom Entertainment, Lds.

NOTES

1. Thanks to Greek Diaspora writer Konstandina Dounis at LaTrobe University in Melbourne, Australia, and Dean Kalimniou, an expert in languages and a lawyer in Melbourne for providing details of usage in the Greek language and as it pertains to the Greek Diaspora. This information benefits from a seminar in diasporas that I gave at LaTrobe University in February 14, 2007, at which I fortuitously met Konstandina.

2. Lawrence M. Friedman. 2001. "Erewhon: the Coming Global Legal Order." *Stanford Journal of International Law* Summer: 2–11; International Monetary Fund. 2000/2001.*Globalization: Threat or Opportunity.* Issues Brief. International Monetary Fund offers some discussion of the economic implications. See also *Globalization and Its Discontents* by Saskia Sassen and Anthony Appiah (New Press, 1999).

3. A useful study of some of the theories of African diaspora is Maggi M. Morehouse, "The African Diaspora: an Investigation of the Theories and Methods Employed When Categorizing and Identifying Transnational Communities," African American Studies, University of California, Berkeley (n.d.), http://ist-socrates.berkeley.edu/~african/morehouse.pdf.

4. Interview for "African Diaspora Knowledge Exchange" conference, Florida Africana Studies Consortium (FLASC), Florida Memorial University, Miami, May 2006. Available on FLASC, DVD Series \#1, 2007.

5. Indeed, the *Encyclopedia Americana* (Danbury, CT: Scholastic Library Publishers, 15 editions, 22 volumes), under its entry on "Diaspora" indicates, "See Jews."

6. See, for example, Joseph E. Harris, "Expanding the Scope of African Diaspora Studies: The Middle East and India, a Research Agenda," *Radical History Review* 87 (Fall 2003): 157–168; Fitzroy A. Baptiste, "African Presence in India — I and II," *African Quarterly* 38:2 (1998): 76–126; *African Presence in Early Asia*, edited by Runoko Rashidi and Ivan Van Sertima (New Brunswick, NJ: Transaction Publishers, 1999); and *Slave Routes and Oral Tradition in Southeastern Africa*, edited by Benigna Zimba, Edward Alpers, and Allen Isaacman (Maputo, Mozambique: Filsom Entertainment, 2005). The most recent contribution in this area has been the conference "The African Diaspora in Asia," held in Goa, India, in January, 2006. See

Ineke van Kessel, "Conference Report: Goa Conference on the African Diaspora in Asia," *African Affairs (Oxford)* (June, 2006). See also the work *The African Diaspora in the Indian Ocean,* edited by Shihan de Silva Jayasuriya and Richard Pankurst (Trenton, NJ: Africa World Press, 2003).

7. See, for example, essays in *The African Diaspora* by Joseph E. Harris, Alusine Jalloh, Joseph Inikori, Colin A. Palmer, Douglas B. Chambers, Dale T. Graden (Austin: University of Texas Press, 1996); Michael A. Gomez, *Reversing Sail. A History of the African Diaspora* (New York: Cambridge University Press, 2005); Gwendolyn Midlo Hall, *Slavery and African Ethnicities in the Americas. Restoring the Links* (Chapel Hill: University of North Carolina Press, 2005).

8. The Universal Declaration of Human Rights, created to ensure the protection of rights and freedoms, was very clear about the need to make a statement on slavery.

9. Cheikh Anta Diop's *Precolonial Black Africa* (Independent Publishers Group, 1990) and the range of Diop's publications are reliable sources of this information based on substantial research. See also Chancellor Williams, *The Destruction of Black Civilization* (Chicago: Third World Press, 1987).

10. Examples of the most egregious of these include apartheid in South Africa, U.S. segregation laws, and Brazil's official processes of "racial democracy," which functioned to disenfranchise the majority African-derived populations.

11. This entire issue of *African Studies Review* on African Diaspora includes essays on Brazil and the Indian Ocean, which, along with the introduction by guest editor, Judith Byfield, "Rethinking the African Diaspora," are important resources in the field of African Disapora studies.

12. See also his recent edition of papers from the first Association for the Study of the Worldwide African Diaspora conference, *Diasporic Africa: A Reader* (New York University Press, 2006).

13. See Carole Boyce Davies and Babacar M'bow, "Towards African Diaspora Citizenship: Operationalizing an Already Existing Geography." In McKittrick, *Black Geographies* (South End Press, 2007).

14. *February 1965: The Final Speeches.*

15. See Web site of the African Union www.african-union.org.

16. A range of Pan-African activists, thinkers, and strategists from the continent and the African Diaspora met repeatedly in Pan African congresses beginning in 1900 and continuing throughout the century to produce the independence of Africa from colonial rule, to produce independent states, and to secure a place for a range of displaced African Diaspora peoples. These include W. E. B. DuBois, Anna Julia Cooper, Sylvester Williams, George Padmore, C. L. R. James, Marcus Garvey, Edgar Wilmot Blyden, Casely-Hayford, Kwame Nkrumah, and others. DuBois, who was at the first Pan African congress, retired to Ghana; he died and was buried there. Padmore was Nkrumah's assistant and a major architect of Pan-Africanism as articulated by Nkrumah in Ghana.

17. African Union Program Summary, Addis Ababa, Ethiopia (CM/Dec. 614 [LXCIV]).

18. See: http://democracy-africa.org/articles/diaspora02.html.

19. See: www.au2002.gov.za/docs/key oau/au act.pdf.

20. See: http://www.whadn.org/.

21. This site, which is now closed, was available at http://diaspora.northwestern.edu.

22. See the conference report, "Goa Conference on the African Diaspora in Asia" by Ineke van Kessel, *African Affairs*, June 6, 2006:1–4.

23. The late Lino de Almeida suggested that it be housed in a place like Brazil.

Maps

———◦———

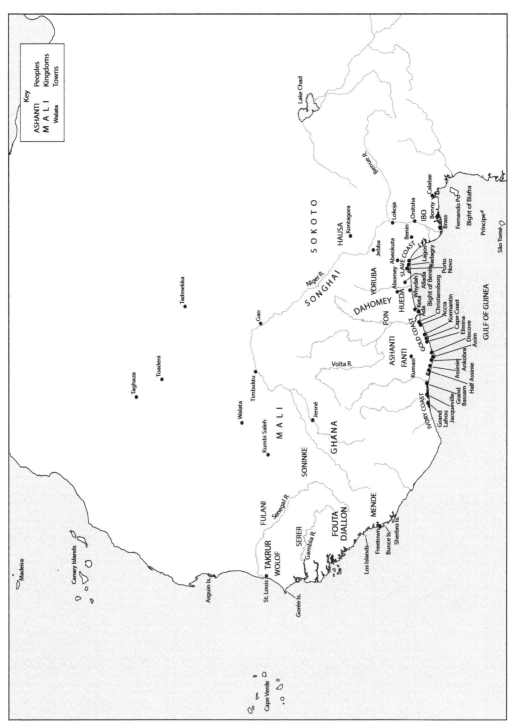

West Africa

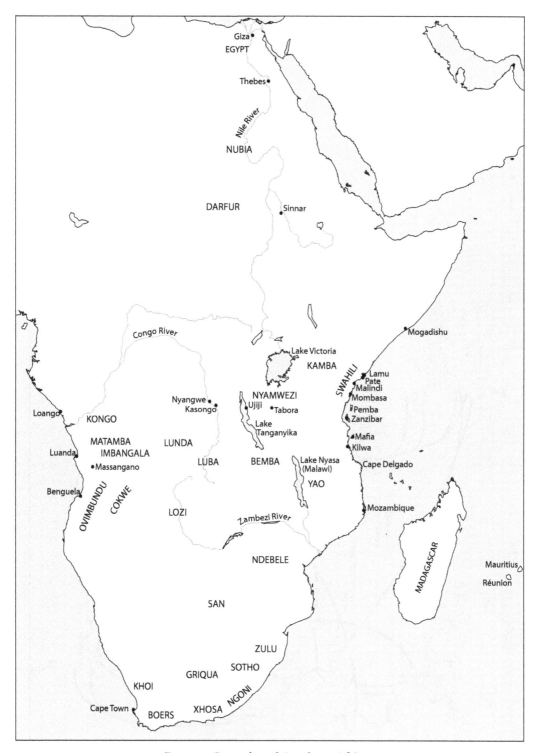

Eastern, Central, and Southern Africa

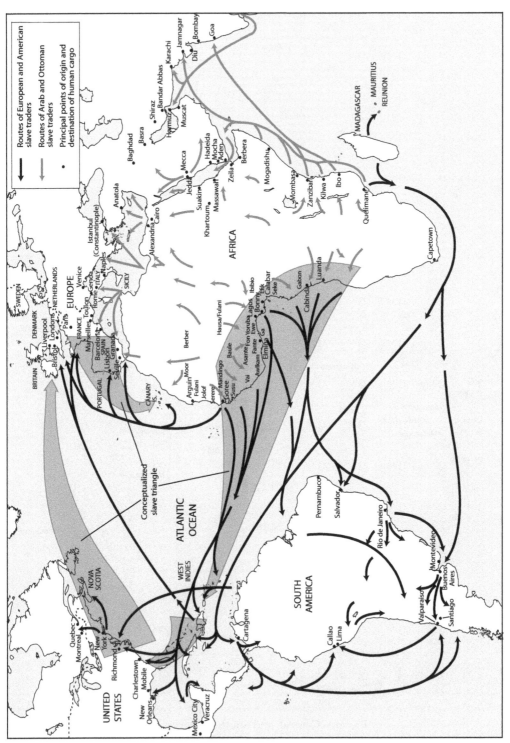

The African Diaspora

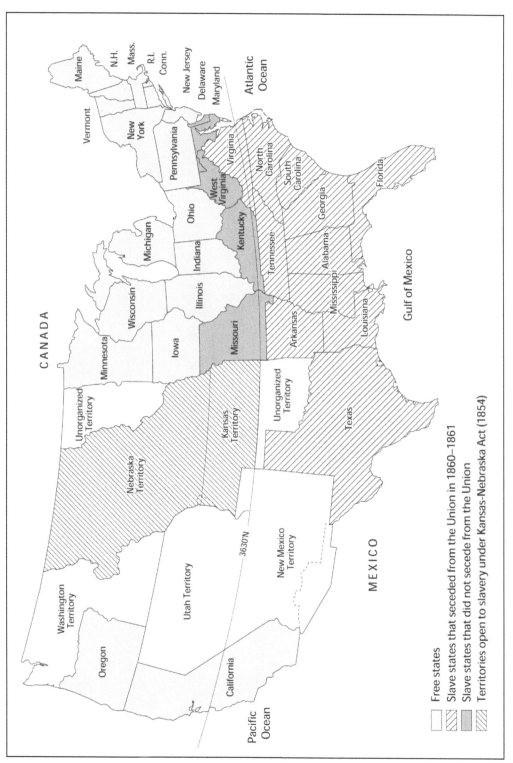

The United States

Free states

Slave states that seceded from the Union in 1860–1861

Slave states that did not secede from the Union

Territories open to slavery under Kansas-Nebraska Act (1854)

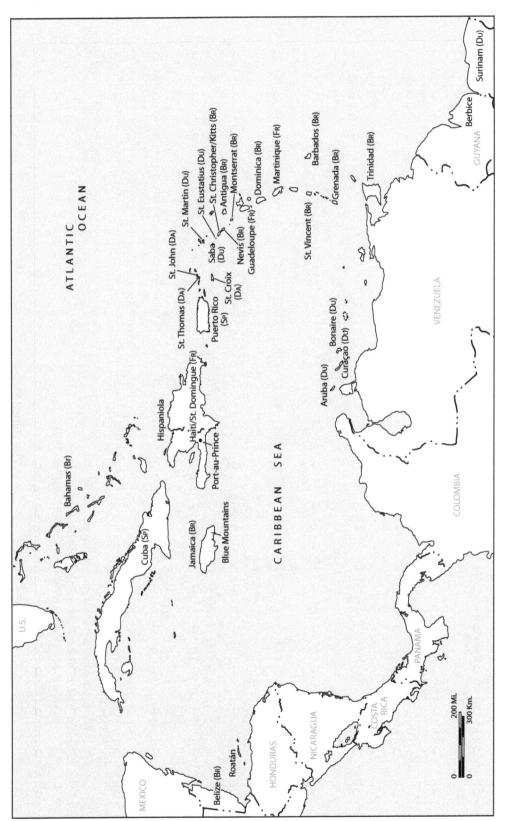

The Caribbean

ENCYCLOPEDIA OF THE
AFRICAN DIASPORA

N

NAACP

See National Association for the Advancement of Colored People (NAACP).

Nascimento, Abdias do (1914–)

Abdias do Nascimento was born in 1914 in the small town of Franca in the state of São Paulo, Brazil. One of seven children, his memories of the life of his parents and grandparents underline his own later development as an activist in the struggle of Afro-Brazilians to regain their humanity, which had been trampled on through years of slavery and subsequent discrimination and marginalization. Before her death, when Abdias was but sixteen, his mother used to tell him stories of their people's incessant suffering, including that of his maternal grandmother, who had been committed to a notorious mental institution, Juqueri, as the direct result of the harsh, horrid life Afro-Brazilians experienced. His mother also related stories about his paternal grandmother, who had been raped by a Portuguese merchant and gave birth to his father.

One event that forever affected his psyche was the story of the Afro-Brazilian abolitionist and writer Luiz Gama, mulatto son of a white aristocrat. Gama's mother, a freedwoman, was a leader of the 19th-century Male insurrection in Bahia. Luiz was born free, but his irresponsible father sold him into slavery in São Paulo to pay off gambling debts. Notwithstanding his bad fortune, Luiz was able to pull himself out of this condition, becoming a leading abolitionist and attorney, and committing himself to the the manumission of slaves until abolition in 1888.

The young Abdias was a brilliant, hardworking student. He was trained as an accountant and served six years in the Brazilian army, which he left as a result of racial discrimination. When he had enlisted in 1930, he was naive and hopeful of finding a good life in the big city of São Paulo. It was during that stint that he received a distressing telegram from home, went absent without leave and arrived to find his mother dead.

Though politically confused, Abdias was firm in his engagement with his black identity. He moved to Rio de Janeiro in 1936 where he worked as a news reporter, studied economics, and got his university degree. His entry into the Afro-Brazilian struggle began with *Frente*

Negra Brasileira (Brazilian Black Front), which was created in the 1920s. He and others organized the first youth gathering, the Afro-Campineiro Congress in 1938. In 1950, *Teatro Experimental Negro* (the Black Experimental Theater, or TEN) organized the first Congress of Brazilian Blacks in Rio. Those organizations and meetings asserted the African presence in Brazil, making blacks aware of their rights and arousing pride in their African ancestry.

Abdias was involved in protest all his life. He joined the integralist movement, a nationalist but hardly pro-black group, because of its anti-imperialist and anticapitalist agenda. There, he met people who became lifelong friends, such as the poet Gerardo Mello Mourão, and progressive bishop Helder Camara, whose name was banned from public reference by the military dictatorship. His time in that movement helped Abdias to understand the intricacy of Brazil's socioeconomic and political realities. As soon as he discovered the racist downside of the movement, he jumped ship and involved himself full time in the Afro-Brazilian movement.

After obtaining his degree in economics, Abdias returned to Rio de Janeiro. His decision to create TEN there was influenced by an experience in Lima, Peru. In 1940, he and some friends had formed the Holy Orchid Brotherhood: they were three Argentines and three Brazilians, poets all, traveling through South America, destitute but surviving on their creative energy. At Lima, they attended a production of Eugene O'Neill's *The Emperor Jones,* in which a white actor in blackface played the title role. There and then, Abdias decided to create a black theater in Brazil.

Before the inception of TEN, however, he was jailed for a club incident for which he had been discharged from the army. There, he founded a convicts' theater, thus wetting his feet as theater director. TEN's objective was to showcase Afro-Brazilian creativity and to use theater as a weapon in the struggle to improve the living conditions of blacks, while emphasizing the excellence of their culture. The doors were open to white participants, as long as they accepted the theater's premises. Abdias summarily rejected any sign of paternalism. His theater was supported by many people, including Eugene O'Neill, whose play was first on the list of productions. The premiere was held at Rio's exclusively for whites Municipal Theater on May 8, 1945, by the order of President Getulio Vargas, Brazil's dictator. TEN's future was tumultuous, victimized by detractors uncomfortable with its agenda. Always unruffled, Abdias and his group published a newspaper, *Quilombo: Black Life, Problems and Aspirations* (1949–1950), which contained a variety of thought-provoking articles and essays, such as Jean-Paul Sartre's "Black Orpheus" on Négritude, and biographical sketches on important black figures, such as Solano Trindade. *Quilombo* means "maroon society," symbol of African resistance, freedom, and survival.

From an early age, Abdias had been irked by his people's absence from the political arena. He got involved in politics in Rio and ran unsuccessfully for office on several occasions. In his opinion, his failure was due to racism. Political success came upon his return from exile in 1981, after the military dictatorship ended. He won elections for the National Congress in 1982, becoming the first African-Brazilian representative explicitly dedicated to advancing Afro-Brazilian concerns. In 1990, he became the first Afro-Brazilian senator in Brazil's National Assembly. In 1991, when Leonel Brizola, the new governor of Rio, created a state secretariat for the defense and promotion of black peoples, he appointed Abdias as secretary.

Abdias's international African Diaspora experience was enabled when he was invited to New York on a grant in 1968. In the United States, he had the opportunity to continue his scholarly, cultural, artistic, and political work and to gain the recognition that was denied him back home. He derived special joy from the attitude of New York City's African American community. He met important figures and participated in demonstrations by black students, joining those at Harvard who were keeping vigil at the president's office for divestment from apartheid South Africa. He visited the Black Panthers' headquarters in Oakland and met Bobby Seale.

Abdias was invited to several institutions as professor, lecturer, and fellow. At the State University of New York at Buffalo, he was named full professor. Notwithstanding all those gratifying successes, the African-Brazilian neither forgot his African roots nor the fact of American racism. He once went to the New York Human Rights Commission to report a woman who refused to rent him an apartment. He was invited twice to speak to the Congressional Black Caucus, in 1980 and 1983, the latter occasion as member of Brazil's National Congress. The U.S. example showed him the sad state of race relations in Brazil. It was also during the American exile that he met and married his wife, Elisa.

Pan-Africanism is well documented in his travels on the African continent, and involvement in many activities on behalf of his ancestral home. He visited Nigeria in 1977 during the FESTAC (Festival of African Culture). Despite the fact that he was excluded from the official Brazilian delegation, Abdias made a name for himself with a fiery statement on Brazilian racism; the text became the seminal book *O Genocídio do Negro brasileiro* (*The Genocide of Brazilian Blacks*).

He was one of the driving forces behind several congresses on black culture held in the African Diaspora. He delivered the inaugural lecture at the W. E. B. DuBois Center for Pan-African Culture in Accra, Ghana, in 1988. The following year, he spent a month in Angola as a United Nations Education, Scientific, and Cultural Organization (UNESCO) consultant. On March 21, 1990, he was present at Windhoek for the ceremony of Namibia's independence, which he considers "the crowning event in these Pan-African peregrinations."

Since his return to Brazil in 1981, Abdias has done much more than participate in politics.

He founded the Afro-Brazilian Studies and Research Institute (IPEAFRO), which sponsored the Third Congress of Black Culture in the Americas (São Paulo 1982). In 1984, the institute, in conjunction with South West Africa People's Organization and the United Nations, organized a seminar on 100 years of Namibia's struggle for independence. It also created the teacher's cultural training program, *Sankofa: Consciousness of African Culture in Brazil*, held at São Paulo's Catholic University in 1983–1984, and at Rio's State University in 1984–1995. He was a keynote speaker at the 2001 World Conference against Racism, in Durban, South Africa.

Abdias is a prolific writer, and his books have been translated into many languages. He has edited two journals, *Afrodiaspora* and *Thoth*. His artwork has been exhibited at several venues, in Brazil and abroad, most recently in Rio (2005). Of the many awards given to him, one of the most memorable was the UNESCO Toussaint L'Ouverture Prize, after his 2004 nomination for the Nobel Peace Prize. His abstract paintings constitute a dimension of his creativity of which many may be unaware. Similar to his writings and thoughts, the art emanates from and is immersed in African culture as the basis for his humanity. Although not a Candomblé initiate, Abdias loves and respects the Orisha, deities of Ifa, traditional African religion, and the figures he portrays, even though abstract in the Eurocentric sense, are filled with symbols of Ogun, Sango, Yemanja, and others.

His Pan-Africanist philosophy is called *quilombismo*, derived from *quilombo*, the independent state established by the maroons who ran away from slave plantations. It is defined and explained in his 1980 book, *Quilombo*. The idea is for all Africans, continental and diasporic, to eschew all forms of bondage and to come together beyond national borders for true liberation, culturally, socially, and economically. The importance of Africa remains the anchor of Abdias's political and cultural program. Throughout his life, he has always sought respect for African Brazilians, and his ultimate goal is to "build an African Brazil."

Femi Ojo-Ade

See also Brazil: Afro Brazilians; Diasporic Marronage; Guyana; Movimento Negro Unificado; Pan-Africanism.

FURTHER READING
Butler, Kim D. 1998. *Freedoms Given. Freedoms Won. Afro Brazilians in Post Abolition Sao Paulo and Salvador*. New Brunswick, NJ: Rutgers University Press.
Nascimento, Abdias do. 1992. *Africans in Brazil*. Trenton NJ: Africa World Press.
Nascimento, Abdias do. 2003. *Quilombo Vida Problemas e Aspiracoes de Negro Edicato*.

Nation of Islam

The Nation of Islam (NOI) has proven to be one of the most influential and longest-lasting black nationalist organizations in the United States and beyond. The organization, originally known as "Allah Temple of Islam," was founded in 1930 by Wallace D. Fard (Master Fard Muhammad) with the aim of restoring black people living in "The Wilderness of North America" to what he viewed as their rightful original position in civilization socially, morally, spiritually, and economically.

According to the fundamental teachings of the NOI, Fard was a traveler from the Holy City of Mecca who had been studying blacks in the United States for well over a decade before he "made himself known" to them as a silk peddler in Detroit, Michigan, on July 4, 1930. Certain scholars argue that Fard joined and/or loosely took part in several major black nationalist groups before founding the NOI, including the Moorish Science Temple of America, the Garvey Movement, and the Hebrew Israelites. A large number of scholars,

most of whom express extremely critical views of the NOI, have strongly questioned Fard's claimed identity and have attempted to show that he has Polynesian or even Pakistani origins. Yet the strongest criticism made about the NOI is its teachings surrounding the concept of "race" (i.e., the black people being the "original" and "chosen" people and the white people being the "devil").

Because of these beliefs principally, both Islamic and non-Islamic scholars have questioned the NOI's legitimacy as a true Islamic community. Yet what has not been taken into context within opposing views on this matter are the greatly intolerant views that the Arab world has by and large adopted against people of other cultures who accept Islam according to their distinct cultural understanding, especially African peoples. Hence, several West African Islamic civilizations were invaded by traditional (i.e., Arab-leaning) Islamic groups before the advent of the transatlantic slave trade because they believed mixing traditional West African customs with Islam was not true Islamic practice.

After Fard mysteriously left the United States in 1934, reportedly to Mexico, the NOI continued under the leadership of one of Fard's most committed students, Elijah Poole (now renamed Elijah Muhammad). It was at this point that Elijah Muhammad no longer taught that Fard was merely a prophet but "Allah in his person." Consequently, Elijah Muhammad was now elevated to the status of "messenger"—the last messenger before the destruction of America, which they believed would come at the hands of Allah himself.

The NOI received considerable notice throughout the 1940s and 1950s as Elijah Muhammad wrote articles for the nationally circulated black-owned newspaper *The Pittsburgh Courier*. However, the NOI rose to prominence and reached a zenith in its membership after the airing of a week-long television special called "The Hate That Hate Produced" with Mike Wallace in 1959. Strongly

A young girl in the company of women of the Nation of Islam listens to Minister Farrakhan's speech at the Millions More Movement march in Washington D.C. in October, 2005. (Noelle Theard)

influencing the NOI's growth at the time was a fiery young minister named Malcolm X, who became the organization's national spokesperson, responsible for building the membership of several temples (mosques) throughout the country.

Malcolm X eventually left the NOI and was assassinated in 1965 by men popularly believed to be NOI members. However, out of the three assassins the only one who was actually caught at the scene was Talmadge Hayer, who was reportedly never a registered member of the NOI. Hayer testified that the other two men who were controversially identified, convicted of and charged with the crime, Norman 3X Butler and Thomas 15X Johnson (both NOI members), were not present at the scene and were not involved in the shooting. Although frequently denied, it has long been suspected that the Federal Bureau of Intelligence (FBI) played a central role in the assassination of

Malcolm X in its well-documented mission to prevent the rise of a "black messiah" as a part of its larger counterintelligence program aimed to "expose, disrupt, misdirect, discredit, or otherwise neutralize" the activities of "radical" movements and their leaders. In 1968, the FBI admitted that it had an agent working in a high position in the NOI.

After Elijah Muhammad's death in 1975 (although certain NOI splinter groups argue that he is still alive), the council chose his son Wallace to become the supreme minister of the NOI. Soon after, Wallace, who changed his name to Al-Imam Warith Deen Muhammad, did away with his father's organizational structure and much of its religious beliefs, and moved the NOI toward Sunni Islam. Many of the farms and successful businesses owned by the NOI were sold.

Several years later, out of dissatisfaction with Warith Deen's leadership, several splinter organizations emerged under the NOI banner. The most successful among them has been led by Louis Farrakhan, who in 1968 became the NOI's second national spokesperson. Under Farrakhan's leadership, the NOI has continued its program of black self-determination and self-improvement. In 1995, Farrakhan organized the historic Million Man March, which was attended by nearly 2 million men. The message of the march was focused on encouraging young black men to reaffirm responsibility at home and in the community. The march inspired the formation of a series of other marches with similar aims (i.e., the Million Women's March, the Million Youth's March, the Million Family March, and most recently, the Millions More Movement: 10th Anniversary of the Million Man March). As Farrakhan has increased the NOI's presence and participation into the mainstream, so has its cultural diversity increased; it now includes a considerable Latino membership, and mosques and study groups are being developed in Canada, England, Africa, and several Caribbean countries.

Antonio Ugalde-Muhammad

See also COINTELPRO; Garvey, Marcus Mosiah (1887–1940); Malcolm X (1925–1965); Male Revolt; Pan-Africanism; Women and Islam.

FURTHER READING
Brent Turner, Richard. 1997. *Islam in the African American Experience.* Bloomington: Indiana University Press.
Gardell, Mattias. 1996. *In the Name of Elijah Muhammad. Louis Farrakhan and the Nation of Islam.* Durham, NC: Duke University Press.
Gomez, Michael. 2005. *Black Crescent. The Experience and Legacy of African Muslims in the Americas.* New York: Cambridge University Press.
Lincoln, C. Eric. 1994. *The Black Muslims in America,* 3rd ed. Trenton, NJ: Africa World Press.
Marsh, Clifton. 1996. *From Black Muslims to Muslims: The Resurrection, Transformation, and Change of the Lost-Found Nation of Islam in America, 1930–1995,* Lanham, MD: The Scarecrow Press.

Muhammad, Elijah. 1992. *Message to the Blackman in America,* United Brothers Communications Systems.

National Association for the Advancement of Colored People (NAACP)

The National Association for the Advancement of Colored People (NAACP), founded in 1909, was one of the first civil rights organizations to take direct action in addressing the issues of disenfranchisement of the African American community during the 20th and 21st centuries. Using the legal system, the organization worked with chapters all across the United States to enfranchise African Americans by ending segregation and enforcing the Fourteenth and Fifteenth Amendments of the U.S. Constitution (Franklin 1967). The multiracial organization also worked to end white racialized violence against blacks (both mob violence and lynching) and to end educational disparities between black and white children.

The organization's founding was sparked by the growing racialized violence against African Americans in the United States, which culminated in race riots in Brownsville, Texas in August 1906; Atlanta, Georgia, in September 1906; and Springfield, Ohio, in 1909. Another spark was provided by William English Walling's article "Race War in the North," which appeared in *The Independent* on September 3. 1908, and chronicled the Springfield riot in which whites went on a rampage, terrorizing the black community. The white mob lynched two African American men, one of whom was 84 years old, and burned black-owned homes and businesses (Franklin 1967, Bennett 1969, Fox 1970, Robinson 1997).

The NAACP was founded by anti-lynching crusader Ida B. Wells-Barnett, chairwoman of the Anti-Lynching League; W. E. B. DuBois, scholar and civil rights activist (DuBois was the only black officer and was the director of publicity and research); New York high school teacher William L. Buckley; Pastor Theodore Dwight Weld and his wife, abolitionist Angelina Grimke; and Bishop Alexander Walters of the AME Zion Church and president of the Afro-American Council. Some participants of the Niagara Movement, such as publisher and activist William Monroe Trotter, initially refused to join the organization because of their distrust of white people (Fox 1970). The white founders of the NAACP included those liberals who were upset by the riot in Springfield, such as civil rights activist and writer Walling, social worker Mary White Ovington, abolitionist Oswald Garrison Villiard, and physician Henry Moscowitz. The white founders of the organization were wary of Wells and Trotter because of their militant stances on lynching and black civil rights. Still, because of DuBois's presence as a board member, the organization was considered very radical and militant (Bennett 1969, Franklin 1967).

The NAACP became a formal organization in 1910. In the 1920s, the group adopted "Lift Every Voice and Sing" as its official anthem. The lyrics were written by James Weldon Johnson, a founder of the NAACP who served as its secretary from 1917 to 1930, and the music was written by his brother, J. Rosamond Johnson.

Two important arms of the NAACP include the *Crisis Magazine*, which reports on the issues and concerns of the black community and calls for change, and the Legal Redress Committee, which takes legal action related to civil rights issues such as segregation. The group has had many legal victories, including a Supreme Court decision banning the grandfather clause and the victory over racial segregation in *Brown v. The Board of Education Topeka*; the latter case was one of 32 won by Thurgood Marshall, who acted as special counsel to the NAACP before being appointed to the U.S. Supreme Court.

Paula Marie Seniors

See also DuBois, William Edward Burghardt (1868–1963); Johnson, J. Rosamond (1873–1954); Johnson, James Weldon (1871–1938); "Lift Every Voice and Sing."

FURTHER READING

Bennett, Lerone. 1969. *Before the Mayflower: A History of Black America.* Chicago: Johnson Publishing Company.

Fox, Stephen R. 1970. *The Guardian of Boston.* New York: Atheneum.

Franklin, John Hope. 1967. *From Slavery To Freedom.* New York: Alfred A. Knopf.

Logan, Rayford W. 1969. *The Betrayal of the Negro: From Rutherford B. Hayes to Woodrow Wilson.* London: Collier-Macmillan.

Robinson, Cedric J. 1997. *Black Movements in America.* New York: Routledge.

Moon, Henry Lee. 1972. *The Emerging Thought of W.E.B. DuBois.* New York: Simon and Schuster.

National Black Feminist Organization (NBFO)

The National Black Feminist Organization (NBFO) was founded in New York in 1973. The NBFO is important to African Diasporan history because it was the first nationally recognized organization that sought to address the simultaneity of oppressions (race, class, gender, and sexual orientation) that affect black women's lives. Even though most black political movements were fought out of the need for people of African descent in the U.S. to be understood and redefined for themselves and by themselves, and women's political movements were fought out of the need to be redefined as women, historically the political agendas of white women and black men had never addressed the specific oppressions experienced by black women. The Civil Rights Movements, other black liberation movements, and the women's movements of the 1950s and 1960s were recent replays of this same dynamic.

By 1970, the lack of positive representation in the media, political agendas, and the overall dehumanization of the black female experience and life in America created a sociopolitical body of scholarship and protest that placed black women at the center of their historical, political, spiritual, emotional, and psychological experiences, making them the focus and subjects of their own relatively defined histories and current realities. Using the donated offices of the National Organization of Women (NOW), a group of 30 Black Feminists gathered in May 1973, to discuss the same issues black women had been discussing for more than 173 years.

The NBFO wanted the black community and the larger society to recognize that there was indeed a black feminist politics that had a long history and current relevance within the black community and larger society. A second aim of the NBFO was to ensure that the black community, black political movements, the contemporary feminist movement, and larger society recognized the importance of looking at oppression through a matrix of domination and simultaneity. More specifically, the NBFO wanted the world to see that racism, sexism, classism, and heterosexism did and do exist in isolation from one another, but they often intersect, which makes their effect on the lives of black women that much more severe. The NBFO also recognized the need for a national organization to address all of these issues in order to finally eradicate them within the national consciousnesses of the United States and the world.

The NBFO fought for minimum wage for domestic workers; raised consciousness about rape and sexual abuse in the black community and larger society; worked with political candidates who supported NBFO issues; and confronted the racist and sexist media, which continually portrayed black women as jezebels, mammies, or tragic mulattoes. The NBFO also fought for reproductive rights for black women; an end to the sterilization abuse of black women and other women of color; equal access to abortion, health care, and child care; welfare rights; an end to anti-imperialist struggles; lesbian and gay rights; an end to police brutality; the preservation of the environment; labor unions; nuclear disarmament; and antiracism issues. The NBFO membership included black women from all classes and addressed issues that pertained to all of them.

The NBFO held its first Eastern Regional Conference in New York in November 1973. For one of the first times in history more than 500 black feminist women from around the world gathered together to form independent chapters of the NBFO. One of the most recognized grassroots chapters that formed out of this conference was the Combahee River Collective (CRC). In 1977, the CRC, which was socialist at its core, issued one of the most publicly recognized position papers on the intersections of race, class, gender, and sexual orientation. The CRC broke new ground in the development of other black feminist organizations.

Even though the NBFO dissolved in 1977, sister organizations, publications, and conferences, such as the first National Conference for Black Women in Otara, New Zealand, in 1980, grew out of it, and a black feminist intellectual and political movement continues to protest and work to eradicate the oppression of black women at the regional, national, and transnational levels.

Kaila Adia Story

See also Combahee River Collective; Cooper, Anna Julia (1859–1964); Davis, Angela (1944–); Feminism: Black Feminist Movement in the United States; Feminism and Black Women in the African Diaspora; Lorde, Audre (1934–1992); Sojourners for Truth and Justice.

FURTHER READING

Cole, Johnnetta Betsch, and Beverly Guy-Sheftall. 2003. *Gender Talk: The Struggle for Women's Equality in African American Communities.* New York: Johnson Publishing Co.

Collins, Patricia Hill. 1998. *Fighting Words: Black Women and Search for Justice.* Minneapolis: University of Minnesota Press.

Giddings, Paula. 1984. *When and Where I Enter: The Impact of Black Women on Sex and Race in America*. New York: HarperCollins Publishers.

Mankiller, Wilma, Gwendolyn Mink, Marysa Navarro, Barbara Smith, and Gloria Steinem, eds. 1998. *Reader's Companion to U.S. Women's History*. New York: Houghton Mifflin Company.

Sheftall-Guy, Beverly. 1995. *Words of Fire: An Anthology of African American Feminist Thought*. New York: New Press.

National Coalition of Blacks for Reparations in America (N'COBRA)

The National Coalition of Blacks for Reparations in America (N'COBRA) defines reparation as a process of repairing, healing, and restoring a people who have been injured by governments or businesses because of their group identity and in violation of their fundamental human rights. Those injured from such inhumanity have the right to obtain from the governments or businesses responsible for the injuries what is needed to repair and heal themselves. In addition to being a demand for justice, it is a principle of international human rights law. As a remedy, it is similar to the remedy for damages in domestic law that holds a person responsible for injuries suffered by another when the infliction of the injury violates domestic law.

Examples of groups that have obtained reparations include Jewish victims of the Nazi Holocaust; Japanese Americans interned in concentration camps in the United States during World War II; Alaska Natives for land, labor, and resources taken; victims of the 1923 massacre in Rosewood, Florida, and their descendants; Native Americans as a remedy for violations of treaty rights; and political dissenters in Argentina and their descendants.

N'COBRA is a grassroots, coalition organization, founded in 1987. Its primary goal is to win full reparations for black African descendants residing in the United States and its territories for the genocidal war against Africans that created the transatlantic slave trade, chattel slavery, and Jim Crow laws and for the continuing vestiges of racial discrimination, which result in dual systems in virtually every area of life, including punishment, health care, education, and wealth, while maintaining the myths of white superiority and black inferiority.

To help win reparations, N'COBRA has initiated several strategic fronts. Its legislative front focuses on lobbying and passing reparations proclamations, resolutions, bills, and laws at all levels (for example, organizations, cities, counties, states, U.S. Congress), while its litigation front files reparations lawsuits of all types for the African holocaust of enslavement and its vestiges, for example, filing against individuals, families, corporations, and the U.S. and other governments. N'COBRA's grassroots and popular support front creates and distributes brochures and holds public forums (for example, town hall meetings and conferences to inform and educate the people of this important movement), while its international front lobbies and petitions international governing bodies, such as the United Nations, the World Court, and the African Union for support.

Although N'COBRA's primary focus is on obtaining reparations for African descendants in the United States, it is part of the international movement for reparations. N'COBRA's International Affairs Commission (NIAC) is the arm of N'COBRA that is responsible for building effective international support, linkages, strategies, cooperation, and partnerships with reparations movements in other parts of the world. Representing N'COBRA, NIAC was very active during the preparatory process for the World Conference Against Racism and the Non-Governmental Organization Forum and government conference held in Durban, South Africa, in 2001. N'COBRA leaders were instrumental in forming the African and African Descendants Caucus during the preparatory process. Under NIAC leadership, N'COBRA played a leading role in the International Front of Africans for Reparations, which was formed at the African and African Descendants Conference in Bridgetown, Barbados, in 2002, and is a founding member of the Global African Congress, which was also organized there.

NIAC is currently cochaired by Aurevouche Dorothy Benton Lewis, a founding member of N'COBRA, former national cochair of N'CO-BRA, and representative to the Global African Congress; and Sababu Shabka, a member of N'COBRA since the mid-1990s and former education adviser to the International Medical Exchange, a health advocacy nonprofit for African health care services. Collectively, both cochairs have travelled extensively in Africa, North and South America, the Caribbean, Europe, and the Middle East. Recently, they worked with international reparations groups in planning an International Reparations Conference that was held in Ghana in July 2006. N'COBRA continues with its organizing activity, conferences and actions, which are all designed to achieve reparations for African descendants victimized by the oppressive systems of enslavement, colonialism, segregation, discrimination, and continuing social and economic inequities.

Kwame K. Afoh

See also Pan-Africanism; Reparations.

FURTHER READING
N'COBRA Web site. www.ncobra.org (accessed January 12, 2008).

Ndyuka Maroons

See Suriname: The Ndyuka Maroons.

Négritude

Négritude, a political and cultural movement and theory of black solidarity and antiracism, was first developed in Paris in the 1930s and 1940s by Aimé Césaire, Léopold Senghor, and Léon Damas. Although the movement attempted to unite all black peoples in the world who had been subjugated by European colonialism and Western racism, it insisted on the centrality of Africa (and hence slavery) in determining black pride. Inspired by the Harlem Renaissance and theorized about often via poetry, the movement led to the 1947 launch of the bilingual journal *Présence Africaine.* Headed by Alioune Diop, *Présence Africaine* was also (and still is) a prolific publisher of literature from across the black world. Through its conferences in the 1950s, Négritude became the reference point for anticolonial and antiracist struggles and debates around the world and helped develop the Pan-Africanist movement.

Senghor had originally taken the idea for Négritude from the 19th-century black American Edward Wilmot Blyden. Blyden was famous for his interest in establishing parallels between the manner in which Jews and African peoples had experienced modernity, a world-comparatist viewpoint that would resurface in Césaire's work. Renowned for its lack of a coherent and agreed definition, the Négritude movement has often been criticized (rather abstractly) as an antiracist form of "racism," as it was perceived to promote black culture as superior to white culture. However, a reading of key texts such as Césaire's 1950 speech *Discourse on Colonialism* shows the character of the movement as merely a stage toward black liberation and the end of racism, rather than an end in itself. Once the cultural imbalance foisted on blacks by European colonialism and slavery, whereby Africa and its Diasporas were deemed inferior to the advanced West, was challenged and redressed, the need for Négritude would, argued Césaire, be "dépassé" (surpassed). This is the tone of Sartre's renowned

1947 essay "Orphée noir," and of the writings of Frantz Fanon. This idea of Négritude as a time-bound movement demanding equality was specifically disputed by Senghor; in a 1976 speech, he claimed, in rather staunch essentialist fashion, that blackness, Négritude, was a fundamental cultural feature of Africa and its Diaspora, and not merely a stage (or tactic) toward liberation. Indeed, Senghor's writings throughout his life underlined his commitment to this essentialist understanding of the idea, writings that link Négritude to humanism and African authenticity in a manner that now seems to have more to do with Senghor's role as father and president of newly independent Senegal than with a theory and practice of antiracist and anticolonial liberation. At the same time, as Arnold (1981) points out, Césaire's *Discourse* displayed an ambiguous form of Marxism that, after the Soviet invasion of Hungary in 1956, became difficult for Césaire to maintain. Indeed, Césaire wrote his famous "Letter to Maurice Thorez," then leader of the French Communist Party, announcing his resignation from the party.

For Fanon, Négritude and its celebration of culture and history did not go far enough, or rather needed to be supplanted by world anticolonialism. As expressed in his book, *The Wretched of the Earth* (1961), Martinican poet, novelist and one-time activist Edouard Glissant is also tactfully and strategically critical of Négritude, insisting that Négritude is a moment, albeit a total one, for the oppressed black, that ceases to exist when the oppressed takes up arms against racial discrimination or colonial oppression. Thus, though adapting the "dépassement" thesis in Césaire's conception of Négritude, Glissant is quick to point to its inability to suggest an alternative world.

Other criticisms of Négritude are apparent. Creole theorists have criticized Négritude for its universalist pretensions, seeing them as mirroring European colonialism's ideology of expansion. A gendered version of the Négritude debate also exists as a specifically female critique of Négritude's masculinist poetics and politics. There have also been a number of Marxist critiques of Négritude, notably by Haitian poet René Depestre.

Having received a powerful rebuttal by Césaire to his criticisms of Négritude in the form of a poem (in 1956), Depestre set out his Marxist critique of Négritude in his famous *Bonjour et adieu à la négritude* (1980). First, he argued, there is a paradox at the heart of Négritude. Formulated to awaken and sustain the dignity of black people, who had been considered worthless animals because of slavery, Négritude had only succeeded in turning pride and self-confidence into a "somatic metaphysics." Rather than arm consciences against underdevelopment, Négritude dissolved its black constituents into a "perfectly inoffensive essentialism," for a "system" (presumably capitalism and/or imperialism) that denies people their identity. "Negrologists," argued Depestre, present Négritude as exclusive to African peoples, whether in Africa or the Americas, and as irrespective of the social, material, and above all class position in society that each black person occupies. Moreover, "recuperated" by neocolonialism, the movement was being used to hide those determinisms in poor black people's lives that were also the conditions of their struggle for liberation: once a form of cultural "marronage," Négritude was now a "state ideology."

Indeed, critics have rightly pointed out that many African and Caribbean rulers since independence have benefited politically from the concept of Négritude, by twisting it to justify their autocratic regimes. Senghor could certainly be accused of this in Senegal not to mention Colonel Mobutu, whose projects of authenticity and "bantuization" of Zaire drew heavily on Négritude. Haiti's François "Papa Doc" Duvalier would similarly use a form of "noirisme." Wole Soyinka, the Nigerian winner of the 1986 Nobel Prize for Literature, also wondered, if the tiger does not need to proclaim its "tigritude," why black people should need to proclaim in words their "blackness"; rather they should act. This position itself has been challenged and revised by Soyinka himself.

Andrew Stafford

See also Blyden, Edward Wilmot (1832–1912); Césaire, Aimé (1913–2008); Maroon and Marronage; *Présence Africaine*.

FURTHER READING

Arnold, A. James. 1981. *Modernism and Négritude. The Poetry and Poetics of Aimé Césaire*. Cambridge, MA: Harvard University Press.

Beti, Mongo, and Odile Tobner. 1989. *Dictionnaire de la Négritude*. Paris: L'Harmattan.

Jack, Belinda Elizabeth. 1996. *Négritude and Literary Criticism. The History and Theory of 'Negro-African' Literature in French*. Westport, CT: Greenwood Press.

Netherlands Antilles and the African Diaspora

The Netherlands Antilles consists of six islands in the Caribbean: Saint Martin, Saint Eustatius, and Saba, which belong to the Leeward Islands (Saint Martin is partly Dutch and partly French), and Curaçao, Bonaire, and Aruba, which are the Windward Islands (Lesser Antilles). The Windward Islands are situated some 900 kilometers from the Leeward Islands, close to the mainland of Venezuela. The islands today have an autonomous position within the kingdom of the Netherlands, which is made up of the three countries: Aruba, the Netherlands Antilles, and the Netherlands.

From 1568 to 1648 the Dutch were at war with Spain. In 1580, Spain conquered Portugal and expelled Dutch traders from the country. This meant that the Dutch had to find an alternative for the Portuguese salt that was used in the herring industry, and the Caribbean seemed to be a good alternative. At the end of the 16th and in the first decades of the 17th centuries, private Dutch merchants and privateers were active in the Caribbean. The Dutch government supported the foundation of the Dutch West India Company (WIC) in 1621 to regulate the trade to Africa and America. The main aim of this company was to extend the war against Spain. After the WIC occupied part of northern Brazil (1624–1654), slave trading became a major factor in WIC's history. Seeking strongholds in the Caribbean in the struggle against Spain, the WIC conquered the island of Curaçao in 1634. The neighboring islands of Aruba and Bonaire followed. In the Leeward Islands, Saint Martin, Saint Eustatius, and Saba also became Dutch colonies. In 1648, Saint Martin was divided into a French and a Dutch part.

During the Brazilian experience the Dutch conquered the Portuguese slave center of Elmina on the West African coast in 1637, which accelerated the nascent Dutch slave trade. From Elmina many Dutch slave ships crossed the Atlantic Ocean to Brazil, Surinam, Curaçao, and Saint Eustatius. Elmina was one of more than 20 Dutch trading posts in West Africa in the 17th century. Curaçao and Saint Eustatius were crucial staple markets for the Dutch slave trade from Africa. Dutch slave exports from Africa from 1620 to 1803 totaled approximately at 550,000 or 5 percent of the whole transatlantic black Diaspora; 64 percent of these slaves were men. Most slaves came from the Gold Coast, the Slave Coast, and the Loango-Angola region. The Dutch West Indian islands were not really suitable for large-scale plantation production, and the WIC saw more possibilities selling slaves from Curaçao and Saint Eustatius to the Spanish and English colonies in the Caribbean. About 92,000 slaves were transported to Curaçao and 29,000 to Saint Eustatius, and from there they were sold to the Caribbean region.

Compared with most of the sugar-producing Caribbean colonies the percentage of slaves in the population was low, and the ratio of whites to slaves was atypical. In 1789, the Dutch Leeward Islands had about 4,256 whites, 785 free "coloreds," and 9,400 slaves. Slaves formed 65 percent of the total population, and the ratio of whites to slaves was 1 to 2.2. In Curaçao there were 3,564 whites, 4,560 free non-whites, and 12,864 slaves in 1789. Slaves made up 61.3 percent of the population and the ratio of whites to slaves was 1 to 3.6. This meant that many slave owners were in direct and personal contact with their slaves. On the largest island, Curaçao, more than 60 percent of the slave owners possessed less then five slaves in the period from 1735 to 1863. In 1764, this island counted 534 owners and 5,534 slaves, but only five masters had more than 100 slaves. Compared with Suriname the slave population in the Dutch Antilles saw a continuous natural increase in the 19th century. This is in sharp contrast with the large plantation societies in the Caribbean. The reasons for this increase were the labor conditions, the nature of slavery, and a higher level of fertility of the female slaves. A proof of these favorable factors are figures from a reliable 1845 report stating that 70 percent of slave children on Curaçao reached the age of 12, while in Suriname only 50 percent survived to this age.

The plantations in the Dutch Antilles did not produce for a world market and that made a big difference in the conditions and treatment of slaves. Dutch travelers tell us that slaves of Curaçao were afraid to be sent to Suriname where slaves were treated far worse. Although the slave situation on these islands was atypical compared with the sugar plantation societies in the West Indies, the social stratification was almost the same. The white elite was formed by Protestant Dutchmen and Sephardic Jews on Curaçao and by British and Dutch settlers in the Dutch Leeward colonies. Most were civil servants, military men, merchants, and planters. Free coloreds and blacks were important for the economy. They formed 20 percent of the Curaçao population in 1789 and 50 percent in 1863. They worked on the land and in the harbors or were artisans or sailors. At the bottom of the social ladder were slaves. They produced corn and sorghum for their masters and the

black community, took care of the cattle, did the hard work in the salt pans of Bonaire and Saint Martin, and served their masters in crafts and in their homes. On Saint Martin and Saint Eustatius slaves were active also on the small sugar plantations. In 1863, slavery in the Dutch colonies was abolished.

In a process of adaptation, mingling, and integration slaves developed local forms of music, traditions, cooking, stories, and a sort of common African language, *guené*, which had long existed as an underground slave language on Curaçao. This process of creolization was not identical in the six islands, because the demographic, social, and economic context was different. The Lesser Antilles had more commercial contacts with Spanish-speaking colonies, and these small societies were influenced by Spanish, Dutch, and African cultural trends. On Aruba, where slavery was not as important as on Curaçao, African influences were not really significant. Latin and Indian features dominate on this island. The African beat and rhythm in dances like *tambú* and tumba in the Lesser Antilles and the belief in evil ghosts or *zumbis* and *eszé* (related to Haitian Voudon) show a more sustained African connection. In the context of this slave society, and in communication with the whites, a new language, Papiamento, started to develop on Curaçao in the 17th century. In this language the *nanzi* (Anancy) stories of the spider as a trickster figure were recounted and adjusted to the local situation.

In matters of religion in the Antilles, the Calvinist Dutch Reformed Church was not really interested in baptizing the slaves. However, the administration tolerated preachers of other religions who did the religious teaching of the slaves, and this was even encouraged in the 19th century. On Aruba, Bonaire, and Curaçao many slaves became Roman Catholics, and on the Leeward Islands many became Methodists, Anglicans, and Roman Catholics. Still, the white elite considered these inferior religions to be specifically for the slaves.

On the Leeward Islands many British settlers influenced the culture and language of the Dutch colonies, and by the 19th century Caribbean English had become the common language of society. In culture and religion the Dutch Leeward Islands show many similarities with the surrounding English-speaking West Indies.

In the Dutch Antilles there were three substantial slave uprisings. In 1750 and 1795 slaves of some plantations rebelled on Curaçao. The 1750 uprising lasted only one day, although 59 slaves and one white overseer were killed by the rebels. The 1795 revolt began August 17 and was more serious. More than 2,000 slaves took part in the rebellion under the leadership of a slave named Tula. After two weeks of negotiations and battles the Dutch soldiers, assisted by civilians and groups of free coloreds and blacks, defeated the rebellious slaves. After both revolts, the punishments for the slave leaders were harsh and cruel. In 1848, the 1,100 slaves of St. Eustatius demanded their freedom. The leaders of the uprising based their demand on the abolition of slavery in the British and French colonies. After some skirmishes, however, the slaves returned to the plantations.

Although there were not such large slave revolts as there were in Haiti or Jamaica, the slaves of the Dutch Antilles were not stereotypically obedient. The many laws to control and regulate the behavior of slaves had to be officially reannounced periodically to remind the white settlers of the black threat. Regulations to prevent slaves from fleeing to foreign colonies were especially strict. Nevertheless, hundreds of slaves still fled from the Lesser Antilles to Venezuela. In 1760, 400 ex-slaves from these islands lived in a city quarter of Coro, Venezuela, where Papiamento was the language commonly used.

Ronald Donk

See also Atlantic World and the African Diaspora; Middle Passage.

FURTHER READING
Most publications about slavery in the Netherlands Antilles are in the Dutch language. In English the following studies can be recommended.

Goslinga, Cornelis Ch., 1971. *The Dutch in the Caribbean and the Wild Coast, 1580–1680.* Gainesville: University Press of Florida.

Goslinga, Cornelis Ch., 1985. *The Dutch in the Caribbean and in the Guyana's, 1680–1791.* Assen, The Netherlands: Van Gorcum Assen.

Goslinga, Cornelis Ch., 1990. *The Dutch in the Caribbean and in Surinam, 1791/5–1942.* Assen, The Netherlands: Van Gorcum Assen.

Postma, Johannes Menne, 1990. *The Dutch in the Atlantic Slave Trade 1600–1815.* Cambridge, UK: Cambridge University Press.

Sypkens Smit, M.P., 1995. *Beyond the Tourist Trap: A Study of St. Maarten Culture.* Amsterdam: Natuurwetenschappelijke Studiekring voor het Caraïbisch Gebied.

Netherlands East Indies: African Soldiers

Between 1831 and 1872, more than 3,000 African recruits sailed from the West African town of Elmina to Batavia (now Jakarta), the capital of the Netherlands East Indies, to serve in the Dutch colonial army. After their contracts expired, some returned to the Gold Coast where the majority settled in Elmina, on a hill still known today as Java Hill. Others, having established families during their long years of army service, opted to settle in the East Indies. They became the founding fathers of the Indo-African communities in the Javanese towns of Purworejo, Semarang, Batavia, Salatiga, and Solo. On Java, the African soldiers and their descendents became known as *Belanda Hitam*—black Dutchmen. The shortage of manpower in the Dutch colonial army, and the high mortality among European troops in the tropics, caused the Dutch government to explore various options for recruitment. Inspired by the example of the British West India Regiments, the Department of Colonies turned to the almost forgotten Dutch possessions on the Guinea Coast, where commercial activity was at a low ebb after the abolition of the slave trade in 1814. It was assumed that Africans would be better equipped to withstand the hot climate and the dreaded tropical diseases in the East Indies.

The 3,080 Africans were recruited in two phases. An experimental phase began in 1831 with the recruitment of a company of 150 volunteers. However, volunteers proved very scarce. Three ships that were sent from Holland in 1831–1832 collected altogether only 44 recruits. This first batch took part in a military expedition in southern Sumatra, and initial reports about their qualities as soldiers were highly favorable: the Sumatrans were reportedly full of awe and admiration for the Africans. In September 1836, an official mission, headed by Major-General Jan Verveer, sailed from the Netherlands with a vast array of presents for the king of Ashanti and instructions to arrange for the enlistment of between 2,000 and 3,000 soldiers. Along the coast volunteers were few and far between, but the Kingdom of Ashanti—a long-standing partner in the slave trade—was seen as the key to solving the manpower problem. In a contract signed on March 18, 1837, the Ashanti king agreed to deliver 1,000 recruits within a year. He received 2,000 guns by way of advance payment, and the promise of 4,000 more to come. Moreover, the Dutch obtained permission to open a recruitment agency in Kumasi. As recruitment was still supposed to be voluntary, slaves offered to the recruiting agent received an advance payment to purchase their freedom. On arrival in Elmina, they were given an act of manumission as proof of their legal status as free men. As part of the deal two young Ashanti princes, Kwasi Boakye and Kwame Poku, accompanied Verveer back to The Netherlands, where they were to receive a Dutch education. Boakye later continued his studies in Delft and became a mining engineer. Contrary to initial plans, he did not go back to the Gold Coast but went to work in the Nether-

lands Indies, where he died in 1904. Kwame Poku did return to Elmina in 1847, where he committed suicide in St. George's Castle in 1850.

Recruitment in Kumasi never met Dutch expectations. All in all, between 1836 and 1842 some 2.280 African soldiers made the journey to the East Indies. Recruitment was first suspended and then abandoned altogether in 1841. The British government had protested that this mode of recruitment amounted to a covert form of slave trading. Moreover, several mutinies by African troops in the Indies had led the colonial administration to doubt the wisdom of the African recruitment scheme.

The African soldiers were counted as part of the European contingent of the army. Their conditions of service were mostly the same as those of Europeans, and considerably better than those of the indigenous soldiers. In due course, the Indo-Africans became part of Indo-European society: they spoke Dutch as their mother tongue, their children attended Dutch schools, and they held Dutch nationality.

The most cohesive Indo-African community lived in the garrison town of Purworejo in central Java, where in 1859 King Willem III allocated them a plot of land. Indo-Africans living outside the main centers tended to assimilate into Indo-European or into Indonesian society, often becoming oblivious of their African roots.

The African soldiers turned out to be no less vulnerable to diseases than their European counterparts. On the other hand, quite a few Africans chose to reenlist for one or more terms of two, four, or six years after their initial contracts expired. They were generally regarded as loyal and courageous, but ill-disciplined in combat. Recruitment was resumed in the late 1850s, but on a much smaller scale and with more precautions to ensure the voluntary nature of enlistment. Between 1860 and 1872, another 800 Africans enlisted in the Dutch army, but recruitment ended in 1872 with the transfer of Elmina to the British.

By 1915, there were no longer any African soldiers in active service in the East Indies. However, many of the sons and grandsons of the African soldiers continued to serve in the Netherlands East Indies Army, establishing colonial control over the vast Indonesian archipelago, fighting the Japanese in World War II, suffering the hardships of prisoner-of-war camps, and ultimately fighting the Indonesian nationalists until the final transfer of sovereignty to Indonesia in 1949. Along with vast numbers of Dutch and Indo-Europeans, most Indo-Africans opted for repatriation to the Netherlands, where they maintained informal contacts with each other. Contact with Ghanaian descendents was established in 2000, when Thad Ulzen, the great-great-grandson of one of the first recruits, Manus Ulzen, attended the 10th Indo-African reunion in the Netherlands. Inspired by the discovery of this unknown family history, the Ulzen family founded the Elmina-Java Museum in Elmina, which has exhibits on the story of the African soldiers of Java.

Ineke van Kessel

See also Ghana; Indian Ocean World and the African Diaspora.

FURTHER READING
Kusruri, Endri. 2002. "Reminiscences of the African Community in Purworejo, Indonesia." In *Merchants, Missionaries and Migrants: 300 Years of Dutch-Ghanaian Relations*, ed. I. van Kessel, 143–149. Amsterdam: KIT Publishers.
Van Kessel, Ineke. 2003. "African Mutinies in the Netherlands East Indies: A Nineteenth-Century Colonial Paradox." In *Rethinking Resistance: Revolt and Violence in African History*, ed. J. Abbink, M. de Bruijn, and K. van Walraven, 141–169. Leiden, The Netherlands: Brill.
Van Kessel, Ineke, 2005. *Zwarte Hollanders: Afrikaanse soldaten in Nederlands-Indië*. Amsterdam: KIT Publishers.
Yarak, L.W. 1996. "New Sources for the Study of Akan Slavery and Slave Trade: Dutch Military Recruitment in the Gold Coast and Asante, 1831–72." In *Source Material for Studying the Slave Trade and the African Diaspora: Papers from a Conference of the Centre of Common-wealth Studies, University of Stirling*, ed. R. Law. Stirling: University of Stirling.

Newton, Huey Percy (1942–)

Huey Percy Newton, a major leader of the Black Panther Party was born on February 17, 1942, in New Orleans, Louisiana. He grew up in Oakland, California, and drifted into patterns of delinquency, which resulted in multiple disciplinary problems, including his dismissal from Berkeley High School and a sentence in juvenile hall. He graduated from Oakland Tech High School and attended Merritt College. His criminal activities yielded multiple criminal convictions before his enrollment at Merritt College. In 1966, he reunited with college friend Bobby Seale to form the Black Panther Party for Self-Defense (BPP) in Oakland, California.

Borrowing heavily from the Declaration of Independence and the U.S. Constitution, drawing from the Deacons for Defense and Justice in Louisiana, and including the teachings of civil rights activists Malcolm X, Robert Williams, and the Lowndes County Freedom organization, Newton and Seale drafted the Ten Point Platform and Program of the BPP. They demanded self-determination, employment, housing, justice, education, exemption from military service, freedom for all black men in federal, state, county, and city prisons and jails. The BPP also demanded an immediate end to police brutality through their paramilitary structure. As the minister of defense of the BPP, Newton advocated "revolutionary suicide," the belief that a revolutionary must accept death as a resolute determination to effect political, economic, and social change.

Newton's imprisonment and subsequent conviction for the 1967 fatal confrontation that resulted in the death of police officer John Frey spawned massive nationwide Free Huey rallies organized by BPP Minister of Information Eldridge Cleaver and Kathleen Cleaver. While in prison, Newton ran unsuccessfully as a political candidate for the 17th District in California on the Peace and Freedom Party ticket. In 1968, the BPP dropped Self Defense from its name to emphasize its transition from a paramilitary stance to an organization focused on implementing a series of social programs that Newton termed "survival programs" by 1970. Newton asserted that the BPP sought natural rights for the people, as reflected in the BPP's slogan "all power to the people." The BPP's free "survival programs" included breakfast programs, sickle cell anemia testing, free food and shoes, medical services, and busing to prisons. Such programs emphasized the self-determination of the BPP's Ten Point Platform and Program.

Upon his release from prison in 1971, Newton advocated his theory of revolutionary "intercommunalism" in a global context. Newton argued that technology created a "global village" that mandated sharing of all wealth produced. The BPP's political organ, The Black Panther Intercommunal News Service (a.k.a. The Black Panther), encouraged international solidarity with the governments of Cuba, Vietnam, China, the Caribbean, and Africa. The BPP's international outreach included facilitating the escape of BPP fugitives, including Eldridge Cleaver, to Cuba and the subsequent establishment of international BPP chapters, especially Cleaver's International Section of the BPP in Algiers in 1970.

Counterintelligence measures fractured the BPP in 1971, exacerbating growing discord. Newton and Cleaver publicly expelled each other from the BPP in 1971 resulting in internal warfare between the New York BPP chapter and other chapters. Some BPP members joined the Black Liberation Army and others moved to Oakland as Newton consolidated the organization to mobilize support for the unsuccessful political campaigns of BPP cofounder Bobby Seale and Elaine Brown, who later became the only chairwoman of the BPP (1974–1977). In 1971, Newton traveled to China to meet with dignitaries, which added to his national and international recognition as leader of the BPP.

In 1972, Newton's business company, Stronghold Consolidated Publications, published the account of George Jackson, who was shot and killed at San Quentin prison on August 21, 1971. He also published his autobiography, *Revolutionary Suicide,* in 1973. Also in 1973, noted author and poet Toni Morrison edited a collection of Newton's writings entitled *To Die for the People: The Writings of Huey P. Newton.*

By 1978, Bobby Seale, Elaine Brown, and other BPP members left the organization. Newton later enrolled at the University of California at Santa Cruz where he earned a doctorate degree. His doctoral dissertation, aptly titled, "War Against the Panthers: A Study of Repression in America," examined the effects of counterintelligence measures against the BPP throughout its history. Drug abuse led to Newton's demise in 1989.

Rose C. Thevenin

See also Black Panther Party; Brown, Elaine (1943–).

FURTHER READING

Newton, Huey P. 1996. *War against the Panthers, A Study of Repression in America.* New York: Harlem River Press.

Newton, Huey P. 1973. *Revolutionary Suicide.* New York: Writers And Readers Publishing Inc.

Newton, Huey P. 1973. *To Die for the People: The Writings of Huey P. Newton.* ed. Toni Morrison. New York: Writers and Readers Publishing Inc.

Seale, Bobby. 1991. *Seize the Time: The Story of the Black Panther Party and Huey P. Newton.* Baltimore: Black Classic Press.

Nicaragua and Honduras: Miskito Indians

See Honduras and Nicaragua: Miskito Indians.

Nichols, Grace (1950–)

Poet, novelist, and children's author Grace Nichols is known for her literary platform, adeptly laced with political undertones, from which she advances the cause for black women's self-worth, acceptance, multiplicity, and resiliency. Born and raised in Guyana, Nichols attended the University of Guyana where she earned a diploma in communications, which afforded her travels to the interior regions of Guyana, where she studied indigenous cultures. She worked as a teacher and journalist before her departure for the United Kingdom in 1977. Her first and only coming-of-age novel, *Whole of a Morning Sky* (1986), chronicles her experiences as a child growing up in Georgetown, the capital of Guyana, and captures the country's tumultuous path to independence and the succeeding migrations of Guyanese.

Nichols is best known for her first and most celebrated poetry collection, *I Is a Long-Memoried Woman* (1983), which won the 1983 Commonwealth Poetry Prize and was subsequently adapted into a film of the same name, directed by Frances Anne Solomon, which was awarded a gold medal at the International Film and Television Festival of New York. This collection is a reliving, a reenactment of the Middle Passage, that chronicles an unnamed African-Caribbean woman's journey from Africa to the Caribbean, from bondage to freedom. This long-memoried woman mourns her past and the loss of her mother tongue, yet remembers and celebrates her ancestral past, preserving these memories in mind, body, and spirit. Having crossed an ocean and lost her tongue, a new tongue that spurts defiance and resistance has sprung, and a New World woman is born.

Nichols claims that her next collection of poetry, *The Fat Black Woman's Poems* (1984), was created out of sheer fun. However, there is a searing critique and questioning of the acceptance of a European standard of beauty—the slim, blue-eyed, blonde European model. Nichols posits the fat black woman as her symbol of beauty, challenging these so-called ideals and subverting so-called established norms. Immersed in self-love the fat black woman becomes the subject of her own discourse as she crowns herself the beauty of all beauties.

Nichols's next collection, *Lazy Thoughts of a Lazy Woman* (1989), can be classified as a sequel to *The Fat Black Woman's Poems.* The lazy woman questions body conformity, or more specifically, beautification of the female body, as she indicts the female tycoons, Mary Kay, Estée Lauder, and Helena Rubenstein, as the mouthpieces of patriarchy and the enforcers of law and order. Moving beyond body commodification and subjugation, the lazy woman reclaims her body sexually and spiritually.

Nichols's poetry collection, *Sunrise* (1996), won the Guyana Poetry Prize in the same year. The Caribbean landscape is celebrated in a lengthy poem about carnival, as an African consciousness is invoked. This carnival atmosphere has far-reaching power as England is Caribbeanized when it is hit with the 1987 hurricane. The hurricane, interestingly, awakens her Caribbean sensibility and sensitivity.

Nichols is also well-known for her children's poetry; the best-known collection is *Come On into My Tropical Garden: Poems for Children* (1988), where she brings to life a lush tropical landscape as she paints a fun-filled Caribbean childhood. She also coauthored, with partner and poet John Agard, *No Hickory No Dickory No Dock: Caribbean Nursery Rhymes* in which she substitutes British fables for West Indian folktales.

Simone A. James Alexander

See also Guyana; Rodney, Walter (1942–1980); United Kingdom: The African Diaspora.

FURTHER READING
Ngcobo, Lauretta, ed. 1987. *Essays by Black Woman in Britain.* London: Pluto.
Nichols, Grace. 1983. *I Is a Long-Memoried Woman.* London: Karnak House.

Nichols, Grace. 1984. *The Fat Black Woman's Poems*. London: Virago.

Nichols, Grace. 1986. *Whole of a Morning Sky*. London: Virago.

Nichols, Grace. 1989. *Lazy Thoughts of a Lazy Woman*. London: Virago.

Nichols, Grace. 1991. *No Hickory No Dickory No Dock: Caribbean Nursery Rhymes*. London: Viking.

Nichols, Grace. 1996. *Sunris.* London: Virago.

Nichols, Grace, and John Agard. 1988. *Come On into My Tropical Garden: Poems for Children*. London: A & C Black.

Solomon, Frances Anne, director. *I Is a Long-Memoried Woman*. London: Women Makes Movies.

Nkrumah, Kwame (1909–1972)

Kwame Nkrumah, the first president and prime minister of Ghana, was born on September 21, 1909, in the village of Nkroful, which is located in the southwestern region of Ghana. He was a member of the Nzimba people and his initial name was Francis Nwia-Kofi Ngonloma.

In 1930, he earned his teacher's certificate at Prince of Wales College in Achimota, Ghana. He continued his studies in the United States where, in 1939, he earned a bachelor's degree in economics and sociology at Lincoln University of the Commonwealth of Pennsylvania. Later, he received his master's in education and philosophy at the University of Pennsylvania in Philadelphia. In 1942, he earned a bachelor's degree in theology at Lincoln Theological Seminary. During his academic studies in the United States, he helped found the African Students Association of America. In 1945, he traveled to London where he intended to earn a doctorate in economics at the London School of Economics. He also enrolled at Gray's Inn to study law.

Nkrumah was secretary and vice president of the West African Student Union, which enabled him to practice his Pan-Africanist and political activist interests. In 1945, he and colleagues Jomo Kenyatta and George Padmore organized the Fifth Pan-African Congress in Manchester, England. In 1947, Nkrumah wrote his first book, *Towards Colonial Freedom*. Later works included *What I Mean by Positive Action* (1950), *Ghana—Autobiography* (1957), *I Speak of Freedom* (1961), *Africa Must Unite* (1963), *Consciencism* (1964), and *Dark Days in Ghana* (1968).

In December 1947, Nkrumah returned to Ghana and became the general secretary and the party treasurer of the United Gold Coast Convention (UGCC). In September 1948, he founded the *Accra Evening News*. In 1957, he also founded the Accra News Agency. In 1949, he left the UGCC and organized the Convention People's Party. Nkrumah's political activism included strikes, boycotts, and campaigns declaring "Positive Action." In January 1950, he was arrested for one of his campaigns that resulted in civil unrest and charged with sedition. In 1951, He was released from prison because he won the elections for the Accra Central seat. Nkrumah held the position of leader of government business, and in 1956, he became prime minister.

On March 6, 1957, Nkrumah declared Ghana's independence. Later that year, on December 31, he married Helena Ritz Fathia, the niece of Gamal Abdel Nasser, the second president of Egypt. The couple had three children, named Gokeh, Samiah Yarbah, and Sekou Ritz.

In 1958, Nkrumah organized the first ACCRA Conference (Conference of Independent African States), which promoted cooperation with African self-governing states and management of their own affairs. On November 23, 1958, he formed the Ghana-Guinea Union (Union of African States) with President Sékou Touré of Guinea. Later, he extended the union to Mali under President Modibo Keita. In December 1958, he also organized an All African People's Conference in Accra, Ghana to confront the issues of uniting all Africans and ending imperialism.

Nkrumah was tenacious about three major objectives: economic planning and integration on a continental basis, a unified military, and a unified foreign policy. In 1960, he declared Ghana as a republic, and in 1964, he declared himself as the life president and Ghana a one-party state. In 1966, Nkrumah was deposed by coup d'etat, while he was abroad in Hanoi, North Vietnam, assisting Ho Chi Minh with solutions on the Vietnam War. Nkrumah suffered from health problems during his exile stay in Conakry, Guinea, where he was made honorary copresident. Subsequently, he was flown to Romania for medical treatment, where he died of cancer on April 27, 1972.

Cheryl Jeffries

See also African Union (AU); Ghana; Lincoln University; Pan-Africanism.

FURTHER READING

James, Cyril Lionel Robert. 1977. *Nkrumah and the Ghana Revolution*. Westport, CT: Lawrence Hill & Co.

Nkrumah, Kwame. 1966. *Neo-Colonialism: The Last Stage of Imperialism*. New York: International Publishers.

Rugamba, Matthew. 2004. "F.N.K. Kwame Nkrumah." Contemporary Africa Database. people.africadatabase.org/en/profile/3196. html (accessed February 24, 2004).

Timothy, Bankole. 1963. *Kwame Nkrumah: His Rise to Power*. Evanston, IL: Northwestern University Press.

Notting Hill Carnival

Notting Hill Carnival—originally transported to London by Afro-Caribbeans, mostly Trinidadians—takes place the last Monday in August, over the bank holiday weekend. What began as a nostalgic celebration of folk memory has proliferated to such an extent that it now has the potential to be used as a model for multicultural integration and instruction in other large European cities. Although this carnival has been ac-

knowledged as "Europe's largest street festival," it takes place primarily in Notting Hill. The carnival has contributed to London's image as a world city because of the economic booster it provides through tourism and its highly professional aesthetic content, which is jointly facilitated by carnival artists from London's different multiethnic groupings.

The Notting Hill Carnival is rooted in Trinidadian carnival: formerly enslaved Africans publicly celebrated emancipation in 1834 by taking to the streets reinstituting their African cultural forms yet simultaneously adopting European festival forms. This historical legacy was transplanted to the global city of London when Caribbean migrants began arriving in London in the early 1950s. However, the literature is sparse and contradictory regarding the actual genesis of the Notting Hill Carnival. Stuempfle states that as early as 1951, a group of 11 steel band players, the Trinidad All Steel Percussion Orchestra, was invited to participate in the Festival of England (Stuempfle 1995, 94). This festival engendered the space for the steel band to become a dominant art form in Caribbean Britain, as it created the possibility not only for homesick Trinidadians to display Trinidadian culture but also to give public prominence to steel band as a Caribbean musical form in Britain. This articulation of Caribbean culture was institutionalized by Claudia Jones, a black Trinidadian writer and activist, who organized the first carnival events. Trinidadians continued to come together to drink rum and "beat pan." The creation of "rum shop culture" in the late 1950s at St. Pancreas created a culture for the genesis of carnival in Britain.

The 1960s saw the public popular demonstration of carnival adopting other features. As early as 1964, a social worker invited the steelband players to participate in the "Notting Hill Festival." Notting Hill was to become the official site for the celebration of carnival, a poor, migrant slum, adjacent to the wealthy streets of Kensington.

In 1965, Notting Hill Carnival appeared in this area for the first time, although there was no financial support from the prestigious Borough of Kensington and Chelsea for this street festival for migrant and other lower class peoples. Rhaune Lazlett, a London-born woman of Amerindian and Russian descent, organized the multiethnic community event. Russell Henderson and other Trinidadians, all members of the Trinidad All Steel Percussion Orchestra, took to the streets with a few masqueraders to celebrate the community event in Trinidadian style. In this way the steel band reclaimed public space for itself in Britain thereby placing carnival at Notting Hill, and initiating Notting Hill Carnival, as we know it today.

At the beginning of the 1970s there were growing racial tensions between the police and Afro-Caribbean youths living in Notting Hill and Ladbroke Grove, which were quite visible in the carnival celebrations. This culminated in the race riots at Notting Hill. Numerous investigations revealed not only opposition from the authorities but also the more serious problem of cultural fragmentation within the different Caribbean groupings, and the clash between black British-born Jamaican youths, who introduced reggae music to carnival. Reggae music is associated with Rastafarianism while soca music is overtly associated with Trinidadian carnival's diverse forms of celebration. With this form of cultural fragmentation, Notting Hill and its carnival thus began to experience a slow transformation from its initial, traditional, Trinidadian Caribbean forms of celebration into a transnational, global site of struggle that was culturally different and differentiated. Nonetheless, the official threat to remove carnival from the streets reverberated deeply among these groups, as Carnival provided the forum for these various groups to coalesce. This form of coming together facilitated a marking out and a shaping of new collectivities and multiple ethno-Caribbean identities in the British mainstream context.

Although becoming a highly politicized event at this point in its existence, Notting Hill Carnival assumed other features. In 1978, a commission was formed to develop and promote the carnival and to raise its profile as a multidiversified, holistic art form embodying dance, music, theater, political commentary, and all the visual arts.

At the start of the 1980s, carnival's reputation began to change as other celebratory forms were introduced. Sound systems appeared officially in carnival. This move created other publicity for carnival, particularly among white British youths, so that by 1986 the population increased, this time with a large number of white British youths.

The 1990s saw the best developments for the economics of the Notting Hill Carnival. As early as 1995, the carnival became known as The Lilt Notting Hill Carnival sponsored by Coca Cola. The Arts Council of Britain also provided financial support for carnivalists. In 1995, in an attempt to raise the national profile of the carnival, the Combined Arts Department of the Arts Council of England provided financial support, in collaboration with Roehampton Institute in London, to develop and compile a publicly accessible National Carnival Database of textual and visual information, and Notting Hill Carnival began to be seen with different eyes. Notting Hill Carnival, enacted out of place in the urban metropolitan setting, has paradoxically transformed this urban place into a highly politicized space that has facilitated the actual development of a culture of carnival in the United Kingdom. This model is now being used in many other cities in Britain as well as elsewhere in Europe, including Sweden; Rotterdam, The Netherlands; Greece; Tenerife, Spain; and Paris, France. The German Carnival of Cultures celebrated in Berlin, Bielefeld, and Hamburg, is one example of how the model of Notting Hill Carnival has been used as a multicultural, multidiversified form of celebration in a homogenous society.

Patricia Alleyne-Dettmers

See also Carnival; Jones, Claudia Cumberbatch (1915–1964); Trinidad and Tobago.

FURTHER READING

Alleyne-Dettmers, Patricia T. 1996. *Carnival: The Historical Legacy*. UK: Arts Council of England.

Cohen, Abner. 1993. *Masquerade Politics. Explorations in the Structure of Urban Cultural Movements*. Berkeley: University of California Press.

Jackson, Peter. 1988. "Street Life: the Politics of Carnival." *Society and Space* 6: 213–227.

Stuempfle, Stephen. 1995. *The Steelband Movement: The Forging of a National Art in Trinidad & Tobago*. Mona, Jamaica and Philadelphia, PA: University of the West Indies and University of Pennsylvania Press.

Nova Scotia and the African American Diaspora

The African American Diaspora in Nova Scotia is the migration, voluntary and involuntary, of blacks from the United States to this British North American colony during the late 18th and early 19th centuries when two separate African American migrations—black loyalists and black refugees—took place. By 1784, after the American Revolutionary War, 3500 black loyalists had immigrated to Nova Scotia and, in addition, 1,232 slaves were brought to the colony by their white loyalist owners. The black loyalists received small allocations of land in a number of widely separated locations, and some of them endured the first race riot in British North American history in 1784. They faced discrimination in terms of employment and an unfair judicial system. In search of better opportunities, nearly 1,200 immigrated to Sierra Leone in 1792–1793 with the aid of British abolitionist John Clarkson. Under similar circumstances during the War of 1812, 2,000 black refugees migrated to Nova Scotia.

Beset by poverty, government inaction, and the hostility of the local white population, the refugees were forced into menial laboring jobs while attempting to farm unfertile land. Both the loyalists and the refugees came north because of military proclamations offering freedom, risked their lives in escaping from slavery, and fought for the British during the wars. Yet there is one important difference between these groups. Unlike the leadership of the black loyalists, the refugee elite opted to stay in Nova Scotia. Thus, despite numerous offers from the colonial government, 94 percent of the refugee population remained in Nova Scotia.

It is important to understand the black loyalists and black refugees in the context of the African American Diaspora. These migrants brought many of their experiences and cultural values to Nova Scotia, such as African churches, the Gullah language, burial ceremonies, and cooking styles. Moreover, African Nova Scotians were keenly aware of events in Afro-America. For example, although slavery had ended in Nova Scotia in the early 19th century, the black population founded the African Abolition Society in 1846. This society's mission focused on the plight of long-lost relatives and friends still laboring in Georgia, South Carolina, and Virginia. As events unfolded during the American Civil War, some African Nova Scotians attempted to aid the cause of freedom through service as seamen. The linkages between Afro-Nova Scotia and Afro-America continued throughout the latter half of the 19th century.

Jason B. Esters

See also Canada and the African Diaspora.

FURTHER READING

Walker, James, 1976. "The Establishment of a Free Black Community in Nova Scotia, 1783–1840." In *The African Diaspora: Interpretive Essays*, ed. Martin Kilson and Richard Rotberg. Cambridge, MA: Harvard University Press.

Whitfield, Harvey Amani. 2004. *From American Slaves to Nova Scotian Subjects: The Case of the Black Refugees, 1813–1840*. Canadian Ethnography Series. Toronto: Pearson Education/ Prentice Hall.

———•———

Nubia

Nubia was an ancient African civilization that endured for almost 5,000 years (3500 BCE– 1323 CE). The long history of Nubia has always been interwoven with that of Egypt, and for this reason, to a great extent obscured by its more well-known neighbor to the north. Ancient Nubia, the land immediately to the south of Upper Egypt, extended about 700 miles into the Nile Valley to modern-day Khartoum. Today, ancient Nubia is partly under the Aswan Dam, partly in Egypt, and partly in the Sudan. Ancient Nubian history is generally divided into the periods of Kerma, the Egyptian Colonization of Nubia, the Kushite Twenty-Fifth Dynasty of Egypt, Napata, and Meroe.

KERMA (2040–1554 BCE)

The Egyptians were aware of Nubia from about 3100 BCE. By Dynasty IV, Egyptian pharaohs were sending occasional expeditions into Lower Nubia for cattle, ebony, oils, copper, diorite stone, incense, ivory, leopard skins, and slaves. Beginning in the Middle Kingdom the Egyptians began to view Nubia as a serious force to be reckoned with. The Twelfth Dynasty pharaohs of the Middle Kingdom constructed a series of massive fortresses in Lower Nubia near the Second Cataract. They were built to oversee the gold mines the Egyptians had started to work in the deserts in Northern Nubia. The fortresses also enabled the Egyptians to control the river traffic in the region. The defensive character of the garrisons, however, indicates the real reason motivating their construction. Located 170 miles south of the fortifications was a strong and flourishing culture the Egyptians called the "Kingdom of Kush." Archaeologists have named it Kerma

after a modern-day town. Kerma was the most powerful state yet seen in Nubia.

Kerma, located in the southern part of Nubia in an area generally referred to as Upper Nubia, had been free of Egyptian control since the end of the Old Kingdom period. It reached its height during the Second Intermediate Period in Egypt, when the Hyskos invaders overran that country. Kerma had developed into a powerful state ruled by a monarchy. There is no more grandiose example of its past glory than the huge circular mounds, as long as football fields, where the rulers of Kerma were buried.

The kings were laid to rest on beds covered with gold. Finely crafted objects in bronze, gold, ivory, and faience were placed around them. The most distinctive feature of royal burials in Kerma was human sacrifice. As many as 400 of the king's close officials and concubines dressed themselves elaborately and were voluntarily buried alive to honor and serve the king in the afterlife.

The arts were free to flower under the stability of Kerma government. Some Kerma artists used Egyptian designs, but they reworked borrowed elements of design and form to create pieces unique to their culture. They were especially skilled in pottery and jewelry making. Beautiful, delicate, and small figurines were the result, made from copper, faience, and mica and taking the form of humans and animals. The most distinctive artwork was a type of pottery, called black topped ware, which had thin, shell-like walls, a black rim, and a brick-red lower section. This delicate, eggshell ware was highly valued in Kerma and was frequently interred along with the dead in royal graves.

NUBIA DURING THE NEW KINGDOM (1554–1080 BCE)

Once the Egyptians returned to power, they concentrated on subduing Nubia. It required 50 to 100 years of military campaigning, but they finally destroyed Kerma, or Kush, as they referred to the country, dominating the region as far as the Fourth Cataract. The Egyptians reoccupied their fortresses at the Second Cataract and began to settle again in Lower Nubia. They governed Nubia by installing an Egyptian official with the title King's Son of Kush.

The Egyptians made strong efforts to acculturate the Nubians. The pharaohs institutionalized the practice of taking young Nubians princes back to Egypt. There they came to adulthood and were steeped in an Egyptian education and culture. As a result, they developed a commitment to Egypt that endured even when they were sent back to govern in their own homeland. The Nubians, for their part, were quite adaptable to Egyptian culture. For instance, they worshipped some Egyptian gods, such as Amun and the goddess Isis. They built small pyramids to bury their royalty and decorated the interiors of their tombs like Egyptian tombs with hieroglyphic texts and wall paintings.

The Nubians engaged in trade activities, worked the gold mines in the desert, and contributed to the Egyptian economy through the enforced tribute and taxes they paid. The Egyptians living in Nubia worked as civil servants, soldiers, merchants, and priests. The Nubians and Egyptians also intermarried, increasing the level of interaction, and the sharing of cultures. After the New Kingdom's decline around 1070 BCE, Egyptian ties and traditions remained strong in Nubia for centuries afterwards.

KUSH (900 BCE–320 CE)

An extensive gap exists in the history of Nubia from about 1000 to 850 BCE. During the eighth century, however, Nubia emerged once again from obscurity with great drama and in triumph. After the New Kingdom declined, Egypt experienced another period of foreign rule known as the Third Intermediate Period (1085–715 BCE). During this period the Nubians gradually moved their center of power further to a site in Upper Nubia called Napata, located just beneath the Fourth Cataract.

Upper Nubia was located between the third and sixth cataracts. This region was the epicenter of the African kingdom in Nubia that the Egyptians called Kush. The Kushite era is divided into two periods known as Napata and Meroe, after sites bearing these names. Kush may have originated at Napata because of the area's importance as an early religious center. Part of the Napatan period is known as Egypt's Twenty-Fifth Dynasty, when the Kushites ruled over Egypt.

About 750 BCE, a Kushite king named Kashta boldly advanced as far as Thebes and conquered Upper Egypt. It is not exactly known how Kashta accomplished this feat. He may have been asked to intervene in Egyptian affairs by the powerful priests of the state god Amun, seeking protection against foreign aggressors. Kashta took the title of pharaoh and his daughter, Amenirdas I, was made divine wife of the god Amun. These important political and religious acts established the Kushite kings as legitimate rulers in Upper Egypt. As a result, they involved themselves in the struggles for political power as new overlords in the country.

Kashta's successor, Piankhy, marched his great army north to do battle with a prince from Libya who had taken over the Western Desert in Lower Egypt (the northern Delta). He soundly defeated the Libyan opposition and conquered all of Egypt. Piankhy left a detailed record of the war and his entry into Egypt's ancient capital, Memphis, on a magnificent victory stele erected in the Great Temple of Amun at Napata. He described himself as raging like a panther against the enemy, but also as a moral and compassionate king with a love for fine horses. He initiated the practice among the Kushite pharaohs of burying entire chariot teams near their royal graves.

For the next 60 years the Napatan royal house ruled both Nubia and Egypt from the old Delta capital of Memphis. Piankhy and his successors comprised the Twenty-Fifth Dynasty in Egyptian history. The Kushite Empire was a cultural renaissance in Egypt, especially in the realm of art and architecture. The

Kushites admired Egyptian culture but were just as proud of being Kushite. They wore the wide armbands, bracelets, and anklets typical of the Kushite south, along with traditional Egyptian dress and royal trappings. They invented a new symbol of royal authority called the Kushite skullcap. It fit close to the head and was encircled by streamers in the back. Two uraie (the sacred asp and insignia of Egyptian royalty) jutted out from the forehead whereas the Egyptians had used only one. The two uraie was the new symbol of Kushite rule over both Egypt and Kush.

Kushite artists fashioned wonderful objects in the fine art of jewelry making. Beautiful pendants, pectorals, earrings, and bracelets exhibited novel design and consummate skill. One of the most splendid was found in the tomb of a queen who was one of the wives of Piankhy. Reflecting an original Kushite conception, a gold Hathor head (goddess of women and beauty) was mounted on top of a perfectly shaped ball made from rock crystal. Architecture constructed during this period was also modeled after Egyptian prototypes. The Kushite pharaohs were mummified and buried near small pyramids. Included in the tomb burials were small Egyptian statuettes, called *shwabti* figures, whose function was to perform any work the gods demanded of the king in the afterlife. The Kushite pharaoh Taharqa (690–664 BCE) had 1,070 *shwabti* figures accompany him into the afterlife (690–664 BCE).

Kushite rule lasted about 100 years in Egypt. The Kushites were forced out when they were defeated by the Assyrians in 671 BCE and were forced to retreat back to Napata. After several attempts to regain the Egyptian throne, they left Egypt for good. Over the next several centuries, the Nubians gradually shifted their focus even farther south. They founded a new political entity and cultural center at Meroe. Located between the Fifth and Sixth Cataracts, the last Nubian state evolved largely in obscurity and independent of foreign invasion.

Meroe (270 BCE–350 CE)

Meroe is frequently described as Nubia's "Golden Age." Its isolation within the difficult Nubian terrain provided protection from the Persians, Greeks, and Romans; the foreign rulers were busy occupying an Egypt whose last native dynasty was put to death by the Persians (ca. 343 BCE). Meroe comprised all of Nubia and extended further south into areas that are now modern-day Sudan. Its significant relations were therefore with other peoples and states within inner Africa. At the same time, they adapted Hellenistic (Greek culture after Alexander the Great) and Roman influences and maintained Egyptian traditions as well.

Meroe achieved its pinnacle of power between 270 and 90 BCE. This era is marked by the large number of powerful queens who wielded political authority. Their special title was a combination of ruler (*Qore*) and "Queen Mother" (*Kandake*). The predominance of queens contributed to Greek and Roman legends about the Nubians and their female queens who they believed were all named Kandake.

Some of the female rulers of Meroe were involved in confrontations with Roman legions during the early part of Meroitic history. Roman rule had supplanted Greek rule in Egypt in 30 BCE, and the hostilities that ensued were over control of the trade routes from India and through central Africa. Eventually, the Meroites and the Romans reached an agreement. It was probably the Kandake Amanirenas (40–10 BCE), who organized a series of negotiations with the Roman emperor Augustus that resulted in a very favorable peace treaty in 21 or 20 BCE. The Meroites were exempted from paying tribute to the Romans. The treaty was honored between Meroe and Roman Egypt until the third century CE, leaving the Meroites to develop their unique civilization in relative peace.

The Meroites experienced glorious cultural achievements. They built large cities and restored old ones. Skilled architects erected a variety of structures, such as Egyptian-like temples, pyramids, mastabas, palaces, and fortifications as well as Roman-influenced taverns, kiosks, and public baths. They used stone and brick. One of the most significant architectural achievements was Musawwarat es-Sufra. This large temple complex consisted of numerous stone buildings. Archaeologists are not certain of its function. However, because of the presence of huge ramps and many elephant carvings and reliefs the Meroites seem to have been involved in the trade of elephants and training these huge animals for warfare in the classical world.

Writing and the arts were other areas of expertise. The Meroites invented their own script. It was based on the Egyptian hieroglyphs but reduced the numerous signs in that language to 23 symbols, to which the Meroites added written vowel notation. By the second century they were writing primarily in their own unique script. However, it remains a mystery as it has not been deciphered. Meroitic can be read, but its meaning is not completely understood.

Meroitic pottery is among the finest examples of ceramics ever produced in the ancient world. Pottery was made by hand and thrown on the pottery wheel. The Meroites created diverse vessels and designs in all shapes and sizes. Painters adorned the surfaces in radiant colors, elegant floral and geometric designs, and with lively animal and human figures.

Meroe came to a gradual end sometime around the middle of the fourth century CE. Increased assaults from desert nomads probably contributed to its demise, in addition to the expansion of the Axumite kingdom (ancient Abyssinia) in northeast Africa. Both of these factors helped to disrupt the economy. The nomads made overland travel hazardous, and they endangered the northern trade routes. And the rise of the Axumites diverted trade routes and activity toward the Red Sea region. The Axumites finally sacked the weakened Meroitic state in 350 CE. Today, the land that was ancient Nubia is divided between the Sudan and Egypt. And in the African Diaspora, it is not unusual to have descriptive reference to Nubia such as that found in the name of the popular singing group, Les Nubians.

Earnestine Jenkins

See also Art in the African Diaspora.

FURTHER READING

Adams, Williams Y. 1977. *Nubia: Corridor to Africa.* London: Penguin.

Conah, Graham. 1987. *African Civilizations.* Cambridge, UK: Cambridge University Press.

Davidson, Basil. 1967. *The African Past.* New York: Grosset & Dunlap.

July, Robert. 1992. *A History of the African People.* 4th ed. Prospect Heights, IL: Waveland Press.

Mokhtar, G., ed. 1987. *Ancient Civilizations of Africa.* Vol. 2, *UNESCO General History of Africa.* Berkeley: University of California Press.

Oliver, Roland. 1991. *The African Experience.* New York: HarperCollins Publishers.

Shillington, Kevin. 1995. *History of Africa.* Rev. ed. New York: St. Martin's Press.

Snowden, Frank. 1970. *Blacks in Antiquity.* Cambridge, MA: Harvard University Press.

Wenig, Steffen. 1978. *Africa in Antiquity: the Arts of Ancient Nubia and the Sudan.* 2 vols. Exhibition Catalogues. Brooklyn, NY: The Brooklyn Museum.

O

Obeah

Obeah (also spelled Obia) is a spiritual and medicinal system of African origin that is practiced throughout the Caribbean. Its important function was to empower, protect, heal and liberate African people. Though it has been argued that the term derives its meaning from various sources, including the term *ob*, the Egyptian term for serpent, and/or *ubio*, the Efik (southern Nigeria) term for a charm used to cause sickness or death (Williams 1934), given the preponderance of Twi-speaking Akan taken to the Caribbean in the transatlantic slave trade, Obeah is more likely etymologically derived from the Akan terms *obayifo*, meaning witch or sorcerer, and/or *bayi*, meaning witchcraft or sorcery.

Early English planters frowned on the practice of what they saw as superstitions and began to stipulate legal sanctions against the practice of Obeah. Europeans also recognized the relationship between African religion and African resistance and attempted to quell any practices that could inspire Africans to revolt and subsequently jeopardize the success of the plantations. The English were particularly suspicious of the religious practices of the Cromanti as they were the leading instigators of

resistance on the island. The success of legendary maroon leaders, Cudjoe (*Kojo*), Queen Nanny (*Nanani*), and Tacky (*Takyi*), was often attributed to the practice of Obeah.

European historians have attached myriad functions to practitioners of Obeah, including medicine men and women, creators of protective amulets and charms, initiators of spells, obtainers of revenge for injuries or insults, peacemakers, enforcers of punishment (particularly of thieves and adulterers), magicians, and fortune-tellers. Most popular and most emphasized of the tasks assigned to Obeah practitioners was "duppy catching." A duppy is a person's shadow, which remains with their corpse upon death and, if not properly buried, can linger and cause harm to people (Stewart 1992).

An analysis of Obeah must place the practice within its proper cultural context, more accurately positioning Obeah as a Caribbean expression of traditional African religious and scientific knowledge. For example, if the terms *obayifo* and/or *bayi* are accepted as the etymological precursors of Obeah, it becomes important to examine their form and function within traditional Akan society. Traditionally, *abayifo* (plural of *obayifo*) are an accepted reality and are recognized as having both positive and negative functions. Reflective of Akan cosmology, which holds that both positive and negative energies are present and necessary in all things, *bayi pa*, translated to mean "good witchcraft," uses spiritual powers to bring good fortune to those who seek its assistance, whereas *bayi boro*, translated as "bad witchcraft," invokes evil spirits for the purpose of bringing disaster to specified individuals (Opoku 1978). Thus, *abayifo* are believed to possess magical powers to provide spiritual blessings and protection or cause harm and injury. In the Western context, however, much of this dual significance of *bayi*, and consequently both *obayifo* and Obeah, are obscured in translation. Furthermore, because of the influence of religions such as Christianity and Islam, much of postcolonial Akan society itself focuses solely on the negative roles of *abayifo* as specialists of *bayi boro*, holding them responsible for much of society's misfortune. From this perception of *obayifo* scholars have drawn parallels to the Obeah practitioners of Jamaica.

Though a necessary part of society, because they have come to be associated more with their negative aspects, *abayifo* operate in secrecy, and if confronted, may deny their participation. Ethnographic research in the Caribbean confirms that there are two kinds of Obeah—one that is negative and deals with evil and witchcraft, and one that is positive, therapeutic, and good (Gottlieb 2000). Thus, Obeah is divested of the negative connotations of black magic and sorcery that are most often given. Obeah practitioners often operate in secrecy and refuse to share the particulars of the practice with outsiders.

Yaba Amgborale Blay

See also Jamaica; Maroon and Marronage.

FURTHER READING

Gottlieb, Karla. 2000. *The Mother of Us All: A History of Queen Nanny Leader of the Windward Jamaican Maroons*. Trenton, NJ: Africa World Press.

Opoku, Kofi Asare. 1978. *West African Traditional Religion*. London: FEP International Private Limited.

Stewart, Robert J. 1992 *Religion and Society in Post-Emancipation Jamaica*. Knoxville: The University of Tennessee Press.

Williams, Joseph J. 1934. *Psychic Phenomena of Jamaica*. New York: Dial Press.

Zips, Werner. 1999. *Black Rebels: African Caribbean Freedom Fighters in Jamaica*. Kingston, Jamaica: Ian Randle Publishers.

Ogou/Ogoun

Ogou/Ogum/Ogun/Gu is one of the most multivalent and well-traveled deities in the African Diaspora. Originating among the Yoruba of present-day Nigeria, his significance quickly spread to the Gbe-speaking people of present-day Benin and Togo where Gbe-speakers worship him as the Vodoun Gu. In the 19th century, wars between the kingdoms of Oyo and Dahomey sent thousands of Africans into the hands of European slave traders. These enslaved Africans brought Ogou/Ogum/Ogun to the Americas.

Among the Yoruba, Ogun is an Orisha associated with iron and warfare, tools, roads and law enforcement. Ogun's signs are the first in the Ifá divination corpus used by *babalao* to discover the individual destinies of their clients. Ogun receives sacrifices of male animals, especially dogs. He was the husband and consort of the Orisha Yemoja. These associations have persisted in the New World.

Ogou is the preeminent Vodoun in the Haitian Vodoun pantheon. His devotees brandish machetes when in the throes of possession trance and offer him *clarin* (raw cane liquor) rum, gunpowder, and animal sacrifice. He has both a cool benevolent avatar in the *Rada* pantheon, named *Ogou Balandjo*, who is identified with the Catholic Saint Joseph, and a hot, demonic manifestation in the *Petwo* pantheon, named *Ogou Ferraille*, who is identified with Saint Jaques Majeur (Saint James). Ogou devotees (called *serviteur*) may walk on hot coals, hold flaming gunpowder in their bare hands, or eat fire to prove the veracity of their manifestation.

In Brazil, Ogum is a prominent Orixá and is honored before all others in the ceremonies of Bahian Candomblé. Candomblé devotees identify him with Santo Antonio (Saint Anthony), while Umbanda practitioners identify him with São Jorge (Saint George). He manifests himself as an Orixá, as a sailor (Ogum Marinho), and as a demonic Exú (Ogum Xoroké). He was the occasionally cuckolded husband of the Orixá of the sea, Yemanjá. He is associated with iron tools, cutting implements, the police, and the opening of roads and clearing of paths. His devotees wear blue while in a possession trance and symbolize their devotion by wearing blue beaded necklaces.

In Cuba the Oricha Ogun is prominent in the orthodox variant of Santería called *Regla De Ocha*. There he is syncretized with the Catholic Saint Peter. As in Haiti his followers brandish machetes while in a possession trance, and as in Brazil, they wear blue garments and blue beaded necklaces.

From these three loci of the slave trade and the efflorescence of African-derived religions, devotion to Ogou/Ogum/Ogun has spread throughout North and South America and the Caribbean.

Brian Brazeal

See also Babalawo; Candomblé; Santería; Vodoun.

FURTHER READING

Apter, Andrew. *Black Critics and Kings: the Hermeneutics of Power in Yoruba Society*. Chicago: Univesity of Chicago Press.

Barnes, Sandra, ed. *Africa's Ogun: Old World and New*. Bloomington: Indiana University Press.

Bascom, William. 1969. *Ifa Divination: Communication Between Gods and Men in West Africa*. Bloomington: Indiana University Press.

Bascom, William. 1984. *The Yoruba of Southwestern Nigeria*. Prospect Heights IL: Waveland Press. (Orig. pub. 1969).

Bastide, Roger. 2007. *The African Religions of Brazil: Toward a Sociology of the Interpenetration of Civilizations*, trans. Helen Seeba. Baltimore: Johns Hopkins University Press (new ed.).

Brown, David H. 2004. *Santería Enthroned: Art, Ritual and Innovation in an Afro-Cuban Religion*. Chicago: University of Chicago Press.

Cosentino, Donald, ed. 1995. *Sacred Arts of Haitian Vodou*. Los Angeles: University of California, Los Angeles, Fowler Museum of Cultural History.

Hurston, Zora Neale. 1938. *Tell My Horse*. Philadelphia: J.B. Lippincott Company.

Okpewho, Isidore (1941−)

Isidore Okpewho is a prolific writer whose accomplishments in creative writing are strongly matched by his outstanding contributions to African literary criticism and scholarship. Quite easily, Okpewho is regarded as the preeminent scholar on African oral performance traditions whose works, such as *The Epic in Africa* (1979), *Myth in Africa* (1983), *African Oral Literature* (1992), and *Once Upon a Kingdom: Myth, Hegemony, and Identity* (1998), and the collections he edited, *The Heritage of African Poetry* (1985) and *The Oral Performance in Africa* (1990), are highly received. As a novelist, Okpewho chronicles some of the social, political, and economic issues facing African societies, such as minority rights, ethnicity, and polygamy.

Okpewho was born on November 9, 1941, in Abraka, in the Delta region of Nigeria. He studied classics at the University of Ibadan, won the Sir James Robertson Prize for best classics student, and earned his bachelor's degree with first-class honors in 1964. In 1974, he earned a doctorate in comparative literature at the University of Denver and another in humanities from the University of London in 2003. Okpewho's literary production effectively began after graduation from college, when he worked as editor in the Lagos office of Longman publishers. While with Longman he published his first novel, *The Victims* (1970), a work that presents a gritty image of African polygamy exacerbated by the demands of contemporary urban life.

Okpewho's two subsequent novels, *The Last Duty* (1976) and *Tides* (1993), fix an unrelenting gaze at the shaping of the modern Nigerian nation state. The former won the African Arts Prize for Literature and the latter, the Commonwealth Writers Prize for Africa.

By the early 1990s, Okpewho's creative and scholarship interests had substantially widened to explore folks arts not only in Africa but also in the African Diaspora, especially in the Americas. In 1994 he had contributed a chapter, "The Cousins of Uncle Remus," to *The Black Columbiad: Defining Moments in African American Literature and Culture*, edited by W. Sollors and M. Diedrich. In 1999 he coedited *The African Diaspora: African Origins and New World Identities* with Carole Boyce Davies and Ali A. Mazrui, followed by a study of the African American poet Jay Wright in the essay, "Prodigal's Progress: Jay Wright's Focal Center" (*MELUS* 23 (3): 187–209). In 2002 his essay "Walcott, Homer, and the Black Atlantic" appeared in the journal *Research in African Literatures*. His novel, *Call Me by My Rightful Name* (2004), marks what could be regarded as the ultimate union of Okpewho's creative imagination with his scholarship, as the novel explores the roots of an African Diaspora identity through a narrative aesthetic that leans heavily on Yoruba oral poetic traditions.

Chiji Akoma

See also Africa.

FURTHER READING

Killam, Douglas, and Ruth Rowe, eds. 2000. *The Companion to African Literatures*. London: James Currey Publishers.

Obiechina, Emmanuel. 1996. "Isidore Okpewho." *Dictionary of Literary Biography*, Volume 157: *Twentieth-Century Caribbean and Black African Writers*, 3rd Series, ed. Bernth Lindfors and Reinhard Sander, 262–276. Detroit: Gale Research, Inc.

Schipper, Mineke. 1989. *Beyond the Boundaries: African Literature and Literary Theory*. London: Allison & Busby with W. A. Allen.

Old Hige

In Jamaica, Ole Hige (also known as Kin Owl) is believed to be an elderly woman or witch who has the ability to take off her skin and fly about the island in a stream of fire. She particularly favors newborn babies, sucking their blood. In earlier times, mothers afraid of Old Hige crossed a knife and fork and put a Bible next to their child's bed, keeping vigil. Infant lockjaw was considered a sign of Old Hige's visitation and much precaution was therefore taken to protect the child. It was believed that after the ninth night, a newborn would be safe from Old Hige.

Known also as "the soucouyant" in the Eastern Caribbean, Old Hige is sometimes thought to be a duppy (or spirit) but has also been imagined as a woman who lives in the community, keeping her secret. She may also have some connection to the Ashanti *obayifo*—a sorcerer who leaves his or her body at night, streaming flames, catching souls, and drinking human blood.

The way to defeat Old Hige is to find her skin and sprinkle it with salt and pepper. The expression, "salt and pepper to yu Mammy," has its origin here, for these words must be repeated to ward off the witch's evil.

Marcia Douglas

See also Jamaica; Obeah.

FURTHER READING

Banbury, Rev. Thomas. 1894. *Jamaica Superstitions; or the Obeah Book*. Kingston: Mortimer C. DeSouza.

Barnes, "Busta" Leslie. 2000. "Rolling Calf." In *Jamaican Folk Tales and Oral Histories*, ed. Laura Tanna. Miami: DLT Associates, Inc.

Hurston, Zora Neale. 1938. "Hunting the Wild Hog." *Tell My Horse: Voodoo and Life in Haiti and Jamaica*. New York: Lippincott Inc.

Moore, Brian L., and Michele Johnson. 2000. "Afro-Creole Belief System I: Obeah, Duppies and Other 'Dark Superstitions.'" In *Neither Led Nor Driven: Contesting British Cultural Imperialism in Jamaica, 1865–1920*, 38–39. Mona: University of the West Indies Press.

Olmos, Margarite Fernández, and Lizabeth Paravisini-Gebert. 2003. "Obeah Myal and Quimbois." In *Creole Religions of the Caribbean: An Introduction from Vodou and Santería to Obeah and Espiritismo*, 131–140. New York: New York University Press.

Olodum

Olodum—short for Yoruba supreme being Olodumaré—is a popular, percussion-based band whose thundering rhythms and social vision have made it the driving force behind the revival of one of Brazil's most African, and most beautiful, cities: Salvador, Bahia. The group's samba-reggae fusion helped put Bahia on the world's musical map, making a mecca of the once-decrepit and dangerous lanes of Salvador's cliffside old town, Pelourinho. The first celebrated Bloco Afro in Carnaval Salvador, Olodum has lured a worldwide following through its layered rhythms and social vision, symbolized by an encircled peace sign set against a backdrop of green, red, yellow, and brown. Free, twice-weekly concerts made it one of the most successful grassroots organizations in the world and a guiding star to thousands of children looking for their musical voice.

Members of Olodum practice in Pelourinho Street, Salvador, Bahia, Brazil. (Ricardo Azoury/Corbis)

Olodum's reggae-samba fusion introduced a new musical voice to the world, inspiring Paul Simon to lease it for his "Rhythm of the Saints" recording, made during a free 1991 summer concert he and Olodum gave in Central Park before an estimated 700,000 people. The group's appeal owes largely to its mesmerizing drumming scheme, which runs the gamut from the fine-sounding *repique* to middle-range *timbao,* the deeper *macasao,* and the big, bass *surdo*.

The band's annual Carnival themes regularly push the envelope on social issues and global trends. Olodum's social activism extends well beyond the pre-Lenten season: the group

led an effort to include a chapter protecting the rights of Afro-Brazilians in Bahia's constitution, held a march of more than 50,000 people to mark the 100th anniversary of slavery's abolition in Brazil, and mounted vociferous opposition to South African apartheid. It dedicated its two platinum records to Nelson Mandela and threw a huge party when Desmond Tutu visited Salvador in 1989.

Proceeds from Olodum's overseas forays have traditionally gone to fund the group's Creative School on Rua das Laranjeiras, which feeds, molds, and ennobles the spirits of musically minded Brazilian children and youth. In addition to mastering an instrument, these students—many former street urchins—study Portuguese, English, dance, and diction. Beneath posters of Malcolm X and Martin Luther King, Jr., they also take courses in human rights issues, self-esteem, racial democracy, nonviolent resistance, and Bahia's Afro-Brazilian heritage. Many make their first public appearance, and assume their first personal commitment, as a member of an Olodum ensemble.

Close to the Creative School lies Olodum House (*A Casa de Olodum*), the group's administrative headquarters and site of the Nelson Mandela Auditorium. The three-story colonial gem, restored by the city of Salvador as part of a neighborhood reconstruction project, emerged from the shell of a structure that dated back to the late 1800s. Its spacious, airy interior was designed by architect Lina Bo Bardi and has welcomed more than 50,000 visitors.

Olodum, which was founded on April 25, 1979, seeks to incorporate blacks and other marginalized members of Bahian society into Brazil's oldest and most traditional Carnival celebration. Voted top *Bloco Afro* in 1985, the group has since appeared in more than 20 countries, yet has never abandoned its commitment to the humble origins of Maciel-Pelourinho, where T-shirt salespeople and other street vendors earn a daily wage selling products emblazoned with the Olodum emblem, which has also become the foremost emblem of Bahia.

Ralph Schusler

See also Brazil: Afro-Brazilians; Cachoeira; Carnival; Ilê Aiyê.

FURTHER READING
Jorge, Joao, et al. 2005. *OLODUM Carnaval Cultura Négritude 1979–2005.* Salvador, Bahia: Bloco Afro Olodum.
Vianna, Hermano. 1999. *The Mystery of Samba: Popular Music and National Identity in Brazil.* Chapel Hill: University of North Carolina Press.

Optiz, May Ayim (1960–1996)

May Ayim Optiz was born to Emmanuel Ayim, a Ghanaian, and Ursula Andler, a German, in Hamburg on May 3, 1960. Her first year and a half were spent in a children's home, after which she was adopted by foster parents who gave her their last name, Optiz. She lived with the Optiz family from 1962 to1979 in North-Rhine Westphalia. She attended schools in Muenster before studying at the University of Regensburg, from which she graduated in 1986. The title of her thesis was *Afro-Deutsche, Ihre Kultur- und Sozialgeschichte auf dem Hintergrund gesellschaftlicher Veränderungen* ("Showing Our Colours, Afro-German Women Speak Out"), which was later published in the book, *Farbe bekennen. Afro-deutsche Frauen auf den Spuren ihrer Geschichte.* It was then translated into *Showing Our Colours: Afro-German Women Speak Out* in England and the United States in 1992. She was one of the founders of the *Initiative Schwarze Deutsche* in 1986. She also cofounded the *Literatur Frauen e. V., Verein zur Förderung der Literaturen der Frauen*. She worked as a speech therapist in a therapeutic pedagogy school for mentally retarded children in 1990 and subsequently wrote a thesis on ethnocentrism and sexism in speech therapy. She further worked on this theme at the Freien Universität Berlin in 1992.

Optiz strove to draw awareness to the plight of the Afro-deutsche and people of African descent living in Germany, presenting her work in forums such as Ghana's PANAFEST (Pan-African Historical Theatre Festival). Her poetry collection, *Blues in Schwarz—Weiss*, was published in 1995. After a series of illnesses, which led to admissions into psychiatric hospitals in Berlin, she committed suicide in 1996. The May Ayim Award (2004) for young Africans initiated by the United Nations Educational, Scientific, Cultural Organization has immortalized her in recognition of her tireless efforts to bring social changes into the lives of people of African descent living in Germany.

Tomi Adeaga

See also Germany and the African Diaspora.

Ortiz, Fernando (1881–1969)

Fernando Ortiz is considered a key figure in the study of 20th-century Afro-Cuban culture. Along with Nina Rodrigues and U. B. Phillips, Ortiz was one of the first intellectuals who studied black societies in the Americas. Born in Havana on July 16, 1881, he was of Spanish descent; his father had Basque roots and his mother was a native Cuban. He studied law at the University of Havana until 1899, when he decided to settle in Barcelona, Spain, to complete his degree. Afterward, he moved to Madrid, where he pursued his doctorate in law and attended classes at the *Instituto Sociológico*, founded by Professor Manuel Sales y Ferré, who introduced him to penitentiary sciences, criminology, and penal law. Between 1902 and 1905, Ortiz lived in different European cities while working for Cuban consulates (Spain, France, and Switzerland). In Geneva, he had the opportunity to attend classes taught by Cesare Lombroso, a well-known medical doctor and psychiatrist who founded the field of criminal anthropology. Ortiz conducted investigations that covered a wide range of disciplines, such as anthropology, law, ethnology, history, folk culture, criminology, linguistics, archeology, art, religion, geography, literature, and identity.

In Latin America, Ortiz created the concept he termed "transculturation," to convey the influence of Africa, other continents, and other races in shaping the culture of the New World. During the early days of the Republic, he was actively involved in Cuban national life as a college professor. He also taught public law at the University of Havana for nine years. Beginning in 1910, and for 50 years on, he was in charge of the *Revista Bimestral Cubana* (Bimonthly Cuban Review) under the aegis of the *Sociedad Económica de Amigos del País* (Economic Society of the Friends of the Country) of which he had become a member in 1907. In 1926, he founded *Sociedad Hispano-Cubana de Cultura*, whose goal was to promote culture: it sponsored the first movie conferences, painting exhibits, and the presentation of major black novelists and poets highlighting the relationship between Hispanic elements and African ones. From 1931 to 1933, he exiled himself in Washington, D.C., to show his opposition to General Machado's dictatorship in Cuba. In 1930, he created *Surco* and *Ultra*, two reviews that dealt with Cuban culture. In 1937, he founded the *Sociedad de Estudios Afro-Cubanos* aimed at analyzing the demographic, legal, religious, literary, artistic, linguistic, and social phenomena generated by the coexistence of different races in Cuba. In 1954, Columbia University awarded him an honorary doctoral degree.

In 1906, Ortiz began his first investigations on the African, Asian, and American culture, which led to the publication of *Los Negros Brujos* (*Black Witch Doctors*); it was the first part of *Hampa Afro-Cubana* (*Afro-Cuban Mob*). This criminal ethnology study analyzed the Cuban society and its ethnic components. In this book, he raised the issue of blackness in Cuba from a scientific, social, and historical point of view. Ortiz believed black Cuban witchcraft was instrumental to the understanding of their idiosyncrasy. This work eventually turned out to be the starting point of his intellectual quest. In 1916, he published *Los Negros Esclavos* (*Black Slaves*), second part of *Hampa Afro-Cubana*, in which he dealt with the Afro-Cuban mob by stressing its anthropological, legal, philosophical, and economic dimensions. Moreover, he brought attention to the geographical origins of Afro-Cubans in their motherland and examined the key features of ethnic groups like the Wolof, Fulani, Mandingo, Lucumi, Arara, Dahomey, Mina, Carabali, and Congo, who constitute the African roots of Cuba to this day. The third part of his work included books on free blacks, and on the Abakuas to complete his study on Cuban delinquency.

In other respects, Ortiz studied and analyzed African oral traditions and mulatto culture. In his opinion, Cuba would not exist without blackness. In 1924, he published *El Glosario de Afronegrismos*, a study on black language in Cuba from a linguistic perspective and was one of the participants in a movement defined as *negrismo*. In 1940, he published the *Contrapunteo cubano del tabaco y el azúcar* in which he mentioned for the first time, the concept of "transculturation" (later used by Bronislaw Malinowski), which reflects the culture shock and the subsequent formation of a synthetic culture. Cultural interpenetration generates the emergence of a new entity. Moreover, the "transcultural method" would make it possible to combine economic, social, and political elements and hereby understand society.

Between 1946 and 1952, Ortiz investigated Cuban music, instruments, theater, dance, and their African roots. In the early 1950s, he published *La Africania de la Música Folklórica de Cuba* (*Africa in Cuban Folk Music*), *Los bailes y el teatro de los negros en el Folklore de Cuba* (*Black dances and theater in Cuban Folk Culture*), and *Los instrumentos de la música afrocubana* (*Afro-Cuban Music Instruments*).

Ortiz died on April 10, 1969, in Havana on L and 23 streets in the Vedado neighborhood where the Fernando Ortiz Library and the *Fundación Fernando Ortiz* are located. The foundation, now chaired by the Cuban writer Miguel Barnet, promotes investigations and knowledge of Afro-Cuban issues. It also awards an annual prize (*L'adya*) that symbolizes Obatala, a Yoruba divinity.

Carlos A. Rabasso

See also Abakuá; Cuba: Afro-Cubans; Obeah; Santería.

FURTHER READING
Iznaga, Diana. 1989. *Transculturación en Fernando Ortiz*. La Habana: Editorial de Ciencias Sociales.
Matos Arevalos, José Antonio. 1999. *La Historia en Fernando Ortiz*. La Habana: Fundación Fernando Ortiz.
Ortiz, Fernando. 1973. *Hampa Afro-Cubana. Los Negros Brujos (Apuntes para un estudio de etnología criminal)*. Miami: Ediciones Universal.
Ortiz, Fernando. 1996. *Los Negros Esclavos*. La Habana: Editorial de Ciencias Sociales.
Suarez, Norma. 1996. *Fernando Ortiz y la Cubanidad*. La Habana: Ediciones Unión & Fundación Fernando Ortiz.

Osun (Oxum/Ochun/Oshun)

The goddess (orisha) Osun is the deity of fresh water, wealth, fertility, and kindness in the indigenous Yoruba tradition called 'Ifa. The Odu *Ose Tura* states that Osun was the only woman among the 17 original Orisa to come from heaven to Earth. Osun was ignored and left out of the serious work of the male divinities because of her gender. Eventually, the male divinities had to appease her in order to have success with their work and efforts. From that point forward Osun/women were no longer to be excluded.

Scholar and priestess of Osun Deidre Badejo identifies Osun as the communal mother of an African World. In this role as communal mother, the Yoruba goddess has given birth to generations of communities in the Diaspora. Through migrations within Africa and through the forced dispersal during the transatlantic enslavement of Africans, those who were able to survive the journeys carried with them their history, their culture, and their traditions.

As Osun manifests in the Diaspora, her children have adapted their worship to fit the various frameworks. Some have even claimed her to be the patron "saint" of their locality. In the Cuban tradition *Santería,* she is *Caridad del Cobre* and is also called *Ochun*; in the Candomblé tradition of Brazil she is *Oxum* or *Pomba Gira*; in Voudoun of Dahomey (Benin) and Voudoun of Haiti she is *Erzulie*. The variations in the names and styles of Osun in traditional practice continue throughout the Diaspora as time and physical distance lend to the adaptations and changes of ancient African traditions.

Statuette of the deity Osun in a Candomblé temple in Olinda, Brazil. (Laurence Fordyce; Eye Ubiquitous/Corbis)

Each Orisa is associated with a color, number, element in nature, and characteristics. Osun's original color is white. Her priests in Nigeria use this as the principal color. During the Osun Osogbo festival, priests, devotees, and participants will wear white. The Osun River, where the festival is held, is said to have medicinal powers, and people crowd the river gathering the waters to fulfill their wishes. She lives in the river, and a popular story of Osun says that she was very tidy and would go to the river constantly to wash her white garment. Eventually, the dress turned yellow from washing in the water, and this is how yellow became one of her colors. She is also associated with gold, representing riches and her position as a queen; green, because of wealth and her relationship with the deity of wisdom, Orunmila; red, because of her relationship with Sango; and pastels (pink, lavender, etc.) representing her lightheartedness and happiness. Osun loves to eat honey, gin, hens, and sweet wine. Her sacred number is five, and her most sacred animal is the fish, according to Osogbo tradition.

Osogbo, Nigeria, is the worldwide center of Osun worship and where the annual Osun festival is held in early August. Osun's highest priestess is called the Iya Osun Agbaye. She lives in the temple in Osogbo. The current Iya Osun is named Omileye Adenle. Osun is also the owner of the Eerindinlogun (16 cowry) form of divination practice, an art she acquired from her husband, Orunmila. Osun continues to morph and travel throughout the Diaspora as her children constantly create and re-create tradition.

Jessica M. Alarcón

See also Candomblé; Santería.

FURTHER READING

Alarcon, Jessica M. 2008. *(Re)Writing Osu: Osun in the Politics of Gender, Race and Sexuality— From Colonization to Creolization*. Miami, FL: Torkwase Press. Badejo, Diedre. 1996. *Osun Seegesi: The Elegant Deity of Wealth, Power and Femininity*. Trenton, NJ: Africa World Press.

Bascom, William. 1980. *Sixteen Cowries*. Bloomington: Indiana University Press.

Fatunde, Fakayode Fayemi. 2004. *Oshun the Manly Woman*. Brooklyn, NY: Athelia Henrietta Press.

Murphy, Joseph M., and Mei-Mei Sanford. 2001. *Oshun Across the Waters: A Yoruba Goddess in Africa and the Americas*. Bloomington: Indiana University Press.

Neimark, John Phillip. 1995. *The Sacred 'Ifá Oracle*. San Francisco: HarperSanFrancisco.

Olajubu, Oyeronke. 2003. *Women in the Yoruba Religious Sphere*. Albany: State University of New York Press.

Oshun State. 2000. *Osun Osogbo Festival*. Osogbo, Nigeria: Oshun State. Booklet.

Washington, Teresa N. 2005. *Our Mothers, Our Powers, Our Texts: Manifestations of Aje in Africana Literature*. Bloomington: Indiana University Press.

Oya

Goddess (Orisha) of wind, lightning, hurricane, and tornado, the chaos that disrupts unjust social orders, and the justifying word, Oya's name is Yoruba for "she tore," signifying her power for upheaval. Because of her penchant to right wrongs and empower the victimized, Oya and her qualities seem to be frequently invoked in the writings of women of African descent throughout the Diaspora. Zora Neale Hurston's *Their Eyes Were Watching God* (1938, republished 1990), Gloria Naylor's *Mama Day* (1993), Simone Schwartz-Bart's *Pluie et vent sur Telumée-Miracle* (1980), and Myriam Warner-Vieyra's *Juletane* (1982) are novels that dramatize the destructive balancing of social hierarchical powers that characterizes Oya's intervention on behalf of downtrodden or mistreated women.

Of all the Yoruba Ifa riverain goddesses whose followers could be venerated as devotees or condemned as practitioners of witchcraft, Oya seems to be the witch/goddess most feared and encrypted throughout the Diaspora. Though she remains Oya of cemeteries, hurricanes, and thunderstorms in Cuban Santería, she surfaces as the feared Ti Kita of Haitian Voudoun, still symbolized by the black cloth she tore in her West African origins, the source of her name, but believed to be relegated solely to a cult dedicated to mysteries of death and destructive magic. In Brazilian Candomblé, Oya seems to be dispersed between the revered Iansá and the benevolent works of women's societies such as the Sisters of the Good Death, her more malevolent powers returned in public worship to her husband, called Xango in Candomblé. Such limitations and identity dispersions are probably best understood in their historical context of chattel enslavement's several hundred years of the binding and silencing impact of the forced intimate intermingling of various traditions, complicated by religious, philosophical, and linguistic suppression. Writing against this tidal legacy, women authors of the African Diaspora are resurrecting Oya with a devastatingly poignant eloquence reminiscent of her own articulate, piercing powers.

Thief of lightning, Oya appropriates traditionally masculine powers in the service of her own disturbance of rigid, oppressive, or ostracizing social orders. A purifying wind that brings storms to shatter the mind and heart and scatter one's enemies, Oya allows afflictions of anguish, despair, or insanity to drive her protagonists to respond to betrayals of the most heinous kinds with spiritual transcendence and even triumph (of an often bloody kind) over their tormentors.

Wife of Shango who resurrected her suicidal husband, Oya carries souls between the lands of the living and the dead. She can gift the infertile with babies and return both the world-weary and their abusers to the spiritual realm, there to live renewed by an insightful understanding of their earthly and otherworldly existences, the purposes of their existence, and the goals for which they struggled all resolved under the leveling influence of Oya's volatile hand. The veil between the worlds is irrevocably sundered by evocation of the goddess who bridges barriers and forces turbulent change.

Alexis Brooks de Vita

See also Candomblé; Osun (Oxum/Ochun/Oshun); Santería; Shango.

FURTHER READING
Brooks de Vita, Alexis. 2000. "Air and Fire, Bringing Rain." In *Mythatypes: Signatures and Signs of African/Diaspora and Black Goddesses,* 101–122. Westport, CT: Greenwood Press.
Fatunmbi, *Awo* Fa'lokun. 1993. *Oya: Ifá and the Spirit of the Wind.* New York: Original Publications.
Fatunmbi, *Awo* Fa'lokun. 1993. *Shango: Ifá and the Spirit of Lightning.* New York: Original Publications.
Gleason, Judith. 1992. *Oya: In Praise of an African Goddess.* New York: HarperCollins.
Harding, Rachel E. 2003. *A Refuge in Thunder: Candomblé and Alternative Spaces of Blackness.* Bloomington: Indiana University Press.

P

Pacific: The African Diaspora

The first African Diaspora to the Pacific region was created tens of thousands of years ago when humans first migrated from the mother continent—Africa—where all people are thought to have originated. DNA studies currently suggest this took place around 65,000 years ago. Some oral traditions suggest that the early peoples of Southeast Asia were black or dark skinned, and this is supported by the African-appearance of peoples living in certain isolated areas, such as the Andaman Islands off the coast of Burma. Later migrations of an Asian branch of humanity moved east and southeast and gradually displaced or absorbed the original populations to produce a physical type that shows characteristics typical of both strains. The eastward movement of these Asians appears to have gone in two main directions: the northern one crossing into the Americas to give rise to the Native American peoples and other groups migrating via a southern route down through the black islands—Melanesia—acquiring some of the genetic markers of those populations before fanning out into the Pacific and colonizing the smaller islands known today as Polynesia. The Polynesians, who show some genetic affinities with their Melanesian neighbors, were the most recent of the early migrants, arriving perhaps 3,000 or 4,000 years ago.

The Melanesian people, the most populous, have the most obvious African ancestral connection. They occupy the larger islands in the southwest region of the Pacific, namely Vanuatu, Fiji, New Caledonia, the Solomon Islands, and Papua New Guinea—so named by Europeans because the people and climate there reminded them of "old" Guinea in Africa. Significant Melanesian populations are also found in the Philippines, Indonesia, and the Torres Strait Islands of Australia. The black or Melanesian countries have the largest landmass areas, the largest populations, and the richest agricultural and mineral resources: gold, copper, nickel, oil, timber, cattle, fish, sugar, cocoa, and coffee are all produced in this region.

ANTIQUITY

Archaeologists assert, on the basis of current evidence, that the present black populations of the Pacific date back 40,000 years for Papua New Guinea, 22,000 years for the Solomon Islands, 20,000 for Vanuatu, and 3,000 for Fiji, and the limits for Black Australians (also known

as Aborigines, which means "original inhabitants," who are considered to be distinct from
Melanesians) have recently been extended from
40,000 to more than 50,000 years. Because there
is no evidence of a land bridge between these
countries, such as the one that connected North
America to Asia during the last Ice Age, the
Black Pacific peoples were most likely the
world's first sailors and navigators. Other evidence of the resourcefulness of these early black
communities is found in Papua New Guinea,
where 9,000-year-old irrigation terraces show
the inhabitants to be among the world's first to
practice agriculture (Bellwood 1980).

EARLY CONTACTS

Modern Pacific history did not begin with the
arrival of Ferdinand Magellan, James Cook, or
Louis-Antoine de Bougainville. For the southwest quadrant at least there appears to have
been ample opportunity for contacts of various kinds in which Africa may have played a
part. During this pre-European period there
were meaningful links and exchanges between
the two regions, including the following:

1. Indonesians sailed across the Indian
   Ocean and made direct contact with
   Africa, probably from the 5th to the
   10th centuries (Verin 1981). Some settled in Madagascar, where their descendants—the Merina or Hova
   people—still speak an Indonesian-
   based language.
2. Indian trade extended from East Africa
   to the southwest Pacific, where Hindu
   religious and political influences have
   been important; evidence for this is
   seen in the Srivijaya Empire in Indonesia and the Hindu religion of Bali.
3. Arab trade likewise extended from East
   Africa into the Pacific, creating important Muslim communities in China,
   Thailand, Malaysia, and the Philippines
   and giving rise to the world's most populous Islamic nation today—Indonesia.

4. Asian trade contacts with Melanesia for
   sandalwood, pearl, and sea cucumber
   had long been in place when a rapid expansion of Chinese commercial and
   political initiative took place early in
   the 1400s under the Muslim admiral
   Cheng He, which reached beyond the
   Pacific, as far as the Red Sea and East
   Africa.
5. Trade and social contacts occurred between black Australians and their
   neighbors to the north, in Indonesia,
   Malaya, and Papua New Guinea. Some
   of these Australians had traveled and
   worked in Southeast Asia long before
   Europeans arrived.

These contacts suggest many opportunities for
interaction among the regions discussed, and
they are currently receiving the attention of a
new generation of world historians whose
careful research promises to develop these possibilities in considerably more depth (Keita
2005).

EUROPEAN HEGEMONY

The European conquest of the Americas and
their encroachments elsewhere reached into
the Pacific, and by the 19th century virtually
every Pacific territory had fallen under the control of outside powers—the Spanish, Portuguese, English, French, German, Dutch, or
American. Pacific peoples suffered greatly, and
many were lured, tricked, or kidnapped from
their homes and sold into servitude or slavery.
Early sugar plantations in Queensland, Australia, were worked by Melanesians, mostly
from Vanuatu and New Caledonia, some of
whom had been recruited while others were
captured by slavers commonly known as
"blackbirders."

AUSTRALIAN PENAL COLONY

African connections to the Pacific are better
documented during the late 18th century as a
result of spillover from the European activities

in the Americas. When the British lost their North American colonies in the U.S. War of Independence (1775–1783), they turned to Australia, a continent in the southwest Pacific with a relatively sparse population, close to Asia and Melanesia. Instead of slavery, the British opted for the forced labor of convicts, and the first 700 of these from English prisons landed in January 1788. Free settlers came later, especially when gold was found in 1851, but for the first few decades of the 19th century convicts were routinely deported to the emerging Australian colonies. When those colonies were united into a federal commonwealth in 1901 it was the policy that only Europeans would be allowed to settle there, but the infamous "White Australia" policy was an oxymoron at best, because Australia was never white to begin with. Furthermore, a good number of the convicts sent there—beginning with the very first fleet in 1788—were people of African descent, and included former slaves or free blacks from the United States, Britain, and the Caribbean (Duffield 1988). Their numbers have been variously estimated to have been from 2 percent to 6 percent of the arrivals at that time. Black convicts continued to arrive well into the 1830s.

BLACK CONVICTS

Evidence for this black presence, although often overlooked, is plentiful in published journals, travel accounts and memoirs of the time, and convict records preserved in various archives. John Caesar, an Afro-Englishman (born either in Africa or the West Indies) living in Deptford, England, was convicted in 1784 (or 1786) for theft and was sentenced to seven years' transportation to the convict colony of New South Wales. Deptford, a town on the Thames River downstream from London, was the site of shipbuilding yards, docks, and a naval base and, like other such towns, already had a black community by the 18th century. Caesar arrived at Botany Bay in January 1788 aboard the ship *Alexander* in the very first shipment of prisoners. He escaped several times,

only to be recaptured. On his last escape Caesar lived free as an outlaw before finally falling victim to bounty hunters in 1796. In the Australian national myth there looms the bushranger, a figure of heroic proportions, a poor settler or ex-convict turned outlaw who rebels against an unjust system and defies it successfully for a while until treachery brings him an untimely end. The Irish-Australian Ned Kelly, a notorious bushranger in the 1870s, is a national icon, but Australia's *first* bushranger was John Caesar, a black man, who preceded Kelly by almost a century (Ward 1958).

Black convicts transported to Australia included British-born blacks, Africans or West Indians living in England, and at least 40 U.S.-born individuals. American slaves who, with the promise of freedom, had joined the British forces during the Revolutionary War and again during the War of 1812 had ended up in Canada or Sierra Leone, while others had settled in England—mostly in port cities. The Afro-British population grew steadily during the 18th century, as Britain's military and commercial influence came to dominate the Atlantic. After 1830, colonial courts began sentencing slaves directly from the Caribbean, and so people from Jamaica, Barbados, Trinidad, and other points were added to the traffic south. Yet another source of black deportees to Australia was the Cape Colony in South Africa, where a new supreme court in 1828 began sentencing petty criminals to transportation, a practice that lasted for about a decade (Duly 1979).

Prison sentences were in multiples of seven; seven years was the minimum and fourteen was the average, although terms could last up to "life." Although some convicts left after their term expired, many stayed, benefiting from the grant of land accorded to new settlers. Black ex-convicts signed on as crew, leaving Australia and returned to Britain or America; some simply went to sea and worked on trade or whaling ships—arduous work that was open to men of all races—while others gravitated elsewhere. Popular tradition in Vanuatu, for example, tells of an African American who operated a successful cotton plantation on Efaté Island in the 1860s. Of the African descendants who remained in Australia there is little trace, as most appear to have been absorbed into the main population, yet in recent years several communities have laid claim to their Afro-Australian ancestral heritage.

GOLD RUSH

The 19th century saw more and more free settlers in the Australian colonies and fewer convicts, so that by mid-century the penal colony system was in its last days. The discovery of gold in 1851 set off a gold rush that by 1852 was joined by settlers, freed convicts, and an influx of immigrants. These came to include adventurers from California, which the United States had acquired from Mexico in the 1848 Treaty of Guadalupe Hidalgo, and which itself had been the scene of a major gold rush in 1849. The Mexican constitution had outlawed slavery in 1829 when California was still a part of Mexico, so that territory had been a destination for African Americans—free or fugitive. After the California gold rush peaked in 1852, a number of prospectors—black and white—pulled up stakes and took passage to Australia. Included in their number were John Jacobs, brother of Harriet Jacobs, author of *Incidents in the Life of a Slave Girl*, and Harriet's son Joseph. Australian newspaper accounts in the 1850s make mention of parties of "coloured Americans," "Jamaican blacks," "an American man of colour," and "a party of American blacks [who] took 500 ounces of gold out of one hole" (Potts and Potts 1985).

EUREKA STOCKADE

African Americans were present at a defining moment in Australian history, when protests against licence fees led to a rebellion against the authority of the British crown. Several hundred miners, a number of whom were black, took up positions in the fortified Eureka Stockade and defied the crown's authority. Redcoat troops stormed the stockade at dawn on December 3, 1854, putting the insurrection down with considerable force but losing their own captain to a rebel bullet. Two black men were among the survivors accused of treason and brought to trial: John Joseph an African American from Baltimore, Maryland (or Boston), and James Campbell, from Kingston, Jamaica. Despite damning testimony against them, both men were acquitted. As the Australian gold rush tapered off some prospectors remained on their claims, still finding the precious metal, some drifted into towns and cities to look for work, and others signed on to ships to try their luck elsewhere. Of those remaining little or nothing is known, unless they distinguished themselves in some way, like Harry Sellars, an African American living in Melbourne, who won the Victorian middleweight boxing championship title in the 1860s (Potts and Potts 1985). Similarly, for the rest of the Pacific, there are no accurate figures for the individuals of African descent who may have left their mark in the region. A footnote to the "Mutiny on the Bounty" story shows that one of the crew was a West Indian, Midshipman Edward Young, born in 1762 (or 1766) in Saint Kitts, who ended his days on Pitcairn Island with Fletcher Christian and the other mutineers.

THE SPANISH-AMERICAN WAR

The next African American contacts with the Pacific were mainly military, coming at intervals of about a half century. The first of these was during and after the Spanish-American War (1898) when the United States sent black troops to help crush the Philippine independence movement. This was the first time since emancipation that the United States had used African Americans in an overseas war, and although black citizens generally welcomed the chance to prove their loyalty and patriotism, there was considerable sympathy for the "little brown brothers" who were falling under American control. African Americans often felt an affinity with the Filipino people, and after black units were withdrawn in 1902 some 500 individuals chose to remain rather than return to the United States (Gatewood 1971).

WORLD WAR II

The next major African American contacts in the Pacific came during World War II, when thousands of "colored troops" were sent to the region, mostly in engineer (labor) battalions. Black troops were with the first wartime convoy to reach Melbourne in February 1942, and by May of that year—a mere six months after the United States had entered the war—there were more than 5,000 in Australia and New Guinea alone. More were to arrive later. One of the U.S. black battalions included John Oliver Killens, who in later years drew on his wartime experiences for his vivid novel *And Then We Heard the Thunder*. This phase of the war was centered in the southwest Pacific, where the Japanese had occupied Malaya, Indonesia, the Philippines, the Solomons, and parts of New Guinea and had bombed northern Australia as a prelude to invasion. Meanwhile, Australia, New Caledonia, and Vanuatu (then known as the New Hebrides) were the centers for the American and Allied buildup, and were the launch points for the actions that would eventually turn back the Japanese.

POSTWAR DEVELOPMENTS

The relative freedom and prosperity that U.S. African Americans seemed to enjoy—in contrast to the colonized peoples of Melanesia and the subject Aboriginal people of Australia—gave many of those Pacific peoples a greater awareness of themselves and an urgent sense that change was needed. Change has come. The U.S. Civil Rights Movement of the 1960s inspired black Australians and galvanized their efforts to finally achieve citizenship in 1967. Since then, most Melanesian countries have become independent: Fiji in 1970, Papua New Guinea in 1975, Solomon Islands in 1978, and Vanuatu in 1980. Independence movements are active in New Caledonia, which is still controlled by France, and West Papua (Western New Guinea), which has been absorbed into Indonesia.

Black Pacific peoples often look to African Americans for inspiration and are intensely interested in events taking place in the United States. Youngsters take cues from music, the reading public seeks African-American writers, and local poets take inspiration from such literary greats as Langston Hughes. Growing political and economic power in Black America is watched with great interest, because Pacific peoples themselves were dispossessed and disadvantaged through colonialism. Even more important is the need to reclaim a heritage and cultural identity that have been badly damaged by events of the past few hundred years. Here too the U.S. African American example has been salient: Pacific people are beginning to talk with pride about the "Melanesian or custom" way and to acknowledge their historical connection to Africa.

RECENT DIASPORA

As a prosperous member of the industrialized Western world Australia has attracted immigrants and refugees of diverse origins to the extent that its population can no longer be characterized as mainly Anglo-Celtic. Black Britons have made their home there as well as refugees from countries like Somalia, Ethiopia, Liberia, Sierra Leone, and Congo, so that now there are small African communities established in most of the major cities. African-born Australians in recent years have included university professors, a beauty queen, and a captain of the national rugby team.

David W. H. Pellow

See also Indian Ocean and the African Diaspora; United Kingdom: The African Diaspora.

FURTHER READING
Bellwood, P. S. 1980. "The Peopling of the Pacific." *Scientific American* 243 (November): 174–183.

Duffield, Ian. 1988. "From Slave Colonies to Penal Colonies: The West Indian Convict Transportees to Australia." In *De la traite à l'esclavage. Actes du colloque international sur la traite des Noirs, Nantes 1985*, vol. 2, ed. Serge Daget, 315–331. Nantes, France: Centre de Recherche sur l'histoire du monde atlantique.

Duly, Leslie C. 1979. "'Hottentots to Hobart and Sydney': The Cape Supreme Court's Use of Transportation 1828–1838." *Australian Journal of Politics and History* 25 (April): 39–50.

Gatewood, Willard B., Jr. 1971. *"Smoked Yankees" and the Struggle for Empire: Letters from Negro Soldiers, 1898–1902*. Urbana: University of Illinois Press.

Keita, Maghan. 2005. "Africans and Asians: Historiography and the Long View of Global Interaction." *Journal of World History* 16:1–30.

Potts, E. Daniel, and Annette Potts. 1968. "The Negro and the Australian Gold Rushes, 1852–1857." *Pacific Historical Review* 37 (November): 381–399.

Potts, E. Daniel, and Annette Potts. 1985. *Yanks Down Under 1941–45: The American Impact on Australia*. Melbourne, Australia: Oxford University Press.

Pybus, Cassandra. 2002. "Black Caesar: our first bushranger was a six-foot African man who arrived on the first fleet." *Arena Magazine* (February 1): 30–35.

Verin, P. 1981. "Madagascar." In *General History of Africa*. Vol. 2, *Ancient Civilizations of Africa*, ed. G. Mokhtar, 693–717. Berkeley: UNESCO, Heinemann and the University of California Press.

Udo-Ekpo, Lawrence T. 1999. *The Africans in Australia: Expectations and Shattered Dreams*. Henley Beach, South Australia: Seaview Press.

Van Sertima, Ivan. 1988. *African Presence in Early Asia*. Revised edition. New Brunswick, NJ: Transaction Books.

Ward, Russel. 1958. *The Australian Legend*. Melbourne, Australia: Oxford University Press.

Padmore, George (1901–1959)

George Padmore, whose native name was Malcolm Ivan Meredith Nurse, was born in 1901 in Trinidad, though there are accounts that give this year as 1902 or 1903. He qualified as "citizen of the world" having through his life expressed interest in the liberation of people under colonial rule as both victims and exploited beings. In 1924, he migrated to the United States after his secondary education in Trinidad to study at Columbia, Fisk, New York, and Howard Universities. Fully trained as a lawyer, political scientist, and journalist, he was a communist convert who rose through the ranks, using his intellect and strong communist influence on the world stage. Padmore traveled to the Soviet Union in 1929, where he became head of the Negro Bureau of the Red International Labour Union, and to Germany in 1931, where he headed the International Trade Union Committee of Negro Workers and published *The Life and Struggles of Negro Toilers*. He wrote extensively as editor of *The Negro Champion* (later *The Liberator*) in Harlem, New York, about injustices in colonial rule and interpreted many world events unfolding at the time with Marxist tools until he left the Communist Party and became a critic of Marxism. In 1955, he wrote that black people should forget about Marxism as a tool of development and should instead free themselves from all European ideologies.

Of all the places he traveled, it was Africa where Padmore's influence became clearer. He met Kwame Nkrumah, Jomo Kenyatta, Tom Mboya, and many of the African students in London and America in the late 1940s, and activists like Garame Kouyate in Paris. He obviously impressed them as an international black activist. When he moved to live in Africa during the decolonization period after Ghana's independence in 1957, he did so as a mentor of Nkrumah and many of the leaders. He had been Nkrumah's representative in London before this, attending to and honoring invitations on his behalf, among them, serving as the best man on Nkrumah's behalf at the sensational London wedding of Joe Appiah, a Ghanaian colonial law student who married the daughter of the Labour chancellor of the exchequer, Sir Stafford Cripps.

Padmore established the International African Service Bureau and the *International African Opinion*, a journal connecting Caribbean and African political activists, trade unionists, and intellectuals. In 1944, Padmore, along with the likes of Nkrumah, Anna J. Cooper, W. E. B. DuBois, Amy Jacques Garvey, and Amy Ashwood Garvey, helped to organize the 5th Pan-African Conference in Manchester, England, which has proven to be one of the most important and strategically decisive conferences held.

While in Ghana, Padmore worked closely with Nkrumah at the Christiansburg Castle, Osu, when Nkrumah was prime minister. Padmore died in 1959, four years after Ghana gained its independence and four years before the Organization of African Unity was founded in Addis Ababa, a project to which he had given great intellectual input. It is significant that Padmore died and was buried in Accra at the Christiansburg Castle, Osu, which is still the seat of government. It seems a fitting symbol of Padmore's contribution to the country of Ghana.

Padmore had helped to establish the Africa Research Library in Ghana; therefore, in the late 1980s his body was exhumed from the Christiansburg Castle and reburied at the library, which was renamed George Padmore Research Library. The library, which was originally built as a monument to Pan-Africanism and a memorial for Padmore, is today a major African research library housing not only Padmore's books and other writings but also a one-stop shop for research on many African countries. Apart from being a reference library with affiliations to U.S. universities and libraries, it is also the storage house of materials of the Bureau of African Affairs, including letters from African leaders to Padmore and Nkrumah as well as information about the strategies that went into many policy works in Africa in the 1950s and 1960s. The library also publishes the *Ghana National Bibliography*.

Ivor Duah

See also Ghana; Nkrumah, Kwame (1909–1972); Pan-Africanism; Trinidad and Tobago.

FURTHER READING
Appiah, Joe. 1996. *The Autobiography of an African Patriot*. Accra, Ghana: Assemblies of God Publishers.
Padmore, George. 1972. *Panafricanism or Communism*. New York : Doubleday.
Padmore, George. 2007. *The Life and Struggle of Negro Toilers*. San Bernadino, CA: Borgo Press.
Tenkorang, Omari Mensah. 2005. Interview with author, May 13.

Palcy, Euzhan (1957–)

Euzhan Palcy is the best-known woman filmmaker of the Caribbean and the most recognized director from Martinique. Her most popular feature is no doubt *Rue Cases Nègres*, or *Sugar Cane Alley*, about a boy trying to achieve an education in the midst of crushing poverty and segregation in 1930s Martinique. Also successful was her drama about apartheid, *A Dry White Season*, and her three-part documentary for French television on Aimé Césaire.

Born in Martinique to a family of musicians and writers, Palcy herself read avidly and began dreaming of filmmaking at age 10 after she read Alan Paton's *Cry the Beloved Country*. When Palcy then read Martinican writer Joseph Zobel's *La Rue Cases-Nègres*, she cried at finally seeing her culture represented on the printed page. For the first time she discovered a black writer from Martinique who wrote about the poor. Though there were no images of Martinique onscreen, Palcy admired the work of Fritz Lang, Alfred Hitchcock, and Orson Welles. At age 17 she made her first film, *Le Messagère* (*The Messenger*), for French television, a black-and-white representation of Martinique's landscape and Creole-speaking people. Though discouraged by those who thought a black girl would never achieve success in France, she left for Paris where she met François Truffaut who supported her efforts to make *Sugar Cane Alley*. Based on Zobel's novel, budgetary constraints allowed for only two well-known actors, yet the film was more successful than *ET* when shown in Martinique. *Sugar Cane Alley* also succeeded in France: it won 17 awards, among them the Silver Lion at the Venice Film Festival. It marked the first time most Martinicans saw their own landscape and culture reflected in cinema. With Palcy's 1989 film, *A Dry White Season*, she became the first black woman to direct a Hollywood film. The big-budget MGM film, starring Marlon Brando, was adapted from Andre Brink's novel about the Soweto riots. Because of producers' initial reluctance to fund a film by a black filmmaker representing South African blacks, Palcy ended up telling the story of two white families. Her most recent film, *The Killing Yard*, concerns the Attica Prison uprising. She was awarded the Sojourner Truth award in 1991 at the Cannes Film Festival. She is currently working on a film version of the Japanese thriller *The Third Lady* and continues to make documentary films and made-for-TV movies.

Gerise Herndon

See also Black Paris/*Paris Noir*; Césaire, Aimé (1913–2008); Zobel, Joseph (1915–2006).

FURTHER READING

Givanni, June. 1992. "Interview with Euzhán Palcy." In *Ex-iles: Essays on Caribbean Cinema*, ed. Mbye Cham, 286–307. Trenton, NJ: Africa World Press.

Herndon, Gerise. 1996. "Auto-ethnographic Impulse in *Rue Cases-Nègres*." *Film/Literature Quarterly* 4 (3): 261–266.

Linfield, Susan. 1984. "*Sugar Cane Alley*: An Interview with Euzhan Palcy." *Cinéaste* 13 (4): 42–45.

Ménil, Alain. 1992. "*Rue Cases-Nègres* or the Antilles from the Inside." In *Ex-iles: Essays on Caribbean Cinema*, ed. Mbye Cham, 156–175. Trenton, NJ: Africa World Press.

Pan-Africanism

Pan-Africanism is an ideology developed by the African-Diaspora and based on the fundamental proposition that people of African ancestry share a common historical experience during the rise of European mercantile expansion and imperial conquest of Africa. Moreover, this common "African" experience provided the basis for the suspension of Africans as the determinant factors in their own historical development and the substitution of European historical development as the determinant influence in the lives of Africans everywhere. In this sense, modern Pan-Africanism is an ideological response to the epoch of European and Arab imperial conquest and their respective slave trades. In 1884, the Berlin conference had established the "Scramble for Africa," which had separated African precolonial nations and ethnic groups and created the artificial borders of colonial and contemporary nation-states.

Whenever one thinks of Pan-Africanism one almost always first think of Marcus Mosiah Garvey, an African-Jamaican native, and Kwame Nkrumah, of Ghana. In the first quarter of the 20th century, Garvey, having moved to the United States, led the largest mass-based movement based on the ideology of black nationalism and Pan-Africanism in the history of the African Diaspora. His organization, the Universal Negro Improvement Association, advocated "Africa for Africans" at the height of European domination of the African continent. Garvey, like Pan-African spokespersons before him, made the connection between the livelihood of Africans in the Diaspora and those on the continent long before European imperialism and the imperialist competition between modern nation-states evolved into modern globalization.

A foremost advocate of Pan-Africanism on the African continent was, of course, Nkrumah. Nkrumah realized that before Africa could achieve economic prosperity Africa must first achieve Pan-African political unity and independence: without Pan-African political unity or union, the economic development of the continent would depend on individual states' relationships to a global economy increasingly dominated by former imperial powers. In short, for Africa to prosper, Africans must return to acting in their own interests and cease operating as a footnote to European development and history. Africans must take control over their own destiny; this, in essence, is the fundamental proposition of political Pan-Africanism.

A great deal of political activity led up to the landmark first Pan-African Conference, organized in 1900 by Trinidadian Henry Sylvester Williams and Haitian Benito Sylvain in London. For example, the West African Students Union empowered a new generation of activists, some of whom would eventually have an impact on the development of African independence movements. Some also see the invasion of Ethiopia by the Italian fascists under Mussolini as a major politicizing event in the advancement of Pan-Africanism. But the first Pan African Conference is credited with establishing the use of the word and concept "Pan-Africanism," bringing together Pan-Africanist thinkers and activists from across the world and giving some concrete structure to this disparate though related set of activities. An organ, *The Pan-African*, was established and a name was given to the movement. A number of other Pan-African congresses would be held in London in 1919, 1921, 1923, and 1927; in Manchester, England, in 1945, and in Dar-es-Salaam in 1975. A more recent conference was held in 1994, organized by a new generation of Pan-African intellectuals and activists.

Tony Martin, a scholar of Pan-Africanism, identifies six dominant ideas that have formed the basis of Pan-Africanism:

1. A global African community
2. Africa as a base
3. A politically unified continent
4. A race-based global movement with a continental united states of Africa
5. Economies of scale
6. Pan-African political impact

Attempts would be made to actualize these principles, either singly or in combination, in various ways through independent nation states, political organizations, and individual scholarship and activity. Some see the more recent organizing of the African Union, which deliberately invokes the politics of Pan-Africanism, as a new possibility for those still caught in bureaucratic nation-state politics but needing a program of action for African peoples on the continent and African Diaspora peoples worldwide.

Dhoruba bin Wahad

See also African Union (AU); DuBois, William Edward Burghardt (1868–1963); Garvey, Marcus Mosiah (1887–1940); Garvey, Amy Ashwood (1897–1969); James, Cyril Lionel Robert (1901–1989); Nkrumah, Kwame (1909–1972); Padmore, George (1901–1959); Ture, Kwame (1941–1998).

FURTHER READING
Garvey, Amy Jacques, ed. 1986. *The Philosophy and Opinions of Marcus Garvey, or, Africa for the Africans*. Dover, MA: The Majority Press. (Orig. pub. in two vols. in 1923 and 1925).
Hooker, James R. 1967. *Black Revolutionary: George Padmore's Path from Communism to Pan-Africanism*. London: Pall Mall.
Martin, Tony. 1984. *The Pan-African Connection: From Slavery to Garvey and Beyond*. Dover, MA: The Majority Press. (Orig. pub. 1983).
Martin, Tony. 2006. *Amy Ashwood Garvey: Feminist, Pan-Africanist and Wife No.1, Or, A Tale of Two Amies*. Dover, MA: The Majority Press.
Mathurin, Owen. 1976. *Henry Sylvester Williams and the Origins of the Pan-African Movement*. Westport, CT: Greenwood Press.

Panama: Afro-Panamanians

Panama has been a region of political importance because of its geographic position. During colonial times, Panama was a strategic place for the Spanish Empire, as a barrier between the Caribbean and the Pacific Ocean, and thus a center of communication between the metropolis and the coasts of the Peruvian Viceroyalty. In the 19th and 20th centuries, it became a commercial point of connection in the Americas. The presence of people of African descent (and other ethnic groups) in Panama is strongly tied to the history of this nation as a place of transit. Throughout Panama's history, there have been five major immigrations to the country, with very different characteristics and from different areas. These migrations have influenced and shaped the construction of the nation in dramatic ways.

Afro-Panamanians can be divided into two major groups: those who landed in Panama as slaves in the 16th century and those who migrated involuntarily or voluntarily to work on different projects in the 19th century. The former are commonly known as Afro-Colonials (or *negros coloniales*) and the latter as West Indians, Afro-Antilleans, *criollos,* or *antillanos* (subsequently called Afro-Antilleans in this entry).

In early colonial history, the Isthmus of Panama was the fundamental commercial link between Spain and western South America. Sixty percent of the total production of silver from the Andes passed through Panama. The isthmus became the first major arrival point for enslaved Africans, particularly those from West Africa. Scholars of the history of Panama do not agree on the specific circumstances of the arrival of the first Africans to the country or on their numeric importance. According to Diez Castillo (1981, 15), the first black slaves to arrive in Panama were brought by the expedition of Diego de Nicuesa, governor of Castilla del Oro in 1509, as a result of the *Capitulación de Burgos,* signed by de Nicuesa and Spain's King Ferdinand on June 19, 1508. Lewis (1980) argues that black slaves first arrived in Panama in 1511. Historians affirm that Pedro Arías de Avila (Pedrarias) was the first to bring slaves to Panama in 1513, as royal governor of Castilla del Oro. There is also contention over the number of slaves present in Panama at any given time. Some scholars argue that black slaves represented 76 percent of the population of the city of Panama in the 17th and 18th centuries (De la Rosa 1993). Others claim that Panama was not a place where slavery was highly important numerically or socially (Guzmán Navarro 1982).

Slavery was transmitted from mother to child and in owners' wills (also known as *esclavitud testada*). In Panama, slavery was not linked, as in other regions of the Americas, to plantation life. Most slaves were brought to Panama to work in the mining industry, by far the most important economic resource of colonial Panama. Use of slaves maximized the profits of Spaniards in the mines of Veracruz, Coclé, and Concepción. Black slaves were also used as a labor force to build cities, towns, roads, churches, and monasteries and as domestic servants.

In colonial Panama, enslaved Africans were considered to be of dubious character and dangerous and were placed in the most arduous tasks. The severe conditions experienced by the enslaved provoked several insurrections and the formation of numerous *palenques* (fortified villages of escaped slaves).

The first known revolt of black slaves in the Isthmus occurred in the city of Panama in 1525; this rebellion was suppressed and the instigators were executed, but it brought about other insurrections and uprisings. By 1533, it was estimated that there were approximately 800 maroons in Panama. Among the most famous maroon leaders, documents mention Felipillo and Bayano or Vallano. By 1533, trips through the King's Highway were highly dangerous because of the assaults and alliances of maroons with pirates such as Sir Frances Drake, Henry Morgan, Edward Vernon, William Parker, and John Oxenham. These attacks continued throughout the 17th century. Colonists lived in a constant state of fear of escaped slaves.

Mechanisms to reduce uprisings included a series of concessions by the Spanish government, physical coercion, and unsuccessful attempts to evangelize the *palenques. Capitu-*

Girls at a carnival celebration in Panama. (Danny Lehman/Corbis)

laciones were among the most important mechanisms against insurrection. Through them, maroons were able to gain recognition, lands, and rights from the Spanish crown if they promised to settle in communities under Spanish control and to pledge allegiance to the crown. Ironically, *capitulaciones* allied the black maroons with the Spanish crown against the *mestizos*. In spite of the success of certain methods of repression of rebellions, maroons continued to be considered threats for Spanish society. "Colonial blacks" (particularly in *palenques)* remained a society apart with their own rituals and ceremonies.

Freedom for Panamanian slaves was a difficult task to accomplish. Some of the mechanisms used included letters of freedom (*cartas de libertad*), given to slaves as a result of a decree by King Ferdinand in 1526, and the *libertad graciosa*, granted to a slave (in some cases, postmortem) due to affection, good services, or illness.

The first Manumission Courts (in charge of providing government funds to collaborate in the payment of individual freedom) appeared in the year 1821 and marked a transition in the history of slavery in Panama. That same year, Panama was incorporated into the Gran Colombia after its independence from Spain. Panama was known as Colombia's "black province" because of its high degree of miscegenation. With this annexation, Panama became subject to the laws of the Gran Colombia. One of these laws was the law of Cúcuta (promulgated July 21, 1821), which established "freedom of the womb" for slaves born after 1821. Slavery gradually waned, and on January 1, 1852, slaves were granted universal freedom in Panama.

One of the most important historical events that produced Panama's second major black experience (Afro-Antilleans) was the famous California gold rush, which started in 1849. The discovery of gold in the region motivated the construction of a railroad that would transport goods and laborers from the East to the West Coast of the United States.

Construction of the Panamanian Railroad began in August 1850 with workers hired from different countries: New Grenada, Jamaica, England, France, Germany, India, Austria, and China. However, organizers of the project were interested in a labor force well adjusted to the environment and with knowledge of the English language. Afro-Antilleans met all these criteria. When construction ended in 1855, thousands of Afro-Antilleans remained in Panama.

A second migration of Afro-Antilleans was the product of the French efforts to build a canal in Panama from 1880 to 1889, under the leadership of Count Ferdinand de Lesseps. By 1884, there were more than 18,000 workers in the project, most of them Afro-Antilleans from Jamaica, Barbados, Santa Lucía, and Martinique (Westerman 1980; cf. Gaskin 1984).

The French project was not successful, and the company displaced more than 18,000 Afro-Antilleans from Jamaica and more than 8,000 Afro-Antilleans from Haiti. From 1881 to 1889, more than 22,000 Afro-Antilleans died of hunger, malaria, and yellow fever. Only 800 from Jamaica and 200 from Haiti survived (Diez-Castillo 1981). Some returned to their island territories, but a large number remained in the country.

The third and largest migration of Afro-Antilleans took place during the first decade of the 20th century when the United States took charge of the construction of the Panama Canal (1904–1914). The Panama Canal Company brought 31,000 men and 9,000 Afro-Antillean women to Panama from 1904 to 1913, most from Barbados. Some of the workers on the U.S. canal had worked for the French Canal Company.

Throughout the construction of these large infrastructural projects, Afro-Antilleans constantly struggled to improve their salaries and working conditions. The conditions that Afro-Antilleans were forced to endure on both canal projects represented a system of semislavery; several strikes to protest these injustices took place between 1881 and 1904.

It is important to mention a fourth migration of Afro-Antilleans to Panama, in this case specifically to the Province of Bocas del Toro, in the northwestern region. Afro-Antilleans arrived in Bocas del Toro during the mid- or late 18th century (accounts vary) to work as slaves of English and Scottish families who had settled in the region after leaving the islands of Providence and San Andres. Adams (1914) suggests that Afro-Antilleans arrived in Bocas del Toro during the 17th century from Jamaica and other British colonies. However, there is no other evidence that confirms this hypothesis.

After slavery was abolished in Panama, Afro-Antilleans in Bocas del Toro became part of a society of independent peasants in small villages on the islands and along the coast. The economy of the Afro-Creole peasant was based on subsistence agriculture, hunting (particularly of turtles), and fishing. This system continued during the 19th century. When the United Fruit Company established large commercial banana plantations in Bocas in 1899, the region became one of the most prosperous in Panama. This triggered another important migration of Afro-Antilleans from the Caribbean and from Panama City and Colon (Reid and Heckadon-Moreno 1980). When the United Fruit Company closed its Atlantic Coast plantations in the 1920s and 1930s (due to outbreaks of the Panama disease and the Great Depression), some Afro-Antillean families were able to buy parcels of land and establish small and medium-sized family farms. This resulted in the unusual development of a black, rural, middle class in the old banana zones. Consequently, the Afro-Antillean experience in Bocas del Toro differs significantly from that of black workers elsewhere in Panama and Latin America.

Relations between "colonial blacks" and Afro-Antilleans have been problematic. Cultural traditions and their history of arrival distinguished "colonial blacks" from Afro-Antilleans: "Colonial blacks" were descendants of Spanish colonial era slaves, spoke Spanish, and were mostly Catholic; Afro-Antilleans were descendants of enslaved Africans from the British colonies, came to Panama mostly as low-paid workers, spoke English, and most were Protestant. "Colonial blacks" and mestizo Panamanians were both prejudiced against Afro-Antilleans, who were perceived as having a distinct culture, an apparent disdain for Latino customs and the Panamanian nation in general, and an envied economic success. The derogatory term *chombo* was used to designate the Afro-Antilleans and differentiate them from "colonial blacks." Afro-Antilleans maintained their Caribbean and British ties, were keen to educate their children in that tradition, and were considered (and in some cases, considered themselves) to be "in transit."

Afro-Antilleans encountered a more overt level of discrimination than Afro-Colonials. After the construction of the Panama Canal, the contradictory and prejudicial policies of the Panamanian government were clearly demonstrated in the way in which migrations were handled. For instance, Law No. 26 of 1931 prohibited migration of Chinese, Libyans, Palestinians, Syrians, Turks, and blacks "whose language was not Spanish." In the Constitution of 1941, Arnulfo Arias Madrid established Hispanic heritage as the "true" heritage of Panamanians, prohibiting migration and citizenship to Afro-Antilleans.

The history of Afro-Panamanians is characterized by rebellion, resistance, and accommodation and by an internal diaspora. Panama prides itself for being a "racial democracy." Although the level of discrimination evident against black and indigenous peoples in other parts of Latin America and the Caribbean is not present in Panama, racism toward black and indigenous populations (regardless of ethnic ascription) is present. Historically, Afro-colonials and Afro-Antilleans struggled for better rights and opportunities—the former as maroons in *palenques*; the latter as workers in infrastructural and other projects—and for

recognition as worthy contributors to the nation. The past has witnessed conflicts between Afro-colonials and Afro-Antilleans, but more recently there have been efforts to present a unified front to represent Afro-Panamanians as a whole. Examples of those efforts include the institution of the Day of Black Ethnicity (*Día de la Etnia Negra*), which has been celebrated nationwide in May since 2000; the creation of the Center for Afro-Panamanian Studies in Panama City; and the organization of the Committee Against Racism.

Cultural connections with other Latin American, and particularly Caribbean, African Diaspora populations are strong and include music (reggae, reggaeton, calypso, jazz, among others), dance, architecture, and religion. Although not commonly known, the Rastafarian movement is present in Panama. Recent government emphasis on tourism has produced an official recognition of the nation's heritage of cultural diversity and the contributions of Afro-Panamanians to this diversity. In addition, it has stimulated a healing of the internal Diaspora between the descendants of Afro-colonials and Afro-Antilleans.

Carla Guerrón Montero

See also Brazil: Afro-Brazilians; Ecuador: Afro-Ecuadorians; Jamaica.

FURTHER READING
Adams, Frederick Upham. 1914. *Conquest of the Tropics: The Story of the Creative Enterprises Conducted by the United Fruit Company*. Garden City, NY: Doubleday, Page and Company.
Castillero Calvo, Alfredo. 1973. *Los Negros y Mulatos Libres en la Historia Social Panameña*. Panama.
Conniff, Michael L. 1995. "Afro-West Indians on the Central American Isthmus: The Case of Panama." In *Slavery and Beyond: The African Impact on Latin America and the Caribbean*, ed. Darién Davis, 147–172. Wilmington, DE: Scholarly Resources.
De la Guardia, Roberto. 1975. *Civilización Occidental: Variedad Panameña*. Panama: Impresora Roysa.
De la Guardia, Roberto. 1977. *Los Negros del Istmo de Panamá*. Panama: Ediciones INAC.

De la Rosa, Manuel. 1993. "El Negro en Panamá." In *Presencia Africana en Centroamérica,* ed. Luz María Martínez-Montiel, 217–292. Mexico: Consejo Nacional para la Cultura.

Diez Castillo, Luis A. 1981. *Los Cimarrones y los Negros Antillanos en Panamá.* Panama: Impr. J. Mercado Rudas.

Gaskin, E. A. 1984. *Blacks Played Significant Role in Improving Life on the Isthmus of Panama.* Balboa, Panama: Gebsa de Panamá.

Grannun de Lewis, Catalina N. 1979. *Los Trabajadores Panameños de Ascendencia Antillana en la Zona del Canal de Panamá: Su Situación Social y Económica.* Panama: CELA.

Guerrón Montero, Carla. 2002. Esclavitud y Relaciones Interétnicas entre Afro-panameños Coloniales y Afro-antillanos en Panamá (Siglo XIX). *Revista Académica Lotería* 442 (3): 79–96.

Guerrón Montero, Carla. 2005. "Voces Subalternas: Presencia Afro-Antillana en Panamá." *Cuadernos Americanos* 111: 33–59.

Guzmán Navarro, Arturo. 1982. *La Trata Esclavista en el Istmo de Panamá.* Panama: Editorial Universitaria, 1982.

Lewis, Lancelot. 1980. *The West Indian in Panama: Black Labor in Panama, 1850–1914.* Washington, D.C.: University Press of America.

Marrero Lobinot, Francisco. 1984. "Nuestros Ancestros de las Antillas Francesas: Interpretaciones Históricas y Sociológicas de Una Minoría Étnica Nacional." 67. Panama.

Reid, Carlos. 1980. *Memorias de un Criollo Bocatoreño,* ed Stanley Heckadon-Moreno. Panama: Litho-Impresora Panamá.

Rodríguez, Frederick. 1981. *Cimarron Revolts and Pacification in New Spain, the Isthmus of Panama, and Colonial Colombia, 1503–1800.* Chicago: Loyola University Press.

Smith, Ronald Richard. 1976. *The Society of Los Congos of Panama: An Ethnomusicological Study of the Music and Dance-Theater of an Afro-Panamanian Group.* Bloomington: Indiana University Press.

Westerman, George. 1980. *Los Inmigrantes Antillanos en Panamá.* Panama: Impresora de la Nación.

Paris Noir

See Black Paris/*Paris Noir.*

Parker, Lawrence Anthony

See KRS-ONE (1965–).

Pattillo, Walter Alexander (1850–1908)

Born into slavery on November 9, 1850, Walter Pattillo was the leader of the Black Populist movement, the largest political movement of rural African-Americans in the late 19th century. Over the course of three decades, Pattillo became one of his state's most important religious, educational, and political leaders, helping to spur the growth of the black Baptist church, establishing the Colored Orphanage Asylum, and serving as a lecturer and national leader of the Colored Farmers Alliance.

After the Civil War, Pattillo drove wagons and worked in a sawmill to support his mother. His father was most likely his mother's slave master. Pattillo joined the General Association of the Colored Baptists of North Carolina at the age of 17 to promote the expansion of the black-led church. Having taught himself how to read and write while a slave, he was determined to get a formal education. In 1870, he married Mary Ida Hart, with whom he would have 12 children. In 1876, he entered Shaw University to study theology. He would go on to preach to dozens of congregations over his lifetime, delivering nearly 3,000 sermons and baptizing more than 3,100 people. He served as a member of the Home Mission Board of the Baptist State Convention in Granville and was elected president of the Middle Baptist Association.

Pattillo's work with the black Baptists brought him into contact with people throughout the state. In the early 1880s, Pattillo ran unsuccessfully for Register of Deeds as a Republican. He became actively involved in public education, not only teaching classes but also serving as Superintendent of Schools in his county and adjoining areas. He established the Colored Orphanage Asylum (later renamed the Central Children's Home), the state's only black orphanage, and served as its general agent in the mid-1880s.

As economic and political conditions deteriorated among African-Americans, however, Pattillo turned his attention to building what would become the largest network of black farmers, the Colored Farmers Alliance. During this period, he edited two newspapers, the *Alliance Advocate* and the *Baptist Pilot*. In his capacity as the elected state organizer and lecturer for the Colored Alliance, Pattillo traveled across the state spreading word of the growing movement and recruiting members into local chapters. His talent as an organizer was in part reflected in the phenomenal growth of the Colored Alliance, which by the early 1890s claimed a membership of some 55,000 black farmers and agrarian laborers.

Recognizing the limits of agrarian organizing without engaging the electoral process itself, Pattillo was among the first to call for the formation of an independent political party, which became the People's Party. After the demise of Black Populism, Pattillo became principal of Oxford High School while continuing to preach to various congregations. In 1906, two years before his death, Shaw University, his alma mater, honored him for his life's work with a doctor of divinity degree.

Omar H. Ali

See also Black Populism (1886–1898).

FURTHER READING
Ali, Omar H. 2002. "The Making of a Black Populist: A Tribute to the Rev. Walter A. Pattillo." *Oxford Public Ledger,* March 28.
Ali, Omar H. 2008. *In the Balance of Power: Independent Black Politics and Third-Party Movements in the United States.* Columbus: Ohio State University Press.
Ali, Omar H. Forthcoming. *Black Populism in the New South, 1886–1898.* Jackson: University Press of Mississippi.

Payada

The *payada* is a form of Creole or folkloric poetry, especially associated with and popular among the gauchos or cowboys of Argentina and Uruguay. Its origins are uncertain, but what is known is that it was already commonly performed in the open air or in the *pulperías* (general stores where gauchos would go to drink) throughout the *campaña* or countryside of the River Plate by the early 1800s. The *payada* takes the form of improvised, sung verses, usually accompanied by a guitar. Common themes intoned by *payadores* included love, the beauty of rural life, and death. A *payada* could be performed as a solo act or as a kind of contrapuntal duel by a duo of *payadores*, as depicted in the Argentine national classic *El gaucho Martín Fierro* (1872), by José Hernández. This answer-and-response contest would end when one of the singers could not poetically retort his adversary.

The *payada,* as was also true with the tango, benefited from the genius of Africans and their descendants. First, Africans enslaved and free worked as horsemen on cattle estates on the River Plate throughout the colonial and national periods, and some even became slave foremen, as was the case with one Patricio de Belén in the Banda Oriental estate of *Las Vacas* (Mayo 1997). They therefore worked and relaxed alongside their white counterparts and shared (and influenced) gaucho culture, including the *payada.* Second, several scholars attest to the importance of Africans in the formation of Creole expressions and language in the River Plate. African Argentines and Uruguayans donated such commonly used terms in Argentina and Uruguay as *quilombo, mandinga,* and *cachimba,* words putatively associated with the Congo-Angola nations (see Britos Serrat 1999). Third, throughout the River Plate (and the Americas), Africans were renowned for their verbal agility, coming up with catchy sales pitches or *pregones* to hawk their wares during the 1700s and 1800s and *cantos de cuna* or nursery rhymes to put infants (their masters' and their own) to bed (for example, "La ronda catonga" by Pereda Valdés 1962, 360).

The chant-and-response nature of the *payada* is common to other verbal and musical expressions throughout Africa and the Diaspora. West Africans, imported to the River Plate certainly brought with them a linguistic and folkloric repertoire inherited from their griots (singers, storytellers, historians). The Mande-speaking peoples of Senegambia made their way to the River Plate via the transatlantic slave trade; among the Mendes (including the Mandinga), griots played an important role in preserving and transmitting ethnic lore and traditions. Their prodigious verbal skills also made them valued advisers to chiefs and kings. In short, West Africans possessed, as an integral element of ancestral culture, "the power of speech" (Bird 1971).

Often performed before large audiences by white and black *payadores* in theaters and circuses in both cities and rural areas in the River Plate, the *payada* is similar to contrapuntal and satiric songs generically called *makawas* and *ibiririmbo* on the African continent. Néstor Ortiz Oderigo compares the *payada* to other African and Afro-American songs found throughout the Americas, including the Brazilian *canto de sotaque*, the Caribbean *canto de gallo*, and the North-American "answer-back songs," for example, rap (Ortiz Oderigo 1974, 108–109).

Just as significant is the role Afro-Argentines and Afro-Uruguayans played in the development of the *payada*. The best *payadores* (just like many of the best early tango musicians) from the city and countryside were black men, notably Luis García, Higinio Cazón, and the greatest of the 19th-century *payadores*, Gabino (Gavino) Ezeiza. Toward the end of the 1800s, these folk troubadours would face off in "cutting contests" throughout Buenos Aires and the interior provinces. Until well into the 20th century, many Argentines nostalgically commemorated Ezieza's birth, and a small monument consisting of a (now weather-faded) bust of Ezeiza can still be found in the old slaughterhouse district of Buenos Aires—one of only three public monuments recalling the Afro-Argentine experience (the other two celebrate the end of the slave trade and the heroism of Falucho, a black hero of Argentine independence).

The *payada* and its performers symbolize yet another African contribution to the culture of the River Plate. The names and performances of legendary *payadores* have endured in the national memory, becoming the stuff of legend. Even the "foundational fictions" of the region have immortalized the black *payador*. Hilario Ascasubi's *gauchesque* classic *Santos Vega* (1850 or 1851) also incorporates the legend of the *Mandinga*; he depicts a verbal duel between Santos Vega and the devil, or *Mandinga*, represented as a black man. Thus, the *payada* truly constitutes an example of *afronegrismos rioplatenses*.

Roberto Pacheco

See also Argentina: Afro-Argentines; Falucho (?–1824); Griots/Griottes of West Africa; Tango, Candombe, Milonga; Uruguay: Afro-Uruguayans.

FURTHER READING
Bird, Charles S. 1971. "Oral Art of the Mande." *Papers of the Manding* 3: 15–25.
Britos Serrat, Alberto, comp. 1999. *Glosario de afronegrismos uruguayos*. Montevideo, Uruguay: Ediciones Mundo Afro.
Lewis, Marvin A. 1996. *Afro-Argentine Discourse: Another Dimension of the Black Diaspora*. Columbia: University of Missouri Press.
Mayo, Carlos. 1997. "Patricio de Belén: nada menos que un capataz." *Hispanic American Historical Review* 77 (4): 597–614.
Ortiz Oderigo, Néstor. 1974. *Aspectos de la cultura africana en el Río de la Plata*. Buenos Aires: Editorial Plus Ultra.
Pereda Valdés, Ildefonso. 1962. "La ronda catonga." In *Lira negra*, ed. José Sanz y Díaz, 360. Madrid: Ediciones Aguilar.
Zabala, Abel. 1998. "El negro Gavino: payador de payadores." *Revista de Historia Bonaerense* 4 (16): 25–26.

People with Their Feet on Backward

People with their feet on backward are figures present throughout the folklore of the Caribbean and other parts of the New World that are often used to instill fear in children so they will not wander off by themselves. For some artists they represent early stages of human growth and even the muse. In Trinidad they are called *douens* (also dwens or duennes) and are said to lead people, especially children, into the forest until they are lost or never heard from again. Associated there with the souls of unbaptized children, they often make sad sounds and are depicted as wearing mushroom hats that hide their faces, although sometimes one can see their eyes glowing like burning coals. Artist Leroy Clarke sees the state of "douendom" as a metaphor for the underdevelopment and psychic morass of New World people, the result of enslavement, colonialism and capitalist expansionism, rendering them "turned around," which is why their feet point backward.

For protection against being completely lost, it is sometimes suggested that you recite some words while you hold a piece of silk from a silk cotton tree in your hand. In Saint Lucia, a similar figure is the bolom, an unchristened dead child with feet on backward like a foetus; they are also described as wearing a hat. Belize has its folk versions of this figure, too. One of them is the *duende* (also *duhende* or *tataduhende*), a small, dwarflike man who wears a big hat, makes a strange noise, and has his feet on backward. He can be a trickster or a guardian of the forest. A motif some versions of the *duende* share with the Sisimite (also Sisimit), a hairy creature who may or may not have its feet on backward or the ability to reverse them, is that they carry off children. In the Dominican Republic, people with their feet on backward are called *ciguapas*. They are supposed to have lived in Hispaniola before the arrival of Christopher Columbus and reside mostly in mountain areas, where they move by taking gigantic leaps. The sound they make is like a hiccup. The women cover themselves with their long hair and come out at night to get food, often stealing it from homes where people are asleep. Though rarely mentioned, male *ciguapas* look like roosters turned upside down and have women's breasts. They make sounds similar to the cries of children. Whoever kills one of them will pay dire consequences for the rest of his or her life. Near the Haitian border they say *ciguapas* kidnap children. To catch a *ciguapa* you need a native dog with five toes and a crescent moon, but it is better to leave them alone because they die of sadness whenever they are caught.

Maria Soledad Rodriguez

See also La Diablesse.

FURTHER READING
Allsopp, Richard, ed. 1996. *Dictionary of Caribbean English Usage.* With a French and Spanish Supplement edited by Jeannette Allsopp. Oxford: Oxford University Press.
Clarke, Leroy. 1981. *Douens. (Poetry collection accompanying an art exhibition, New York, 1974–1979).* New York: KaRaEle.
Estrella Veloz, Santiago. 2001. "La ciguapa: entre la decadencia y el olvido." *[A]hora* 30 (23 de abril): 30–31.
Parham, Timothy, and Mary Gomez Parham, eds. 2000. *If Di Pin Neva Ben: Folktales and Legends of Belize.* Benque Viejo del Carmen, Belize: Cubola.
Walcott, Derek. 1996. "Afterword: Animals, Elemental Tales, and the Theater." In *Monsters, Tricksters and Sacred Cows: Animal Tales and American Identities*, ed A. James Arnold, 269–277. Charlottesville: University Press of Virginia.

Peru: Afro-Peruvians

People of African descent constitute between 6 and 10 percent of the Peruvian population. Afro-Peruvian communities are concentrated mainly on the coast, in the zones surrounding the plantations and in the major cities, most notably Lima; however, people of African descent can also be found in the highlands. The contribution of Afro-Peruvians to national culture has been highly significant and is evident in culinary, artistic, sporting, and religious traditions, yet most Afro-Peruvians experience poverty, marginalization, and racism in their daily lives and tend collectively and individually to possess little sense of ethnic identity. There is little national recognition that Afro-Peruvians constitute a community with particular problems and goals. In response, a number of Afro-Peruvian individuals and organizations have been working to build a social movement whose aim is full achievement of equal rights and the recognition of Afro-Peruvian culture.

History and Origins

Africans first arrived in Peru during the Spanish conquest, as colonized people forced to participate in the military defeat of the Incas. Africans were imported in large numbers throughout the colonial period, and slave labor was essential to the rural and urban economies. Africans brought skills and techniques in agriculture, metallurgy, craftsmanship, and manufacturing, and they occupied roles as domestics, laundresses, wet nurses, artisans, tailors, and construction workers. By the late 16th century, peoples of African descent formed 50 percent of the Lima population. There was no direct slave trade to Peru; Africans arrived via other American ports and, as a result, were already used to European culture and integrated more easily into the new culture. Daily interactions in the cities between people of African descent, indigenous peoples and Hispanic creoles led to the creation of unique customs. Africans played a particular role in the development of popular religion. The procession of Señor del Milagros (Our Lord of Miracles), today considered to be one of the three most important religious festivals in Latin America, originated in the practices of an African religious fraternity, while Martín de

Porras, a black cleric famous in colonial society for his acts of healing among the poor, was canonized after inspiring popular worship. Female food vendors spread a taste for dishes of African origin throughout the city, and elite society came to consider that a table was not well-set without the inclusion of soups and savories made by an Afro-Peruvian cook.

Resistance and Palenques

Active resistance to slavery was a permanent condition of life among people of African descent in Peru and was chiefly expressed in the flight of slaves and the formation of *bandas de cimarrones* and *palenques*. The most famous refuge for runaway slaves was *El Palenque de Huachipa* on the central coast, which was led by Francisco Congo. Although relations between Africans and indigenous people were largely characterized by resentment and distrust, a result of the role played by Africans in the Conquest, on occasion alliances did develop, most notably the relationship between African rebel leader Juan Santos Atahualpa and indigenous chief Tupa Amaru in the 1780 insurrection: the first to demand the liberation of all slaves.

People of African descent played a key role in the struggle for independence; in particular, Afro-Peruvian battalions playing a decisive role in the crucial battles of Junín and Ayacucho. Participation was a strategy for emancipation: Simón Bolívar had decreed freedom for all slaves who served against Spain in 1821, and the Peruvian Constitution of 1823 legislated freedom for all children born of slaves. Yet these gains were followed by a shameful reversal of policy in the face of landowner agitation, and in 1840 slavery was reestablished and remained in place until 1854. Final abolition brought little change in the economic position of ex-slaves and, after the initial flight from the haciendas, racial discrimination and economic depression forced many black people to return to the same kinds of positions they had held during slavery. The lack of change in conditions prompted two major 19th century rebellions by Afro-Peruvian peasants: the Chincha uprising in 1879, and the Cañete rebellion in 1881.

RECENT TRENDS

In the early 20th century, there was significant Caribbean migration to the Amazonian region of Peru, most notably that of laborers from Jamaica and Barbados to the rubber plantations of the Putumayo, where they were subject to severe abuse. Many Caribbeans stayed in Peru after the end of the rubber boom: the black community of Las Lomas in Northern Peru is said to have been founded by Afro-Jamaicans.

The first half of the 20th century saw no major revaluation of the cultural legacy of Afro-Peruvians, and elites and intellectuals— including the socialist and proindigenous intellectual José Carlos Mariategui—continued to present blackness as a negative trait in Peruvian culture. From the 1950s, an Afro-Peruvian protest voice emerged to challenge this perception, first through dance and theater groups, such as Cumana, Union Santa Cruz, Gente Moreno and Peru Negro, which sought to revalidate Afro-Peruvian artistry, and later through social groups influenced by the Civil Rights Movements in the United States. The most famous articulator of an Afro-Peruvian consciousness is Nicomedes Santa Cruz. He championed the *decima*—a form of poetry based on African norms. His most famous 1964 work, *Cumana,* dealt with black problems in Africa and the Americas and caused great controversy, as it represented the first time an Afro-Peruvian had vocally drawn attention to such issues. Contemporary Afro-Peruvian consciousness groups, such as Movimiento Francisco Congo, Agrupación Palenque, and Asociación Pro-Derechos Humanos del Negro, view their goals within a nationalist framework and hope to use their organization to strengthen Peruvian democracy by creating greater economic and politics rights for people of African descent.

Nicola Foote

See also Bolivia: The African Presence; Chile: Afro-Chileans; Ecuador: Afro-Ecuadorians.

FURTHER READING

Aguirre, Carlos, ed. 2000. *Lo africano en la cultura criollo.* Lima: Fondo Editorial del Congreso del Peru.

Busto Duthurburu, José Antonio del. 2001. *Breve historia de los negros del Peru.* Lima: Fondo Editorial del Congreso del Peru.

Luciano, José, and Humberto Rodriguez Pastor. 1995. "Peru." In *No Longer Invisible: Afro-Latin Americans Today,* ed. Minority Rights Group, 271–286. London: Minority Rights Group.

Santa Cruz, Nicomedes. 1971. *Antología: décimas y poemas.* Lima, Peru: Campodonico-ediciones.

Petwo

Petwo is the fiery component of Haitian Vodoun that is composed of *lwas* (spirits) and practices that are considered Kreyol (creole) or indigenous to Haiti; according to scholars they were inspired as an enraged response to atrocities engendered by chattel slavery on the isle of Saint Domingue. The origin of the Petwo rite is somewhat shrouded in mystery. It is attributed by some to a Spanish-speaking man of African descent, Don Pedro, a powerful *oungan* (ritual specialist) whose name appears in many Vodoun songs. The Petwo component of the Haitian Vodoun complex is derived from his name. The religious practice Petwo is also considered the result of a request by enslaved Africans for African "medicine" that would aid in combating and overthrowing the conditions of servitude in Haiti (St. Juste, personal communication). A Petwo rite conducted at Bois Caïmon is considered the catalyst that fueled Haiti's 1791 revolution, freeing enslaved Africans from chattel slavery and simultaneously gaining Haitian independence. Petwo is considered the active, aggressive side of Haitian Vodoun (Deren 1953).

Many of the *lwa* of the Petwo nation are, according to Herskovits, associated with Angola and some are believed to be Congo deities (1937). It is generally accepted that the Petwo *lwas* are ferocious and can be prone to acts of violence, severely punishing negligent devotees. Some aspects of Petwo, however, parallel the Rada component of Vodoun; there is some overlap in the names of Petwo and Rada *lwas*. Rada *lwa* names are sometimes used in conjunction with Petwo descriptors. The Petwo part of their names usually indicates aggressive, fiery temperaments—terms such as *je wouge* (red eyes) or *la flambeau* (torch). Petwo ezulis, for example, include Ezuli Je Wouge and Ezuli Danto and are described as aggressive and violent. Compared with the sweet and flirtatious actions of Rada *lwa* Ezuli Freda Dahomey, Deren describes the sounds made by Ezuli Je Wouge as "half groan, half scream" (Deren 1953).

The date designated for Petwo is July 24, the height of summer with its accompanying heat. Fire is always a component of Petwo ceremonies in that it is sacred to Petwo *lwas*; bathing in ritually prepared flames is part of Petwo services for the *lwas*. Petwo drums, energetic singing, and dancing for the *lwas*, a ritual specialist adept in managing the protocol that underlies Petwo rites, food for the lwas and congregation, as well as altars and implements that are favored by Petwo *lwas* are all necessary elements for a Petwo ceremony. The ceremonies are hot, due in part to the fires that are kept throughout the service. They are hot also because of the intense spirited rhythms and actions of ceremony participants.

Joan Hamby Burroughs

See also Haiti; Vodoun.

FURTHER READING

Brown, Karen M. 1991. *Mama Lola: A Vodou Priestess in Brooklyn.* Berkeley: University of California.

Davis, Wade. 1988. *Passage of Darkness: The Ethnobiology of the Haitian Zombie.* Chapel Hill: University of North Carolina Press.

Deren, Maya. 1953. *The Divine Horsemen.* New York: Thames & Hudson.

Dunham, Katherine. 1969. *Island Possessed.* New York: Doubleday.

Fouchard, J. 1981. *The Haitian Maroons,* trans. A. F. Watts. New York: Theo Gaus, Ltd.

Frank, Henry. 2002. "Haitian Vodou Ritual Dance and Its Secularization." In *Caribbean Dance from Abakuá to Zouk,* ed. S. Sloat, 109–113. Gainesville: University Press of Florida.

Herskovits, Melville. 1937. *Life in a Haitian Valley.* New York: Alfred A. Knopf.

Laguerre, Michel. 1980. *Voodoo Heritage.* Beverly Hills, CA: Sage.

Metraux, Alfred. 1972. *Voodoo in Haiti,* trans. H. Charteris. New York: Schocken Books.

Rigaud, Milo. 1985. *Secrets of Voodoo,* trans. R. B. Cross. San Francisco: City Lights Books.

Phi Beta Sigma

Phi Beta Sigma is an African-American Greek letter fraternity that was organized to "exemplify the ideals of brotherhood, scholarship, and service" among college-educated young men. As one of the nine predominately African American Greek letter organizations in the Pan Hellenic Council, Phi Beta Sigma has a membership of more than 110,000 members and more than 700 chapters throughout the continental United States, Hawaii, the Caribbean, Europe, Asia, and Africa.

Phi Beta Sigma was founded on January 9, 1914, on the campus of Howard University in Washington, D.C. On April 15, 1914, Phi Beta Sigma became the first Greek letter organization formally recognized on the campus of Howard University. A. Langston Taylor, a Howard University student, along with fellow students Leonard F. Morse and Charles I. Brown, envisioned an African American fraternity that would promote a greater sense of fellowship between exceptional, yet diverse, men of color who would unite for the cause of service to humanity.

The founders conceived Phi Beta Sigma as a mechanism to deliver services to the general community. Rather than gaining skills to be used exclusively for themselves and their immediate families, the founders of Phi Beta Sigma held a deep conviction that they should return their newly acquired skills to the communities from which they had come. This deep conviction was mirrored in the fraternity's motto, "Culture for Service and Service for Humanity." On January 31, 1920, Phi Beta Sigma was incorporated in Washington, D.C., and became Phi Beta Sigma Fraternity, Incorporated.

Phi Beta Sigma implements its mission of service through its three national programs of Bigger and Better Business, Education, and Social Action. Bigger and Better Business became a key interest during the 1924 Conclave held in Philadelphia, Pennsylvania, when the fraternity hosted exhibits from 25 African American business establishments. It is also the first and only fraternity to own and operate a Credit Union for its members.

In 1934, Phi Beta Sigma instituted a program that was primarily concerned with the well-being of minority groups. Past social action projects have focused on national and state anti-lynching legislation, abolition of Jim Crow laws, fair wage and working conditions legislation for minorities, full citizenship rights for all citizens, and Project SADD (Students Against Drunk Driving). Phi Beta Sigma was also instrumental in providing leadership, organization, and resources for the Million Man March in Washington, D.C., in 1995 and the Million Family March in 2000.

The purpose of Phi Beta Sigma's education program is to help graduates, undergraduates, and the community at large attain the highest scholastic achievement possible. Its membership boasts a large percentage of educators, including former U.S. Secretary of Education Ron Paige.

As an international organization, Phi Beta Sigma was the first Greek letter organization to establish chapters in the continent of Africa and was the first to have presidents of other countries in its membership, such as Kwame Nkrumah, past president of Ghana, and Nelson Mandela, past president of South Africa. Other notable members of Phi Beta Sigma are scientist George Washington Carver; Alain Locke, philosopher and first African American Rhodes scholar; Harlem Renaissance writer James Weldon Johnson; Black Panther cofounder Huey P. Newton; A. Philip Randolph, founder of the Brotherhood of Sleeping Car Porters; and Nnamdi Azikiwe, past president of Nigeria.

Jason Esters

See also Nkrumah, Kwame (1909–1972); Zeta Phi Beta.

FURTHER READING

Ross, Lawrence C., Jr. 2002. *The Divine 9: The History of African-American Fraternities and Sororities.* New York: Dafina Books.
Savage, Sherman W., and Lawrence D. Reddick. 1957. *Our Cause Speeds on an Informal History of the Phi Beta Sigma Fraternity.* Fuller Press.

Philip, Marlene Nourbese (1947–)

A versatile writer, poet, essayist, fiction writer, and playwright, Marlene Nourbese Philip is known as much for her trenchant critiques of Canadian society and analyses of the legacies of slavery and colonialism in the Afrospora, as she calls the Diaspora, as she is for her haunting poetry. Several of Philip's works have been especially influential: her novel for adolescents, *Harriet's Daughter* (1988) has become a classic; her first collection of essays, *Frontiers: Essays and Writing in Racism and Culture* (1993), and her monograph, *Showing Grit: Showboating North of the 49th Parallel* (1993), engaged a variety of debates over racism and culture with an uncompromising clarity and directness that shook the Toronto cultural establishment. Her third poetry collection, *She Tries Her Tongue, Her Silence Softly Breaks* (1988), which won the Casa de las Americas prize for that year, contains an evocative poetic argument about the nature of language in the African Diaspora that has fueled considerable theorizing and debate.

Born in Tobago, Philip moved to Trinidad as a child. She graduated from the University of the West Indies in Economics. Her master's degree in political science (1968) and her law degree (1973) were obtained at the University of Western Ontario. After seven years practicing family and immigration law in Toronto, where she still lives, Philip turned to writing full time. Her first collection, *Thorns*, appeared in 1980, and her second, *Salmon Courage*, three years later. In 1991, Philip published *Looking for Livingstone*, in which a fictional traveler pursues the historical Livingstone for eons, on her journey meeting a series of tribes whose names are anagrams of the word silence. A second collection of essays, *A Genealogy of Resistance and Other Essays* (1997), gathers work written over a number of years; it contains one of Philip's finest pieces, "Dis Place—The Space Between," a mixed-genre essay on women, women's bodies, and slavery and its aftermath that moves between argument and poetry and ends in a play. Philip had earlier concluded the second edition of *Showing Grit* with a farcical and exhilarating dramatic postscript (1994). Her major foray, *Coups and Calypsos* (1999), has been produced in Toronto and London; it depicts the dissolution of a mixed marriage (an African and a South Asian) against the backdrop of the 1990 coup in Trinidad. More recently, her script of *Harriet's Daughter* has received workshop productions.

Philip's awards include a Guggenheim Fellowship in Poetry in 1990, a McDowell Fellowship in 1991, the Toronto Arts Award in Writing and Publishing in 1995, the Elizabeth Fry Society Rebels for a Cause Award in 2001, the YWCA Woman of Distinction in the Arts Award in 2001, and the Chalmers Fellowship in Poetry in 2002.

Leslie Sanders

See also Canada and the African Diaspora; Trinidad and Tobago.

FURTHER READING

Deloughrey, Elizabeth. 1998. "From Margin to the (Canadian) Frontier: 'The Wombs of Language.'" In *She Tries Her Tongue, Her Silence Softly Breaks,* ed. M. Nourbese Philip, 121–144. *Journal of Canadian Studies* 33 (1).

Mahlis, Kristin. 2004. "A Poet of Place: An Interview with M. Nourbese Philip." *Callaloo* 27 (3): 682–697.

McKittrick, Katherine. 2000. "'Who Do You Talk To, When a Body's in Trouble': M. Nourbese Philip's UnSilencing of the Black Bodies in the Diaspora." *Journal of Social and Cultural Geography* 1 (2): 223–236.

Philosophers and the African American Experience

Only about one percent of all academic philosophers in the United States are African American, and in the past the percentage was even lower. Moreover, before the 1970s, and because of segregation, most African American philosophers taught at the historically black colleges and universities (HBCUs).

In 1895, the *Afro-American Encyclopedia* presented William D. Johnson's article, simply titled "Philosophy." Johnson defines philosophy and outlines its tasks and scope with only secondary commentary about the black experience (Johnson 1895). Even more strongly, William A. Banner (Harvard PhD, 1946) has consistently argued against the very idea of a distinctive African American or black philosophy. Others, such as Marxist philosopher Eugene C. Holmes (Columbia PhD, 1942) and Rhodes Scholar Alain Locke (Harvard PhD, 1918), wanted to directly adjoin philosophy with the black experience. Locke and Holmes both discussed the subject of the aesthetics of African American literature and more generally issues about black culture.

In turn, Richard I. McKinney, former chair of the Department of Philosophy at Morgan State University, expressed his intellectual interest in black life as early as the submission of his bachelor of divinity thesis, *The Problem of Evil and Its Relation to the Ministry to an Under-privileged Minority*, at Newton Theological Seminary in 1934. McKinney's doctoral dissertation (although in education rather than philosophy), *Religion in Higher Education Among Negroes*, at Yale University (1942) clearly indicates his abiding concern with the African American religious experience. In contrast, John M. Smith pursued a PhD in philosophy rather than education, although his area of specialty was in the philosophy of education. Smith's dissertation topic was *A Comparison of Plato's and Dewey's Educational Philosophies*, and he received a doctorate from the University of Iowa in 1941. Smith went on and taught at the HBCU Elizabeth City State University in North Carolina. It should be noted that some African American philosophers decided to get their doctorates in religion/theology or education rather than in philosophy because they considered their roles as philosophers to be ineluctably tied to the educational aims of the HBCUs.

Thus, in addition to McKinney, Francis A. Thomas, the long-time chair of philosophy at Central State University (Wilberforce, Ohio), also received his doctorate in education. Thomas, whose doctoral dissertation was about *Philosophies of Audio Visual Education as Conceived of by University Centers and by Selected Leaders* (Indiana University 1960), functioned as both chair of philosophy and director of audio visuals at Central State University. In fact, combining administrative duties with teaching became the plight of several African American philosophers, and such burdens associated with the survival of HBCUs often re-stricted their needed time and energy for research and publication. Among those serving as presidents of HBCUs were Joseph C. Price at Livingston College (North Carolina), John Wesley Edward Bowen at Gammon Theological Seminary (Georgia), Willis Jefferson King at Gammon Theological Seminary and Samuel Houston College (Texas), John H. Burrus at Alcorn A & M (Mississippi), Richard I. McKinney at Storer College (West Virginia), Marquis L. Harris at Philander Smith (Arkansas), William Stuart Nelson at Shaw University (North Carolina) and Dillard University (Louisiana), Broadus Butler at Dillard University, Gilbert Haven Jones and Charles Leander Hill at Wilberforce University (Ohio), and Benjamin Mays at Morehouse College (Georgia). Among those in the capacity of chairs of philosophy departments, along with the aforementioned McKinney and Thomas, were Louis Baxter Moore, Alain Locke, Eugene C. Holmes, Winston K. McAllister, and William A. Banner at Howard University; James L. Farmer at Wiley College; William T. Fontaine at Morgan State University; and Samuel W. Williams at Morehouse College.

An advocate of the philosophy of nonviolence with social democratic leanings, Samuel W. Williams was a key mentor to Martin Luther King, Jr., and King gained a philosophical foundation for his views on nonviolence from Williams. George D. Kelsey was another faculty member in the philosophy and religion department of Morehouse who contributed to the development of King's notions about nonviolence as a philosophical perspective. King directly consulted Kelsey for advice when writing the classic text *Stride Toward Freedom*. Kelsey, who received a PhD from Yale in 1946, would go on to publish an important book representative of the Christian idea of nonviolence, titled *Racism and the Christian Understanding of Man*.

William Stuart Nelson not only advised King during the Montgomery bus boycott on Gandhian principles of nonviolence but also developed the first academic course on the philosophy of nonviolence at a higher educational institution, namely Howard University. Nelson held several positions at Howard, including dean of the School of Religion and vice president. Nelson also founded and was editor of *The Journal of Religious Thought*, which remains a major source for intellectual discussion in the philosophy of religion. Both Benjamin Mays and James Farmer also taught at Howard's School of Religion, and Nelson, along with Mays, actually met with Gandhi in India. Thus, for a sizable group of African American philosophers, especially at the HBCUs, religion was intractably tied to philosophy, and this was especially prominent with the institutionalization of departments/programs that combined religion and philosophy. Charles Leander Hill, who was a minister in the African Methodist Episcopal Church, specifically comments on the role of religion in education. In fact, Hill was an internationally renowned expert on Philip Melanchthon, the Protestant co-reformer with Martin Luther.

As late as 1973, in a report to the American Philosophical Association, African American philosopher William R. Jones makes a public note of religion's detrimental effects on the development of black philosophy students for graduate study in the discipline. Even today in contemporary African American history there are far more preachers and theologians than philosophers.

The first two African Americans holding doctorates in philosophy were Patrick Francis Healy and Thomas Nelson Baker; both men were former slaves and ordained ministers. Although Baker attended Hampton Institute, neither he nor Healy taught at HBCUs. Healy earned his doctorate from the University of Louvain in Belgium in 1865. Healy was one of a handful of African American scholars during the 19th century to teach at predominantly white or all-white institutions. Ordained a Catholic priest, Healy was on the faculty at Holy Cross, St. Joseph College (Philadelphia), and Georgetown. Healy was the first African American to earn a PhD in philosophy. Patrick Healy being very fair in complexion (his father was white) decided to pass for white. Patrick Francis eventually became the president of Georgetown at a time when this school did not admit black students.

Thomas Nelson Baker became the first African American to earn a PhD in philosophy from an institution in the United States. Baker's doctorate in philosophy came in 1903 from Yale. Born on a plantation, just five years before Healy got his doctorate, Baker was 33 when he received his first degree from Boston University. He later received a bachelor's degree in divinity from Yale before getting his terminal degree. Yale also has the distinction of being the institution to grant the first PhD in philosophy to an African American woman. Joyce Mitchell Cook was the first African American woman to serve in the capacity as an academic philosopher. Cook earned her doctorate from Yale University in 1965. Her dissertation in axiology (value theory) was entitled *A Critical Examination of Stephen C. Pepper's Theory of Value*. Faced with racism and sexism, Cook taught at Howard University but was also employed outside academia because of restricted opportunities. Unlike fellow pioneers Healy and Baker, Cook was not engaged in philosophy from a religious standpoint.

This was not the case for John Wesley Edward Bowen; he was interested in questions related to religion and philosophy. Bowen earned a PhD from Boston University in 1887 and taught philosophy at several HBCUs. Yet he received his degree in historical theology rather than outright in philosophy. Bowen's dissertation topic was *The Historic Manifestations and Apprehensions of Religion as an Evolutionary and Psychological Process*. Bowen received a bachelor's degree from the University of New Orleans in 1878 and a bachelor's of divinity from Boston University in 1885. Bowen's academic career included teaching at Central Tennessee College, Morgan State College, Howard University, and Gammon Theological Seminary in Atlanta, and he was the first African American to hold a professorship at Gammon Theological Seminary.

In the first decades of the 20th century, at best only a few African American philosophers acquired visiting positions at white universities. Resistance to black philosophers as faculty has had a long history. For example, after receiving his doctorate from the University of Chicago in 1933, Albert M. Dunham was assigned to teach a summer class in the philosophy department. The appointment was to be a gateway to full-fledged membership with the philosophy faculty. However, more than half of the students dropped the class when they discovered that their professor was a black man. Although the administration managed to gather enough students to continue the class, the idea of Dunham joining the Chicago faculty was quickly abandoned. After Alain Locke recruited him, Dunham went on to teach at Howard University. The decision not to hire Dunham at Chicago ultimately proved too much for him to handle. He suffered a nervous breakdown and subsequently died in a mental institution.

It should be noted that, during the 20th century, Cornelius Golightly became the first philosopher to break the race barrier as a regular faculty member with a department of philosophy on a white campus. With a doctorate from the University of Michigan, awarded in 1941, and primarily through the support of the Rosenwald Fund, Golightly was hired at Olivet College in 1945. In 1946 Francis Monroe Hammond joined the philosophy department at Seton Hall. Hammond was not only the first African American on the Seton Hall faculty, but he was also the first black person to ever serve as chair (1946–1951) of a philosophy department at a white college. Remarkably, in 1953, Hammond also became chair of the department of psychology at Seton Hall. Hammond's capacity to take on this dual role was in no small measure due to the fact that his doctoral dissertation, *La Conception Psychologique de la Société selon Gabriel Tarde*, was an interdisciplinary undertaking positioned within both philosophy and social psychology.

One year after Hammond came to Seton Hall, William T. Fontaine entered the philosophy department at the University of Pennsylvania as a lecturer, and in 1949 he was promoted to assistant professor. Fontaine advanced to associate professor in 1963 and thus acquired the distinction of becoming the first African American professor to receive tenure at the University of Pennsylvania. Despite these advances, the door to philosophy departments at white colleges and universities remained primarily closed for most black philosophers.

A glaring example is the experience of Broadus N. Butler. After finishing his doctorate in philosophy at the University of Michigan in 1952, Butler (a former Tuskegee airman) applied for a job at a white college. He was told in a rather emphatic manner, "Why don't you go where you will be among your own kind" (Harris 1983). Also in 1952, Forrest O. Wiggins (University of Wisconsin PhD, 1938) was dismissed from his position as an instructor in the philosophy department at the University of Minnesota. Wiggins was hired in 1946 as the first African American faculty member at Minnesota. However, racism and political ideology combined to lead to his firing. The president of the university, James L. Morrill, acknowledged that because Wiggins was black he would be under close watch. Subsequently, Morrill fired Wiggins despite the fact that the philosophy department and a considerable number of students supported Wiggins's continuance on the faculty at Minnesota. In fact, before being fired Wiggins received three consecutive merit pay raises. Officials in the state legislature called for Wiggins's dismissal after he gave a lecture on

"The Ideology of Interests." Wiggins argued that capitalist and military interests were at the foundation of the Korean War. Undoubtedly, in addition to racism, the influence of McCarthyism and Cold War politics played no small part in Wiggins's departure.

Along with Wiggins, philosophers Charles Leander Hill and Marc M. Moreland directly spoke out against the dangers of McCarthyism and the Cold War. Moreland, a professor of philosophy at Morgan State, in his article "The Welfare State: Embattled Concept" thus challenged the undemocratic character of loyalty oaths and the Justice Department's use of "subversive lists." In turn, Hill joined in the countrywide efforts of some 365 people of various ideological and professional backgrounds to repeal the Subversive Act of 1950 and later united with 100 concerned citizens, scholars, and clergy in calling for world peace in opposition to the nuclear arms buildup.

Pressing issues connected with political and social reality were not remote from the actual context of the academic work pursued by African American philosophers. For a substantial number, the African American experience was the crucially situated object of philosophical inquiry. William T. Fontaine was a Rosenwald Fellow (1942–1943) and did his research on "A Study of the Mind of the Negro as Revealed in Imaginative Literature." Fontaine continued along the path of exploring African American philosophy in several articles, and this culminated with his book, *Reflections on Segregation, Desegregation, Power, and Morals*. Carlton L. Lee, who taught philosophy and religion, explicitly focused on the black experience. Lee's doctoral dissertation (submitted to the University of Chicago Divinity School in 1951) was on *Patterns of Leadership in Race Relations: A Study of Leadership Among American Negroes*. Although Broadus Butler wrote on the topic of *A Pragmatic Study of Value and Evaluation*, for his terminal degree in philosophy from the University of Michigan, he was nevertheless a prolific writer on issues facing African Americans. Many

of his articles not only appear in numerous mainstream (white) publications but also in black journals such as *Negro Digest* and *The Crisis*. Butler did work on W. E. B. DuBois and in 1964 published a booklet titled *Another 1963 American Tragedy: Dr. W.E.B. DuBois*.

Though DuBois did not pursue graduate study in philosophy, he did major in it as an undergraduate. Among other notable philosophers, DuBois studied with William James, the Harvard philosopher/psychologist and cofounder of pragmatism. Several African American philosophers have commented on DuBois. In the Afro-American journal *Freedomways*, Eugene C. Holmes wrote on the topic, "W. E. B. DuBois—Philosopher." Holmes argued that DuBois was a materialist. Robert C. Williams (PhD Columbia University, 1975) wrote an essay, "W. E. B. DuBois: Afro-American Philosopher of Social Reality."

Berkley Eddins initiated discussion around philosophy and black studies in a major mainstream (white) journal of philosophy with his "Philosophia Perennia and Black Studies," and Charles A. Frye devoted a complete text on the subject, *Towards a Philosophy of Black Studies*. Frye, who earned a doctorate from the University of Pittsburgh (1976), was also committed to formulating theoretical grounds for developing black philosophy with *Level Three: A Black Philosophy Reader*.

A former student of Eugene C. Holmes, Percy E. Johnston started the *Afro-American Journal of Philosophy* in 1982. This was the first academic journal dedicated to philosophy and the black experience. Other efforts along the lines of the philosophy of the black experience include William R. Jones's pioneering essay, "The Legitimacy and Necessity of Black Philosophy: Some Preliminary Considerations." In another article, "Crisis in Philosophy: The Black Presence," Jones developed a crucial report on the status of black philosophers, which he presented to the American Philosophical Association (APA). This report was the catalyst for one of the most significant institutional changes in professional philosophy; namely the advent of the Committee on Blacks in Philosophy within the APA.

Furthermore with the rise of black studies, philosophers not only carried out research in this field but also began serving as administrators. Carlton L. Lee founded and was the first director of Black Americana Studies at Western Michigan University; he held that post from 1970 until his death in 1972. William R. Jones was the long-time director of African American Studies at Florida State University. Additionally, Robert C. Williams was acting director of Afro-American Studies at Vanderbilt University and Charles A. Frye was director of a similar program at the Southern University at New Orleans from 1991 to his untimely demise in 1994.

Before the aforementioned philosophers and even going back to the 19th century, the philosophy of the black experience was on the agenda of African American philosophers. Alexander Crummell graduated from Cambridge University in 1853 and studied with William Whewell, one of the Cambridge Platonists. Crummell founded the American Negro Academy (ANA) in 1897 and among its members were W. E. B. DuBois, J. W. E. Bowen, and George Washington Henderson. Henderson was a graduate of the University of Vermont and first black person in the country to be inducted into Phi Beta Kappa.

Four years before the ANA, Rufus L. M. Perry published his "The Cushite or the Descendent of Ham as Found in the Sacred Scriptures and in the Writings of the Ancient Historians and Poets from Noah to the Christian Era." Perry, a former slave, graduated from Kalamazoo Seminary in 1861. A precursor to what today is known as the public intellectual, Perry's contributions to philosophy earned him an honorary doctorate in philosophy from the State University of Louisville in 1887.

Perry's son, Rufus Lewis Perry Jr., also pursued philosophy, although he was a lawyer. Perry was an 1891 graduate of New York University and a member of the French scholarly association, Société Academique d'Historie Internationale. In addition to his work titled "L'Homme d'après la Science et le Talmud," he published a history of Western philosophy, which was the first published by an African American. Perry's *Sketch of Philosophical Systems* (1899) was principally concerned with Greek philosophy. Later, in 1954, George G. M. James's *Stolen Legacy* critiques the standard presentation about Greek origins of the history of philosophy. James argues that Greek philosophy amounts to no more than plagiarized Egyptian philosophy. Three years before James's book, there appeared another text on the history of Western philosophy written by an African American philosopher.

Instead of a spotlight on classical Western philosophy, Charles Leander Hill published *A Short of History of Modern Philosophy from Renaissance to Hegel*. The second African American to earn a doctorate in philosophy from The Ohio State University (1938), Hill served as president of Wilberforce University from 1947 to 1956. Hill's primary motivation for writing his book was to provide his students with a suitable introductory text in the history of philosophy.

It should be noted that the teaching of philosophy was a central concern of philosophers at the HBCUs. This becomes transparent with Richard I. McKinney's essay, "Some Aspects of the Teaching of Philosophy." Later Berkley B. Eddins made inroads into the philosophy of history. In this subfield, Eddins remains one of the foremost African American philosophers. His scholarly articles, "Does Toynbee Need Two Theories of History?" and "Speculative Philosophy of History: A Critical Analysis," and his book *Appraising Theories of Histories* are representative of a larger corpus.

This essay is only the tip of the iceberg with regard to the history of African American philosophers. Undoubtedly there remains a considerable wealth of valuable materials that are yet to be unearthed and that will surely provide the needed material for historical reconstruction of the intellectual legacy left by African American philosophers.

John H. McClendon III

See also African Diasporic Sociology; "African" in African American History; Black/Blackness: Philosophical Considerations.

FURTHER READING

Belles, A. Gilbert. 1969. "The College Faculty, the Negro Scholar, and the Julius Rosenwald Fund." *The Journal of Negro History* 54 (4): 383–392.

Blakely, Allison. 1974. "Richard T. Greener and the 'Talented Tenth's Dilemma." *Journal of Negro History* 59 (4): 305–321.

Butler, Broadus N. 1962. "In Defense of Negro Intellectuals." *Negro Digest* 11 (August): 41–44.

Cook, Joyce Mitchell. 1977–1978. "On the Nature and Nurture of Intelligence." *The Philosophical Forum* 9 (2–3): 289–302.

Crummell, Alexander. 1897. *Civilization: The Primal Need of the Race.* Occasional Papers, III. Washington, D.C.: American Negro Academy.

Eddins, Berkley B. 1971. "Philosophia Perennia and Black Studies." *The Southern Journal of Philosophy* 9 (2): 207–210.

Fontaine, William T. 1967. *Reflections on Segregation, Desegregation, Power, and Morals.* Springfield, IL: Charles C. Thomas.

Frye, Charles A. 1978. *Towards a Philosophy of Black Studies.* San Francisco: R & E Research Associates.

Harris, Leonard. 1983. *Philosophy Born of Struggle.* Dubuque, Iowa: Kendall/Hunt Publishing Co.

Hill, Charles Leander. 1955. "William Ladd, the Black Philosopher from Guinea: A Critical Analysis of His Dissertation on Apathy." *The A.M.E. Review* 72 (186 October-December): 20–36.

Holmes, Eugene C. 1950. "The Main Philosophical Considerations of Space and Time." *American Journal of Physics* 18 (59): 560–570.

James, George G. M. 1954. *Stolen Legacy.* New York: Philosophical Library.

Johnson, William Decker. 1895. "Philosophy." In *Afro-American Encyclopedia,* ed. James T. Haley. Nashville, TN: Haley and Florida.

Johnston, Percy E. 1969. "Black Theories of History and Black Historiography" *Dasein* 9 (1 and 2): 27–38.

Jones, William R. 1973. Report of the Subcommittee on the Participation of Blacks in Philosophy. Crisis in Philosophy: The Black Presence. *Proceedings and Addresses of the American Philosophical Association.* 47: 118–125.

Jones, William R. 1977–1978. "The Legitimacy and Necessity of Black Philosophy: Some Preliminary Considerations." *The Philosophical Forum* 9 (2–3): 149–60.

Locke, Alain L. 1935. "Values and Imperatives." In *American Philosophy, Today and Tomorrow,* ed. Horace M. Kallen and Sidney Hook, 313–336. New York: Lee Furman. (Reprinted in Leonard Harris, ed. 1983. *Philosophy Born of Struggle.* Dubuque, Iowa: Kendall/Hunt Publishing Co.)

McClendon, John H. 1982. "The Afro-American Philosopher and the Philosophy of the Black Experience: A Bibliographic Essay on a Neglected Topic in Both Philosophy and Black Studies." *Sage Race Relations Abstracts* 7 (4): 1–53.

McClendon, John H., III. 2004. "The African American Philosopher and Academic Philosophy: On the Problem of Historical Interpretation." *APA Newsletter on Philosophy and the Black Experience* 4 (1; Fall): 2–9.

McKinney, Richard I. 1960. "Some Aspects of the Teaching of Philosophy." *Liberal Education* 5 46 (463): 366–379.

Titcomb, Caldwell. 2001. "The Earliest Members of Phi Beta Kappa." *The Journal of Blacks in Higher Education* 33 (Autumn): 92–101.

Williams, Robert C. 1976a. "W. E. B. DuBois: Afro-American Philosopher of Social Reality." In Bicentennial Symposium on Philosophy. New York: City University of New York Graduate Center. (Reprinted in Leonard Harris, ed. 1983. *Philosophy Born of Struggle.* Dubuque, Iowa: Kendall/Hunt Publishing Co.)

Williams, Robert C. 1976b. "Afro-American Folklore as a Philosophical Source." *Journal of the West Virginia Philosophical Society* (Fall): 1–6.

Williams, Robert C. 1985. "Ritual, Drama, and God in Black Religion: Theological and Anthropological Views." *Theology Today* 41.4 (January): 431–443.

Photography and the African Diaspora

African Americans shaped the practice of photography from its origin in 1840 and have participated in its history as practitioners and subjects. Six months after the public announcement of the process in Paris, Jules Lion (1810–1866), a free man of color, a lithographer and portrait painter, exhibited the first successful daguerreotypes in New Orleans. The African-American public was interested in making likenesses (which we now call photographs). These were numerous free black men and women who established themselves as daguerreans, photographers, inventors, artists, and artisans who had gained local and national recognition in their respective cities. Portraits of prominent and lesser-known African Americans were produced regularly in galleries and studios throughout the country. The portraits of well-known African Americans soon became popular, and the practice of private photography—photographing individuals for personal collections and albums—became more and more the artistic method for creating a likeness.

In the last half of the 19th century in Africa, Europe, the Caribbean, and the Americas, photographs were created for scientific studies, ethnographic portraits, portraiture, art, pornography, documentation, families of all classes, and those who thought it important to have their likenesses preserved for posterity. French photographers began photographing in French colonies as early as 1839. The earliest photography in Africa was concentrated in the north.

During photography's early history, images produced by African, Caribbean, and African American photographers presented portraits of noted men and women and family members in dramatic settings. Some of the most noted early and mid–20th century African portrait photographers in Africa include Mama Casset (1908–1992), Meissa Gaye (1892–1982) (Senegal), Daniel Attotumo Amichia (1908–1994) (Ghana and the Ivory Coast), Alphonso Lisk-Carew (Sierra Leone) (1887–1969), Seydou Keita (1923–2004), Malick Sidibe (Mali, b. 1936), and Samuel Fosso (Cameroon, b. 1962). In North America, black photographers such

as J. P. Ball (1825–1905), Augustus Washington (1820–1875), C. M. Battey (1873–1927), Arthur Bedou (1882–1966), Florestine Collins (1895–1987), Elise Forrest Harleston (1891–1970), and James VanDerZee (1886–1983) made photographs to celebrate special occasions in the sitter's life—such as marriage, birth, graduation, confirmation, and anniversaries—or the achievement of a particular social or political success.

One of the earliest known photographic studies in America of African American physiognomy was conducted in 1850 by Harvard scientist Louis Agassiz and J. T. Zealy, a white daguerreotypist in Columbia, South Carolina. The latter was hired to take a series of portraits of African-born slaves on nearby plantations. The daguerreotypes were anatomical studies of the faces and the nude upper bodies of African men and women. A French photographer, Prince Roland Napoleon Bonaparte, trained as an ethnologist, made a career out of ethnographic photography. Much of the work of 19th-century black photographers was in sharp contrast to these scientific and stereotypical images.

From the turn of the century to the mid-1920s, photography expanded in a variety of ways. Newspapers, such as *The Negro World*, published by the Universal Negro Improvement Association, incorporated photographs from around the world; journals such as the National Association for the Advancement of Colored People's *Crisis* and books published photographic images of black subjects and events. Courses in photography were offered in schools and colleges, and correspondence courses were also available. C. M. Battey, an accomplished portraitist and fine-art photographer, was a noted educator in photography. Battey founded the photography division at Tuskegee Institute in Alabama in 1916. Battey did the most extensive portrait series of African American leaders produced in the 19th century and early 20th centuries. His photographic portraits of John Mercer Langston, Frederick

Douglass, W. E. B. DuBois, Booker T. Washington, and Paul Laurence Dunbar were sold nationally and reproduced on postcards and posters.

In 1911, Addison Scurlock (1883–1964), who was Howard University's official photographer, opened a studio in Washington, D.C., which he operated with his wife and his sons, Robert and George, until 1964. In New York City, James VanDerZee, undoubtedly the best known black studio photographer, began capturing the spirit and life of New York's Harlem in the 1920s and continued to do so for more than 50 years.

In the 1920s, young black photographers who viewed themselves as artists moved to larger cities in search of education, patronage, and support for their art. Harlem was a cultural center for many of these photographers. In 1921 the New York Public Library's 135th Street branch in Manhattan (now known as the Schomburg Center for Research in Black Culture) organized its first exhibition of work by black artists, entitled "The Negro Artists." Two photographers, C. M. Battey and Lucy Calloway, displayed six photographs in this exhibition of more than 65 works of art. The Harmon Foundation was one of the first philanthropic organizations to give attention, cash awards, and exhibition opportunities to black photographers. These awards came to be known as the William E. Harmon Awards for Distinguished Achievement Among Negroes. In 1930 a special prize of $50 for photographic work was added in the name of the Commission on Race Relations.

Elise Forrest Harleston (1891–1970) of Charleston, South Carolina, and P. H. Polk (1898–1985) of Tuskegee, Alabama were also notable photographers. Harleston opened a photography studio with her painter husband, Edwin Harleston, after studying with Battey in 1922. Polk opened his first studio at Tuskegee in 1927.

During the depression, numerous images were taken of the lives of African Americans.

The Resettlement Administration, later known as the Farm Security Administration (FSA), was created in 1935 as an independent coordinating agency; it inherited rural relief activities and land-use administration from the Department of the Interior, the Federal Emergency Relief Administration, and the Agricultural Adjustment Administration. From 1935 to 1943, the FSA photography project generated 270,000 images of rural, urban, and industrial America. Many of the heavily documented activities of the FSA were of black migrant workers in the South. In 1937, Gordon Parks, Sr., decided that he wanted to be a photographer after viewing the work of the FSA photographers. He was hired by the FSA in 1941, and during World War II he worked as an Office of War Information correspondent. After the war he was a photographer for Standard Oil Company. In 1949 he became the first African American photographer to work on the staff of *Life* magazine.

Roy DeCarava (b. 1919) is the forerunner of contemporary urban photography. In 1955, DeCarava collaborated with Langston Hughes in producing a book entitled *The Sweet Flypaper of Life,* which depicted the life of a black family in Harlem. In 1952, DeCarava became one of the first black photographers to receive a Guggenheim Fellowship. In 1954 he founded a photography gallery that became one of the first galleries in the United States devoted to the exhibition and sale of photography as a fine art. DeCarava founded the Kamoinge Workshop for black photographers in 1963.

From the 1930s through the 1960s photographers began working as photojournalists for local newspapers and national magazines marketed to African American audiences, including *Our World, Ebony, Jet, Sepia,* and *Flash,* among others. Only a few African-American photojournalists, most notably Gordon Parks, Sr., Richard Saunders, Bert Miles, and Roy DeCarava, were employed for the larger picture magazines, such as *Life, Look, Time, Newsweek,* and *Sports Illustrated.* Most had learned photography while in the military and had studied photography in schools of journalism. This period also marked the beginning of reportage and the documentation of public pageantry and events. In the 1930s, smaller handheld cameras and faster film helped photographers express their frustration and discontent with social and political conditions within their communities. The Civil Rights Movement was well documented by photographers such as Moneta Sleet, Jr. (1908–1998) (New York and Chicago), Jack T. Franklin (b. 1922) (Philadelphia), Charles "Teenie" Harris (Pittsburgh), and U.S. Information Service Agency photographers Saunders and Griffith Davis.

From 1935 to the early 1990s musical pioneers were the frequent subjects of photographers. Chuck Stewart (b. 1927), Milt Hinton (1910–2002), DeCarava, and Bert Andrews (1931–1993), for instance, photographed performing artists in the studio, onstage, and in nightclubs.

During the active years of the Civil Rights and Black Power movements—the early 1960s through the 1970s—a significant number of socially committed men and women became photographers, documenting the struggles, achievements, and tragedies of the freedom movement. Student Nonviolent Coordinating Committee photographers Doug Harris, Elaine Tomlin, and Bob Fletcher were in the forefront in documenting the voter registration drives in the South; Robert Sengstacke (b. 1943), Howard Bingham, Jeffrey Scales (b. 1954), and Brent Jones photographed the activities of the Black Panther Party and desegregation rallies in the North and on the West Coast. In 1969 Moneta Sleet, Jr., was the first African American photographer to receive a Pulitzer Prize for his photograph of Coretta Scott King and her daughter at the funeral of the Rev. Dr. Martin Luther King, Jr.

In South Africa, Peter Magubane (b. 1932) photographed the atrocities of the apartheid regime. His photographs were published in *Drum Magazine*, a South African magazine that was established in the early 1950s. The magazine published photographs of black urban life and culture as well as the political climate of South Africa.

In the 1970s, universities and art colleges began to offer undergraduate and graduate degrees in photography, and African American photographers began studying photography and creating works for exhibition purposes. Others studied in community centers and workshops. The symbolic and expressive images of the works produced in the 1980s and 1990s offer sociological and psychological insights into the past, as well as examinations of contemporary social themes, such as racism, unemployment, child and sexual abuse, and death and dying. Most of these works are informed by personal experience. Significant contributors to the development of this genre are Jeanne Moutoussamy-Ashe (b. 1951), Albert Chong (b. 1958), Hank Sloane Thomas (b. 1976), Roland Freeman, Todd Gray (b. 1954), Chester Higgins (b. 1946), Jeffrey Scales (b. 1954), Coreen Simpson, Lorna Simpson (b. 1960), Carrie Mae Weems (b. 1950), Carla Williams (b. 1965), Noelle Theard (b. 1979), and Willie Williams (b. 1950) in the United States; Magubane, George Hallett, Zwelethu Mthewa (b. 1960), Santu Mofokeng (b. 1956), Rashid Lombard, and Andrew Tshabangu (b. 1966) in South Africa; David A. Bailey, Joy Gregory, Roshini Kempadoo (b. 1959), Ajamu, and Rotimi Fani-Kayode (1955–1989) in the United Kingdom; Rene Pena Gonzales (Cuba, b. 1957), David Davidson (Martinique, b. 1963), Radcliffe Roye (Jamaica, b. 1970), Rose-Ann Marie Bailey (Canada, b.1971), and Terrie Boddie (b. 1965) (Nevis) in the Caribbean; and Anisio C. De Caravalho (b. 1930), Bauer Sa (b. 1950), Eustaquio Neves (b. 1955), Vanten Pereira, Jr. (b. 1960), Walter Firmo (b. 1937), Carla Osorio (b. 1972), Denise Camargo (b. 1964), and Luiz Paulo Lima (b. 1955) in Brazil.

Many of the photographers working currently respond to social issues, political issues, culture, family, and collective history. They also explore the impact of sexuality, colonialism, stereotyping and the female body. The issues addressed in contemporary photography create a revised interpretation of the visual experience through digital technology and in genres including portraiture, landscape, and documentary photography.

Deborah Willis

See also Drum; Harlem.

FURTHER READING
Crawford, Joe. 1973. The Black Photographers Annual, Brooklyn, NY: (self-published by the editor and the black photographers annual).
Simon, Njami. 1998., *Anthology of African & Indian Ocean Photography*. Paris: Editions Revue Noire.
Willis, Deborah. 2000. *Reflections in Black: A History of Black Photographers 1840–Present*. New York: W.W. Norton.

Pointe du Sable, Jean Baptiste (1745–1818)

See du Sable, Jean Baptiste Pointe (1745–1818).

Portalatin, Aida Cartagena (1918–1994)

Aida Cartagena Portalatin is the most recognized woman writer in 20th century Dominican literature. She is the author of *Del sueno al mundo* (poetry, 1944); *Vispera del sueno* and *Llamale verde* (poetry, 1945); *Mi mundo el mar* and *Una mjer esta sola* (poetry, 1956); *La voz destada* and *La tierra escrita* (poetry, 1961); *Escalera para Electra* (novel, 1982); *Yania tierra* (poetry, 1982); *En la casa del tiempo* (poetry, 1984); and *Culturas africanas: rebeldes concausa* (essays, 1985).

Widely acknowledged and respected for the quality and militancy of her poetry, Portalatin's better-known works are *Una mujer esta sola*, the first openly feminist poem published in the Dominican Republic, and *La voz desetada* and *La tierra escrita*, poems of angry protest against racial discrimination and exploitation. After retiring from her work as a college professor, Portalatin continued to live in the Dominican Republic and engaged in literary activities until she passed away in June 1994.

See also Dominican Republic.

FURTHER READING
Cocco de Filippos, Daisy. 1995. "Aida Cartagena Portalatin: A Literary Life." In *Moving Beyond Boundaries*. Vols. 1 and 2, *International Dimensions of Black Women's Writing*, ed. Carole Boyce Davies and Molara Ogundipe-Leslie. London: Pluto Press.
Cocco de Filippos, Daisy, ed. & trans. 1988. *From Desolation to Compromise: The Poetry of Aída Cartagena Portalatín*. Santo Domingo: Ediciones Montesinos. No. 10.

Présence Africaine

Présence Africaine—the magazine and the publishing house—were successively founded by Alioune Diop, a Senegalese intellectual (1910–1980), to promote exchanges between African and European intellectuals. In November 1947, the first volume of the magazine appeared simultaneously in Paris and Dakar, Senegal. In his first editorial, entitled *"Niam N'goura vana niam m'paya"* ("Eat so you can live not so that you can fatten"), Diop explains that the idea goes back to 1942–1943 in Paris where some students from "out of sea" or "overseas" (the former appellation for territories under French domination), who were living in a Europe anxious about its essence and the authenticity of its values, decided to get together to study the situation and the characteristics that defined them.

These intellectuals from the French colonies found themselves on their own and caught in the trap of leaving home and finding Paris an alienating though exciting city. Hence, the magazine allowed them to define themselves. Writings of intellectuals such as Leopold Sédar Senghor, Jean-Paul Sartre, Albert Camus, and Theodore Monod were frequently featured in its columns. In 1949, Diop founded the Présence Africaine publishing house. Although the beginning was very difficult, books such as Cheikh Anta Diop's *Nations Nègres et Culture* and Aimé Césaire's *Discourse on Colonialism* were very successful and established the house's reputation throughout the black world. Seydou Badian's *Under the Storm* propelled *Présence Africaine* to its height, selling 30,000 copies.

While the eruption in the African literary landscape of powerhouse publishing companies such as L'Harmattan, Silex, and Karthala threaten the venerable *Présence Africaine*, it continues to stand, just like an African baobab extending its branches with roots plunging deep in the African literary soil.

Among the historical achievements of *Présence Africaine* is the organization of the first international congress of black writers and artists. Organized in the heart of Eurocentric production of knowledge, the congress announced the beginning of the contestation of European intellectual supremacy and gave *Présence* its institutional dimension. Although Eurocentric critics have dismissed the success of the congress because it focused more on questions of imperialism and colonialism and less on literary issues, their arguments amply demonstrate their ignorance of the duality of literature and political engagement in African Diaspora knowledge production. These analyses fail to see the refusal by the United States of exit visas to W. E. B. Dubois and Paul Robeson as precisely the criticism they levied against *Présence Africaine*.

Decolonization and the rejection of Europe's place at the top of the intellectual hierarchy were considered legitimate subjects of literature. Creating that unruptured link between creativity and political liberation, *Présence Africaine* has always stood for African writers and artists, encouraging them to make it a duty and an obligation to play their roles in the process of liberation then and now. Today, after the death of Alioune Diop, and after more than 50 years in existence, *Présence Africaine* is managed by Alioune Diop's wife, Christiane Yandê Diop, an intellectual and his creative partner from the start.

Babacar M'Bow

See also Négritude; *Paris Noir*.

FURTHER READING
Mudimbe, V. Y., ed. 1992. *The Surreptitious Speech: Présence Africaine and the Politics of Otherness 1947–1987*. Chicago, IL: University of Chicago Press.
Présence Africaine: Cultural Review of the Negro World. 1947-present.
Ojo-Ade, Femi. 1977. *Analytical Index of Présence Africaine*. Washington, D.C.: Three Continents Press.

Primus, Pearl E. (1919–1994)

Pearl Primus was a worldwide authority on dance of the African Diaspora and pioneer of modern dance. Born November 29, 1919, in Trinidad, Primus determined her ancestry as Ashanti. Her family moved to New York City when she was two years old, where she grew up. She received her bachelor of arts in biology, health, and physical education from Hunter College in 1940. Intending to become a doctor, she was denied access to medical school because of racism. She also experienced racism as a graduate student of sociology and health education when she was denied access to a laboratory job and to a swimming program.

Racism was not a deterring factor but a motivational one leading her to the YWCA (Young Women's Christian Association) in Harlem, where she found her first dance home and began a career devoted to dance study, research, teaching, and choreography. In 1943, Primus made her first and highly successful professional dance presentation at the New York City 92nd Street YMCA/YWCA while continuing to perform at Café Society Downtown, an integrated nightclub (*Life Magazine*, October 11, 1943). Her research in the Caribbean and the southlands of the United States led to the interpretative dance pieces from Langston Hughes's "The Negro Speaks of Rivers" (1943), Lewis Allen's "Strange Fruit" (1943), and the music of Josh White, Sr.'s, "Hard Time Blues" (1943). Her powerful interpretation of other people's words and music continued until as late as 1979, when she memorialized the racially motivated bombing of a church in Birmingham, Alabama, producing a piece to "Michael, Row Your Boat Ashore" in 1979.

From 1945 to 1947, Primus studied education at Columbia University while also performing professionally with her own dance company and in the Broadway revivals of "Showboat" (1946) and "Emperor Jones" at the Chicago Opera House (1947).

In 1948, she was awarded the last of the Julius Rosenwald Foundation grants and began a 28-month fellowship to study dance in Africa. Primus lived throughout West and Central Africa observing and recording African dance and ceremonies.

Primus performed internationally in 1951 by special invitation for King George VI and Queen Mary of England, and in 1952, she performed at the second inauguration of Liberian president William V. S. Tubman as well as in Israel and France. In 1953, she met her husband Percival S. Borde, a Trinidadian dancer and choreographer. Together they founded what was to become the Primus-Borde Dance Language Institute, developing methods for cross-cultural education in elementary schools through dance. In 1956, the Primus Company went on a world tour in 1956 to Belgium, Italy, India, Indonesia, India, and Liberia. In 1959,

the Oni (king) of Ife, Adesou Adermi II, spiritual head of the Yoruba people of modern Nigeria, officially adopted Primus as his daughter and named her Omowale "child returned home."

Upon returning from overseas, Primus completed a master of arts in educational sociology from New York University in 1959 followed by another research travel grant to Africa in 1962 from the Rebecca Harkness Foundation. The tour included command performances for heads of state plus 28 other performances.

From 1959 to 1961 Primus founded and directed the first performing arts center in Liberia, called "Konama Kende" (A New Thing Living), where she was called "Jay Bonu" (The Boss Lady) and her husband, Percival, was nicknamed "Jangbanolima" (a man who would rather dance than eat). Her interpretive dance from Liberia "Fanga" (1949) became her signature piece, resulting in the award of the "Star of Africa" from the Liberian government.

Other highly recognized works are "African Ceremonial" (1944), "Impinyuza" (The Incomparable") (1951), and "The Wedding" (1979), from her dance repertoire totaling an astounding 150 works over a 52-year career. Primus taught and influenced dancers and choreographers who have continued to build on her work, including the late Alvin Ailey, Judith Jamison, Donald McKayle, and Talley Beatty, among many others.

Primus was awarded a PhD in anthropology in 1978 from New York University. It was the first time African dance was allowed to meet the language requirement for a doctorate.

Her works have been performed worldwide. In the United States performances and reconstructions of her work have been conducted by and through Alvin Ailey Dance Theater, Phildanco, Jacob's Pillow, Lincoln Center, Carnegie Hall, and Urban Bush Women. In 1992, a gala 50 Year Celebration of Dance was held in Primus's honor at the Kennedy Center for the Performing Arts in Washington, D.C.

Pearl Primus depicts lynching through expressionistic dance, 1951. (Hulton-Deutsch Collection/Corbis)

Primus has held a number of teaching positions, including the Five College Consortium in Massachusetts, Howard University, New York University, and State University of New York. Her awards include the Distinguished Service Award from the Association of American Anthropologists (1985) and honorary doctorates from Spelman College (1988), and the New School for Social Research (1992). In 1991, she was awarded the National Medal of Arts from President George H. W. Bush and the American Dance Festival's (ADF) first Balasaraswati/Joy Ann Dewey Beinecke Chair for Distinguished Teaching. She was posthumously awarded the ADF Scripps Award for Lifetime Achievement in Choreography. One of her last public appearances was in the spring of 1994 at the University of Utah in Salt Lake City, where she was awarded the Olaudah Equiano Award of Excellence and Pioneering Achievement.

Primus taught and choreographed up to her death in October 1994. In December 1995 her ashes were taken to Barbados and scattered across the ocean by her son, master drummer Onwin Babajinde Borde, so she could forever touch the shores of Africa. The nonprofit Kuumba Cultural Arts Resource Center, in Lumberton, North Carolina, run by codirectors Louis D. Ramos II and Veleria

Thompson-Ramos, continues to perpetuate the legacy of Pearl Primus.

Louis D. Ramos II
Veleria Thompson-Ramos

See also Dance in the African Diaspora; Trinidad and Tobago.

FURTHER READING

Ahye, Molly. 1978. *Golden Heritage: The Dances of Trinidad and Tobago*. Petit Valley, Trinidad: Heritage Cultures.

Alladin, M. P. 1979. *Folk Dances of Trinidad and Tobago*. Maraval: National Cultural Council.

Emery, Lynne. 1985. *Black Dance in the United States from 1619 to 1970*. Palo Alto, CA: National Press Books. (Orig. pub. 1972).

Green, Richard. 2002. "(Up) Staging the Primitive: Pearl Primus and 'the Negro Problem' in American Dance." In *Dancing Many Drums*, ed. T. DeFrantz, 105–139. Madison: University of Wisconsin Press.

Haskins, James. 1990. *Black Dance in America: A History Through Its People*. New York: T.Y. Crowell.

Welsh-Asante, Kariamu, ed. 1998. *African Dance: An Artistic, Historical, and Philosophical Inquiry*. Trenton, NJ: Africa World Press.

Web sites:
www.geocities.com/pearlprimus/
www.geocities.com/kuumbaculturalarts/

Prince, Mary (1788–?)

Most of the available biographical and historical information about Mary Prince comes from her own account, *The History of Mary Prince: A West Indian Slave Related by Herself* (1831). Published by the Anti-Slavery Society in London and Edinburgh, it ran to three editions that year alone and was crucial in rousing public support for the abolitionist cause. In 1829, Prince had presented a petition to Parliament appealing for manumission from her owner, James Wood of Antigua. Prince's petition was unsuccessful but was part of a multipronged and powerful campaign that was to culminate in the passing of the Emancipation Act in 1833.

Mary Prince's *History* remains unique being the only account published in Britain by a female slave, relating in first-person narrative the experience of West Indian slavery. Her history was written while Prince was a servant to Thomas Pringle, secretary of the Anti-Slavery Society. Susanna Strickland, later Susanna Moodie, transcribed the narrative, and Pringle, who was also a poet, edited the transcription. Prince details the emotional suffering of slavery, the physical and sexual abuse, as well as her many resistances, thus exploiting the roles of both the "good slave" and the noble rebel. Written in the mode of Romantic abolitionist discourse, the *History* achieves the effect of sounding like the unmediated voice of Prince directly appealing to the British public, truthful eyewitness and spokesperson whose task is to inform the public of slave suffering and of the moral turpitude of the plantocracy.

Prince was born in Bermuda in the Devonshire parish in 1788 into the ownership of a farmer, Charles Myners. Her mother was a household slave and her father was a sawyer, and they had other children. When Myners died, Prince passed into the possession of Captain Williams. Until the age of 12, when the estate was sold off and the Prince family dispersed, Prince was a companion to Williams's daughter. Prince was bought by Captain Ingham of Spanish Point. After five years of severe abuse Prince was sold at her own request to a Mr D. He owned land on the remote Turk's Island where the salt industry supplied Bermuda with its main income. For about ten years Prince labored in the gruelling salt ponds until D returned to Bermuda. At around the age of 30, Prince asked to be sold to the Woods family, and they took her to Antigua, a relatively liberal environment for British slaves. In the Woods's household Prince faced another violent regime, yet she took steps toward freedom. She saved money through huckstering and hints at the relationship she had with a white man, Captain Abbot, who tried to buy her freedom. Prince never mentions having any children. She later joined the Moravian Church where she met her future husband, a free black named Daniel James. In her mid-forties Prince came to England with the Woods hoping they would free her. The Woods were intransigent. Prince was forced to leave them and came under the direction of the Moravians and the Anti-Slavery Society. Sustaining many injuries incurred by her masters' violence, by her middle age Prince had arthritis, was lame, and was going blind. She is described in a court transcript of 1833 in which Woods won a case of libel against Pringle over the *History's* content. After this there are no further records. It is uncertain whether she was able to rejoin her husband in Antigua as a free woman. She remains a key figure of slave resistance.

Kerry Sinanan

See also Feminism and Black Women in the African Diaspora; Salt and the African Diaspora.

FURTHER READING

Ferguson, Moira. 1992. *Subject to Others: British Women Writers and Colonial Slavery, 1670–1834.* London: Routledge.

Prince, Mary. 1986. *The History of Mary Prince: A West Indian Slave.* 1831. London: Pandora Press.

Prince Hall Masons

Prince Hall Masons are an official branch of the worldwide fraternal order of Free and Accepted Masons, commonly referred to as Freemasons. It was founded as a refuge of manhood for African American men by Cambridge, Massachusetts, minister Prince Hall, a man believed to be of Caribbean origin. It is the only American branch of Freemasonry that received its charter directly from the Grand Lodge of England.

In 1775, Hall journeyed to Boston Harbor, Massachusetts. to fulfill his desire to become a Mason. Hall was initiated in the rites of Freemasonry at British Lodge No. 58, an army lodge connected to a regiment stationed under General Gage, thus becoming the first person of African decent who was initiated into the order of Freemasonry in the American colonies. On March 6 of the same year a number of other men were initiated, passed, and raised to the degree of Master Mason in the same lodge. These 15 Masonic brothers were issued a dispensation by the lodge so they could meet and organize (but not initiate new Masons) until they were authorized by an official charter to establish their own lodge. On July 3, 1775, Prince Hall dedicated the first Lodge of Colored Americans, African Lodge No. 1, at a lodge room he had prepared on Water Street in Boston. He also became their first lodge leader, or Worshipful Master.

Prince Hall was not content with the limited powers contained in the dispensation from the army lodge and wanted African Lodge No. 1 to enjoy the full Masonic rights and powers of other Masonic bodies in the country. Hall's many requests and petitions for an autonomous charter were summarily rejected by his white counterparts in the Masonic order, most times on the basis of color. Yet, solely because of Hall's persistence, African Lodge received a charter from the Grand Lodge of England 10 years later on March 2, 1784, establishing the lodge officially as African Lodge No. 459. Hall became the only Mason in America who held a warrant directed to himself from the Mother Lodge in England.

The warrant to African Lodge No. 459 of Boston is the most significant and highly prized document known to the Prince Hall Masonic Fraternity. Through it, Masonic legitimacy among free black men is traced and on it, more than any other factor, rests their case. That charter, which is authenticated and in safekeeping, is believed to be the only original charter issued from the Grand Lodge of England still in the possession of any lodge in the United States.

In later years, the fact that Hall obtained his charter from the Grand Lodge of England itself, along with the right and executive power to establish other Lodges of African American Masons, became a point of contention for some white Masons in America. The question of extending Masonry arose when Absalom Jones of Philadelphia, Pennsylvania, appeared in 1791 in Boston. He was an ordained Episcopal priest and a Mason who was interested in establishing a Masonic lodge in Philadelphia. Delegations also traveled from Providence, Rhode Island, and New York to establish the African Grand Lodge that year. Prince Hall was appointed Grand Master, serving in this capacity until his death in 1807.

Prince Hall served in the American Army during the Revolutionary War and was instrumental in appealing to George Washington for the right of all men of color to be allowed to fight in the Revolutionary War. The resulting resolution from that meeting ensured that freemen of color (including those in African Lodge No. 459) would be allowed to become soldiers.

Shortly after his death, the name of African Lodge No. 459 was changed to Prince Hall Grand Lodge in honor of the man who made it possible for men of color to unite under the Masonic Order in North America. The Prince Hall Masons, though rarely a topic of discussion, have invariably had a strong presence throughout the centuries in shaping the destiny of black people in the Americas and representing cross-diaspora collaborations. Prince Hall Masons helped a young Ida B. Wells keep her orphaned family together before she became a leader in the antilynching movement. In its 200-plus years, the Prince Hall Grand Lodge has spawned more than 44 other Grand Lodges. Today, the Prince Hall fraternity has more than 4,500 lodges worldwide, forming 44 independent jurisdictions with a membership of over 300,000 Masons.

Jason Esters

See also Garvey, Marcus Mosiah (1887–1940).

FURTHER READING

Cass, Donna. 1957. *Negro Freemasonry and Segregation.* Chicago: Ezra A. Cook Publications.

Grimshaw, H. 1995. *Official History of Freemasonry Among the Colored People in North America.* Kila, MT: Kessinger Publishing. (Orig. pub. 1902).

Wallace, Maurice O. 2002. *Constructing the Black Masculine Identity and Ideality in African American Men's Literature and Culture, 1775–1995.* Durham, NC: Duke University Press.

The Provincial Freeman

The black abolitionist paper *Provincial Freeman* (1853–1859) was the third black newspaper published in Canada. (The first black newspaper in Canada, *The British American,* was first published in March 1845.) Its inaugural issue—born out of controversy with Canada's second black paper, the *Voice of the Fugitive* (1851–1853) published in Windsor, Canada West—appeared on March 24, 1853. Cofounded by Samuel Ringgold Ward and Mary Ann Shadd, the antislavery *Provincial Freeman* supported "the elevation of the Colored people," temperance, and women's rights. The paper was a broadsheet with seven columns per page. It included material such as reprinted poetry from the *National Era,* addresses from various antislavery associations, a letter by Harriet Beecher Stowe, news of a black singer in Buffalo, and recipes. The second issue of the *Provincial Freeman* appeared one year later.

Beginning March 25, 1854, the newspaper was published weekly in Toronto. Its prospectus, attributed to Shadd, stated the paper's devotion to "Anti-Slavery, Temperance and General Literature." The masthead added Shadd as publishing agent. Scholars recognize that naming Ward editor was a guise to protect Shadd from gendered assaults on her capabilities as publisher and editor. Furthermore, Ward toured Europe for much of the period during which his name appears on the masthead, which seems to support the evidence that Shadd was the primary editor.

In its first year, the *Freeman* promoted black emigration to Canada and criticized the Refugee Home Society, which was locally administered by former *Voice of the Fugitive* publisher Henry Bibb, and the Dawn Institute, which was managed by Josiah Henson and John Scoble. The paper questioned the success of white American and Canadian abolitionism and sought support from the Toronto Ladies Association for the Relief of Destitute Colored Fugitives, which, to Shadd's frustration, held a fund-raiser in support of *Frederick Douglass' Paper*. Articles advocating women's rights were also of prominence in its pages. Pieces on suffrage, letters from women readers discussing the paper's acceptance of female correspondence, and a column entitled "Women's Rights" all appeared in the paper's first year. The *Freeman* also reprinted literature from prominent women writers such as Fanny Fern (Sara Parton) and Frances E. Watkins Harper.

By its first anniversary as a weekly, in March 1855, the *Provincial Freeman* had added emigration to its list of causes—second on the nameplate after antislavery—and authorized Isaac D. Shadd (Mary Ann's brother) "to receive subscriptions." By June of that year, Mary Ann Shadd announced her departure from the paper's editorship, transferring it to Baptist minister and active member of the Provincial Union, William P. Newman, though Shadd continued to write and raise funds for the paper.

Publication paused until August while the *Freeman* moved to Chatham where it was met with antiblack resistance. In November 1855, African American journalist William Howard Day became the paper's corresponding editor. Facing legal challenges, the *Freeman* continued publication into 1857, though it was pleading for funds. Extant copies do not exist for the remainder of 1857. The history of the paper after this period is incomplete, and it is unclear how

many issues were printed. Extant copies exist from January and June of 1859.

Andrea Stone

See also Shadd Cary, Mary Ann (1823–1893).

FURTHER READING
Heath, Leila. 1987. "Black Ink: An Historical Critique of Ontario's Black Press." *Fuse* 11 (1): 20–27.
Murray, Alex L. 1959. "*The Provincial Freeman*: A New Source for the History of the Negro in Canada." *Ontario History* 51 (1): 25–31.
Murray, Heather. 2002. *Come Bright Improvement. The Literary Societies of Nineteenth-Century Ontario.* Toronto: University of Toronto Press.
Rhodes, Jane. 1998. *Mary Ann Shadd Cary: The Black Press and Protest in the Nineteenth Century.* Bloomington: Indiana University Press.

Puerto Rico: Afro-Puerto Ricans

Borikén or *Boriquén,* as the indigenous Tainos called the island of Puerto Rico, is situated to the east of Hispaniola, now the nations of Haiti and Dominican Republic. On his second voyage (1493) Christopher Columbus sighted *Boriquén* and called it *San Juan Bautista.* The island was renamed Puerto Rico in 1506 and followed the pattern of colonization of Spanish territories in the Americas. Spain implemented a colonial system in which indigenous people and later enslaved Africans supplied the labor force in the development of the colony and thus formed an important element of the island's social composition.

HISTORY

Puerto Rican historiography asserts that Africans arrived on the island both as slaves and *libertos* (free people). Some of these *libertos* were domestic servants and conquerors; such was the case of Juan Garrido, who participated in the conquest of Mexico, Florida, and the West Indies (Alegría 2004). These *conquistadores* lived in the Iberian Peninsula and became *ladinos* or Christianized Africans. In addition to Juan Garrido, other *ladinos* arrived in Puerto Rico by 1500. Francisco Piñon and Francisco Mexia were among them. Both were engaged in mining. Piñon and Mexía were also *encomenderos*. Their descendants are the founders of black communities on the island, such as Piñones and Loíza (Sued Badillo and López Cantós 1986, 23–32). Hence, the presence of Africans in Puerto Rico was established from the conquest of the island.

During the colonial period, the Spanish established an economy that required more labor than could be supplied by indigenous people, mainly because the Taino population had decreased from exploitation and mistreatment by settlers. In Hispaniola the Tainos rebelled in response to this mistreatment. In some instances they joined with Africans to establish maroon communities. This union placed the colonizers on alert against any alliance between indigenous people and Africans. Despite attempts to exploit the indigenous population as the main source of labor, advocators for the rights of indigenous people shifted the balance against Africans. In 1501, Spain granted *asientos* (licenses) to Portuguese merchants to bring captive Africans to the Indies. Among the requirements, Africans brought to the Spanish colonies were to be Christianized. Juan Ponce De León, first governor of Puerto Rico, imported the first captive Africans to the island in 1508. However, these Africans were brought under special circumstances as it was not until 1510 that a Dutchman named Geronimus introduced enslaved Africans as stipulated by an *asiento* (Díaz-Soler 2000, 30). There was very little settlement in the first decades after 1501, and the island's population was modestly low. The census of 1530 shows Africans and Indians in the majority (1,523 slaves, 1,148 Indians, and 369 whites).

The *asientos* granted to Portugal lasted from 1595 to 1640. During this period the Spanish colonies received thousands of enslaved Africans from Portuguese domains (Cape Verde, Angola, and Minas) in Africa. Documents related to this particular period have helped to establish that the captive Africans brought to Puerto Rico during the late 16th and throughout the 17th century came mainly from Angola. In 1598, British forces under the command of Sir George Cumberland occupied the city of San Juan; in his diary Cumberland confirms the Angolan factor. Cumberland notes that while he was there a slave ship arrived in Puerto Rico with Angolans; they were confiscated (Díaz Soler 2000, 78). Another account by Bishop Damián López de Haro, who visited the island in 1644, observed that in addition to the few Portuguese and Spanish residents in the city of San Juan, Angolan slaves made up the majority of the population (López Cantos 1986, xlv).

The increasing number of Africans enslaved or free was a key factor in the development of the Puerto Rican society. Several census reports suggest that throughout the Spanish colonial period the free African descent population outnumbered whites. The *padrón* (census) of 1673 shows 1,791 free blacks, 820 whites, and 667 slaves (Figueroa 1979, 103). The increasing number of *libertos* on the island might be also explained by the fact that in 1664, the Spanish crown began to enact *cédulas*; these granted political asylum to runaway slaves from the British and Netherlands colonies. These self-emancipated Africans were granted freedom in exchange for embracing Catholic faith and taking an oath of loyalty to the king of Spain (Brau 2000, 145). They established new communities on the outskirts of the city San Juan (*Santurce*) and composed the new free black class while the local enslaved population remained in bondage.

In the 18th century, the economy and society were founded. The existing *haciendas* depended on enslaved labor. As the colonial period took its course, political developments involving succession to the throne in Spain resulted in neglect of its colonies. Lack of proper oversight and the proper regulation of trade encouraged contraband and smuggling with other European dependencies. In addition to acquiring basic commodities for survival, many *hacendados* (planters) smuggled captive Africans, mainly from the British, Dutch, and French, contravening the *asiento* agreement. Consequently, there were close ties with the rest of the Antilles, which contributed to the making of the Afro-Caribbean community (Morales Carrión 1952).

The large number of free people of color resulted from the ambivalence of the Spanish colonial system, which maintained a segment of the African-descended population in bondage, while free people of color made significant gains in the colonial social structure. A good case is Miguel Enríquez, who was born a free mulatto. His grandmother was an African from Guinea. In the early days he worked as a shoemaker and learned to read and write. Later he emerged as a corsair, sailor, smuggler, and military man. Enríquez participated in the defense of the island of Vieques against the British in 1718 by loaning the Spanish his fleet of ships. Hence, he received accolades for the defeat of the British. As a result of the success of his business and his military service, Spain granted Enríquez the honorific title of "Caballero de la Real Esfinge" and a license to become a *corsario* (corsair or coast guard). Through this Enríquez accumulated considerable wealth. Reports indicate that when the *situado* or cash trading from Mexico was delayed, Enríquez made loans to the colonial government to cover the military payroll. Consequently, many mulatto soldiers emulated Enríquez, who also became a target of envy and had to be protected by the local government. In the end, a plot orchestrated by some Spanish colonial officers and the white elite stripped Enríquez of all his wealth; he fled to Saint Thomas where he died in 1743 (López Cantos, 1994).

For many years it has been debated whether the *haciendas* and slave labor complex in Puerto Rico was very different from that of the rest of the Caribbean. It was assumed that the development of slave trade and sugar plantation economy was not interrelated. This paradigm made it difficult to establish the role of the enslaved population in the island's economy and society. This continued until the 1970s when efforts were still being made to assess the role of slavery in Puerto Rican history. The tendency was to deny the importance of the enslaved labor in the development of sugar production and in fact their organic contribution in the island (Díaz Soler 2000).

This paradigm was virtually unchallenged until the early 1980s when a study focusing on the Ponce region (southern part of the island) demonstrated that the growth of the slave plantation complex was a logical result of the collapse of Spanish mercantilism and its replacement by a new colonial relationship in which foreign trade, imported capital, and African slave labor played dominant roles (Scarano 1984). The work adopted another interpretation of the Puerto Rican sugar industry, presenting it as a counterpoint to the Cuban model.

Another important study on slave labor and the development of the plantation economy focused on the municipality of Vega Baja between 1800 and 1873. The study traced the history of the agrarian property and social weaving that slavery created. According to the study, slavery permitted the rise of the sugar economy at the beginning of the 19th century, and enslaved Africans were pivotal. It was only because of the demands and external pressures to end slave trade that the planters forced the peasants or *jornaleros* to do this labor (San Miguel 1989, 84). The historiography of the plantation system in Puerto Rico also sheds light on the social aspect of slavery. Slaves lived in barracks or huts, yet they were able to establish families. According to the 1869 census, 34.4 percent of slaves worked in the fields and nearly 8 percent worked as domestic servants and artisans. In their spare time slaves had social gatherings where they played *bomba,* an Afro-Puerto Rican musical genre. In many instances during these *bomba* gatherings slaves plotted and organized uprisings (Baralt 1982; Díaz Soler 2000). Drum playing (an African Diaspora phenomenon) became a tool of communication that caused fear among the plantations.

Slave resistance on the island and racial relations are subjects of the new historiography, which disputes the belief that there were few insurrections and that the island did not provide topographical characteristics for maroon communities similar to those in Jamaica (Díaz Soler 2000). On the contrary, it has been established that in the early 16th century the Spanish government kept records of many Africans who fled to the interior of the island. Some returned to work; on occasion, they formed a group engaged in "petit maroonage." Enslaved persons in Puerto Rico did not depend on maroonage to be free, however. They resorted to the legal system to complain against the physical abuse of their masters (Nistal Moret 2000, 17–18). In other instances they purchased their own freedom through *coartación* (a system that allowed slaves to purchase freedom in installments). However, *coartación* was limited and depended on the character and goodwill of the masters.

The slave population was under constant surveillance, and Spanish authorities increased their vigilance and repression after the revolt in Haiti. The records the colonial authorities kept on slaves' activities are a good source for study in this area. These records include the name of people involved, type of offense, and legal outcome. To prevent widespread revolution, the Spanish authorities opted to deny these events or simply to report them as uprisings (Baralt 1982). Another strategy of social control was the implementation of *bandos* or codes, such as *Bando contra la raza africana* of 1848, which attempted to institutionalize racial control among the enslaved and free black population.

Research on the racial discourse in Puerto Rico has shown that during Spanish colonial administration racial tensions and race discrimination against the African population were pervasive. As early as the 1760s Friar Abbad y La Sierra stated that people of African descent had suffered constantly because of their origins (Abbad y La Sierra 1975, 399–400). Discrimination against people of African descent is closely linked to the fact that the island was a slave society and the social colonial structure perpetuated the stigma of associating slavery only with Africans.

In Puerto Rico, racial and class struggles also have their history in slavery and abolition. In 1864, the issue of slavery in Puerto Rico assumed new urgency. The founding of the *Sociedad Abolicionista* put pressure on the Spanish government to abolish slavery. In November 1865, after the liberal monarchists came to power in Spain, Cuba and Puerto Rico were invited to send representatives to the *Junta Informativa* (an advisory, fact-finding group) in Madrid the following year. Interestingly, Spain had neglected this group for decades. The reasons why Spain changed its policy are unknown, but some have speculated that the government was under pressure from England and local abolitionist groups to end slavery. Others believed Spain's invitation to the colonies was spurred by the fear that the expansionist mood displayed earlier by the United States would continue once the Civil War ended (Jiménez 1998, 158). Regardless of Spain's motives, the Cuban and Puerto Rican delegates welcomed the opportunity to represent their homelands in Madrid. The group of Puerto Rican attendees included five liberal abolitionists and one conservative. The delegation argued that Puerto Rico, unlike Cuba, depended almost entirely on its free labor force for its agricultural production.

As a result of this meeting and the outbreak of the first war of independence in Cuba, in 1870, the *Ley Moret* was enacted to abolish slavery gradually. The *Ley Moret* created a system of *patronato,* or apprenticeship. Plantation owners also attempted to flout the law by changing the ages of the slaves to keep them in bondage for a longer period. In addition, the Ten Years' War in Cuba delayed the complete implementation of the law. At the end of it, the newly created *Partido Liberal Reformista,* with its antislavery platform, pushed for a serious solution to the problem of slavery in Puerto Rico. As a first measure to legitimize the process in 1868 and 1872, two censuses were taken, which indicated a reduction of the slave population—a fact that abolitionists used as their final attack (the 1869 census showed a figure of 323,454 whites; 237,710 free colored; and 39,069 slaves). Finally, in March 22, 1873, slavery was abolished in Puerto Rico. African descendants began to construct alternative communities, and most of them would later shape the Puerto Rican working class.

The status of African descendants after emancipation is relevant to the understanding of the strategies used by the working classes during the first 20 years of the American occupation of 1898. Recent scholarship on the topic of the post-emancipation period, particularly in the Caribbean, has provided a comparative framework for study among different Caribbean colonies (Beckles and Shepherd 1996). In the case of Puerto Rico, the most recent research sheds light on the life of free black Puerto Ricans after emancipation. It examines how freed slaves used new forms of "contracts" as mechanisms to reunite with their relatives. The study also contributes to the understanding of the socioeconomic structures of the 19th century and the different social developments that took place during that period; these include the emergence of urban identities, artisanship, labor movement links, and political party struggles (Mayo Santana, Negrón Portillo, and Mayo López 1997).

Historians agree that the labor movement concept began in the late 1860s and early 1870s. The first group that formed a "worker-oriented organization" was the *artesanos,* who organized themselves in the urban centers. These organizations were characterized by the creation of clubs, societies for mutual help, and

cooperatives. Initially, the *casinos,* or artisan clubs, imitated the social activities of the Creole class, but later they were transformed into organizations that fostered the intellectual growth of its members (García and Quintero 1982). With the American occupation workers sought advancement of their group by affiliating with the American Federation of Labor and established cross-class alliances. An example of these cross-class alliances was reflected by the leader of the Republican Party José Celso Barbosa, an Afro-Puerto Rican with a medical degree from the University of Michigan. Despite his political convictions of the eventual annexation of Puerto Rico to the United States, Barbosa was respected by all social groups. His birthday (July 27) is one of the island's national holidays.

As in the case of workers' organizations in the Caribbean, Puerto Rican unions established political cross-class alliances to advance their agenda. From mid 1910 to the beginning of the 1920s, the labor movement in Puerto Rico evolved from guilds and exclusive groups to political parties, which had the goal of obtaining better social and economic conditions. A recent study indicated that in 1920 a chapter of the Universal Negro Improvement Association (UNIA) was established in San Juan. The founding of a UNIA chapter in Puerto Rico demonstrates another contribution of Afro-Puerto Ricans to the labor movement and demonstrates that Afro-Puerto Ricans used labor unions as vehicles in the struggle against economic oppression and racial discrimination (Román 2003).

CULTURAL CONNECTIONS

Racial discrimination became more evident when the African-descended population reaffirmed its cultural link with Africa. One of the debates in Puerto Rican historiography is the cultural contribution of Africans. It was the held view that Afro-Puerto Ricans lost all connection with their African traditions and rituals. Furthermore, it was suggested that African traditions were absorbed by the Indian and the Spanish race (Díaz Soler 2000, 173). Although the island is mainly Catholic, traces of African religions are seen in different spiritual practices. It is not a surprise seeing an altar dedicated to *Shangó*, *Ochún*, or *Yemaya* in a Puerto Rican household; at the same time the person is a devotee of the Catholic faith. On the island it is common to visit a *santero* to receive guidance while making a visit to the church and praying before an image of the Virgin Mary. It is not a contradiction to make a trip to the *botánica* to purchase special lotions and herbs prescribed by the *santero* to chase away evil spirits. Thus, the so-called syncretization of European and African religions in Puerto Rico is a clear evidence of the Africanization of the island's culture.

The previous example challenges the misconceptions that on the island there is no trace of the African culture. In the early 1970s a debate on this issue was sparked with the publications of the two volumes of *Narciso descubre su trasero, El negro en la cultura puertorriqueña* (Zenón Cruz 1974) and *El elemento afronegroide del español en Puerto Rico* (Alvarez Nazario 1974). In *Narciso* the concept of black Puerto Rican is defined and the political, economic, and cultural contributions of African-descended people on the island's national identity are described. *El elemento afronegroide* is a linguistic study of the African presence in Puerto Rico in the Spanish spoken on the island. Both seminal works attempt to articulate the concept of Afro-Puerto Ricanness that has been missed in the island's national discourse. A similar claim emerges from a Marxist point of view in the seminal essay *El país de cuatro pisos* (*The Four-Storeyed Country*). It establishes that Africans and *Afrocriollos* were the precursors of nationalism, which Puerto Rican intellectuals now associate with *el jíbaro* or the peasant (González 1980). The *jíbaros* are seen as deriving from European immigrants that settled in the rural areas. This debate about the *jíbaro* can

be traced back to the end of the 19th and beginning of the 20th century when Puerto Rican intellectuals romanticized the *jíbaros* and identified them as the initiators of Puerto Rican culture. While the European, particularly the Spanish race, was exalted (Hispanophilia), the African-descended population was excluded from the island's national identity.

Recently, the discussion on the role of Africans in the island's national identity has become a vehicle through which issues of race and racism among Puerto Ricans are directly addressed. However, because this critical scholarship is mainly produced by members of the Puerto Rican Diaspora in the United States, particularly in relation to the brand of racism they experience there, its impact in Puerto Rico has been limited and gradual (Duany 2002).

The degree of denial over racism in Puerto Rican society is so profound that textbooks and other literature on the history of Puerto Rico downplay the fact that in the 1950s the group *Liga para Promover el Progreso de los Negros en Puerto Rico* (League to Promote the Advancement of Blacks in Puerto Rico) denounced racist practices in the private and government sectors. Juan Falú Zarzuela founded this group, which is modeled after the principles of the National Association for the Advancement of Colored People. The exclusion of this civil rights group from Puerto Rican social history by the Puerto Rican elite illustrates how in several intellectual circles the attempt to dilute the problem of race makes it difficult for black people to organize and mobilize against racial oppression.

The U.S. presence in Puerto Rico has exacerbated political tensions on the island. Manifestations against American imperialism were channeled through the creation of political parties such as the *Partido Nacionalista* (1922). Its leader, Pedro Albizu-Campos, an Afro-Puerto Rican, fought for the island's independence. He also advocated for preserving the island culture by using a contemporary strategy that consisted of embracing Catholicism and *hispanofilia* (cult of Hispanic culture). Some scholars have argued that Albizu's approach was a denial of the island's African past; whereas others contend that his approach was merely a reliable strategy to resist U.S. imperialism. Albizu and his party followers were persecuted by the Federal Bureau of Investigation and the local government; he was in and out from prison until he died in 1965.

Today the discussion related to the African presence in Puerto Rico is being raised with relative openness. Private institutions, such as the Banco Popular of Puerto Rico, contributed to the making of a documentary recognizing the Afro-Puerto Rican musical genre *bomba* and *plena*. A new trend was established by the descendants of Juan Falú Zarzuela, founder of the *Liga*: by using research and DNA they were able to trace their family roots to Senegal. Inspired by this outcome, another Afro-Puerto Rican family (the Richardsons) also traced their roots to Nigeria. Another admirable effort is the alliance among the traditionally black communities and members of the academia. Their hard work and activism have sparked the interest of the Afro-Puerto Ricans citizens to celebrate their African heritage. Overall, the search of the *tercera raíz* (third root) has given voice and agency to Afro-Puerto Ricans in the conceptualization and construction of Puerto Rican identity.

Milagros Denis

See also Cuba: Afro-Cubans; Dominican Republic; Febres, Mayra Santos (1966–); Garvey, Marcus Mosiah (1887–1940); Haiti; Mexico: African Heritage; Santería.

FURTHER READING

Abbad y Lasierra, Fray Iñigo. 1975. *Historia geográfica, civil y natural de la isla de San Juan Bautista de Puerto Rico*. Annotated by Isabel Gutiérrez del Arroyo. Rio Piedras, Puerto Rico: Editorial Universitaria.

Alegría, Ricardo. 2004. *Juan Garrido: el conquistador negro en las Antillas, Florida, Mexico y California*. 2nd ed. San Juan: Centro de Estudios Avanzados de Puerto Rico y del Caribe.

Alvarez Nazario, Manuel. 1974. *El elemento afronegroide en el español de Puerto Rico*. San Juan, Puerto Rico: Instituto de Cultura Puertorriqueña.

Baralt, Guillermo. 1982. *Esclavos rebeldes. Conspiraciones y sublevaciones de esclavos en Puerto Rico (1795–1873)*. Rio Piedras, Puerto Rico: Ediciones Hiracán.

Beckles, Hilary, and Verene Shepherd, eds. 1996. *Caribbean Freedom. Economy and Society from Emancipation to the Present*. Princeton, NJ: Markus Wiener.

Brau, Salvador. 2000. *Historia de Puerto Rico*. Rio Piedras, Puerto Rico: Editorial Edil.

Diaz Soler, Luis M. 2000. *Historia de la esclavitud negra en Puerto Rico*. Río Piedras: Editorial de la Universidad de Puerto Rico.

Duany, Jorge. 2002. *The Puerto Rican Nation on the Move: Identities on the Island and in the United States*. Chapel Hill: University of North Carolina Press.

Figueroa, Loida. 1979. *Breve historia de Puerto Rico*. 2 vols. Rio Piedras, Puerto Rico: Editorial Edil.

Garcia, Gervasio L., and A.G. Quintero. 1982. *Desafío y solidadridad: breve historia del movimiento obrero puertorriqueño*. Rio Piedras, Puerto Rico: Ediciones Huracán.

González, José Luis. 1980. *El pais de cuatro pisos y otros ensayos*. Río Piedras, Puerto Rico: Ediciones Huracán.

Jiménez de Wagenheim, Olga. 1998. *Puerto Rico. An Interpretative History from Pre-Columbian Times to 1900*. Princeton, NJ: Markus Wiener Publishers.

López Cantos, Angel. 1994. *Miguel Enríquez: corsario Boricua del siglo XVIII*. Puerto Rico, Puerto Rico: Ediciones Puerto.

Mayo Santana, Raúl, Mariano Negrón Portilla, and Manuel Mayo López. 1997. *Cadenas de esclavitud y solidaridad. Esclavos libertos en San Juan, siglo XIX*. Rio Piedras: Universidad de Puerto Rico.

Morales Carrión, Arturo. 1952. *Puerto Rico and the Non-Hispanic Caribbean: A Study in Decline of Spain's Exclusivism*. Rio Piedras: University of Puerto Rico.

Nistal Moret, Benjamín. 2000. *Esclavos prófugos y cimarrones. Puerto Rico, 1770–1870*. Rio Piedras, Puerto Rico: Editorial Universitaria.

Román, Reinaldo L. 2003. "Scandalous Race: Garveyism, the Bomba, and the Discourses of Blackness in 1920s Puerto Rico." *Caribbean Studies* 31 (1, January-June): 213–259.

San Miguel, Pedro. 1989. *El Mundo que creó el azúcar. La haciendas en Vega Baja, 1800–1873.* Rio Piedras, Puerto Rico: Ediciones Huracán.

Scarano, Francisco. 1984. *Sugar and Slavery in Puerto Rico. The Plantation Economy of Ponce, 1800–1850.* Madison: University of Wisconsin Press.

Sued Badillo, Jalil, and Angel López Cantos. 1986. *Puerto Rico Negro.* Río Piedras, Puerto Rico: Editorial Cultural.

Zenón Cruz, Isabelo. 1974. *Narciso descubre su trasero: el negro en la cultura puertorriqueña.* 2 vols. Humacao, Puerto Rico: Editorial Furidi.

Pushkin, Alexander Sergeevich (1799–1837)

Heralded as Russia's most beloved writer, Alexander Sergeevich Pushkin was born into a family of wealth and serf-abusing privilege, a fact that many Soviet revolutionaries were willing to overlook. Because his maternal great-grandfather, Ibrahim Petrovich Gannibal, was an African slave from present-day Eritrea, who became the godson, chief engineer, army general, and court favorite of Czar Peter the Great, some of Pushkin's biographers have wrongly asserted that he was an "octoroon." Following aristocratic tradition of intermarriage, his parents, Nadja and Sergei, were related by blood, and both were the descendants of the famous Ibrahim. Thus, Pushkin's African ancestry came from both sides of his family.

Pushkin's poems began to appear in public when he was 15. By the time he graduated from the Imperial Lyceum three years later, Russia's leading literary figures acknowledged him as a rival. His extensive repertory of poetry and prose is revered for its intrinsic "Russianness." Though he experimented with Shakespearean styles in romantic tragedy and Byronic styles in poetry, he rejected popular literary trends from France and Germany. For the most part,

he wrote about Russian people, Russian culture, and Russian values.

Pushkin settled in Petersburg, where he wrote extensively. He also sold the serfs he inherited in order to live a life of youthful hedonism, drinking heavily and taking many mistresses, including married women. During this time, he gradually developed a sense of political consciousness and a taste for social reform. Thus, he occasioned the czar's disfavor in 1820, resulting in his banishment from Petersburg to Ekaterinoslave in southern Russia. While in exile, he visited the Caucasus and the Crimea. In 1823, he was transferred to Odessa, where his drinking, womanizing, and literary energy continued. He also wrote many personal letters, one of which was intercepted and forwarded to the czar. Because the letter contained the sentiments of an atheist, he was exiled once more, this time to his mother's estates in the village of Mikhaylovskoe in northern Russia, where he was kept under constant surveillance.

Pushkin was proud of his African ancestry. Indeed, before his untimely death, he had begun composing a novel in homage to his grandfather, entitled *The Blackamoor of Peter the Great.* Marriage and court intrigues plagued him consistently in the last years of his life. Determined to marry "the most beautiful woman in Russia," he met Natalya Goncharova in 1829 and married her in 1831. Wedlock did not discourage Natalya's many admirers. Czar Nicholas I had two reasons for summoning the handsome couple to court. First, he wanted to control the content of Pushkin's publications. The prolific writer could publish nothing without the czar's official permission, not even a newspaper editorial. Permission, if forthcoming, took as long as four years. Second, he enjoyed the company of the coquettish Natalya. Pushkin was certain that Nicholas conferred him with a court title to facilitate Natalya's attendance at lavish balls and other court functions. Yet these troubled years, 1831 to 1837, proved to be Pushkin's most productive literarily.

In 1834, Madame Pushkina met Georges-Charles d'Anthès, a young French émigré, and the adopted son and paramour of Baron Jacob von Heeckeren, a Dutch diplomat. Their intimacy was less than private, and when Pushkin learned of it in 1837, he challenged the Frenchman to a duel. This was not his first duel but it was his last. Court society sided with d'Anthès but the Russian people rendered him the most hated personality in the history of their literature. For the sake of mob control, the czar ordered a small, well-guarded funeral, by invitation only. With reason to fear for his life, d'Anthès fled to Paris, where he pursued a career in politics. Natalya remarried in 1844.

The Pushkins had four children: Alexander, Grigory, Natalya, and Marya Alexandrovna. Pushkin's descendants include the actor Peter Ustinov and Prince Philip Mountbatten, Duke of Edinburgh, consort of England's Queen Elizabeth II. Of Pushkin's work, Serena Vitale, one of his recent biographers, puts him, as many Russians have, in the company of Shakespeare.

Joseph Dorsey

See also Europe and the African Diaspora.

FURTHER READING
Blagoi, D. D. 1982. *The Sacred Lyre: Essays of the Life and Work of Alexander Pushkin*. Moscow, Russia: Raduga Publishers.

Creighton, Laura G. 1999. *A Bibliography of Alexander Pushkin in English: Studies and Translations*. New York: Mellon Press.

Evdokimova, Svetlana. 2003. *Alexander Pushkin's Little Tragedies: The Poetics of Brevity*. Madison: University of Wisconsin Press.

Pushkin, Alexander. 1936. *The Works of Alexander Pushkin: Lyrics, Narrative Poems, Folktales, Plays, and Prose*. New York: Random House.

Pushkin, Alexander. 1943. *Poems, Prose, and Plays*. New York: Random House.

Pushkin, Alexander. 1999. *Collected Stories*. New York: Everyman's Library.

Sandler, Stephanie. 1989. *Distant Pleasures: Alexander Pushkin and the Writing of Exile*. Palo Alto, CA: Stanford University Press.

Vitale, Serena. 2000. *Pushkin's Button*. Chicago: University of Chicago.

Q

Quilombhoje

São Paulo–based Quilombhoje (Quilombo today) was the first African Brazilian writers' collective. Founded in 1980 by Cuti, Owaldo Camargo, Paulo Colina, Abelardo Rodrigues, and others, the group's main objective is to discuss and critically analyze the Afro-Brazilian experience in literature and to create space for Afro-descendants to discuss issues of identity, inclusion, citizenship, and self-esteem.

The first meeting of the collective took place at the now-defunct Bar Matamba, a bohemian tavern popular among intellectuals, located downtown in the city of São Paulo. Soon after its creation, the group took over the task of publishing and promoting *Cadernos Negros*. *Cadernos Negros*, the first publication by, about, and for an Afro-Brazilian audience, has been published annually since 1978, with editions featuring poetry and short fiction alternatively.

In the mid–1980s the group went through its first major crises and schism, resulting in the departure of Camargo, Colina, and Rodrigues. These writers were very critical of the literary quality of the early material published by *Cadernos Negros*, which at time privileged social politics of community building over dis-

embodied literary aesthetics. It was also during this period that the group was joined by some young writers, who would later become major names in contemporary Afro-Brazilian literature, such as Miriam Alves, Abilio Fereira, Esmeralda Ribeiro, Márcio Barbosa, Sônia Fátima da Conceição, and Oubi Inae Kibuko. The new, revitalized Quilombhoje grew and reached out to the entire country, becoming the central space for the maturation of the contemporary Afro-Brazilian literary voices.

Currently run by Esmeralda Ribeiro, the president, and Márcio Barbosa, the vice president, more recently, Quilombhoje has embraced a broader editorial mission to promote and market Afro-Brazilian literature and culture at large. Among other titles, the group has published a collection of critical essays entitled *Reflexões sobre a Literatura Afro-Brasileira* (*Reflections about Afro-Brazilian Literature*) (1982) and a book about issues of race and self-esteem, called *Gostando Mais de Nós Mesmos* (*Liking Ourselves Better*) (1999). Quilombhoje also runs a Web site, www.quilombhoje.com.br, with updated information about Afro-Brazilian literature, upcoming cultural events, and new releases. Although more recent editions have been cosponsored by partnerships with private and public institutions, the collective has remained an independent and self-supporting institution staffed by volunteer members.

Rick J. Santos

See also Brazil: Afro-Brazilians.

FURTHER READING
Afolabi, Niyi, Marcio Barbosa, and Esmeralda Ribeiro, eds. 2007. *The Afro-Brazilian Mind*: *Contemporary Afro-Brazilian Literary and Cultural Cricticism*. (Bi-Lingual). Trenton, NJ: Africa World Press.
Cadernos Negros (journal). 1979–present. Sao Paulo: Quilombhoje.

Quilombhoje's website. www.quilombhoje.com.br.

Quilombismo

See Brazil: Afro-Brazilians; Diasporic Maroonage; Maroon and Maroonage; Nascimento, Abdias do (1914–), *and* Zumbi of Palmares.

R

Rada

Rada, one of the two prominent ritual components of the Haitian religion Vodoun, is largely a product of an ancient African civilization located in Dahomey (now Benin), West Africa. More specifically, the word "Rada" is a shortened version of the name of the Dahomey town, Arada, from which many aspects of Haitian Vodoun were transported and transformed (Desmangles 1992; Metraux 1972).

Enslaved Africans in Haiti organized themselves according to the territory they occupied in Africa and their common languages. Haitian Vodoun includes a complex of several ritual groups that were originally organized in that manner; hence, place names like Congo, Arada, or Siniga (Senegal) or cultural designations like Ibo, Nago, or Bambara identified groups of people in Haiti (Herskovits 1937; Metraux 1972). Those groupings are referred to as nations and were instrumental in the organization of Vodoun's religious structure. Each nation held on to beliefs and practices from its ancestral culture, and those practices became a part of the larger complex that is referred to as Vodoun. According to Leslie Desmangles (1992), at least 17 nations of Lwas have been identified in Haiti. Many of them are now in-corporated into the two major ceremonial groups of Haitian Vodoun, Rada and Petwo.

Rada Lwas, compared with the Lwas of Petwo, are considered "cool" spirits who are often associated with water and the air. Among the Rada pantheon are Lwas such as Danbala Wedo, Ayida Wedo, Ezuli Freda Dahomey, Papa Legba, and Aizan, to name a few. Each Lwa has specific attributes that include some aspect of nature, personality traits that are similar to those of human beings, and control over some domain of human existence.

Rada ceremonies facilitate interchanges among people and the Lwas, providing links to cultural heritage while affording opportunities for creating harmony between spirit and material realms. Ritual specialists aid in this process by creating an environment that encourages interaction between humans and Lwas. The ritual specialist (*oungan* or *manbo*) coordinates all components of Rada ceremonies. Those components include musical instruments played by skilled specialists; altars and items dedicated to the Lwas; ritual expressions that include speech, songs, and dances that are carried out by the ritual specialists and members of the congregation; and food for Lwas and the congregation. Each Lwa has specific objects, colors, food, songs and dances that they favor. The presence of those items, in addition to favorable drumming, singing, dancing, and proper protocol, increases the potential for Rada Lwas attending services in their honor.

Joan Hamby Burroughs

See also Haiti; Petwo; Vodoun.

FURTHER READING

Burroughs, Joan. 1995. "Haitian Ceremonial Dance on the Concert Stage: the Contextual Transference and transformation of Yanvalou." Ph.D. diss., New York University.

Deren, Maya. 1953. *The Divine Horsemen*. New York: Thames & Hudson.

Desmangles, Leslie. 1992. *The Faces of the Gods*. Chapel Hill: University of North Carolina Press.

Dunham, Katherine. 1969. *Island Possessed*. New York: Doubleday.

Fleurant, Gerdes. 1996. *Dancing Spirits: Rhythms and Rituals of Haitian Vodun, the Rada Rite*. Westport, CT: Greenwood Press.

Frank, Henry. 2002. "Haitian Vodou Ritual Dance and Its Secularization." In *Caribbean Dance from Abakuá to Zouk*, ed. S. Sloat, 109–113. Gainesville: University Press of Florida.

Herskovits, Melville. 1937. *Life in a Haitian Valley*. New York: Alfred A. Knopf.

Laguerre, Michel. 1980. *Voodoo Heritage*. Beverly Hills, CA: Sage.

Metraux, Alfred. 1972. *Voodoo in Haiti*, trans. H. Charteris. New York: Schocken Books.

Wilcken, Lois. 2002. "Spirit Unbound." In *Caribbean Dance from Abakuá to Zouk*, ed. S. Sloat, 109–113. Gainesville: University Press of Florida.

Raizales

OVERVIEW

The English-speaking Afro-descendants of the Archipelago of San Andrés, Old Providence (Providencia) and Kathleena, Colombia, self-described as natives and indigenous people, were finally recognized in the 1991 Colombian Constitution as "raizales." However, these Caribbean people, principally of African and British descent, who built the communities on the Archipelago, have different origins, history, cultural identities, language, traditions, religious beliefs, institutions, and social organizations from the rest of their fellow Colombians. The Archipelago, presently a United Nations Educational, Scientific, and Cultural Organization world biosphere reserve, includes three inhabited islands, located in the Caribbean Sea, southwest of Jamaica, 110 miles east of Nicaragua, and 480 miles northwest of mainland Colombia. Politically, it is a province of Colombia.

HISTORY

In 1627, a group of Puritans landed on San Andrés and Providence, followed during the next decade by more ships bringing slaves from Bermuda and Jamaica. But in 1641, because of the wars between England and Spain, the Spaniards cleared the islands of British settlers, taking the slaves as spoils of war and sending the Pilgrims back to England. Within years, however, British colonists were back, reestablishing settlements in the Archipelago. They bought slaves from Jamaica to work the tobacco and cotton farms.

In 1822, the native people of the Archipelago agreed to become part of the Gran Colombia (Colombia, Venezuela, and Ecuador). Basically, they were left alone to till their soil, practice their religion (Protestantism, mainly Baptist), speak their language (English), and develop their own culture. After slavery was outlawed, the demarcation between master/mistress and slave blurred, and blacks and whites mixed freely. They produced local musical, dance, and culinary blends as well. Evolving over three centuries, this English/Creole-speaking, Afro-Anglo-Miskito-Latino mixture is the unique native culture of the Archipelago. Family names such as Bowie, Downs, Forbes, Hudgson, May, and Pomiere from San Andrés, and Archbold, Henry, Howard, Livingston, Newball, Robinson, and Taylor from Old Providence are common on the Archipelago.

Beginning in 1912, Colombia changed its laissez-faire policy and implemented laws to colonize and Colombianize the ethnic natives. In 1953, the state declared San Andrés a free port, thereby initiating uncontrolled immigration, overpopulation, and tourism that promoted economic activity benefiting the nonnative community at the expense of the raizales. In the 1970s, the state built three bases for all branches of the Colombian military armed forces on San Andrés and Providence.

CURRENT SITUATION

Today, with a population of more than 100,000, San Andrés has the highest population density in the Caribbean—more than 3,000 persons per square kilometer. Overpopulation has resulted in severe stress on government services, which in turn has resulted in ecological degradation of the islands and the surrounding coral and oceanic biosphere. To this end, the Afro-descendants—churches, ethnic movements, small foundations, and the native community abroad—founded an umbrella organization: Archipelago Movement for Ethnic-Native Self-Determination (AMEN-SD), whose mission is to bring dignity to the ethnic people of the islands. In this effort, the Seaflower Archipelago Development Agency was formed to help the native islanders living in the United States and on the Archipelago improve their social well-being and economic opportunities and to work against discrimination and social exclusion.

Ernestina Martinez and
Claire A. Nelson

See also Colombia: Afro-Colombians.

FURTHER READING

Archipelago Movement for Ethnic-Native Self-Determination, www.amensd.org.

"Articulo 310, Titulo XI, Capitulo 2." *Constitución Política de Colombia 1991*, 2nd ed. Bogotá: Escuela Superior de Administración Publica ESAP, 125.

Eastman Arango, Juan Carlos. 1992. "Creación de la Intendencia de San Andrés y Providencia: La Cuestión Nacional en sus Primeros Años." *Revista Credencial Historia* 3 (January-December): 25–36.

Petersen, Walwin Godfrey. 1995. "Brief Review of the Archipelago's Colonization." In *This Is San Andrés*, 8–30. Bogotá, Colombia: Ediciones Gama.

Yelvington, Kevin A. 2001. "The Anthropology of Afro-Latin America and the Caribbean: Diasporic Dimensions." *Annual Review of Anthropology* 30:227–260.

Randolph, Asa Philip (1889–1979)

A. Philip Randolph, born in 1889 in Cresent, Florida, was one of the early leaders of the Civil Rights Movement. When Randolph was young, his family moved to Jacksonville, Florida, and soon after graduating Bethune-Cookman College, Randolph migrated to New York City in 1911, where he worked several jobs, including an elevator operator. Experiencing job exploitation, Randolph created an Elevator and Switchboard Operators Union, thus gaining early experience in labor organizing. Randolph also attended the City College of New York, although he never received his bachelor's degree.

Randolph received an education in politics on the streets of New York. There he heard soapbox speakers such as Eugene V. Debs and the black socialist Hubert Harrison preach the gospel of socialism. Taken by their class analysis, Randolph became convinced that there were numerous benefits for working-class African Americans in industrial unionism. After meeting Chandler Owen and studying Marxism, both men became members of the Socialist Party, arguing that racism was rooted in capitalist exploitation and the Socialist Party was the best means of liberating the black masses. In 1917, Randolph and Owen started the first black Socialist journal in the country, *The Messenger*.

In 1925, Randolph became involved in the 12-year fight of the Brotherhood of Sleeping Car Porters (BSCP) to win the right to collectively bargain with its employer, the Pullman Company. The company used a host of intimidating tactics, including firing workers, persuading religious leaders and many of the black middle class to publicly denounce the Brotherhood, and organizing a company union to undermine the Brotherhood's legitimacy. However, Randolph, the organizers, and members of the BSCP persevered. Randolph and the BSCP did not only turn to porters to win recognition but also relied on support from community and civic organizations. In particular, Randolph requested and received support from many in the various black religious communities. Labor organizations, including the American Federation of Labor, supported the BSCP. Finally, in 1937, the union won recognition after the passage of the Emergency Railroad Transportation Act (ERTA) and the National Industrial Relations Act (NIRA) gave workers the right to organize and collectively bargain.

Eventually, the Railroad Mediation Board ordered an election for employee representatives for the porters, and the BSCP overwhelmingly won. By the summer of 1935, the Brotherhood began formal negotiations with the Pullman Company. But it should be noted that although it was because of the ERTA and the NIRA that the BSCP eventually received recognition, the fact that Randolph and the members of the BSCP "stayed the course" and did not fold led to the union's victory. Moreover, the BSCP should be seen as more than a labor organization. Randolph and leaders of the organization interpreted their struggle as a civil rights one. Throughout his public career, Randolph argued that civil rights must be linked to the rights of working people, and in numerous speeches and letters he contended that the battle for recognition was to win dignity and respect for black people.

Randolph remained active in the fight for labor and civil rights. By the early 1940s Randolph had established the March on Washington Movement (MOWM), which helped organize thousands of people of African origins in the United States to march on the nation's capital in 1941 demanding that President Franklin Roosevelt ban discrimination in the arms industry. The threat of thousands of black people coming to Washington, D.C. to protest convinced Roosevelt to issue an executive order banning discrimination in defense plants. The president also created the Fair Employment Practices Committee to help ensure that defense manufacturers would not practice racial discrimination. In 1948, Randolph also forced President Harry S. Truman to desegregate the United States Armed Forces. By 1963, as civil rights campaigns were taking place throughout the nation, Randolph again called for a march on Washington for jobs and freedom. The historic march took place in August 1963, bringing more than 250,000 people to the nation's capital.

Clarence Taylor

See also Bethune-Cookman University.

FURTHER READING
Anderson, Jervis. 1974. *A. Philip Randolph: A Biographical Portrait.* New York: Harcourt Brace.
Pfeffer, Paula F. 1990. *A. Philip Randolph, Pioneer of the Civil Rights Movement.* Baton Rouge: Louisiana State University Press.

Rap/Rappin'

As an African linguistic tradition, rap or rappin' is a speech act that has existed before the time of hip-hop and has several lexical entries. Smitherman (1994, 1977), Green (2002), and Keyes (2002) define rap as (1) a casual way to converse that involves the exchange of greeting, salutation, and some inquiry into the person's well-being; (2) to engage in a duel of ritual insults such as signifyin', or playin' the dozens where the victor belittles his or her opponent by constructing an insult that is either fluid or rhythmic, but above all else funny; (3) to have an affectionate, flirtatious way with words and an ability to gain favor with the opposite sex, to have game; and (4) a poetic and rhythmic type of braggadocio speech that is chanted over music.

The word *rap* itself has a fairly recent history. It entered into the English language late in the 16th century with the meaning to talk vigorously or or to say suddenly. Most scholars agree that use of rap in the African American community appeared in the mid to late 1960s. However, the word was in use as early as the 1940s and is most likely familiar to the blues genre. The word can be traced to Chicago where blues musician Peter Chatman (Leroy/Memphis Slim), who hailed from Memphis, Tennessee, frequently worked at a nightclub called the "Rap Club," rappin' the blues.

The success of hip-hop is due in part to rap being a part of daily life and the reciprocal relationship that hip-hop artists have with Africans throughout the Diaspora. Before the 1979 commercial release of "Rapper's Delight" by New York's Sugar Hill Gang, "sistahs" were rappin' on every community corner and took part in rap sessions where they performed call-and-response chants called "cheers." All-female neighborhood drill teams were formed. They performed these cheers in competitions and were featured in neighborhood parades and talent shows. Two of the most popular cheers were "Roll Call" and "Hollywood Swingin'(ers)."

The performance of "cheer" among young adolescent women is a national pastime in the African American community. Like the legendary "baaad man" toasts such as Dolemite and Stagolee, cheers have numerous renditions and vary from region to region. They are called *cheers* or *games* in the Midwest, *steps* in the Northeast, and *ring games* in Jamaica.

Rap is also incorporated into greeting rituals. In U.S. barbershops, historically regular patrons would announce their arrival by rhyming a rap about themselves upon entering. Rap was also incorporated into the greetings ritual among young men who engage in a friendly competition forming couplets about one another. Although this practice is competitive in that the person with the cleverest couplet is declared the winner, the aim is to pay the other the greater compliment, alluding to his coolness while at the same time downplaying one's own coolness. In the end, both speakers are complimented and the ritual exchange demonstrates their camaraderie.

Rappin' is a common day-to-day speech act in the African American community. The rap found in hip-hop is not the product of gang street culture or the conditions of urban poverty; instead, it is part of the traditional discourse practices of the African Diaspora. In fact, most of the linguistic features found in hip-hop may be found in some form in communities throughout the African Diaspora, from the Spanish to English code switching stemming from Afro-Latin to the "rude boy" Patwa rants found in Jamaica sound systems and to Ebonics.

In *You Know My Steeze,* Samy Alim (2004) shows that hip-hop artists use more African American linguistic features in their lyrics than they do in their day-to-day speech. His study shows that hip-hop artists are making a conscious effort in choosing linguistic forms to capture the attention of black people who are most attuned to the African Diasporic speech community. Alim's study recorded an increase in final consonant cluster deletion and simplification, such as "r" deletion in the word "car" pronounced "Kaw" or the simplification of the final consonant cluster "ty" in the word *fifty* pronounced as "fifd." There was also an increase in the production of sentences with zero copulas, as in "John bugging," which means, "John is bugging" in European American English. Most languages in West Africa do not have words that end with consonants, or what linguists call word final consonants. Like many West African languages, the African American language uses several phonological rules transforming the English language into an African phonological form.

Afrika Bambaataa is right when he states that rap has always been present and has played a crucial role in sustaining the African American community; keeping alive its traditions and customs; and chronicling its hardships and triumphs. Many progressive intellectuals who have taken on the question concerning rap in hip-hop all acknowledge its African linguistic attributes. Most scholars agree that hip-hop's aesthetics of rhyme forms an intricate part of the African Diaspora and is merely sounding off on what hip-hop immortal Afrika Bambaataa describes as being the continuation of an African-derived bardic tradition (Perkins 1996, Keyes 2002, Kelly 1996, Rose 1994, Fricke & Ahearn 2002).

Tracing the origins of hip-hop's African-derived bardic traditions, Keyes (2002) and Kelly (1996) explore this topic extensively. In his article "Kickin' reality, Kickin' Ballistics" Kelly situates hip-hop's narrative style within the tradition of signification and traces its usage through the lineage of African American performers from the 20th century back to the 19th century. He cites performers such as Lightnin' Rod (Jalal Uridin of the Last Poets), Lloyd Price, Screamin' Jay Hawkins, and the baaadman tales of the 19th century (Kelly 1996, 119). Also included in this tradition are the earliest known tales of lion and Brer Rabbit whose trickster insignia can be seen in the lyrical performances of hip-hop's own Trick Daddy and Lil' Kim. Their lyricism embodies the trickster figure who possesses a cunning intellect and gifted wordsmiths that both appropriately sashay "Aye wan' sum su-ga on my tongue" in Trick Daddy's video "Suga."

Keyes goes further back than Kelly to show how hip-hop's narrative styles are similar to Dogon's bardic tradition in Mali. She also indicates that several scholars noticeably observed that the Dogon concept of *Nommo* functions in the cultural practices throughout the African Diaspora (Keyes 2002, 22). *Nommo* is the concept that "the power of the word" can make a difference and change the world. Keyes also documents the symmetry between hip-hop and the Dogon's rhythmic speech performance and suggests that both are done "in a chant like fashion" (Keyes 2002, 20). She offers as evidence of hip-hop's linkage to African bardic traditions the memoir of a Moroccan traveler in the 14th century who reported while visiting Mali the performance of poetry over the playing of drums (Keyes 2002, 19). In view of these examples, hip-hop is the latest derivation of an African tradition that was revolutionized by its abductees who were violently injected into the New World. The language underwent evolution after evolution as the abductees survived the atrocities associated with the ethos of the New World to become New Africans. These New Africans spoke Africanized languages throughout the African Atlantic. Hip-hop inspired the vitalization and resurgence of African languages by those of African descent who under European linguistic colonization were characterized as autistic.

For many, the popular belief is that hip-hop is a product of urban street culture born during the time many have characterized as the postindustrial era. The desolate conditions that define the era were caused by a dramatic change in the economy where the flight of industries from major metropolitan areas led to unemployment in large portions of the population, and this loss of industry led to urban decay. Coupled with Reagan's administration policies, which changed the focus from welfare to warfare, an approach many have come to call "benign neglect" meant the loss of programs aimed at helping the poor. Indeed, times were hard during hip-hop's development; however, these conditions do not account for its emergence. There are no empirical connections between poverty and a particular form of art.

The notion that poverty is in any way responsible for hip-hop is unfounded. Rap originates from African American language and therefore rap and hip-hop are products of the African American community. In many respects, when defining the African American community, its populace can never be identified stagnantly by limiting its pedigree to the United States, thus defining hip-hop as an American art form. Instead, one must look toward the African Diaspora. The demands of the slave trade and the industrial market and the forced emigration and migration of Africans within the Americas constantly revitalized its populations and created a fluid mixture of African-derived cultures. So in all respects, to cite William Eric Perkins's quote of Kool Herc, hip-hop is at its core "very African."

The epistemology where hip-hop gets its genius is distinctly African. When the first generations of Africans landed in the New World as slave laborers they brought with them their own epistemology. Although African languages were banished, African modes of thought continued to survive in European mediums of communication such as English, Spanish, Portuguese, and French. The juncture of African knowledge with European communication systems revolutionized strategies for conducting speech acts in European language systems among Africans in the Diaspora; the Indo-European had become Africanized. This transformation or Africanization of European languages underwent evolution as it was transmitted from generation to generation. As a result of this intergenerational transmission, the vocal aesthetics of rhyming evolved from field hollers, work songs, and spirituals to the praise songs of gospel to the blues, jazz, bebop, jive talk, and signifyin' to, finally, rappin'.

Walter Sistrunk

See also Bambaata, Afrika (1957–); Blues: A Continuum from Africa; Griots/Griottes of West Africa; Hip-Hop Culture in the African Diaspora; Jazz; Rapso.

FURTHER READING

Alim, Samy H. 2004. *You Know My Steeze: An Ethnographic and Sociolinguistic Study of Style Shifting in a Black American Speech Community.* Los Angeles: American Dialect Society, no. 89.

Di Poalo Healey, Attonette, ed. 2004. *The Dictionary of Old English Corpus in Electronic Form.* Toronto, Canada: Center for Medieval Studies, University of Toronto.

Fricke, Jim, and Charlie Ahearn, eds. 2002. *Yes, Yes Y'All: The Experience Music Project Oral History of Hip-Hop's First Decade.* New York: Da Capo Press.

Green, Lisa J. 2002. *African American English: A Linguistic Introduction.* Cambridge, UK: Cambridge University Press.

Harris, Sheldon. 1979. *Blues Who's Who: A Biographical Dictionary of Blues Singers.* New Rochelle, NY: Arlington Publishers.

Kelly, Robin D. G. 1996. "Kickin' Reality, Kickin' Ballistics: Gangsta Rap and Postindustrial Los Angeles." In *Droppin' Science: Critical Essays on Rap Music and Hip Hop Culture,* ed. William Eric Perkins, 117–158. Philadelphia: Temple University Press.

Keyes, Cheryl L. 2002. *Rap Music and Street Consciousness.* Urbana: University of Illinois Press.

Labov, William. 1972. *Language in the Inner City: Studies in the Black English Vernacular.* Philadelphia: University of Pennsylvania Press.

Perkins, William Eric. 1996. "The Rap Attack: An Introduction." In *Droppin' Science: Critical Essays on Rap Music and Hip Hop Culture,* ed. William Eric Perkins, 1–47. Philadelphia: Temple University Press.

Rose, Tricia. 1994. *Black Noise: Rap Music and Black Culture in Contemporary America.* Middletown, CT: Wesleyan University Press.

Rickford, John. 1999. Introduction. "Phonological and Grammatical Features of African American Vernacular English (AAVE)." In *African American Vernacular English,* 3–14. Oxford: Blackwell.

Smitherman, Geneva. 1994. *Black Talk: Words and Phrases from the Hood to the Amen Corner.* New York: Houghton Mifflin Company.

Smitherman, Geneva. 1977. *Talkin and Testifyin: The Language of Black America.* Detroit, MI: Wayne State University

Rapso

Rapso is the power of the word, the rhythm of the word, the truth, and the light; therefore, pure rapso is the living experience of the voice. It is a vocal manifestation of the hopes and fears and aspirations of a people struggling for true liberation. Rapso then has its historical toots in the ancient African traditions of the *djeli djali* or griot. Therefore, the practitioners of rapso are considered the vessels of speech, the storehouse of knowledge and history, and the teachers and communicators for this new generation. The rapso poet—man or woman—is one who lives and practices the art of the word.

In its initial creation, rapso was born from a deliberate study of the African oral forms, like the *djeliya*, and African Caribbean forms, like the chantuelle, calypso, and other oral traditions. The rhythms used included steelband, calypso, orisha, Shouter Baptist, the spoken forms of robber talk, pierrot grenade, calypso, and other aspects of Caribbean oral tradition, including the spoken rhythms of Rastafari.

Rapso's earliest progenitors, including Lancelot Layne, Brother Resistance, Cheryl Byron, and Eintou Pearl Springer, are identified as deliberately studying African and African-Caribbean oral culture and applying these to the creation of a distinctive form of Caribbean spoken word. Beginning with Layne, other noteworthy performers have been Sister Ava; Kareiga Mandela, known for his "Rapso Soldier"; Ataklan; 3 Canal, with the popular "Talk Yuh Talk"; Sister Shaquila of "Weep Not My Child"; and Sheldon Blackman, son of Ras Shorty I. Brother Resistance's "Book So Deep" has been anthologized in *Voiceprint*.

Thereby "the power of the word/the riddum of the word" as the shorthand summary of what is rapso repeats itself in all discussions of this form. Its political origins, in the Caribbean Black Power Movement of the 1970s, also infuses it with the politics of liberation. Brother Resistance, today's foremost exponent of Rapso, defines it as the voice of the people in the heat of the struggle for true liberation and self-determination. The music form is called rapso riddum and represents the synthesis of voice rhythm with rhythm of drums (drums of skin and drums of steel). Rapso's advent is simultaneous with dub poetry in Jamaica and rap in the United States. A conscious link with those poets is articulated—Baraka, Mikey Smith, Gil-Scott Heron, and Oku Onuora are all outgrowths of black power struggles in those countries. For resistance, they come to the same end, from different directions, including the socially and politically conscious lyrics of some U.S. soul singers like Curtis Mayfield and James Brown.

Today, calypso tents in Trinidad feature some rapso artists, notably Brother Resistance, and there is a conscious cultivation of new generations in the annual "Breaking New Ground," during which poems are created in workshops and then presented in a final public performance.

Carole Boyce Davies

See also Calypso; Griots/Griottes of West Africa; Hip-Hop Culture in the African Diaspora; Rap/Rappin'; Reggae.

FURTHER READING

Brother Resistance. 1986. *Rapso Explosion*. London: Karia Press/New Jersey.

Brown, Stewart, Mervyn Morris, and Gordon Rohlehr, eds. 1989. *Voiceprint: An Anthology of Oral and Related Poetry from the Caribbean*. London: Longman Caribbean.

Rapso (Booklet). 1999. Trinidad and Tobago.

Webb, Dexter. 1998. "Beyond Lancelot Layne. A Survey of Rapso Music 1969–1998." Undergraduate thesis, Caribbean Studies, University of the West Indies.

Rastafarianism

Rastafarianism can best be described as an African-oriented, Judeo-Christian–influenced, religious social movement that originated in Jamaica in the early 1930s. It was inspired by the crowning of Haile Selassie I as emperor of Ethiopia in 1930. Haile Selassie I was formerly known as Rastafari Makonen before he was crowned, and from there the name "Rastafari" that defines this movement originates.

Haile Selassie I is widely considered to have a lineage that is traceable to King Solomon of Israel and Queen (Makeda) of Sheba from Ethiopia. He is cited as being 225th in the line of Ethiopian monarchs that stretch back to King Solomon (see the *Kebra Negast*). In this respect, one of the central tenets of Rastafarianism is that Haile Selassie I is a descendant of King David, which the Bible cites as one of the necessary criteria for the returned Messiah (Revelation 5:5). When Ras Tafari was crowned Emperor Haile Selassie I, he was bestowed the titles king of kings, lord of lords, conquering lion of the tribe of Judah, elect of God, and light of the world.

The founders of the Rastafari movement were Leonard Howell, Joseph Nathaniel Hibbert, Robert Hinds, Archibald Dunkley, and Altamont Reid, who preached (tirelessly around the island of Jamaica) that Haile Selassie I was the returned Messiah that the Bible spoke about in the book of Revelation. Remarkably, all of them preached this message independently of each other (except for Hinds who was effectively Howell's lieutenant). Out of all these pioneering Rastafari preachers, Howell was clearly the most prominent and, in hindsight, the most successful of the early Rastafari proponents. Howell was so prominent with his teachings, in fact, that he quickly came to the attention of the then colonial Jamaican government. He was arrested in Kingston, Jamaica, in December 1933, for using what was considered seditious and blasphemous language to boost the sale of pictures of Haile Selassie I. He was sentenced to two years in prison, but upon his release went right back to preaching the divinity of Haile Selassie I (Rastafari) (Smith et al. 1960; Chevannes 1994).

Rastafarianism is widely considered to be a continuation (and natural evolution) of Ethiopianism, which had been refined and widely disseminated by Marcus Garvey (Jamaica's first national hero). Ethiopianism in a very fundamental sense is an interpretation of Psalm 68:31, which reads: "Princes shall come out of Egypt and Ethiopia shall soon stretch forth her hands unto God." Garvey's interpretation of this piece of biblical scripture was that glory was soon to come to the black man and woman, and redemption for Africa and Africans was at hand. In addition to providing an Ethiopianist ideology that provided the theological and ideological foundation for the Rastafari movement, Garvey also developed a political ideology— Africa for the Africans at home and abroad— which helped to lay the foundational basis for the principle of repatriation that is so central in the Rastafari belief system (Barnett 2003).

From its very early stages, the Rastafari movement has always been a polycephalous, heterogeneous, decentralized movement. It consists of various denominations, better known as houses or mansions of Rastafari. The largest and most pervasive mansions are the Twelve Tribes of Israel, the Nyahbinghi, and the Boboshante, known officially as the Ethiopian African Black International Congress.

Though there is some doctrinal diversity between the mansions, some principles are common to all. These common principles of the Rastafari belief system, which are based largely on a typology provided by Winston Williams (2000), are detailed below, and have been adapted to nine key principles:

- The first principle is that Haile Selassie I is divine.
- According to the second principle, Marcus Garvey is considered to be a prophet and patriarch and, in the case of the Boboshante House, is also considered to be divine.
- The third principle outlines how Rastafari are committed to the fight against oppression, wherever it may be and against whoever is committing it. Out of this principle comes the concept of "Babylon," which for Rastafari is a term

that epitomizes all agents of oppression, whether a nation-state, a group of nation-states, a government, an oppressive institution, the police, or even the military.

- According to the fourth principle, Ethiopia is a holy and sacred land (the equivalent for Christians would be Jerusalem). Rastafari also consider Ethiopia to be the cradle of civilization and the birthplace of humanity.
- The fifth principle, which addresses repatriation and reparations, is another important aspect of the Rastafari belief system. Most Rastafari consider their real and natural home to be Africa, which they refer to synonymously as Ethiopia (the land from which their ancestors were forcibly taken, only to experience the tortuous journey of the Middle Passage). They refer to it as Zion, the land God promised to his chosen people. As such, Rastafari strive to repatriate to the continent en masse and are agitating for reparations from the former European colonial powers, as well as the United States, to facilitate this. Some, like the Shashamane community, have already returned and now make their home in Ethiopia following a land grant from Haile Selassie after his visit to Jamaica.
- The sixth principle is that of "Itality," which is essentially striving to live a natural lifestyle, both in terms of appearance (for example, dreadlocked hair) and food (which is termed an "Ital diet"). There are degrees of variation, however, among the various houses. Thus, not every Rasta has dreadlocks (for example, some members of the Twelve Tribes of Israel House and the Coptic House) and not every Rasta is a vegetarian (for example, the Twelve Tribes of Israel House). However, pork is strictly prohibited as is the processing of one's hair.

- The seventh principle is that of the "I and I" concept. For Rastafari, a divine essence is considered to lie in everyone. All one has to do is tap into that essence to realize one's potential godliness. The divine essence is considered to constitute the large I for Rasta, while the small I is considered to constitute one's base physical self.
- The eighth principle is that marijuana is a holy sacrament for Rastafari (as opposed to being a recreational drug). Rastafari adherents smoke it, drink it, and even eat it to facilitate connecting the small I with the large I.
- The ninth principle is the way of reason. This is the way Rastafari reach the intersubjective truth and come to a consensus on important community issues. (Reasoning highlights the collective aspect of the movement.)

The Rastafari movement consistently reconnects Africans of the Diaspora with continental Africa and its inhabitants. The fundamental philosophical and ideological orientation of the Rastafari movement is firmly rooted in the concept of the African Diaspora as a displaced populace, whose homeland and geographical base is ultimately Africa. Rastafari has also spread to the continent; there are communities in various African nations, including Zimbabwe, and a community of Jamaicans who returned to Ethiopia and are now residing in Shashamane, Ethiopia. The continent of Africa is not only central to Rastafari from a geographical perspective, it is also central in terms of the formulation of identity for Rastafari, who see themselves as displaced Africans in general, and, in some specific cases, as Ethiopian Israelites.

Michael Barnett

See also Africa; Garvey, Marcus Mosiah (1887–1940); Jamaica; Marley, Robert Nesta (Bob) (1945–1981); Pan-Africanism; Reparations.

FURTHER READING

Barnett, M. A. 2003. "Intra-Racial Encounters in Defining African Identity in the Americas." A Comparative Analysis of Black Leadership and Social Movements." *Ideaz* 2 (1): 32–41.

Barnett, M. A. 2005. "The Many Faces of Rasta: Doctrinal Diversity within the Rastafari Movement." *Caribbean Quarterly* 51 (2): 67–78.

Chevannes, Barry. 1994. *Rastafari: Roots and Ideology.* New York: Syracuse University Press.

Smith, M. G., Roy Augier, and Rex Nettleford. 1960. *The Rastafari Movement in Kingston, Jamaica.* Mona, Jamaica: University of the West Indies.

Williams, Winston. 2000. *The Seven Principles of Rastafari.* Caribbean Quarterly Rastafari Monograph. Mona, Jamaica: University of the West Indies.

Rayner, John Baptis (1850–1918)

John Baptis Rayner, the black populist leader from Texas, was born on November 13, 1850, in Raleigh, North Carolina to a black slave, Mary Ricks, and a white planter, Kenneth Rayner. Raised by his great-grandparents, "J. B." Rayner worked on the family plantation before his father, a Whig congressman and leader of the Know Nothing Party, gave him the support to attend Shaw University and St. Augustine's Normal and Collegiate Institute. During Reconstruction, Rayner became active in the Republican Party, through which he was elected to several local offices, including deputy sheriff, magistrate, and constable. In the early 1880s he led a migration of black farmers and agrarian workers to Texas and settled in Calvert.

Rayner became active in the Texas campaign for prohibition in 1887, which brought him back into politics. In 1892, as the Populist movement sweeping the South was making its transition from building farmers' alliances toward engaging the electoral process itself, Rayner joined the newly formed People's Party.

Becoming a leading advocate of political independence in Texas, he traveled up and down the state establishing black chapters of the People's Party and was credited for bringing at least 25,000 African Americans into the party's ranks.

Known as the "Silver Tongued Orator of the Colored Race" for his erudition and effectiveness as a political organizer, in 1894 he was elected to the People's Party state executive committee as a member-at-large and a member of its platform committee, through which he strengthened the party's position on black civil and political rights. He continued organizing across the state until 1898, before black Populism began its precipitous decline under fierce attacks by the Democratic Party and its local paramilitary apparatus—notably, the White Man's Union.

After the collapse of the independent movement, Rayner returned to the Republican Party. Earlier he had married Susan Clark Staten, with whom he had two children. After she died, he then married Clarissa S. Clark, with whom he had another three children. Rayner became a professional fund-raiser for black education initiatives, including Conroe College (for which he served as president) and the Farmers' Improvement Society School. By the turn of the century he reversed his position on prohibition and campaigned against it. While Rayner worked publicly for accommodation—currying favor with the lumber magnate John Henry Kirby, who contributed to his educational projects and occasionally employed him as a labor recruiter—privately he wrote of "the white man's hallucinated idea of his race superiority." Rayner died at the age of 68 in his home in Calvert on July 14, 1918.

Omar H. Ali

See also Black Populism (1886–1898).

FURTHER READING

Abramowitz, Jack. 1951. "John B. Rayner: A Grass-Roots Leader." *Journal of Negro History* 36 (April): 160–193.

Ali, Omar H. 2003. "Black Populism in the New South, 1886–1898." Ph.D. dissertation, Columbia University.
Cantrell, Gregg. 2001. *Feeding the Wolf: John B. Rayner and the Politics of Race, 1850–1918*. Wheeling, IL: Harlan Davidson.

Reagon, Bernice Johnson (1942–)

Bernice Johnson Reagon, cultural historian, singer, songwriter, producer, and founder of the internationally renowned a cappella group, Sweet Honey in the Rock, began her illustrious career as an activist in the Student Nonviolent Coordinating Committee as a field secretary and a member of the Freedom Singers with her former husband, the late Cordell Reagon, in the early 1960s. She was raised in rural Albany, Georgia, the daughter of a Baptist minister father, and was a singer most of her life. Reagon sang in the choir while attending Albany State College, where she was studying Italian arias and German lieder as a contralto vocalist. In December 1961, the first civil rights march occurred and Reagon joined the struggle, realizing that the songs she had learned in her childhood had laid the foundation for struggle during the movement. In 1968, she founded and directed the historical Harambee Singers in Atlanta, Georgia.

After relocating to the Washington, D.C., area with her family, daughter Toshi and son Kwan, Reagon became the vocal director for the DC Black Repertory Theater from 1972 through 1977. During those years, Reagon joined the Smithsonian Institution as program director, curator, and folklorist, heading up the Program in Black American Culture of the National Museum of American History. During her tenure, Reagon pioneered the institution's annual tribute to Martin Luther King, Jr., "Of Songs, Peace and Struggle," held at the museum each January. She became curator emeritus at the Smithsonian in 1993.

Reagon is the producer of the groundbreaking joint venture between the Smithsonian Institution and the National Public Radio series, *Wade in the Water: African American Sacred Music Traditions*, which began broadcasting in 1994. She was also curator of the accompanying traveling exhibition produced by SITES (Smithsonian Institutions Traveling Exhibition Service).

At Spelman College, Reagon created a live performance production, *Lord! I've Got A Right to the Tree of Life! A Tribute to Early African American Sacred Song*, and produced a CD and video documentary based on the production. She has served as musical consultant, composer, and performer on several films and video projects, such as the award-winning *Eyes on the Prize*, the Emmy-winning *We Shall Overcome*, and the PBS special *Roots of Resistance: A Story of the Underground Railroad*, as well as *Frederick Douglass: The Lion Who Wrote History*. In 1992, Reagon was featured in the Emmy-nominated documentary *The Songs Are Free: Bernice Johnson Reagon with Bill Moyers*.

In 1973, Reagon created the vocal group Sweet Honey as an outgrowth of her vocal workshops and wrote for, performed with, and directed the group until her retirement in February 2004. She is the composer/librettist for *Temptations of Saint Anthony*, a musical by Robert Wilson based on the 19th-century work of Gustav Flaubert (*Madame Bovary*), which premiered in Dulsberg, Germany in 2003. She also continues to collaborate with her daughter, Toshi, on projects including *Beah: A Black Woman Speaks*, produced by Jonathan Demme and LisaGay Hamilton, which premiered in Los Angeles in 2003 and showed on HBO during 2004. Reagon has released numerous solo recordings: *River of Life* (1986), *Give Your Hands to Struggle* (1975, rereleased by Smithsonian Folkways records in 1997), and *Still on the Journey* (1993) among others.

Eve Ferguson

See also Jazz and Blues Singers, Black Women; Sweet Honey in the Rock.

FURTHER READING

Reagon, Bernice Johnson. 1983. *Songs That Moved the Movement*. Washington, D.C.: New Perspectives.

Reagon, Bernice Johnson. 1986. *Compositions One: The Original Compositions of Bernice Johnson Reagon*. Washington, D.C.: Songtalk Publishing.

Reagon, Bernice Johnson, ed. 1992. *We'll Understand It Better By and By: Pioneering African American Gospel Composers*. Washington, D.C.: Smithsonian Press.

Reagon, Bernice Johnson. 1993. *We Who Believe in Freedom: Sweet Honey in the Rock: Still on the Journey*. New York: Anchor Books.

Sweet Honey in the Rock. 2000. *Continuum: The First Songbook of Sweet Honey in the Rock*. Washington, D.C.: Contemporary A Cappella Publishing.

Reggae

"A type of music developed in Jamaica about 1964, based on Ska usually having a heavy four-beat rhythm, using the bass, electric guitar, and drum, with the scraper coming in at the end of the measure and acting as accompaniment to emotional songs often expressing rejection of established 'white man' culture." That early definition of reggae, from the 1980 second edition of the *Dictionary of Jamaican English* (Cambridge University Press), points to the politics of reggae as well as its technical qualities. The social, cultural, and political resonance of reggae in the mid–1960s Jamaica is evident in the gloss on "skengay" given by Professor Rex Nettleford, who is quoted in the dictionary: "the sound of the guitar simulates gun-shots ricocheting in the violence-prone backlanes of the depressed areas of Kingston, hence 'skeng' means a gun or 'iron.' The link between the music and the realities of contemporary ghetto life gives the words a particular

cogency at this time." Thus, the music encodes violence, the language of musical expression onomatopoeically representing the sounds and pressures of ghetto life. In the entries on reggae and rocksteady, the *Dictionary of Jamaican English* cites a *New York Magazine* article of November 4, 1975 written by Jacobson: "Rock Steady is perhaps the slowest and most deliberate-tempoed popular music within memory. But the madness of 'new' Kingston couldn't be fully expressed in the simple grind of Rock Steady. A more complicated structure evolved to carry the weight of the lyrics, which were increasingly political (songs like 'Burning and Looting Tonight'). Sinuous music contrasted with cut-throat lyrics."

The classic 1971 movie *The Harder They Come*, a major cultural force in the worldwide spread of reggae, documents the role of the music as an expression of cultural resistance to systemic exploitation of the dispossessed. The soundtrack is an explosive celebration of the defiant human spirit that refuses to be suppressed: "As long as the sun will shine/ I've got to get my share, what's mine/ So the harder they come, the harder they fall/ One and all." Not much has changed in Jamaica since Jimmy Cliff, in the role of "Rhygin," sang the angst of a generation of sufferers. So reggae music continues to be one of the weapons of choice for the urban poor whose "lyrical gun"—to quote Shabba Ranks—earns them a measure of respectability. The contemporary dance hall deejays are heirs to a long tradition of engaged music—a reggae tradition in which the dread sensibility of Rastafari trodding the steep and narrow path of righteousness fuses with the mystical consciousness of kumina and revival.

Outside of Jamaica, reggae has spread globally as the music first accompanied migrant Jamaicans to Britain and North America and then became more broadly incorporated into the global economy of the multinational entertainment industry. Fusion with other musical styles, such as rock, was an inevitable consequence of this globalization. Bob Marley's career illustrates the repackaging of indigenous reggae music to suit a "flower power" rock market that was ready to test the power of the new holy herb, marijuana, and the music that sacralized it. As a critical statement about safeguarding, recognizing, and promoting the art form, a Global Reggae Conference was held for the first time at the University of the West Indies, Mona, Jamaica, in February 2008, bringing together scholars and exponents of reggae and related forms from around the world.

Carolyn Cooper

See also Jamaica; Marley, Robert Nesta (Bob) (1945–1981); Rastafarianism.

FURTHER READING

Bradley, Lloyd. 2004. *Reggae. The Story of Jamaican Music.* London: BBC Worldwide.

Cooper, Carolyn. 2004. *Soundclash. Jamaican Dancehall Culture at Large.* New York: Palgrave Macmillan.

Davis, Stephen. 1981. *Reggae Bloodlines. In Search of Music and Culture in Jamaica.* London: Heinemann. (Orig. pub. 1977).

Hebdige, Dick. 1987. *Cut 'N' Mix. Culture, Identity and Caribbean Music.* London: Routledge.

Reparations

The end of the 20th century saw increased calls for reparations across the African Diaspora. African descendants living in the West, along with several African nations, continued to emphasize the importance of reparations for slavery and colonial land grabs at the start of the 21st century as a means of addressing the historic injustices of Western Europe and the United States. African Diasporans point out that the reparations provided by Germany to the Jewish victims of Nazism, and reparations awarded by the United States to Japanese citizens interned during World War II, reflect the moral imperative that European nations provide restitution or compensation for land taken during the colonization of Africa and that the United States provide reparations to African Americans for the harm caused by the transatlantic slave trade.

In 2001, the 53rd session of the Sub-Commission on the Promotion and Protection of Human Rights of the United Nations addressed the issue in a resolution entitled "Recognition of responsibility and reparation for massive and flagrant violations of human rights, which constitute crimes against humanity and which took place during the period of slavery, of colonialism and wars of conquest." This resolution pointed out the need for the international community to consider the consequences of historic incidences of slavery, colonialism, and conquest. Later that year, the World Conference against Racism, Racial Discrimination, Xenophobia and Related Intolerance determined that slavery and the transatlantic slave trade constituted crimes against humanity and called on concerned states to "take appropriate and effective measures to halt and reverse the lasting consequences of those practices." Furthermore, in 2005 the United Nations specifically addressed this issue through the "Basic Principles and Guidelines on the Right to a Remedy and Reparation for Victims of Gross Violations of International Human Rights Law and Serious Violations of International Humanitarian Law." These principles present specific obligations on states found guilty of committing gross human rights violations, including compensation, restitution, reconciliation, and apology as well as retribution against responsible parties.

Despite United Nations resolutions and declarations, efforts to obtain reparations for slavery have largely been unsuccessful. In the United States, in the early 2000s, courts dismissed several reparations lawsuits filed by slave descendants against corporations that profited from slavery. Claimants seeking redress for more recent injustices, however, have met with slightly more success. In 1994, the Florida Legislature provided a $2.1 million reparations award to the victims of a 1923 race riot in Rosewood, Florida. The award allotted up to $150,000 payments for victims of the violent riot that claimed eight lives and demolished a southern black town. In 1997, the African National Congress–led government of South Africa began implementing a broad reparations program for the victims of apartheid that included restitution, compensation, and reconciliation programs. Restitution programs include the provision of land or compensation for those stripped of their land rights under apartheid, and reconciliation programs include numerous memorials, educational awareness programs, and a national holiday commemorating reconciliation. As compensation, the roughly 19,000 victims of apartheid who testified before South Africa's Truth and Reconciliation Committee received a one-time payment of close to $4,000 at a total cost of approximately $85 million. In 2006, the German government offered roughly $25 million to Namibia for the massacre of the Herero and Dama populations during its colonial period, which saw the loss of tens of thousands of lives. So far, Namibia had not accepted the offer, which fell far below the billions of dollars sought by the surviving members of those groups.

Carlton Waterhouse

See also African Americans and the Constitutional Order; The National Coalition of Blacks for Reparations in America (N'COBRA).

FURTHER READING
Basic Principles and Guidelines on the Right to a Remedy and Reparation for Victims of Gross Violations of International Human Rights Law and Serious Violations of International Humanitarian Law. www.ohchr.org/english/law/remedy.htm (accessed 2/18/08).
Brooks, Roy L., ed. 1999. *When Sorry Isn't Enough: The Controversy Over Apologies and Reparations for Human Injustice.* New York: New York University Press.
Report of the World Conference Against Racism, Racial Discrimination, Xenophobia and Related Intolerance. www.unhchr.ch/huridocda/huridoca.nsf/(Symbol)/A.Conf.189.12.En? Open document (accessed January 20, 2008).

Winbush, Ray, ed. 2003. *Should America Pay: Slavery and the Raging Debate on Reparations.* New York: Amistad/HarperCollins Publishers.

The Republic of New Africa

The Republic of New Africa (RNA) is an African American nationalist and separatist organization created on March 31, 1968, when more than 200 black nationalists came together in Detroit, Michigan, to draft a Declaration of Independence. The NRA plan was to establish an independent nation for African Americans. The RNA attempted to negotiate peacefully for freedom from the United States, at times seeking the help of other countries (Congo-Brazzaville, Tanzania) to negotiate. The RNA declared itself "an African nation in the western hemisphere struggling for complete independence" and adopted the following as the nation's oath: "For the fruition of Black Power, for the triumph of Black Nationhood, I pledge to the Republic of New Africa and to the building of a better people and a better world, my total devotion, my total resources and the total power of my mortal life."

The RNA partially derives from the Revolutionary Action Movement (RAM). RNA and RAM belong to the lesser-known African American nationalist organizations that often remained small and isolated and perhaps, more importantly, remained independent of both the white Left and the mainstream Civil Rights Movement. Heavily influenced by Malcolm X, these organizations took an international and anticapitalist analysis and understanding of the world, with a particular interest vested in working-class struggles and issues of race and poverty in urban contexts. The RNA, unlike RAM, did launch active armed self-defense campaigns and offered self-defense classes.

Beyond the creation of the RNA, the goal of the organization was to ultimately set up the

United States of Africa through the consolidation of the African continent into five parts: North Africa, East Africa, South Africa, Central Africa, and West Africa. This state would be governed through the African Peoples Economic Congress headquartered in Central Africa and constituting the top command legislative body, made up of 5,000 members elected worldwide from every country of 50,000 or more Africans; the review body named OAS (Organization of African States); the United States of Africa, the elected executive body; and finally, the local states constituting the local/district body of government.

The RNA advocates reparations to African Americans for the wrongs of slavery, segregation, discrimination, institutional racism, and white supremacy. After the abolition of slavery, the failed Reconstruction never successfully guaranteed the 40 acres and a mule promised then to former slaves. The RNA was willing to settle for $10,000 for every African American (asking for $400 billion to sustain the new nation during its first years). The money would help establish the new nation. Out of this amount, only a portion ($4,000) would go directly to the individual; the remainder was to go to the government. Influenced by Third World liberation movements, revolts, and uprisings, the anticapitalist leaders of the RNA modeled its economic system after the newly independent Tanzania's socialism. All the citizens of the RNA were subjected to disciplinary guidelines, among which were the prohibition of narcotics, marijuana, and alcoholic intoxication; the compulsory payment of taxes; and the right for men to have several wives. Citizens must also submit to political education classes and maintain a respectable but firm attitude.

The founders of RNA, Gaidi and Imari Obadele (formerly known as Milton and Richard Henry), were two brothers who were followers of Malcolm X. They were originally from Philadelphia, Pennsylvania, where they were active in local civil rights groups. The pair later moved to Detroit, Michigan, where they established the Group of Advanced Leadership (GOAL), a local civil rights organization. Invited by the organization for an address in 1963, Malcolm X delivered his famous "Message to the Grassroots." After the death of Malcolm X, GOAL renamed itself the Malcolm X Society and fully embraced the idea of an independent black nation as the ultimate expression of black nationalism. In the manifesto establishing the organization, the RNA called for the creation of an independent black nation, the RNA, to be carved out of five Southern states. The manifesto also called for the payment of $400 billion in reparations. The RNA asserts that Africans in the United States have a right to self-determination, which ought to have been afforded to them after the Civil War in the form of a plebiscite. Instead, blacks were incorporated de jure into the United States by the Fourteenth Amendment. Thus, the first goal of the RNA was a United Nations–supervised election among African Americans to determine whether they wished to form a separate nation. If this vote was to turn out favorably to the RNA's claims and demands, the aim of the organization would then have become to force the U.S. government to cede the national territory to create the new nation and transfer blacks in the Northern states to the new land and the whites in the five Southern states to the remaining parts of the United States. The Republic of New Africa demanded five states in the South of the United States (the Black Belt), namely Alabama, Georgia, Mississippi, Louisiana, and South Carolina, to establish its new nation. These states were perceived as the land rightfully belonging to African Americans, given the history of the United States and the fact that this is where African Americans had mostly lived, toiled, and farmed. These states represented a tenth of the U.S. territory; they also symbolized the fact that at the time (1968), African Americans made up 10 percent of the total U.S. population.

In 1971, Imari Obadele I became president of RNA and moved its headquarters to Jackson, Mississippi. Once established there, the

RNA consecrated its capital in Hinds County, Mississippi, where the organization had bought 20 acres of farmland from a black landowner. There was founded the nation's capital city of El Hajj Malik Shabazz (Malcolm X's adopted name after his departure from the Nation of Islam). On that day, 13 citizens of the RNA were arrested on charges of concealed weapons and possession of marijuana. The same year the Federal Bureau of Investigation (FBI), as part of its COINTELPRO (counter-intelligence program) of political repression, conducted an early-morning raid on the Jackson offices of RNA, and in an ensuing gun battle, a Jackson police officer was killed while another officer and an FBI agent were wounded. Obadele I and several other RNA leaders were sentenced to long prison terms, but as a result of protest and litigation Obadele I was freed after five years and resumed his leadership of RNA.

In March 1972, the RNA presented for enactment to both Houses of the U.S. Congress its "Anti-Depression Program of the Republic of New Africa to End Poverty, Dependence, Cultural Malnutrition, and Crime among Black People in the United States and Promote Inter-Racial Peace." As indicated in its title, the program proposed a variety of solutions to some of the issues faced by African descendants in the United States. The program was never scheduled for debate in any of the Houses, however.

The police and FBI raid on the headquarters of the RNA in 1971 left the group in disarray. It later moved its headquarters to Washington, D.C. In 1984, the national membership was between 5,000 and 10,000. Because of state repression, RNA reconstituted itself as the New Afrikan Movement, and since 1987 it has continued to press for reparations through N'COBRA (National Coalition of Blacks for Reparations in America), a coalition of black organizations dedicated to building a mass movement for reparations and a plebiscite for separations.

Maboula Soumahoro

See also "African" in African American History; Black Power Movement in the United States; COINTELPRO; Malcolm X (1925–1965); The National Coalition of Blacks for Reparations in America (N'COBRA).

FURTHER READING
Bracey, John. 1970. *Black Nationalism in America.* Indianapolis: Bobbs-Merrill.
Chokwe, Lumumba, Imari Abubakari Obadele, and Nkechi Taifa. 1993. *Reparations Yes!* Baton Rouge, LA: House of Songhay.
Davenport, C. 2005. "Understanding Covert Repressive Action: The Case of the United States Government Against the Republic of New Africa." *Journal of Conflict Resolution* 49 (1): 120–140.
Imari Obadele. 1975. *Foundations of the Black Nation.* Detroit: House of Songhay.
Kelley, Robin D. G. 2002. *Freedom Dreams: The Black Radical Imagination.* Boston: Beacon Press.

Ribeiro, Esmeralda (1958–)

A journalist by profession, Esmeralda Ribeiro stands out as one of the most important Afro-Brazilian women writers of today. Her works, similar to those by Miriam Alves, Alzira Rufino, Geni Guimarães, and Conceição Evaristo, find their inspiration and are created within spheres that tend not to be part of the national literary mainstream. Ribeiro is very active in promoting the works of Afro-Brazilian women writers. Today, together with Márcio Barbosa, she is especially known as the editor of the *Cadernos Negros* series, a collaborative enterprise and collection initiated in 1978 to serve primarily as a space of literary expression for black writers in Brazil.

Most of her poems and short stories are a part of this collection. Ribeiro reaffirmed her commitment to black writing when she joined the literary-activist organization Quilombhoje. An endeavor created by Cuti (Luiz Silva),

Quilombhoje started in 1980, the third year of the annual *Cadernos Negros* anthology series, in a collaborative effort with Oswaldo de Camargo, Abelardo Rodrigues, Paulo Colina, and Mário Jorge Lescano.

Ribeiro had a short novel, *Malungos e Milongas,* published in 1988. She is also one of the authors of *Gostando mais de nós mesmos* (1999). To date, her poems and short stories have appeared in *Cadernos Negros* 5 (1982), 7 to 26 (1984–2003), *Cadernos Negros: Os Melhores Poemas (Black Notebooks. The Best Poems)* (1998), and *Cadernos Negros: Os Melhores Contos (Black Notebooks. The Best Short Stories)* (1998) (Ribeiro and Barbosa 2003, 140–142).

Ribeiro's writings have been published in Portuguese and English. They appear in various other anthologies and collections: *Pau de sebo. Coletânea de Poesia Negra* (organized by Júlia Duboc, Brodowski: Projeto Memória da Cidade, 1988); *Moving Beyond Boundaries. International Dimension of Black Women's Writing* (edited by Carole Boyce Davies and Molara Ogundipe-Leslie, London: Pluto Press, 1995); *Enfim . . . Nós/Finally . . . Us: Contemporary Black Brazilian Women Writers* (edited by Miriam Alves and Carolyn R. Durham, Colorado Springs, Colorado: Three Continent Press, 1995); *Callaloo* vol. 18, number 4, 1995; *Ancestral House* (edited by Charles H. Rowell, Boulder, Colorado: Westview Press, 1995); *Quilombo de Palavras-a literatura dos afro-descendentes* (organized by Jônatas Conceição and Lindinalva Barbosa, Salvador: CEAO/UFBA, 2000); and *Fourteen Female Voices from Brazil: Interviews and Works* (edited by Elzbieta Szoka, Austin, Texas: Host Publications, 2002).

Ribeiro has produced several articles that reflect on the experience of writing in relation to issues of race, women, and the black movement in Brazil: *Gênero e representação na literatura brasileira. Vol. II* (organized by Constância Lima Duarte, Eduardo de Assis Duarte and Kátia da Costa Bezerra, Belo Horizonte: UFMG, 2002); "A escritora negra e seu ato de escrever participando," in *Criação*

Crioula Nu Elefante Branco. I Encontro de Poetas e Ficcionistas Negros Brasileiros (organized by Cuti, Miriam Alves, and Arnaldo Xavier, São Paulo: Secretaria do Estado da Cultura, 1987); and "Reflexão sobre Literatura Infanto-juvenil" in *Reflexões. Sobre a Literatura Afro-Brasileira* (Quilombhoje/Conselho de Participação e Desenvolvimento da Comunidade Negra, 1985).

Dawn Duke

See also Quilombhoje.

FURTHER READING
Ribeiro, Esmeralda. 1988. *Malungos e Milongas.* São Paulo, Brazil: Quilombhoje.
Ribeiro, Esmeralda, and Márcio Barbosa. 2003. *Cadernos Negros Volume 26. Contos Afro-Brasileiras.* São Paulo, Brazil: Quilombhoje.

Robeson, Paul (1898–1976)

Paul Leroy Robeson, well-known athlete, politician, singer, actor, and orator, was born on April 9, 1898, in Princeton, NJ. His mother was killed when he was six, leaving his Protestant minister father the sole provider. The family lapsed into abject poverty forcing his father to work in menial jobs. Paul graduated high school with honors. After earning 15 baseball, basketball, and track varsity letters and twice being named All-American football team member, he graduated valedictorian and Phi Beta Kappa from Rutgers University. Robeson completed a law degree at Columbia University, but chose theater rather than jurisprudence. He joined the Provincetown Players Company where Eugene O'Neill was resident playwright. O'Neill cast Paul as lead in *All God's Chillun Got Wings* and *Emperor Jones.*

Robeson chipped away at the seemingly insurmountable national political and social structure that made African Americans disenfranchised second-class citizens and became a respected and admired "world citizen." Singing in 25 languages, his deep baritone voice touched people worldwide. He made more than 300 recordings and brought spirituals into classical music (Blockson 1998). Significant in classical theatre, film, and the music industry, Robeson brought African Americans to the forefront in theater when he starred as Othello in Shakespeare's *Othello* (1943–1944). In 1944, he won the Donaldson Award for best actor. His film debut, silent film *Body and Soul* (1925), was directed by African American pioneer film director Oscar Micheaux. Robeson starred in 11 films; his well-known movies include *Emperor Jones* (1933), *Song of Freedom* (1936), *Jericho* (1937), *Big Fella* (1937), and *Proud Valley* (1939). Robeson refused to accept a destiny of discrimination, inequality, and hypocrisy by becoming an activist, and he ultimately risked all as he fought social injustice.

In 1921, Robeson married Eslanda Goode and they had one child, Paul Jr. Concerned about the oppressed, especially people of color worldwide, he embraced empowerment ideologies and socialist philosophy. As the chairman of the Council of African Affairs, Robeson, along with W. E. B. DuBois, Oliver Cox, Claudia Jones, and several African American scholars, was considered un-American and potentially dangerous. His civil rights activism resulted in castigation, physical endangerment, and the loss of a career that affected tremendously the artistic milieu of the United States. He was one of the top ten concert draws early in the second quarter of the century and was making an annual salary of approximately $100,000, but his earning had dropped to approximately $6,000 annually by the late 1940s. Hollywood, Broadway, concert halls radio, and television blacklisted him. His passport was revoked from 1950 to 1958 (White 1998).

In 1956, congressional interrogators asked Robeson why he didn't move to Russia since he embraced its people, politics and social ideology. He replied, "Because my father was a slave, and my people died to build this country . . . I'm going to stay here and have a part of it just like you. And no fascist-minded people will drive me from it! Is that clear?"

In 1958, Robeson recovered his passport and published his autobiography, *Here I Stand*. In celebration of Robeson's achievements and presence at Rutgers University, the student union is named in his honor. Robeson died on January 23, 1976. He received a posthumous Grammy Award in 1998. In February 2004, the U.S. Postal Service recognized him with a commemorative stamp.

Valerie Smith

See also Black Cinema; Cox, Oliver Cromwell (1901–1974); Du Bois, William Edward Burghardt (1868–1963).

FURTHER READING
Apheker, Herbert. 1997. "Personal Recollections: Woodson, Wesley, Robeson and DuBois." *The Black Scholar* 27(2): 42–45.
Blockson, Charles L. 1998. "Paul Robeson, Melody of Freedom." *American Vision* 13 (1, Feb/Mar): 14–19.
Brown, Lloyd L. 1997. *The Young Paul Robeson.* Boulder, CO: Westview Press.
Brown, Lloyd L. 1997. *On My Journey Now.* Boulder, CO: Westview Press.
Foner, Philip S., ed. 1978. *Paul Robeson Speaks. Writings, Speeches, Interviews 1918–1974.* New York: Citadel Press.
Howard, Wendell. 1996. "Paul Robeson." *Midwest Quarterly* 38 (1, Autumn): 102–116.
Robeson, Paul, Jr. 2001. *The Undiscovered Paul Robeson.* New York: John Wiley and Sons.
White, Timothy. 1998. "Paul Robeson's Song of Freedom." *Billboard*, April 11.

Rodney, Walter (1942–1980)

Walter Rodney was born on March 23, 1942, in Georgetown, Guyana, to a working-class family. He attended the Queen's College on an open exhibition scholarship, and his distinguished high school career culminated with his winning a scholarship to the University of the West Indies in Mona, Jamaica, in 1960.

While in Jamaica, Rodney was an active supporter of Caribbean Unity, and he traveled extensively in Jamaica supporting the West Indian Federation during the referendum of 1961. Three years later, he obtained a degree in history with first class honors. As an undergraduate, Rodney was already writing and contributing to scholarly journals on the issues of slavery and capitalism, and speaking in the defense of the poor.

In 1963, Rodney received yet another scholarship, to study African history at the School of Oriental and African Studies at the University of London. There, he became a member of the group of Caribbean workers and students who studied and debated with C. L. R. James. Rodney participated in the discussions at Hyde Park Corner. His doctoral research work took him to Spain, Portugal, and Italy and, in the process, Walter learned Portuguese and Spanish. In 1966, at the age of 24, Rodney received his PhD. His doctoral thesis was published in 1970 as *A History of the Upper Guinea Coast, 1545–1800*.

Rodney's first job in the academy was as a lecturer in history at the University of Dar es Salaam, in Tanzania, East Africa. At that time, Tanzania was the headquarters of the Organization of African Unity Liberation Committee. In 1964, the Zanzibar revolution had radicalized the politics of East Africa, and in 1967, the Tanzanian government launched the Arusha Declaration. Che Guevara had also traveled through Tanzania on his way to fight in the Congo.

In 1968, Rodney returned to Jamaica to lecture at his alma mater and became deeply involved in the rise of mass political activity on the island. He worked closely with poor people and "grounded" with Rastafarians in Kingston and other parts of the country. Though constantly under surveillance, Rodney was not intimidated. Scholarly work accompanied his work with the ordinary people.

In October 1968, Rodney attended the Black Writers Conference in Montreal and was barred from Jamaica upon his return. The ban had massive repercussions as students and ordinary people, angry at the expulsion, began a massive popular uprising. Some of the public presentations Rodney gave in Jamaica were published in a small book, *The Groundings with My Brothers* (1969).

After his expulsion from Jamaica, Rodney spent time in Toronto and traveled to Cuba. In early 1969, he returned to Tanzania, where he resumed teaching at the University of Dar es Salaam. At this time, the University of Dar es Salaam was a magnet for all of those in Africa who were thinking through the issues of liberation and freedom. It was in this intellectual milieu that he published his best-known work, *How Europe Underdeveloped Africa* (1974). Rodney's numerous writings on the subjects of socialism, imperialism, working-class struggles, Pan-Africanism, and slavery contributed to a body of knowledge and an intellectual tradition that came to be known as the Dar es Salaam School of Thought. He traveled extensively throughout East Africa and was one of the founders of the History Teachers Workshop of Tanzania. This workshop assigned members the task of rewriting the textbooks for high school students in Tanzania.

In 1974, Rodney moved with his family back to Guyana, and he was appointed professor of history at the University of Guyana. The government of Guyana, however, canceled the appointment as his political activity increased. Out of paid work, he refused to leave the country. Instead, over the next six years he threw himself into independent research and political organization. He increased his work as an international scholar, teaching and researching on a full-time basis, working full-time as an activist in the Working People's Alliance (WPA), and remaining committed as a serious scholar.

Rodney's study of the Guyanese working people included a study of Guyanese plantations in the 19th century and a three-volume study of the Guyanese working people; however, before the latter was complete, Rodney was assassinated on June 13, 1980, by a bomb concealed in a walkie-talkie. After his assassination, the first volume, *A History of the Guyanese Working People, 1881–1905* was published by Johns Hopkins University Press. This book provided the historical foundations for the political movement that he played a central role in founding and that he led until his death, the WPA. More than anything else, the WPA was committed to the politics of reconciliation among all racial groups in Guyana, beginning with the working people. It was Rodney's view that only when children learned proper history and respect for others that the struggles against racial insecurity could be overcome. Two children's books were produced, *Kofi Baadu Out of Africa* and *Lakshmi Out of India* (1980).

Rodney was not just a Guyanese figure. He was also known worldwide, especially in the Caribbean and Africa, where he enjoyed great popularity for his solidarity with the struggles of the working people. For this reason, Eusi Kwayana, the Guyanese politician and coleader of the WPA, termed him as the prophet of self emancipation.

Horace Campbell

See also Caribbean Black Power; Guyana; Pan-Africanism.

FURTHER READING

Campbell, Horace. 1991. "The Impact of Walter Rodney and Progressive Scholars on the Dar es Salaam School." *Social and Economic Studies* 40 (2): 99–135.

Kwayana, Eusi. 1991. *Walter Rodney*. Wellesley, MA: Calaloux Publications.

Lewis, Rupert. 1998. *Walter Rodney's Intellectual and Political Thought*. Detroit: Wayne State University Press.

Rodney, Walter. 1974. *How Europe Underdeveloped Africa*. Washington, D.C.: Howard University Press.

Rodney, Walter. 1980. *Kofi Baadu, Out of Africa*. Georgetown, Guyana: S.N.

Rodney, Walter. 1981. *A History of the Guyanese Working People, 1881–1905*. Johns Hopkins Studies in Atlantic History and Culture. Baltimore: The Johns Hopkins University Press.

Rodney, Walter. 1990. *Walter Rodney Speaks: The Making of an African Intellectual*. Trenton, NJ: Africa World Press.

Rodney, Walter. 2000. *Lakshmi Out of India*. Georgetown, Guyana: Guyana Book Foundation.

Rogers, Joel Augustus (1880–1966)

Over the span of 50 years, preeminent writer, historian, and anthropologist J. A. Rogers traversed continents, unearthing the suppressed and forgotten fragments of his people's past in an effort to reclaim humankind's most vital contributions as African. Born Joel Augustus Rogers on September 6, 1880, Rogers spent his formative years in Jamaica. The trajectory of Rogers's career was not cemented until his immigration to the United States in 1906 and his exposure to the hypocrisy of a nation in debt to slavery, yet socially and politically crippled by xenophobia. With his remarkable lens, Rogers applied his many talents toward historiography, assessing the extent to which the victimization of Africans on the continent, in the Americas, and throughout the Diaspora could be directly attributed to Western history's depiction of them as an ahistoric, barbarous, and relatively inferior people.

Rogers became a naturalized U.S. citizen in 1917, and after a brief stint in Chicago, established a home base in the heart of Harlem at the inception of the Harlem Renaissance and Marcus Garvey's Universal Negro Improvement Association's (UNIA) back to Africa movement. Hence, at the time Rogers embarked on his career, he had not only gained insight into the many scientific and theoretical theses that debunked the pseudoscience that rationalized racism, he resided in an environment where evidence of African genius was ubiquitous. His *From Superman to Man* (1917) and *As Nature Leads* (1919), signaled his use of anthropological research to begin an early scientific challenge of the logic of the concepts of race and racism, and thereby the demystification of the construction of a "master race." Through his scholarship, Rogers collapsed the great divide between whites and blacks and recast the world in shades of grey. His three-volume work entitled *Sex and Race* and his *Nature Knows No Color Line* attest to his achievement in this regard.

Throughout the 1920s, much of Rogers's work was centered on the burgeoning African American art forms and innovations, as popularized during the Harlem Renaissance. The masterfully poetic tribute entitled "Jazz at Home," featured in Alain Locke's *The New Negro* (1925), both showcased the versatility of his talent and situated this work within this colorful and complex diasporic space. His orations edified members of Garvey's various UNIA chapters, and as a means of publicity, Rogers shared excerpts from his many works with academics and laypeople alike. As a journalist and correspondent, Rogers lent himself to the sociopolitics of the milieu, covering Garvey's 1923 trial, the 1930 coronation of Haile Selassie I, and Italy's invasion of Ethiopia. His publication, *The Real Facts about Ethiopia* (1935), revealed the details of the war from a perspective like no other, and afforded the Diaspora access to such realities as the role of women in the war and the predominance of fascism, veritably informing about Mussolini's maneuverings.

The 1930s and 1940s were Rogers's most prolific, and his works demonstrated his tool of choice against the rise of leaders such as Mussolini and Hitler. Although local threats to Africans in America persisted, Rogers took the opportunity to use the evidence he accrued during his travels to Europe to quell the new wave of anti-African sentiment. Combining his knowledge of art and architecture with archival resources, Rogers produced *Hitler and the Negro*, a short piece documenting the role of Africans in German history, as well as Europeans' reverence of black icons, such as the Madonna. To further emphasize the significance of Africans in Euro-

pean and world history, Rogers completed *World's Greatest Men and Women of African Descent* (1931), *100 Amazing Facts About the Negro, with Complete Proof* (1934), and *World's Great Men of Color, 3000 B.C to 1946 A.D.* (1946). Rogers, however, kept his finger on the pulse of racial politics back home where conditions were no less pernicious. Racist notions popularized by the eugenics movement still held currency, and the legislative decision regarding desegregation instigated the sponsorship of anti-integrationist press and media. His recognition of the shifting climate and fear of further bombings, riots, and other physical threats directed at the African American community engendered the creation of *Africa's Gift to America* in 1959 and *Five Negro Presidents* in 1965.

His writings as a columnist for the *Negro World*, *Pittsburgh Courier*, *The Crisis*, *Survey Graphic*, and *American Mercury*, were but a few of his many contributions. Rogers was also an active member of the Société d'Anthropologie, the American Geographic Society, and the American Academy of Political Science. In addition to the years he spent conducting research in Europe and countless other locales, Rogers sojourned to the Sudan, Egypt, and Morocco and documented the realities of populations as varied as the maroons of Jamaica and those of South America.

Janice Giles

FURTHER READING

Rogers, Joel Augustus. 1920. *The Approaching Storm and How It May Be Averted*. New York: self-published.

Rogers, Joel Augustus. 1925. "Jazz at Home." *Survey Graphic*. Reprinted in *Doubletake. A Revisionist Harlem Renaissance Anthology*, ed. Venetria K. Patton and Maureen Honey, 127–133. New Brunswick, N.J.: Rutgers University Press, 2001.

Rogers, Joel Augustus. 1957. *From Superman to Man*. New York: Helga M. Rogers.

Rogers, Joel Augustus. 1972. *World's Great Men of Color*. New York: The Macmillan Company.

Rogers, Joel Augustus. 1989. *Africa's Gift to America*. St. Petersburg, FL: Helga M. Rogers.

Rogers, Joel Augustus. 1990. *Sex and Race.* St. Petersburg, FL: Helga M. Rogers.

Simba, Malik. 2006. "Joel Augustus Rogers: Negro Historian in History, Time and Place." *Afro-Americans in New York Life and History* 30.2: 47–68.

Smith, Jessie Carney, ed. 1998. *Notable Black American Men.* Detroit: Thompson Gale.

Rolling Calf

In Jamaica it is believed that duppies (i.e., spirits of the dead) have the ability to appear in very particular forms. One such form is the rolling calf. This spirit is most often understood to be the duppy of a dishonest person (usually a shopkeeper) but has also come to include various bloodthirsty characters such as murderers and butchers.

Rolling calves roam at night and frequent the roots of cotton trees during the day. As the name suggests, the rolling calf takes the physical form of an animal; however, its most distinguishing feature is a chain tied around its neck. When the rolling calf makes its presence known, the chain can be heard dragging on the ground. This rattling sound, accompanied by the spirit's terrible roar, has made the rolling calf legendary for instilling fear. The rolling calf is in fact unique in that it is most often heard rather than seen. Those who claim to have seen this duppy report its fiery eyes as well as its fear of the moon or any type of light. Some have reported that they have chased this spirit away by turning on the headlights of a car. It is notable, however, that in the old days, there were more ceremonious ways as well. One interviewee who grew up in the 1940s in the parish of Clarendon, reports rumors of escape via a pen knife, a cross, and a bottle of white rum. The method was as follows: (1) Draw a cross on the ground with a pen knife; (2) sprinkle rum over the entire area; and (3) set the rum on fire. When the rolling calf smells the rum it would attempt to lick it and would become trapped by flames.

Appearances of the rolling calf are particularly frequent during the Christmas season. Most Jamaicans associate the word "rolling" with the calf's tendency to wander, though the term may also refer to the thunder of its roar. Beyond that, the rolling calf's origin remains sketchy. Could there be some larger significance to the sound of chains dragging on the ground? This question incites imagination and imagination incites ancestral memory. In the novel *Madam Fate*, for example, the nature of the rolling calf is reimagined as the tormented and sad spirit of a runaway slave boy, an iron chain still anchored to his neck.

Marcia Douglas

See also Jamaica; Old Hige.

FURTHER READING
Douglas, Marcia. 1999. *Madam Fate.* New York: Soho Press.

Ross, Jacob (1956–)

Jacob Ross teaches creative writing at Goldsmith University in London and is acclaimed as a short story writer par excellence. Born in Grenada, Ross migrated to Europe where he attended the University of Grenoble, France. He moved to England in 1984 and has lived there since.

Ross's first collection of short stories, *Song for Simone and Other Stories*, published in 1986, evokes the Grenadian space of his childhood. Like other stories about adolescent life in the Caribbean, Ross's collection is framed by a rapidly changing social world. The child protagonists in this collection struggle to maintain the simplicity and carefree innocence of childhood, yet they are faced with many adult responsibilities and endure many adult experiences in a society that is being tested by political instability. *Song for Simone* has earned Ross many accolades and has been translated into German and Spanish. The collection has often been compared to George Lamming's *In the Castle of My Skin,* a coming-of-age novel that links the development of a male adolescent protagonist to the development of an island nationalism. Ross, like Lamming, succeeds in conveying themes that are powerful in their messages yet evocative in their rendition. The issue of alienation and the struggle to retain one's individualism in the face of social constraints is portrayed in the title story about a young girl's psychological journey to adulthood and is reinforced in the other stories in the collection.

Ross's second volume of short stories, *A Way to Catch Dust,* continues to explore the relationship between the individual and society. This book confirms Ross's prowess as a skillful story teller. Although the characters depicted are older than those in Ross's first collection of short stories, they are similarly struggling to come to terms with a society that is constantly and dramatically changing.

Ross has also been coeditor of literary anthologies of Caribbean diasporic writings. In 1998, with the Grenadian poet Joan Amin-Addo, he coedited an anthology entitled *Voices, Memory, Ashes: Lest We Forget.* He also coauthored *Behind the Masquerade, the Story of the Notting Hill Carnival* with the Ghanaian cultural activist, Kwesi Owusu, and has contributed to *Storms of the Heart: An Anthology of Black Arts and Culture,* the anthology edited by Owusu. Ross has served as editor of *Artrage Intercultural Arts* magazine. This popular British magazine, originally called *Echo,* focuses on the visual, literary and performing arts.

Ross has an abiding interest in photography, and this interest reveals itself in some of the pictures in the book. In a photo essay "Photographing Carnival, Catching the Spirits," Ross describes his experience of carnival and how he comes to photography as an imaginative springboard to capture the sociopolitical drama of the cultural reality of the black Briton as it is being wrought in the pageantry of carnival.

Ross has done many international lecture tours and creative writing workshops. He has taught his craft in universities as far as the University of Jordan in the Middle East and as close as St. George's University in Grenada.

Antonia MacDonald-Smythe

FURTHER READING
The Jacob Ross website.
  freespace.virgin.net/jacob.ross/ (accessed March 10, 2005).

Rufino, Alzira (1949–)

Activist, feminist, author, poet, essayist, and *ialorixá* (priestess of Candomblé, the Afro-Brazilian religion), Alzira Rufino stands out as one of the leaders of Afro-Brazilian feminist consciousness today. Currently residing in Santos, São Paulo, Brazil, she is known as the founder and director of the Casa de Cultura da Mulher Negra (Black Women's Cultural Center), an entity she has headed since its formation in 1986. Inspired by Rufino, the Casa started as a group effort, a collective, bearing the name Coletivo de Mulheres Negras da Baixada Santista (the Baixada Santista Black Women's Collective). The expression "Baixada Santista" refers to the lower coastal plain upon which the port city of Santos is located. Four years later, in 1990, the coletivo evolved into the now well-known Casa de Cultura da Mulher Negra. To date, Rufino remains the central figure and driving force behind the Casa and all its endeavors. Interviewed and written about at home and abroad (Royster 1988; Haje 2000; Duke 2003), the activist Rufino is very well known in São Paulo as head of one of the most prominent nongovernmental organizations and as a very outspoken leader who fights for the rights of women.

Rufino has written literary and political studies and publications on the historical and contemporary experiences of Afro-Brazilian women: her 1988 anthology entitled *Eu, Mulher Negra, Resisto* (*I, Black Woman, Resist*) and *Muriquinho Piquininho* (1989), a book-length poem that traces the experience of enslavement from Africa to the Americas through the eyes of a child. Some of her poems can also be found in *Cadernos Negros* 19 (1996). Today she is editor-in-chief of the biannual magazine published by her organization, entitled *Eparrei*, and the monthly *Eparrei Online Bulletin*.

As part of this larger venture, Rufino has published several important essays and short works on women. Published in 1986, *Mulher Negra Tem História* (*The Black Woman Has a History*), the result of a collaborative project, is a biographical compilation of 30 Afro-Brazilian women who left their mark on Brazilian history. Her 1988 collection of essays, *Articulando* (*Articulating*), focuses on a wide range of issues, such as African politics, the black movement, and the status of black women, while her 1997 text, *O Poder Muda de Mãos Não de Cor* (*Power Changes Hands Not Color*), is a comparative study about the status of white and black women in Brazil over two decades. Domestic violence is another issue that is important to her, as can be seen in "Violência contra a mulher, uma questão de Saúde Pública" (Violence Against Woman, a Question of Public Health), which is found in the *Annals of the II National Meeting of Popular Organizations*. "Atravessando o muro das lamentaç ões contra o racismo" (Crossing the Wall of Lamentations Against Racism) was written on the occasion of the International Conference on Racism in Durban, South Africa in 2001.

Today Rufino continues to make strides in the district of Santos and on the national scale in the following arenas: the creation of shelters (2000); the elaboration and implementation of laws against racism and domestic violence; and the creation of the National Law of Compulsory Notification of Domestic Violence in Public and Private Services of Health (November 24, 2003). Her successes in the areas of cultural rescue, the creation of judicial and psychological services for victims of violence, and income generation have influenced other organizations to initiate similar work in the cities of Três Corações (Minas Gerais), Goiânia (Goiás), São Sebastião (São Paulo), and Duque de Caxias (Rio de Janeiro).

Dawn Duke

See also Brazil: Afro-Brazilians.

FURTHER READING

Duke, Dawn. 2003. "Alzira Rufino's *Casa de Cultura da Mulher Negra* as a Form of Female Empowerment: A Look at the Dynamics of a Black Women's Organization in Brazil Today." *Women's Studies International Forum* 26 (4, July-August): 357–368.

Haje, Bahiji. 2000. "Entrevista com Alzira Rufino. Poucas Mulheres Negras Superam as Barreiras da Cor no Mercado de Trabalho." *Mulheres*, 7–11.

Royster, Jacqueline Jones. 1988. "Brazilian Writer/Activist Alzira Rufino: A Resonant Voice From the Dark and Narrow Space." *SAGE* 2 (Fall): 77–78.

Rufino, Alzira. 2000. "10 Anos de (R)Existência." *Emparrei. Jornal da Mulher Negra*, April: 12.

Rufino, Alzira, Nilza Iraci, and Maria Rosa Pereira. 1986. *Mulher Negra Tem História*. Santos, São Paulo, Brazil: Alzira Rufino, Nilza Iraci, Maria Rosa Pereira.

Ruiz, Antonio

See Falucho (?–1824).

S

Salsa

"Salsa" is a catchall term currently used to describe every kind of Afro-Cuban musical genre, including *guaracha, mambo, cha-cha, rumba, danzon*, but predominantly *son*. The styles of *son* and *casino* in particular have had the greatest influence on salsa music and dance as it is known today. Rumba is an umbrella term for related music, dance, and song styles that originated in Cuba, with significant influences from African drumming and Spanish poetry and singing. Rumba is the essence of the popular Cuban rhythms now referred to as salsa.

Casino refers to the Casino Deportivo in Havana where it was created and popularized as a successor to the syncopated *son*. Both *son* and *casino* are themselves related to earlier dance forms, particularly folkloric rumba (with its essential clave beat). *Son* and *casino* differ in terms of the movements they accent, the styles and patterns of steps, and the complexity with which partners' arms are intertwined. *Casino* also tends to be faster and more high-energy than *son*.

Unlike *son*, *casino* can be danced in a circle or *rueda* (wheel), where two or more couples respond to the call of a leading male dancer, and male partners exchange female partners

through previously learned dance patterns associated with each call. These patterns have specific and amusing names related to local sayings or typical romantic situations—but usually from a male perspective, as traditionally men are the callers.

Salsa, which means "sauce" in Spanish, was first used as a catchall term in 1930s Cuba, and in 1933 it was mentioned in the song "Echale Salsita" by Cuban composer Ignacio Piñero. In the song, Piñero refers to the "spiciness" of the famous restaurant "El Congo" in Havana and at the same time the "in-the-groove" feel of the music.

After the revolution in 1959, Cuba—once the Latin American version of Las Vegas—was isolated from the rest of the world, although new Cuban sounds and dance styles continued to emerge. Celia Cruz, the undisputable Queen of Salsa, and La Sonora Matancera, Perez Prado, Machito, and several other renowned Cuban musicians decided not to return to their now communist homeland and established themselves in Puerto Rico, Mexico, Venezuela and New York, where they signed long-term contracts.

Meanwhile, Puerto Ricans had become the largest Spanish-speaking population in New York City. Puerto Rican artists were playing and dancing to Cuban beats at the famous Palladium and started to mix in their own interpretations, adding to the jazz sounds from the Chano Pozo era. Scholars argue about who was the first to use salsa as a brand name. Among three big names in the industry, Jimmy Sabater released a record with a name "Salsa and Bembé" in 1962; in 1974, Tito Puente stated, "Esto es una gran Salsa," literally, "This is a big Sauce" in reference to the music experimentation they were playing at the time; and Larry Harlow (creator of the Fania All-Stars) released his album "Salsa" in 1973.

In the 1970s, and particularly in New York City, salsa eventually became known as its own dance style rooted in the Cuban dance forms of *son* and *casino*. The term "salsa" also helped popularize, brand, and commercialize all Latin American music. In 1985, Cuban singer Gloria Estefan and Miami Sound Machine set the basis for the crossover boom of Latin music with their international hit song "Conga." Marc Anthony, La India, Victor Manuel, Isaac Delgado, and Gilberto Santa Rosa, to name a few, represent the 1990s trend: the romantic salsa, where ballads with passionate lyrics took over the rhythm.

During the growing, international salsa craze, salsa not only maintained its connection to its African roots but also drew on African Diasporic musical traditions of the countries where it was embraced. Even in African countries like Senegal (with the band Africando), Congo, and Nigeria, salsa was embraced and flavored with other popular and traditional styles. Meanwhile, the sounds, rhythms, and dance movements of rumba and other Cuban styles were echoed in the popular music played in urban Latino neighborhoods across the United States.

ANTECEDENTS

An important geographical factor must be considered with salsa: Cuba is the biggest island in the Caribbean and was the last to abolish slavery. With two important ports (Havana and Santiago de Cuba), the island served as a holding and trade center of enslaved Africans from diverse parts of Africa during Colonial times. And slave shipments can be traced as late as the 19th century. All these ethnic groups from Africa, and particularly the Bantu, Carabali, and Yoruba, brought their rich performance traditions to the island, and these in time mixed with those of the Spaniards and Europeans. Moreover, the Haitian Revolution against France spurred an important immigration of French and Haitians to Oriente (east of Cuba), adding to the already complicated polyrhythms inherited by Cubans of African descent.

For each Cuban rhythm there is an associated dance. Historically, musicians have competed to monopolize the attention of the dancers in a country where music and dance are an integral part of society. Ignacio Cervantes, Miguel Failde, Trio Matamoros, Ignacio Piñeiro, Benny More, Felix Chapottin, Arsenio Rodriguez, and Enrique Jorrin are only a handful of the renowned groups whose songs are still played all around the world.

In today's Cuba, *timba*, a new version evolved from the *son*, replaced the popularity of *casino*. Orquesta Revé, Los Van Van, Charanga Habanera, and Adalberto Alvarez represent some of the more popular bands in the genre. *Timba* is a complex fusion of *son* with Afro-Cuban beats: bata drums, songo, rumba, and so on, called street dance in New York. Although dancing to *timba* does not require a partner, *timba* rescues the old sensuality of the *son*. Even now the story repeats: Cuban artists have left the island in search of freedom and opportunities, and with them, *timba* has spread around the world. The world was recognizing the Cuban rhythms now constantly syncretized with other genres such as *cumbia,* jazz, merengue, *plena,* samba, the Spanish "*Cante Jondo,*" the American hustle, swing, and so on. In all corners of the world—from Asia, the Middle East, Africa, and Europe to the rest of the Caribbean and Latin America—thousands of dance lovers had come to worship salsa.

Neri Torres

See also Afro-Cuban Music; Cruz, Celia (1924–2003); Cuba: Afro-Cubans.

FURTHER READING
Boggs, Vernon. 1992. *Salsiology: Afro-Cuban Music and the Evolution of Salsa in New York City*. Westport, CT: Greenwood Press.
Orovio, Helio. 1992. *Diccionario de la Música Cubana*. 2nd ed. Havana, Cuba: Letras Cubanas.
Orovio, Helio. 2003. *Cuban Music from A to Z*. Durham, NC: Duke University Press.
Ortiz, Fernando. 1965. *La Africanía de la Música Folklórica de Cuba [1950]*. 2nd rev. ed. Havana, Cuba: Editora Universitaria.
Ospina, Hernando Calvo. 1995. *Salsa! Havana Heat, Bronx Beat*. New York: Latin American Bureau for Research and Action.

Salt and the African Diaspora

In spite of the many health concerns associated with salt consumption, African Diaspora peoples enjoy an intimate relationship with salt, at the levels of culture and consciousness. The discussions, fictional and historical, of the salt trade and salt as a tool of oppression are numerous. In *The History of Mary Prince: A West Indian Slave* (1987), Prince claims that she and other slaves lived in constant fear of being sent to mine salt in the salt bogs. Salt, as both a material and metaphorical substance, has been a source of great ambivalence in an African diasporic context. It has been used as an instrument of punishment (i.e., "seasoning," or the agony of a whipped slave whose bleeding wounds are rubbed in salt or washed with brine), was a source of wealth in 18th-century Africa, and was a necessary ingredient for sufficient seasoning of foods. Salt can cause harm, as does the salt sea to the unsuspecting swimmer, fisherman, hurricane survivor, refugee, or rebellious African.

Perhaps the source of this ambivalence to salt lay in the trauma of the Middle Passage, among enslaved Africans, male and female, who chose to dive into the ocean rather than endure bondage in a foreign land, or among the children many threw overboard for the same reason. In this case, taking on the ocean and its salt sustains/preserves the spirit against degradation. An examination of the history of the salt trade in West Africa provides insight into the importance of salt among continental Africans. In his studies of the 18th-century history of the coastal states of west-central Africa and of the colony of Saint Domingue, cultural anthropologist Hein Vanhee noticed the use of salt for symbolic reasons. He indicates that Capuchin missionaries traveling in the kingdom of Kongo often met people indigenous to the region who asked them for salt, or *anamungoa*. These people used salt in rituals (called baptism by Vanhee). Often, after receiving the salt, they would rush off before the missionaries could apply water. He contends that although the historical information is scarce, it can be presumed that salt was used in other non-Christian initiation ceremonies. It could also be argued that they rushed off to hoard the valuable commodity before the missionaries could dilute it.

Although Vanhee's research did not yield information on the uses of salt in Saint Domingue among the African-born slaves working on plantations toward the end of the 18th century, much has been written on the use of salt for symbolic reasons in Vodoun ceremonies in Saint Domingue. Anthropologist Wade Davis's *The Serpent and the Rainbow* contains information on symbolic uses of salt in Vodoun rituals in 20th-century Haiti (Davis 1985, 180). Salt is used to baptize a child, because an unbaptized child could be taken by the devil. To release the child from the devil's grasp, a bit of salt is placed on its tongue. Salt is believed to be the antidote for tetrodotoxin, the poison that initiates the zombification process. As in Haiti, Steven Buhnen (1996) submits salt was used as an antitoxin during the 18th century in what is now the Republic of Guinea.

Still, salt has contradictory meanings across the Diaspora. In contrast with the beneficial uses of salt, much sociological work has been done on the damaging effects of salt on African American communities in the United States. Thomas W. Wilson's 1986 study, "Africa, Afro-Americans, and Hypertensions: An Hypothesis," argued for what has become known as the "slavery hypothesis for hypertension." Wilson posited that the prevalence of high blood pressure among African American populations in the United States is the result of (1) salt deficiency in West Africa, (2) the physical trauma of the Middle Passage, and (3) conditions of slavery in the United States, specifically the high salt content of food slaves were forced to eat. Recent research has found that African American peoples born in the United States are more sensitive than white Americans to increases in dietary salt and that when injected with saline solutions, African Americans retained intravenous sodium longer than white Americans did.

These observations have prompted the medical community to look to the African past for genetic evidence of hypertension. In "The Slavery Hypothesis for Hypertension Among African Americans," historian Philip Curtin contends, however, that this hypothesis is both inaccurate and ahistorical (Curtin 1992). Curtin's position answers and raises several questions. First, he provides ample evidence that one of the primary elements of Wilson's hypothesis, that Africans brought to the Americas during the Middle Passage came from salt-poor regions of Africa, is incorrect. In addition, salt was easily obtainable in 18th-century West Africa. Paul Lovejoy, who has researched the salt trade in the western Sudan extensively, asserts in *Salt of the Desert Sun: A History of Salt Production and Trade in the Central Sudan*

A worker harvests salt from evaporative ponds in Fachi, Niger, in 1999. (Michael S. Lewis/Corbis)

(1986) that in the region including the Lake Chad basin, the south-central Sahara Desert, the Benue River basin, and the Niger Valley, from the Benue northward to the Sahel, the salt trade extended into present-day Ethiopia, Chad, Benin, Nigeria, Mauritania, Ghana, Sierra Leone, and Senegambia. Imported and locally made sea salt had been traded in the region as early as the 18th century.

Lovejoy has traced 16 different types of salt, each with very specific purposes and uses for culinary, medicinal, industrial and other purposes (Lovejoy 1986, 16–17). These salts can be broken down into two major classifications: salt and natron. The former consisted predominately of sodium chloride. The latter was a combination (sometimes erroneously referred to as potash) that included high concentrations of sodium carbonate, sodium sulphate, and other chemicals (Lovejoy 1986, 15).

Lovejoy also provides a discussion of the culinary uses of salt in 18th- and 19th-century Central Africa. Whereas salt was used as a condiment, usually sprinkled on food after it was cooked, Africans seasoned their foods with salt before cooking, using it to enhance the flavor of food (Lovejoy 1986, 18).

Although Curtin determines that slave mortality had little to do with salt (and water) depletion and more to do with respiratory illness (Curtin 1992), it seems highly likely that slaves died from a combination of the two, along with the various other illnesses to which they were susceptible. Although there may be no evidence that the dietary trauma experienced during the Middle Passage is the source of African Americans' difficulty in metabolizing salt, it is also logical to explore the possibility that dietary habits forced on slaves during the period of enslavement initiated dietary habits that, having persisted in the present day, account for the high incidence of hypertension among African Americans and Caribbeans. Salted meats and fish continue to be a staple of African Diasporic cuisine, even though many are moving toward more healthful foods. In addition, the socioeconomic conditions of most Africans in the Americas limit them to the very types of food that are least healthful, precisely because they are inexpensive and thus often the only ones that they can afford. Fresh fruits and vegetables and unprocessed, low-sodium foods tend to be extremely expensive and are often not offered in large supply in the communities in which they live.

Besides its relationship with health concerns, salt can also be read in connection with spiritual health and well-being at the level of protection from evil. *Drums and Shadow: Survival Studies among the Georgia Coastal Negroes* (Georgia Writers Project 1986) contains several accounts by African American southerners of salt being used to prevent or dissipate evil, complete with the African origins of some of these beliefs, such as methods for keeping witches and evil spirits away. The root of this belief is found in a narrative amongst the Vai of Liberia: "when a witch comes to your house to ride you at night, he takes off his skin and lays it aside in the house. It is believed that the witch may be killed by sprinkling salt and pepper in certain portions of the room, which will prevent the witch from putting on his skin. Just before they go to bed it is a common thing to see Vais people sprinkling salt and pepper about" (Georgia Writers Project 1986, 264). This is probably one of the roots of the mythology of the "soucouyant" of Trinidad, or the "witch women" of Jamaica, who slip out of their skins at night and travel about as glowing balls of flames, usually sucking the blood of unsuspecting men, women, and children. In her essay "Hoodoo in America: Conjure Stories," Zora Neale Hurston (1931) told of a good woman who after discovering a witch waited until she took off her skin and left it lying on the floor. The good woman then sprinkled salt and pepper on the witch's skin (Liggins-Hill et al. 1998, 66).

The narrative of flight, which permeates African diasporic folklore and spirituals, often includes a discussion of salt as an impediment to spiritual flight. In tales of "flying Africans," the consumption of salt prevents enslaved Africans from escaping bondage by making their spirits too heavy to fly. Earl Lovelace uses a version of a flying Africans tale in relationship to salt to begin his famous novel entitled *Salt* (1996, 3). References to salt abound, beyond the biblical, into African, African American, and Caribbean literature—including Toni Cade Bambara's *The Salt Eaters* (1980), Edouard Glissant's *Black Salt* (1999), and Nalo Hopkinson's *The Salt Roads* (2004)—and figure prominently in rituals of West African origin. Lorna McDaniel provides a discussion of salt as a hindrance to spiritual transcendence and as a means of persecution in *The Big Drum Ritual of Carriacou: Praisesongs for Rememory of Flight* (1998). In the various rituals connected with the Big Drum, food offerings to ancestors and river and sea orisas are not prepared with salt.

Participants can consume salt, but only in small amounts (Liggins-Hill et al. 1998, 66). McDaniel argues that overconsumption of salt is as much a part of African diasporic physical history and consciousness as is the insistence on avoidance of it. Again, salt makes the spirit too heavy to fly. Although the consumption of salt would be necessary under the conditions of slavery (for the purpose of water retention in the hot sun), overconsumption also leads to hypertension and various other health problems.

The issue of salt, then, is very important for African diasporic representations of flight. In African diasporic mythology, spirits are the only beings that can travel all over the world, and they do not eat salt. In several belief systems (Shango, Candomblé, Santería), foods prepared for the ancestors never contain salt. This belief in the spiritual benefits of avoiding salt is also held by Rastafarians and participants in the Kumina tradition, according to Clinton Hutton and Nathaniel Samuel Murrell (1998), who argue that many Rastafarians believe the salt-heavy diet imposed on enslaved peoples in plantation society was designed to adulterate their minds and render their spirits too heavy to fly home free to Africa. Many Kumunists believe ancestral spirits do not need or eat salt for this reason (Hutton and Murrell 1998, 46).

These multiple metaphors/narratives of flight and the usage or nonusage of salt unite African diasporic cultural traditions, mythology, and ritual. African Diaspora experience is characterized by constant negotiation between a past marked by constant upheaval, adversity, and struggle, and a present and future filled with the legacy of creative, practical, linguistic, and psychological resistance. Fully aware of the "salt of hardship" in all of its forms, African-descended peoples have mastered the art of separating out of this hardship just what is needed for survival.

Meredith M. Gadsby

See also Middle Passage; Sugar Cane and the African Diaspora.

FURTHER READING

Bambara, Toni Cade. 1980. *The Salt Eaters*. New York: Random House.

Buhnen, Stephen. 1996. "Brothers, Chiefdoms, and Empires: On Jan Jansen's 'The Representation of Status in Mande.'" *History in Africa*, Vol. 23, 111–120.

Curtin, Philip. 1992. "The Slavery Hypothesis for Hypertension Among African Americans: The Historical Evidence." *American Journal of Public Health* 3 (12): 1681–1686.

Davis, Wade. 1985. *The Serpent and the Rainbow*. New York: Simon and Schuster.

Ferguson, Moira. 1987. *The History of Mary Prince: A West Indian Slave*. London: Pandora.

Georgia Writers Project. 1986. *Drums and Shadows: Survival Studies Among the Georgia Coastal Negroes [by the] Savannah Unit, Georgia Writers' Project, Work Projects Administration*. 1940. Athens: University of Georgia Press.

Glissant, Edouard. 1999. *Black Salt*. Ann Arbor: University of Michigan Press.

Hopkinson, Nalo. 2003. *The Salt Roads*. New York: Warner Books.

Hurston, Zora Neale. 1931. "Hoodoo in America: Conjure Stories." *Journal of American Folk Lore* 44: 404–405.

Hutton, Clinton, and Nathaniel Samuel Murrell. 1998. "Rastas Psychology of Blackness, Resistance, and Somebodiness." In *Chanting Down Babylon: The Rastafari Reader,* ed. Nathaniel Samuel Murrell, William David Spencer, and Adrian Anthony McFarlane, 36–54. Kingston, Jamaica: Ian Randle Publishers.

Liggins-Hill, Patricia et al. 1998. *Call and Response: The Riverside Anthology of the African American Literary Tradition*. Boston and New York: Houghton Mifflin.

Lovejoy, Paul. 1986. *Salt of the Desert Sun: A History of Salt Production and Trade in the Central Sudan*. New York: Cambridge University Press.

Lovelace, Earl. 1996. *Salt*. London: Faber and Faber.

McDaniel, Lorna. 1998. *The Big Drum Ritual of Carriacou: Praisesongs for Rememory of Flight*. Gainesville: University Press of Florida.

Murrell, Nathaniel Samuel, William David Spencer, and Adrian Anthony McFarlane, eds. 1998. *Chanting Down Babylon. The Rastafari Reader*. Kingston, Jamaica: Ian Randle Publishers.

Perinbam, Marie. 1996. "The Salt-Gold Alchemy in the Eighteenth and Nineteenth Century

Mande World: If Men Are Its Salt, Women Are Its Gold." *History in Africa* 23: 257–278.

Wilson, Thomas W. 1986. "Africa, Afro-Americans, and Hypertensions: An Hypothesis." *Social Science History* 10: 489–500.

Wilson, Thomas W. 1986. "Salt Supplies in West Africa and Blood Pressures Today." *Lancet* 1: 784–786.

Wilson, Thomas W., and C. E. Grim. 1991. "Biohistory of Slavery and Blood Pressure Differences in Blacks Today: A Hypothesis." *Hypertension* 17 (suppl 1): 122–128.

Salvador da Bahia

São Salvador da Bahia de Todos os Santos, generally known as Salvador, or simply Bahia, is the capital of the northeastern Brazilian state of Bahia. It is located at 13° south latitude and 38° west longitude, at the tip of the peninsula that divides the Bay of All Saints (*Bahia de Todos os Santos*) from the Atlantic Ocean. The population of urban Salvador in 2007 is estimated at approximately 2.9 million inhabitants, and a total of approximately 3.7 million inhabitants live in the entire metropolitan region. This makes Salvador the largest city in the Brazilian northeast, the fourth largest city in Brazil, and one of the ten largest cities in Latin America.

Salvador is famous throughout Brazil and throughout the world as a center of Afro-Brazilian music, religion, cuisine, and culture. It is home to millions of Brazilians of African descent and has been known at least since the 1930s as the Black Rome (*Roma Negra*) of the Americas. Today, black movement activists call it "an African nation called Bahia."

Salvador's first known European settler was Diogo Alvarez, known as Caramuru, a shipwrecked sailor who married an indigenous Tupinambá princess (later christened Catarina Paraguassú) and facilitated the city's early colonization by the Portuguese. European settlement began in earnest in 1549 with the arrival

of Tomé de Souza's embarcation. Salvador remained the largest city and the capital of Portugal's American colony until 1763 when the capital moved to Rio de Janeiro. Salvador was invaded and briefly occupied by the Dutch in 1624. In 1823, the city was the site of Bahia's brief war of independence from Portugal (the rest of Brazil had already won its independence in 1822).

The importation of enslaved Africans to the city of Salvador began in the mid 16th century. It entered its most intense period from 1790 through 1831 when slavery was officially banned. A clandestine trade in African slaves extended until 1850 and beyond, however. Salvador was a major market for enslaved Africans especially from the regions around the Bight of Benin as well as the kingdom of Kongo and Angola. In 1888, Brazil became the last American country to ban slavery. Most of the Africans imported to Bahia worked in the sugar cane and tobacco plantations of the fertile Recôncavo region around the Bay of All Saints. The sugar produced in Bahia was shipped out through Salvador's bustling ports and provided the city's wealth in its colonial heyday. The enslaved and free Afro-Brazilians in the city of Salvador itself performed a bewildering variety of occupations, working as porters, stevedores, barbers, musicians, domestic servants, street vendors of food and farm products, skilled artisans, tailors, and dockworkers. Many of Salvador's enslaved people worked for pay and were eventually able to purchase their own freedom. This, along with other roads to freedom, precipitated the growth of a class of free Brazilians of African descent. These individuals were crucial for the development of Salvador's Afro-Brazilian religious institutions and the leadership of its slave insurrections.

In addition to this class of free Afro-Brazilians, the peripheral neighborhoods and forests around Salvador were home to many communities of escaped slaves called *quilombos*. Salvador saw a series of slave rebellions in the early

19th century, the most famous of which was the Malê Revolt of 1835, led by African Muslims.

The 19th century also saw the rise of Candomblé in Salvador and the Bahian Recôncavo. The city is home to the most famous temples of Candomblé in Brazil. These *terreiros* attract followers and clients from throughout the country and throughout the world. Famous priestesses of Candomblé, like Menininha de Gantois and Aninha de Opô Afonjá, called Salvador home.

Salvador's African heritage also gave it an extraordinarily rich musical culture. Many of Brazil's famous musical styles, including samba, afoxé, axé music, samba reggae, pagode, and even MPB (or Brazilian popular music) arose in the city or its immediate hinterlands and carnival. Salvador's culinary tradition incorporates many recipes and ingredients of African provenance, including peanut flour, dried shrimp, red palm oil (*dendé*), and okra.

Salvador is divided into a lower city (*Cidade Baixa*), home to the bulk of the city's industry, markets, ports, and commercial districts, and an upper city (*Cidade Alta*), which has most of the residential districts. The two are joined by steep alleys called *Ladeiras*, funicular inclined planes, and the famous landmark, the *Elevador Lacerda*.

Salvador's historic center was restored from decrepitude and transformed into a tourist district after being designated a United Nations Educational, Scientific, and Cultural Organization World Heritage Site in 1985. As part of this push to restore the historic center to its colonial beauty, many of the neighborhood's Afro-Brazilian residents were forced from their homes and relocated to urban slums or distant, impoverished suburbs. The *Pelourinho*, as the tourist district is known today, takes its name from the pillory or whipping post where African and Afro-Brazilian slaves received public punishment for infractions against their masters.

Like most of Brazil, the city of Salvador is characterized by vast disparities of wealth, which is reflected in the city's geography where both gleaming apartment buildings and slums exist.

These inequalities coincide largely (though by no means completely) with differences in skin color. The vast majority of Salvador's urban poor are phenotypically darker than its elite. Bahia's system of racial classification is often described as being based on a continuum. Interactions among people of different skin colors are largely cordial giving rise to the phenomenon of "cordial or cynical racism" in which color prejudice is maintained in education, access, the job market, and in the city's elite public spaces.

Brian Brazeal

See also Brazil: Afro-Brazilians; Cachoeira; Candomblé; Carnival; Filhos de Gandhy; Ilê Aiyê; Lino Alves de Almeida, José (1958–2006); Middle Passage; Olodum; Transatlantic Slave Trade.

FURTHER READING

Freyer, Peter. 2000. *Rhythms of Resistance: African Musical Heritage in Brazil.* Hanover: Wesleyan University Press.

Instituto Brasileiro de Geografia e Estadística www.ibge.gov.br/english/ (accessed January 22, 2008).

Mattoso, Katia. 1991. *Bahia, Século XIX: Uma Provincia no Império.* Rio de Janeiro, Brazil: Editora Nova Fronteira.

Pierson, Donald. 1942. *Negroes in Brazil: A Study of Race Contact at Bahia.* Chicago: University of Chicago Press.

Reis, João José. 1991. *A Morte é Uma Festa: Ritos Funebres e Revolta Popular no Brasil do Século XIX.* São Paulo: Compania de Letras.

Reis, João José. 1993. *Slave Rebellion in Brazil: The Muslim Uprising of 1835 in Bahia,* trans. Arthur Brakel. Baltimore: Johns Hopkins University Press.

Sansone, Livio. 2003. *Blackness Without Ethnicity: Constructing Race in Brazil.* New York: Palgrave.

Samba

Samba is the popular song and dance form of Brazil in a syncopated 2/4 time with emphasis on the second beat. Traditionally played by strings, such as the *cavaquinho* (a small four-stringed guitarlike instrument), and percussion, such as the *pandeiro* (a tambourine) and *tamborim* (a smaller *pandeiro* played with a stick), samba is characterized by the persistent drumbeat of African spiritual ceremonies and a repertory of lyrical themes. As one of the more famous cultural expressions of Africans in Brazil, samba embodies the ideas of solace, celebration, culture, identity, philosophy, and tradition. Samba and its informal samba gathering are at once popular music, a genre, and an urban phenomenon that emerged in the *favelas* (impoverished areas) of Rio de Janeiro at the start of the 20th century.

The origin of the term "samba" is said to be "semba," an expression found in the Kôngo-Angola region of west central Africa where many of the enslaved Africans in Brazil were acquired. The historical evidence suggests that samba was not created in 20th-century Rio de Janeiro, as the term was used in 19th-century Brazil to generally refer to a polyrhythmic dance accompanied by percussion, and that those who are credited with samba's emergence in Rio de Janeiro came from Bahia in northeast Brazil. Movement from northeast Brazil to Rio de Janeiro when slavery was abolished in 1888 allowed for the development of "houses" that functioned as sites of socialization and culture. One of the principal houses was that of Hilária Batista de Almeida (also known as Tia Ciata), who was a practitioner of Candomblé and one of the key persons responsible for samba and carnival in Rio de Janeiro. Samba coexisted with the transmission of the spiritual values and practices of Candomblé, an African-derived spiritual system adhered to in Brazil.

The musical genre of samba was crystallized with the 1917 carnival hit "*Pelo Telefone*" (On the Telephone) by Donga. Regarded by most as the first samba recording, this song was composed at Almeida's house and soon carried the new music outside the *favelas*. Houses like Almeida's were gathering sites for musicians of African descent, and many of the famous *sambistas* (those who compose, sing, or play samba) were assiduous visitors. Notable *sambistas* include João da Baiana, Pixinguinha, Sinhô, Caninha, Heitor dos Prazeres, Nelson Cavaquinho, Clara Nunes, Noel Rosa, Adoniran Barbosa, Paulinho da Viola, Martinho da Vila, Cartola, and Bezerra da Silva. The traditional form of samba in Rio de Janeiro came to be known as *samba de morro* (samba of the impoverished hillside areas). *Samba-exaltação* (samba of praise) and *samba-canção* and the efforts of white Brazilian composers to popularize songs for white middle-class consumption overshadowed *samba de morro*. Several samba musicians countered this longstanding cooptation by the larger society with cultural resistance in the form of a dual *samba-pagode* current; the first current of the 1970s and 1980s reflected the roots of samba, while the other more commercialized current of the early 1990s replaced the older styles in the media. The latter current represents an international African-Brazilian aesthetic, while the former embodies a national, tradition-bound African-Brazilian expression. The current forms of samba in Brazil, including *samba-reggae* and *samba de roda*, exist in the domain of popular culture, while *escolas de samba* (Samba schools) or large-scale, organized carnival parade groups are exploited by the tourism industry. The stereotypical icons of samba lyrics, that is, the *malandro* (smooth-talking hustler), *mulata* (sensual black woman), and *otário* (utterly unintelligent person), underscore the issues of race, the paradox of African cultural life in Brazilian society, and samba as a site for simultaneous cultural innovation, resistance, and cooptation.

Kwasi Konadu

See also Brazil: Afro-Brazilians; Carnival; Salvador da Bahia; Samba Schools.

FURTHER READING
Guimarães, Fernando. 1978. *Na roda do samba.* Rio de Janeiro, Brazil: Funarte.

Shaw, Lisa. 1999. *The Social History of the Brazilian Samba*. Brookfield, VT: Ashgate.

Sodré, Muniz. 1998. *Samba, o dono do corpo.* Rio de Janeiro, Brazil: Mauad.

Samba Schools

Samba is Brazil's national rhythm. Once repressed and marginalized because it belonged to the oppressed Afro-descendants, it has become a natural treasure, Brazil's national identity, and the centerpiece of carnival. Its presence in the festival is ultimate proof of the Africanity of carnival. Samba schools are big associations constituted into *Liga das Escolas de Samba do Rio* (League of Rio Samba Schools) governed by special law. The competition is astonishingly competitive for the annual prize as champion of carnival. The schools are divided into two groups: schools in the Special Group parade on Sunday and Monday, and schools in the Second Division parade on Friday and Saturday. The winner is announced on Ash Wednesday after the jury's deliberations. A queen is also elected annually. The importance of the event is comparable to the final of the World Cup competition in football (soccer), a sport synonymous with Brazil. Each school, mostly cariocas, has about 4,000 members. Some participants from elsewhere in Brazil, or from foreign countries, also join, and each member pays about $1,000 for a fancy dress, without which one cannot parade. A structure called the *sambodromo*, which was specially constructed by Oscar Niemeyer, the architect who created Brazil's gorgeous capital, Brasilia, was unveiled in 1984; it serves as a viewing point of the parade and the culmination of the festival. If Rio's carnival is a spectacle of endless love, or orgy, with beautiful women baring their breasts and lustful men ogling and hugging them, if it is the quintessential moment of merriment marked by the syncopated and pulsating beat of the samba, it is also the epitome of capitalistic commercialism. It is an industry bringing in foreign currency to the tune of billions.

It is interesting to note that the rhythm of samba has evolved over the years according to the demands and dictates of the carnival parade, and heated debate has always been attached to the "real roots" of the music. One aspect has remained constant: samba has resisted the use of electric instruments and other forms of "modern" music. The crystallization of the music occurred in Rio within the carnival-parading samba schools in the 1930s. Thus, *samba de morro* (referring to the hills where the ghettos, or *favelas*, were located) became a national cultural symbol, and sambistas have traced its origin back to Africa.

The first parade of a samba school took place in 1929, when *Deixa Falar* (Free Speech) was led by "people of ill repute" on horses furnished by the military police. From then on the schools were given government subsidies. By 1935, samba schools' parade was a fixture on officialdom's published program. Rio's major newspaper, *O Globo*, became sponsor, establishing regulations, including the requirement that each group must have women dressed as Baianas (legendary women wearing traditional dress from the Afro state of Bahia).

In 1937, the nationalist dictatorship of Getúlio Vargas decreed that samba schools must present, as part of their dramatized parade, didactic themes based on history and patriotism. That model was later extended to other parts of the country. As the population became more culturally aware and more politically progressive, beyond the restricted vision of the dictatorship, African themes came to enter the horizon of depiction.

Samba schools have long attracted foreign cultural figures, such as Walt Disney, Josephine Baker, and the Japanese painter Tzuguharu Fujita, who, upon returning to his country, founded a samba band at the National School of Fine Arts. Samba schools have been invited to play at presidential events. In recent times, samba schools have honored Brazil's superstars of music. Not only are they included in the parade, but themes are created in their honor: such was the case at the 1994 carnival when one of the most respectable schools, *Mangueira*, paid homage to the Bahian musicians Gilberto Gil (currently minister of culture), Gal Costa, and Maria Bethânia. Indeed, samba is Brazil's national music, and samba schools are an integral and essential aspect of almighty carnival.

Femi Ojo-Ade

See also Brazil: Afro-Brazilians; Carnival; Samba.

FURTHER READING
Vianna, Hermano. 1999. *Samba.* Chapel Hill: University of North Carolina Press.

Samedi/Baron Samedi

Baron Samedi is an immensely popular deity in the Haitian Vodoun pantheon. He is the most commonly seen member of the *Gede* family of Haitian *Loa* who are often considered to be spirits of the dead. He presides over cemeteries and crossroads and the spirits of the dead. His typical iconography includes a black top hat and long black coat, his face painted like a skull, glasses or sunglasses, and a cane often adorned with an erect phallus. The name Baron Samedi is probably a Haitian Creole (*Kreyol*) derivation from the French words for Saturday and cemetery.

The Baron possesses his followers (called *serviteurs*) at parties and in ritual contexts and they don some version of the aforementioned clothing. He is the last to arrive at a Vodoun ceremony but few Vodoun ceremonies end without an appearance of the Baron and the other *Gede*. His typical possession behaviors include singing and dancing lewdly, making lascivious comments to spectators in his typi-

cal high-pitched nasal voice, miming coitus, eating gluttonously, drinking heavily, and smoking cigars, pipes, and cigarettes.

But the Baron is taken very seriously. He may offer his clients and devotees helpful advice on a range of problems from romantic difficulties to employment. He advises them of when they are under the influence of witchcraft, and he can be invoked to wreak revenge on his follower's enemies. He is well loved and deeply feared.

Baron Samedi often serves as a social censurer. He insults all and sundry at possession parties, but especially the rich. He exposes hypocrisy and illicit affairs. He condemns the ungenerous. He is also the deity most often invoked in witchcraft and black magic.

His devotees offer him candles and copious amounts of *clarin* (raw sugar cane liquor) and rum as well as candy and coins at cemeteries and crossroads. The Baron's altars are adorned with crosses, iron chains, and wooden penises. All Souls' Day (November 1) is the Baron's holiday par excellence. He leaves the cemetery and goes out into the world. On one occasion in the 1950s a troop of *serviteurs* possessed by Baron Samedi and other *Gede* processed to the governmental palace in Port-au-Prince, Haiti, and demanded money from the president, who promptly paid up.

Baron Samedi is also invoked in the creation of *Zombis*. Haitian *Zombi* are not necessarily the soulless walking dead depicted in North American horror movies. In some aspects of the mythology, they are spirits of the dead, caught in bottles and used to help their owners. Baron Samedi must be invoked before graves can be opened to get the bones that are essential ingredients of such *Zombi*.

Although Haitian Vodoun is usually thought to be derived from the Vodoun religions of old Dahomey (present day Benin and Togo), Baron Samedi is a uniquely Haitian deity without any obvious parallels elsewhere in the religions of the African Diaspora. François "Papa Doc" Duvalier, dictator of Haiti from 1957 to 1971, intentionally adopted the imagery and the voice of Baron Samedi in his public appearances and even in his cabinet meetings to signal his devotion to the malevolent forces of Vodoun and strike fear into the hearts of his people and his government ministers.

Brian Brazeal

See also Haiti; Vodoun.

FURTHER READING
Ackerman, Hans, and Jeanine Gauthier. 1991. "The Ways and Nature of the Zombi." *Journal of American Folklore* 104 (414): 466–494.
Cosentino, Donald, ed. 1985. *Sacred Arts of Haitian Vodou*. Los Angeles: University of California, Fowler Museum of Cultural History.
Cosentino, Donald, ed. 1987. "Who Is that Fellow in the Many Colored Cap?: Transformations of Eshu in Old and New World Mythologies." *Journal of American Folklore* 100 (37): 261–275.
Dunham, Katherine. 1969. *Island Possessed*. New York: Doubleday.
Hurston, Zora Neale. 1938. *Tell My Horse*. Philadelphia: J.B. Lippincott Company.

San Mateo de Cangrejos

San Mateo de Cangrejos was a Puerto Rican town founded by maroons from neighboring Caribbean islands. In 1664, while under Spanish rule, Puerto Rico began recognizing escaped slaves from non-Spanish islands as free men and women, on the condition that they swore loyalty to the Spanish king and agreed to be baptized into the Catholic faith. Most of those seeking refuge came from English or Dutch islands. In time a community of runaway slaves developed in an area located near the capital city of San Juan. By 1710 more than 80 people inhabited this area, and in 1714 Governor Juan de Rivera officially granted this land to the refugees. Each man was given the usufruct of two cuerdas (1.94 acres) of land and materials to build a home. Most became cassava farmers. In 1773, Cangrejos became a town. By this time, more than 800 people were living in the area. The same year, an auxiliary militia unit was created with men living in the area. Known as the "Morenos de Cangrejos," they distinguished themselves in battle against invaders. Today the area of San Mateo de Cangrejos is called Santurce.

Lorraine Rivera-Newberry

See also Puerto Rico: Afro-Puerto Ricans.

FURTHER READING
Puerto Rico Reconstruction Administration. 1940. *Puerto Rico, a Guide to the Island of Borinquen*. New York: The University Society.
Tovar, Federico R. 1973. *A Chronological History of Puerto Rico*. New York: Plus Ultra Educational Publishers.

Sancho, Ignatius (1729–1780)

Ignatius Sancho was born aboard a slave ship off Guinea (West Africa) in 1729 and baptized with the name Ignatius at Carthegena, where he was taken to the Spanish West Indies with his parents, both of whom died shortly after, his mother of "a disease of the new climate" and his father by suicide. At a little over the age of two, Sancho's master took him to England where he became the property of three disagreeable sisters living at Greenwich who surnamed him Sancho after an imagined resemblance to the squire of Cervante's *Don Quixote*. In the belief that African ignorance was the surest insurance for his obedience, the three sisters shut the doors of education against the young Sancho. But Sancho was soon to be rescued by the Duke of Montagu who, on accidentally seeing him, immediately took a liking to him and frequently brought him home to Blackheath where he encouraged his wife to tutor Sancho in reading, much to the annoyance of his mistresses who threatened to send him back to African slavery. After the death of Montagu, Sancho fled to the duchess for protection. There he remained a butler until her death, when he found himself favored by a bequest of 70 pounds and an annuity of 30 pounds from her will.

Sancho married a young West Indian woman whom he loved dearly, and he frequently mentions her in his letters. Toward the end of 1773, "repeated attacks of gout, and a constitutional corpulence" forced him to retire from the duke's family and to set up a grocery shop with his wife. Through hard work and thrift, they were able to raise a large family and live a fairly decent and stable life. However, Sancho died in December 1780.

The letters of Ignatius Sancho, written mainly during his years as a grocer, were published in London in 1782 under the title, *Letters of the Late Ignatius Sancho, An African, to which are prefixed Memoirs of His Life by Joseph Jekyll, Esz., M.P.* The letters cover a wide variety of subjects and reflect the philosophy of the Age of Enlightenment and its neoclassical style. They reveal a mind nourished by intense and sensitive reading and understanding of the writings of his contemporaries (such as Alexander Pope and Laurence Sterne) and the classical greats they often imitated. Sancho also wrote poetry in the neoclassical style and even attempted two pieces for the stage, but these have not been located as yet. In addition, he composed and published music (described in *Ignatius Sancho—An Early African Composer in England*) and distinguished himself as an art critic. Although he barely discusses slavery, black freedom, his Africanness, and his experience of racism, the eloquence, clarity, sophistication, humor, and philosophical insights of his letters seem to have provoked many English readers to reconsider their prejudices toward Africans and the African World.

Chukwuma Azuonye

See also United Kingdom: The African Diaspora.

FURTHER READING
Azuonye, Chukwuma, and Steven Serafin, eds. Forthcoming. *The Columbia Anthology of African Literature.* New York: Columbia University Press.

Dathorne, O. R. 1974. *The Black Mind: A History of African Literature.* Minneapolis: University of Minnesota Press.

Gikandi, Simon, ed. 2003. *Encyclopedia of African Literature.* New York: Routledge.

Herdeck, Donald E. 1974. *African Authors: A Companion to Black African Writing, Volume 1: 1300–1973.* Washington, D.C: Inscape Corporation.

Irele, F. Abiola, and Simon E. Girkandi, eds. 2004. *The Cambridge History of Africa and Caribbean Literature.* 2 Vols. Cambridge, UK: Cambridge University Press.

Jahn, Janheinz. 1968. *Neo-African Literature: A History of Black Writing.* New York: Grove.

Jahn, Janheinz, Ulla Schild, and Almut Nordmann. 1972. *Who's Who in African Literature: Biographies, Works, Commentaries.* Tübingen, Germany: Horst Erdmann Verlag.

Killam, Douglas, and Ruth Rowe, eds. 2000. *The Companion to African Literatures.* Bloomington: Indiana University Press.

King, Reyahn, et al. 1997. *Ignatius Sancho: An African Man of Letters.* London: National Portrait Gallery.

Sancho, Ignatius. 1782 (1803). *Letters of the Late Ignatius Sancho, an African: to which are prefixed Memoirs of His Life by Joseph Jekyll.* London.

Sankofa

The film *Sankofa,* written and directed by Ethiopian-born filmmaker Haile Gerima, was made in 1993 under his own Mypheduh Films and was coproduced by his wife, filmmaker Shirikiana Aina. The film took its title from an Akan concept that means "one must return and repair the past in order to move forward." The groundbreaking independent film tells the story of Mona (played by Oyafunmike Ogunlano), a high fashion model who, while being photographed at Cape Coast Castle in Ghana, is reproached by an old man for forgetting her past. Instantly, she is transported back to the days of slavery where she becomes Shola, a house slave whose lover, Shango (played by Jamaican dub poet Mutabaruka), is caught up in the quest for freedom. The African-born slave Nunu (Alexandra Duah), whose mulatto son attempts to thwart their efforts, leads the struggle for freedom on the plantation. Shola, who is constantly abused by the master, eventually takes her fate into her own hands.

Sankofa explores the multiple social levels of slavery in the United States, including the issues of division and loyalty within the slave communities, maroons (escaped slaves recreating African communities), and the schism between African and Western ways.

The feature-length film was produced for less than $1 million and, despite critical acclaim, received no interest from major studios for distribution. This was attributed to the controversial content along with the fact that no major stars appeared in the film.

With knowledge of the difficulties of distributing independent films with a distinctly black perspective, Gerima and Aina initially rented a theater, where the film played for an unprecedented 11 weeks. They used the profit to create copies of the film to be shown in alternative venues, such as the Museum of Fine Arts in Boston, where it became an international phenomenon. The initial success of *Sankofa* was due largely to word of mouth among those who had viewed the movie, which eventually traveled to Chicago, Los Angeles, Detroit, and Atlanta. The dramatic film won the 1993 Best Cinematography Award at FESPACO and the 1993 AGIP Grand Prize at the African Cinema Festival in Milan, Italy, among other awards.

Eve M. Ferguson

See also FESPACO and African Film Festivals; Gerima, Haile (1946–); Mulatta; Mutabaruka (1952–); Shango.

FURTHER READING

Alexander, George. 1993. *Why We Make Movies: Black Filmmakers Talk About the Magic of Cinema.* New York: Harlem Moon.
Sankofa. 1993. Washington, D.C.: Mypheduh Films.

Santería

Santería is a Spanish word for the belief system of Yoruba heritage that developed among Cuba's African and African-derived populations. But it refers also to the similar system practiced in places like Puerto Rico, the Dominican Republic, and Latino communities in the United States. The word *Santería* comes from the Spanish "*santos*" or "saints" and means "of the saints" or "the religion of the saints" in English. The religion was created by enslaved Africans as they confronted Roman Catholic Church teachings. It is important to note that both Catholic and African religious understandings included the belief that the Supreme Being could make his desires known through the saints.

Santería members report alternative names for Santería: *Lukumí, Yoruba, Ocha,* and *Regla de Ocha. Ulukumí,* although not thoroughly substantiated, is thought to be a place, region, or city in ancient Yoruba-land, southeastern Nigeria and the Republic of Benin today (Castellanos in Lindsay 1996, 39–41). Eventually, the regional designation became a term for the many types of related Yoruba groups who left West African ports and landed in Cuba as *Lukumís* or *Lucumís.* In Cuba, the word *Lukumí* became a way of greeting friends, as well as an alternative name for the Spanish *Regla de Ocha*—literally, "The *Oricha* Order or Rule/Law" (see Brandon 1993 for *Santería* history). Although Santería is not always the preferred term, all refer to one West African worship practice of Yoruba heritage in which the Orishas are present.

Researchers have noted intra-African as well as Catholic-African syncretism among the religions that formed in the Americas, including Santería (Walker 1980; Daniel 2005). An example of intra-African syncretism can be seen in the interspersed prayers, songs, and dances, or sometimes whole rites, from Kongo-Angola or central African tradition into Yoruba settings or in the interchange of Yoruba and Arará (another West African religion of Cuba) names. Often, time and attention are given to "old Congo spirits" when they arrive in a public Santería service or when they are invoked in private as a separate part of Yoruba practice. At times, names of Yoruba *orichas* are interchangeable with Palo spiritual entities (*nkisis*), for example, Ogun and Sarabanda, or with Arará spiritual entities (*vodunes*), like Chango and Gebioso. Historically, intra-African syncretism is caused by joining two or more differing religions in one family, usually one from the maternal and the other from the paternal side. Children then practice both religions, and over time, practices combine as members try to be respectful to both ancestral traditions.

SANTERÍA, LUKUMÍ, AND YORUBA BELIEFS

Worshipers within this and similar African American religions understand Santería as a balancing of spiritual and material energies, individual and cosmic concerns, and practical and theoretical philosophies. They surround themselves with or attend carefully to nature (plants, herbs, animals, wind, earth, fire, and water) and combine natural objects with spiritual objectives. They perform devotional prayers of praise and follow a priestly caste of male and female leaders, called *santeros (as)*, who pray for and advise, heal, and cure the extended religious family. These spiritual leaders also acknowledge a higher caste of divining priests, called babalawos, who study the philosophic principles of the oracle of Ifa and who counsel and direct religious practice also. Some Santería members express allegiance to Santería, but rely mostly on their Roman Catholic devotion and the Catholic clergy.

More often, members are born into Santería or initiated in as *iyawos*. They construct and maintain altars for the saints in their homes. An *iyawo* studies for several months before initiation ceremonies, for one year after initiation, and fully completes obligations after seven years of service to the ritual community. At the time of death, members are ritually incorpo-

rated into the ancestor realm (to live with the most ancient ancestors called Eguns) through organized funereal services.

Orichas, the Yoruba divinities, were transported from their home territories in what are now Nigeria and Benin, across the Bight of Benin, to the Caribbean and Latin America (particularly Haiti, Cuba, Brazil, and Trinidad); there, they were transposed into or at least discussed in terms of *santos* or saints. A huge difference between Yoruba-land religious practices and those in the Americas was the joining of all the *orichas* into one religious liturgy, as opposed to worshipping each *oricha* on his or her own soil. This profound reconfiguration of African religious thought into an African American religion called Santería occurred in Cuba, but Yoruba beliefs and practices are now found within niches of transnationality in the United States and elsewhere around the globe—from Canada to Chile to Finland to Japan.

Two prominent characteristics of Santería (and Roman Catholicism also) are beliefs in life after death and the existence of divine, human-like spirits or saints. Santería worshipers believe that the life force or *ache* that is within everyone and everything comes from God, or the Supreme Being, in Catholic terms, and from Olofi, Oludumare, or Olorun, and others in *Santería*. The saints or *orichas* have influence with the Supreme Being and are "more available" or close to the human community. Worshipers believe nothing truly dies at death, but lives on in different realms and forms within the universe. They believe that the *orichas* live in Orun, a cosmic realm of the universe, and that they come to earth when invoked properly or when needed, in accordance with their function of guiding and protecting the religious community. Worshipers believe humans may leave their bodies in the human realm at death, but their *ache* goes to live with the ancestors. Therefore, the dead are alive in the ancestor realm, a different location in the Yoruba worldview than the human realm (Bascom 1969; Daniel 2005, 81–82, 84–85).

Like all of the dominant religions, Santería has spiritual transformation as its objective. The ideal and most preferred transformation is from an ordinary human to a godly or spiritual being, and transformation is the goal of many Santería services; also, ideally, the experience of transformation should linger beyond a single religious service and should affect behavior and attitudes in other nonreligious settings. In Santería, this idea is expanded to the idea of an extended family of believers within the social world. It begins and ends, however, with the believing individual in her or his relationship with nature and a very populated spiritual world.

Santería devotees believe in multiple aspects of God, just as many Judeo-Christians believe. In their view, different aspects of God are responsible for particular domains of social life. For example, Oludumare is the creative aspect of God; he or she is not the dimension of God that they would call on for troubles with their agricultural or business concerns or for protection against imminent danger. She or he is thought to be too far away, while the *orichas* Yemanyá or Ogún would be invoked more quickly. Worshipers' methods of efficient spiritual communication are through musical and danced invocations, as well as through prayer and sacrifice—sometimes the sacrifice of the animals that are thought to be associated with each *oricha*. Worshipers say they are "feeding" the *orichas*, but they also treat the spilling of blood as a symbol of serious purpose and commitment (similar to Christians' views of symbolically "eating the body and drinking the blood of Christ" during communion in both Protestant and Catholic religions).

Santería has often been analyzed in terms of its transformative power through ceremonial "spirit possession." The term "possession" is problematic, however, in that it fosters a pejorative estimation of a legitimate African, as well as a legitimate religious, belief. Thoughtful worshipers speak of "manifesting" spiritual energy and "incorporating" or "embodying" the *orichas*. These terms are preferred to the one colonial authorities used to describe culturally-different behaviors among Africans.

RELIGIOUS SERVICES OR CEREMONIES

Private, prayerful services account for much of Santería worship; however, semi-public dance and music ceremonies invoke the *orichas* to commune with the entire religious community. Ceremonies, called *toques* or *bembes* in Spanish or *wemileres* in Yoruba, punctuate a calendar year with celebratory "birthdays" of the *orichas*, as well as "birthdays" or initiation anniversaries of worshipers. *Toques* are structured liturgies that combine drumming, singing, praying, dancing, and divining. As a result, Santería is often regarded as a "dancing religion," and a great number of baptized drummers, drums, and initiates gather for regular services between sunrise and sunset; after sunset other *abericula* (nonbaptized) drums are usually played for services.

Worshipers interpret the life histories of the *orichas* as lessons for human behavior. Proper social relationships and appropriate behaviors are outlined and retold in chants, proverbs, folk tales, and religious liturgy as well as oral, written, and danced histories. These relationships and behaviors are vividly repeated through codified gestures, expressive movement sequences, and a range of kinesthetic responses. Spiritual communication, physical healing, and societal solidarity are confirmed within danced religious services.

In the dances of Santería, the physical body becomes the social body, both the repository of knowledge from the collective memory of a variety of Yoruba ethnic groups and the sensitized reactor to contemporary transnational culture. While in performance, the body is dressed in memory and spiritual clothing; it drinks of archaic chants and ancient rhythms, as well as from synthesized and electronic sound concoctions. It digests and displays organic movements of old, as well as contemporary gestures, until it generates a power within that is capable of transforming self and others.

The *batá* are a group of three drums from the Yoruba culture in Nigeria. (islapercussions.com)

The music liturgy is led by the *akpwon* or lead singer and a chorus of males and females singing in responsorial or call and answer form. They sing a huge vocal literature that is organized into sections for the *orichas*, called *trataos*. Vocalists work simultaneously with trained musicians who play *batá* (or two-headed drums), *güiro* (or beaded gourds), or *Iyesa* drums (specific Yoruba nation drums) from a huge percussion repertory (Amira and Cornelius 1992). And, the dancing is also codified according to the *orichas*.

CONCLUSION

Santería maintains the following features within its worldview: a highly structured initiation process, specifically organized divining and funereal procedures, a richly textured sound, visual and gesture complex, and a sup-porting social kinship or extended family organization. While the worship changed with the transatlantic crossing, many Yoruba principles and precepts on which it was grounded have survived in contemporary devotional communities. Worshipers believe that through initiation, divination, offerings, routine celebrations, and funeral services a believer can grow toward greater spiritual strength, maintain balance in the material world, and learn from the wisdom of the *orichas*. Rites of adoration and petition, including dance, song, and drumming, permit a transformation, a manifestation, or in other views a reincarnation of specific *orichas* or *santos*—and the *orichas* arrive within the body of a worshipping dancer. As drums voice each *oricha's* particular set of rhythms, as chants are sung in archaic ritual languages, and as the worshipping bodies dance, African religious orientation continues as Santería in the Diaspora.

Yvonne Daniel

See also Àshé; Candomblé; Vodoun.

FURTHER READING

Adefunmi, I, Oba Osejiman Adelabu. 1982. *Olorisha, A Guide Book into Yoruba Religion.* Oyotunji Village, SC: Great Benin Books.

Amira, John, and Steven Cornelius. 1992. *The Music of Santería; Traditional Rhythms of the Batá.* Crown Point, IN: West Cliffs Media.

Barnes, Sandra T., ed. 1989. *Africa's Ogun: Old World and New.* Bloomington: Indiana University Press.

Bascom, William. 1950. "The Focus of Cuban Santería." *Southwestern Journal of Anthropology* 6 (1, Spring): 64–68.

Bascom, William. 1969. *Ifa Divination: Communication between Gods and Men in West Africa.* Bloomington: Indiana University Press.

Bascom, William. 1972. *Shango in the New World.* Occasional Publication of the African and Afro-American Research Institute, No. 4. Austin: University of Texas.

Bascom, William. 1980. *Sixteen Cowries: Yoruba Divination from Africa to the New World.* Bloomington: Indiana University Press.

Bolívar, Natalia. 1990. *Los orichas en Cuba.* La Habana, Cuba: Ediciones Union.

Brandon, George. 1993. *Santería from Africa to the New World: The Dead Sell Memories*. Bloomington: Indiana University Press.

Cabrera, Lydia. 1940. *Cuentos negros de Cuba*. Havana, Cuba: La Verónica.

Cabrera, Lydia. 1957. *Anagó: Vocabulario Lucumí*. Havana, Cuba: Ediciones C.R.

Cabrera, Lydia. 1974. *Yemaya y Ochun*. New York: Colección del Chichereku.

Cabrera, Lydia. 1983. *El monte*. Miami: Colección del Chichereku. (Orig. pub. 1954).

Canizares, Raul. 1999. *Cuban Santería*. Rochester, VT: Destiny Books.

Carnet, Carlos. 1973. *Lucumí. Religión de los Yorubas en Cuba*. Miami: AIP Publications Center.

Castellanos, Isabel. 1996. "From Ulkumí to Lucumí." In *Santería Aesthetics in Contemporary Latin American Art*, ed. Arturo Lindsay, 39–41. Washington, D.C.: Smithsonian Institution Press.

Daniel, Yvonne. 2005. *Dancing Wisdom: Embodied Knowledge in Haitian Vodou, Cuban Yoruba, and Bahian Candomblé*. Champaign: University of Illinois Press.

Edwards, Gary, and John Mason. 1985. *Black Gods: Orisa Studies in the New World*. Brooklyn, NY: Yoruba Theological Archministry.

Gleason, Judith. 1987. *Oya, In Praise of the Goddess*. Boston: Shambhala Publication.

Gonzalez-Wippler, Migene. 1973. *Santería: African Magic in Latin America*. New York: Julian Press.

Gonzalez-Wippler, Migene. 1992. *The Santería Experience: A Journey into the Miraculous*. St. Paul, MN: Llewellyn Publications.

Lachatánere, Rómulus. 1942. *Manuel de Santería*. La Habana, Cuba: Editorial Caribe.

Lindsay, Arturo, ed. 1996. *Santería Aesthetics in Contemporary Latin American Art*. Washington, D.C.: Smithsonian Institution Press.

Lucas, Olumide. 1948. *The Religion of the Yorubas*. Lagos, Nigeria: CMS Bookshops.

Mason, John. 1985. *Four New World Yoruba Rituals*. New York: Yoruba Theological Archministry.

Murphy, Joseph. 1988. *Santería: An African Religion in America*. Boston: Beacon Press.

Murphy, Joseph, and Mei-Mei Sanford, eds. 2000. *Osun Across the Waters: A Yoruba Goddess in Africa and the Americas*. Bloomington: Indiana University Press.

Ortiz, Fernando. 1985. *Los bailes y el teatro de los negros en el folklore de Cuba*. La Habana, Cuba: Editorial Letras Cubanas. (Orig. pub. 1951).

Sandoval, Mercedes Cros. 1975. *La religión de los orichas*. Hato Rey, Puerto Rico: Colección Estudios Afrocaribeños.

Simpson, George. 1980. *Black Religions in the New World*. New York: Columbia University Press.

Vega, Marta. 2000. *The Altar of My Soul*. New York: Bantam Books.

Walker, Sheila. 1972. *Ceremonial Spirit Possession in Africa and Afro-America*. Leiden, Holland: E. J. Brill.

Walker, Sheila. 1980. "African Gods in America: The Black Religious Continuum." *Black Scholar* 11 (8): 45–61.

Santiago de Cuba

There is extensive literature on the African roots of Cuban culture. Historians agree that African culture remained a stronger presence in Cuban culture, largely because of the continuance of the "illicit slave trade" up through the end of the 19th century. Thus Yoruba and Congolese religious practices, and the Abakua secret society were able to maintain a certain currency. Larry Crook (1992) traces the origins of the enslaved Africans who were transported to Cuba as being primarily from West and Central Africa. They represented varied ethnic groups, including the Lucumi (Yoruba), Arara (Dahomean), Abakua (Carabali), and various Bantu (Congo) peoples.

HISTORIC DEVELOPMENTS

Santiago de Cuba was founded in 1514 and was the first capital of Cuba, from 1522 to 1589. It was only a few years after Santiago became the capital of Cuba that the first enslaved Africans were transported there. They were the ancestors who sowed the seeds of African matrix cultural traditions in Cuba. Rafael D. Jiménez (2000) affirms that the first *bozales*, that is, Africans born in the continent of Africa, arrived in the village of Santiago in 1522.

Cuba's strategic location in the Caribbean and its large size made it a vital port during the transatlantic enslavement trade. There was a diverse flow of imports and exports that included enslaved Africans who were transported from Africa, other Caribbean islands, South and Central America, and the United States. This allowed for a renewed flow of continental enslaved Africans who constantly replenished African cultural traditions in Cuba during the 350-year transatlantic slave trade. Jimenez estimates that 1.3 million enslaved Africans were imported to Cuba during that period, which endured legally until 1886. Thus Santiago de Cuba, like Salvador da Bahia in Brazil, is one of the African diasporic sites where the African imprint is strongest, and is expressed in the material, spiritual and cultural identity of its people.

The historic background of the extensiveness of the transatlantic slave trade in Cuba can be seen by the large concentration of Africans imported to Cuba. This extensiveness also highlights the constant African cultural renewal that continued past the official 1886 abolition of slavery. Therefore, it also explains the rich and varied African matrix expressions evident in Cuba. Judith Bettelheim (1993) provides further insight into the significance of Santiago de Cuba's contribution to the economic, social, and cultural realms that eventually led to Cuban national identity and cultural traditions. She invokes the recollection of the socioeconomic implications of the enslavement and plantation system in the establishment of Santiago de Cuba in a position of central importance for more than half of the island. In addition, Santiago de Cuba was fundamental in effecting profound cultural changes fundamental to the configuration of a national culture for all Cuban people.

The dominant input in Cuban national culture is African, given the marked presence of African-descended people that have been bearers of the African matrix culture. This prominent African influence in Cuba was attained through the maintenance of African matrix cultural traditions and expressions. Antonio Benítez Rojo (1999) asserts that African music as reinterpreted in the African diaspora was the driving force in creating modern Cuban nationality. In Cuba, national culture is centered on music and dance. Rafael Brea López (1997) attests to the multidimensional significance of music and dance in the Caribbean. He proclaims music and dance to be the most popular artistic expressions in the multicultural Caribbean. López similarly argues for the importance of dance, song and percussion in the structuring of a cultural system that also has existence in the realm of ideas, philosophy and religiosity.

CONTEMPORARY SANTIAGO DE CUBA

As of July 2004, statistics on Cuba indicate an estimated population of 11,308,764. The province of Santiago de Cuba has a population of 1.2 million and the city of Santiago's population is 554,000. Cuba's population is estimated to be 62 percent African descended, including the black and mulatto census categories. Therefore, significantly more than half of Cuba's population can be considered porters of African matrix cultural heritage.

Santiago de Cuba is known to have the best carnival celebrations in Cuba. There are also numerous festivals, which are mostly African matrix cultural productions. The descendants of the African cultural porters who survived the transatlantic enslavement process managed to preserve what can be referred to as African matrix cultural expressions.

Alicia M. Sanabria

See also Abakuá; Cuba: Afro-Cubans.

FURTHER READING

Bettelheim, Judith. 1993. *Cuban Festivals: An Illustrated Anthology*. New York: Garland Publishing.

Boggs, Vernon, ed. 1992. *Salsiology: Afro-Cuban Music and the Evolution of Salsa in New York City*. New York: Excelsior Music Publishing Company.

Crook, Larry. 1992. "The Form and Formation of the Rumba in Cuba."

Jimenez, Rafael A. D. 2000. *Africa en Santiago de Cuba en su 485 Aniversario*, ed. Guadalupe R. Hechavarria. Palma Soriano, Cuba: Gráfica Haydee Santamaria.

Lopez, Rafael Brea. 1997. "Africania de la Danza Caribena." *Del Caribe* 26: 37.

Rojo, Antonio Benitez. 1999. "The Role of Music in the Emergence of Afro-Cuban Cultures." In *The African Diaspora: African Origins and New World Identities*, ed. Isidore Okpewho, Carole Boyce Davies, and Ali A. Mazrui, 197–203. Bloomington: Indiana University Press.

Schomburg, Arturo Alfonso (1874–1938)

A writer, an activist, and a historian, Arthur Schomburg is a major contributor to the development of a body of knowledge and research sources on the African Diaspora. His large rare collection of literature and artifacts has been used by scholars of the African Diaspora worldwide for almost a century.

Bibliophile Arturo Schomburg, who was of Puerto Rican descent, in an undated photo. The Schomburg Center for Research in Black Culture in Harlem is named after Schomburg, who was an avid collector of materials related to African Diaspora peoples and their experiences. (Bettmann/Corbis)

He was born Arturo Alfonso Schomburg in Santurce (a community in San Juan), Puerto Rico, on January 24, 1874. His mother, Maria Josefa, was a freeborn black native of Saint Croix, U.S. Virgin Islands, and his father, Carlos Federico Schomburg, was a mestizo with German heritage. Arturo identified himself as an "*Afroborinqueño*" (Afro-Puerto Rican).

Schomburg's activist life began when he was a child and his fifth-grade teacher adamantly argued that people of African descent had no history, made no contributions to society, and were basically insignificant. Schomburg became committed to challenging these popular portrayals of his people. He developed an "insatiable thirst" for knowledge about the histories and cultures of people of Africa. Schomburg chose to study at St. Thomas College in the Virgin Islands after studying painting at the San Juan Institute in Puerto Rico.

In April 1891 he moved from Puerto Rico to Harlem, New York. He immediately connected with the Latin American community and joined El Sol de Cuba Lodge No. 38, the Spanish-speaking Masonic lodge. Between 1892 and 1896 he actively participated in the political club Las Dos Antillas, which advocated for independence for Cuba and Puerto Rico. In 1911 Schomburg cofounded the Negro Society for Historical Research and was one of its earlier secretaries. This organization published several scholarly documents on the African Diaspora experience. In 1914, Schomburg was inducted into the American Negro Academy, which championed black history and fought against the "scientific racism" of the day. He later became the president of the academy.

In 1904, Schomburg published his first article, "Is Hayti Decadent?" in *The Unique Advertiser*. In 1925, he wrote "The Negro Digs Up His Past." During that period he became a prolific writer, publishing multiple articles in the *New York Times*, the *Crisis*, *Opportunity*, and other journals and magazines. He was a very important figure in the Harlem Renaissance and was friends with many of the artists and activists in both the Harlem Renaissance and within the Afro-Latino Diaspora community.

Schomburg was awarded the William E. Harmon Award in 1927 for outstanding work in the field of education. From 1931 to 1932, he was curator of the Negro Collection at the Fisk University library (Nashville, Tennessee). In 1932, Schomburg traveled to Cuba, collected materials, and met Afro-Cuban artists and writers. From 1932 to 1938 he served as curator of the Schomburg Collection of Negro Literature and Art housed at the 135th Street Branch. He remained there, doing what he loved, until his death on June 8, 1938. Schomburg's assessment of the importance of African and African Diaspora history and culture is best summarized in the three tenets that were articulated in his article "*The Negro Digs Up His Past*" and that guided his life:

- The Negro has been throughout the centuries of controversy an active collaborator, and often a pioneer, in the struggle for his own freedom and advancement.
- By virtue of their being regarded as something "exceptional," even by friends and well-wishers, Negroes of attainment and genius have been unfairly disassociated from the group, and group credit lost accordingly.
- The remote racial origins of the Negro, far from being what the race and the world have been given to understand, offer a record of creditable group achievement when scientifically viewed, and more important still, they are of vital general interest because of their bearing upon the beginnings and early development of culture.

Valerie Smith

See also Harlem Renaissance; Puerto Rico: Afro-Puerto Ricans; Schomburg Center for Research in Black Culture.

FURTHER READING
AfricaWithin.com. "Arturo (Arthur) Alfonso Schomburg (1874–1938), Bibliophile, Historian, Writer, Collector." www.africawithin.com/schomburg/schomburg bio1.htm (accessed January 22, 2008).

Ortiz, Victoria. 1986. "Arthur A. Schomburg: A Biographical Essay" in The Legacy of Arthur A. Schomburg: A Celebration of the Past, A Vision for the Future. Exhibition catalog. New York: The New York Public Library.

Schomburg, Arthur A. 1925. "The Negro Digs Up His Past." Harlem Number *The Survey Graphic* (March): 70–72. etext.lib.virginia.edu/harlem/SchNegrT.html (accessed January 22, 2008).

Schomburg (Arthur A.) Papers, 1724–1895 (1904–1938). New York Public Library Digital Library Collection.

The Arthur A. Schomburg Papers. 1991. The New York Public Library, Astor, Lenox and Tilden Foundations.

Sinnette, Elinor Des Verney. 1989. *Arthur Alfonso Schomburg: Black Bibliophile & Collector*. New York: The New York Public Library.

Schomburg Center for Research in Black Culture

Many consider the Schomburg Center for Research in Black Culture to be the world's leading research facility devoted to the preservation of materials on the global African and African Diaspora experiences. It serves as a focal point for Harlem's cultural life, a source of inspiration and education for the populace, and the national research library in the field. The original collection that formed the foundation of the center, which evolved over time, was purchased in 1926 from Arturo (Arthur) Alfonso Schomburg for $10,000 by the New York City Public Library. The collection reached international acclaim soon after its purchase and has served as a major repository of materials and artifacts of African and the African Diaspora peoples for more than 80 years. Originally, the library system housed the materials in a poorly lit dusty row house in Harlem, and they were accessible by appointment only.

The breadth and scope of the collection is impressive, and at times overwhelming, because there is such a wealth of scholarly content and rich history. The collection was ultimately moved to a beautiful new building that serves as a library, research center, and museum, and it became known as the Schomburg Center for Research in Black Culture. The center houses permanent and temporary exhibits, as well as traveling exhibits. It contains databases, digital collections, and African American church collections, including the African Methodist Episcopal Church collection. The materials in the center are organized in five collections:

- Art and Artifacts Division: Includes traditional African and Diaspora artifacts, such as masks, statuary, traditional dress, sculptures, paintings, and adornments and archival materials on the subject. The 20th-century works are emphasized.
- General Research and Reference Division: Holds and provides access to books, serials, and microforms containing information by and about the people of Africa and the Diaspora. Particular emphasis is placed on the social sciences, humanities, and the arts of sub-Saharan Africa, the Americas, and the Caribbean.
- Manuscripts, Archives and Rare Books Division: Contains one-of-a-kind and rare books, archival materials, and a variety of manuscripts.
- Moving Image and Recorded Sound Division: Contains collections of records and other audiovisual materials, including a gallery collection.
- Photographs and Prints Division: Contains documents and photos that provide in-depth study of the

experiences of Africans and the African-descent peoples.

The Schomburg Center for Research in Black Culture is a gathering place for cultural events, a major research center for scholars of the African and African Diaspora experience, and an educational center with the goal of increasing knowledge about the African American peoples and their experiences and cultures.

Valerie Smith

See also "African" in African American History; Schomburg, Arturo Alfonso (1874–1938).

FURTHER READING
Schomburg home page,
www.nypl.org/research/sc/sc.html.

SCLC

See Southern Christian Leadership Conference (SCLC).

Scott, Hazel (1920–1981)

Hazel Scott was one of America's foremost pianists. Under the guidance of her mother, Alma, she began playing piano at the age of two. Hazel began formal music training after the family moved from Trinidad and Tobago to the United States in 1924. She made her American debut at New York's Town Hall two years later and, by 1929, Scott had acquired six scholarships to Juilliard School of Music in New York City. At 14, she was too young to attend Juilliard, so she joined her mother's All-Woman Orchestra, playing piano and trumpet. By 16, Hazel was a radio star on the Mutual Broadcasting System and playing at the Roseland Dance Hall with the Count Basie Orchestra. Her combination of two approaches to piano—classical and jazz—made Scott an outstanding contributor to the genres. In the late 1930s, she appeared in the Broadway musicals *Singing Out the News* and *Priorities of 1942*. Her films include *Something to Shout About, I Dood It, Tropicana, Broadway Melody, The Heat's On* (1943), *Broadway Rhythm* (1944), and *Rhapsody in Blue* (1945). During the early 1950s, she became the first black woman to have her own television show, but due to accusations of her being a communist, her show was canceled. Scott defended her position in fund-raising events, fighting for groups in the name of equal rights. She was widely recognized for her efforts in the struggle for racial freedom and justice. After living in Paris, she returned to America in 1967, and appeared on the television shows *Julia* and *The Bold Ones*. In 1978, she was inducted into the Black Filmmakers Hall of Fame. In October 1940, she starred at the opening of Barney Josephson's Cafe Society Uptown, off Park Avenue, and ever since that date, her pianistic pyrotechnics have been acclaimed throughout the United States and Europe. Hazel was married to the Rev. Adam Clayton Powell, Jr., noted Congressman, preacher, and editor. Her most famous hit was "Tico Tico" released on her album *Relaxed Piano Moods*, with Charles Mingus and Max Roach, and is most highly regarded by critics today. Her style was stride and boogie woogie, popular in the 1940s. Scott continued to perform until her death in 1981.

Joan Cartwright

See also Jazz and Blues Singers, Black Women; Trinidad and Tobago.

FURTHER READING
The African American Registry. "Exceptional Talent and Appeal, Hazel Scott." www.aaregistry.com/african american history/946/Exceptional talent and appeal Hazel Scott (accessed January 22, 2008).
Caribbean Hall of Fame. "Hazel Scott" caribbean.halloffame.tripod.com/Hazel Scott.html (accessed January 22, 2008).
Harrison, Daphne Duval. 1988. *Black Pearls: Blues Queens of the 1920s*. New Brunswick, NJ: Rutgers University Press.

Seychelles Islands

The Seychelles Islands, or the Republic of Seychelles, is an archipelago of islands, with at least six defined groups of islands (Groupe d'Aldabra, Groupe de Farquhar, Groupe d'Alphonse, Groupe des Amirantes, Iles Proche, Groupe des Iles Australes) off the coast of East Africa in the Indian Ocean, in closest proximity to the islands of Mauritius and Reunion. The Seychelle islands, especially Mahe, the biggest, and Victoria, the capital, served as symbols of Anglo-African relationship in precolonial rule: Africa's resistance to colonial rule and British exiles or dissidents to the islands. The Seychelles Islands today are populated partly by descendants of enslaved Africans who have influenced the history, politics, and culture of the country representing an important relationship between Africa and the Diaspora. In many ways, the Seychelles mirror the Caribbean islands, on the other side of the world with similar geographies, colonial histories, land and sea scapes, peoples and cultural production.

With a population of 90,000 spread among 115 small islands covering an area of 107 square miles, the Seychelles was initially colonized by the French in 1756 and administered as part of Mauritius. In 1814, the British signed the Peace Treaty of Paris with the French and became the new colonizers.

Between 1814 and 1920, the British used the islands as political prisons for the leaders who resisted colonial rule. The exiled leaders were from Palestine, but also (and most significantly) Cyprus (Archbishop Makarios), Malaysia (the Sultan of Perak), and Maldives (Afif Didi). Among the African political prisoners were King Mwanga and King Kabarega from the powerful kingdoms of Uganda; others were from Malawi, Somalia, Zanzibar, and Egypt.

One prisoner who became world famous, however, was the 20-something-old King Nana Prempeh I of Asante who preferred exile to British destruction of his kingdom's capital, Kumasi, in 1896. He was exiled the longest— 24 years in Mahe (almost equivalent to Nelson Mandela's stay at Robben Island) with his mother Nana Yaa Akyea and 54 other chiefs and relatives.

Prempeh's imprisonment, like those of the others, was a strategy of weakening traditional political systems in the colonies while the period of exile was used for political and cultural indoctrination and dispossession. The prisoners became Christians under duress and chose their denominations. They were baptized and given Christian names. Prempeh converted to Anglicanism and was given the name Edward after King Edward of England. He, like the others, ended practices such as polygamy and wearing the traditional *Ntam* or African cloth. Instead, he was made to wear suits and taught to read and write in English.

In 1924, when Prempeh I returned to Kumasi, and contrary to British expectation that his exile had weakened the kingdom and would make him the embodiment of a British ruler, his people, the Asantes, who had waited for 24 years and rejected British-appointed kings and chiefs in the interim, restored him as an asantehene or king of the Asantes. Though colonial intentions and systems largely succeeded with imposition of a Westminster type of parliamentary government, traditional institutions in Asante and parts of Africa where some of the exiles came from did not die completely and are today part of the local government structures.

Today, while a high degree of tourism marks the beautiful Seychelle Islands, the people of Seychelles see themselves as one of the world's exponents of creole language and cultures. A Creole Festival (Festival Kreol) organized by the Creole Institute (Institut Kreol) is held every year in the capital city of Victoria during the month of October. It is meant to showcase the cuisine, music, dance, film, knowledge production in general of Creole Culture (the blend of African, European, Asian cultures) in this part of the world. Another group, L'association Banzil Kreol, is headquartered there and is meant to coordinate activities of creole cultures across the islands in the Indian Ocean and beyond.

Ivor Agyeman-Duah

See also Ghana; Mauritius.

FURTHER READING
Agyeman-Duah, Ivor. 1999. *Memories of History in Seychelles*. Kumasi, Ghana: CIR Publishers.
Festival Kreol. www.seychelles.net/festivalkreol (accessed February 9, 2008).
Mahoune, J. C. P. 1999. *One Century Ago—An Asante King in Seychelles!* Kumasi, Ghana: CIR Publishers.
Villiers, Les de. 2002. *Africa 2002*. Connecticut: The Corporate Council on Africa.

Shadd Cary, Mary Ann (1823–1893)

Teacher, activist, lecturer, publisher, editor, recruiter, and lawyer, Mary Ann Shadd was born on October 9, 1823 to a free black family in Wilmington, Delaware. Founder of Canada's third black newspaper, Shadd became the country's second woman newspaper editor. She was the first African American woman enrolled in law school in the United States.

Shadd taught school in Delaware, Pennsylvania, and New York. Critical of black material ostentation, she published *Hints to the Colored People of the North* (1849). In 1851 she attended an antislavery convention at St. Lawrence Hall in Toronto, where prominent black abolitionist delegates Henry Bibb, Samuel Ringgold Ward, and Martin Delany were in attendance. That year, she emigrated to Canada West to open an integrated school for children and adults in Windsor. In financial need for her project, Shadd enlisted the help of the Rev. Alexander McArthur and the American Missionary Association. Shadd promoted black immigration to Canada West and published *A Plea for Emigration; or, Notes of Canada West* (1852).

Increasingly, Shadd's support for integration and free black emigrants and her opposition to the Refugee Home Society cast her as a rival of Henry Bibb, local administrator of the Refugee Home Society and publisher of the black abolitionist biweekly *Voice of the Fugitive* (1851–1853), and his wife Mary, cofounder and teacher of a school for fugitives. Scholarship on Shadd and Bibb tends to underscore an "integrationist versus separatist" ideological divide between them and portrays the community as falling into either camp; however, competition for school funds, public accusations of malfeasance, and gendered attacks on character all informed the animosity between the high-profile leaders and suggest that neither the rivalry nor the community's response to it was so neatly split.

Shadd approached Samuel Ringgold Ward for help in starting a second black abolitionist newspaper in Canada West, the *Provincial Freeman* (1853–1859). Over the newspaper's lifetime, Shadd worked as editor, writer, fund-raiser, and spokesperson. In 1856, she married Thomas Cary, a Toronto barber, antislavery activist, and father of three children from a previous marriage. They had two children, though, as Shadd had moved to Chatham by 1855, there is no evidence the two shared a residence. Shadd added Cary to her name and signed her editorials "M.A.S.C." Thomas Cary died in 1860.

Shadd Cary edited Osborne Perry Anderson's memoirs, entitled *A Voice From Harpers Ferry* (1861). She received Canadian citizenship in 1862. In 1863, Shadd Cary recruited black troops for the Union Army. To this end, she traveled through the United States, primarily in the perilous Midwest. Although Shadd Cary had returned to Canada West at the end of the Civil War, she moved back to the United States after the passage of the Fourteenth Amendment. She lived in Detroit and, in 1869, moved to Washington, D.C., where she wrote for the *New National Era* promoting black employment and women's suffrage. She worked as a teacher and school principal. Shadd Cary enrolled in Howard Law School and graduated in 1883, after which she practiced law in Washington. She died of stomach cancer in 1893.

Andrea Stone

See also Canada and the African Diaspora; *The Provincial Freeman*.

FURTHER READING
Bristow, Peggy, coordinator. 1994. *"We're Rooted Here and They Can't Pull Us Up": Essays in African Canadian Women's History.* Toronto: University of Toronto Press.
Cooper, Afua Ava Pamela. 2000. "Doing Battle in Freedom's Cause: Henry Bibb, Abolitionism, Race Uplift, and Black Manhood, 1842–1854." PhD Diss. University of Toronto.
Rhodes, Jane. 1998. *Mary Ann Shadd Cary: The Black Press and Protest in the Nineteenth Century.* Bloomington: Indiana University Press.
Shadd, Mary Ann. 1998. *A Plea for Emigration; or, Notes of Canada West,* ed. Richard Almonte. Toronto: The Mercury Press. (Orig. pub. 1852).
Silverman, Jason. 1984. "'We Shall Be Heard!' The Development of the Fugitive Slave Press in Canada." *Canadian Historical Review* 65 (1, March): 54–69.

Shakur, Assata Olugbala (1946–)

Assata Olugbala Shakur (born Joanne Chesimard) was a prominent member of the Black Panther Party for Self-Defense and the author of an autobiography that changed the way resistance and women's participation in revolutionary struggles have been conceptualized. Born in Jamaica, New York, on July 20, 1946, to a predominately Southern, female-led family, Shakur describes herself as being an ordinary revolutionary—someone who rises up to face the challenges of life for herself and her community. In Swahili her name means, "She who struggles," "Love for the people," and "the Thankful" (Shakur 1986)

Exerting her independence at a young age, her life was filled with challenges to racism, sexism, and classism. She is a political activist who was falsely accused, tried, and persecuted by the U.S. government, specifically by the state of New Jersey, for allegedly killing a New Jersey State trooper. Depicted as a fearsome leader of the Black Liberation Army, Shakur was victimized by J. Edgar Hoover's Federal Bureau of Investigation campaign to criminalize black nationalist organizations and their leaders (COINTELPRO or Counterintelligence Program).

As a black activist woman, she was forced underground and made a fugitive for several years before her eventual arrest, during which she was shot at, physically and mentally tortured, and denied any and all human rights, even during her pregnancy in prison. Her case and the trials she was made to endure were highly publicized because of the blatant disregard for humanity she experienced in the hands of the U. S. criminal justice system. The charges against her included: armed robbery, bank robbery, kidnap, murder, and attempted murder—all of which have been proven false. As a result of this persecution, she spent more than 10 years in men's and women's detention centers in the United States before her liberation from prison and subsequent escape and exile to Cuba.

In 1986, her autobiography, *Assata*, was published, revealing her own account of her life experiences including her capture and false arrest. She described the brutality she endured while incarcerated and a powerful background narrative that lays out her awakening as a black revolutionary grounded in a history of critical awakening. Several films about Shakur and her life story have been produced, such as *Eyes of the Rainbow* by Cuban filmmaker, Gloria Rolando. Recording artist Common wrote and produced "A Tribute to Assata," which was featured on his *Like Water for Chocolate* album (2000). In addition to several interviews with Shakur, other significant publications include an autobiography written by Evelyn Williams, Shakur's aunt, confidante, and lawyer. Campaigns to "Free Assata" were launched worldwide by organizations from South Africa to Cuba. Periodically, since her exile in Cuba, the New Jersey state government has offered substantial bounties for Shakur's arrest. Despite protests and other actions to try to protect her, in May 2005, the state of New Jersey posted an international bounty on her for $1 million. In response, several student organizations of universities and colleges in the New York and New Jersey area displayed posters saying "Assata Is Welcome Here."

Keshia Abraham

See also Abu-Jamal, Mumia (1954–); Black Power Movement in the United States; Cuba: Afro-Cubans.

FURTHER READING

AfroCuba Web. www.afrocubaweb.com. (Accessed February 21, 2008).

Bin-Wahad, Dhoruba, Assata Shakur, and Mumia Abu-Jamal. 1993. *Still Black, Still Strong*. New York: Semiotext(e).

Shakur, Assata. 1986. *Assata*. New York: Lawrence Hill Books.

Williams, Evelyn A. 1993. *Inadmissible Evidence: The Story of the African American Trial Lawyer Who Defended the Black Liberation Army*. New York: Lawrence Hill Books.

Shakur, Tupac Amaru (1971–1996)

Tupac Amaru Shakur was a talented and gifted rap artist, actor, and poet. Tupac Amaru means "shining serpent" from the ancient Inca civilization of South America and Shakur means "thankful to God" in Arabic. His birth name was Lesane Parish Crooks and he was born in Manhattan, New York, on June 16, 1971. His mother, Alice Faye Williams (Afeni Shakur), was a political activist and a member of the New York Black Panther Party. His father was William Garland. A creative child, Shakur struggled growing up poor in the Bronx and Harlem, but learned to express his thoughts and feelings about his childhood, sexism, racism, and violence through his poetry. He was a member of a Harlem theater group, the 127th Street Ensemble, when he was 12 years old and later studied ballet and acting at the Baltimore School for the Performing Arts. He was a member of Leila Steinberg's writing circle when he was 19 years old.

In the early 1990s, Shakur left Digital Underground where he was a dancer and rap artist to strike out on his own. He succeeded in recording 13 albums and starring in eight films. His books and albums include *Tough Love* (1996), *The Rose That Grew from the Concrete* (1999), *Tupac Resurrection* (2003). In 1992, he made his first solo debut album, *2Pacalypse Now*. Later, he made *Strictly 4 My N.I.G.G.A.Z.* (1993), *Me Against the World* (1995), *All Eyez On Me* (1995), and *2 PAC Outlawz: Still I Rise* (1999). Even after his death, his phenomenal creative musical output has continued into the 21st century. Shakur's strong and salient performance talent opened the door for his acting career. He starred in the movies *Juice* (1992), *Poetic Justice* (1993), and *Above the Rim* (1994).

Shakur's immersion into rap accompanied his thug image in the media and in reality. On April 5, 1993, he was sentenced to 10 days in jail for assaulting a local rap artist with a baseball bat at a concert in Lansing, Michigan. On October 31, 1993, he was also charged for shooting two off-duty Atlanta police officers, but the charges were dropped. On November 29, 1993, he was facing 25 years for charges of sodomy and sexual abuse of a 19-year-old woman, as well as weapons possession, for which he was largely acquitted on December 1, 1994. On March 10, 1994, he was charged for assaulting Allen Hughes, the director of the film *Menace to Society*, after being dropped from the movie cast. On November 30, 1994, he survived being shot five times during a suspected plotted robbery at a Times Square recording studio in New York. On February 14, 1995 he was sentenced to four and a half years at the New York Rikers Penitentiary. He spent eight months in a New York prison and in October 1995 Marion "Suge" Knight, the chief executive officer of Death Row Records, posted a $1.4 million bond to release him. Shakur became a member of Death Row Records and began to release albums.

On September 7, 1996, he was shot four times in the chest in a drive-by shooting, after watching the Mike Tyson–Bruce Seldon fight with Suge Knight in Las Vegas. On September 13, 1996, he died after being in critical condition for six days. He was 25 when he died, and his murder remains unsolved. A poet of Shakespearean proportions to his generation, he conveyed a message of black self-love in his creative brilliance.

Cheryl Jeffries

See also Hip-Hop Culture in the African Diaspora.

FURTHER READING
Dyson, Michael Eric. 2001. *Holler If You Hear Me*. New York: Basic Civitas Books.
Jones, Quincy. 1998. *Tupac Shakur*. New York: Three Rivers Press.
"A TupacHQ—Life History— 2pac Tupac Amaru Shakur Makaveli." www.tupaq.com/lifehistory.shtml.

Shange, Ntozake (1948–)

Ntozake Shange wrote her most famous work, *For Colored Girls Who Have Considered Suicide/ When the Rainbow is Enuf* in 1975. The following year, the play opened at the Henry

Street Settlement's New Federal Theatre in New York, thrusting Shange into immediate prominence. That same year, and 17 years after the phenomenal run of Lorraine Hansberry's *A Raisin in the Sun*, *Colored Girls* became the second play by a black woman to reach Broadway. Through this play, Shange popularized a poetic style that sought to revive and tap from the nonverbal paradigms that inform her ancestral oral traditions. To preserve this ceremonial ideal, she devised an avant-garde stage—the choreopoem—to overcome the limitations of dialogue and realism. In her pursuit of a vibrant theatrical form, Shange initiated a revolutionary phase in the African-American quest for a functional theater.

To fully explore black music, dance, and other nonverbal resources, Shange rejected conventional theater practices and promoted a rich interdisciplinary form that appealed to all the physical senses. Reconstructing standard English usage, Shange used language to reinforce her theatrical liberty and further reject standard practice. Using a colloquial, metaphoric, and rhythmic style that agreed with her poetry, she deliberately distorted the English language by breaking away from conventional spellings and pronunciations. Using her chosen "language," Shange addressed a wide range of themes, including, among others, racism, the unique position of black woman, stereotypes, the black middle class, the disregard for black artists, and black survival. Central to her themes was a black feminist and Pan-Africanist consciousness that emerged in her antiracism and anti-imperialism stance, her rejection of Western cultural hegemony, and her commitment to recuperating marginalized black traditions. The intensity of Shange's drama is perhaps best expressed in her adaptation of Frantz Fanon's combat breath theory. Her combat breathing implies the opening of wounds that would be left to bleed as part of a healing process, inspiring solidarity, and seeking the spiritual transcendence of a corporal existence where women are vulnerable.

Born Paulette Williams to Paul T. and Eloise Williams, a surgeon and a psychiatric social worker, in Trenton, New Jersey, on October 18, 1948, her early childhood, first in upstate New York and later in St. Louis, was extremely sheltered and comfortable. Shange was 13 when her family returned to New Jersey where she completed high school. In New Jersey, she became increasingly aware of the constraints imposed by sexism and racism.

Shange earned a bachelor's degree with honors in Afro-American music and poetry from Barnard College in 1970 and a master's degree in American studies from the University of Southern California in 1973. In 1971 she dropped the name Paulette Williams and adopted the African (Zulu) name, Ntozake Shange. Ntozake means "she who comes with her own things" while Shange means "one who walks like a lion." The new names pointed to her new identity and artistic direction.

From 1972 to 1975, Shange taught at Sonoma State College, Mills College, and the University of California Extension. While teaching at Sonoma State College, she began writing poetry in earnest. She also found time to dance and perform her poetry with the Third World Collective, Raymond Sawyer's Afro-American Dance Company; the West Coast Dance Works; and her own company, then called For Colored Girls Who Have Considered Suicide. She also participated in poetry readings at San Francisco State College and with the Shameless Hussy poets. Her involvement with African-type dance was enhanced by her participation in the activities of Halifu Osumare's The Spirit of Dance, a small troupe of black women. Shange also worked with dancers and musicians who practiced Santería. Taking advantage of her rich dance background, she reapplied this knowledge in the body language of *Colored Girls* with stunning effectiveness.

At the age of 27, Shange moved to New York where, in July 1975, *Colored Girls* was professionally produced at Studio Ribea in New York

City. This was the beginning in a series of 867 performances, 747 on Broadway. Beginning by relying almost absolutely on the choreopoem form, Shange gradually shifted to less rigid choreopoem-related formulas. The significance of her stylistic shift lies in her awareness of the creative restraints resulting from the formulation of rigid dramatic techniques. This shift is evident in *Colored Girls*, *Boogie Woogie Landscapes* (1979), *Spell #7* (1979), *A Photograph: Lovers in Motion* (1977), and *Daddy Says* (1987).

Overall, Shange played a key role in expanding the black literary focus on racial and cultural identity so that it embraced a sexual revolution. Having lost faith in the ability of men to respond effectively to female subordination, she furnished the American stage not just with a significant black presence but also a feminine one. Shange thus made pronounced contributions to the black aesthetic and its efforts to break down conventional walls.

Phillip Effiong Uko

See also Feminism: Black Feminist Movement in the United States.

FURTHER READING

Brown-Guillory, Elizabeth. 1988. *Their Place on the Stage: Black Women Playwrights in America*. New York: Greenwood Press.

DeShazer, Mary K. 1989. "Rejecting Necrophilia: Ntozake Shange and the Warrior Re-Visioned." In *Making a Spectacle: Feminist Essays on Contemporary Women's Theatre*, ed. Lynda Hart, 86–100. Ann Arbor: University of Michigan Press.

Richards, Sandra L. 1983 "Conflicting Impulses in the Plays of Ntozake Shange." *Black American Literature Forum* 17 (2, Summer): 73–78.

Shange, Ntozake. 1975. *For Colored Girls Who Have Considered Suicide/When the Rainbow Is Enuf*. New York: Macmillan Publishing Co.

Shange, Ntozake. 1979. Interview. In *In the Memory and Spirit of Frances, Zora, and Lorraine: Essays and Interviews on Black Women Writing*, ed. Juliette Bowles, 23–26. Washington, D.C.: Institute for the Arts and the Humanities.

Shange, Ntozake. 1984. *See No Evil: Prefaces, Essays & Accounts*. San Francisco: Momo's Press.

Wilkerson, Margaret B. "Music as Metaphor: New Plays of Black Women." In *Making a Spectacle: Feminist Essays on Contemporary Women's Theatre*, ed. Lynda Har, 61–75. Ann Arbor: University of Michigan Press, 1989.

Shango

Shango (in Brazil, spelled Xango) is a significant orisha in the pantheon of Yoruba cosmology. Shango came to the Americas via the enslaved Africans brought there by the Middle Passage. His presence today is greatest in Brazil, Trinidad and Tobago, and Cuba. His story of unification, upward mobility, and resurrection seemed to resonate with the enslaved, who hoped to do the same. According to various oral accounts from western Africa, Shango began as the fourth alafin of the city of Oyo, the center of Yoruba spiritual and political strength. An alafin was both a religious and dynastic leader, a divine king who ruled by divine right. As alafin, Shango unified the Yoruba peoples after years of bloody civil wars. Shango himself was a great soldier and the epitome of Yoruba masculinity. Once he had achieved unity by means of war, he thought he needed the thrills of battle to keep on being successful. Thus, in order to renew civil war and to recapture his momentum, Shango commanded his own brothers to fight each other. In the melee that ensued, one brother murdered the other. This new grim reality came as a shock to Shango, who hanged himself from an iroko tree. This death was not the final curtain for Shango, of course; his main wife, Oya, brought Shango back to life as an orisha through magical invocations. Shango transformed from dead ruler to orisha by admitting his failure and learning his lesson about the evils of arbitrary and selfish uses of absolute power. His example warned future alafins about abusing their subjects for self-image or self-gratification.

After his resurrection, in nearly all versions of the story, Shango reconnected with his father, Obatala, who undergirded the moral values of Yoruba cultures. This reunion gave Shango the ethical insights to judge the actions of others, particularly other alafins. His displeasure with their policies or behaviors could lead to omens of lightning and fire, signs of Shango's presence and his imminent enforcement of providential decisions. White, the color of lightning, and red, the color of fire, became associated with the veneration of Shango. In Cuba, enslaved Africans paired Shango with the Catholic Saint Barbara in part because both of their transcendent journeys involved lightning and fire and, thus, both the male African orisha and female Catholic saint were connected to the colors white and red. In Brazil, Xango was paired with the male Saint Jerome, whose own life story included fiery rhetoric and lightning-sharp flashes of revelation.

Charles H. Ford

See also Brazil: Afro-Brazilians; Cuba: Afro-Cubans; Middle Passage; Oya; Santería.

FURTHER READING

Brandon, George. 1993. *Santería from Africa to the New World: The Dead Sell Memories.* Bloomington: Indiana University Press.

Canizares, Baba Raul. 2000. *Shango: Santería and the Orisha of Thunder.* Bronx, NY: Original Publications.

Fatunmbi, Awo Fa'lokun. 1991. *Iwa-pele: Ifa Quest.* Bronx, NY: Original Publications.

Warner-Lewis, Maureen. 1996. *Trinidad Yoruba: From Mother Tongue to Memory.* Tuscaloosa: University of Alabama Press.

Siddis in North Karnataka, India: Biomedical Status

The Siddis are an Afro-Indian ethnic group that settled in north Karnataka, especially in the Uttara Kannada district and bordering regions of the Belgaum and Dharwad districts. They have marked similarities to Africans, from whom they originate, and are popularly known as "Siddis" among the African Diaspora in India; they are found mainly along the west coast of India (Lobo 1984). The Portuguese and English refer to them by various other names, such as Caffre, Abyssinian, and Habshi (Burman 1984; Chauhan 1995).

According to records and scholars, the Siddis are descendants of Africans who were brought to India mainly by Arab, Portuguese, and Dutch voyagers (Kamat 1985). The slave trade between western India and East and Southeast Africa throws light on the origin of the Siddis.

Each Siddi settlement has about 5 to 40 houses, 8 to 10 settlements within 10 kilometers from the village sangha or Grameena *sangha*. Three or four village *sanghas* constitute a cluster *sangha* (which need not correspond to the *taluka*). Presently, there are nine cluster *sanghas* (Idagundi, Kotemane, Gunjavati, two at Arbail, Malagoan, Bhagvati, Mudalgeri, and Gavegal). In all the 28 Grameena *sanghas* there are 189 settlements, according to a 1996 survey. A *sangha* means "association" or "group"; *Taluka* means "block headquarters." Many villages put together constitute a *taluka*. Many *talukas* put together constitute a district. Many districts form a state. The words "*sangha*" and "*taluka*" are in local language, Kannada. However these terms have the same meaning in most of the languages in India, including the national language, Hindi.

Apart from their common ethnic stock and economic condition, there are three religious groups among the Siddis themselves: Hindu, Muslim and Christian. Physically they resemble each other.

A lot of work has been done on the history of migration of African Diaspora peoples who settled in Goa, Karnataka, Maharashtra, Gujarat (along the coast), and Andhra Pradesh. Sociological aspects of the Siddis have also been studied extensively, especially by T. C.

Palakshappa in 1976 and Cyprian H. Lobo (now Kiran Kamal Prasad) in 1984. Few anthropometric studies have been done and little work has been done to study the biomedical status of the Siddis.

We studied the nutritional status, oral health, and general health of the Siddi community. Non-Siddis of the same socioeconomic status who lived in the same environment served as controls. A total of 526 Siddis and 346 non-Siddis were registered for health examination. All subjects submitted for physical examination but some did not consent to a blood examination. Hence it was not possible to examine all the people for all the parameters.

Height and weight for age were compared with the 50th percentile values of the National Centre for Health Statistics to determine nutritional status (Lavoipierre 1983). The Siddi children showed a better nutritional status compared with non-Siddi children ($x^2 = 13.732, df = 4, P<.01$) The nutritional status of Siddi adults was better than that of non-Siddi adults ($x^2 = 13.422, df = 1, P< .001$)

CURRENT STATUS AND CONCLUSIONS

- Better nutritional status observed among the Siddis could be attributable to their food habits, as they consume nonvegetarian food. The low incidence of dental caries in Siddis (10.13 percent in adults and 13.67 percent in children) compared with non-Siddis (20.23 percent in adults and 16.8 percent in children) could be attributable to the inherently greater resistance to caries in African races.
- Very low incidence of lice infestation among Siddis (0.57 percent) compared with non-Siddis (21.95 percent) could be attributable to the curly nature of their hair, where the nits (lice eggs) may not be able to get firmly attached as well as different hair-grooming standards.
- Scabies and tinea infections were slightly lower among the Siddis (0.57 percent

and 2.68 percent, respectively) compared to non-Siddis (1.22 percent and 3.96 percent, respectively), which could be attributable to poor personal hygiene.
- In blood groupings the Siddis exhibited a higher frequency of A gene (19 percent) than B gene (16.01 percent), whereas among the non-Siddis, the frequency of A gene was lower (20.77 percent) than B gene (23.01 percent).
- The frequency of Rh negative gene was higher in Siddis (27.38 percent) than in non-Siddis (19.44 percent).
- Sickle cell disease and thalassemia were not detected, probably indicating loss of the gene for these abnormal hemoglobins.

Prakash V. Patil and Pramod B. Gai

See also India and the African Diaspora.

FURTHER READING
Anbalagan, K. 1985. *Electrophoresis: A Practical Approach*, 81–90. Madurai, India: Life Science Book House.
Burman, Roy B. K. 1984. *Census of India: Bibliography on Scheduled Castes, Scheduled Tribes, and Selected Marginal Communities of India, Part XI (IV A)*. New Delhi: Office of the Registrar General, 1191. 1961.
Chauhan, R. S. S. 1995. *Africans in India: From Slavery to Royalty*. New Delhi: Asian Publication Services.
Dacie, J. V., and S. M. Lewis. 1991. *Practical Hematology*. 7th ed. Edinburgh: ELBS with Churchill Livingstone.
Henry, J. B. 1989. *Clinical Diagnosis and Management by Laboratory Methods*. 17th ed. Philadelphia: WB Saunders Co.
Kamat, S. U. 1985. *Gazetter of India Karnataka State*, 53. Bangalore, India: Government of Karnataka.
Lavoipierre, G. J. 1983. *Measuring Change in Nutritional Status*, 75–86. Geneva, Switzerland: World Health Organization.
Lobo, C. H. 1984. *Siddis in Karnataka*. Bangalore, India: Centre for Nonformal and Continuing Education.
Palakshappa, T. C. 1976. *The Siddhis of North Kanara*. New Delhi: Sterling Publishers.

Signifying

"Signifying" is the term used to characterize different forms of verbal play common in African American communities in which cleverly contrived comments are used to make subtly veiled commentary or witty insults are used to make not-so-subtly veiled criticisms. In America's climate of racial segregation and violence, the coded literacy and secret skillful articulation of signifying is one Africanism that survived in the Americas as a means to cope with and resist the silencing oppression of slavery and its legacy. It is a means to suggest a critique while simultaneously sidestepping a direct response or even acknowledging any malicious intent. In short, signifying uses both irony and indirection to express ideas and opinions.

Above all, signifying is a ritualistic practice that serves various functions in different African American discursive and communal spaces. Some scholars define signifying as primarily a male-dominated activity (the female version is called "specifying"). African American men in this verbal art form focus their anger, aggression, and frustration into a relatively harmless exchange of wordplay where they can establish their masculinity in verbal "battles" with their peers. This form of signifying lends itself to validating a pecking order style of dominance based on the result of the verbal exchange. Geneva Smitherman (1975) sees signifying as a humorous means to produce well-meaning social critiques for the good of the community at large. Therefore, all members of the community can participate in its formation and, if necessary, its correction.

Each participant depends on the verbal text of the other from which he or she will extract some idea in order to construct a new level of meaning, thereby enriching the wordplay and revealing new ideas. Practitioners of signifying often display a mastery of rhythm and rhyme, social awareness, cultural critique, and a high level of improvisational ability.

Parties who signify on one another are usually aware that they are entering an arena of verbal wordplay, where the most quick-witted, versatile, artful, playful, and layered rhetorician/speaker is often acknowledged as the victor through the response and acceptance of the audience. The opposing party can either "lose" through his or her lesser quality of skillful verbal play or by "losing his cool" by taking an artful slight too personally. These guidelines are readily apparent in various forms of signifying such as "playing the dozens," "snappin" on somebody, telling "yo momma" jokes, or rhyming in a street corner hip-hop cipher.

Henry Louis Gates (1988) suggests that signifying in literature is a rhetorical trope that embodies the African-American vernacular essence of the trickster character in African mythology. African American literary works and authors systematically pay homage to the literary tradition by "signifying back" to their literary forbears, establishing connections, revisiting themes, expanding their meaning and significance, and ultimately affirming their significance.

Sometimes signification may occur by inverting a name or meaning, "turning it inside out" to express social commentary. Toni Morrison does this in her novel, *Song of Solomon*, where the street named for a prominent African American doctor who has been rejected by the town's white society is called "Not-Doctor Street." In today's national politics, politicos and cultural critics in the African American community signify on Supreme Court Justice Clarence Thomas's name by inverting it, calling him "Tom-Ass Clarence."

Signifying can affirm, critique, or build community through the involvement of its participants. It depends on the bending, recycling, reshaping, revising, and reinventing of old ideas into new perspectives through instantaneous verbal engagement, which must meet the approval of the larger community witnessing the signifying event to be construed as valid. Though the witticisms expressed through signifying can be as sharp, pointed, and painful, as they are funny, it constitutes a set of rhetorical techniques that plays a vital role in the communication practices of African American communities.

Jason Esters

See also Rap/Rappin'.

FURTHER READING

Gates, Henry Louis. 1988. *The Signifying Monkey.* Oxford, UK: Oxford University Press.

Mason, Theodore O. 1997. "Signifying" In *The Oxford Companion to African American Literature,* ed. William L. Andrews, Frances Smith Foster, and Trudier Harris. New York: Oxford University Press.

Smitherman, Geneva. 1975. *Black Language and Culture: Sounds of Soul.* New York: Harper.

Smitherman, Geneva. 1977. *Talkin and Testifyin: The Language of Black America.* Boston: Houghton.

Simone, Nina (1933–2003)

Nina Simone, a classically trained pianist, singer, and songwriter, was born Eunice Kathleen Waymon in Tryon, North Carolina, on February 21, 1933. A child prodigy at the piano by the age of four, Simone's musical talent blossomed at the African Methodist Episcopal church where her mother was a minister and where Simone played piano and sang in the choir. Simone continued her musical education and studied classical piano at the Juilliard School of Music in New York where she prepared for entrance in the Curtis Institute of Music in Philadelphia. When she was not accepted, Simone attributed her rejection to racism. By this time her family had moved from Tryon to Philadelphia, and to support them as well as to finance private music lessons Simone worked as an accompanist.

In the summer of 1954, Simone took a job at the Midtown Bar and Grill in Atlantic City where she cultivated a fan base. By 1957, she had found an agent, and in 1958, Simone's first album, *Jazz as Played in an Exclusive Side Street Club* (later known as *Little Girl Blue*) was issued on the independent label Bethlehem Records. The single, "I Loves You Porgy," from *Porgy and Bess,* her only Top 20 hit, sold over a million copies.

After Simone's second album on Bethlehem, *Nina Simone and Her Friends* (1959), she signed with the national label Colpix (Columbia Pictures Records) and released nine albums, among them several important live ones, including *Nina Simone at Town Hall* (1959), *Nina Simone at The Village Gate* (1962), and *Nina Simone at Carnegie Hall* (1963). Simone briefly married Don Ross in 1958, and divorced him the next year. A second marriage to Andy Stroud, a former police detective who became her recording agent and with whom she had a daughter, Lisa Celeste, lasted from 1960 to 1970.

Like Abbey Lincoln, who often traveled in Simone's circle of artist friends, including James Baldwin, Langston Hughes, and Lorraine Hansberry—significantly all writers—Simone's musical repertoire shifted away from show tunes and ballads to original songs about America's racial problems. Simone was often called the voice of the Civil Rights Movement because of songs like Simone's album "Mississippi Goddam" (featured on the 1964 album *Nina Simone in Concert*), which was written after the assassination of Medgar Evers in Mississippi (June 1963) and the bombing of a Baptist church in Alabama that killed four black girls (September 1963), "Old Jim Crow," and "To Be Young, Gifted and Black." The latter, composed with the keyboardist Weldon Irvine, Jr., honored playwright Lorraine Hansberry (who was writing a play with the same title at the time of her death), which became an anthem for the growing Black Power Movement and was recorded by numerous artists, among them Aretha Franklin.

Simone also performed a plethora of songs that explicitly named sexual desire, such as "I

Want A Little Sugar in My Bowl," "Gimme Some," "Chauffeur," "Take Care of Business," and "Don't Take All Night." Simone's recordings of sexual blues bear significance in that they draw on and expand on the musical tradition of the early blues of the Jim Crow and Great Migration era. By revising old blues imagery and combining it with the social themes of her time, Simone represented a different kind of black female symbol—sexual, nurturant, authoritative, and committed to racial uplift.

One of the first artists to wear her hair natural, Simone rejected bee hives and supper club gowns wearing instead short, natural hair, often corn-rowed or braided, and African clothes—what she considered symbolic representation of her racial pride. Her song, "Four Women," in which she creates stark representations of black womanhood throughout American history by describing each woman's skin tone and hair style in relation to her victimization and objectification, reflected the exclusion of black women from dominant Eurocentric representations of beauty.

In 1967, Simone was named the Female Jazz Singer of the Year by the National Association of Television and Radio and became the first woman to win the Jazz Cultural Award. However, embittered by racism, Simone renounced the United States as her homeland in 1969 and would live, over the next two decades, in several countries, including Barbados, Liberia, the United Kingdom, Switzerland, and the Netherlands.

Joining a tradition of African American artists such as Josephine Baker, Sydney Bechet, James Baldwin, Chester Himes, and Richard Wright, Simone adopted France as her home in 1991. That same year she published her autobiography, *I Put a Spell on You,* and her music was featured in the film *Point of No Return.* Here, Simone, like the black artists before her, experienced the freedom to explore new aesthetic and social perspectives in her music. In 1992, Verve Records released *Let It Be Me! Nina Simone at the Vine Street Bar & Grill in Hollywood.*

On April 21, 2003, 10 years after Elektra released her last album, *A Single Woman,* Nina Simone, recipient of honorary doctorates in music and humanities and composer of more than 500 songs, died at Carry-le-Rouet, France.

LaShonda Katrice Barnett

See also Jazz and Blues Singers, Black Women.

FURTHER READING
Acker, Kerry. *Nina Simone.* 2004. New York, N.Y. Chelsea House Publications.
Hampton, Sylvia, with David Nathan. 2004. *Nina Simone: Break Down and Let It All Out.* London, England: Sanctuary Publishing Ltd.
Simone, Nina, with Stephen Cleary. 1991. *I Put a Spell on You: The Autobiography of Nina Simone.* New York: Da Capo Press.
Nina Simone, Obituary, *New York Times,* April 22, 2003.

SELECTED DISCOGRAPHY
Baltimore (Sony 57906).
Black Gold (BMG International 659624).
Feeling Good: The Very Best of Nina Simone (Universal International 522747).
Folksy Nina/Nina with Strings (Collectables 6208).
Nina Simone in Concert/I Put a Spell on You (Verve/Polygram Records 846543).
Nina Simone Sings Nina (Verve/Polygram Records 529867)

Sistren

The Sistren Theatre Collective is a women's theatre group from the Caribbean island of Jamaica. In 1977, some women employed as street cleaners performed a play at the Annual Worker's Week Celebrations with the assistance of Honor Ford-Smith, staff tutor at the Jamaica School of Drama. This resulted in the play *Downpression Get a Blow* about garment workers unionizing to defend their rights. Many of the women had been teenage mothers and were the sole breadwinners for their families.

After the worker's week the women met Ford-Smith and persuaded her to help them devise performances based on their life experiences. This marked the beginning of the Sistren Theatre Collective ("sistren" means "sisters" in Jamaican creole), a grassroots theatre group that has become a model for politically committed postcolonial dramaturgy.

Sistren's first major production, *Bellywoman Bangarang* (1978), dramatizes the life stories of young girls marking their passage to womanhood as single mothers. Members' testimonies were subsequently published in *Lionheart Gal: Life Stories of Jamaican Women* (1986). The group later performed *QPH* (1982) focusing on life narratives of elderly destitute women. This play was based on research and interviews with women in Kingston. Yet another play, *Nana Yah* (1979), examines the role of women in Jamaican history by invoking the legendary figure of Nanny, leader of the maroons or runaway slaves, who led them into battles against colonial authorities. The strength of contemporary women in battling sexual violence and capitalist exploitation is presented in *Muffet in a all a wi* (1983). Many of these plays use African and Caribbean rituals and folklore as essential elements to convey the message of struggle.

Another aspect of Sistren's work in feminist struggle and resistance was their community outreach workshops and performances. Their attempts to network with women's and popular theater groups in Jamaica and the Caribbean resulted in productions such as *Domestick, Ida Revolt inna Jonkonnu Stylee, Sweet Sugar Rage, Tribute to Gloria Who Overcame Death,* and *The Case of Iris Armstrong* from 1982 to 1985. During this period, Sistren established a research unit and its newsletter became a magazine covering important issues such as domestic and sexual violence, the social effects of economic liberalization, and legal provisions for the protection of women. However, in 1987, the group made the regrettable decision to abandon outreach work in developing women's groups. After Sistren's reorganization in 1987, it has continued under the leadership of some of its founding members. Because the scale of its work is much reduced it is difficult to assess its current impact in Jamaica and the Caribbean, but there is no denying the continued relevance of the work it undertook from the 1970s to the 1990s.

Kanika Batra

See also Jamaica.

FURTHER READING
Ford-Smith, Honor. 1989. *Ring Ding in a Tight Corner: A Case Study of Funding and Organizational Democracy in Sistren 1977–1988.* Toronto, Canada: Women's Program.
Sistren with Honor Ford-Smith. 1986. *Lionheart Gal: Life Stories of Jamaican Women.* London: Women's Press.

Slave Trade

See Transatlantic Slave Trade.

Smith, Dante Terrell

See Mos Def (1973–).

Sojourners for Truth and Justice

The Sojourners for Truth and Justice was an all African American women's progressive civil rights group that sought to give black women an independent voice in the emerging postwar black freedom movement and to build ties of political solidarity with women across the African Diaspora during the early 1950s.

Veteran progressive activist Louise Thompson Patterson (1901–1999) and Mississippi-born actor-poet Beah Richards (1926–2000) formed the short-lived, New York–based organization in 1951. The group named itself after Sojourner Truth, the notable 19th-century African American abolitionist and women's rights advocate. Inspired by a tradition of African American women's resistance and drawing from the Marxist-Leninist positions of the American Communist Party (CPUSA) on racial and gender oppression, the Sojourners developed a radical black feminist program. The stifling Cold War political atmosphere in the United States and the ambivalence of the CPUSA toward the Sojourners contributed to the organization's demise by 1953. Although practically forgotten today, the Sojourners anticipated radical black women's organizations of the 1970s and 1980s.

The Sojourners emerged at a moment of intense activity in progressive African American political circles around the cases of Willie McGee, the Martinsville Seven, the Trenton Six, and Rosa Lee Ingram during the late 1940s and early 1950s. The McGee case involved a black Mississippi truck driver who was falsely accused of rape by a white woman in 1945. The Martinsville Seven case involved seven African American men falsely accused of gang raping a white woman in Martinsville, Virginia, in 1949. The Trenton Six case involved a group of young African American men who were sentenced to death on a bogus charge of murdering an elderly white shopkeeper. Ingram, a black Georgia sharecropper, was sentenced to death in 1948 for defending herself from the sexual advances of a white man. The cases generated international attention. Despite the efforts of the Civil Rights Congress to build amnesty movements around these cases, McGee and the Martinsville Seven were executed in 1951.

The idea for organizing the Sojourners originated during the summer of 1951, but was stimulated by a poem Beah Richards

penned in 1950, "A Black Woman Speaks of White Womanhood, of White Supremacy, of Peace." The piece powerfully critiqued the discourse of chivalry that justified the raping of black women and lynching of black men on the grounds of defending white womanhood. The poem asserted that systems of racialized sexual violence and white supremacy not only subjugated black women but also made white women the property of white men. Richards gained notoriety for the poem after reading it before the left-wing Women for Peace group in Chicago. Although not a communist, Richards was a Progressive Party activist, and she moved in left-wing circles. For Patterson, a long-time member of the Communist Party and the Civil Rights Congress, the poem was a clarion call for action. She approached Richards about forming an all-African American women's civil rights group. By early September, the two women had formed the initiating committee for the Sojourners for Truth and Justice. The committee issued "A Call to Negro Women" for the group's inaugural meeting in Washington, D.C. from September 29 to October 1, 1951.

The Call stands as an important expression of 20th-century black feminism. The statement reflected the group's understanding that African American women faced multiple oppressions and that mobilizing black women was essential for realizing equality and justice for all. The statement condemned Jim Crow, police brutality, lynching, the death penalty, sexual violence against African American women, and the impoverishment of black Americans. The group called on the federal government to enforce the Thirteenth, Fourteenth, and Fifteenth Amendments and to protect civil liberties. The group stepped directly into Cold War politics, charging that racism was the United States' Achilles' heel on the global stage. They demanded the end to the Korean War. The final section called on African American women "to dry your tears, and in the spirit of Harriet Tubman and Sojourner Truth,

ARISE" and attend the group's opening meeting in Washington (FBI, Sojourners for Truth and Justice Files, 100–384225—2, October 1, 1951, n.p.).

More than 130 women attended the Sojourners for Truth and Justice meeting in Washington. The event represented a coming together of a politically and socially diverse group of black women activists. Some of the notable attendees included veteran progressive activists/intellectuals Louise Thompson Patterson, Dorothy Hunton, Shirley Graham DuBois, and Eslanda Robeson, all of whom were members of the Council on African Affairs. New York–based community activist Angie Dickerson, the militant editor of the *California Eagle,* Charlotta Bass, actor Frances Williams, and playwright Alice Childress also took part in the proceedings. In addition, Rosalie McGee, the 28-year-old, working-class wife of the recently executed Willie McGee; Bessie Mitchell, a sister of one of the Trenton Six defendants; Amy Mallard, whose husband had been murdered in Georgia for voting; and Josephine Grayson, widow of one of the Martinsville Seven attended the meeting. The Sojourners recognized that these women served as powerful symbols of racial injustice meted against black people. The group also encouraged these women who had no previous experience as political activists to become leaders in the struggles for racial justice.

The convention issued the "Proclamation of the Sojourners for Truth and Justice," which reiterated many of the points in the Call. The group selected Bass as president and Patterson as executive secretary. The highlight of the meeting came on its final day. Delegations of Sojourners burst into the Pentagon, White House, and State Department. They demanded civil rights, protection of civil liberties, the end of the Korean War, and the respect of African American women. That evening Sojourners led a candlelight vigil for human rights and peace outside the White House.

After the inaugural meeting, Sojourners attempted to build a black women–led, mass movement for racial equality and the dignity of black womanhood. The organization founded branches in New York; Baltimore; San Francisco; Los Angeles; Chicago; Cleveland; Richmond, Virginia; and North Carolina. The assassination of Henry Moore, the leader of the Florida branch of the National Association for the Advancement of Colored People, and his wife, Harriett, on Christmas morning 1951 became a major rallying cry for the group. The Sojourners called for 5,000 African American women to march in Washington on February 12, 1952, Abraham Lincoln's birthday, to protest the deaths of the Moores. Protestors were instructed to come dressed in black and in veils. However, the Sojourners were unable to stage the event.

The group held its last major gathering, the Eastern Seaboard Conference, in Harlem, New York, on March 23, 1952. The proceedings reveal the influence of Communist Party positions on the "triple oppression" of black women, popularized by party leader Claudia Jones, who was also a member of the Sojourners. The group drafted a constitution, organized a youth auxiliary, and debated strategies to bring black women into the labor movement. The delegates also discussed how to build ties with progressive white women.

The Sojourners' efforts to forge ties of political solidarity with female antiapartheid activists in South Africa highlight the group's diasporic vision. Sojourners sent letters condemning apartheid to the South African ambassador to the United Nations. The group took part in antiapartheid protests in front of the South African consulate in Manhattan. Sojourners also corresponded with female antiapartheid activists and labor organizers in South Africa. These actions illustrate that the Sojourners viewed black women's oppression in internationalist terms and were attempting to build political alliances with progressive women in Africa.

Cold War political repression was largely responsible for the Sojourners' demise by early

1953. FBI surveillance reports highlight the government's tendency to view the group as a subversive, communist front. From the beginning, FBI informants riddled the organization. In little more than a year, the FBI collected more than 400 pages of detailed files on the organization. In the context of U.S. efforts to win the allegiance of emerging Third World nations against the Soviet Union, the efforts of groups like the Sojourners to bring international attention to Jim Crow were of particular concern to cold warriors. Government repression of the group illustrates the devastating effects McCarthyism had on black female progressives.

The Communist Party's ambivalence toward the Sojourners also contributed to the organization's end. Party officials never fully embraced the Sojourners as the former viewed the latter as a divisive manifestation of racial and gender separatism. Although she never formally nor publicly broke from the CPUSA, Patterson gradually moved away from it by the early 1950s because of the party's cool response toward the Sojourners.

The Sojourners has recently attracted the attention of scholars interested in black feminism and African American women's activism. The group anticipated radical black feminist organizations of the 1970s and 1980s, such as the Third World Women's Alliance, National Black Feminist Organization, Combahee River Collective, and Sisters in Support of Sisters in South Africa. Despite its short existence, the Sojourners for Truth and Justice stands as an important social protest organization in the African Diaspora during the mid–20th century.

Erik S. McDuffie

See also Feminism and Black Women in the African Diaspora; Jones, Claudia Cumberbatch (1915–1964); National Black Feminist Organization (NBFO).

FURTHER READING
Boyce Davies, Carole. 2008. *Left of Karl Marx. The Political Life of Black Communist Claudia Jones*. Durham: Duke University Press.

Federal Bureau of Investigation. "Sojourners for Truth and Justice" Files. October 6, 1951.

Green, Ben. 1999. *Before His Time: The Untold Story of Harry T. Moore, America's First Civil Rights Martyr*. New York: Free Press.

Hamilton, Lisa Gay. 2003. *Beah: A Black Woman Speaks*. Televised film, Clinica Estetico and LisaGay Inc for HBO/Cinemax. Videocassette. 90 minutes.

Horne, Gerald. 1988. *Communist Front? The Civil Rights Congress, 1946–1956*. London: Associated University Presses.

McDuffie, Erik S. 2003. "Long Journeys: Four Black Women and the Communist Party, USA, 1930–1956." Ph.D. diss., New York University.

Louise Thompson Patterson Papers. Special Collections, Robert W. Woodruff Library, Emory University, Atlanta, GA. Boxes 15, 27.

Shapiro, Linn. 1996. "Red Feminism: American Communism and the Women's Rights Tradition, 1919–1956." Ph.D. diss., American University.

Soukous

The word *soukous* is a derivation of the French *secouer*, which means "to shake." It is used to describe a popular rhythm of the Democratic Republic of the Congo (formerly Zaire and the Belgian Congo). The antecedents of this fast-paced beat are Afro-Cuban music, Congolese rumba, and West African highlife, all brought together in various forms in the exciting history of African music.

Congo music, as other Africans call the rhythm of the Congo, dates back to the work camps of European companies in the 1930s, where musicians used guitar, bottles, and *likembe* (*sanza*) to play and sing songs in traditional forms combined with Cuban (*son*, the mother of rumba, *pachanga*, *charanga*, mambo, bolero, salsa, and so on) and West African highlife. The advent of radio in the 1940s, and the later opening of studios brought to life various Congo music groups. The one Congolese constant was the language of songs,

Lingala; in East Africa the music was known as Lingala music. Franco's influence was indelible: the guitar was a fixture, accompanied by rhythm guitar, double bass, congas, clips, and later a third guitar (misolo), and brass and woodwinds.

A good number of the protégés of Franco, one of Soukous's leading exponents, and his contemporaries branched out to form their own bands in the late 1960s and early 1970s. A common trend among them was the desire to speed up the rhythm of the rather slow rumba. They were listening to music from other places, such as highlife, rock and roll, and soul. Among them were students calling themselves Zaiko Langa Langa. Their music was fast paced and their dressing style was sophisticated. To the music they added dance steps. One of their leaders was Pepe Kalle, who went on to create the band Empire Bakuba. Others were Koffi Olomide and Tshala Muana.

Because of the bad political situation in their country under dictator Mobutu, some musicians went into exile in Kenya where their fast music influenced the local dance craze, *cavacha*, and rhythm. A part of the remarkable phenomenon of soukous is that it affected popular music development in Francophone West Africa, and that influence has not abated, but has expanded to the Anglophone sector, too. Soukous really became a distinct genre in the 1980s as Congolese musicians, still suffering from the sociopolitical turmoil of their nation, left for Paris and London. Although some bands retained the old format of starting off a track in the sweet, slow mode of the rumba, reminiscent of Franco, others eschewed the slow beat and went directly into the speedy beat, inviting everyone to the dance floor. Paris-based Kanda Bongo Man pioneered this beat. His compatriot, Papa Wemba, had two bands, Viva la Musica for soukous, and another, including French session players, for his brand of pop.

Kanda Bongo Man invented a dance for his soukous, *kwassa kwassa*. Other artistes have fol-

lowed suit, and soukous has become inextricably linked to dance. In Central and East Africa, it is known as *soukous ndombolo*. In the new millennium of videos, bands produce CDs and DVDs, or CVDs, and the stage is packed by an array of musicians, instrumentalists, singers, and dancers, both male and female. The dancers, and often the singers and players, too, perform specially choreographed steps, with booty-shaking and hip-swinging a regular feature. Soukous's popularity has spread across the Atlantic, and soukous bands regularly tour Canadian and American cities, playing in places such as Central Park, New York.

Femi Ojo-Ade

See also Highlife; Salsa.

FURTHER READING
Manuel, Peter. 1990. *Popular Musics of the Non-Western World: An Introductory Survey.* Oxford, UK: Oxford University Press.
Nidel, Richard. 2004. *World Music: The Basics.* London: Routledge.
Rough Guide to Congolese Soukous. 2000. World Music Network (Audio CD)

Soul Music

Soul music was an outgrowth of the citified rhythm and blues that had moved up from the Deep South, particularly the Mississippi Delta, into the chilly North of New York City, the icy Midwest of Chicago, and the balmy Mudtown of Watts, Los Angeles, fused with the God-seeking cry of gospel. During soul music's glory days in the 1960s and the early 1970s, Motown, Atlantic, Stax, and Arista Records were played 24 hours a day on radio stations devoted to soul, such as the Los Angeles KGFJ, an all–African American station whose byline was "The Sound of Success."

Soul music became the expression of young African America coming out of the explosive dawning of the Civil Rights Movement and the blighted faith of the great migrations North, Midwest, and Far West. Popping its fingers rhythmically in groups of two to five on street corners, doing a lot with simple lyrics and a repetitive chorus for the main message, and belting out that characteristic climax holler that had been racially strained out of the integrated new blues and jazz, soul took the deliberate buildup and full-voiced bellow of gospel music beyond rhythm and blues and singers like Lou Rawls, Brook Benton, and Johnny Mathis. Instead, soul was the raw cry of a broken heart full of the passion and suffering of a wrong relationship, because nothing else in the crumbling world of riots, assassinations, and arrests could possibly offer any happiness. The new combination of sacred musical patterns with profane, sensual lyrics was shocking, limitless, and profoundly satisfying.

By the time rhythm and blues legends such as Ray Charles and Otis Redding had cut new songs for the new generation, young men and women in groups with names like the Drifters, Chubby Checker, Little Anthony and the Imperials, Martha Reeves and the Vandellas, the Four Tops, the Temptations, and the Supremes were already on the scene. African American businesspeople with a sharp ear for opportunity were picking up these young artists, recording their original songs, and putting their music out on the segregated radio waves. Enraptured young African American listeners headed for the corner record shops in droves to buy the new 45s (a single song on a plastic disc).

When a young Marvin Gaye started cutting singles, he sang with a yearning that brought vivid images to the mind and a vibrant urgency to the body that demanded emotive movement. There was the unembarrassed showmanship of a prizefighter and a preacher overcome by the spirit in each of James Brown's hollered-out raspy songs, whether they were about how men did not want skinny women or about how no man with black pride

should still be straightening his hair. By the mid–1960s, everyone had gone from doing the twist to doing the mashed potato, the jerk, and the Watusi, because that is what these singers told you it was time to do. And African American disc jockeys had set the nation a new standard, shouting at young people to "be there" when the new soul singers hit the big stadiums, or "be square."

Soul filled the airwaves with shameful secrets, gut-wrenching disillusionment, and pain-filled love all expressed in flawless rhyme, with a trumpet or saxophone solo, a shout-and-response chorus, and a holler climax that brought soaring catharsis. These formulas applied even to the smooth serenade harmonies of Little Anthony and the Imperials, the Delfonics, the Chi-Lites, the Urhythmics, the Miracles, Herb Melvin and the Blue Notes, the Dells, the Naturalistics, and the earliest Temptations and Supremes. Riskier voices described unblushing need and grating pain: the Four Tops, Al and Jackie Wilson, "Wicked" Wilson Pickett, Jimmy and David Ruffin, Jerry Butler, Gladys Knight and the Pips, Irma and Carla Thomas. But soul could get downright raunchy; Millie Jackson, the Ohio Players, and eventually loner Chaka Khan brought that kind of soul on home in their very different ways. Raw voices, wrenching in their unrestraint, such as those of Aretha Franklin, Bobby Womack, Stevie Wonder, Al Green, and Bill Withers experimented with more abstract expressions of how that familiar old heartache sounded beside a new philosophical outlook, with deeply moving results. Holland, Dozier, and Holland made up a songwriting team whose lyrics could not fail a performer. Power and polish combined in the new soul that evolved in singers such as Luther Vandross and Barry White. Even single-song stars such as Fontella Bass and Ann Peebles had their place and their fame.

Only one generation removed from the jazzy sound of big-city bands, jazz soul groups like Booker T. and the MGs, the Bar-Kays, and

Junior Walker and his All-Stars brought trumpet or sax riffs with rare and highly repetitive lyrics—or no lyrics at all—to a new level of youthful accessibility and success. Families too, such as Sly and the Family Stone, the Jackson Five, the Staple Singers, the Isley Brothers, the O'Jays, and finally the retro-jazz Pointer Sisters all made it big.

Now the music drove the movement. Afro hair products including a fisted pick stuck straight in the back of the head, complex corn-row braids, huge hoops of silver and gold in the ears and on the wrists, and Dashiki shirts over tight hip-hugger bell bottoms proclaimed a confident new look that was all about racial self-invention and self-acceptance.

As the protest eras of the 1960s and 1970s cooled into what would become the decades of conservative political backlash in the 1980s and 1990s, perhaps soul was hit by the Euro-American business spotlight. Like spirituals, ragtime, blues, and jazz before it, people whose ethnicities and interests lay outside African American communities seemed to have discovered that soul was a moneymaker. Solo artists emerged as Smokey Robinson abandoned the Miracles, as Eddie Kendricks left the Temptations, and the Commodores surrendered their lead singer, Lionel Richie, to soloism. Al Green preempted his last soul concert by using it to announce his return to gospel.

A few consummate performers made chameleon changes, bringing as much joy to African American audiences as ever, such as Michael Jackson (formerly of the Jackson Five), Diana Ross (former lead singer of the Supremes), and Marvin Gaye, who had already risen once from the ashes of the death of his partner and lover, Tammy Terrell. Now Gaye, before his own death, briefly carried on in the wave of cooling male reflection that included such artists as Isaac Hayes and Curtis Mayfield. But the incomparable Sam Cooke had long before been shot dead like a common thief, just trying to get into his own motel room, killed like freedom-fighting political leaders of the time. Disenchantment with the dream was setting in. The rhythmically gifted teens who had spawned and supported soul were now dispersed and a little older. Some determined young adults had taken the Civil Rights Movement at face value and forged a way into colleges, universities, and professionalism. Many had moved on to a struggling maturity via commitments such as marriage, babies, and jobs, all with their own challenges. A younger group was now teetering on the brink of community implosion brought about in the wildfire growth of gangs that arose after the Black Panthers were hunted down.

What remained of soul in this era faded as passing single hits grew cute rather than emotive. New Age message jazz artists and musical groups, like Herbie Hancock; Quincy Jones; Earth, Wind and Fire; and Parliament were able to bridge to the subsequent artistic movements. Still in each generation, including hip-hop, new versions appear, from the neo-soul contributors like India Irie to Alicia Keys, from Maxwell to Johnny Legend. And soul music would create echoes in the African Diaspora from the soul movement among Afro-Brazilians, Caribbean, African, and Black British youth to the more recent Heather Headley from Trinidad and Tobago.

Alexis Brooks de Vita

See also Black Panther Party; Blues: A Continuum from Africa; Hair; Hip-Hop in the African Diaspora.

FURTHER READING
Baraka, Amiri. 2002. "The Phenomenon of Soul in African-American Music." In *Jubilee: The Emergence of African-American Culture*, ed. Howard Dodson. Washington, D.C.: The National Geographic Society.

Lornell, Kip. 2002. *Introducing American Folk Music: Ethnic and Grassroot Traditions in the United States.* Boston: McGraw-Hill.

Marsh, Dave. 1992. *It Tears Me Up: The Best of Percy Sledge.* Audio Cassette. New York: Atlantic Recording Corporation.

Sellman, James Clyde. 1999. "Soul Music." In *Africana: The Encyclopedia of the African and*

African American Experience. New York: Basic Civitas Books.

Southern Christian Leadership Conference (SCLC)

In January 1957, 60 African American leaders from major cities across the South met at Ebenezer Baptist Church in Atlanta, Georgia, and founded the Southern Leadership Conference on Transportation and Nonviolent Integration. Most were members of the National Association for the Advancement of Colored People (NAACP), but they believed a more well-rounded approach that included appeals to government legislation and to the larger public consciousness would lead to social justice. The organization met again in New Orleans, Louisiana, on February 14, 1957, where it elected an executive board of directors and shortened its name to the Southern Leadership Conference. Most of the elected leaders were Baptist ministers. Rev. Wyatt T. Walker was the organization's first executive director, but it was its first president Rev. Dr. Martin Luther King, Jr., who provided the organizational vision, inspirational leadership, and essential philosophy. Like King, several of the leaders, such as Rev. Ralph D. Abernathy, T. J. Kempson, and Fred Shuttlesworth had recently led bus boycotts in their communities in order to win better treatment for black people in public transportation.

During its first convention in Montgomery in August 1957, the organization was renamed the Southern Christian Leadership Conference (SCLC) and adopted its primary objective: to achieve full citizenship and equality for African Americans through nonviolent protest. They believed this objective would appeal to public sympathy and would serve as an initial step in healing American society through "redemptive love."

The two weapons chosen to wage the war on the social, political, and economic system that enforced the second-class citizenship of African Americans were direct social action and voter registration. The Prayer Pilgrimage to Washington in 1957, the organization's first demonstration, attracted 25,000 people. The success of this march led to the youth marches for integrated schools in 1958 and 1959, which together had 40,000 participants.

However, it was not until several students in Greensboro, North Carolina, staged the first successful sit-in that the SCLC leaders found a method of direct action dramatic enough to build a coherent strategy around. The SCLC, along with other organizations, worked to pressure the government into desegregation of public services and staged several effective sit-ins that were televised by national media outlets. The NAACP, which had an older leadership constituency, was a bit reticent about the approach initially.

During its peak years, the SCLC had 85 local affiliates. The SCLC played a key role in organizing and supporting several additional campaigns to fight segregation and secure voting rights. This included the Citizenship Education Project, sit-ins across the state of Georgia, the Birmingham Confrontation, and the 1964 Saint Augustine fight against segregation and the Ku Klux Klan. When the Congress of Racial Equality launched the freedom rides in 1961, SCLC leaders, including King, Abernathy, Lawson, and Shuttlesworth, provided their expertise. By mobilizing blacks, organizing marches, and filling jails with nonviolent protesters, a worldwide television audience observed the violent acts of southern whites against African Americans. Influenced by the SCLC's mass protest movement, Congress passed the Civil Rights Act of 1964.

However, during nonviolent protest actions organized in Selma, Alabama, in 1965 the SCLC faced several challenges. The organization began to clash with the Student Nonviolent Coordinating Committee (SNCC) over

Flag-bearing demonstrators march from Selma to Montgomery in the historic March 1965 voting rights protest. Organized by the Southern Christian Leadership Congress, the march led directly to the 1965 Voting Rights Act, which outlawed Southern states' attempts to prevent African Americans from voting. (Library of Congress)

tactics, which many students believed were becoming stagnated; the limitations of the non-violent philosophy; and the perceived notion that SCLC members took undue credit for the success of regional protests that SNCC had actually initiated. During the Selma to Montgomery March in 1965, as approximately 600 marchers attempted to cross Selma's Edward Pettus Bridge and pray, 200 state troopers attacked them with whips, cattle prods, clubs, tear gas, and horses. Television crews recorded the battered protesters as they fled the area, and national media coverage dubbed the encounter "Bloody Sunday."

The resulting violence from Selma prompted President Lyndon B. Johnson to urge the passage of the Voting Rights Act of 1965, and the SCLC quickly registered 85,000 new voters within four months. Despite the success of the march, the Federal Bureau of Investigation

(FBI) spent most of its time trying to undermine the SCLC, which FBI Head J. Edgar Hoover saw as a communist front organization. Another unfortunate circumstance was that societal and racial violence continued to mar the national landscape. The Watts race riot in 1965, the call for "black power" by Stokely Carmichael on the Meredith march in 1966, the war in Vietnam, and the Detroit race riot in 1967 caused the SCLC to address a larger range of issues. In 1967, the SCLC organized the Chicago Freedom Movements and Operation Breadbasket, but these forays into galvanizing the protest movement in northern urban centers posed different challenges than the movements in the South in addition to significant white resistance. King was also speaking out against the Vietnam War, which detracted from his broad-based appeal and popularity.

In 1968, the SCLC organized the Poor People's March on Washington as a civil disobedience action. While taking time out from this campaign to support sanitation workers in Memphis, Tennessee, King was assassinated in April 1968. The campaign continued, but the movement had lost much of its vigor. Abernathy succeeded King as president of SCLC and led the Poor People's March on Washington, a demonstration at the Republican National Convention, and a sanitation workers' strike in 1968. In 1977, Joseph E. Lowery, the chairman of the SCLC's board of directors, was unanimously chosen as Abernathy's successor. Lowery served as president of the SCLC for 20 years coordinating efforts against South African apartheid, extending the Voting Rights Act of 1965, and fighting the epidemic of drugs and violence in African American communities. He also grappled with the difficulty of maintaining the relevance of the organization in the post–civil rights era, which has plagued all succeeding leaders.

Jason Esters

See also King, Martin Luther, Jr. (1929–1968); Ture, Kwame (1941–1998).

FURTHER READING

Peake, Thomas R. 1988. *Keeping the Dream Alive: A History of the Southern Christian Leadership Conference from King to the Nineteen-Eighties.* New York: P. Lang.

Riches, William T. Martin. 2004. *The Civil Rights Movement: Struggle and Resistance,* 2nd ed. Palgrave Macmillian: New York.

"Southern Christian Leadership Conference." 1992. *Encyclopedia of African-American Civil Rights: from Emancipation to the Present,* ed. Charles D. Lowery and John F. Marszelek. New York; Greenwood Press.

Soyinka, Akinwande Oluwole (1934–)

Akinwande Oluwole Soyinka, who became Africa's first Nobel laureate in literature in 1986, was born in July 13, 1934, in Abeokuta, western Nigeria, a predominantly Yoruba region. After attending University College in Ibadan, Nigeria, from 1952 to 1954, Soyinka traveled to the University of Leeds, remaining in the United Kingdom for five years while obtaining a bachelor's degree in English with honors in 1957. He worked as a play reader at the Royal Court Theatre in London and wrote and directed his own plays. He returned to Nigeria in 1960, the year of its independence from Britain, to research drama in West Africa by virtue of a Rockefeller grant. Soyinka's return found him deeply involved not only in theater, beginning with the Orisun Theatre Company in 1964, but also in the country's struggle for self-governance.

Soyinka's literature reflects his role as a political activist and his concern with individual human rights and experiences. Arrested twice and detained in solitary confinement for two years, Soyinka has worked to develop Nigerian independence and stability. Just as his literary works delve into the evaluation and reconstruction of African culture and knowledge, Soyinka has participated in the tumultuous Nigerian political evolution from colonial governance to self-governance. His criticism of Nigerian leaders has placed him in both voluntary and involuntary exile from the country on numerous occasions.

His extensive works include drama and poetry, fields in which he writes most comfortably, but also personal memoir, novels, literary criticism, and political commentary. His most recognized plays, such as *The Road* (1965) and *Death and the King's Horseman* (1975), examine the relationship between social institutions and individual knowledge, using the intersection of African and Western traditions to explore sources of strength and conflict within communities. Although Soyinka features Yoruba gods and traditions in many of his works, he writes primarily in English and incorporates non-African tales in his plays, such as in his rewriting of *The Bacchae of Euripides* (1973). His investigation of the connection between the material and the spiritual worlds emphasizes similarities of tradition throughout cultures and highlights African artistry as it contributes to human history and development. A critic of the Négritude movement, believing it contributes to a false dichotomy of European rationalism and African emotionalism, Soyinka promotes a revaluation of African thoughts and values as they have developed both before and in conjunction with Western relationships. His works explore the usage of myth and collective history in determining individual lives.

Soyinka returned to Nigeria in 1998 after the death of its military leader. He has held positions at universities throughout the world, including Cornell University and the University of Ife. He continues to write and work for political equality for Africans.

Soyinka's plays include *The Lion and the Jewel* (1963), *A Dance of the Forests* (1963), *Three Short Plays* (1969), *Madmen and Specialists* (1971), *Opera Wonyosi* (1981), *A Play of Giants* (1984), and *From Zia with Love and A Scourge of Hyacinths* (1992). His poetry includes *Idanre and Other Poems* (1967), *A Shuttle in the Crypt* (1971), *Ogun Abibiman* (1976), and *Mandela's Earth and Other Poems* (1988). His novels include *The Interpreters* (1965) and *Season of Anomy* (1973). His autobiographical writing includes *The Man Died* (1972), *Aké: The Years of Childhood* (1981), *Isara: A Voyage Around "Essay"* (1989), *Ibadan: The "Penkelemes" Years, A Memoir, 1946–1965* (1994), and *You Must Set Forth at Dawn* (2006). His essays and critical works include *Myth, Literature and the African World* (1976), *Art, Dialogue and Outrage: Essays on Literature and Culture* (1988), and *The Burden of Memory, the Muse of Forgiveness* (1999).

Amanda Conrad

See also Africa.

FURTHER READING
Jeyifo, Biodun. 2001. *Conversations with Wole Soyinka*. Literary Conversations Series. Jackson: University Press of Mississippi.

Gibbs, James, ed. 1980. *Critical Perspectives on Wole Soyinka*. Washington, D.C.: Three Continents Press.
Maja-Pearce, Adewale, ed. 1994. *Wole Soyinka: An Appraisal*. Oxford, UK: Heinemann.

Spelman College

Spelman College, founded in 1881, is a private four-year liberal arts college for African American women in Atlanta, Georgia. Offering bachelors of arts and bachelor of science degrees, it remains the oldest historically black women's college in the United States. It is a founding member of the Atlanta University Center (AUC), the largest consortium of historically black colleges. Dedicated to scholastic achievement, community involvement, and social leadership, Spelman features research centers and initiatives in the sciences, humanities, and business, including the Women's Research and Resource Center and the Center for Biomedical Research.

Established by two white teachers from New England, Sophia B. Packard and Harriet E. Giles, Spelman opened as the Atlanta Baptist Female Seminary. In Atlanta, at the request of Dr. Shaver, a black ABHMS school teacher, Giles and Packard met with Pastor Frank Quarles, the minister of Friendship Baptist Church. Quarles was a staunch supporter of Packard and Giles, often calling on local ministers to provide them with further assistance. On April 11, in the basement of Friendship Church, the school opened with 11 students. The following week they had 25. With a growing student population, additional funds were needed to hire teachers, purchase supplies, and procure a new building.

In 1882, Rev. George King, whom they met on a trip to New England, introduced Giles and Packard to John D. Rockefeller who provided substantial aid to the school. Spelman's desperate need for more land was answered when ABHMS purchased former Union Army quarters in the West End area in 1883, including nine acres of land and five frame buildings. Here they opened the "Model School," a student teacher training facility, which provided much needed instruction to fill positions opening in new urban and rural black schools.

Spelman's struggles, however, were not just financial. Dr. Henry L. Morehouse hoped the property would be shared with the Atlanta Baptist Seminary (Morehouse College). Packard and Giles opposed the proposals to unite the schools, arguing for independent women's education. Rockefeller provided them with financial aid, allowing Spelman to remain independent. Moving enabled Spelman to offer new courses, increase the student body, and house boarders. Among other changes, in 1884, the Atlanta Female Baptist Seminary was renamed Spelman Seminary to honor John D. Rockefeller's wife, Laura Spelman Rockefeller, and her parents, Harvey Buel Spelman and Lucy Henry Spelman, antislavery activists. In 1887, Spelman graduated its first class, conferring high school diplomas to six young women. Granted a charter by Georgia in 1888, Spelman became incorporated under a board of trustees consisting of 16 members, two of whom were African Americans. Spelman maintained organizational independence from Morehouse, but several students took college courses there.

The 1890s marked another period of expansion: buildings were constructed and additional land was acquired. The formation of a missionary training program established international links by sending Spelman students to African countries and bringing African students to Spelman. Its college department opened in 1897, and Spelman granted its first college degrees to Jane Granerson and Claudia T. White five years later. Lucy Tapley's presidency at Spelman Seminary was marked by the completion and dedication of Sister's chapel in 1927. Under Tapley's administration Spelman Seminary changed its name to Spelman College. Its expansion and growth as a college oc-

curred under President Florence Read (1927–1953). Not only did Read increase the school's endowment, but she also redirected its focus from vocational training to liberal arts education. In 1930, Spelman received accreditation from the Association of American Colleges.

Albert Manley became Spelman's first African American president in 1953. The late 1950s–1960s marked a period of growing activism among Spelman students. Like their counterparts in Greensboro, North Carolina, Spelman students challenged segregation by organizing sit-ins, demonstrations, economic boycotts, and lawsuits. Spelman students along with students from other AUC schools drafted an "Appeal for Human Rights," which received national attention. Spelman students were founding members of the Student Nonviolent Coordinating Committee and Committee on Appeal for Human Rights. Spelman established its first black studies program in 1969.

The 1970s marked tension between administration and students who desired a black female president. They achieved their goal when Dr. Johnetta Cole, Spelman's first black female president, was elected in 1987. The school's endowment grew substantially under her administration; Dr. William (actor Bill Cosby) and Camille Cosby contributed $20 million to the college. Spelman's first alumna president, Audrey Forbes Manley (class of '55) was appointed in 1997. In 2002, Dr. Beverly Tatum became Spelman's third black female president. The college has produced numerous conferences and intellectual activities that link women scholars across the Diaspora, such as the journal *Sage*, the ongoing work of the Women's Research and Resource Center, and a conference on women and AIDS in 2003.

Folashadé Alao

See also Feminism and Black Women in the African Diaspora; Morehouse College.

FURTHER READING
Cohen, Rodney. 2000. *The Black Colleges of Atlanta*. Charleston, SC: Arcadia Publishing.

Corley, Florence Fleming. 1985. "Higher Education for Southern Women: Four Church Related Women's Colleges in Georgia, Agnes Scott, Shorter, Spelman and Wesleyan, 1900–1920." PhD thesis, Georgia State University.

Guy-Sheftall, Beverly, and Jo Moore Steward. 1981. *Spelman: A Centennial Celebration, 1881–1981*. Charlotte, NC: Delmar.

Lefever, Harry G. 2005. *Undaunted by the Fight: Spelman College and the Civil Rights Movement, 1957–1967*. Macon, GA: Mercer University Press.

Manley, Albert. 1995. *A Legacy Continues: The Manley Years at Spelman College, 1953–1976*. Lanham, MD: University Press of America.

Read, Florence Matilda. 1961. *The Story of Spelman College*. Princeton, NJ: Princeton University Press.

Vanlandingham, Karen Elizabeth. 1985. "In Pursuit of a Changing Dream: Spelman College Students and the Civil Rights Movement, 1955–1962." Master's thesis, Emory University.

Spiritual Shouter Baptist Religion

Spiritual Shouter Baptist is a mystical religion, indigenous to the Caribbean, in particular, Trinidad and Tobago. The religion was established and sustained as a cultural response to colonial domination in slavery, a system that dehumanized and degraded African identities. Africans, however, while inculcating a diasporic consciousness, greatly retained their spiritual understanding of the world as manifested in their rituals and practices. Thus, for four centuries, beginning in the 15th century, Africans, with their fear of oppression, repressed many of their religious practices. By the 19th century, and particularly after emancipation, Africans began to be extremely forceful in exposing their spirituality in forms of religions like the Spiritual Shouter Baptist. The visibility of its members in worship was remarkable in the late 19th century when they began to conduct their religious activities openly, while they faced both society's contempt of their rituals and practices and the colonizers' challenge at imposing Christianity on them. The result was the legal constraint of the Shouter Prohibition Ordinance of 1917 in Trinidad and Tobago. However, the Spiritual Shouter Baptists, in a remarkable manner, continued not only a religious but also a political struggle: the right to freedom of worship and the right to social justice.

The progress of the Spiritual Shouter Baptist religion exemplifies a movement of resistance. It enabled many Africans to gain control of their identities, both as spiritual and political beings, and enabled communities to become solidified in their commonality as African descendants in the Diaspora.

According to the ideologues of this religion, Europeans plagiarized Christianity from its origins, Egypt. Thus, for the Spiritual Shouter Baptists, boundaries of African (Yoruba) and Christian ideologies can overlap. Therefore, the lead role European Baptists played in Christianizing enslaved Africans during the centuries of slavery was not entirely a threat in a diasporic African religious redevelopment. Africans, overall, were better able to re-create their past identities seeing that some Christian practices, handed to them by the colonizers, were not alien to them. However, the African content of their religion had to be masked or covert, because of the colonizers' brutally punitive measures to restrain African forms of worship. Many Africans, however, believed their own cultural expressions were natural and empowering; thus, they persisted relentlessly with their religious practices. The perseverance of the Spiritual Shouter Baptists is remarkable, for, as African people, European Christianity could not contain them. They strongly maintain their claim to a lineage from John the Baptist, a reputable Biblical figure.

The Spiritual Shouter Baptists experienced significant rejection by the state of Trinidad and Tobago because of their openness in worship; their singing, which noisily proclaimed manifestations of praise; and their vibrating body movements. Therefore, society named these believers "Shouters." However, they failed to understand why the state persecuted them. They argued that many of their religious practices, for instance, baptism, the act of bell ringing, the use of the Bible, and the "Mourning Ground" for spiritual rejuvenation, were similar to practices in other faiths. Added to that, they claimed they carried out instructions that the Bible decreed. Yet the state criminalized members of this religion by enacting a law, the Shouters Prohibition Ordinance of 1917. The Shouters became a direct target of race and religious discrimination.

Consequently, the Spiritual Shouter Baptists strategized their survival through their political consciousness. That is, they sought allies among people who showed dissidence toward colonial rule; those who practiced Protestant Christianity; and lawyers, politicians, and activists who were engaged in the labor movement to improve the welfare of the workers in Trinidad and Tobago. They displayed a high level of political consciousness, which enhanced the quality of their leadership, and their debates articulated the broader struggle in the 1940s. The many believers, at that time, who pioneered the struggle on behalf of the Spiritual Shouter Baptist religion, did extraordinary work. Among those engaged in politics were Archbishop Elton Griffith, Archbishop Glanville Williams, and Tubal Uriah Buzz Butler. Others, such as Samuel Ebeneza Elliot (Papa Neza) and Maka Leanie Brezian, were active in the healing and medicine power (Clarke 2005). In the 1940s, political mobilization, with supporters such as Philip Granger and Elma Francois, was the stimulus that helped them maintain their awareness and knowledge of the radical democratic changes that were taking place locally and globally. Events at that time, such as the anthropological research of Melville J. Herskovits in Trinidad, which legitimized rituals and practices of this religion; the constitutional changes, like universal adult suffrage in the Caribbean, which arose from the Moyne Commission Report in 1951; and the 1948 Universal Declaration of the Human Rights, would precipitate their success in repealing the Shouters Prohibition Ordinance in 1951.

The Spiritual Shouter Baptist community has been notable for a very impressive presence of Caribbean women. Many of the women, who form the axis of this church, maintain impressive leadership in religious and secular roles. The religion, however, draws from the Bible to assert gender conventions. On the one hand, this faith recognizes "there is neither male nor female; for you are all one in Jesus Christ" (Galatians 3:28) (Jacobs 1996, 172) as an egalitarian doctrine. While, on the other hand, it points to 1 Corinthians 11:3: "But I would have you know, that the head of every man is Christ; and the head of the woman is the man; and the head of Christ is God." In reality, these contradictions are truths in this religious context. Studies show that women conduct their responsibilities in religious practices with fortitude, yet the church, including the women, defer to men on an everyday basis, as men receive the standard respect and privileges accorded to them in society (Laitenen 2002, 14).

Caribbean women in this religion have exercised supremacy to articulate social issues as they affect the lives of people of African descent. As a result, they engage in community organizing, in political debates, and often, in a personal way, ensure that caring and nurturing services are made available to those in need. Thus, such words as "pillars holding up the earth" (Lovelace 1986, 131), when used to describe these Caribbean Spiritual Shouter Baptist women, suggest that they distinguish themselves because of their heightened spiritual consciousness and their ability to pioneer religious and social movements. Generally, the religion regards these women as holding "dominance in the Spiritual realm" (Laitenen 2002, 11), as findings of several studies indicate their longevity in the Spirit as believers, worshippers, and servers. Thus, with accumulated knowledge and experience they can sustain highest authority.

The Spiritual Shouter Baptist faith is one that is imbued with the power of the Spirit. Belief in the Spirit makes them independent and guides their roles in healing, inspiring, comforting, and helping those in need. Examples abound of their work with the homeless, the incarcerated, the sick and so on. Therefore, many leaders (archbishop, mother, reverend, bishop), in making meaningful their religious responsibilities, have strengthened the links between religion and social justice and human rights in the societies in which they reside.

Believers of the Spiritual Shouter Baptist faith acknowledge the significance of sustaining African nationalism as a hallmark of their identity. They have rationalized that the persecution they have experienced for centuries and largely still encounter is due to their blackness. Though they believe in forgiveness, they feel the need to project theirs as a distinct mission to sustain an African identity totally as a means of respect to their ancestors and themselves. Nevertheless, many believers of this faith embrace other faiths, such as Hinduism and Orisha, as a reflection of their understanding of the Christ and the Spirit. Today the Spiritual Shouter Baptists are an officially recognized religion in Trinidad and Tobago.

The Spiritual Shouter Baptist faith has had an influence on the calypso culture and rhythm of Trinidad and Tobago, and thus on the national community. Their hymns have pronounced African rhythms, which calypsonians borrowed and fused with the calypso to produce pulsating recordings that the public readily appreciated and purchased. Sometimes calypsonians dramatized and sensationalized the experiences of members of the faith in their renditions; at other times they, through ridicule in their lyrics, supported those in society who showed contempt and scorn toward this religion.

The Spiritual Shouter Baptist Religion is a phenomenon of the dynamics in cultural and political resistance in Trinidad and Tobago, and indeed, the Caribbean region. Historically, domination and oppression created the battle for religious freedom, which this religion won and has remarkably sustained. Thus, the story of their journey offers strategies to resist colonizing forms of hegemony. Theirs was a successful goal to construct an oppositional religious entity that would keep them linked to issues that endanger the rights of African people. Therefore, communities of this religion flourish in many locations where diverse descendants of Africans in the Caribbean and its Diaspora become more and more attracted to the spiritual and to the social and political vitality it grants to society.

Yvonne Bobb-Smith

See also Trinidad and Tobago.

FURTHER READING

Bisnauth, D. 1989. *History of Religions in the Caribbean.* Kingston, Jamaica: Kingston Publishers.

Clarke, Anthony. 2005. *A Spiritual Shouter Baptist 2005 Sacred Solar Calendar.* Port of Spain, Trinidad and Tobago: Gordon Rohlehr.

Henry, Frances. 2003. *Reclaiming African Religions in Trinidad.* Kingston, Jamaica: University of the West Indies Press.

Herskovits, Melville. 1947. *Trinidad Village.* New York: Alfred Knopf.

Houk, J. 1995. *Spirit, Blood and Drums: The Orisha Religion in Trinidad.* Philadelphia: Temple University Press.

Jacobs, Carl M. 1996. *Joy Comes in the Morning: Elton George Griffith and the Shouter Baptists.* Port of Spain, Trinidad and Tobago: The Caribbean Historical Society.

Laitenen, Maait. 2002. *Aspects of Gender in Spiritual Baptist Religion in Tobago: Notes from the Field.* Working Paper series no. 6. Saint Augustine: University of the West Indies, Centre for Gender and Development Studies.

Lovelace, Earl. 1986. *The Wine of Astonishment.* London: Heinemann.

Rohlehr, Gordon. 1990. *Calypso and Society in Pre-Independence Trinidad.* Port of Spain, Trinidad and Tobago: Gordon Rohlehr.

Said, Edward. 1993. *Culture and Imperialism.* London: Chatto and Windus.

Taylor, Patrick, ed. 2001. *Nation Dance: Religion, Identity and Cultural Difference in the Caribbean.* Bloomington: Indiana University Press.

Sport and the African Diaspora

RACE AND SPORT IN THE BRITISH EMPIRE: THE CARIBBEAN

Sport, that is, the institutionalized physical practice of internationally, rule-governed competitive games, emerged in its modern form during the 19th century. Most of the world's most popular sports such as cricket, football (soccer), and rugby, derived their formal codification in Victorian Britain. The diffusion of Western sports attempted to supplant indigenous games and sports, also competitive, rule-governed, and international at times, with a Western systematization of activities that were thought to be morally superior. British colonial elites viewed sports as a pedagogical tool, able to teach native peoples the values of fair play, respect for rules and authority, and notions of teamwork and sacrifice. However, the imposition of sports was met with degrees of resistance. For example, in the Caribbean, cricket came to articulate the wider politics of anticolonial struggle against British imperialism. As the Trinidadian intellectual C. L. R. James observed, the campaign during the 1950s to have a black player appointed captain of the West Indies cricket team mirrored and helped to produce a wider politics of black empowerment and political consciousness. From the late 1970s until the mid 1990s, the success of the West Indies cricket team came to be seen as a form of black pride and achievement not only for Afro-Caribbeans but also for black peoples throughout the African Diaspora. Today, cricket in the English-speaking Caribbean is no longer the cultural dominant it was during the 20th century. Because of American-ization, young Caribbeans are as likely to be interested in sports such as basketball and American football as they are cricket. And although cricket remains an important site for the production of a pan-Caribbean identity, some commentators suggest that the collectivist forms of solidarity that cricket used to create have now been replaced by a more individualist ideology that focuses on the individual achievements of players such as Brian Lara, rather than cricket embodying the aspirations of the region as a whole.

RACE AND SPORT IN THE UNITED STATES

The first black athletes were either horse racing jockeys, as enslaved Africans were given the task of caring for, training, and then riding their owners' horses, or boxers who would, quite literally, fight their way to freedom. White slave masters would sometimes select physically able black men to box under their guidance and then bet on the outcome. However, the Jim Crow laws meant that the early African American experience in sport was marked by discrimination and exclusion. An important milestone in the history of African American sports history occurred in 1908 when the Texas-born Jack Johnson became the first black Heavyweight Champion of the World. Johnson's successes, which attracted worldwide attention, publicly challenged the "obviousness" of white supremacy. In an effort to restore the symbolic order of white supremacy, when Johnson finally lost his world title the so-called "color line" was redrawn, which prevented black boxers from competing for world titles. The later successes of African American stars, such as the athlete Jesse Owens and boxer Joe Louis in the 1930s, the baseball player Jackie Robinson in the 1940s, and the tennis player Althea Gibson in the 1950s, served a similar role in representing black cultural achievement in the midst of white racism. The 1960s marked a shift in how black athletes were perceived in America. The black-gloved (Black Power) salute by Tommie Smith and John Carlos at the 1968 Mexico Olympic Games remains an iconic and more militant image of black sporting struggles for freedom. Smith and Carlos were part of a wider campaign for human rights that included not only addressing the forms of racial segregation and discrimination still operating within U.S. sports at that time, but also challenging the lack of Civil Rights for African Americans more generally and highlighting the plight of black South Africans and the continued injustices produced by apartheid. With the emergence of self-conscious and politically aware athletes such as Muhammad Ali, sports came to be seen as an important site for articulating cultural politics engaged in exposing and challenging racial injustice. Today, athletes like tennis stars Venus and Serena Williams offer different images to young black people, showing a new, empowered form of black femininity, or what might be called a "ghetto fabulous" style. Black athletes in America have come a long way since the days of Jack Johnson and are now global celebrities, like Tiger Woods in golf and Michael Jordan in basketball, able to earn millions of dollars in endorsements and earnings.

RACE AND SPORT IN AFRICA

Much of the limited research on sport in Africa has tended to focus on the politics of race and sport in South Africa. The 1977 Gleneagles agreement and the campaign to isolate South Africa through a sporting boycott is widely viewed as making an important contribution to the eventual downfall of apartheid. It is important to note for those studying South Africa, an ongoing concern has been how sport was used during the apartheid regime to further racial segregation and how, since the African National Congress came to power, sport is now being used as a way to develop a new, multicultural imagery for South Africa. In 1995, Nelson Mandela's embrace of the Springboks, the South African national rugby union team, seen for many decades as the sport and team of white Afrikaners, was a public example

of sport's role in articulating a postracial democratic settlement in that country. Similarly, the achievements of black runners at international sporting events such as the Olympics have produced national pride in countries such as Ethiopia and Kenya. However, this success has come at a cost in reproducing biological discourses of absolute racial difference and perpetuating myths concerning the supposed "natural athleticism" of African bodies. Indeed, there is a widespread anthropological curiosity, which demonstrates the continuation of colonial frameworks in viewing Africa itself, with the constant media and academic fascination with Kenyan long-distance runners in particular and the concomitant search for racio-biological explanations for their success.

The sporting success in recent years of soccer teams such as Nigeria, Ghana, Cameroon, and South Africa has shown the talent and progress that African countries have made, leading some commentators, such as the Brazilian soccer star Pelé, to predict that an African country will win the men's football World Cup in the near future. South Africa's successful bid to stage the 2010 men's football World Cup finals is seen as an important moment in the sporting history of Africa in terms of demonstrating the continent's ability to host a major sporting event and positioning Africa itself as a central player within world sport.

RACE AND SPORT IN THE 21ST CENTURY

The future politics of sport within the African Diaspora will be as varied as the sports played and the regions they are played in. More attention needs to be paid to the experiences and achievements of black female athletes. As structural barriers to girls' and women's access to sporting opportunities slowly decline, the 21st century is likely to see the politics of race and sport played out through the lives and achievements of female athletes. However, alongside these success stories, black athletes in various parts of Europe continue to experience both verbal and physical racial abuse. The success of black athletes, many from various locations across the African Diaspora, reveals the contradictory nature of race and sport as these players are often regarded as local and national heroes and have played a vital role in helping Europe itself come to recognize, accept, and even celebrate its multicultural present and future. Although many of these athletes celebrate victories under particular nation-state flags, their success also lends itself to another reading in terms of increasing black participation and success in selected and available sports. Sometimes these are read as the breaking of barriers, as in speed skating. Thus, just as European colonialism reshaped the landscape of Africa, black athletes are now reconfiguring the contemporary political and cultural realities of what it means to be a European.

Ben Carrington

See also "African" in African American History; Brazil: Afro-Brazilians; Jamaica; James, Cyril Lionel Roberts (1901–1989).

FURTHER READING

Armstrong, G., and R. Giulianotti, eds. 2004. *Football in Africa: Conflict, Conciliation and Community*. Basingstoke, UK: Palgrave.

Carrington, B., and I. McDonald, eds. 2001. *"Race," Sport and British Society*. London: Routledge.

Edwards, H. 1969. *The Revolt of the Black Athlete*. New York: Free Press.

Hoberman, J. 1997. *Darwin's Athletes: How Sport Has Damaged Black America and Preserved the Myth of Race*. Boston: Mariner Books.

James, C.L.R. 1963. *Beyond a Boundary*. London: Serpent's Tail.

Sri Lankan African Diaspora

The presence of people of African descent in Sri Lanka draws attention to the eastward migration of Africans across the Red Sea and the Indian Ocean, a topic that has received less attention than the westward migration across the Atlantic. Although Abyssinians (modern-day Ethiopians) were trading in fifth-century Sri Lanka when the island was an emporium in the Indian Ocean, historical evidence so far suggests that the African presence in Sri Lanka coincides with colonial activity. Portuguese colonizers were saved from defeat by an emergency reinforcement of African soldiers sent from their base at Goa. The Dutch who followed the Portuguese also increased the African presence on the island. The British presence on the island predated Britain's Abolition of Slavery Act. The British Empire also drew on African manpower.

The population census reports of 1871 to 1911 list Africans as Kaffirs (a word the British adopted from the Portuguese word *cafre*, which the Portuguese adopted from the Arabic *qafr*, which means "nonbeliever"). Intermarriage with other ethnic groups is common, but there are physiognomically identifiable Afro–Sri Lankans in several parts of the island. The largest number are in Puttalama in the North-Western Province: Puttalama Town, Sellan Kandel, and Sirambiyadiya.

The lyrics of their songs, which they call *manhas* (apparently a contraction of the Portuguese word *marchinhas*, meaning "little marches") are in the Indo-Portuguese of Ceylon (nowadays called Sri Lanka Portuguese Creole). Creole was the lingua franca of the island for almost 350 years before English replaced it. Today Creole is mainly heard during singing sessions. Elderly Afro-Sri Lankans use Creole as a secret language. No attempt is made to teach their children Creole (unlike the Portuguese Burghers in Batticaloa and Trincomalee in the Eastern Province) but despite "out-marriages" the children learn *manhas* early in life. They do not compose new *manhas* and only sing the songs that have been handed down to them through an oral tradition. Homemade instruments (two halves of dried coconut shells and a piece of wood, a spoon and a fork, a spoon and a bottle), *rabana* (a drum), and tambourine are used. A few decades ago the mandolin was played but the instrument is now less common. African cultural retentions are evident in their music and dance. The arm, hip, and body movements and postures are particularly significant in this context. The music is rhythm driven. Music, song, and dance give Afro–Sri Lankans a collective identity.

Shihan de Silva Jayasuriya

See also Creole, Creolity, Creolization; India and the African Diaspora; The African Diaspora in Asia (TADIA).

FURTHER READING

De Silva Jayasuriya, Shihan. 2001. "Les Cafres de Ceylan: le chaînon portugais." *Cahiers des Anneax de la Mémoire* (3): 229–253.

De Silva Jayasuriya, Shihan. 2003. "Les femmes et l'esclavage au Sri Lanka." *Cahiers des Anneax de la Mémoire* (5): 99–122.

De Silva Jayasuriya, Shihan. 2003. "The African Diaspora in Sri Lanka." In *The African Diaspora in the Indian Ocean*, ed. Shihan de Silva Jayasuriya and Richard Pankhurst, 251–288. Trenton, NJ: Africa World Press.

Goonatilleke, Miguel. 1983. Report of an Interview with the Portuguese Speaking Community in Puttalam. Colombo, Sri Lanka: Department of National Archives.

Steelpan

The steelpan, the national instrument of Trinidad and Tobago, familiarly called 'pan' by its many aficionados, is the only innovative musical instrument of the 20th century.

HISTORY

The early history of the steelpan is closely tied to the carnival period and the freed slaves who participated in the pre-Lenten activities, especially in the postemancipation period of 1834 to 1838. Activities included the beating of African drums, which the Colonial administration later outlawed with Ordinance One of 1884 after the second Cannes Brulées Riots. However, the drums were subsequently replaced by the tambour (tamboo)-bamboo bands, which consisted of cut bamboo stems of various widths and lengths. Four different types of bamboo were selected. The largest or thickest in circumference was used for the bass or boom. There was also the fuller or foule, the chandler and the cutter. When these stems were struck on their sides or beaten on the ground they produced a variety of sounds that provided the rhythmic clatter for the procession of revelers. These tamboo-bamboo bands with their homemade instruments had supplied the background rhythms for the chanting of bongo and *kalinda* songs, which had traditionally accompanied the stick (*bois*) fights in the *gayelles*. The tamboo bamboo's durability was effected by peeling the outer material of the stem and splitting the bamboo.

For a brief transitional period in the mid 1930s some of the expressly tamboo-bamboo bands changed their format and became hybrid bands, which would offer the woody sound of the original tamboo-bamboo mixed with a new metallic sound produced by a range of discarded metal objects, creating a repertoire of instruments that also expanded to include the bugle, and the empty bottle struck with a spoon. This eclectic ensemble took over musically as the rhythmic base to accompany the singing of popular songs and calypsos. The metal surfaces of improvised containers also allowed some variation of sound if they were struck in different areas of the object.

The emergence of the steelpan would come about in a series of small, significant, and in many cases accidental steps. Between 1936 and 1941, it was the ingenuity of a number of pioneering individuals who were trying to improve on the limitations of the instruments of the day in the interest of increasing the range and variation of the percussive sounds required for their street parades. These players

The steelpan, or steel drum, is purported to be the only musical instrument created in the 20th century. (iStockPhoto)

competed for musical dexterity and bragging rites among themselves and only later on did they discern the possibilities of playing simple melodies, as the number and range of notes became available. Much of this innovation occurred within a relatively small area in Port-of-Spain and its environs, especially, but not exclusively, in the area known as Behind the Bridge. There was much networking and constant adoption of new ideas along with further and ongoing experimentation by the pioneers' proletarian musical community.

Initially, the metal surfaces had no defined notes and were struck with shortened broomsticks. This repeated striking caused the metal surfaces to fracture from the hard, sharp surfaces of the sticks. It was discovered that two different sounds could be produced by beating one part of the pan more often than the other. So, in those early days the players were actually beating pan, a term that is now considered

quite patronizing and insulting to describe the action of playing the instrument. Later on, someone would shorten a small, 15-gallon, steel drum by removing a greater part of the side, called the skirt, and pounding the surface outward. A hammer was then used to sink three separate parts of the now convex playing surface. This action produced a pan with three notes. These pans were 15 to 20 inches in diameter and had a skirt of 12 to 14 inches from the rim. Moreover, it was realized that the reverse process of sinking the bottom in and the notes out would produce a better tonal quality. This method, credited to Ellie Mannette, has since become the standard for making a steelpan. Subsequent research has confirmed that this intuitive process was in fact scientifically correct.

Before long, for the greater convenience to the performer, these pans would be strapped on the side or around the neck of the player who was then able to use two sticks instead of one to beat the pan. The pannist's hands were now freed to play the pan rather than supporting the pan with one hand, while beating it with the other. Coincidental with these developments was the introduction of the rubber-covered, lighter sticks or mallets, which allowed a better quality sound to be produced while also protecting and promoting the longevity of the pan's playing surface. From these early beginnings came the evolution of three (1944), five (1945), and nine (1946) note pans, in relatively quick order, as a number of early pan tuners began using larger steel drums, which the demand for more musical notes had mandated. By 1951, there were 23 notes on the tenor pan. The increase in the number and variety of notes at this juncture would facilitate the playing of more complex melodies and, indeed, many musical exponents expressed surprise and amazement when the early pannists began to exhibit such range.

STEELBAND

A typical steelband in these early days would consist of four or five lead pans, then called ping pongs, scratchers, kittle drum, and bass drum (cuff boom), which were considered background pans, and an iron percussion section, which has been expanded into what is now affectionately called "the engine room." Today, a steelband consists of a variable number of steelpans of assorted types and may range from as few as four or five drums to as many as 200 or more pans, as is demonstrated at the annual Panorama competition in Trinidad, regarded as the premier pan event in the island or in the rest of the world.

Today, steelpans are manufactured from specifically made 55-gallon steel drums, replacing the discarded oil drums of a previous era. These customized drums can better accommodate the hammering and stretching required for creating quality pans. The process of pan manufacture involves the following: the drum is cut to length for the particular pan type; after sinking and marking off the notes, backing occurs, the pan is grooved, its surface is heat treated, and the notes are tuned and blended.

Any steelband, however, must consist of a number of basic units. First, there are the soprano, lead, melody, or tenor pan; a double second pan; a cello-pan; and a bass section in addition to an engine room consisting of a variety of percussion instruments such as the iron and scratcher.

Each pan has a playing surface of various notes with a surrounding enclosure called a skirt, which acts as a resonator and varies in length for the different types of pans. The sizes of the pans are defined to a great extent by the length of the skirts, and this has important implications not only on the quality of the sound produced but also on the portability and transport requirements of the different instruments.

Each pan is played with a different pair and kind of pan stick or mallet from the small, light sticks topped with rubber tubing for service on the tenor pans to the larger, longer sticks each topped with a rounded rubber ball for the bass pans. Some sticks use plain or polished wood with rubberized grips, and others use bamboo or aluminum rods. Further experimentation and development has led to electronic sticks, interchangeable sticks, and chord sticks. Iron and scratcher sections augment the sound of the band.

Pan stands were introduced in 1956, followed in the 1960s and '70s by yet another series of improvements for the steelpan, when road pans on wheels appeared, allowing greater mobility. This modernization was soon followed by the introduction of racks with canopies to protect the stretched metal playing surface from the effects of the sun, steelbands on floats (1965), the nine bass (1971), the rocket pan (1972), the 12 bass (1973), the quadraphonic pan (1974), the triple tenor harmony arrangement (1976), and the pan harmony comprising six pans (1977). The widespread adoption of chromed lead pans would soon follow. This originality would also have the dual function of increased protection of the playing surface while improving the pan's aesthetic appeal.

The pan yard is the main hub or locus of steelband functionality at the community level. It is thus used for a variety of activities such as storing the instruments, pan racks, for pan practice sessions, liming, and within recent times the staging of concerts, fetes, exhibitions, classes in music with emphasis on the pan, even religious gatherings, and limited commercial activity by vendors from the surrounding neighborhood. Some of the earlier pan yards were previously used as *gayelles* or *Orisha palais*, as these spaces represented the natural and historical gathering places in the communities. Since then pan yards have evolved from cramped enclosures that accommodated a few pans and a motley crew of panmen, to those of today, which are often spacious, organized, and owned, leased, or freehold properties on which the steelband men and women of various ages and social backgrounds can practice and hone their craft.

PAN ACROSS THE DIASPORA

In 1951, a group of top panmen was selected for a tour of Europe. This panside was called Trinidad All Steel Percussion Orchestra, which departed Trinidad for England in July of that year to perform initially at the Festival of Britain. This trip by all accounts led to the internationalization of the instrument and led an appreciative acceptance at home. Concurrently, there was the formation of one of the first all-female Girls Pat Steel Orchestra, which successfully toured British Guiana (now Guyana) and Jamaica in 1952. Along with developments in Trinidad steelbands were established across the Caribbean. Steelbands now exist in many cities across the world. There are also school steelbands in Trinidad with the government-sponsored Pan in the Classroom projects as well as eclectic ensembles and exclusive family bands. International exploitation of this resource is beginning, and in the United States,

major universities and schools, including historically black colleges and universities, like Florida Memorial University in Miami, are engaging in research and/or have created their own orchestras. In 1979, Trinidadian steelband had a major impact at the Festival of African Culture in Nigeria (FESTAC), leading to steelband developing in Africa.

Standardization of the pan and intellectual property rights for the instrument are issues as in 2002, the U.S. government granted two Americans a patent for supposedly being the first to make a steelpan using a hydro forming press, a process already discovered by Dr. Clement Imbert and Eugene McDavid at the University of the West Indies, Saint Augustine, in the 1970s. In addition, a grooveless pan is being patented by Phil Solomon from Guyana; a patent was granted in 2004 to a Trinidadian-born American, Trevor King, for a circle of fifths tenor pan, an instrument previously designed and developed by Anthony Williams, the leader of the famous Pan Am North Stars Steel Orchestra.

Neila Todd

See also Calypso; Trinidad and Tobago.

FURTHER READING

Gonzalez, Sylvia. 1978. *Steelband Saga: A Story of the Steelband (the First 25 Years)*. Trinidad and Tobago: Ministry of Education and Culture Publication.

Horne, Louise. 2003. The *Evolution of Modern Trinidad and Tobago*. Eniath's Printing Company (ISBN 976–8193–11–5).

Johnson, Kim, Helene Bellour, Milla Cozart Riggio and BP Trinidad and Tobago. 2002. *Renegades: The History of the Renegades Steel Orchestra*. New York: Macmillan.

Slater, John. 1995. The *Advent of the Steelband (and My Life and Times with It)*. Rev. Ed. Lintho Press Printers.

Steumpfle, Stephen. 1995. *The Steelband Movement: The Forging of a National Art in Trinidad and Tobago*. Kingston, Jamaica: University of the West Indies Press.

Thomas, Kenrick. 1999. *Panrica-Tacarigua's Contribution to the Evolution of the Steelband Phe-*

nomenon in Trinidad and Tobago. Washington, D.C.: Original World Press.

Stono Rebellion

The Stono Rebellion occurred in the low country of South Carolina about 12 miles south of Charleston in St. Paul's Parish on September 9, 1739. Despite the celebrated history of slave rebellions in the American South, the uprising was one of only two organized slave rebellions in English-speaking North America that ever came to fruition. Although the hardships of plantation life are often looked at as the sole pretexts for slave uprisings, the Stono Rebellion and the events surrounding it illustrate the complex set of factors that the Stono rebels attempted to negotiate. In that year the white colonists were plagued by a yellow fever epidemic that was claiming the lives of six South Carolinians daily, and they were also threatened by the possibility of war with the Spanish. Furthermore the Spaniards guaranteed the freedom of escaped slaves from British North America and in 1738 established a settlement for fugitives entitled Gracia Real de Santa Teresa de Mose (Fort Mose) north of Saint Augustine, Florida. Throughout the course of that year many slaves attempted to escape to Florida and some were successful.

The revolt began in the early morning of September 9, 1739. A group of about 20 slaves gathered, made their way across the Stono Bridge, and under the command of a slave named Jemmy seized weapons and powder from a local store after decapitating the two storekeepers. Now armed, the conspirators made their way toward Georgia killing whites that they confronted along the way. Some slaves voluntarily joined ranks with the group as they encountered them; reportedly, others were forced to join.

Lieutenant Governor William Bull by chance came in full view of the rebellious lot and was successful in avoiding their wrath. With swelled numbers, the rebels made their way to an open field where they began to celebrate. By four o'clock that evening, the white militia had organized under the leadership of Lieutenant Governor Bull. The better-armed militia took the rebels by surprise, rapidly disbanding the group. Though the uprising was contained by nightfall, many of the conspirators who were not captured that day were hunted down in bloody skirmishes.

The characteristics of low-country plantation society helped to shape the atmosphere for the uprising. The colonists were familiar with African slavery from its very beginning. Some immigrants arrived in the colony from Barbados and the wider British Caribbean sometimes bringing slaves. Still the economy of the colony in its earliest years was based on deerskins, which the colonists acquired through trade with Native Americans. Another important undertaking of early South Carolinians was cattle raising, which provided limited economic success and fostered an environment of relative autonomy for blacks who worked on ranches.

However, the economic structure of the colony changed once the colonists achieved success at growing rice primarily for Caribbean (primarily for slave consumption) and European markets (particularly Holland, Spain, and Portugal). In 1695, the colony had produced 500 pounds of rice. By 1704, the lands of low-country South Carolina yielded 800,000 pounds of rice. The dependence on African labor to work the rice plantations of the South Carolina low-country led to a commensurate rise in the African population. Rice planting required appreciably more labor than the tobacco plantations of the Virginia Chesapeake. In 1690 there were 1,500 slaves in South Carolina, and in 1710 there were 4,100. A small proportion were of Native American descent but the number of Native American slaves in Colonial South Carolina decreased as plantation society matured. By 1730, the black population had increased to 20,000.

Colonial South Carolina's dependency on enslaved African labor necessitated that the merchant-planter coalition that dominated South Carolina plantation society institute laws to draw sharp lines of distinction between the free and enslaved, and subject Africans to a perpetual state of servitude. In 1717, South Carolina passed a law relegating any white woman to a period of seven years of indentured servitude for giving birth to a mixed-race child. In 1721 and 1734, patrol acts were passed to keep a close eye on Africans on surrounding plantations. Among the most restrictive of these laws was the the Negro Act of 1735, which forbade slaves from wearing clothes "above the condition of slaves," denied them access to trade houses, and limited the extent to which they could sell their services.

The enslaved practiced several forms of resistance to vent their opposition, but in early Colonial South Carolina what stands out is the frequency with which slaves "voted with their feet" by running away. It was not uncommon for slaves to flee South Carolina plantation society in hopes of reaching Spanish Florida. However, the possibilities of achieving freedom by flight decreased considerably with the establishment of the British colony of Georgia (1732) to the south, between South Carolina and Florida.

The timing of the rebellion could perhaps be attributed to the increased workload of the enslaved Afro-Carolinian population. The rice crop of 1739 was larger than any before it and twice that of 1738. As the labor supply was not proportionally increased, the labor demands on each slave were greatly increased. September was a period of the cycle of rice production where labor tasks were extremely arduous. Using a 15- to 25-pound mortar and pestle, processing and dehusking was usually a sun-up to sundown task that was mostly done from September to April.

The 1739 Spanish invasion threat, the inducements of slaves in British colonies, the implementation of restrictive laws backed by harsh punishments, greater labor demands, and the attenuation of the white minority by disease likely dictated the timing of the rebellion. The slaves were responding to New World circumstances that affected their lives. Thus, the Stono rebels were seeking to liberate themselves from enslavement in an increasingly oppressive plantation society of Colonial South Carolina.

Perry Kyles

See also African Americans and the Constitutional Order; "African" in African American History; Capitalism and Slavery; Haitian Revolution.

FURTHER READING

Carney, Judy. 2002. *Black Rice: The African Origins of Rice Cultivation in the Americas*. Cambridge, MA: Harvard University Press.

Pearson, Edward A. 1996. "'A Countryside Full of Flames': A Reconsideration of the Stono Rebellion and Slave Rebelliousness in the Early Eighteenth-Century South Carolina Lowcountry." *Slavery and Abolition* 17 (2): 22–50.

Wood, Peter. 1974. *Black Majority: Negroes in Colonial South Carolina from 1670 through the Stono Rebellion*. New York: W.W. Norton & Company.

Sugar Cane and the African Diaspora

Sugar cane is perhaps unrivalled among other crops in its tremendous impact upon the landscapes, cultures, ecologies, economics, and politics of the New World. For centuries most of the sugar cane in the Americas was grown in the Caribbean, but it has historically been produced in substantial amounts in northeastern Brazil, Central and South America, and the southern United States. However, the role of Europe and Africa is just as critical to the historical study of sugar cane in the Americas, in that the growing consumption of sugar in Europe, the accumulation of wealth from the sugar colonies, and the vast extraction of human capital from Africa, significantly affected the sugar cane industries of the New World. Sugar cane has emerged not only as a crop but also as a poignant illustration of external economic and political influence over former colonies, environmental transformation and degradation, social and race relations, and modern demographics in the Americas.

Originally introduced to Hispaniola on Christopher Columbus's second voyage and brought by successive expeditions to other areas, sugar cane in the 15th and 16th centuries was a relatively small-scale commercial enterprise in the Spanish colonies and northeastern Brazil. Subsistence farming characterized agricultural production in the early centuries of colonization, though it was eclipsed in the mid-17th century by monoculture production of cash crops—namely sugar, but also tobacco, cacao, indigo, and coffee—for export to European markets. Sugar cane did not rise to the prominence it would enjoy for several centuries until British and French colonies in the Caribbean began large-scale cultivation in the Lesser Antilles, following the Dutch introduction of sugar cane to Barbados in 1640 via Brazil. By the 18th century, Saint Domingue (present-day Haiti) and Jamaica were the largest producers of sugar cane, while the economies of colonies like Barbados and Guadeloupe were based almost entirely on sugar. During the 18th century, the increasing popularity of this former luxury was evidenced by changes in the eating habits of many Europeans, due to increased availability, which in turn led to a surge in production of sugar in the colonies. Sugar cane production and demand suffered and declined at various times during the 19th century with the end of slavery and the emergence of new producers of cane sugar, and in the 20th century with free market trade in Europe and competition from beet sugar and other sweeteners. The production of sugar has decreased significantly today and is chiefly controlled by governments and a few large corporations. However, the continued dependency on North American and European markets suggests that the outward orientation of the sugar cane production remains an important part of the legacy of sugar in the Americas.

The sugar cane industries in the Americas monopolized land and created settlement patterns whose nuclei were the plantations, mills, and factories—or the centers of production. The harvesting of sugar cane requires careful coordination as it must be milled within one day to maintain the optimal sugar content, so efficient production of sugar depended on the close proximity of mills and factories. During the zenith of sugar production in the New World, extraction of wealth from the plantation societies also funded colonial endeavors, including further acquisition and occupation of land. Several scholars have argued additionally that the raw materials produced in the colonies stimulated the Industrial Revolution by providing capital, as well as viable models of agro-industry based on a combination of technical knowledge, coordination, and division of labor that would later characterize industrialized Europe. In this way the production of sugar is also closely tied to the development of capitalism.

Labor is one of the most important aspects of the discussion of the American sugar industries, and one whose legacy is visible today. Both the limited indigenous population and European indentured laborers proved less than satisfactory for the demands of increasing plantations. Because sugar could be produced at a much cheaper cost with the use of slave labor and, in doing so, give colonies an advantage over sugar from the East, the African slave trade provided a solution to the lack of adequate labor. The labor-intensive cultivation and harvesting of sugar cane would come to rely on the importation of enslaved Africans to work on the plantations, dramatically changing the racial composition of the Americas. Of the more than 10 million enslaved Africans forcibly taken to the New World, roughly half labored in the Caribbean, where they constituted the majority of the population, governed by a small population of whites. Today, the demographics of the Americas, most notably the Caribbean and northeastern Brazil, reflect large populations of descendants of Africans. After emancipation and largely unsuccessful attempts at encouraging European and free African immigration, indentured laborers, primarily from India, were brought to the Caribbean to replace slave labor. Of the approximately 500,000 Indian laborers, most went to the newer sugar-producing colonies of Trinidad and British Guiana, although the French Caribbean also recruited a significant number. Chinese laborers were also brought to the New World, many of whom worked on sugar plantations in Cuba. These groups have all contributed to the diverse cultural geography of the Americas, linked by the common thread of labor in sugar production.

The cultivation of sugar cane has had serious environmental implications resulting from the removal of forest cover, erosion, and soil degradation. The uneven patterns of land ownership created by the sugar cane industries have concentrated landholdings in the hands of a few, dispossessing many. The structure of plantation societies has had long-term effects on the social relations within territories and on the political and economic relationships between former colonies and colonial powers. Sugar cane has likewise been responsible for the migration of millions of peoples, whether free, coerced, or enslaved, and as such has had a major impact on the racial and cultural composition of the Americas.

Hillary Scott

See also Atlantic World and the African Diaspora; Capitalism and Slavery; Salt and the African Diaspora.

FURTHER READING

Galloway, J. H. 1989. *The Sugar Cane Industry: An Historical Geography from Its Origins to 1914.* Cambridge, UK: Cambridge University Press.

Mintz, Sidney. 1986. *Sweetness and Power: The Place of Sugar in Modern History.* New York: Penguin Books.

Richardson, Bonham C. 1998. *The Caribbean in the Wider World, 1492–1992: A Regional Geography.* Cambridge, UK: Cambridge University Press.

Williams, Eric E. 1994. *Capitalism and Slavery.* Chapel Hill: University of North Carolina Press.

Suriname: The Ndyuka Maroons

HISTORY

The first permanent European settlements in Suriname were founded in 1651 by the British, but they passed to Dutch control after 1667. These relatively modest plantations used only small slave components, but after the Indian wars (1676–1686) they developed into large-scale agro-industries, producing mainly sugar for the world market. Colony Suriname grew into a voracious consumer of slaves: inhumane working conditions, including the climate of the marshy lowlands, and the dramatic expansion of the plantation system required ever more enslaved Africans. In 1688, there were 23 plantations with 564 slaves; 50 years later, there were 430 plantations with 50.000 slaves. Between 1650 and 1700, 52 percent of the imported slaves were Loangos or Kongos. During the next 35 years the great majority of slaves were imported from West Africa; after 1736, Central Africa provided one-third of the slaves (Price and Price 1999, 278). Thus, a large arc of the African coast from present-day Senegal to Namibia, for hundreds of miles inland, lost part of its population to Suriname and contributed to the evolution of Ndyuka culture and that of the Suriname maroons in general.

From the beginning, enslaved Africans escaped the plantations, some to found free communities in the interior. Many of these runaways successfully battled the planters and their mercenaries. In southeast Suriname, between 1720 and 1730, the Ndyuka nation coalesced out of a number of such groups. In Central Suriname, another powerful coalition of runaways achieved recognition as the "Saramaka."

During the 1750s, the Ndyuka posed such a threat to the colony that Dutch authorities offered them their freedom and regular shipments of goods if they would stop their attacks on the plantations and return to the planters any slaves that escaped later. The peace treaty, concluded in 1760, created an independent black nation, more than a century before the abolition of slavery in Suriname (1863). Thereafter, some runaways were returned to the planters, but most were integrated into Ndyuka communities. Dutch authorities attempted to restrict the Ndyuka to the country's interior, but the planters needed them as lumberers. Gradually, hundreds of maroons settled in the plantation colony proper. From 1880 to 1925, Ndyuka and other maroons became important as boatmen transporting thousands of gold miners to places deep in French Guiana.

About 10.000 Ndyuka still inhabit their old heartland along the Tapanahoni River, a tributary of the Marowijne (Maroni) River, which separates Suriname from French Guiana. Others have settled in the capital, Paramaribo, in the eastern part of Suriname's coastal zone and in French Guiana. Several thousands live in the Netherlands. Today's widely dispersed Ndyuka (estimated at 50.000 total) battle the forces of disintegration with the loyalties of kinship and religion.

KINSHIP

The dominant principle of Ndyuka social organization is matrilineality. All Ndyuka know to which of the 14 matrilineal clans (*lo*) they belong. Most Ndyuka villages are clan-owned. Clans are divided into matrilineages (*bee*), which can be subdivided into matrisegments (*wan mama pikin*). As is usual in matrilineal societies, other principles help structure kinship relations. Bilateral consanguineal kin

groups (*famii*) play an important role. Whether lineage or family, kinship is crucial: when two unfamiliar Ndyuka meet, they first determine if and how they are related. One concern is to determine whether their respective kin groups had a bad relationship in the past: certain actions by one's matrilineal ancestors may have aroused a fury (*kunu*) in the other's matrilineage. In such cases, especial respect and decency should be shown toward that party, for the avenging spirit or ghost is easily provoked to inflict misfortune, illness, even death. Hence, precise genealogical data are imperative among Ndyuka in their heartland and in the diaspora (Köbben 1967; van Wetering and Thoden van Velzen 2002).

GODS AND ORACLES

The second integrative force of Ndyuka society is even more important. The Ndyuka believe in a variety of gods and spirits. Central to every village both geographically and ritually are the ancestor shrines: the mortuary (*kee osu*) and the ancestor pole (*faakatiki*). Every morning village elders congregate at the *faakatiki* to beg their ancestors for the well-being of the community and speedy recovery of the sick; libations are poured and village affairs are discussed.

Ancestors are respected but known entities. But the domain of the gods is largely unknowable. Ndyuka recognize numerous gods (*gadu*) who are powerful and immortal beings, though generally not considered omniscient and omnipresent. Topping the supernatural hierarchy is Masaa Gadu (the Lord God), the creator. Immediately below him in spiritual power are the great deities: *Gaan Gadu* (great deity) or *Gaan Tata* (great father), *Ogii* (danger), and *Gedeonsu*. These intervene directly in human affairs, take sides in conflicts, and punish humans for their sins. Unlike *Masaa Gadu*, who protects all humankind equally, the great deities are tribal or national gods. *Gaan Tata* led the Africans on the plantations out of slavery, fighting alongside his people like Yahweh among the Jews, and is still seen primarily as the Ndyuka's staunchest defender against their enemies, especially against the most dangerous, witches (*wisiman*). *Gaan Tata* insists that every corpse be carried through the village and examined for evidence of witchcraft. If a witch is so discovered, or even if mere contamination with witchcraft is detected, the deceased's possessions are confiscated by *Gaan Tata's* priests, and the corpse is dumped at some unholy spot in the forest.

Ogii is the king of the forest spirits and *Gaan Tata's* host. When the rebel slaves arrived on the Tapanahoni River, infant mortality was high. *Gaan Tata*, a stranger to the Amazonian rain forest, begged *Ogii* for assistance. The king of the forest assigned *Gaan Tata* a small army of forest spirits to assist him and his people, on condition that *Gaan Tata* would behave as a proper guest, not spoiling the environment. During the 1970s, *Ogii's* medium decided that *Gaan Tata* had condemned so many (mainly innocent) deceased Ndyuka of witchcraft that Ogii's forest, river, and creeks had become polluted. That medium ruled the Ndyuka heartland for almost 10 years, desecrating *Gaan Tata's* places of worship, forbidding the carrying of the corpse, and substituting periodic screening of the living population for witchery. For those found contaminated, a simple cleansing ritual was considered sufficient. Today, a generation later, *Gaan Tata* is again being venerated.

Gedeonsu is considered a shielding, comforting deity. In their prayers, the Ndyuka say: "When we are hungry, we know where to run to. You will always be there to take care of us, to offer us solace." Every three or four years pilgrimages are held to *Gedeonsu's* forest shrines. Hundreds of Ndyuka men and women, from both the interior and the city, partake in these sacred treks.

There is no formal cult for *Masaa Gadu*, but worship of the great deities is organized with shrines and priests. Secular offices, such as chief and captain (village headman), are often combined with priestly ones. "Carry oracles," tabernacles tied to a plank carried by two priests, dominate religious practice. The plank's movements answer questions put to the oracle. All major problems are discussed this way. Any new spirit medium seeking legitimacy makes his or her first trip to one of those oracles. During the civil war (1986–1992), when hundreds of young Ndyuka men joined the resistance against Suriname's military junta, the oracles were consulted to see whether the gods would support them. *Gaan Tata* told the guerrillas that they should have consulted him earlier and not to ask him to support a decision they had made by themselves. At the same time, the god criticized the military for their rough handling of the Ndyuka people. But followers of *Ogii*, the forest deity, openly supported the insurrection. Before every military action by the insurgents, a carry oracle was consulted. Before being allowed to join the guerrillas, every volunteer was checked by the carry oracle for witchcraft or intent to betray the cause (Thoden van Velzen and van Wetering 2004).

Although almost all maroon societies in the Americas have disappeared, the Ndyuka and the Saramaka continue to exhibit considerable cultural vitality and autonomy (Price 1996).

Approximately 100 miles separate the Ndyuka heartland from the coast where most economic activity takes place. It is common knowledge that the authorities in Paramaribo seek an agreement with certain influential Ndyuka to open the terrain between the Tapanahoni River and the coast to exploitation by international mining and logging interests. Opposition to these projects, which would destroy the virgin rain forest, is spearheaded by the *Gaan Tata* oracle. The oracle operates not by directly rejecting government proposals, but making accusations of witchcraft against the recently deceased relatives of those who favor the wholesale exploitation of Suriname's forests, thus undermining the reputation of those families.

H.U.E. Thoden van Velzen
and W. van Wetering

See also Maroon and Marronage.

FURTHER READING

Köbben, A. J. F. 1967. "Unity and Disunity: Cottica Djuka Society as a Kinship System." *Bijdragen tot de Taal-, Land-en Volkenkunde* 123 (1): 10–52.

Price, Richard. 1996. *Maroon Societies: Rebel Slave Communities in the Americas.* Baltimore: The Johns Hopkins University Press.

Price, Sally, and Richard Price. 1999. *Maroon Arts: Cultural Vitality in the African Diaspora.* Boston: Beacon Press.

Thoden van Velzen, H.U.E., and W. van Wetering. 2004. *In the Shadow of the Oracle: Religion as Politics in a Suriname Maroon Society.* Long Grove, IL: Waveland Press.

Van Wetering, W., and H. U. E. Thoden van Velzen. 2002. "Ndyuka." In *Encyclopedia of World Cultures*, ed. Melvin Ember, Carol R. Embers, and Ian Skoggard, supplement, 222–227. New York: Macmillan Reference USA.

Sutherland, Efua Theodora (1924–1996)

Efua Morgue (her maiden name) Sutherland, Ghanaian playwright and community activist, founded PANAFEST (PanAfrican Festival), the coming together of Africans of the Diaspora to celebrate the arts, and made significant contributions to drama in Ghana.

Sutherland was born on June 27, 1924 in Cape Coast, in the central region of Ghana, then the Gold Coast, a British colony. After primary and secondary schooling there, she received her bachelor of arts in education at Homerton College, Cambridge University, and later studied linguistics, African languages and drama in the School of Oriental and African Studies in London. She returned to teach at her alma mater, St. Monica, and other learning institutions, including the prestigious Achimota School. In 1954, she married William Sutherland, an African American, and had three children.

Sutherland was a woman of vision and creativity. In 1957, she helped organize the Ghana Society of Writers and later, the Ghana Experimental Theater Co. In 1959, she founded *Okyeame*, a literary journal, and in 1960, she founded the Ghana Drama Studio, a fixture in the University of Ghana in the Institute of African Studies, where she served as a research associate. In 1968, she developed Kusum Agromba, a performance group who entertained in various venues, including churches, schools, and colleges, all across the country. She also aided in developing the Ghana National Children's Commission.

As a writer, Sutherland focused on using her works as a means of educating and motivating Ghanaians to be politically involved, prideful, and agents in their country's progress, all the while instilling pride in the different cultures and people of Ghana. Her play *Foriwa* (1967) is a drama set in the newly independent country of Ghana where the main female character, Foriwa, is a southerner who marries Labaran, a visionary northerner. Significant to their uniting is the role of the female, as Foriwa's mother plays a critical role by embracing Labaran as a suitable mate for her daughter. Sutherland, who was also quite influenced by the Greek classics, penned *Edufa* (1967), her re-creation of Euripides' *Alcestis*.

Another celebrated play, *The Marriage of Anansewa* (1975), reveals Sutherland's interest in and commitment to African oral culture and myth. Here, the Ananse trickster figure takes the role of a father who attempts to trick the various suitors of his daughter, Anansewa, so that he may gain wealth through her bride price. Important to this work is what Sutherland calls *mboguo*, which, much like a Greek chorus, is the act of audience members commenting on the development of the play through music and dance. Sutherland also wrote children's books, including *Playtime in Africa* (1962), *Vulture! Vulture!* (1968), *Tahinta* (1968), *The Roadmakers* (1961), and *The Voice in the Forest* (1983). Sutherland worked with and influenced Ghanaian artists such as Ama Ata Aidoo, Joe de Graft, and many more.

During the 1980s, Sutherland served as adviser to Ghanaian president Jerry Rawlings and helped establish the W.E.B. DuBois Memorial Center for Pan African Culture. Sutherland died on January 21, 1996.

Miriam C. Gyimah

See also Feminism and Black Women in the African Diaspora.

FURTHER READING
Brown, Lloyd. 1981. *Women Writers of Black Africa*. London: Greenwood Press.
Odamtten, Vincent. 2003. "Sutherland, Efua Theodora." *Encyclopedia of African Literature*. New York: Routledge.
Who's Who in African Literature: Biographies, Works, Commentaries. 1972. Germany: Becht-Druck & Co.
Wilentz, Gay. 1992. *Binding Cultures: Black Women Writers in Africa and the Diaspora*. Bloomington: Indiana University Press.

Swahili

The Swahili (singular *Mswahili*, plural *Wa-Swahili*) are a historically ancient group of coastal peoples stretching more than 2,000 miles along East Africa's coast. Distinctly Swahili communities with a shared but regionally variant Swahili culture and language were already well established by the seventh century CE. The Swahili language of the northeastern Bantu family is today one of the most widely spoken African languages. Kiswahili is a lingua franca in more than eight modern East and Central African countries and is also widely known throughout parts of the African Diaspora and the rest of the world. With antecedents reaching back as far as seven millennia, Swahili civilization arose gradually, starting perhaps more than 2,000 years ago, producing lasting stone architecture by the seventh century CE, and extending through several major periods of cultural efflorescence.

Swahili culture produced a set of distinct yet overlapping local communities with a common language and material culture featuring particular regional variants. Swahili villages, towns, and cities can be found in ecological niches: low-lying coastal areas, such as Malindi, Kenya or Mogadishu, Somalia; nearby islands often accessible at low tide, such as Mombasa or Manda in Kenya; and offshore islands, like Pemba, Zanzibar, and Mafia in Tanzania, accessible only by deep-sea vessel. Local production, trade, and cultural exchange form the economic basis of Swahili civilization. This cultural exchange connected coastal communities from Somalia to Mozambique in what Richard Wilding (1987) called the "coasting trade," and it also connected the entire Indian Ocean world with hinterland and interior communities throughout East Africa and the continent beyond. The Swahili language, part of the northeastern Bantu linguistic stream, is widely accepted to be about 75 percent Bantu-based and 25 percent Arabic, with small influences from several other African and Asian linguistic groups. In the past century, Kiswahili has become a lingua franca in most of East Africa, including Kenya, Tanzania, and much of Uganda, Congo, the offshore Indian Ocean islands of the Comoros archipelago and Mozambique, as well as in numerous Afro-Diasporic communities throughout the world.

EARLIEST CONTRIBUTORS TO PROTO-SWAHILI CIVILIZATION

Most histories of the Swahili written during and since the colonial era (1880s to 1960s) wrongly emphasized the primacy of Arab influences in Swahili antiquity, largely because of diffusionist and racial tendencies in Western anthropology and science that attempted to deny African history and agency. However, recent linguistic, archaeological, and historical investigations, especially those of African scholars trained in postindependence African contexts, have largely overturned this perspective, important though Arab connections were.

The earliest inhabitants of the East African coast were late Stone Age African foragers, whose hunter-gatherer descendants still live in pockets of the East African culture-scape. These peoples also engaged in fishing, hunting, and complex long-distance trade. Southern and eastern Cushitic-speaking and eastern Nilotic-speaking agro-pastoralists were the next major populations in the region, reaching as far south as present-day Tanzania. The historical influence of these groups on Swahili culture, particularly its northern half, has been underestimated by most scholars, but was provocatively suggested by James de vere Allen (1993) and Richard F. Wilding (1987). Their modern descendants include the Gabbra, Borana, and Oromo peoples,

As Allen and Wilding suggested, this connection is crucial to understanding the influence of Axum and other Ethiopian cultures, as well as Sudanese and Egyptian states, on the Swahili world to the south. Much of the ancient world's incense trade originated within this region, between the interior of the Horn of Africa and the Ethiopian highlands, and the extensive trade networks that emanated from both. More than 9,000 years ago, predynastic Egypt imported most of its resinous incense (used in embalming and other rituals), as well as precious stones and other goods from a land they called Punt, which researchers speculate lay on the African side of the southern Red Sea, or along the East African coast further south, if not generically referring to the whole of this pre-Swahili region. Together with gold and cinnamon, East Africa–derived incense was probably among the three most valued commodities of the ancient world, placing the earliest Swahili world at the center of global economic ties.

Bantu-speaking people bearing sophisticated iron technology and intensive agricultural and hunting practices spread into Central and then Eastern Africa throughout the first millennium BCE, and reached the coastal regions in the ear-liest centuries of the first millennium CE. It is still unclear whether they blended with, displaced, or absorbed an existing agricultural coastal population that existed by exploiting the marine environment, but the new Bantu-speaking populations expanded quickly and forged social relations with the pastoralists and hunter-gatherers in their midst. The latter, for example, usually were members of the secretive and ritualized well-sinking guild that provided water for all coastal inhabitants and their livestock. The northeastern branch of the Bantu-speaking family, known as Sabaki, ultimately formed the basis of the widely spoken Swahili language, a particular Sabaki variant with up to 25 percent loan words from Arabic as well as a smattering of influences from Persian, Urdu, Hindi, Portuguese, Malagasy, and Cushitic language groups, and more recently from English as well.

After the possibility that Egyptian and Phoenician vessels reached East Africa 2–6 millennia ago, there are good written records of Greek, Roman, and Arab travelers' and geographers' accounts of East Africa from the third century BCE. What was to later become the Swahili coast was at this time already an integral part of worldwide systems of trade and cultural contact. Dated to the first century CE, the *Periplus of the Erythrean Sea* is a Greek guide to the East African coast, known to them as Azania; it describes an already thriving and vital mercantile city known as Rhapta, whose location today remains a mystery despite speculation about the Rufiji and Lamu delta basins as probable sites. Arab ties with the East African coast began during this period as well, and Islam came to the Swahili coast from as early as the seventh century CE. The Arabic word for the coast and its people was *Zanj,* and the term *Swahili* is itself an Arabic term for coast (from *Sawahil*), much like the term *Sahel,* which refers to the southern "coast" or edge of the Sahara. Small numbers of Arab immigrants assimilated into coastal cultures over the centuries, intermarrying with local people and forming a part of local communities, while engaging in trade.

THE APEX OF SWAHILI CIVILIZATION

A florescence of distinctive stone architecture dates to this period, being already well established by the seventh century in cities from Mogadishu and Shanga in the north to Kilwa in the south. From the 8th to the 15th centuries, the Swahili coast entered a long period of florescence, with a major expansion in the number of cities and stone towns, reaching a total of more than 400 at its apex. Old and new cities grew in size; interior populations were drawn to the coasts and islands; and international trade, as well as trade with interior regions of the continent, expanded at steady rates. The 13th and 14th centuries may have been the penultimate apex of this development for the East African coast as a whole, although complex regional variation remained the norm. While this corresponds neatly with known developments elsewhere within the 13th century world system, the Swahili coast is often neglected in conventional world histories, although it clearly deserves to be seen as an integral part of Old World economies and cultural systems. It is possible that the Swahili world and its transoceanic allies to the east provided an important outlet for a southern shift of world systems into the Indian Ocean while the Mongol invasions wreaked havoc on societies across the whole of the Old World from the north.

These global connections underwrote a rich cultural assemblage along the coasts of East Africa, with distinct multistoried stone and coral architecture, indoor plumbing, diversified crafts such as silversmithing and wood carving, and dense urban cores in the midst of elaborate multiethnic and multilingual cities that encompassed pastoralists and agriculturalists as well as merchants both foreign and local. The *siwa*, or side blown horn, became a distinct Swahili customary item, and ritual sword fighting, also still in practice today at ceremonies, stems from this era if not earlier. The ivory trade was growing in this period, as African ivory was preferred to Asian varieties, and a trickle of slaves continued to flow east and north as well. Iron and mangrove poles were also large-scale exports, and East African iron, being more malleable, was exported in massive quantities to India where it was found to be of the best quality for the new process of making the galvanized steel that was being smelted in Asia. It can even be suggested that this East African iron thus led to the creation of swords so superior to all others that when one found its way into Europe, where they were exceedingly rare at first, its power led to the creation of the Excalibur myth. Gauging from the quantity and importance of these trade items alone, it should be clear that the coast exported more than just luxury goods, as has often been suggested, even if gold from the Great Zimbabwe region, gems from various regions, turtle shells, and animal skins continued to occupy important places within trade economies. Other cultural elements, some of which were also exported, were less material, such as the language, oral history, and epic poetry that date to this era of Swahili history and were influential throughout the region. These provide lasting works of art as well as detailed historical accounts of the social history of the coast.

TRADE AND THE ARRIVAL OF EUROPEANS

Trade that had existed for millennia by this time became larger in scale and more regularized than it had ever been before. Oman, Yemen, the Arab world, Persia, and India were the main trade partners across the Indian Ocean, and their cultural influences were also felt along the length of the East African coast. More distant lands, including Cambodia, Indonesia, China, Rome, and Nabatea constituted additional trading partners and sources of cultural exchange. The pottery of these places is often found in archaeological digs from this era, among a vast majority of locally produced wares, usually known as incised Tana wares, named for the Tana River. This pottery base clearly indicates the foundations of Swahili society in local interior cultures reaching thousands of miles inland mainly along riverine valleys. Overland and trickle trade is also known to have existed with distant regions of the African continent, though this has been downplayed and less researched until the past decade or two, with the promise of exciting new discoveries to be made in the near future by local archaeologists such as Chapurukha Kusimba and Felix Chami. African trade partners with the Swahili coast included, at various times and places, Egypt, Sudan, Ethiopia, Central Africa, the Great Lakes region, the eastern and central Saharan caravan routes, Great Zimbabwe, and southern Africa. But as Wilding made clear, the bulk of Swahili trade was in fact intra-Swahili trade between regions like Mogadishu, Mombasa, and Malindi in the north; Zanzibar, Pemba, and Kilwa in the middle; and Mozambique, Great Zimbabwe, the Comoros, and Mapungubwe (in South Africa) in the south.

The arrival of the Portuguese after 1498 did not destroy Swahili culture and trade as much as it posed a regular source of prolonged disruption. Swahili economies nevertheless managed to grow even during the 16th, 17th, and 18th centuries despite the predations and violence Europeans began visiting on the region. Omanis, especially the Mazrui Dynasty, established themselves in major coastal cities such as Mombasa and Pate, usually in close concert with inland peoples such as the Mijikenda or Oromo whom they relied upon as trade and military partners and allies. It was only with the advent of the Busaidi Omanis, who relocated the capital of their empire to Zanzibar from Muscat and rapidly conquered the coast in the first decades of the 19th century, that this balance was permanently disrupted and more exploitative relations became the norm. The 19th century saw an unprecedented skewing of coastal power relations, with the rise and massive expansion of Atlantic-style slave trading and plantations, underwritten by European naval power aligned with the Busaidi, Swahili elites, and Banyan financiers from India. During this period social relations were profoundly reordered and, as was entailed in all colonial processes, history itself was largely rewritten to reflect the new social structure.

QUESTIONS OF ORIENTATION AND BIAS IN SWAHILI HISTORIOGRAPHY

From this period then originates the so-called Arab (or Persian) myth of Swahili origins, predicated on the racial assumption that African accomplishments could not reflect African cultures and so must derive from outside the continent. It was now claimed that Arabs had conquered or colonized the supposedly empty coast from the earliest times, bringing with them all of the lasting elements of Swahili civilization, especially stone architecture. While extreme versions of this biased perspective have been definitively overturned since the end of formal colonial rule in East Africa, vestiges of it remain in otherwise critical works of scholars even today. Nonetheless, Muslim and Arab settlers occupied numerically small proportions of coastal populations until the 19th century and generally fit themselves within existing social and hierarchical orders. Syncretism between Islam and indigenous cultures was the norm, and coastal cultures absorbed settlers and incorporated them for the most part, rather than the other way around. Conversion to Islam was rare beyond certain neighborhoods of the coastal cities, again until the 19th century. Biases toward a larger than historically justified role for Islam and Arabs in East Africa remain, in part, because of the effects of colonial dislocation on the production of knowledge. Few local coastal peoples other than Arabs and Swahili have produced social science scholars to represent their perspectives in the academy.

These questions of bias are also pertinent to discussions of the slave trade. The British in particular blamed slavery, in exaggerated forms, on existing Arab cultures in the Indian Ocean, but these were not chattel forms of slavery, until this was introduced in the 19th century under European influence from the Atlantic system where it had gradually been limited. Far more slaves, now chattel slaves for the most part, were exported from East Africa in the 19th century than in the preceding two millennia. Some reached the Atlantic system via the French colonial islands in the southwest Indian Ocean, but most were destined for Egypt, the Ottoman Empire, Arabia, and India. Local Swahili and Omani elites were able to retain nominal autonomy throughout this period, though British and French rule was encroaching rapidly, and with the advent of the machine gun and the scramble for Africa, formal territorial colonialism began in the 1880s and 1890s. Abolition in East Africa, as it had been in West Africa in the preceding century, became largely a tool to undermine local elites and supplant them with European rule.

The Swahili Today

Swahili scholars and others have correctly pointed out that Swahili peoples at the coast have been marginalized in the postcolonial period, despite relative prominence and freedom during the colonial years (1895–1963 in Kenya). Investors from the interiors of Kenya and other East African countries, combined with the influx of foreign capital, have displaced the Swahili from the burgeoning tourist industries that have become leading sectors of postcolonial economies such as Kenya. Mijikenda and other non-Swahili coastal peoples, historical partners in earlier Swahili civilizations, also point out that they are even further displaced within the schema, being marginal to the Swahili who are themselves being marginalized from the centers of postcolonial state power. Much as elsewhere in the world, the colonial- and slave-era hierarchies set up in the past two centuries continue to a large extent to organize coastal social relations today. Swahili are marginalized economically vis-à-vis the state, tensions exist between what some refer to as pure versus innovated (i.e., African influenced) Islam, as well as between Muslims and non-Muslims in some parts of the coast, and many racial and slave-based terminologies are still used as ethnic labels.

At the same time, many of the egalitarian and cross-cultural elements of Swahili history are still in full effect in coastal communities, and such tendencies continue to assert themselves in numerous ways, in cross-class marriages, business partnerships, and community and women's organizations. Many non-Swahili coastal residents have and continue to undergo a process of what they might call Swahilization, an adoption of Swahili dress, linguistic inflection, comportment and mannerism, and styles of living. Such subtle shifts ensure that Swahili culture expands and allows mobility into Swahili industries such as fishing, boat trades, and urban commerce. Although these arenas are under competition from modern industries and postcolonial newcomers, they continue to assert their presence in contemporary cities and towns throughout East Africa. Numerous regional Swahili traditions continue unabated, such as the arrival each year of dhows from the Comoros Islands to celebrate the New Year or Maulidi each year in far away Lamu. Study-abroad programs bring new groups of students to learn about Swahili language and culture, and tourism continues despite the setbacks of recent geopolitical events. Swahili merchants still trade their wares, and Swahili fishermen continue to draw immense hauls of fish from the sea each day. Historical sites are being preserved for future generations and in turn are becoming tourist sites in their own right. Many chapters of Swahili history remain to be written in future years, and fertile debates about the past continue to produce new insights of this rich and complex history. The Swahili remain at once a global and a local, an African and an Indian Ocean, people.

Jesse Benjamin

See also Incense; Indian Ocean and the African Diaspora; Zanj (Zinj, Zang).

Further Reading

Abungu, George, and Henry Mutoro. 1993. "Coast-Interior Settlements and Social Relations in the Kenya Coastal Hinterland." In *The Archaeology of Africa: Foods, Metals, and Towns*, ed. Thurstan Shaw, Paul Sinclair, Bassey Andah, Alex Okpoko, and contributors. London: Routledge.

Allen, James de vere. 1993. *Swahili Origins: Swahili Culture and the Shungwaya Phenomenon*. London: James Curry.

Chami, Felix A. 2002. "The Graeco-Romans and Paanchea/Azania: Sailing in the Erythraean Sea." London: British Museum, Society for Arabian Studies.

Cooper, Frederick. 1980. *From Slaves to Squatters: Plantation Labor and Agriculture in Zanzibar and Coastal Kenya, 1890–1925*. Nairobi: Kenya Literature Bureau.

Glassman, Jonathan. 1995. *Feasts and Riot: Revelry, Rebellion and Popular Consciousness on the Swahili Coast, 1856–1888*. Portsmouth, NH: Heinemann.

Kusimba, Chapurukha M. 1999. *The Rise and Fall of Swahili States*. Walnut Creek, CA; London: AltaMira Press.

Mazrui, Alamin M., and Ibrahim Noor Shariff. 1994. *The Swahili: Idiom and Identity of an African People*. Trenton, NJ: Africa World Press/Red Sea Press.

Mkangi, Katama. 1995. "The Perception of Islam by the Mijikenda of Kenya Coast." In *Islam in Kenya: Proceedings of the National Seminar on Contemporary Islam in Kenya*, ed. Mohamed Bakari and Saad S. Yahya. Nairobi, Kenya: Mewa Publications.

Pearson, Michael N. 1998. *Port Cities and Intruders: The Swahili Coast, India, and Portugal in the Early Modern Era*. Baltimore: Johns Hopkins University Press.

Wilding, Richard F. 1987. *The Shorefolk: Aspects of the Early Development of Swahili Communities*. Occasional Papers #2. Mombasa, Kenya: Fort Jesus.

Willis, Justin. 1993. *Mombasa, the Swahili, and the Making of the Mijikenda*. Oxford, UK: Clarendon Press.

Sweet Honey in the Rock

Sweet Honey in the Rock, the legendary a cappella female vocal group, took its name from Psalm 81:16, where God promises the people will be fed by honey out of the rock. The symbolism of its name is an apt metaphor for African American women; honey, the ancient substance with myriad medicinal uses, is both sweet and nurturing, and rock represents strength and endurance against time and the elements. One of the group's first performance songs was a rendition of the traditional song "Sweet Honey in the Rock" based on the biblical parable and became the inspiration for their name.

The ensemble was created in 1973 by Bernice Johnson Reagon as an offshoot of her vocal workshops for the D.C. Black Repertory Theater Company. Its wide-ranging repertoire has its roots firmly planted in the African American musical legacy. Sweet Honey performs traditional gospel hymns, blues, spirituals, reggae, rap, African chants, poems, hip-hop, folk songs, jazz improvisations, and ancient lullabies solely through the use of the human voice or accompanied by minimalist hand percussion instruments such as *shekeres* and calabashes. The ensemble specializes in the sacred music of the black church, where the Civil Rights Movement, and the protest songs it inspired, was born. Sweet Honey's songs, whether traditional or original compositions, cry out against struggle and injustice and instill hope and peace on a global level.

Sweet Honey in the Rock began recording two years after it was formed; after a performance at the folk festival of the University of Chicago, the group signed with Flying Fish Records. On the second recording, *B'lieve I'll Run On*, in 1978, the group worked with Redwood Records before returning to Flying Fish for most of their later albums. In 1989, the ensemble won a Grammy Award in the category of Best Traditional Folk Recording for their version of Leadbelly's "Grey Goose" on the 1988 compilation album, *Folkways: A Vision Shared*. The group has also received several Grammy nominations for its own recordings. Sweet Honey in the Rock has also received numerous CARA (Contemporary A Cappella Recording) awards. Sweet Honey in the Rock released its 17th recording, *And the Women Gather,* in 2003. In 2007, they released "Experience 101," which targeted a youth audience.

The multimember ensemble has included more than 20 women since its inception more than three decades ago. Originating as a quartet, the group has grown to six members, including Shirley Childress Saxton, who has provided American Sign Language interpretation of Sweet Honey's songs for the hearing impaired audience since 1980.

In 2004, Bernice Johnson Reagon retired from the group, which was celebrated in their 30th-anniversary collaboration with Bernice Reagon's daughter, Toshi, and her band, Big Lovely, entitled *Eveningsong.* The historic celebratory performance played to rave reviews in 13 cities throughout the United States. In 2003, Sweet Honey triumphantly returned to England and Scotland with a six-city tour that took them to London's Royal Festival Hall, Exeter Cathedral, and Edinburgh's Usher Hall. The group also regularly performs at the Michigan Womyn's Festival and has traveled around the world carrying the message of love, peace, and struggle.

In the autumn of 2003, the Smithsonian Institution paid tribute to the group by requesting the donation of artifacts reflecting the group's history for its permanent collection in the National Museum of American History. Sweet Honey signed an official deed of gift covering the costumes, instruments, posters, and recordings donated to the performing arts collection, where the items will be housed alongside other musical history artifacts such as Michael Jackson's glove.

In appreciation of Sweet Honey in the Rock's popularity nationwide, the group received the Award of Merit from the Association of Performing Arts Presenters. The ensemble was also honored in their hometown of Washington, D.C., with a star on the Warner The-

ater's walk of fame, which was feted by scores of local community members with an event surrounding the ceremony.

To conclude its 30th anniversary, Sweet Honey in the Rock created and performed a concert featuring the Sweet Honey in the Rock Community Choir; Endings and Beginnings was based on original compositions. The 150-member chorus, trained and directed by original Sweet Honey member Ysaye Barnwell, was developed during a semester course, "Vocal Community" at the University of Maryland. The one-time concert also featured the premiere of an a cappella suite composed by Sweet Honey based on the biblical text in Luke 2:1–21, *The Nativity.* During its 31st season, PBS aired *A Song for Everyone,* documenting Sweet Honey in the Rock's history by Emmy award-winning filmmaker Stanley Nelson.

See also Blues: A Continuum from Africa; Feminism and Black Women in the African Diaspora; Jazz and Blues Singers, Black Women; Rap/Rappin'; Reagon, Bernice Johnson (1942–).

FURTHER READING
Reagon, Bernice Johnson. 1993. *We Who Believe in Freedom: Sweet Honey in the Rock: Still on the Journey.* New York: Anchor Books.
Discography
The Women Gather (2003)
Still the Same Me (2000)
. . . Twenty Five (1998)
Selections (1976–1988) (1997)
Sacred Ground (1996)
I Got the Shoes (1994)
Still On the Journey (1993)
In This Land (1992)
All for Freedom (1989)
Live at Carnegie Hall (1988)
Breaths (1988)
The Other Side (1985)
Feel Something Drawing Me On (1985)
We All . . . Every One Of Us (1983)
Good News (1981)
B'lieve I'll Run On (1978)
Sweet Honey in the Rock (1976)
Videos
Sweet Honey in the Rock: Singing For Freedom

T

TADIA

See The African Diaspora in Asia (TADIA).

Tango, Candombe, Milonga

The tango is a musical genre (primarily music and dance, but also song) that originally developed in the slums and brothels (*orilleras* and *arrabales*) of downtown Buenos Aires, Argentina, and Montevideo, Uruguay between the 19th and early 20th century; it was especially popular at first with the urban lower class. The tango is musically related to the *habanera*, an Afro-Cuban rhythm in a moderate 2/4 time, having the same meter but with traditionally a faster pace. By the early 20th century, the tango had transcended its original artistic, social, and national boundaries, becoming popular with dancers and performers of all classes in the River Plate and eventually winning audiences throughout Latin America, Europe, and beyond.

Although it is certainly true that in its modern form the tango is in fact inspired by some European rhythms and forms, what is not as commonly known is that the tango also owes a debt of gratitude to African and Afro-Platine musicians for its origins and development. In Argentina and Uruguay, as across the Americas, Africans bestowed a rich musical legacy; from the earliest arrivals in the New World, Africans used music and dance (often in conjunction with religious worship) to preserve their ancestral culture(s) and resist the hegemonic traditions of their European masters. For example, African instruments in Argentina and Uruguay used to accompany dancers included the *mazacalla* (a kind of two-headed rattle), the *marimba* or xylophone, and, of course, the drum or *tamboril*.

Folkloric dances in the River Plate attributed by specialists to African descendants include the *calenda* or *caringa*, the *bambula*, the *chica* or *congo*, the *gato*, the *pericón*, the *charanda* or *zemba*, and even the gaucho (cowboy) *malambo*. However, the *candombe*, which featured syncopated drum beats and improvised dance steps, was the favored rhythmic expression of Africans in the River Plate from the 18th until well into the 19th century. The traditional *candombe* is a highly choreographed or pantomimic dance between men and women, often involving folkloric characters such as the *gramillero*, the *escobillero* or *escobero*, and the *tata vieja*, as well as drummers or *comparsas*. Couples danced in file, side by side, as the "king" and "queen" supervised the performance. In the end, the king would raise his ceremonial scepter and call an end to the drumming and dancing (Carámbula 1995, 41–50).

Candombe dances took place in Buenos Aires and Montevideo inside *salas* or outside in *ranchos* or *rancherías*. Holidays—especially Corpus Christi, the Feast of the Epiphany or festival of San Baltasar on January 6, and Christmas—and Sundays were commemorated by dances sponsored by the different African *cofradías* (Roman Catholic lay brotherhoods) and ethnic "nations," such as the Cabindas, Molembos, and Minas, among many others. Colonial and early national elites feared the possibility of unrest and the social meaning of these dance festivals, which allowed large numbers of slaves and free blacks to come together and assert their agency and culture. Several times throughout the colonial and early national periods, white elites petitioned the government to ban *candombes*, and eventually African social organizations had to register with the police commissioner of their respective towns (see Andrews 1980, 157 for Buenos Aires). The echo of the *candombe* can still be heard today in Montevideo's *llamadas* (drum playing) during carnival and the festival of San Baltasar, as well as almost daily in the city's many *conventillos* or tenement housing (Goldman 1997).

In addition, more than one academic has maintained that the *candombe's* secret attraction rested in its religious content, a meaning often disguised by Africans in the River Plate (Lanuza 1967, 49–51). Some parallels between the dance steps of the *candombe* and those of *Oxalá* and *candomblé* in Brazil seem to exist. Regardless of whether or not the *candombe* contained religious connotations, the dance became an integral part of the black communities of Argentina and Uruguay for more than 200 years. Some scholars believe that the *candombe* was a distant precursor of the tango.

In Buenos Aires's traditional black zones, San Telmo, Montserrat, and Concepción, known as the "*barrios del tambor*" (neighborhoods of the drum), the *candombe* eventually gave way to another popular dance called the *milonga* or *baile de corte y quebrada* (cut-and-break dance) by the middle of the 1800s. The dance halls (*academisas de baile*) and brothels of both Buenos Aires and Montevideo were often located in black neighborhoods and attracted the urban demimonde of lower-class whites and *gente de color* (African descendents), who came to drink and dance (and more often than not, fight). Buenos Aires police records from 1856 document about 12 such establishments in Montserrat, Concepción, and El Retiro. The *milonga* originated as a dance of the so-called *compadritos* (street toughs), who were imitating (and taunting) the steps of the *candombe*. Even though in the traditional Afro-Platine *candombe* the dancers were apart from one another, the *milonga* nonetheless borrowed from the former many characteristic steps. An 1883 description of the *milonga* noted its relationship to the *candombe*, while Andrews quotes an old Afro-Argentine woman who in 1902 recalled how the *compadritos* invented the *milonga* based "on our music" (Andrews 1980, 166). Rossi (1958, 125–128) also concluded that the dance was created by Africans.

By the end of the 19th and beginning of the 20th century, the tango replaced the *milonga* as the favorite music and dance of the urban poor. Some suggest that the word "tango" itself is an African (possibly Kimbundu or Kikanga) word for drum, dance, or festival (see, for example, Gobello 1976 for more on this topic). According to Rossi (1958, 144–147), the first reference to tango dances comes from 1808; in the Montevideo of the mid-1860s, furthermore, the tango was known as "*el Chicoba*." The tango imitated the *milonga*, including its characteristic *ombligada* (the partners' intimate embraces) and *culeada* (swiveling hips). Over time, however, as the tango became Europeanized, the torsos of the dancers stiffened and the *cortes* and *quebradas* became slower and more grave, eventually giving way to the modern-day tango with its "filigrees" and intricate steps. But as George Reid Andrews (1980, 165) asserts, whenever couples lock their bodies tightly together and sway back and forth, the descent of the tango through the *milonga* is manifest, and the "steps of the tango form a kinetic memory of the candombe."

Moreover, despite the popular opinion that tango's white *guardia vieja* (old guard) were the only ones responsible for its development, black musicians in the River Plate played an important role in tango's evolution during the late 19th and early 20th centuries. Among early Afro-Argentine tango musicians and composers were "El Negro" Casimiro, "El Mulato" Sinforoso, and "El Pardo" Sebastián Ramos Mejía. Casimiro was a celebrated composer and violinist, known for his "*picardía morena*" (or black wit, reminiscent of Afro-Platine *payadores* such as Gabino Ezeiza), while Ramos Mejía was an early exponent of the accordion. Other African Argentine tango musicians were "El Pardo" Jorge Machado, José Santa Cruz, and the most celebrated tango pianist of his day, Anselmo Rosendo Mendizábal. Mendizábal composed the earliest known modern tangos, including "Reina de Saba," "Don José," and, most famously, "El Entrerriano." Thus, from its earliest days, the tango gained from the musical genius of black musicians on both sides of the River Plate (Natale 1984, 209–220).

Similar to what Robin Moore (1997) has discussed regarding popular (i.e., Afro-Cuban) music in early 20th-century Havana and labeled as the "nationalizing of Blackness," John Chasteen (2000) writes that by the 1920s, tango became recognized as an "unofficial national symbol" in Argentina (and, one could add, Uruguay). What is significant about this is Chasteen's timing of tango's nationalization to the 1920s. Rather than ignoring or forgetting the tango's African heritage, as early as 1926 Vicente Rossi was already affirming and defending (his paternalism and sometimes questionable racial views notwithstanding) the black contributions to this "national" musical genre's birth and evolution.

Roberto Pacheco

See also Argentina: Afro-Argentines; Dance in the African Diaspora; Payada; Uruguay: Afro-Uruguayans.

FURTHER READING
Andrews, George R. 1980. *The Afro-Argentines of Buenos Aires, 1800–1900*. Madison: University of Wisconsin Press.
Carámbula, Rubén. 1995. *El candombe*. Buenos Aires, Argentina: Ediciones del Sol.
Chasteen, John C. 2000. "Black Kings, Blackface Carnival, and Nineteenth-century Origins of the Tango." In *Latin American Popular Culture: An Introduction*, ed. William H. Beezeley and Linda A. Curcio-Nagy, 43–59. Wilmington, DE: SR Books.
Gobello, José. 1976. "Tango, vocablo controvertido." In *La historia del tango: sus orígenes*. Vol. 1, ed. Manuel Pampín, 134–144. Buenos Aires, Argentina: Ediciones Corregidor.
Goldman, Gustavo. 1997. *¡Salve Baltasar! La fiesta de reyes en el barrio Sur de Montevideo*. Montevideo, Uruguay: Impresora Federal Nuevosur.
Lanuza, José Luis. 1967. *Morenada: una historia de la raza africana en el Río de la Plata*. Buenos Aires, Argentina: Editorial Schapire.
Moore, Robin. 1997. *Nationalizing Blackness: Afrocubanismo and Artistic Revolution in Havana, 1920–1940*. Pittsburgh, PA: University of Pittsburgh Press.
Natale, Oscar. 1984. *Buenos Aires, negros y tango*. Buenos Aires, Argentina: Peña Lillo Editor.
Rossi, Vicente. 1958. *Cosas de negros*. Buenos Aires, Argentina: Librería Hachette. (Orig. pub. 1926).

The African Diaspora in Asia (TADIA)

The African Diaspora in Asia (TADIA) is a network of scholars who were previously working in isolation on different areas of Asia and in diverse academic disciplines. Formed in 2002 by Jean Pierre Angenot and Shihan de Silva Jayasuriya, TADIA attempts to break down the compartmentalization that exists within institutions and pool the academic resources of its members. TADIA aims to seek out Afro-Asian communities and bring them to the attention of the academic world. It aims to investigate the educational, employment, and organizational needs of contemporary Afro-Asian communities. TADIA's activities revolve around interconnected programs of academic research, cultural activities, educational needs, and socioeconomic and organizational workshops. The acumen of the academic community will be enhanced through conferences and the proceedings will be published and disseminated. TADIA is now a project associated with the United Nations Educational, Scientific, and Cultural Organization.

The cultural activities include bringing together African musicians, dancers, and other artists so that they are aware of other similar diasporas and the significance of African retentions such as music, song, and dance, in molding African identity. This involves Afro-Asian artists performing outside their countries as well as artists from other African Diasporas performing in Asia. Socioeconomic workshops would be held, initially in India, bringing together leaders of Afro-Indian communities. This would also provide a forum for Afro-Indians from various parts of India to meet and discuss how they would like to organize themselves in the future, for example by establishing an All India Siddi Federation. Organizational workshops are also planned in India to help the communities. TADIA's first conference was held in January 2006 in Goa, India.

A nongovernmental organization is being formed in India to receive grants from funding bodies to pay for the activities TADIA has earmarked to enhance Afro-Asian communities. The work is currently led from India, but there are also larger numbers of Afro-Asians in Pakistan. Currently, the number of Afro-Indians is estimated at more than 50,000 whereas there are one and a half million Afro-Pakistanis.

TADIA membership currently exceeds 300 scholars who maintain an interest in Afro-Asiatic communities. These scholars are affiliated with more than 200 institutions throughout the world. The diverse cultural systems faced by the African who migrated eastward and the complex interactions with the host societies who had ancient religions, many languages, and various customs require the attention of scholars who would approach the Diaspora from many facets. The scholar needs to be a historian, a linguist, an archaeologist, a biologist, an ethnologist, a psychiatrist, an anthropologist, and a specialist in oral tradition to analyze this Diaspora. It is not possible for any particular scholar to be a specialist in all these disciplines, so TADIA is gathering the expertise in order to develop the field and enhance the welfare of the Afro-Asian communities.

Shihan de Silva Jayasuriya

See also India and the African Diaspora; Indian Ocean and the African Diaspora; Sri Lankan African Diaspora.

FURTHER READING
Baptiste, Fitzroy A. 1998. "African Presence in India (1 and 2)." *African Quarterly* 38 (2): 76–90, 91–126.
De Silva Jayasuriya, Shihan and Richard Pankurst, eds. 2003. *The African Diaspora in the Indian Ocean.* Trenton, NJ: Africa World Press.
Harris, Joseph. 2003. "Expanding the Scope of African Diaspora Studies: The Middle East and India, a Research Agenda" *Radical History Review* 87: 157–68.

Thiong'o, Ngugi wa (1938–)

Ngugi wa Thiong'o has led Kenyan struggles for literary and political autonomy for more than four decades. A writer and critic from the

Gikuyu ethnic group, he is best known for historical novels depicting crises in Kenya's quest for independence, from the Mau-Mau rebellion of the 1950s to the semidictatorial regime of Daniel Arap Moi that ended in 2002. Thiong'o's insistence on writing in African languages and his ideas about the place of culture and literature in postcolonial societies have influenced writers throughout Africa and beyond.

Born in Limuru, Kenya, Thiong'o was educated in English at Christian colonial schools in Kenya, at Makerere University in Uganda, and at the University of Leeds, England. His family, members of the ethnic group most prominent in the Mau-Mau rebellion, suffered greatly after being accused of sympathies with the rebels. Thiong'o was radicalized during those years and during his subsequent study in England, where he came into contact with other ex-colonial subjects and imbibed the liberatory Marxism of Frantz Fanon.

Thiong'o wrote his first novel, *Weep Not, Child* (1964), under his birth name, James Ngugi. During the remaining years of the 1960s and 1970s, he slowly shed the trappings of his colonial upbringing and replaced them with his indigenous African heritage. He adopted the name Ngugi wa Thiong'o and became increasingly dedicated to cultivating his mother tongue, Gikuyu. In 1967, he published *A Grain of Wheat*, another examination of the Kenyan fight for independence.

Thiong'o taught at Nairobi University from 1968 to 1977. During the last years of the government of Jomo Kenyatta, Thiong'o became vocal about the imminent rise to power of Daniel Arap Moi, then the vice president of Kenya. Thiong'o's play *Ngaahika Ndeenda* (*I Will Marry When I Want*; 1977), written and produced with fellow Gikuyus, so incensed Moi that he was jailed without charge for one year. While in prison he wrote *Petals of Blood* (1978), his last novel in English.

Thiong'o claimed that by writing in English rather than African languages, writers had been propagating the "neocolonial slavish and cring-ing spirit" that had convinced Africans that they could neither govern themselves nor foster a sufficiently rich indigenous culture (1986, 26). He pointed out that writing in English effectively excluded the African proletariat from cultural transactions. The shift from English to African languages (primarily Gikuyu, but Swahili as well) provoked a great deal of praise and condemnation from other writers who argued that he had effectively denied anyone but the Gikuyu the privilege of reading his books. In 1980, he published the first novel in Gikuyu, *Caitaani Mutharabaini* (*Devil on the Cross*).

Continued friction between Thiong'o and Moi led Thiong'o to flee Kenya for London and then the United States, where he has lived for the last two decades. Thiong'o taught at Yale University, New York University, and the University of California at Irvine, where he is now a Distinguished Professor of Literature.

Thiong'o returned to Nairobi triumphantly in August 2004 and began a hugely popular tour of Kenya to promote his novel *Muroogi wa Kigogo*, a Gikuyu work five years in the making. He also planned to reconsecrate his marriage to his wife Njeeri under Gikuyu traditional rites. The homecoming turned tragic just two weeks after he arrived, when armed assailants broke into Thiong'o's apartment, stole money and a computer, and raped his wife. Ngugi and Njeeri defiantly continued with their planned ceremony later that month. At the end of August they returned to California, vowing to return to Kenya "again and again," despite the ordeal they had faced.

Graeme Wood

See also Fanon, Frantz (1925–1961); Kenyatta, Jomo (1889–1978).

FURTHER READING
Gikandi, Simon. 2000. *Ngugi wa Thiong'o*. Cambridge, UK: Cambridge University Press.
Thiong'o, Ngugi wa. 1986. *Decolonising the Mind: The Politics of Language in African Literature*. London: Heinemann.
Sicherman, Carol. 1990. *Ngugi wa Thiong'o: The Making of a Rebel*. New York: Hans Zell.

Thomas, Piri (1928–)

Piri Thomas (also known by his birth name, Juan Pedro Tomas or John Peter Thomas) was born in Harlem, New York, of a white Puerto Rican mother and a black Cuban father. Initially, Thomas identified solely with his Puerto Rican identity; however, the urban barrio of Harlem gave Thomas a mixture of experiences. An important way he has developed his identity is through interactions with various characters in memoir. They present Thomas with complex, differing attitudes with regard to identity, giving special attention to his name, color, and language/accent, eventually leading him to self-understanding.

In the memoir *Down These Mean Streets*, Thomas covers a span of 15 years, from 1942 to 1957, in which he discloses detailed episodes of his life and his desire to come to terms with his place within the social schema of America. In particular, he battles questions such as "Am I black? Puerto Rican? Or just American?" This journey takes Thomas from a static, stagnant center toward a fluid, conflictive, and ultimately peaceful inner space that resembles his trajectory in life. He goes from the barrio, around the world, to prison, and back to Harlem, but with a new determination to succeed and a new awareness of his black/Puerto Rican identity.

As a native Harlemite and New Yorker, Thomas's life was affected by the social structure of the United States, which contributed to Thomas's bout with self-definition. Yet, despite the strong claim of U.S. multiculturalism, the two-tiered system of racial classification, in which people are viewed as either black or white, can cause confusion, especially as dark-complexioned immigrants attempt to apply concepts of racial identity familiar to them in their countries of origin to the social framework of America (Duany 1998, Torres-Saillant 1998).

Various sources that address identity in Latin America argue that a major difference between the construction of identity in the United States and the construction of identity in Latin America is that in Latin America the emphasis is placed on nationality first and race second. In the United States, race supposedly takes precedence over nationality and is based on one's genotype as opposed to phenotype.

In *Down These Mean Streets*, Thomas's encounters with discrimination occurred mainly because he did not "look" Latino, speak Latino, or have a name that people perceived to be "Latino." Juan Flores in his book *From Bomba to Hip-Hop* (2000) discusses the reaction to this label, and asserts that "Latino" is an "imagined community" that is continuously being defined by interior and exterior forces, but according to Flores, the "outside representation" has the upper hand.

Though there may be a difference between methods of constructing identity in the United States and Latin America, one should not assume that Latin America's nationality-first model of classification signifies unity among all people in each separate Latin American country. There are distinctions between groups within individual countries. In Puerto Rico, for example, there are sublabels for different Puerto Rican people and a strong sense of color consciousness that divides groups. An illustration of this comes from Marta Cruz-Janzen's article "Latinegras" (2001) where she addresses the truth about the blunt colorism and discrimination in Puerto Rico. In her article she provides a few subcategories based on shade of skin, color and shape of eyes, and textures and hues of hair that operate in Puerto Rico:

Darkest: Negras, Morenas, and Prietas
Brown/golden: Cholas and Mulatas
Wheat colored; Trigueñas
Light-skinned with black features: Jabas
White features without straight hair: Grifas
Spanish looking: Criollas
Indigenous blood: Zambos

Cruz-Janzen's article exposes the multiple levels of blunt racism and color stratification in

Puerto Rico and abroad. Evidence of this is reflected in Thomas's memoir, where the frequent internal monologues, conversations, and events he recounts betray conflicting attitudes toward race and nationality.

Thomas goes through various stages in finding his racial identity (innocence, awareness, questioning/testing, rebellion, and acceptance), and through his travels he eventually learns to come to terms with Puerto Rican, American, and black identity. His experiences teach that nationality and language do not exclude people from being discriminated against; all around the world people are color stricken.

Jessica M. Alarcón

See also Puerto Rico: Afro-Puerto Ricans; Salsa.

FURTHER READING

Cruz-Janzen, Marta. 2001. "Latinegras: Undesirable Mothers, Daughters, Sisters, and Wives." *Frontiers* 22 (3): 169–182

Duany, Jorge. 1998. "Reconstructing Racial Identity: Ethnicity, Color and Class among Dominicans in the United States and Puerto Rico." *Latin American Perspectives* 25 (3): 147–173.

Flores, Juan. 2000. *From Bomba to Hip-Hop*. New York: Columbia University Press.

Thomas, Piri. 1967. *Down These Mean Streets.* New York: Vintage Books.

Thomas, Piri. "Biography." The Official Piri Thomas Web site. www.cheverote.com/piri.html (accessed November 10, 2004).

Torres-Saillant, Silvio. 1998. "The Tribulations of Blackness: Stages in Dominican Racial Identity." *Latin American Perspectives* 25 (3): 126–147.

Till, Emmett (1941–1955)

Emmett Louis Till, born in 1941, was a 14-year-old boy from Chicago who was mutilated and murdered in Mississippi in the summer of 1955, in a racial persecution ritual of hanging, dragging, maiming, and burning in some combination, traditionally known as lynching. Till had come down for the summer to Money, Mississippi, to visit his mother's relatives. Because Till allegedly whistled at a white woman, a deadly lynching took place: local white men kidnapped the teenager from his great-uncle's house, beat and mutilated him all about the face and head, chopped off much of his skull, shot him, tied a cotton-gin fan around his neck with barbed wire, and threw his body into the Tallahatchie River.

The case gained international attention because of the unusual determination of Till's mother, his surviving family members, and their supporters. As a unit, they refused to be cowed or silenced by fear of reprisal. Above all, Mamie Elizabeth Bradley, as Till's mother was known at the time of his death, brought both national and international attention to the horrors enacted upon her child by insisting that his body be returned to her in Chicago from Mississippi.

Young Till's lynching exposed the nightmarish frequency with which African Americans still faced the lynching phenomenon in the Jim Crow South. For, when the Tallahatchie River was dragged to recover Till's body, the bodies of two African Americans, George Lee and Lamar Smith, were also found. The two were religious leaders and political activists who had mysteriously disappeared shortly before Till's murder. The Delta Region has been identified as having the highest number of lynchings in the period 1880–1930 and therefore the highest in the nation.

News media covered the collapse of Till's 33-year-old-mother when faced with her son's casket at the station. Standing between the two bishops who supported her, she called on God to witness. The day she received her son's remains, Bradley violated the agreements imposed on her and her representatives by Mississippi officials who had declared that the body could not be viewed but must be buried in a locked casket affixed with the seal of the

Emmett Till and his mother, Mamie Till Mobley. The 14-year-old Till was murdered by vigilantes in Mississippi in 1955. (Library of Congress)

state in which her son had been murdered. Bradley had the funeral director break the lock and seal and prepare the body so she could identify her child. The funeral director had to hose away massive quantities of lime, which had been placed there to speed up disintegration and destroy evidence of the tortures that had been inflicted on the teen.

Of the three bodies pulled from the river, Bradley's uncle, Papa Mose, had managed to identify this particular body as Till's because of a ring the boy wore that had been his father's. Now, Bradley was only able to confirm that the body returned to her was her son's by close inspection of his ankles and knees, the perfection of his two remaining teeth, and the color of his remaining eye. In an unprecedented bid to force the watching world to witness America's tolerance of racist depravity, Bradley insisted on a glass-casket viewing of her son's unrecog-

nizable remains at the Rayner Funeral Home, followed by an open-casket funeral on September 3, 1955. In the course of four days, roughly 100,000 people came to bear witness to what had been done to Till. *Jet* magazine and the *Chicago Defender* circulated photos of his remains, with his mother's pictures of him taken the previous Christmas taped to the velvet of his casket. Though the figure in the casket was cleaned up and suited, with the worst protrusions removed and the front and back of his head sewn together, the body was not readily identifiable as human.

The trial of Till's murderers brought international attention to the Civil Rights Movement—And its casualties—in Mississippi. Like Mississippi-born activist Ida B. Wells-Barnett, who exposed to an international community the barbarity of ritual lynching in her pamphlets *Southern Horrors* (1892), *A Red Record*

1895), and *Mob Rule in New Orleans* (1900), Till's family and witnesses risked their own lives to make sure that an international audience was once again forced to confront Euro-America's rites of racial oppression. Civil rights leader Medgar Evers, field secretary for the Mississippi branch of the National Association for the Advancement of Colored People, gathered evidence for the case against Till's murderers by assuring witnesses for the prosecution that they would have safe passage out of Mississippi. Even as she attempted to enter the courtroom to testify to her son's character, Till's mother was badgered by hostile local media. In an extraordinary act of courage, Till's great-uncle Moses Wright became the first African American man in the state of Mississippi documented to have accused Euro-American men of hate crimes in a court of law.

A jury of 12 Euro-American men returned a unanimous verdict of "not guilty" after one hour's deliberation. This bald act of injustice ensured the escalation of racist persecution and activist resistance, as the Civil Rights Movement gained momentum. Two documentary films on Emmett Till have been made, and there have been media coverage and investigative journalism on programs like *Sixty Minutes*. In 2005, it was announced that Emmett Till's body was being exhumed for further evidence and that new trials would take place.

Alexis Brooks de Vita

See also African Americans and the Constitutional Order; Jim Crow; Wells-Barnett, Ida B. (1862–1931).

FURTHER READING

Beauchamp, Keith, producer and director. 2005. *The Untold Story of Emmett Louis Till.* Till Freedom Come Productions.

Campbell, Bebe Moore. 1993. *Your Blues Ain't Like Mine.* New York: Ballantine Books.

Hampton, Henry, and Vecchione, Judith, producers. 1987. *Eyes on the Prize: Awakenings 1954–1956.* Boston, MA: Blackside.

Moody, Anne. 1976. *Coming of Age in Mississippi.* New York: Laurel.

Nelson, Stanley, producer. 2003. *The Murder of Emmett Till.* Written by Marcia A. Smith. PBS American Experience.

Till-Mobley, Mamie, and Christopher Benson. 2003. *Death of Innocence: The Story of the Hate Crime That Changed America.* New York: Random House.

Wilkinson, Brenda. 1997. *The Civil Rights Movement: An Illustrated History.* New York: Crescent Books.

Williams, Juan. 1987. *Eyes on the Prize: America's Civil Rights Years 1954–1955.* New York: Viking Penguin.

Tolson, Melvin Beaunoris (1898–1966)

Melvin Tolson was a poet, essayist, and teacher. At times a controversial figure, through his work he explored the meaning of African American identity and was especially interested in the intersections between African American, European, and African culture. Though best known for his poetry, he was also an influential newspaper columnist and teacher who pioneered interracial college debates.

The son of a Methodist minister, Tolson was born in 1898 in Missouri. After graduating from Lincoln University in Pennsylvania in 1923, Tolson was hired as an English professor by Wiley College, a black liberal arts school in Marshall, Texas. Committed to the civil rights struggle, Tolson spoke out frequently against racial and economic injustice, both on campus and off and in the newspaper column, "Caviar and Cabbage," he wrote for the *Washington Tribune* from 1937 to 1944. While at Wiley, Tolson started a debate team that participated in the first recorded interracial college debate in the United States, held in 1930 against the University of Michigan and had numerous victories over black and white colleges, including Harvard University. In 1947, Tolson left Wiley for Langston University in Oklahoma, where he remained the rest of his career.

Tolson's first collection of poems, *Rendezvous with America*, published in 1944, brought him great acclaim. In 1947, Tolson was named the poet laureate of Liberia and began writing the celebratory *Libretto for the Republic of Liberia*, published in final form in 1953. In 1965, Tolson published *Harlem Gallery: Book I, The Curator*. In this work, he continued his exploration of African American identity, especially the role of the black artist in American society.

In his work, Tolson sought to integrate a number of influences and traditions, both scholarly and folk, epic and lyric, African American and American, and African and European. In *Harlem Gallery* especially, he blended African American cultural references, slang, oral traditions, folk humor, and blues forms with the complex syntactic patterns and esoteric allusions of modernist poetry. Tolson acknowledged the difficulty of his work, but insisted that it could be appreciated by a wide range of readers and that it illustrated the cultural amalgam he saw as at the heart of both African American identity and the American experience. In May 1966, four months before his death, Tolson was awarded the annual poetry prize by the American Academy of Arts and Letters. A film of Tolson's activity as a demanding but inspiring teacher and community activist in Marshall, Texas, particularly his work with the legendary debate team, has been made as *The Great Debaters* produced by Oprah Winfrey's Harpo Productions and directed by Denzel Washington, who also played the role of Tolson. It was released in 2007 to great acclaim.

David Gold

See also Jim Crow; Langston University and HBCUs; Lincoln University.

FURTHER READING
Flasch, Joy. 1972. *Melvin B. Tolson*. New York: Twayne.
Farnsworth, Robert M. 1984. *Melvin B. Tolson, 1898–1966: Plain Talk and Poetic Prophecy*. Columbia: University of Missouri Press.
Gold, David. 2003. "'Nothing Educates Us Like a Shock': The Integrated Rhetoric of Melvin Tolson." *College Composition and Communication* 55 (2, December): 226–253.
Tolson, Melvin. 1982. *Caviar and Cabbage: Selected Columns by Melvin B. Tolson from the Washington Tribune, 1937–1944*, ed. Robert M. Farnsworth. Columbia: University of Missouri Press.
Tolson, Melvin. 1999. *"Harlem Gallery" and Other Poems of Melvin B. Tolson*, ed. Raymond Nelson. Charlottesville: University Press of Virginia.
Tolson, Melvin, Jr. 2001, February 25. Interview with the author.
Washington, Denzel. 2007. Director. "The Great Debaters." 123 minutes. Chicago, IL: Harpo Films.

Tonton Macoutes

The Tonton Macoutes were a private militia created by former Haitian president François Duvalier, who maintained and protected his authority through brutal methods of lawlessness. Their very name incited fear amongst the Haitian people. In Haitian folklore, the Tonton Macoute is a bogeyman who puts bad children in his knapsack. Duvalier established this new militia out of the fear that he could not trust members of the national army. Clémont Barbot, Duvalier's right-hand man, led the Tonton Macoutes. They remained a semisecret entity until the first of many failed attempts to overthrow Duvalier from power. After this attempted coup, Duvalier uniformed his militia with denim shirts, blue jeans, red armbands, and their trademark dark sunglasses so that they would be easily recognized. However, the macoutes were best known for the vicious manner in which they hunted Duvalier's adversaries, at times decimating entire families, including women and children. They often left evidence of their crimes visible as a warning to others who might rebel against the president.

Many joined Duvalier's militia for the status and the fear that was associated with the Tonton Macoutes. Although members of Duvalier's militia did not receive a salary, they did receive other perks—their children were given priority for admission to schools as well as scholarships, for example. After Duvalier's death in 1971, the Tonton Macoutes continued to serve under his son Jean-Claude Duvalier. Although their title was changed to the Volunteers of National Security to separate them from their violent acts, the Tonton Macoutes continued to terrorize the Haitian people until they were disbanded in 1986 when Duvalier fled the country.

Nadia I. Johnson

See also Haiti.

FURTHER READING

Diederich, Bernard, and Al Burt. 1986. *Papa Doc and the Tonton Macoutes.* Port-au Prince, Haiti: Henri Deschamps.
Ferguson, James. 1987. *Papa Doc, Baby Doc: Haiti and the Duvaliers.* Oxford, UK: Basil Blackwell.

Tosh, Peter (1944–1987)

Peter Tosh, born Hubert Winston McIntosh on October 19, 1944, in the small fishing village of Belmont in the parish called Westmoreland, Jamaica, is probably best known for founding the legendary Reggae group the Wailing Wailers, along with Bob Marley and Bunny Livingstone, in 1963 in the Kingston ghetto of Trench Town. In addition to his rich baritone, Tosh brought to the Wailers his versatile musicianship and songs such as "Get Up, Stand Up" (written with Marley) and "Stop That Train."

The group shot to international prominence in the early 1970s. All three founding members eventually became superstars and arguably exerted as much influence on world music as the Beatles did. Aside from practically helping to invent reggae music, the Wailers were a force to contend with and influenced many different genres of music from jazz to rhythm and blues to rock to pop, from the 1970s right up to the present.

Tosh was by far the tallest of the three original Wailers (he was about six feet, four or five inches tall), and he was undoubtedly the most militant. Tosh was an outspoken, defiant, fiery, unwavering protest artist. He was a true product of 1960s Jamaica in all its "rude-bwoy" aspects. The quality that stood out most in Tosh was the one that probably ensured him an untimely death: he was very politically committed and serious about social change. He was the ultimate role model of the politically conscious Rastafari adherent and exemplified the political potential of the Rasta movement.

Tosh released his first album, "Legalize It," in 1976 on the CBS label. The title track continues to this day to be the biggest-selling single in Jamaican history despite the fact the release was banned in Jamaica, because of the album's pro-marijuana stance. Tosh's songs were centered on topics like equal rights, the antiapartheid struggle, police brutality, and other human and civil rights issues.

Tosh, an undeniable human rights and civil rights activist, had quite dramatically almost lost his life after a vicious police beating in 1978, not long after the famous One Love Concert. After criticizing the Jamaican government during this historic concert he had become a marked man. He made history at the concert by first calling down fire and brimstone on the rulers of Jamaica, Michael Manley, Edward Seaga, and other government (and opposition) officials in attendance. At the concert Tosh performed the song "Equal Rights" for the first time.

The titles of Tosh's songs graphically illustrate the various topics and issues he addressed: "Equal Rights," "Downpressor Man," "400 Years," "Apartheid," "Stand Firm," "Recruiting Soldiers," "African," "Legalize It" (marijuana), and "Get Up, Stand Up (for your Rights)." These are just some of the politically charged songs Tosh wrote. It is evident from just this small sample that Tosh was an ardent campaigner for equal rights and justice for African/black people in particular and for poor people in general. His now classic "African" is recognized for its affirmation of African identity worldwide. "No matter where you come from/As long as you're a Black man/You're an African."

Tosh also experienced, in his own words, nine assassination attempts before he was murdered in his home. The mysterious circumstances around Tosh's murder clearly raise the question as to whether the government orchestrated the assassination. The gunmen who invaded his house on that fateful night of September 11, 1987, took no money, jewelry, or any other material valuables. They simply killed Tosh in cold blood.

Tosh was a forward thinker. He was not in search of a perfect world, but one that afforded its citizens a better modicum of equal rights and justice. Tosh dedicated his life to humanity and was a foot soldier in the loftiest of struggles. Tosh will always be remembered as a champion of equal rights and justice. Not only was he an acclaimed musician, but he was also an uncompromising activist in the tradition of the Rastafari elders who forged the Rastafari movement in a violently hostile social environment.

Michael Barnett

See also King, Martin Luther, Jr. (1929–1968); Malcolm X (1925–1965); Marley, Robert Nesta (Bob) (1945–1981); Rastafarianism; Reggae; Wailer, Bunny (1947–).

FURTHER READING

Campbell, Nicholas. 1992. *Stepping Razor Red X: the Peter Tosh Story.* Amherst, MA: Northern Arts Entertainment.

Scott, Ricardo A. 1999. *On the Night He Was Betrayed: Peter Tosh, the Man, the Prophet, the Legend.* New York: Cornerstone Productions, Inc.

Tosh, Peter. 1997. *Mark of the Beast* (Honorary Citizens Box Set). Sony Music Entertainment.

Tosh, Peter. 2002. *Stepping Razor Red X.* DVD. Canada. Video Service. 103 minutes.

Transatlantic Slave Trade

By the middle of the 15th century, the artistic, trade, and academic centers of the ancient West African empires of Mali, Ghana, and even the military Songhay had been weakened by centuries of expansionism and combat with Islamic North Africans when the first Europeans—Portuguese—landed on the West African coast seeking gold. West, North, and East Africa all had significant histories of trade and flourishing kingdoms. Thus, the Europeans circumventing the usual North African routes to come directly to the West African coast were treated with the usual ritual hospitality and openness to consider exchange that traditionally characterized continental African encounters with those who were not recognized enemies. Historians, aware of traditional customs that constrained West Africans to consider trade and offer hospitality when initially encountering European profiteers and pirates, now challenge the idea that African cooperation was due to ignorance, childlike trust, worship of the European, or self-surrender.

The earliest story of Europeans taking up the Arab interest in capturing Africans seems to begin with a Captain Gonzales sent by a Prince Henry to West Africa in 1441. Arriving on the West Coast, Gonzales and his men captured three people. The captives offered to exchange themselves for 10 others. Gonzales accepted the three-for-ten trade and took his 10 prisoners back to Portugal as gifts. Portugal set itself up in trade on the Guinea Coast in 1444. By 1482, King Ansa of the Fanti granted the Portuguese permission to occupy the coast and take part in the gold trade. The Portuguese constructed a fort called El Mina that soon became a prison for more captives.

In 1503, a Dominican priest pointed out to a Spanish king that a shipload of Africans enslaved in Spanish gold mines in San Domingo (Haiti) survived the brutal treatment and harsh conditions better than the indigenous population. The king therefore ordered that another 50 Africans be brought to Spain's Caribbean gold mines in 1510. Thus, a sovereign's exploitative acquisitiveness and a religious courtier's sycophancy launched what would become the defining economic, sociopolitical, cultural, philosophical, and moral movement of the modern world: the Atlantic slave trade.

Throughout its 400-year history, the Roman Catholic pope would remain an advocate and arbiter of Europe's rapidly growing slave trade economies. As European nations dismantled African civilizations by depleting populations and inciting wars of survival, succeeding popes dispensed permissions to dominate the trade alternately between Portugal, Spain, and England, who competed with Holland, France, Sweden, Denmark, and the colonies that formed the United States.

From 1500 through 1870 from 12 million to 15 million Africans are conservatively estimated to have been captured and transported across the Atlantic Ocean as forced unpaid laborers in the economic ventures of Europe's American and Caribbean colonies. The highest estimate is approximately 75 million captives. Because of the less-than-straightforward strategies used to capture, retain, transport, and profit from these human beings during this wildly fluctuating period of international relations, arriving at a provable estimate of the numbers of people actually taken from the African continent is probably impossible. For example, there is the impossibility of adequately calculating the numbers of captives who left the African coast but died of disease or violence or who were thrown overboard during the Middle Passage so that ships' crews might avoid arrest, pillage, tariffs, starvation, thirst, disease, rebellion, or piracy. There is no adequate way of accounting for all the captives

who therefore never reached Caribbean island docks to be "broken" or prepared for continental American plantations during the heyday of Europe's Atlantic slave trade.

These cargoes of enslaved African laborers followed invading waves of European soldiers now armed with exploding gunpowder in projectile equipment, which allowed them unimpeded encroachment into the Americas and the Caribbean. Such weaponry complemented the European concept of honorable warfare as the mass projection of destructive matter on distant opponents not similarly armed, as opposed to the death-toll constraints imposed by pre-explosive face-to-face or hand-to-hand combat. Together with new access to the Chinese invention of explosive warfare, the Atlantic slave trade made possible Europe's collective ambition to competitively appropriate the temperate world's resources while suffering the least expenditure of its own, thereby establishing the bases of modern global economic and political imbalances.

Portugal dominated the first 200 years of the Atlantic slave trade, transporting at the very least 1.7 million people from the Congo-Angola region to the Caribbean and Brazil. Another 3.5 million (at minimum) people were soon brought not only from Congo-Angola but also from the Bight of Benin, the Bight of Biafra, the Gold Coast, Senegambia, and upper Guinea. As human beings came to be the predominant export from the rapidly disintegrating social systems of the African continent, political and ideological motives for making war against one's neighbors were increasingly replaced by economic considerations and the threat of annihilation. What began as the profitable export of prisoners of war, or those considered social deviants, such as adulterers, murderers, sorcerers, or traitors, or those sold in times of crisis such as drought and famine to feed surviving family members, escalated into the development of warlike African states whose commerce depended on the capture and sale of their neighbors. In the early 1700s, King

Agaja established the sale of human beings as the principal commerce of the growing West African kingdom of Dahomey. In the 1750s, King Agaja's son, King Tegesibu, is known to have sold more than 9.000 people a year into the chattel slavery of Europe's colonies.

Spain, Portugal, the Netherlands, England, and France brought shiploads of textiles, beads, rum, firearms, and gunpowder to the African coast. These European trading companies built forts along the coast to keep competing Europeans from stealing their African captives. The captives were then transported to the Caribbean to be "broken" and thence to Europe's colonies in the Americas to be sold into gold and silver mining camps or agricultural slavery. Having unloaded and profited exponentially from the sale of their human cargo, European and colonialist ships then left the Americas bound for European markets with loads of gold, silver, cotton, coffee, tobacco, and rice to feed the new urban and industrial economies developing in Europe, a financial engine powered by European and U.S. investment in human bondage. This "triangular trade" (or "rectangular" according to Asante and Mattson 1992) established a lucrative link between the formerly somewhat isolated regions of Europe, Africa, the Caribbean, and the Americas. As contact, profit, and genocide kept pace with each other, the exigent compromises of morality and humanity that made participation in the Atlantic slave trade possible also necessitated development of the socioeconomic, political, and philosophical rationalizations about racial superiority that characterized Europe's emergence from feudalism into "Enlightenment."

Records indicate that most of these captives were the victims of African or Arab raids perpetrated on villages in the African interior. These newly enslaved people, therefore, had usually never seen Europeans before being sold to them on the coast, branded to mark which European company now owned them, imprisoned in fortresses, and detained in the holds of European ships for transport across the Atlantic Ocean. Many captives thought their European jailors were demons or spirits, not people, and that these "skinless" beings planned to eat or otherwise consume or befoul their African prisoners. This often proved to be a reasonable expectation, as a wide variety of physical and sexual abuses and degradations were practiced upon captive men, women, and children during these transatlantic voyages lasting five to eight weeks. Besides being subjected to rape, the lash, or more inventive methods of intimidation, subjugation, and control, captives reported being left to lie in their own and others' bodily secretions, including effluvia from healthy as well as dying bodies trapped in close proximity in the hold; being underfed or deprived of water; or seeing fellow captives leap or be thrown overboard. Though imprisoned with strangers whose languages they often could not speak, individuals and several shiploads of Africans did manage organized revolts before their enslavers reached their destinations. When successful revolts did not take place, records indicate that many of the enslaved who were transported across the Atlantic were relieved to discover that what was expected of them in the land of their captors was work, however harsh. Yet there were equal numbers of captives who reportedly would have preferred death to their new lives of chattel enslavement, including as it did institutionalized rape and various acts of extreme terrorism and torture, used to discourage revolt and escape.

As far as European colonizers were concerned, it is likely that importing foreign laborers unfamiliar with the terrain, wildlife, and languages of the Americas, and therefore hampered by disorientation should they try to escape the mines or plantations where they were enslaved, proved to be an effective method of retaining an imprisoned workforce. Importing Africans who, for whatever combination of reasons, had a likely chance of actually surviving the creative inhumanity of European chattel enslavement in the colonies was also an effective means of stemming the profit-eating tide of enslaved Native American deaths. Throughout the colonies, indigenous peoples, enslaved and free, were soon decimated in genocidal numbers not only by explosive weaponry but also by unprotected exposure to virulent European diseases.

By the time it was outlawed, the international trade in enslaved Africans had already brought monumental wealth and, thereby, unprecedented international power to both the colonizing and formerly slave-trading countries of Europe and their satellite colonies. In this way modern slave societies fostered the rapid and powerful growth of an elite new wealthy European and Euro-American middle class. Many who did not participate directly in the trade benefited from the production, transportation, or sale of iron, cloth, lumber for ships and buildings, chocolate, coffee, tea, rice, cane for sugar and rum, and a wealth of other products made possible by exploiting the resources of the temperate zones.

Many of the Euro-American colonists were by now in revolt, demanding autonomous control of what remained of their capital-producing human and natural resources. Concurrently, the African aristocracy that had formerly benefited from the trade in human beings became dismantled and dramatically disempowered as the chaos engendered by European colonialist expansionism overran the African continent. Indeed, some of the African military potentates who had made a livelihood from capturing and selling their neighbors, such as the aforementioned Dahomean king Tegesibu, found themselves hunted down and enslaved in the second half of the 18th century, as desperation grew on the continent to feed the European demand for human lives or be consumed into the market or colonized into homeland slavery in one's own turn. Holocaust levels of destabilization devastated the African continent after more than three and a half centuries of the aggressive deportation of the childbearing and arms-bearing preservers of disparate communities' social orders. By the beginning of the 19th century, slave trade prey and predator alike, even as far as North Africa, found themselves equally vulnerable to European colonialism's encroachment onto the African continent, with its Enlightenment disdain for and appropriation of Africa's ancient peoples, monuments, and autonomous governments. By far, the most economically and militarily empowered new class of the Atlantic world's elite in the 19th century were those who descended from European slaveholders in North, Central, and South America and the Caribbean, or from European and American shipping magnates and merchants who had served stints as slave transporters late in the previous century.

The Act of 1807 outlawed international trade in human beings. Britain's African Squadron patrolled the Atlantic to enforce the new ban on a practice from which England no longer benefited, having lost some of its most profitable colonies to the formation of the United States. By the time of the ban, records conservatively indicate that more than 10 million African people had been forced across the Atlantic in at least 36,000 voyages to Europe's American and Caribbean colonies. The great bulk of this human cargo, perhaps half of the documented captives, had been taken from Angola-Congo to South America, predominantly to Brazil. Most of the captives who actually survived the Middle Passage and reached chattel enslavement were young men aged 14 through 30. It is estimated that about a fourth of the surviving captives were young women.

More than a million captive Africans from various regions ended up in the island colony that eventually became Haiti. Nearly as many Africans arrived in each of the island colonies that became Cuba and Jamaica. Conversely, fewer than half a million captives from all over West, Central, and East Africa, as evidenced by the cultural retention of folklore characters such as East Africa's "Kaka Sungura" or Br'er Rabbit, found themselves in the North American English colonies that would become the United States.

Paradoxically, it seems that the Anglo-American preference for the increasingly incestuous production of one's own enslaved progeny shifted English colonists' appetite from the importation of acculturated Africans to the circulation of racially and culturally Anglicized Afro-Americans. This taste for sexual usage of the indentured or enslaved African population in the English colonies that became the United States was not at all curtailed by outlawing marriage between those of European and those of African descent. Racist theorizing developed proportionately with the profits made by enslaving those of African descent in the English colonies, whether born enslaved, free, or indentured. Before the end of the 17th century, Virginia had outlawed marriage between European colonists and Africans. In 1705, Massachusetts determined that Africans participating in interracial marriages would be whipped and sold out of the colony into slavery. Pennsylvania adopted a similar law in 1726, specifying that it applied to free persons. While such measures to discourage legitimate, sanctioned, and protected sexual and reproductive relations between Europeans and Africans increased in number, region, and severity, concurrent laws to enslave the children of Europeans born to enslaved women were also enacted. In short, Anglo-American law favored the sexual usage of those of African descent by European men, rewarding these men who raped, coerced, or seduced their enslaved population by turning the responsibilities normally owed children into wealth owned by the European father. Anglo-American men were thus increasingly legally encouraged to rape the African women in their charge and enslave their own Anglo-African children who resulted from such unions. Such children were then subjected to sale, rape, and the continuing cycle of inbreeding Anglicization of the African population in the American colonies.

The Anglo-American contribution to the insemination of its own enslaved Anglo-African population facilitated a superficial de-Africanization of the widely divergent ethnic groups brought together in the colonies that became the United States. These mixed-race and home-grown Anglo-Africans had been imported in only one-tenth the number that reached Brazil but were then spread thinly across as great a stretch of land. Racially and culturally Anglicized, increasingly light-skinned native English-speaking African Americans, enslaved by their English-American parents, siblings, distant relations, and neighbors, seemed to display an equally diluted grasp of the philosophical self-concepts, modes of combat, and familiarity with non-Christian religious theories and deities that problematized the importation of Africans among the severely race-conscious English colonists, in the first place. It is important to recall that many of the United States' abolitionists were not so much opposed to the notion of chattel slavery as to the presence among Anglo-Americans of Africans. Now that enslaved Africans had made the United States one of the potentially wealthiest nations in the Atlantic region, many abolitionists now wanted America's African population to simply disappear. They therefore argued in favor of shipping the originally imported Africans' now deculturated descendants back to the African continent that they had never seen and could only abstractly consider home. English colonial laws that adapted to favor an enslaver's rape of African women and the economically profitable enslavement of that Englishman's own children when born of such rape contrasted with French law and Latin denial in other colonies struggling with the efficacy of freeing, educating, and gainfully employing children descended from both slaveowner and enslaved.

The historically unprecedented numbers of Africans exported as chattel laborers into Europe's American colonies, and European colonizers' needs to justify and continue to profit from the extraordinary human rights abuses such genocidal activity necessitated, conflicted with Europe's own philosophical disenchantment with its medieval feudal and aristocratic systems of government. While French citizens overturned aristocratic rule in their home country, their colonies struggled with concepts of racial versus class hierarchy. Although the French preference for a system of privilege seemed to be toward one that preferred class, meaning that children born of unions between the enslaved and their enslavers could initially be born into a free and privileged mixed-race middle class in the French colonies, racial hierarchy predominated and conflicted with this French approach in English, Spanish, and Portuguese colonies. The idea that national progress and self-improvement required that one *blanquearse* or whiten oneself led to literal and cultural African genocide in former Spanish colonies such as Argentina. This series of ideological conflicts has led to the modern development of sociophilosophical systems that historians call modern slave societies, modeled on slave societies of European antiquity but bolstered by hierarchical racial rationalizations. These justifications of drastic systems of inequality are driven by a European colonial equation of wealth and explosive military power with divine right.

From the 1500s through the early 1800s, European religious dogma, including Anglican and Nordic departures from Catholicism, developed the self-serving concept that Europe's Christian Godhead wanted the rest of the world to sacrifice itself to the apparently insatiable materialist drives of Europe and, eventually, to Europe's revolting colonial descendants. As the African population in the colonized Atlantic increased, and slaveholding became the predominant symbol identifying social status and power, other socially sanctioned interactions began to mirror the extremity of the master-slave relational skew. Thus, dependence on stabilizing and justifying the chattel enslavement of the majority of the colonies' populations eventually reshaped the pro-colonialist European philosophical mind away from egalitarianism and the fluidity of a power-wielding nonaristocratic class toward racial absolutism and racialized authoritarianism. By the time the Atlantic slave trade was no longer financially profitable and therefore ended, European and Euro-American philosophers and theologians had taught their populations to believe, in the main, that these systems of inhumanity were ordained and sanctioned by nature as well as by a Christian god.

Alexis Brooks de Vita

See also Abolitionism in the African Diaspora; Atlantic World and the African Diaspora; Middle Passage.

FURTHER READING

Asante, Molefi K., and Mark T. Mattson. 1992. *Historical and Cultural Atlas of African Americans.* New York: Macmillan Publishing Company.

Berlin, Ira. 1998. *Many Thousands Gone: The First Two Centuries of Slavery in North America.* Cambridge, MA: The Belknap Press of Harvard University Press.

Dodson, Howard, ed. 2002. *Jubilee: The Emergence of African-American Culture.* Washington, D.C.: The National Geographic Society.

Everett, Susanne. 1996. *History of Slavery.* Edison, NJ: Chartwell Books.

Eze, Emmanuel Chukwudi, ed. 1997. *Race and the Enlightenment.* Malden, MA: Blackwell Publishing.

Franklin, John Hope. 2000. *From Slavery to Freedom: A History of African Americans.* New York: Alfred A. Knopf.

Giddings, Paula. 1988. *When and Where I Enter: The Impact of Black Women on Race and Sex in America.* New York: Bantam.

Horton, James Oliver, and Lois E. Horton. 2005. *Slavery and the Making of America.* New York: Oxford University Press.

James, C. L. R. 1989. *The Black Jacobins: Toussaint L'Ouverture and the San Domingo Revolution.* New York: Vintage Books.

McEvedy, Colin. 1980. *Atlas of African History.* New York: Facts on File.

Osagie, Iyunola Folayan. 2003. *The Amistad Revolt: Memory, Slavery, and the Politics of Identity in the United States and Sierra Leone.* Athens: University of Georgia Press.

Sweetman, David. 1984. *Women Leaders in African History.* Oxford, UK: Heinemann Educational Books.

Transition

Transition, a cultural magazine founded in Kampala, capital of Uganda, in 1961, by the Ugandan-Indian Rajat Neogy, had its name changed to *Ch'indaba* in 1976 under the editorship of Wole Soyinka, was discontinued in 1976, and was revived in 1991 by Henry Louis Gates Jr., Anthony Appiah, and Wole Soyinka, thereby moving its base to the United States. The development of debate represented in its contents from its beginnings to the present; the impact of the fortunes of its editors on the vicissitudes of its existence; the shifting of its editorial base from Uganda to Ghana under state pressure; and its discontinuation on account of funding challenges, which led, eventually, to its revival in the United States, are indicative of fundamental aspects of the progression toward self-actualization of the African intelligentsia and the relationship of this striving to similar efforts in the African Diaspora in the United States, which, since the end of the 20th century, has come to represent the geographical and cultural axis around which the most prominent members of the black intelligentsia gravitate.

Transition became a focus for the exploration of pivotal issues in the constitution of African identity, as realized both on the African continent and in the Diaspora. The formulation of the questions through which these issues were defined and the various modes of engagement with these questions represent some of the earliest efforts at charting the cultural frameworks that were coming into existence in Africa in the 1950s and 1960s, a cultural efflorescence inspired by the creative energies released in Africa in relation to the struggles for, and the subsequent freedom from, colonial rule.

This shift in the geographical location of its editors and the journal itself, as well as the circumstances that brought that about, reflects the power balance between the north and the south that has characterized their relationship from the 19th to the 21st centuries, a balance reinforced by the experience of working with lean resources that motivated its first two editors to seek and get financial assistance from outside Africa.

The debate on the linguistic and larger cultural identity of African literature that received particularly incisive exploration from a variety of perspectives in *Transition*, foregrounded questions central to cultural self-determination vital to all states where cultural and social institutions have been affected by colonialism, questions that are still being revisited on account of the permanently transformative character of the colonial experience.

In its reemergence in the United States, *Transition's* essays came to epitomize the lines of debate that characterize reflection on black identity, even though the magazine does go further afield to explore issues and works by scholars whose concerns do not directly involve the black world. A reading of the anniversary issue of *Transition*, the combined 75th and 76th issues, published in 1997, is vital to grasp the development of the magazine. It reprints key articles from its earlier volumes, with an essay by Michael Vazquez, the current executive editor, that reviews the history of the magazine, and another, by Wole Soyinka, the second editor in the magazine's history (1974–1976) and present chairman of the editorial board, that, from an autobiographical perspective, contrasts the idealism of the magazine's earlier birth with the painful realities associated with its development.

Toyin Adepoju

See also Drum; Présence Africaine; Soyinka, Akinwande Oluwole (1934–).

FURTHER READING

Benson, Peter. 1986. *Black Orpheus, Transition and Modern Cultural Awakening in Africa.* Berkeley: University of California Press.

James, Louis. 1969. "The Protest Tradition: Black Orpheus and Transition." In *Protest and Conflict in African Literature*, ed. Cosmo Pieterse and Donald Munro, 109–124. London: Heinemann.

Tribe and Tribalism

Tribe is a problematic term that lacks a consistent meaning. A tribe can be a social group of families, clans, or generations united by common descent, or the term can describe a group of people with similar characteristics or interests. In African contexts, a tribe is often considered to be an ethnic group with a shared language or culture. However, given the millions of people who speak the same African languages and share the same cultures, the term tribe is often an inappropriate description that obscures realities. Tribe is used erroneously to describe many different groups, from nine million Zulu speakers in South Africa to a small band of Americans competing in a remote setting on the popular television show *Survivor*. There can be smaller tribes inside of larger tribes or large language/ethnic groups that run across vast regions as say the Yoruba, which became an empire with extensions now in the Americas and articulated through a variety of Orisa pratices. Some of these groupings were actually precolonial nation states disrupted by slavery and colonialism. Therefore, if a tribe can be just about anything, it serves as an unsatisfactory and contradictory label.

As a unit of analysis, tribe is pervasive in the Western anthropological mindset. Many Westerners consider all Africans to be "tribal." When classifying others, Westerners tend to look for tribes in Africa but not in other parts of the world, including the former Yugoslavia. Africans themselves have reinforced the stereotype of Africa as tribal in their usage of the word "tribe" (Lowe 1997) to capture their own ethnic belonging, assuming that outsiders are unfamiliar with African terms used in its place. Speakers of the Shona language in Zimbabwe, for instance, might use the term *rudzi* among themselves instead to denote a type or kind of group. One main problem with the term tribe is that it fails to be specific and describe the subtleties of many situations. The term also carries many negative connotations by reinforcing an image of the primitive and conveying a static sense of timelessness. For many, "tribe" suggests links to irrationality or superstition, and it carries misleading historical and cultural assumptions (Lowe 1997). The call to avoid using the term is an attempt to be more accurate about Africa and the Diaspora.

Identities are expressed in many ways throughout Africa and the Diaspora. Although at times invented, identities are indeed very real, be they ethnic, linguistic, religious, national, regional, or local. Many scholars of Africa use the term "ethnic group" in place of tribe, given the stereotypes that surround tribe. To be even more specific, terms used to describe a particular group include lineage, clan, village, town, chiefdom, community, kingdom, political unit, state, or language group. Often, a combination of these terms is needed to describe sophisticated social identities within a complex social order. As Africans moved throughout the Atlantic world, their fluid ethnic identities traveled with them and remained central in their lives. The work of scholars has demonstrated that distinct, hybrid ethnic identities existed in slave societies in the Americas as certain African languages and cultures dominated particular slave ships and were present in large concentrations at various destinations (Thornton 1998). Research has revealed that the Bambara and others from Senegambia reestablished a Bambara culture as Africans in Louisiana, for example, while the Twi served as leaders in Jamaican communities (Caron 1997; Morgan 1997). In Bahia, Brazil, most slaves came from the Bight of Benin, and the practice of Candomblé in Brazil has clear connections with Yoruba religion and culture in West Africa. Numerous aspects of African ethnic identities and "nations," including creative variations of these identities, appeared in expressive forms of African culture in the Diaspora.

Ethnic consciousness is not simply some sort of deep primordial allegiance; rather, it is created and re-created as an ongoing process.

People draw on historical memories and oral traditions to foster and alter ethnic identifications. Identities are diverse, ambiguous, complicated, messy, and fluid. Ethnic identities tend to take on a powerful salience because they *appear* to be natural and primordial, as evidence from Rwanda chillingly revealed during the genocide in 1994. However, ethnic identity or "tribalism" is often manipulated in the pursuit of power. This was the case in Rwanda, where the two main identities, Hutu and Tutsi, were once quite fluid but became fixed during the colonial period. Although Hutu and Tutsi speak the same language (Kinyarwanda) and share the same religion and clan affiliations, European colonial officials favored the Tutsi over the Hutu and issued identity cards during the colonial period as part of their quest to sort and label Africans. Thus, rather than reflecting "ancient tribal rivalries," the violence in Rwanda in 1994 was the result of more recent power struggles where extremists used the "tribal card" to spur members of the Hutu majority to kill their fellow citizens. Ethnic identities may arise at any given time, but they are most famous for leading to violence when they are used to satisfy group aspirations at the expense of others (Wilmsen and McAllister 1996).

In the African setting, it is widely understood that Africans and Europeans transformed ethnic identifications through social, political, and ideological means during the colonial and postcolonial eras (ca. 1890–present). Some scholars have argued that modern "tribalism" in Africa is the result of European and African "creations" of ethnic identities during the colonial era. While there is no doubt that much tampering with ethnicity occurred during the colonial period, recent research has revealed the existence of earlier roots of ethnic consciousness throughout Africa. Just as colonial officials manipulated ethnic identities, so did precolonial African leaders.

After independence, there was much concern that ethnicity would act as a divisive force and subvert nationalist tendencies on the African continent. In some countries ethnic realities were ignored in favor of integration and nationalist agendas. The first president of Mozambique, Samora Machel, declared soon after independence, "We are all Mozambicans!" Zambia's slogan was "One Zambia, One Nation." However, the denial of ethnic realities and social trajectories in the postcolonial era led not only to disintegration but also to discontent among many African populations. Anger and frustration throughout the continent over acts of exclusion and domination served to strengthen the identities and agendas of many subnation groups. The Igbo of southeast Nigeria seceded soon after independence in 1967 to create the Republic of Biafra, but a civil war for over two years ended in defeat and national reconciliation. Eritrea, on the other hand, seceded from Ethiopia and successfully became an independent nation after a protracted struggle.

Given the artificial formation of Africa's national boundaries, there is a dire need today to examine both the constraints and possibilities of existing ethnic identities on the continent (Nnoli 1998). In the popular media and political arenas Africans are debating the implications of their history of tribalism. Despite the relatively useless meaning behind the term tribe, the phenomenon of tribalism continues to haunt postcolonial Africa.

Elizabeth MacGonagle

See also Africa; Atlantic World and the African Diaspora.

FURTHER READING
Caron, Peter. 1997. "'Of a Nation Which Others Do Not Understand': Bambara Slaves and African Ethnicity in Colonial Louisiana, 1718–60." *Slavery and Abolition* 18 (1): 98–121.
Forrest, Joshua B. 2004. *Subnationalism in Africa: Ethnicity, Alliances and Politics.* Boulder, CO: Lynne Rienner.
Lowe, Chris, with Tunde Brimah, Pearl-Alice Marsh, William Minter, and Monde Muyangwa. 1997. "Talking about 'Tribe':

Moving from Stereotypes to Analysis." Africa Action Background Paper. www.africaaction.org/bp/ethall.htm (accessed April 30, 2005).

Morgan, Philip D. 1997. "The Cultural Implication of the Atlantic Slave Trade: African Regional Origins, American Destinations and New World Developments." *Slavery and Abolition* 18 (1): 122–145.

Nnoli, Okwudiba, ed. 1998. *Ethnic Conflicts in Africa.* Dakar, Senegal: CODESRIA.

Thornton, John. 1998. *Africa and Africans in the Making of the Atlantic World, 1400–1800.* 2nd ed. Cambridge, UK: Cambridge University Press.

Wilmsen, Edwin, and Patrick McAllister, eds. 1996. *The Politics of Difference: Ethnic Premises in a World of Power.* Chicago: University of Chicago Press.

Trinadade, Solano (1908–1974)

Solano Trindade is considered the greatest black poet that Brazil has ever known. He was born in Recife in 1908. His father was a cobbler and a dancer of the folk music *pastoril* and *bumba-meu-boi.* His mother, Emerenciana, a laborer and tidbit seller, used to have him read popular stories and romantic poetry to her. Thus, although he did not have much of a formal education, Trinadade grew up living and admiring Afro-Brazilian popular culture, while experiencing firsthand the joy and pain of his people. His career as a militant began indirectly in 1930, with his first poems dealing with the Afro-Brazilian condition. In 1932, he created in Recife the *Frente Negra Pernambucana* (Pernambucan Black Front), a movement that did not last.

In 1934, Trinadade participated in the first and second Afro-Brazilian congresses, in Recife and Salvador, respectively. In 1936, he founded the Center of Afro-Brazilian Culture with the goal of disseminating intellectual and artistic production. He moved to Belo Horizonte in 1940 and, with the poet Balduino, formed a group for popular art. That was his first attempt at creating popular theater, another failure, because a flood swept away all the material. After a short return home to Recife, he left for Rio de Janeiro, where many Afro-Brazilian artists and activists lived.

Trinadade frequented Café Vermelhinho, a meeting point for young artists, poets, intellectuals, journalists, and politicians. One of those in attendance was another Afro-Brazilian artist-activist, Abdias do Nascimento, with whom Trinadade would collaborate in *Teatro Experimental Negro* (TEN). The 1945 premiere of TEN's production would later spark a racist reaction from the white Rio community. Trinadade was already listed as a troublemaker by authorities: in 1944, after the publication of his poem, "Tem gente com fome" (You have hungry people), he was arrested, and his book, *Poemas de uma vida simples*, was seized. Such harassment did not deter Trinadade in his commitment to his people's cause. In 1950, he realized one of his most cherished dreams: he collaborated with the socialist Edson Carneiro to found the *Teatro Popular Brasileiro* (Brazilian Popular Theater). Five years later, he added the dancing group, *Brasiliana*, which toured several European countries performing and promoting Afro-Brazilian culture. Trinadade was the first to produce on stage the classic play "Orfeu" (Black Orpheus) by Vinicius de Morais, which was later adapted into film by Marcel Camus.

Trinadade was the architect of the cultural transformation of the town of Embu, about an hour away from São Paulo, into a center for black artists to live. There, memories are alive of Solano as an artist, researcher and promoter of black popular culture, theatrical director, and Bohemian, an Afro-Brazilian for whom art is the essence of life. In his Popular Theater, Trinadade taught dance and diction, and his students were mostly laborers, students, and the unemployed, in short, the mass of the people. He moved to Embu upon his return from Europe in 1955, and in 1967 he met a brother in struggle, the Négritude cofounder, Leopold Sedar Senghor. It was as a result of Trinadade's efforts that Embu has become what it is today, a market and a home for artists welcoming a constant influx of tourists. Trinadade was nicknamed "the patriarch of Embu."

In Prague, Trinadade produced the documentary *Brazil Dances*. As an actor, he worked in several films, such as *Misterios da Ilha de Venus* (Mystery on the Island of Venus) and *Santo Milagroso* (Miraculous Saint). He coproduced the film *Magia Verde* (Green Magic), which was given an award at the Cannes Film Festival.

Trinadade suffered immensely for his blackness. Wrongly accused of gun possession in the 1950s, and also because of his membership in the Communist Party, he was thrown in jail, while his ailing son, Liberto, was detained. In 1964, another son, Francisco, died in prison, a victim of the Brazilian dictatorship. His material poverty was never a deterrent in his work, and it remains striking how such a great talent lacked enough support. His theater eventually collapsed, and by 1970, his health was deteriorating. He died in Rio in 1974, penniless.

After death, Trinadade seems to have found some recognition, particularly among critics. After his first poems in 1944, he published two other collections, *Seis tempos de poesia* (1958) and *Cantares ao meu povo* (1961). Trinadade the poet has been compared to the Cuban Nicolás Guillén, and to the African American Langston Hughes.

Trinadade was exceedingly proud of his African ancestry. His poems are songs of Afro-Brazilian freedom, struggle, and survival. The 21st century activists of Brazil's *O Movimento Negro Unificado* (United Black Movement) and poetry collectives like Quilombhoje owe a great deal to Trindade, among others.

Femi Ojo-Ade

See also Brazil: Afro-Brazilians; Guillén, Nicolás (1902–1989); Hughes, Langston (1902–1967); Nascimento, Abdias do (1914–); Négritude; Quilombhoje.

FURTHER READING
Nascimento, Abdias do. 1992. *Africans in Brazil.* Trenton, NJ: Africa World Press.
Butler, Kim D. 1998. *Freedoms Given. Freedoms Won: Afro Brazilians in Post Abolition Sao Paulo and Salvador.* New Brunswick, NJ: Rutgers University Press.

Trinidad and Tobago

Trinidad and Tobago is a twin island state that covers only 5128 square kilometers and contains a population of only 1.3 million persons. The two islands lie at the south of the Caribbean Sea near the coast of Venezuela, which is about seven miles away. But it has made contributions to the African Diaspora through political icons like Henry Sylvester Williams, George Padmore, C. L. R. James, Eric Williams, Claudia Jones, and Kwame Ture; through cultural enrichments in the forms of calypso, steelpan, and carnival; and through Olympic-level athletes and world-class entertainers far beyond what would be expected of a country of that size and population.

HISTORY

In 1962, the two islands gained their independence from the United Kingdom as one nation. The nation became a republic in 1976 but has remained within the British Commonwealth and is a member of the United Nations, the Organization of American States, CARICOM (Caribbean Community), and other international organizations.

The original inhabitants were so-called Caribs and Arawaks (of the same line as the Amerindians of the Americas). They established fishing and agricultural communities and pursued their distinctive social and cultural development. There is undeniable evidence that the natives had greeted people from Africa to their shores long before the arrival of Spaniards. This ancient meeting of the early African Diaspora with the indigenous people of the islands was to continue with the subsequent coming of additional Africans on the slave ships. The Europeans who came to these islands after the voyages of Columbus from 1492, were in general initially greeted by the native population with customary hospitality. Those natives, however, who did not die at the cruel hands of the Europeans lived only to regret their display of kindness.

To replace the supply of labor that was depleted through inhuman treatment of the natives, the Europeans turned to Africa. This was the start of the permanent African Diaspora in the islands of Trinidad and Tobago. People were snatched from several parts of Africa, especially from the west coast, and taken across the dreaded Middle Passage of the Atlantic Ocean to work on the plantations of the New World.

Postslavery African additions to the population of these islands has been minimal, except for the arrival of black ex-soldiers from the East Coast of the United States who had been recruited by the British army in the War of American Independence. These African Americans settled in the southern part of Trinidad; one of these settlements still bears the name of Fifth Company.

At the end of the slave trade in 1807, and with the abolition of slavery in 1833, the population of the country changed its ethnic makeup with the arrival of indentured laborers, from India in particular. Other additions to the labor force also came from China and Portugal. In 1797, when the British took the country, the population was 14,250—10,000 Africans, 2,086 Europeans, 1,082 free people of color and 1,082 Amerindians—the present population of 1.3 million has an ethnic/racial makeup of 39 percent Africans, 39 percent East Indians, and small percentages of Chinese, Syrians, mixed, and local whites (often called

French Creoles). The mixed and French Creole groups comprise people with varying percentages of African, European, and of diverse ethnic combinations, particularly African and Indian, called pejoratively "douglas." No country in the world has a larger percentage of Afro-Indians who identify more closely with their African than with their Indian origins than does Trinidad and Tobago. Many mixed-race persons also claim Amerindian ancestry.

RELIGIONS

The religious breakdown of the population is 30 percent Roman Catholic; 24 percent Hindu; 10 percent Anglican; 6 percent Muslim, including Black Muslims; 4 percent Presbyterian, Evangelical, and other small Christian denominations; and a small but unspecified percentage following African-derived religions such as Orisha and Shango. The latter group includes the Spiritual Shouter Baptists. The religion with the strongest African retentions practiced in the country is Orisha, which in its earlier manifestations was called Shango. Adherents to this religious faith, along with the Spiritual Shouter Baptists, were, until recently, prohibited by law from practicing their religious rites. But that law was repealed, and the number of the African Diaspora who are able to openly practice their religion, has increased tremendously. Spiritual Shouter Baptist Liberation Day has been proclaimed as a national holiday on March 30. All other religions except Hindu have large representations from among the African Diaspora. One Muslim sect gained notoriety for an attempted overthrow of the government in 1990.

LANGUAGES

English is the official language of the country, which has a 98 percent literacy rate. But as in other parts of the English-speaking world, it has its own peculiarities, particularly accent, grammatical structure, and local vocabulary. Alongside Standard English, a Creole English is widely used, increasingly at the popular level. The version of Creole English spoken in Trinidad and Tobago has evolved from the interaction of languages spoken by the various peoples who came to this land. Thus, although essentially English in syntax and vocabulary, the Creole English has distinct African retentions, along with French, and to a lesser degree Spanish and Hindi. This is the language of the Calypso—the typical "folk" song of the country. Spanish is now taught extensively in schools as the government intends that it be a second language.

The African retentions in the popular language, which is used by all in varying degrees, relate to different features of society, especially food. Local dishes like *pelau, coo coo, payme, calaloo, souse,* roast corn, *fufu, eddoes,* and styles of seasoning and cooking can be traced back to Africa. The bongo drum and its use in wakes, the word "obeah" as a term of witchcraft, and *sousou* as a system of collective saving of money are all African derived.

CULTURAL EXPRESSIONS

By far the best-known cultural expression of the people of Trinidad and Tobago is the calypso. This popular form of music and dance had its origins in the minds and bodies of those first Africans who were brought seminaked to this part of the world on slave ships. Calypso evolved from the rhythm and chant of the Kalinda of the Yoruba people, and the word *kaiso,* its traditional name, has been traced directly to African linguistic systems. Every year a new batch of calypso is prepared, sung, and danced during the carnival season. The calypsoes deal with all the issues people consider important. No one, no subject is exempt. Calypso is the voice of the people. It is well recognized that the only new musical instrument invented in the 20th century is the steelpan. Trinidad and Tobago and particularly the local African Diaspora are very proud of their invention and development of this musical instrument.

Carnival can be considered another notable contribution of the African Diaspora of Trinidad and Tobago to world culture. This cultural festival is celebrated just before the start of the Catholic Lenten season. Only the carnival of Rio de Janeiro rivals in artistic and cultural magnificence. It is the time of the year when the African Diaspora flocks to the islands to participate in this "greatest show on earth." Although some say it is derived from ancient Roman festivals, there is concrete evidence that carnival evolved from ceremonies and masquerades in Africa. This local festival has been exported to numerous cities in the United States, Canada, and the United Kingdom. Several masquerade festivals still take place in Africa.

The celebration of Emancipation Day on August 1, a national holiday, is second only to carnival for the outpouring of the cultural expressions from the African Diaspora in Trinidad and Tobago. On that day, people of African descent display great pride in their African ancestry with parades in the finest African wear, singing, chanting, drum beating, conferences, artistic exhibitions, cultural shows, historical reenactments, and African religious ceremonies. Trinidad and Tobago is the first country to proclaim its day of emancipation as a national holiday. Local Africa-affiliated organizations such as the Caribbean Historical Society and especially the Emancipation Support Comittee have been successful in prompting other countries to give such recognition to emancipation. Both organizations came out of the National Joint Action Committee's efforts in the Black Power Movement of the 1960's.

AFRICAN DIASPORA ICONS

Trinidad and Tobago has produced numerous recognizable African Diaspora icons. These include Henry Sylvester Williams (b. 1869), who organized the first Pan-African Conference in 1900. He had a great influence on W. E. B. DuBois, Kwame Nkrumah, and other Africanists like George Padmore and C. L. R. James. Muzumbo Lazare, a Trinidadian attorney in London, helped organize this first Pan-African

Conference (later to be called Congress), which brought delegates from Africa, the West Indies, the United States, and Canada. In London he ran unsuccessfully for Parliament, but was later elected to the Marylebourne Borough Council in 1906. He finally returned to his native land of Trinidad where, until he died in 1911, he energetically pursued his Africanism and nurtured the growth of the African Diaspora with outstanding zeal. George Padmore, who gave the greatest thrust to Pan-Africanism as we know it today, was born in the same Tunapuna/Arouca area of Trinidad as Sylvester Williams and C. L. R. James.

One of the most influential but controversial icons of the African Diaspora born in Trinidad and Tobago is C.L.R. James. Claudia Jones has the distinction of being the founder of the first London carnivals and the first major black newspaper in England, the *West Indian Gazette* (1958). And, among the scholars in the African Diaspora, Eric Eustace Williams stands out for his intellectual output and political achievements. Kwame Ture, who was born in 1941 in Port of Spain, Trinidad and changed his name from Stokely Carmichael, is another noted activist who contributed significantly to U.S. African American struggles like voter rights, and the larger Panafricanism movement.

John Jacob Thomas (b. 1840) distinguished himself as a teacher in the early postemancipation days by trying to provide education to Africans recently liberated from the trauma of slavery. Thomas wrote *The Theory and Practice of Creole Grammar*, which was a revolutionary attempt to dispel feelings of inferiority related to language. His greatest work, however, was *Froudacity*, which he published in 1889 the year of his death. It was a masterful counterattack against the contempt displayed for the people and society of the time by an English writer and historian, J. J. Froude, in his book *The English in the West Indies*.

Hazel Scott was born in Trinidad in 1920 and played the piano at three years old, performed in New York City at eight years, and eventually became an outstanding pianist, performing at Carnegie Hall. She was married to Rev. Adam Clayton Powell, Jr., who was accused of being a communist sympathizer and spoke out vehemently against racial injustices.

Winnifred Atwell (b. 1913) gained universal recognition as both a classical and jazz pianist with performances at illustrious venues like the Royal Albert Hall in London and before the Queen of England. During World War I, Audrey Jeffers (1898–1968) served with the West African troops and organized a West African Soldiers Fund. Returning home, she founded the Coterie of Social Workers and was the first woman to be elected to the City Council of Port-of-Spain and later to the nation's Legislative Council in 1946.

Tubal Uriah Buzz Butler (1895–1977) was born in Grenada but lived most of his life in Trinidad and Tobago. As a labor leader and politician, he distinguished himself as the champion of the worker and the poor and led the 1930s labor riots in the oilfields, which eventually brought independence to the country. He formed the Butler Party and was elected to the Legislative Council in 1950. He is recognized throughout the African Diaspora for his valiant battles for the people and against colonialism.

POLITICAL AND SOCIAL STRUCTURE

Since independence from the United Kingdom in 1962, the country has been operating as a parliamentary democracy with general elections every five years. The bicameral Parliament consists of the 31-seat Senate and the 36-seat House of Representative; the president is head of state and the prime minister is head of government. For the administration of the country there are nine county councils, two city and three borough corporations, and the special Tobago House of Assembly. The People's National Movement has been the dominant political party since it brought the country into independence under the leadership of Eric Williams.

This party has a strong African association while the opposition parties, including the present United National Congress, tend to have strong East Indian backing. The social structure of the country is essentially stratified according to income, but the demarcation lines are not very strong or rigid. Race, color, and particularly education are significant determinants of social classification.

ECONOMY

Trinidad and Tobago has the largest gross domestic product (GDP) of the Anglophone Caribbean, one of the highest per capita GDPs among the nations of the Western Hemisphere, and one of the highest standards of living in the developing world. The major sectors of the economy are natural gas, petroleum and petrochemicals, construction, services, and agriculture. Oil reserves at the current rate of extraction are expected to last approximately 10 years, but the islands enjoy large reserves of natural gas. The exploration of natural gas is steadily surpassing petroleum in its contribution to the GDP. New petrochemical plants, which are being constructed using the country's natural gas resources, include ammonia, urea, and methanol. These large industrial projects are located at the newly built Point Lisas industrial park, which, along with the park's new iron and steel plant, provide Trinidad and Tobago with an industrial base that is unmatched throughout the Caribbean. Tourism, which is rather undeveloped compared with other Caribbean islands, is concentrated in the sister isle of Tobago. The agricultural sector has been suffering a long decline,

Even with cyclical growth, the citizens of the country have been benefiting from a quality of life that surpasses that not only of most other Caribbean islands but also of other Western Hemisphere oil exporters, such as Mexico and Venezuela. The country also enjoys a 98 percent literacy rate, which is higher than Italy's, a per capita energy consumption rate that exceeds Britain's, a per capita newspaper circulation above that in several Western European countries, an income distribution comparable to that of the United States, and access to electricity and potable water that is better than most developing countries. Life expectancy is 71, and primary and secondary school enrollment ratio is 94 and 85 percent, respectively. Nevertheless, the country also suffers problems associated with more developed societies, including pollution, obsessive consumption, entrenched labor disputes, growing drug abuse, and a recent escalation in crimes, especially kidnapping. As in other Caribbean countries, chronic unemployment is a major social problem.

Trinidad and Tobago has a mixed economy that allows for a level of government involvement second only to that in Cuba among the countries of the Western Hemisphere. The large role in the economy of subsidies, transfers, and joint ventures between the government and the private sector creates an intertwining of the public and private sectors that often blurs distinctions between them. The government is the largest single employer in the country. Although Trinidad and Tobago is a country where capitalism generally flourishes, free enterprise, especially in the foreign sector, is highly regulated by the government.

Trinidad and Tobago is a very open economy, dependent on the export of oil and gas to purchase large amounts of imported food, consumer goods, and capital goods. It is the most important exporter of oil and gas to the United States from the Caribbean Basin. Unlike virtually every other Caribbean country, it generally enjoys yearly trade and balance of payments surpluses. It depends on the United States for roughly 50 percent of its trade, but the islands also maintain important trade relations with the European Economic Community and CARICOM.

Michael Alleyne

See also Carnival; James, Cyril Lionel Robert (1901–1989); Jones, Claudia Cumberbatch (1915–1964); Padmore, George (1901–1959);

Pan-Africanism; Steelpan; Transatlantic Slave Trade; Ture, Kwame (1941–1998); Williams, Eric Eustace (1911–1981).

FURTHER READING

Anthony, Michael. 1988. *Towns and Villages of Trinidad and Tobago*. Port-of-Spain, Trinidad and Tobago: Circle Press.

Augier, F. R., and S. C. Gordon. 1962. *Sources of West Indies History*. London: Longmans.

Bereton, B. B. Samaroo, and G. Taitt. 1998. *Dictionary of Caribbean Biography*. Mona, Jamaica: University of West Indies Press.

Elder, J. D. 1988. *African Survivals in Trinidad and Tobago*. London: Karia Press.

Simpson, George E. 1965. *The Shango Cult in Trinidad*. Rio Piedras, Puerto Rico: Institute of Caribbean Studies, University of Puerto Rico.

Van Sertina, Ivan. 1976. *They Came Before Columbus*. New York: Random House.

Williams, E. 1963. *History of the People of Trinidad and Tobago*. London: Andre Deutsch.

Trinidad and Tobago: African Impact on the Social Order

The impact of Africa and Africa-originated populations on the social order of Trinidad and Tobago is a microcosmic part of the controversial question that, for several centuries, European historians, scientists, and administrators have attempted to answer without facing the facts. From the Greek historian Herodotus (484–425 BCE) to the Festival of African Culture (1977 CE) the question "What have Africa and the Africans contributed to world civilization?" has challenged scientists, researchers, travelers, and historians to produce reliable, valid answers.

The early formulations of African cultural survivals have been the subject of academic dispute between social scientists debating the questions of white/black assimilation and segregation in the New World societies. Indeed, one of the most critical social scientists who opposed the view that Africans in the Dias-

pora had retained at least some of their culture was Franklin Frazier, a product of the Chicago Sociological School. And this question is crucial to the subject: If New World Africans had retained nothing of their ancient African culture, as Frazier and others argued, there are no grounds on which to propose that they had any cultural impact on the New World social order as Melville Herskovits and later Africanists were obliged to admit.

To understand the paradox of Frazier, a black man, denying the retention of Africanisms (African cultural traits) by New World blacks and locking horns with Herskovits over the question of an African cultural heritage in the Americas and the West Indies, one must recall that Frazier had set out initially to oppose Herskovits's theories, all of which were based on genetics and physiology and purported to show Africans as being of a race different from Europeans and incapable of assimilation into European society. Because this was the position taken by the physical anthropologists under Franz Boas, Herskovits's teacher, Frazier, who opted for integration, had to argue that the culture of Diaspora Africans was a product of their new environment, that they were Americans in culture and therefore as qualified for equality of opportunity as white Americans.

But the fight over African cultural survivals took more serious shape after Herskovits returned from his field research in Dahomey, Nigeria, Suriname, Haiti, and Trinidad and flooded the world with his reports on what he termed the "tenaciousness of African culture" under conditions of "culture contact." From his field materials he developed theories about cultural transmission—about the three ways in which acculturation takes place, reinterpretation, accommodation, and assimilation—and about the impact he had seen the African cultural heritage exerting on the social order of the New World, especially the Caribbean. Herskovits died fighting the battle of cultural relativism by which he had hoped to change the attitude of the white

World to African culture. But the evil of centuries of anti-African theorizing had already done damage; even in Herskovits's works ethnocentricism and bias turn up in unexpected places.

The task of clinching the argument in favor of African survivals in the New World was thrown to a succeeding generation of scholars as for many groups of African ancestry, Africa was associated with a negative rather than a positive regard for their racial past and their cultural roots and origins. In the Trinidad and Tobago social order, research has revealed the dimensions of African culture in demography, worldview (cosmogony), religion, social organization, economics, property, work, art, craft, politics, and social control.

DEMOGRAPHY

The most significant African input is the injection of a variety of human ethnic groups, each with its unique genetic history generally classified under Negroid and Bantu. The potential reproductive capability with which this input has endowed the Caribbean population as a whole has not been evaluated. However, the African migration created a number of gene pools and hereditary types in an ecology in which the indigenes were gradually decimated. Further, the cross-fertilization of races in Trinidad and Tobago, small as it is, in the African, Caucasian, and Oriental sectors, has given rise to new "marginal types" of ethnics, thus canceling out or at least reducing the probability of genetic death through monozygous imbalance in the population. The straight nose bridge and silken smooth black skin of the Fulani/Hausa, the high cheekbones and brilliant white eyes of the Yoruba, the musculature of the Congo people, and the light tan shade of the Ibos—all of these physical characteristics and others of the black people of this country are transmitted through race-crossing to the people of Oriental and Caucasian origin, thus creating a distribution of ethnic variations seen in few lands.

WORLDVIEW RELIGION

This heading includes metaphysical activities, moral and ethical systems, divinatory rituals, and beliefs about the dead and the gods. From West Africans like the Mandingoes, the Radas, the Yorubas, the Ibos, and the Hausas a religious system has developed in which there are a recognized Supreme Being (Olodumare, Chukwu Aro, and so on), and a pantheon of divinities of equal status who are active among humans to the point of possessing them spiritually.

From them derives a system of sacrifice (blood), a body of sacred narratives by which the "faithful" are guided in their relations with the Orishas. From the West Africans, Trinidad and Tobago received a cosmogony in which the concept of fate, the afterlife, and judgment are central in the morality system. Connected with this belief in the other world is the belief in reincarnation and the active intervention of the living dead (compare with the Catholic saints) and the ancestors in the affairs of the living. One can, without fear of contradiction, account for the basic religiosity of the people of this nation by reference to the fundamental place of religion and its moral codes in traditional African civilizations. For these civilizations there is no generation gap: the older a person gets the nearer he or she is to the ancestral gods and the more his or her words become oracular.

In this connection, in the Christian religion, my research has shown nothing in terms of belief, ritual acts, and dogma about the cosmos that can be demonstrated as being superior to African religions. From inside Africa, reports from the field show many native peoples refusing to accept Christianity on the grounds that it has nothing the native religion does not supply. (See Herskovits et al. 1959.) It is widely accepted that it is in the area of religion that Afro-Caribbean culture resembles most closely the traditional African cultures. It should be noted here, that the Mandingoes (Mende) and the Hausas were the first ethnics to introduce the Islamic religion into Trinidad.

SOCIAL ORGANIZATION

Social organization includes kinship systems, social ranking on the basis of blood or affinity, family typology, residence, and descent rules. Many of the cultures from which the blacks of Trinidad and Tobago came practice patriliny— that is, descent is reckoned through males. In Trinidad and Tobago it is the male ancestral authority upon which people call in the disposal of immovable property like land. In a sense, just as in Nigeria, it is the land (ancestral) that claims the male child. The patrilineal extended family of West Africa is still very much with us as is the matrifocal family.

The extended family, consisting of a man, his wife, his unmarried sons and daughters, and some of his grandchildren, resident in the old primary family household is an undying social institution that urban migration has reinforced, not to mention bad housing problems. Today, a woman may be the head of that extended family household and just as easily its primary authority figure.

Another feature of social organization retained from ancient African customs is the fictive kin, whereby persons unrelated by blood or affinity may ask for and receive kinship status in a family and enjoy all the privileges and perform all the duties of a kinsperson. These kinspeople include godparents, *portez*, grannies, and nannies. This method of extending the corporate family group certainly substitutes for the several secret and social groups (for example, Ogboni cult, Oro) that traditional African communities used to give solidarity to their social relationships and impregnability to their lineage.

In rural villages of Tobago all adults are addressed by the lateral kin term *cousin*. In fact, this status carries a duty of surrogate parent and mentor for the young of the community. Serial polygyny without proper controls loses all of its potential social value and functionality. Many females in the society would die without fulfilling their aspirations of sharing their life "as a natural woman" with a human being who is her offspring were it not for this breach of Christian monogamy prescriptions. It is an abomination to be infertile by nature or by accident; just so, any social restriction on the black woman in respect of her right to reproduce her kind is illegal in this cultural framework.

Inside Africa, given names continue to be received by a person even after death. Such names, apart from the clan name, are indicative of the conditions and circumstances surrounding the birth and/or conception of the child. Names are therefore very significant and carry important signals about a person's status and descent. Among the Trinidad and Tobago peasant black population this custom is very viable. It is common to hear names like Pretty Miss, Bright Man, Little Man, Pin-Pin, Oldman, Braveman, Bigman, Tryamsee, Giftson, Dearson, Comfort, Content, Hardtime, Corntime, Workman Bear All, and Oneseed. Related to this are nicknames or funny-names, which are given to children to baffle the evil spirits who can call infants, especially *abiku*, and lead them away to destruction. All the taboos about name-calling in Nigeria have been noted by field researchers among African descendants in Trinidad and Tobago.

ECONOMICS

Labor, savings, corporate productive groups, bride service, property, inheritance rules, and so on are included under this heading. Living on and off the land (subsistence agriculture) is the major form of production among the majority of African descendants in Trinidad and Tobago. The family, as in Africa, is the basic economic productive unit. Often the earnings of the family are supervised by the oldest male in the household. The mother often advises as to how this money (wealth) should be disbursed. As in Africa, black women are the true traders and are given much say in buying and selling transactions, although they will claim that their husbands have the last say.

Work on the land is carried out on a cooperative basis; able-bodied men form work-corvees (lend-a-hand, brothers, partners, task-workers) to cultivate or farm each other's fields in succession over a number of days, each owner providing food for his "partners." In some cases, just as is done in West Africa, music is provided to help the workers perform. Women perform the light work on the family farm.

Bride-price has not survived in the black social organizations of Trinidad and Tobago, but there is bride-service among peasants. A son-in-law, even a prospective one, must do some work on his wife's parental homestead and hold himself ready to give to his in-laws some assistance with work all through his married life.

Among the rural folk and the tradespeople in towns, there is the custom of cooperative saving (savings clubs calls *susu*, from the Akan "esusu"), by which very large items may be purchased by an individual through pooling small sums along with his friends. This is an African custom that has persisted among all Afro-Caribbean societies, but Trinidad and Tobago people hold that it is peculiar to them. The talent system, involving a small capital advance, is another rural black economic institution.

A common method of trading in Trinidad and Tobago is called "exchange," in which payment in kind may be made for services received or there may be outright bartering of goods, ground provisions, and vegetables. Fishermen may "exchange" their fish for vegetables or fruits. A mutually accepted scale of values ("standards") exists between such traders. This kind of economic arrangement has antecedents in Africa, although most service has been noted among rural villages in some remote communities on both islands.

ART, CRAFT

These include the vernacular forms of the arts—such as local culinary arts, folk music and dance, and dramatics. Most of the African-derived music of Trinidad and Tobago is ritual in function, for example, music for Orisha worship (Shango). The obituary music for

dead-wakes (bongo, singing, *velorios*), the music for invocation of ancestors (Tobago–reel dance music), the music of the independent Baptists (jubilees), the hymns and chants of the Spiritual Baptists (groaning, throne-of-grace) all represent modified structural and performance or stylistic features of African traditional music. The emphasis on percussion and quadruple tempo, polyrhythm, and contrapuntal singing styles, together with the organization of the performing group (whether choral or orchestral) on a strictly labor "division" between leader and chorus, are definitely retained stylistic traits from African tradition. Many musical instruments found among black folk musicians in Trinidad and Tobago are identical with their counterparts inside Africa, for example the *sanza* (mbira), *emele* (omelet), *dun-dun*, and *shekere*.

The traditional uses of music by Africans to accompany work, to induce trance-states in devotees, to palliate the gods and ancestors, and to drive out evil spirits from the sick can be found still among the blacks of this country. Music to accompany work on land and sea takes the form of digging songs, woodmen's music, harvesting (reaping) songs, and planting songs, exactly as happens in West African communities. Satiric music and music to convey abuse and condemnation of social conditions are hereditary.

The plastic arts derived from Africa constitute a very small part of the present corpus, but there is a small residue of wood carving and calabash carving that does not by any means approach the sophistication of the traditional carvers at Oyo in Nigeria. Post carvings, like those decorating the entrance to the Institute of African Studies, Unibadan, has been attempted in some Trinidad rural villages; however, they may be modern imitations of commercial pieces from present-day Africa. At Plymouth in Tobago, one sees house-wall decorations executed by fisherman brush (billy) with chip-chip shells, exactly as the Fulani people of Kano State, Nigeria, do to their mud walls with snail shells.

Thatching techniques executed with cane straw and palm fronds in Tobago villages bear a clear similarity to the straw work on mud-walled houses in Asaba and Onitsha in Iboland (Nigeria). Straw-plait motifs seen among the Fulanis have been noted at Mundo Muevo and at O'Meara Road among Afro-Hispanic hybrids. The mats made from balisier leaf-stalks for spreading cocoa to dry are identical to the prayer mats commonly used in Nigeria by the Hausa Islamic devotees, who carry them about rolled up under their arms. Of course, the materials used differ from Hausaland to Trinidad and Tobago. The weaving technique and designs however, show marked similarities across the two societies.

Wood carving in Trinidad and Tobago shows a marked resemblance to that in some Nigerian localities, chiefly in articles like food mortars, cutlass and hoe handles, hope chests, and food platters or bread boards. Attempts at zoomorphic designs on these articles tie them with the African plastic arts tradition. Some carved masks have been turning up in the Best Village Fair, but their connection to African ancient traditional artists is unclear.

Within the Trinidad and Tobago Carnival, African-derived ceremonial artifacts include the Ju-ju masquerade (witch doctor) and the Perrot Grenade costume, which closely resembles the costume of the *Egungun* ancestral figure, seen annually in Yoruba towns and villages. The head mask of the African figure, since 1881, has been debarred from the Trinidad and Tobago Carnival costume. The *Egun* ancestor death mask of Yorubaland must not expose any part of the body whatever because it encloses the ancestor-spirit and is very sacred. The dragon beast mask of the carnival reminds me of the Cross River water python monster mask. The intricate carnival netalwork of Ken Norris has African antecedents.

Sophisticated ancestral hair styles have been re-created in the contemporary period across the African diaspora. The common one seen is the corn-row or cane-row, very commonly

Moko jumbies, African Diaspora stilt dancers, in Trinidad Carnival. (Wolfgang Kaehler/Corbis)

used for decorating heads of little Nigerian girls. The head tie known as the *gele* among the Yoruba, has been imitated in this country, and French Creole women have made the head tie a symbol related to courtship. It goes under other names, such as *tete-marlin, madras, daizen.* In Nigeria, it is indicative of ethnic and class distinction instead.

Only a few of the traditional culinary arts of West Africa have persisted among Trinidad and Tobago blacks. The pounded yam of the Nigerians has been replaced by the pounded plantain. The roasted plantain is eaten as a special sweetmeat, while fried ripe plantain (*dodo* in Nigeria) is served with breakfast. Callaloo (*kararu* in Africa) has been retained, although it has been modified by adding salted pork, land crabs, and spices. Cassava meal is used in Trinidad and Tobago to prepare cassava-coocoo, a stiff paste very similar to the Nigerian *garri*, which is the standard meal for high- and low-class folk in Nigeria. In Trinidad and Tobago for a long time, only the lower economic class ever eats cassava coocoo. Corn coocoo, however, is a ritual meal for Shango in Trinidad and Tobago, while *fungi* is a nonritual delicacy. These have become now part of the national ethnic menus, available in major hotel chains and as delicacies in receptions and Sunday and holiday meals.

Snails are eaten in Nigeria but not Trinidad. The welks (welkin) from the rocky coast and the blue land crabs, however, are delicacies for the peasants. Although one type of monkey is eaten in Trinidad, it is an abomination to eat monkeys in Nigeria. Some Nigerians eat dogs, a sacred animal to Ogun, the god of Iron, but in Trinidad and Tobago this custom is unheard of. Iguana is eaten in this country, but in Nigeria the chameleon is the most sacred beast in the bush and is never eaten, not even ritually. As in Nigeria, the manicou or giant rat is eaten here.

A few items of clothing have survived the passage from Africa. The *buba* and the *lappa* can be seen among Tobago peasant women. A long skirt resembling the Fulani coat and called a *koti* has been noted among some rural villages both in Trinidad and Tobago.

Body marks and decorative tattooing of the erogenic body parts have completely disappeared among New World blacks, especially the face marks indicative of tribal or ethnic membership. However, ceremonial marks (with very little scarification) are placed on initiates of the Shango and the Spiritual Baptist. Some black people still place identical "body marks" upon their infants. This custom is positively traditional for West Africans. Of course, in Trinidad and Tobago these marks are not by any means "decorative" compared with the circumcision marks placed on Ibo girls when they are age graded. Both male and female circumcision have disappeared among African descendants in Trinidad and Tobago.

POLITICS, SOCIAL CONTROL

This last area of the social order to be examined for African cultural influence concerns politics and the political institutions operative in this country, whether at the formal or informal level or organization or within the national communal or domestic sector. Political organization is concerned with the maintenance of social order within a territorial framework by the organized exercise of coercive authority through the use, or possibility of use, of physical force. Because of the predominance of the British constitutional system in Trinidad and Tobago, one must remember that politics is a very broadly defined institution. This allows researchers to recognize certain marginal conventions that are very effective in achieving the objectives of social control and even in administering what some anthropologists have termed regulated vengeance and repressive justice. Both of these popular functions of politics can be found among certain ethnic groups other than Africans in this country and, in terms of the subject under discussion, one can logically ask whether the Africans originally brought any of these popular political institutions to Trinidad and Tobago.

Think of the *kingole* of the Kikuyu and the *injoget* of the Nandi people, by which individuals who had offended against the community were put to death or otherwise punished by popular ostracism, banishment, or other psychological privations. Think of the divine kingship system of West Africa, by which *obas* and chiefs hold on to their positions on the basis of charisma, through ancestral authority, and traditional rules of succession. Have any of these political traditional "conventions" persisted? For instance, is there anything in the politics of Trinidad and Tobago at the national level (or at the private communal level) that resembles the Ogboni society of kingmakers whose support or lack of it can make or break even the *oba*?

It must be admitted that the African "secret societies" as such were not included in the cultural baggage of those Africans who came to Trinidad and Tobago, at least not in sufficient strength to give them a new lease on life. History shows, however, that the Mandingoes and the Congoes did attempt to organize themselves, especially around Port of Spain, into politicoeconomic groups, but unlike their African counterparts in Haiti they failed. Nothing like the East Indian *panchayat* evolved among the Africans in Trinidad and Tobago.

Africans in Trinidad and Tobago have retained nothing of the level of the traditional elders' councils that are so powerful in peasant society in West Africa. Hence, there are no pseudopolitical integrative popular institutions among the black peasantry of this country whereby public opinion can be communally mobilized by a local leader.

European culture, through the colonial system, was late in making its impact on the West African traditional lifeways before the 19th century, in spite of the inroads of the South Atlantic slave trade. Thousands of Africans transported from their homes would have been untouched by any European-type political institution before their migration. This can be seen in the case of the Haitians who retained their institutions of social control. Why did the Trinidadian blacks lose the elders' council, the *Ogboni*, the *Oro*, and other suchlike "social regulators"? Of course something of the West African divine king syndrome can be seen in the founder/president institutions common to political parties, friendly societies, and of late, village councils in Trinidad and Tobago. In Nigeria, an *oba* (*oni*, king, ruler) who the populace decides has outlived his viability as a ruler is advised to "go to sleep" by either taking poison himself or having one of his several "mothers" (wives) administer it. To indicate their will, the kingmakers and the *oba mogba* (king's friends) send him a calabash of parrot eggs. In modern times he is assassinated but in ancient times he was induced to die "in his own house" as a good man must do, according to Yoruba values.

It is interesting to note that several modern African politicians have come up against the European political parliamentary system, which runs counter to the "settled indigenous (political) systems" of authority and leadership. The African traditional image of authority means permanent or hereditary leadership, as against the transient rotational image of authority in Western parliamentary systems. There is, therefore, a cultural basis for the "crisis in parliamentary democracy" inside many African countries. It may be that Trinidad and Tobago has retained this old African concept of permanent authority in its political system, which clashes with the Western institution of "rational leadership." It is hardly reasonable to wonder why Africans exerted so slight an influence on the political institutions of Trinidad and Tobago. European political philosophy has swamped Africans both in Africa and in the New World. The situation in Africa is mitigated by the tenacity with which the Africans have held on to traditional law and their chieftaincy system, which operates through the basic patri-clan system. In the New World, where the kinship system and its jural and political powers were eroded, there was nothing upon which the blacks could erect anything like popular government structures. Moreover, the loss of the powerful religious systems of authority by the Diaspora Africans can be held accountable for the almost complete absence of anything African in the Trinidad and Tobago political system, except maybe the use of clientage and the respect for charismatic leadership.

CONCLUSION

Despite the academic controversies over the question of whether the African people who migrated under force to the Caribbean brought their culture with them and, more importantly, to what extent, if at all, they have influenced the social order of Trinidad and Tobago, it is admitted that it is materially impossible for a people to live in contact with other ethnic groups without influencing them in a variety of ways. In the case of Trinidad and Tobago, it is a matter for pride that several marks of the African tradition have evidently been left on the social order—on the physical form of the people, on the music and the dance, on the language and the literature, on the social control mechanisms, and on the political institutions, small as this may be.

J. D. Elder

See also Carnival; Steelpan; Trinidad and Tobago.

FURTHER READING

Elder, J. D. 1969. "The Yoruba Ancestral Cult in Gasparillo: Its Structure, Organization and Social Function in Community Life." *Caribbean Quarterly* 16 (3):5–20.

Herskovits, Melville. 1947. *Trinidad Village*. New York: A. A. Knopf.

Herskovits, Melville, et al. 1959. "The Pakot Resistance to Change." In *African Cultures*, 144–167. Phoenix.

Martin, Tony. 1983. *The Pan-African Connection: From Slavery to Garvey and Beyond*. Cambridge, MA: Schenckman Publishing Co.

Warner-Lewis, Maureen. 1991. *Guinea's Other Suns: The African Dynamic in Trinidad Culture*. Dover, MA: The Majority Press.

Tropiques

The Martinican cultural revue *Tropiques* was founded in 1941 by Aimé and Suzanne Césaire with the significant collaboration of René Ménil and Aristide Maugée. In 14 issues (12 volumes) published until 1945, the literary and cultural revue pressed for the construction of a new Martinican cultural identity. The contributors focused primarily on the island's folklore, flora, politics, poetics, history, and cultural diversity (from Catholicism to Hinduism to Animism) as well as its African, Asian, European, and Latin American origins. But they also explored the potential influences of European theorists, such as the German ethnographer Leo Frobenius, and of French poets and writers, such as Lautréamont, Rimbaud, Mallarmé, and André Breton for a new literature. They turned as well to the Americas for inspiration, studying Venezuelan and Haitian poetry, exalting the Cubans Wilfredo Lam and Alejo Carpentier, and examining the impact of the Harlem Renaissance, particularly the work of Langston Hughes and Claude McKay. With its apparently apolitical cultural focus, the revue initially thrived in a period of unusual censorship, racism, and oppression during the Vichy regime in France, the repressive reign of Vichy representative Admiral Robert in Martinique, and the resulting American blockade of the island. Though the revue was briefly forbidden in 1943 for being revolutionary and racial, the collective's authors prevailed in publishing increasingly radical cultural works until the end of the war.

Tropiques' critical engagement in the question of cultural identity marked a profound revolution in Caribbean poetics. The writers of *Tropiques* challenged a culture of attempted assimilation that had resulted in a literary sterility they decried. Suzanne Césaire, for example, indicted the sort of Caribbean poetry taught in schools in Martinique in 1942 as a literature of "sugar and vanilla," a form of "tourism" that must die in order for a true Martinican poetry to be born. In their quest for a new literature, the writers explored different movements, in particular surrealism and Négritude—being among the first to embrace a black identity and an African origin for the island's culture—as tools for constructing a new poetics.

The French surrealist André Breton stumbled across the first issue of the revue while exiled in Martinique in 1941, an experience that led to his subsequent dissemination of Aimé Césaire's hitherto-unknown *Notebook of a Return to My Native Land* in New York and Paris. In many ways *Tropiques* revitalized surrealism at a time when its main European practitioners were silenced and scattered. Likewise, in embracing the earlier works of the Harlem Renaissance, the revue also introduced them to a whole new audience. As it explored outside influences, the revue's allegedly folkloric focus became increasingly radical, racially grounded, and political, a shift evident in its later essays on the socioeconomic and cultural impact of colonization for people of color in Martinique.

Kara Rabbitt

See also Césaire, Aimé (1913–2008); Césaire, Suzanne (1915–1966); Harlem Renaissance; Négritude.

FURTHER READING

Kesteloot, Lilyan. 1974. *Black Writers in French: A Literary History of Négritude*, trans. Ellen Conroy Kennedy. Philadephia: Temple University Press.

Ménil, René. 1978. "Pour une lecture critique de *Tropiques*." *Tropiques* 1: 25–35.

Michel, Jean-Claude. 2000. *Black Surrealists*. New York: Peter Lang.

Richardson, Michael, and Krzysztof Fijalkowski. 1996. *Refusal of the Shadow: Surrealism and the Caribbean*. London: Verso.

Truth, Sojourner (ca. 1797–1883)

Sojourner Truth stands as a hero among the most prominent and towering figures in the 19th-century abolitionist and feminist struggles in the United States. She brought vigor, vitality, and strength to the antislavery movement through her natural charisma and charm and her political activism in antebellum America. Sojourner Truth was born about 1797 in Ulster County, New York, not too long after the end of the American Revolution. She was named Isabella Bomefree and lived with her parents, James and Elizabeth Bomefree, in her early childhood. She spoke Dutch as her first language because it was the language of her parents' slave masters. But by the time Isabella was about nine she was sold away after her master's death to non–Dutch-speaking slaveholders. Before then, her parents had already lost 10 or 12 children to the slave trade.

Isabella was bought by John Dumont in 1810. She worked for 17 years for the Dumont family practically until her emancipation in 1827 by an antislavery and abolitionist law promulgated in the state of New York. This statute promised to give legal freedom to all New York slaves under the age of 40 by 1827. Isabella married Thomas, a fellow slave, while she lived with the Dumonts; they had five children: Diana, born about 1815; Peter, born about 1821; Elizabeth, born about 1825; Sophia, born about 1826; and one who could not be identified. Thomas was much older then Isabella as was often the case on most slave plantations, and Isabella rarely saw her husband. She left him when she went away with her baby to work for Isaac and Maria Van Wagenen. The Van Wagenens shared the ideals of equality and simplicity that would eventually steer Isabella to the Methodist Church, where she became a preacher in the service of her Lord Jesus Christ and the cause of human freedom.

In August 1831, Isabella became a servant of Pierson. In 1832 she would later join a religious commune in which her new master was an active member. This commune, called the "Kingdom," was led by Prophet Mathias. Isabella, however, left the commune after three years when suddenly the Kingdom found itself in crisis upon the death of Pierson in 1834 in suspicious circumstances. Isabella was accused by the *New York Times* of being a witch who had been responsible for the death of Pierson. She successfully sued the *Times* and forced them to retract their story. She then asked her Lord for a new name after she got tired of being called Bell by her slave masters. Isabella believed that through a religious conversion the Lord had given her a new name, which did not include the last name of a slave master. That name would be "Sojourner Truth," because she was by this time very much convinced that the Lord's last name was Truth. At the age of 46, and in a state of heightened religious conversion and zeal, she traveled on foot throughout the length and breadth of New England delivering speeches to various audiences and constantly evoking the truths of biblical scriptures. Truth had no permanent address at this rather nomadic period in her life. She often stayed with prominent members of the women's movement when she traveled, such as Susan B. Anthony and Elizabeth Cady Stanton.

Her speeches were often a blend of religion and critical comments on contemporary political and social issues. Around this time Sojourner Truth began to embark on a path of personal autonomy that would make her an active participant in the abolitionist and women's movement during that period. However, Truth had already demonstrated a spirit of defiance against the status quo of her times when in 1826 John Dumont sold her son Peter to one of his in-laws. The child landed in Alabama where slavery was not expected to end soon. Truth went to court and got the return of her son. There can be no doubt that this legal action was indicative of a strong woman who would fight to dislocate the structures of plantation and chattel slavery in the United States.

Truth joined the Northampton Association for Education and Industry in the 1840s. Around this time she came into contact with antislavery advocates and feminists. In the late 1840s she met William Lloyd Garrison and many of his followers in the abolitionist movement. She also met Olive Gilbert and collaborated with her in 1850 to write and publish her autobiography, called the *Narrative of Sojourner Truth*. Between 1850 and the Civil War, she gained fame and notoriety on the feminist lecture circuit. At the so-called "Mob Convention" on women's rights held in 1853 in New York, Truth warned that the time was near when women would gain full equality with men.

Truth met Abraham Lincoln on October 29, 1864, during which time they deliberated on the most outstanding and burning issue facing the nation, which was of course the Civil War and the issue of slavery. During this meeting, she asked Lincoln to sign her book of life, a collection of signatures and photographs. Truth

later became a counselor to the freeman society of Arlington, Virginia, assisting freed slaves from the South to resettle in the West. She remained in Washington, D.C. while she carried out her work among slave refugees from the Civil War. Truth died in November 1883 in Battle Creek, Michigan, in the house she had shared with her daughters.

Tarnue Johnson

See also Feminism and Black Women in the African Diaspora; Sojourners for Truth and Justice.

FURTHER READING
Clift, Eleanor. 2003. "And Ain't I a Woman?" *Newsweek* 142 (18): 1–3.
Lerner, Gerda. 1997. "Mother, Mystic, Myth." *Nation* 264 (2): 25–28.
Painter, Nell Irvin. 1994. "Representing Truth: Sojourner Truth's Knowing and Becoming Known." *Journal of American History* 81 (2): 461–493.
Painter, Nell Irvin. 1997. *Sojourner Truth. A Life, A Symbol.* New York: Norton.
Painter, Nell Irvin. 1998. *Narrative of Sojourner Truth.* Harmondsworth, UK: Penguin Books

Ture, Kwame (1941–1998)

Kwame Ture, a leading figure in the progression of the African Diaspora struggles from the Civil Rights and anticolonial movements to Black Power and Pan-Africanism, was born Stokely Carmichael on June 29, 1941, in Port of Spain, Trinidad. He moved to New York at an early age and attended the famous Bronx High School of Science. Upon graduation he received scholarship offers from many Ivy League colleges but chose to attend Howard University where he received a bachelor's degree in 1964. He later received an honorary doctorate (1971) from Shaw University. While at Howard University he joined the Student Nonviolent Coordinating Committee (SNCC), a leading student organization in the desegregation Civil Rights Movement in 1960. He was active with SNCC in Greene and Lowndes counties in Alabama, including the Lowndes County Freedom Organization, better known as the Black Panther Party (BPP). His participation in sit-ins and freedom rides, organizing peasants and literacy campaigns, as well as battles with the Klu Klux Klan, Federal Bureau of Investigation, and Central Intelligence Agency throughout his life placed him at the forefront of the struggle for black human rights.

In Mississippi he was involved in the Mississippi Freedom Democratic Party. He put his life on the line, like so many, facing torture, jail, and endless abuses in the quest for a better quality of life. Undying love for the people describes his attitude and work. He raised and popularized the call for "black power" at the Meredith march in Mississippi in 1966 after his election as chairman of SNCC in June. During his tenure as Chairman of SNCC, he first traveled to Cuba.

In 1967 he became honorary prime minister of the Black Panther Party in a gesture of unity between the SNCC and the BPP. His call for an African United Front with the Southern Christian Leadership Conference, National Association for the Advancement of Colored People, Nation of Islam, Black Caucus, and other groups was his trademark demand. His increased ideological development guided him from Havana to Hanoi to Tripoli and beyond in support of and as part of the struggles of the oppressed peoples around the world. Under Ture's leadership, SNCC played a vanguard role in building mass support in attacking numerous imperialist wars, including Vietnam. His stance on behalf of the Palestinian people in denouncing the Zionist aggression in 1949 and the 1967 Israeli war expanded African people's understanding of the machinations of imperialism and European settler zionism. His historic support of the demands of the Chicano/Mexican/Native American struggles via the American Indian Movement, La Raza Unida, International Indian Treaty Council,

Stokely Carmichael (Kwame Ture), an effective leader of the Student Nonviolent Coordinating Committee (SNCC), brought the concept of Black Power into the U.S. civil rights struggle. In 1967, an advocate of militancy rather than nonviolent cooperation, he broke with SNCC and joined the more radical Black Panthers. In 1978, he changed his name to Kwame Ture to honor African leaders Kwame Nkrumah and Ahmed Sékou Touré. (Library of Congress)

and so on, including their demand for the liberation of their homeland, the Americas, made him revered by indigenous peoples throughout the Western Hemisphere.

In 1967, he coauthored with Charles V. Hamilton, *Black Power, the Politics of Liberation in America*. That same year, as a manifestation of an ongoing political struggle, Ture was disassociated from SNCC, and he became the prime minister of the Black Panthers, headquartered in Oakland, California. He soon became disenchanted with the Panthers and moved to Guinea, West Africa.

While residing in Africa, the late President Ahmed Sékou Touré bestowed on him the name "Kwame Ture" to honor Osagyefo Kwame

Nkrumah, who led Ghana to independence from Britain, and, Sékou Touré, who was president of Guinea and his mentor. For more than 30 years, Ture led the All-African People's Revolutionary Party and devoted the rest of his life to Pan-Africanism as a movement to uproot the inequities of racism for people of African descent and to develop an economic and cultural coalition among the African Diaspora.

Under the tutelage of these two great Pan-Africanists, Ture recognized that organization and constant political education are the keys to the liberation of Africa and African people. The first study cells of the All African People's Revolutionary Party (AAPRP) had been created by Kwame Nkrumah in Conakry in 1968. In 1969, Ture undertook the assignment to revisit North America and the Caribbean to build the AAPRP under Nkrumah's organizational direction.

Ture traveled all over the world building the AAPRP and supporting the just struggles against exploitation and oppression. Over the years, he met and worked with progressive and revolutionary leaders and with many national and international organizations representing Arab, Indian, Chicano, Irish, and other oppressed peoples.

Although restricted by the effects of his illness and treatment for cancer, Ture continued to speak on college campuses until he returned to Guinea, determined to continue his chosen work with the AAPRP until the end. Even in his last days he was organizing against the Cuban and Libyan embargos/travel bans and promoting an African United Front. As he was fighting the battle against cancer, Ture received an outpouring of love and support from individuals, organizations, and governments.

In 1980, Ture, together with the Sisters in the AAPRP, called for the formation of the All African Women's Revolutionary Union, the largest formation within the AAPRP. This would ensure that African women assumed a vanguard role in eliminating not just national (race) and class oppression but also sexism.

Ture made immense contributions to the struggles of African people worldwide. He was a fearless, humble organizer in the service of the African Revolution. Ture's dedicated and tireless work earned him the love and admiration of the struggling people everywhere. To the end he answered the telephone, "Ready for the Revolution."

Kwame Ture died on November 15, 1998. His earlier marriages to Miriam Makeba and Guinean physician Marlyatou Barry had both ended in divorce. He is survived by his mother, two sisters, two sons, and his extended family throughout the world.

Macheo Shabaka

See also All-African People's Revolutionary Party (A-APRP); Black Panther Party; Howard University; Pan-Africanism; Trinidad and Tobago.

FURTHER READING

Carmichael, Stokely, and Charles V. Hamilton. 1967. *Black Power: The Politics of Liberation in America.* New York: Random House.

Thelwell, Ekwueme Michael, Stokely Carmichael, and John Edgar Wideman. 2003. *Ready for the Revolution: The Life and Struggles of Stokely Carmichael (Kwame Ture).* New York: Scribner.

Turkey: Afro-Turks

Afro-Turks are Turkish citizens who are of African ancestry. They are the descendants of Africans who were taken to the part of the world which is today Turkey during the Ottoman period as slaves. The ethnic composition of the population of Turkey is very diverse and the population of every region of Turkey differs from the others. The ethnic composition of the Aegean and the Mediterranean coast area includes people of African ancestry along with other groups. Therefore, it may be claimed that there exists an African Diaspora in Turkey, which is a constituent of the African Diaspora in Asia.

Research on the African Diaspora in Turkey is of great importance in order to be able to clarify the position of the histories of the Ottoman Empire and the Turkish Republic within world history and within the system of global relations. Herewith, the position of the African Diaspora in Turkey within the African Diaspora in the world and its importance would be determined as well.

In spite of the paucity of research on Ottoman slavery, which produced the Afro-Turks, there are attempts to achieve more knowledge. For example, the discourse on Ottoman slavery is gradually becoming part of the slavery discourse in other societies through studies done by both Turkish scholars and scholars of other countries. A comparative overview of the studies on slavery in general and slavery in the Ottoman Empire would also reveal how studies on Ottoman slavery are lagging behind in the overall discourse on slavery which is currently generating interest and gaining significance in intellectual circles (Toledano 1998, 138).

Besides, both in the Ottoman era, as well as the Republican era Africans have been considered as Turks/Muslims. Consequently, Afro-Turks are virtually statistically non-existent in the official demographic records of the Ottoman and Republican eras of Turkish history. Little wonder, therefore, that Afro-Turks are absent from state reference sources such as yearbooks (salname), indexes (rehber), and statistics (Günes 1999, 4).

Another reason for the neglect of people of African origin who lived or still live in this part of the world in both Ottoman and Turkish historiography is the fact that foreign research institutes still dominate the study of "Anatolia's ancient and modern history and culture." Thus there is an "absence of the development of a homebred intellectual scientific potential with a rationalist, competitive and revisionist quality to oppose conservatism" (Sahin 1995, 208). In this manner, there are almost no referable scholarly works in Turkish.

Information on the lives of these people after the demise of slavery in the Ottoman Empire or in the Turkish Republic is very scarce.

It is also impossible to obtain information on the lives of the descendants of the Africans, i.e., the African Turks today, as no questions were/are asked concerning race, ethnic origins or religion in the population censuses in Turkey. Besides using archive material, the only way to obtain information is using sociological/anthropological methods.

Esma Durugönül

FURTHER READING

Andrews, Peter Alford. 1989/1992. *Türkiye'de Etnik Gruplar (Ethnic Groups in the Republic of Turkey.* Wiesbaden: Dr. Ludwig Reichert Verlag, and Istanbul: Ant Yayinlari.

Durugönül, Esma. 2003. "The Invisibility of Turks of African Origin and the Construction of Turkish Cultural Identity: The Need for a New Historiography." *Journal of Black Studies*, Vol. 33:3 (January): 281–294.

Erdem, Y. Hakan. 1996. *Slavery in the Ottoman Empire and Its Demise 1800–1909.* London: Macmillan Press.

Günes, Günver. 1999. "İzmir'de Zenciler ve Zenci Folkloru." *Toplumsal Tarih*, Şubat: 4–10.

Martal, Abdullah, 2000. "Afrika'dan İzmir'e: İzmir'de Bir Köle Misafirhanesi." *Kebikeç* 10: 171–186.

Olpak, Mustafa. 2005. *Kenya-Girit-İstanbul Köle Kiyisindan İnsan Biyografileri.* Istanbul: Ozan Yayincilik.

Planhol, Xavier de. 1958. *De la plaine Pamphylienne aux lacs pisidiens. Nomadisme et vie paysanne.* Paris: Librarie Adrien-Maisonneuve.

Şahin, Sencer. 1995. "Türkiye Genelinde Eskiçağ Bilimleri ve Eskiçağ Tarihi Temel Bilimleri." *Arkeoloji Dergisi III.* Ed. Hasan Malay, Ege Üniversitesi Edebiyat Fakültesi Yayinlari: 203–214.

Toledano, Ehud R. 1982. *The Ottoman Slave Trade and Its Suppression, 1840-1890.* Princeton, New Jersey: Princeton University Press.

Toledano, Ehud R. 1998. *Slavery and Abolition in the Ottoman Middle East.* Seattle and London: University of Washington Press.

Turner, Nat (1800–1831)

Nat Turner was the leader of the most successful slave rebellion, which signaled the beginning of the end of chattel slavery within the United States. Turner was born on October 2, 1800, in Southampton County, Virginia, on Benjamin Turner's plantation. Turner, the son of slaves, was the property of Benjamin Turner, a prosperous plantation owner. Nat Turner's mother, Nancy, and grandmother were Africans brought to the United States. A mature and intelligent child, Turner was considered a prophet, accepted Christianity, and became very religious. Turner grew up sharing his mother and grandmother's hatred of slavery. Taught to read by Benjamin Turner's son, Samuel, Nat developed deep religious beliefs. He read the Bible, avoided participating in society, and spent most of his free time fasting and praying.

In 1821, Turner ran away from his overseer, returning after 30 days because of a vision in which he was instructed to return to Benjamin Turner. The next year, following the death of his master, Samuel Turner, Nat was sold to Thomas Moore. In 1824, Nat Turner had another vision about obtaining freedom.

Between 1825 and 1830, Turner preached to other slaves, teaching them self-respect, to struggle for justice, and to resist and struggle against slavery. His preaching and charisma gave him many followers who believed he was a prophet. He considered himself chosen by God to deliver African Americans from slavery and to kill whites with their own weapons.

In 1830, Turner was moved to the home of Joseph Travis. His official owner, however, was now a child named Putnum Moore. In February 1831, there was an eclipse of the sun that Turner took as the sign he had been promised. He confided his plan to start the slave rebellion to the four men he trusted the most. They decided to hold the insurrection on the symbolic date of July 4; however, they had to delay the rebellion because Turner was sick. On August 13, 1831, there appeared a bluish-green sky that Turner considered the last sign to begin the rebellion. Turner and his men met in the woods to make their plans. He took the title of General Cargill. Around two in the morning, on August 21, 1831, they went by horseback to the Travis household, where they killed the entire family as they were sleeping. They went from house to house killing all of the whites they encountered. Turner believed this show of force would encourage other slaves to join the rebellion, while frightening whites. Turner's plan worked to an extent because his force grew to more than 40 slaves, most on horseback. On August 22, 1831, Turner went toward Jerusalem to acquire weapons. By this time, Turner's forces had grown to 60 or 70 people as they continued to move from one house to another. However, as their size increased, Turner's force became disorganized and lost the element of surprise. Whites learned of the rebellion and formed a militia of more than 100 people that confronted Turner and his rebels who scattered. After spending the night near some slave cabins, Turner and his men attempted to attack another house but were forced back. Some of the men left Turner to return to the plantations, and some of the rebels were captured. The remaining force then met the state and federal troops in their final struggle, in which one slave was killed and many escaped, including Turner. The rebels had shot, clubbed, and stabbed 57 whites to death. On October 30, 1831, Turner was found and arrested. He made a statement to his court-appointed attorney, Thomas R. Gray, in which he admitted to leading the rebellion, but pleaded not guilty. On November 5, 1831, Nat Turner was sentenced to death in the Southampton County Court. He was hanged and skinned.

The state executed 55 African Americans, banished numerous others, and acquitted a few. After the rebellion, close to 200 African Americans, many of whom were innocent, were murdered by white mobs. In addition, slaves as far away as North Carolina were falsely accused of having a connection with the rebellion and were subsequently tried and executed.

Aaron Ogletree

See also Haitian Revolution; Stono Rebellion.

FURTHER READING
Aptheker, Herbert. 1966. *Nat Turner's Slave Rebellion, Together with the full text of the so-called "Confessions" of Nat Turner made in prison in 1831*. New York: Humanities Press.
Bennett, Lerone, Jr. 1968. *Pioneers in Protest*. Chicago: Johnson Publishing Company.
Clarke, John Henrik, ed. 1968. *William Styron's Nat Turner: Ten Black Writers Respond*. Boston: Beacon Press.
Foner, Eric, ed. 1971. *Nat Turner*. Englewood Cliffs, NJ: Prentice Hall, 1971.
Tragle, Henry Irving, ed. 1971. *The Southampton Slave Revolt of 1831*. Amherst: University of Massachusetts Press.

Tuskegee Institute/Tuskegee University

Tuskegee Institute was founded by Booker T. Washington in 1881 at the bequest of African American craftsman Lee Adams, who guaranteed the black vote to white legislator W. F. Foster for his support to start a school for black youth in Tuskegee, Alabama. It became one of the most successful of the historically black colleges and universities in the United States. Lee was able to secure $2,000 from the state legislature to establish the school. Hampton graduate and formerly enslaved Booker T. Washington was hired as the chief administrator and principal of the school (Logan 1969; Washington 1900). Washington used the Hampton model of industrial education (for example, farming, domestic work) and combined it with "practical knowledge," such as hygiene and etiquette, and the Victorian morals of economy, hard work, and financial prudence. The objective at Tuskegee was to send students back to the rural

and plantation districts as teachers to educate black people in these communities (Washington 1900).

Using Hampton's model of coeducation, Washington included black women in his educational model—as students, teachers, and principals (Washington 1900). In 1882, Fannie N. Smith, Washington's first wife, worked with him to include students and teachers in their home life. She also organized conferences to uplift African American women in U.S. society. Hampton graduate Olivia A. Davidson joined Washington as a teacher at Tuskegee Institute and became his wife after Smith died in 1884. In 1890, Margaret James Murray, a Fisk University graduate, began working at Tuskegee Institute as a "lady principal." She eventually married Washington after the death of Davidson (Washington 1900).

By 1906, the 25th anniversary of Tuskegee Institute, the college had become one of the most important and thriving black educational institutions in the world with assets of $3 million. Housed on a 100-acre farm, the facilities grew from a shack to more than 10 large buildings, a women's college, and more than a dozen instructors (Washington 1900). Black scientists like George Washington Carver had an academic home for his research on the peanut. Board members included President William Taft and President Theodore Roosevelt. In 1985, Tuskegee Institute became a university, and by 2005 the school was valued at $500 million.

Paula Marie Seniors

See also Hampton Institute/Hampton University.

FURTHER READING
Harlan, Louis R. 1983. *Booker T. Washington: The Wizard of Tuskegee 1901–1915*. New York and Oxford: Oxford University Press.
Harlan, Louis R., and Raymond W. Smock. 1988. *Booker T. Washington in Perspective*. Jackson and London: University Press of Mississippi.
Logan, Rayford W. 1969. *The Betrayal of the Negro: From Rutherford B. Hayes to Woodrow Wilson*. London: Collier-Macmillan.

Washington, Booker T. 1900. *Up from Slavery: An Autobiography of Booker T. Washington.* New York: Bantam, Doubleday, Doran & Company.

———

Tynes, Maxine (1949–)

Recipient of the Milton Acorn People's Poet Award in 1988, Maxine Tynes is immensely popular in her native Nova Scotia, where her four collections of poetry are best-sellers. Tynes's style comes alive in performance; her often intricate rhythms and realistic images are both moving and appealing. A particular preoccupation in her work is her sense of complex social location: as a diasporic black woman, as a Nova Scotian, as a feminist, and as a disabled person. Her topics are various: black Nova Scotian history and culture, women's lives and gender relations, poverty, global politics, the difficulty of navigating the world for people with physical disabilities, deeply personal tributes to family and friends, and love.

Tynes's voice is unique in black Canadian literature, particularly because of her insistent orality. She takes up oral tradition, not by interpolating a dialectal voice or sayings, but rather by recourse to declamatory forms, lists, litanies, and exhortations. Orality is her register, and apparent directness and simplicity her mode in the tradition of a Langston Hughes or a Nikki Giovanni. Long neglected by scholars, Tynes is now attracting scholarly attention.

Born in Dartmouth, Nova Scotia, to a working class family, Tynes attended Dalhousie University and later became the first African Canadian member of its board of governors. Most of her working life has been as a high school teacher in the Dartmouth schools. Tynes's poetry collections came in rapid succession: *Borrowed Beauty* (1987); *Woman Talking Woman* (1990); *Save the World for Me* (1991), a book for children; and *The Door of My Heart* (1993). In 1990, a room of the new Dartmouth Public Library was named for her. She has also received an honorary doctorate from Mt. St. Vincent University.

Leslie Sanders

See also Canada and the African Diaspora.

FURTHER READING

Fuller, Danielle. 1999. "'Raising the Heart': The Politics of the Popular and the Poetics of Performance in the Work of Maxine Tynes." *Essays in Canadian Writing* 67: 76–112.

Stone, Marjorie. 1997. "The Poet as Whole-Body Camera: Maxine Tynes and the Pluralities of Otherness." *Dalhousie Review* 77 (2): 227–257.

U

Uncle Tom and Tom Shows

The fictional character of long-suffering Christian slave Uncle Tom was created by Harriet Beecher Stowe after the passage of the Fugitive Slave Law in 1850, in a story that appeared in 41 installments between June 1851 and April 1852 in the Washington, D.C.–based abolitionist periodical *The National Era*. The story captivated Northern readers and, within weeks, *Uncle Tom's Cabin, or, Life among the Lowly* was published in book form by John P. Jewett of Boston. An unprecedented 300,000 copies sold before the end of 1852 in the United States. Almost immediately several editions were published in England where the story and representation of the characters in a variety of the popular art formats became a cultural phenomenon.

In the story, Uncle Tom is sold down the river, away from his loving family and life on the Kentucky plantation where he had always lived. Even in the face of beatings by the cruel slavemaster Simon Legree, Uncle Tom remains devout and committed to his faith in a benevolent God; ultimately, though, he is beaten to death by Legree. As an ill-treated victim of an evil system, slavery, Uncle Tom was a sympathetic figure to the abolition-minded, and because he was

a Christian who believed he would share eternity with Christ, he held enormous appeal for evangelical Christians.

"[A] strong, powerfully built man," wrote Stowe in describing Uncle Tom. In Hammatt Billings's engravings for the original 1852 publication Uncle Tom was a father in the prime of life with dark hair and broad shoulders. The renowned English illustrator George Cruikshank drew Uncle Tom for an English edition that first year. By the 1860s, especially after emancipation of slaves in 1863, Uncle Tom was almost always rendered as an elderly man.

Staged renditions of Harriet Beecher Stowe's antislavery novel *Uncle Tom's Cabin* became known as "Tom Shows." As they had for the blackfaced minstrel shows, popular since the 1840s, white actors performed all the roles, including the slave roles, for which they darkened their skin with burned cork. George C. Howard's premiere production of *Uncle Tom's Cabin*, set to George Aiken's script, was mounted in New York City on July 18, 1853. Soon after, P. T. Barnum presented a version by Henry J. Conway at the American Museum and the Bowery Theater with minstrel star Thomas Dartmouth "Daddy" Rice in the role of Uncle Tom. By 1879, 49 touring Tom Shows were listed in the *New York Daily Mirror*.

In Harry Birdoff's 1947 description of Tom Shows, it is clear that they had evolved into an entertainment that bore less resemblance to Stowe's original novel and had more in common with blackfaced minstrel shows or melodramas. The posters and flyers, which preceded a troupe's arrival in small towns across the country, highlighted favorite scenes. "Eliza pursued across the ice by the hounds," "Topsy doing a breakdown," or, in his "grandiloquent" pose, "lawyer Marks," a rather insignificant character from the novel, who through actors' bombast onstage had become a hit. When the mulatto mother Eliza escaped over the frozen Ohio River in the novel, there had been no dogs in hot pursuit, but on stage, showing hounds lapping at the heels of the desperate runaway was fraught with heart-stopping thrills. Over the years more and bigger dogs became part of productions. Nor had the rowdy slave child Topsy danced a breakdown in the book per se. Yet this dance, along with the cakewalk, stump speeches, and pathetic songs, were minstrel show mainstays, and Topsy's role had expanded in response to audience reactions.

In the Howard-Aiken play, the producer's daughter, Cordelia Howard, became a star as Eva, the white child who befriended the slave Uncle Tom. G. C. German had been reluctant to take the role of Tom, presuming it would be what he called a "Jim Crow Darkey" and not a dramatic role. That a *New York Daily Times* (July 27, 1853) review called German's characterization "a strong, black, labouring man" indicates that he successfully avoided the minstrelsy stereotype. German played Tom from July 18 to August 22, 1853. Subsequently, J. Lingard played Tom as an older man. Meanwhile, at the Bowery Theater, Thomas D. Rice, the very performer who had in 1828 originated the black-faced character Jim Crow, the rustic old slave with the quirky jumping dance, was expected to perform Tom as an old man. An 1873 photograph shows the famous stage actor David Belasco costumed for his San Francisco performance as Tom. He appeared to be elderly, bald with a fringe of white hair. Belasco was then 20. In 1878, Sam Lucas became the first African American performer to portray Tom. The production was not successful. Tom Shows continued to be performed throughout the country well into the middle of the 20th century.

By the 20th century, Uncle Tom was a familiar icon as an old man on playbills and posters for staged versions and motion pictures based on the story. As a stoop-figured old slave, Uncle Tom has become an icon evoking nostalgia for the Old South, a stereotypical figure of a loyal servant. During the American Civil Rights movement of the 1960s into the Black Power/Black Pride era of the 1970s, to be called an "Uncle Tom" or a "Tom" was perhaps the most severe insult one could receive from a fellow African American, derogatory shorthand for a fawning sycophant, "yassuh-ing" the (white) man at the expense of his own dignity. The sobriquet continues in use. Supreme Court Justice Clarence Thomas was called "Uncle Thomas" for his ultra-conservative opinions.

Jo-Ann Morgan

See also Jim Crow.

FURTHER READING
Ammons, Elizabeth, ed. 1980. *Critical Essays on Harriet Beecher Stowe*, Boston: G. K. Hall.
Birdoff, Harry. 1947. *The World's Greatest Hit "Uncle Tom's Cabin."* New York: S. F. Vanni, 1947.
Gossett, Thomas F. 1985. *"Uncle Tom's Cabin" and American Culture.* Dallas: Southern Methodist University Press.
Hedrick, Joan D. 1994. *Harriet Beecher Stowe—A Life.* New York: Oxford, 1994.
Moody, Richard. 1955. "Uncle Tom, the Theatre, and Mrs. Stowe." *American Heritage* 6 (October): 29–33. 102, 103.
Morgan, Jo-Ann. 2004. "Picturing Uncle Tom with Little Eva—Reproduction as Legacy." *Journal of American Culture* 27 (1, March): 1–24.
Toll, Robert C. 1974. *Blacking Up—The Minstrel Show in Nineteenth-Century America.* New York: Oxford.

Underground Railroad

See Canada and the African Diaspora.

United Kingdom: The African Diaspora

Evidence of the black presence in Great Britain and Ireland (the United Kingdom) is scattered for the British never legalized segregation and so there are no lists of black people. Black people lived in Britain from the moment of the earliest written records—when the Romans under Julius Caesar added England to their empire 2,000 years ago. Some of the troops who controlled the pagan tribes were African. After these came other black people, traveling with returning pilgrims and Crusaders from the Holy Land; on ships that had ventured to the tropics; and as members of visiting groups, generally from Europe. African men and women were at the Scottish court in 1505 and at the English court where an African musician is noted in 1507 and depicted in a painting from 1511.

Five Ghanaians came to London in 1555 to learn about and then assist with British trading activities in western Africa. British desire for Africa's gold expanded within a decade to participation in the transatlantic slave trade.

Africans also worked on ships trading with Africa and the Caribbean. At first recruited abroad, sailors settled in British ports. Coercion, slavery, and bondage played their part but the black men and women who lived in Britain were sometimes documented in baptism and other civic records, receiving money in wills, and entertaining Queen Elizabeth I (1575).

A continuing black presence in Britain should be dated from 1596. In 1596, the queen suggested that "blackamoores" should be exchanged for prisoners of the Spanish. In 1601, she wanted to expel "the great numbers of negars [sic] and Blackamoores which . . . are crept into this realm." Elizabeth's wishes did not lead to legislation, however. Despite racial laws in the colonies, in the United Kingdom interracial marriage was never illegal; there were no segregated schools or churches. Property ownership remained influenced by financial restraints not racial ones (some leases had antiblack clauses, but how many is unknown). The growth in British economic strength, underwritten by profits from the slave trade and plantation sugar, encouraged individuals from Africa and the Diaspora to seek their fortune in the United Kingdom.

Samuel Pepys's London diaries of the 1660s note black servants (male and female), and paintings of members of high society included black servants (the Duchess of Portsmouth, 1682; Lady Elizabeth Murray, 1779). Francis Barber's portrait by Joshua Reynolds (1767) was painted 17 years after Barber left Jamaica—he was now valet and secretary to literary giant Samuel Johnson. Ignatius Sancho's portrait was painted by Thomas Gainsborough (1768); the African had been sold in England at the age of two. He worked for the Duke of Montague who became his patron. Married to an Afro-Caribbean woman, Sancho ran a shop, wrote music, and had his letters published after his death in 1780. Other paintings and illustrations of London life included black subjects. Most are nameless.

Considerable evidence of the black presence has been located in the parish records of city churches near docks. Liverpool has a dock church's baptism records of August 6, 1795, listing the son of "a native of Savannah" and the son of a man from Antigua. Both fathers may have been white, however, and a dilemma for historians of the black presence in the United Kingdom is the near-absence of any note of a person's ethnicity or race. We know that in 1768 Thomas Richmond and George Dorlton sailed on James Cook's voyage, which brought knowledge of New Zealand and Australia to the British.

Other slave-servants accompanying West Indian employers often broke from their bonds when in Britain, and they found support among Britons in all walks of life. Colonials placed announcements in the British press: missing "Negro slaves" have been identified from 1659 to the 1790s. This documentation supports a view that Britain's black population resulted from slavery and shipping, which ignores self-motivated travelers (notably African leaders and traders) and craft workers (leatherwork, weaving, lace making, tailoring, carpentry, or work with horses: all occupations providing mobility). Servants in country houses attended their employers in London and when traveling, extending the black presence into distant corners of the kingdom. Some settled locally and married: rural church burial registers might note "from Africa" or "a native of Barbadoes [sic]" decades later. The rural presence of Africans outside the country houses is largely conjecture except for one woman in 17th-century Dorset.

Revenues from slave-labor colonies discouraged government action over slavery, and affected the judiciary when colonial owners sought to recover human property. The status of slaves within the United Kingdom remained legally unclear, but a network of Africans assisted runaways and encouraged publicity. The case of James Somerset, owned by a Massachusetts official, brought greater awareness in 1772, and exposed the tyranny of the slave trade. So did an insurance claim by ship owners 10 years later. More than 130 slaves going to Jamaica on the *Zong* were thrown overboard because the ship was thought to be low on water: an English court ordered the insurers to pay the claim. Through Olaudah Equiano, a Nigerian enslaved in Barbados who settled in England in 1777, and Granville Sharp, these events encouraged the Anti-Slavery Society.

In 1838 slavery was abolished in Britain's empire. Abolitionist publicity named black people and provided their histories. So too did late 18th century efforts to remove unemployed sailors, including black Americans (mainly born in Virginia and the Carolinas), to a new life in Sierra Leone.

Caesar Picton is missing from lists of ex-slaves and the "Black Poor," for he used an inheritance from an employer to become a coal merchant in Kingston on Thames in 1788. He died rich. There were also largely nameless black street vendors, entertainers, beggars, and soldiers (often musicians).

Descriptions of those charged with crimes has led to nearly 600 black people being identified as prisoners removed to Australia from 1787. Names have surfaced through other legal cases. Examination of cases reveals that judgments were similar for every criminal: society was otherwise not concerned with color.

Black men and women were involved in less spectacular, more everyday, matters, earning a living and raising families. Joseph Emidy, a musician in Falmouth, Cornwall, established a family there in the 1800s (one strand migrated to the United States in the 1890s). Hampshire-born Thomas Birch Freeman worked as a gardener (he knew the Latin names of plants) when, in the 1830s, he became a Methodist missionary in Ghana for decades. But for his impact there, Freeman, like his father, would be an unknown black Briton.

More visible individuals include Poland-born violinist George Polgreen Bridgetower. He played for British royalty in the 1790s, greatly impressed Beethoven, and died in London in 1860. Norwich-born William Darby (1796–1871) was famous as "Pablo Fanque" the circus proprietor. Georgia-born Bill Richmond boxed in and around London from 1805; Virginia-born Tom Molineaux was another successful boxer between 1810 and 1815. There has been a continuous black presence in British boxing ever since.

The radical tradition includes William Davidson, who was executed for his role in plans to assassinate members of the government in 1819, and fellow-Jamaican Robert Wedderburn, whose speeches and publications led to a prison sentence. Social unrest in 1830–

1848 involved the Chartists, in which England-born William Cuffay took a leading role—he was one of three black men duly transported to Australia. Joseph Jackson Fuller (1825–1908) of Jamaica moved with his father to Africa and became a major influence in the Baptist church in Cameroon. From the 1880s he lived in London, speaking at conferences. His son by his English wife worked in the Congo; a grandson was a shoe repairer in London. His son by his first wife studied engineering in Norwich.

Nineteenth-century documentation includes New York–born actor Ira Aldridge, black sailors in paintings of the death of Admiral Nelson in 1805, and photographs of Dejatch Alamayu of Ethiopia, Cetshwayo of the Zulus, Bishop Samuel Ajayi Crowther, and the Jamaican nurse-author Mary Seacole. Nameless people appear in photographs, illustrations, and publications promoting charities, notably Barnardo's orphanage.

There were "savage entertainers," touring the United Kingdom presenting an image of Africa. Minstrel groups came from the United States. Black individuals also appear in numerous illustrations, in diaries and letters, and on posters and in books: the "Hottentot Venus" from South Africa, William Lane ("Master Juba"), and the Zulus seen by Charles Dickens. Dickens noted black servants in London as did fellow novelist Anthony Trollope.

The release and computerization of British census records of 1881 and 1901 suggests that a search based on place of birth will reveal the black population. As New Yorker Aldridge is listed in the 1841 census as being from Africa, and a 1901 enumerator wrote "Siberia" instead of "Liberia," this source has dangers. "Race" is not listed, so American author Henry Downing is not identified as black in the London census of 1901. Among other black models, Jamaica-born Fanny Eaton sat for numerous painters in London from 1859. A seamstress in 1861, she was the widow of a cart driver, mother of seven, and a cook in the Isle of Wight in 1901.

Africa and the Caribbean provided limited educational opportunities, so blacks came to England to acquire skills. James Horton qualified as a doctor in the 1850s and became a pioneering African nationalist. Theophilus Scholes, a Jamaican doctor who had also studied in Scotland, worked in both the Congo and Nigeria, retiring to London in the 1890s where he wrote four books critical of imperialism. Joseph Casely Hayford studied at Cambridge, worked in Africa and Britain, and wrote law books and a novel; and fellow England-educated Ghanaian John Mensah Sarbah's *Fanti Customary Laws* was in a second edition by 1904.

Two medical students from Sierra Leone show, by their different careers, the range of possibilities. Daniel Taylor, a London graduate of 1874, was a failure and unemployable by the authorities while John Randle, a graduate of St. Andrews University in Scotland, worked in Nigeria. He married Victoria Davies, the African goddaughter of Queen Victoria. Mrs. Victoria Davies Randle was educated in Cheltenham, often visited the queen, was proudly Yoruba, and supplied a Yoruba drum theme to the illegitimate son of Dr. Taylor—Samuel Coleridge-Taylor (1875–1912), the London-born composer. He used it in his *Twenty-four Negro Melodies*, published in Massachusetts in 1905 with a preface by Booker T. Washington. It was through Mrs. Randle that the composer met the Casely Hayfords in London.

African Americans sought support in the United Kingdom for the abolition of slavery. In 1878, Virginia-born Thomas Johnson and his brother-in-law Calvin Richardson (and their wives) moved to Cameroon after Baptist college training. Other Americans toured Britain, gathering funds and sympathy for their struggles: Frederick Douglass, the best known, toured in 1845–1847 and 1859–1860. William Brown, who escaped slavery in a box, wrote his autobiography and reenacted his escape in British theaters. Ida B. Wells toured in the 1890s on an anti-lynching campaign. Booker T. Washington visited twice, and W. E. B. DuBois made several visits, on vacation and for conferences (starting with the Pan-African conference in London in 1900).

Liverpool is Britain's longest-established black community as Liverpool merchants dominated Britain's share of the slave trade. Some captives came to the city and were sold to be servants. Up to 70 boys and girls attended a school for black children by the 1780s. Some stayed, some sent their children to the city, and the community grew. James Cleveland (died 1791) a Liverpool-educated child of a Sierra Leonean mother followed his father's occupation as a slaver in Africa, whereas Otto Ephraim of Nigeria benefited from a sea captain patron. Family recollections have provided much of the history of black Liverpool.

Names emerge from the mists when a relative achieves. Because Liverpool-born John Archer became a borough mayor in London in 1913 we know of his brother and their Barbados-born father. Folkestone-born sportsman Walter Tull became a lieutenant in the army in 1917 (his brother was a dentist). George William Christian was one of six children of an Antigua-born sailor long settled in Liverpool: Christian was a merchant in Nigeria; two sisters migrated to Canada; and the third, Octavia Christian, had five sons, including Sir Herbert Gladstone McDavid, chief executive officer of two major shipping lines in the 1950s.

Concern for others of African birth or descent led Archer to participate in the Pan-African conferences of London (1900, 1919) as did Trinidad-born Edinburgh University graduate Dr. John Alcindor (1873–1924): both were to lead the London-based African Progress Union. They were friends of Coleridge-Taylor, DuBois, and visiting and resident black folk.

Britain's immigration law of 1905 was aimed at reducing migration from eastern Europe, but *King's Regulations*, the army's handbook, had long imposed a color bar: no "aliens, negroes, &c" could be officers. This was ignored in the case of ranker Tull, promoted in France.

London-trained Sierra Leonean lawyer Samuel Lewis was knighted in the late 19th century. Ghanaian Samuel Brew (who died in London in 1915) had the ambition to be elected to parliament. Rhodes scholar Alain Locke (author of *The New Negro* [1925]) became a friend of Pixley Seme (officer of South Africa's African National Congress) at Oxford in 1908, and British and Irish colleges continued to train lawyers and doctors, writers, musicians, nurses, and historians.

Trinidad-born, London-qualified lawyer Henry Sylvester Williams (1869–1911) was elected a member of a London borough, but is known through his publication, *Pan-African*, and the 1900 conference. Snubbed by his white wife's parents (as was Dr. Alcindor), he worked in Africa and the Caribbean. James Jackson Brown, a Jamaica-born medical student in London in the 1900s, had support from his wife's family, qualifying after their sons were born and running a solid practice for decades.

Brown and Alcindor were refused by the Royal Army Medical Corps (Brown refused to be a sergeant as he was a qualified doctor—and therefore should merit officer; Alcindor was awarded a Red Cross medal for his work with the wounded in London train stations). There are West Indian troopers' graves in Sussex; more than 600 black South Africans are named on a memorial near Southampton, and in cemeteries in France honoring World War I dead, black and white lie side by side.

In 1919, race riots hit British cities: unemployed soldiers blamed black people when they could not find jobs. Archer's African Progress Union employed Oxford University graduate Edward Nelson (an Afro-Guyanese who was elected to the local council from 1913 to his death in 1940) in defense. This link between the professional black establishment and the poor had existed when Equiano alerted Sharp about the Zong, and in the settlement of Sierra Leone, and with Cuffay in the Chartists.

Britain continued to receive ambitious settlers, including Jamaican Marcus Garvey who died in London, and fresh generations of nationalists took up the writings of Horton and Edward Blyden, and challenged imperialism. Some lived to see the political independence of

African and Caribbean colonies (Guyanese Ras Makonnen, Jomo Kenyatta, Julius Nyerere, Eric Williams) while others (Garvey, Sol Plaatje from South Africa, Aggrey of Ghana, Scholes) left influences in Britain that survived long after their deaths.

The 1920s and 1930s saw black entertainers at the highest levels: Americans Paul Robeson, Roland Hayes, and Lawrence Brown performed in concert recitals. From 1919 to 1921 the American-led Southern Syncopated Orchestra toured, featuring both New Orleans clarinetist Sidney Bechet and Dr. Horton's violin-playing grandson. Royal Academy of Music graduate, South Carolina–born Edmund Jenkins (1894–1926) led high society bands. Café society had Grenada-born Leslie Hutchinson and the American duo Turner Layton and Clarence Johnston (who sold millions of discs).

The 1930s understanding that jazz was a black creation enabled Guyana-born, England-educated Ken Johnson to lead a band of instrumentalists born in Cardiff, London, Trinidad, Panama, Jamaica, and Sierra Leone. It was in a tradition that owed a great deal to Coleridge-Taylor's friend, choir leader Frederick Loudin, whose Fisk Jubilee Singers toured for decades from the 1870s—making spirituals accepted as a black musical achievement. The League of Coloured People, led from 1931 by Jamaica-born and London-qualified Dr. Harold Moody, publicized achievement and discrimination in Britain and the tropical empire.

War brought black men and women to Britain (and African American soldiers, whose British children numbered around 1,000) to serve in the anti-Nazi effort. Alcindor's soldier son rose to be a captain, and Africans and Caribbeans, including Trinidadian ace Ulric Cross, flew airplanes.

Postwar depression in the colonies and the need to rebuild British cities led veterans to consider migration, and in 1948 the *Empire Windrush* reached England from Jamaica. For many, this is the United Kingdom's first black settlement.

From the 1950s West Indian and then African migration to the United Kingdom had a colossal impact—the lands from which they came were denuded of ambitious and talented people. Views that "lower standards" would affect Britain became widespread. Accommodations, jobs, and promotion were restricted, but schools and universities were not. The migrants were generally anxious to get on, dreaming, as migrants always do, of a successful return to their natal lands. Settlement led to specialist shops, newspapers like the *West Indian Gazette* and *Afro Asian Caribbean News* and major festivals like the Notting Hill Carnival. As far as churches go, black participation in Christian worship is currently perhaps five times that of whites. Ugandan lawyer John Sentamu's appointment to be Archbishop of York in June, 2005, makes him the second most senior official in the Church of England (Anglican Church).

Political unrest and economic inequalities on the continent encouraged African settlement: regime changes were planned in London and refugees found a haven, still with the ongoing tension manifesting as well in overt racist attacks at times. A great deal of activism however had taken place in the 70's, 80's and 90's with journals like the *Black Liberator,* edited by Alric Cambridge, and the Black and Third World Book Fair organized by John La Rose of New Beacon Books. Poetry by writers like Linton Kwesi Johnson, Benjamin Zephaniah, and Dorothea Smartt offered another aesthetic that echoed Caribbean origins. And new waves of immigrants from former colonies create an amazing mix of post-colonial peoples now resident in England. The children, the first substantial number of British-born black people, and now grandchildren, have made an impact across the United Kingdom, and, despite the legend that the few black Britons before the *Windrush* were sailors, students, and servants, are participating in the rescue of their history. Britons aware of a black ancestor are making that public. Francis Barber's descendants live in

Staffordshire, Joseph Fuller's near London, and Coleridge-Taylor's near Croydon. The recovery of the lengthy history of Britain's black population is in its early years.

Jeffrey Green

See also Abolitionism in the African Diaspora; Europe and the African Diaspora; Pan-Africanism.

FURTHER READING
Costello, Ray. 2001. *Black Liverpool. The Early History of Britain's Oldest Black Community 1730–1918*. Liverpool, UK: Picton Press.

Fryer, Peter. 1984. *Staying Power: The History of Black People in Britain*. London: Pluto Press.

Gerzina, Gretchen Holbook, ed. 2003. *Black Victorians / Black Victoriana*. New Brunswick, NJ: Rutgers University Press.

Green, Jeffrey. 1998. *Black Edwardians: Black People in Britain 1901–1914*. London: Frank Cass.

Marsh, Jan, ed. 2006. *Black Victorians: Black People in British Art 1800–1900*. Aldershot, UK: Lund Humphries.

Myers, Norma. 1996. *Reconstructing the Black Past. Blacks in Britain 1780–1830*. London: Frank Cass.

Smith, Graham. 1987. *When Jim Crow Met John Bull. Black American Soldiers in World War II Britain*. London: I. B. Tauris.

Universal Negro Improvement Association (UNIA) and African Communities League

See Garvey, Marcus Mosiah (1887–1940).

The University of Woodford Square

During the mid–1950s Dr. Eric Williams began a remarkable strategy of popular education that would propel the people of Trinidad and Tobago on a path toward self-determination and national independence and would indefinitely transform the meaning of democracy and public engagement during the postcolonial period. Williams offered a series of free university-style lectures on philosophy, international politics, and Caribbean race relations, many of which, after June 21 1955, were held in Woodford Square, a public park in the heart of the nation's capital, Port of Spain. The lectures drew their intellectual grounding from Williams's own scholarship. They reflected a belief in the revolutionary power of the intellect and education used as a tool that could rescue the people of Trinidad and Tobago from the humiliations of the past (Lamming 1997, 732): ideas that had been reinforced for Williams through his interactions with African American intellectuals and activists during his years at Howard University.

Thousands traveled to hear "De Doc" at what he renamed the "University of Woodford Square" and its associated "colleges" in outlying areas. At a time when education was a privilege, Williams offered political instruction that focused on placing Trinidad and Tobago within the global context of other movements advocating democracy and self-government (Williams 1962, 243). Such a strategy not only provided the people with a language through which political demands for independence could be articulated but it also empowered them to believe in their potential as arbiters of their own destiny. The popularity of Williams's lectures helped secure his position as leader of the People's National Movement and his appointment as head of government after winning the 1956 general election.

Although Williams is credited with a rare willingness and ability to engage the electorate in political dialogue, some commentators have pointed to a tension within his political leadership between this populist tendency and his own position as prime minister, "father of the nation," and "professor" (Cudjoe 1997).

Eric Williams at *The University of Woodford Square,* by Adrian Camps-Campins, 1956. (Courtesy Adrian Camps-Campins)

This tension is witnessed in the lasting impact of Williams's popular education strategy and the meaning assigned to Woodford Square as a public space for political participation. Before Williams, Woodford Square had been variously appropriated as a site of colonial authority (where military processions were performed and rebellious slaves were violently punished) and, after its redesign in 1813, pleasure (as a park where the wealthy and powerful could promenade and relax). Williams radically transformed these colonial meanings and, by renaming the park the "University of Woodford Square," claimed it as a nationalist space where the marginalized majority could meet to participate in educational activities and political dialogue. So successful was his strategy that when the National Joint Action Committee (Black Power movement) began to protest Williams's leadership in 1970, they took their meetings to Woodford Square. A series of destabilizing events and mounting urban violence, culminating in a national state of emergency, left Williams—initially responsible for igniting a popular spirit of public political engagement—with little choice but to padlock the gates to Woodford Square between April 21 and November 20, 1970.

The University of Woodford Square is now marked by a sign: a faint reminder of the significance of Williams's educational strategy to Trinidad and Tobago's struggle for self-determination. To this day, however, Caribbean politics, religion, and philosophy continue to be debated in the park by small groups of people, many of whom remain marginal to the mainstream political and educational process.

Clare Newstead

See also Capitalism and Slavery; Trinidad and Tobago; Williams, Eric Eustace (1911–1981).

FURTHER READING

Anthony, M. 1997. *Historical Dictionary of Trinidad and Tobago*. Latin American Historical Dictionaries Number 24. London: The Scarecrow Press.

Cudjoe, S. R. 1997. "Eric Williams and the Politics of Language." *Callaloo* 20 (4): 753–763.

Lamming, G. 1997. "The Legacy of Eric Williams." *Callaloo* 20 (4): 731–736.

Williams, E. W. 1962. *The History of the People of Trinidad and Tobago*. Port of Spain, Trinidad and Tobago: PNM Publishing.

Williams, E._W. 1969 *Inward Hunger: The Education of a Prime Minister*. London: Andre Deutsch.

Uruguay: Afro-Uruguayans

Afro-Uruguayans greatly contributed to their country's economy, society, and culture. First, they were the slaves, peons, and artisans whose toils allowed for Uruguay's economic development between the 17th and 19th centuries. Second, African Uruguayans were the soldiers whose blood and sacrifices forged an independent nation-state from a Spanish colony and defended that independence from foreign invaders, first Great Britain and then Brazil, during the first decades of the 19th century. Third, black Uruguayans were the musicians, writers, and artists whose works enriched, enlightened, and entertained their fellow citizens from colonial times to the present. Moreover, even the very symbols of nationhood in the River Plate, namely, the tango and the *gaucho* (cowboy), were influenced by the genius of Africans and their New World descendants.

HISTORY AND ORIGINS

Some of the earliest African arrivals in the Americas came not only as slaves but also as conquerors. *Ladino* (or acculturated) servants such as Juan Cortés and Juan Garrido, both of whom assisted Hernán Cortés in the defeat of the Aztec Empire, and Juan Valiente, who accompanied Pedro Valdivia to Chile in 1536 and was awarded with an estate near what would become Santiago de Chile, experienced extraordinary social mobility as armed retainers of their Spanish masters (Rout 1976, 75–77; Restall 2000). African-born slaves or *bozales* made their initial appearance in the River Plate in 1534 with Pedro de Mendoza. As in Mexico and Peru, enslaved Africans facilitated the colonization of the River Plate; Africans in the company of Governor Hernando Arias collaborated in settling the Banda Oriental (later Uruguay) in 1608 (Montaño 1997, 25).

For most of the colonial period, the port of Buenos Aires served as the exclusive entry point for enslaved Africans in the River Plate. Spanish mercantilism sought to limit the ready access of slaves and other goods entering the New World by strictly regulating trade. Slaves entering the port of Buenos Aires, after passing a health inspection, were then regularly shipped inland, to Córdoba and the northwestern provinces of Salta and Tucumán, across the Andes Mountains to Chile, and to the mines of Potosí in Alto Perú (now Bolivia). The dearth of native workers in the region (unlike in Mexico and Peru), the Spanish elite's disdain for manual labor, the need for domestic servants as social-status symbols, and the constant demands for manpower in the mines of Potosí combined to stimulate the transatlantic and internal slave trades in the River Plate during the 16th and 17th centuries. Exact figures of African slave arrivals in Uruguay for the 16th and early 17th centuries are imprecise, largely because of the contraband slave trade.

Despite Spain's best efforts, slave smuggling was endemic for most of the colonial period, owing in part to the proximity of Brazil, especially Colônia do Sacramento. For instance, of the 12,778 slaves recorded as entering the River Plate by way of Buenos Aires from Brazil between 1606 and 1628, only 288 did so legally (with licenses), and 8,932 slaves (worth 1,404,709 *pesos*) were confiscated from smugglers during the same period and resold by royal authorities. In 1611, the Council of the Indies in Seville, Spain, received information from colonial agents that more than 15 Dutch and English ships laden with contraband enslaved Africans had entered the port of Buenos Aires (Scheüss de Studer 1984, 91–92, 102; Pacheco 2001, 16–17).

The slave trade—legal and contraband—continued unabated in the viceroyalty of the River Plate throughout the 1600s and 1700s. Enslaved Africans came from West, Central, and East Africa, especially from what are today Senegal, Ghana, Ivory Coast, and Angola. The Spanish monarchy successively bestowed permits or *asientos* to the Portuguese, French, and English for slave procurements and shipments to their colonies in the Americas. More often than not, however, European slave traders were unable to meet the demands of Spanish colonists for slave labor, which further encouraged contraband trade. Frustrated by the lack of compliance of European slavers and by slave smuggling, and owing to political and economic reforms within the Spanish bureaucracy in the 1770s, Spain freed its trade in the late 18th century. In 1779, Montevideo, with its excellent natural harbor, was designated as a port of entry for enslaved Africans, supplementing the trade through Buenos Aires. In Montevideo, the slave trade gained in importance and volume during the late 18th and early 19th centuries. Pereda Valdés calculates that between 1751 and 1810, 20,000 slaves arrived legally in the port of Montevideo (Pereda Valdés 1965, 31–32).

Centuries of the slave trade influenced the makeup of the population of Uruguay. For the first half of the 19th century, John Hoyt Williams (1987) highlights the racial composition and demographics of Montevideo and its countryside. Of a total population of 2,501 in 1800, for instance, people of color, free and slave, accounted for 817. By 1810, the numbers of Africans and their descendants had increased to 2, 518. In Montevideo's hinterland (places such as Las Piedras, Pantanoso, and Toledo), moreover, Williams documents a population of color of close to 200 out of a total of less than 1,000 (Williams 1987, 415–416, 421).

In the Banda Oriental, as in the rest of the New World, Africans labored in a host of jobs and under diverse conditions. Most slaves in Uruguay worked in and around the major cities, especially Montevideo, as domestics and day laborers. Female African slaves worked as seamstresses, cooks, laundresses, wet nurses, and duennas in elite homes. Male slaves were often hired out by their owners and worked in both skilled and unskilled jobs, regularly keeping for themselves a portion of their income. Black men occupied the lower artisan levels, laboring as tailors or shoemakers. Africans also monopolized several unskilled jobs throughout the cities, including pest exterminators, dock workers, water porters, and load bearers. Both slave men and women worked in meat-salting plants, slaughterhouses, workshops, bakeries, and *pulperías* (general stores) in and around Buenos Aires and Montevideo. What is often overlooked, however, is that slaves also labored as peons and *gauchos* in the countryside, and some even became slave foremen on cattle estates in the River Plate. Such was the case of Patricio de Belén, whose horsemanship and administrative skills allowed him to become the slave administrator of the cattle ranch of Las Vacas in the Banda Oriental (Pacheco 2001, 46–47, 48, 51; Mayo 1997).

There were generally few large-scale plantations employing African slave labor in the River Plate; the Society of Jesus or Jesuits were among the largest slave owners in the region, owning sugarcane estates in Argentina's Northwest. Because of this and the largely urban and domestic nature of slavery in the River Plate, scholars have often described the slave regime in Argentina and Uruguay as mostly benign.

RESISTANCE AND MAROONAGE
Given the nature of the peculiar institution, even under the mildest of situations, African bondsmen in Uruguay resisted their servitude

in various ways. For example, slave and free Africans often resorted to cattle theft as a means of gaining income and subsistence and as a show of resistance against the powers of the state and landowners. Slave theft and malingering constitute examples of what scholars call *petit maroonage*, which were common throughout the New World. John Chasteen records the stealing of cattle from large estates by poor blacks in Uruguay well into the 1890s (Chasteen 1995, 70–72). African and New World slaves in the River Plate also practiced cultural *maroonage*, routinely gathering in the *salas* (halls) of ethnic "nations," for example, Benguelas, Congos, Mandingas, and Minas, among several West African and Central African peoples, and used ancestral rites, music, and dance to assert their agency.

Acts of *grand maroonage*, or large-scale slave rebellions such as the Haitian Revolution (1794–1804), were uncommon in the River Plate. Nonetheless, colonial and early national officials in Buenos Aires and Montevideo feared slave uprisings by *negros alzados*. One of the largest slave revolts in the River Plate occurred in Montevideo in 1803. Twenty slave and free African Uruguayan men met in secret to plan their flight from the city. Taking their wives, children, and a few possessions, the rebels settled on a small island in the River Yi and founded a maroon colony. The colonial regime responded and attacked the slave settlement. The slaves and freedmen resisted but were ultimately defeated. The slaves were returned to their masters, and some of the free blacks were executed as a warning to others (Rama 1969, 21–22; Montaño 1995, 412, 423–427).

EMANCIPATION AND BEYOND

In addition to flight and resistance, enslaved Africans in the Americas had other, institutional means of procuring their freedom and that of their relatives. Medieval Spanish law, deriving from *Las Siete Partidas* (1251–1265) of Alfonso X of Castile and León ("The Wise), recognized the humanity and rights of slaves.

Regardless of the strict *sociedad de castas* adhering in Spanish America throughout the colonial period, slaves had personal rights. Under the *Recopilación de Leyes de Indias* of 1680, slaves were given the right to acquire their own freedom and that of their family. Additionally, on May 31, 1789, the Spanish crown issued a royal decree on the treatment of slaves in its New World holdings. The *Código Negrero* of 1789 (not to be confused with King Louis XIV of France's *Code Noir* of 1685) contained 14 chapters, outlining in detail the treatment, education, occupations, and rights of bondsmen and bondswomen in Spanish America. Slaves were entitled to legal representation by way of public defenders (or *protectores de esclavos*) in cases of grievances against their masters. Manumission, purchased and freely given by owners, although rare in Montevideo, nonetheless represented a legal means of slave freedom guaranteed under Spanish law.

Slavery's legal demise in the River Plate began with the promulgation of "free womb" laws in the early 1810s and the legal termination of the slave trade in the 1830s. However, slavery persisted in Uruguay into the 1840s and 1850s via contraband slave trading from Brazil. Also, de facto slavery continued in the form of the *patronato*, which extended the period of servitude for slaves born under free-womb legislation by placing them under the tutelage of owners for a specified period of time (which was often abrogated and illegally extended). In December 1842, President Joaquín Suárez formally abolished slavery. By 1846, former president Manuel Oribe and all political sides in Uruguay's years-old civil conflict agreed to do away with the peculiar institution in the nation. Final emancipation for Uruguayan slaves, however, did not happen until 1853, when the *patronato* was constitutionally abolished. In effect, ultimate emancipation in the River Plate made de jure what had in fact long been de facto; by the first half of the 19th century, slavery had lost its raison d'etre in Uruguay. Abolition in the early national period was therefore very much a fait accompli in the River Plate (Pacheco 2001, 72, 74–75).

Another legal means of emancipation available to African Uruguayan men before the formal termination of slavery was military service during the River Plate's seemingly interminable independence and civil wars during the 19th century. Afro-Uruguayans fought faithfully against Native Americans (the *Charruas*, *Guaranies*, and *Tapes*, among others) during the conquest and colonization, as well as against the foreign invasion of the River Plate by the British in 1806–1807. They also sided with José Gervasio Artigas (the father of the Uruguayan nation) against the Spanish during the independence struggles between 1816 and 1820. In 1821, after Brazil's capture of the Banda Oriental, the "Immortal 33" fought for and helped reassert the independence of Uruguay by 1825. Among the Immortal 33 who fought to free Uruguay from Brazil were several African and Afro-Uruguayan slaves, including two bearing the important last names of Artigas and Oribe, indicating their owners (Rout 1976, 170). Although few Afro-Uruguayan soldiers achieved lasting fame, "Ansina," Joaquín Lenzina or Lencina (or was he Manuel Antonio Ledesma?), fought heroically with General Artigas and followed him into exile in Paraguay, earning the sobriquet the "fiel payador of Artigas" (Montaño 1998, 113–120). Moreover, African Uruguayans fought on both sides of the *Colorado-Blanco* civil wars of the 19th century.

After independence and the abolition of slavery in the first half of the 19th century, Afro-Uruguayans gradually assimilated to the national society (Rama 1969). Despite the displacement of the rigid social hierarchy of the colonial and early national periods, which limited the rights and privileges of blacks in Argentina and Uruguay (for example, they could not hold certain jobs or receive a higher education), African Uruguayans continued to face various degrees of alienation and discrimination. For instance, Afro-Uruguayans continued to live in poor tenement houses known as *con-*

ventillos. Among the more popular of these slums in Montevideo were those of Medio Mundo, Palermo, and Reus.

RECENT TRENDS

For black Uruguayans, political participation was practically nonexistent in the late 19th and first decades of the 20th centuries. As a result, African Uruguayan intellectuals united and formed their own cultural and political organizations and publications, notably the journal *Nuestra Raza* (founded in 1917, reestablished in 1933, and enduring until the middle of that century) and the political party *Partido Autóctono Negro* or PAN (founded in 1937 by Ventura Barrios, Elemo Cabral, and Salvador Betervide). Unfortunately, PAN never developed a coherent political program. Sadly for PAN's leadership, it misjudged the support of the political movement's natural constituency. Afro-Uruguayans simply did not vote for the party in several elections, opting instead to cast their ballots for the traditional *Colorado* or *Blanco* parties. By 1944, PAN disbanded (Pereda Valdés 1965, 195–196). Another notable Afro-Uruguayan cultural institution was the *Teatro Negro Independiente*, founded by playwright Andrés Castillo in the 1950s and enduring until 1982. The company sought to celebrate black cultural contributions to Uruguay (Cordones-Cook 1996). In the 1990s, and into the present day, Afro-Uruguayans and others have organized a network of people and organizations called *Organizaciones Mundo Afro* to promote black culture and fight against racism (Pacheco 2001, 112–113).

Despite the ignorance of some of their compatriots, Afro-Uruguayans have played a critical role in the evolution of national culture. Black Uruguayans either created or helped shape Platine music and dance, especially the *candombe*, the *milonga*, and that quintessential Argentine-Uruguayan art form, the tango. Music and popular religion intersect in Montevideo during the holidays (especially during carnival and the festival of San Baltasar) and

Members of a *comparsa* dance to the *candombe* during the *Llamadas* parade in Montevideo, Uruguay on February 6, 2004. The *Llamadas,* which date back to colonial times, started as a custom of the slaves in Montevideo, and actually are an important part of the longest running carnival in the world. (Andres Stapff/Reuters/Corbis)

are especially influenced by the *llamadas* of white and black drummers (Goldman 1997). Furthermore, folklore also evidences uniquely African elements. For example, the legend of the Mandinga is common to both sides of the River Plate, especially among country folk. Legend has it that Satan or the devil (depicted as a black cowboy or *gaucho*) roams the isolated rural parts of Argentina and Uruguay in search of souls to steal.

In addition, popular speech in the River Plate has incorporated many words of putative African origin according to linguists, including *cacunda, mandinga,* and *quilombo,* among many others. The *payada* is a chant-and-response verbal duel similar to contrapuntal and satiric African songs known as *makawas* or *ibiririmbo*

on the African continent and common among black communities throughout the Americas. Prominent Afro-Uruguayan/Afro-Uruguayanist writers and artists of the 20th century include Ildefonso Pereda Valdés, Juan Julio Arrascaeta, Carlos Cardoso Ferreira, Cristina Rodríguez Cabral, José Emilio Cardoso, and Julio Guadalupe. The two most widely acclaimed black writers were Pilar Barrios, who dwells on the sufferings of the black race in *Piel morena* (1947), and Virginia Brindis de Salas, who stresses black pride and liberation in her *Pregón de Marimorena* (1974). Visual artists include the 19th-century "impressionist" Pedro Figari, a white painter enamored with the culture of the *conventillo* and the *candombe,* and in recent times Rubén Galloza. Furthermore, Afro-

Uruguayan entertainers, such as Rey Charol and Rubén Rada, and athletes, especially footballers, have proudly represented their nation on the world stage (Pacheco 2001, chapter 6).

Many scholars assert that blacks in the River Plate are "forgotten." They insist that a hegemonic state has "whitewashed" the history books to exclude them, marginalizing African Uruguayans as the "other." There is a germ of truth to this; however, this is only a partial truth. Persistent problems with racism and discrimination notwithstanding, Afro-Uruguayans (about 6 percent of the population, mostly located in Montevideo, but also in the departments of Artigas, Rivera, Cerro Largo, Treinta y Tres, and Rocha) have by and large successfully integrated into national society. Africans in the River Plate were in reality subjected to demographic and social pressures that favored their biological and cultural assimilation. In fact, Afro-Uruguayans (although not to the extent of Afro-Argentines) have been rendered largely invisible as a result of centuries of miscegenation and acculturation. Black elites in the River Plate have nonetheless fought against the agents of their subordination and marginalization. To recognize black participation in the building of the nation is to acknowledge contributions entitling African Uruguayans to civil rights and full equality with whites, thereby ending their invisibility.

Roberto Pacheco

See also Ansina (1760?–1860); Argentina: Afro-Argentines; Chile: Afro-Chileans; Ecuador: Afro-Ecuadorians; Tango, Candombe, Milonga.

FURTHER READING

Chasteen, John C. 1995. *Heroes on Horseback: A Life and Times of the Last Gaucho Caudillos.* Albuquerque, NM: University of New Mexico Press.

Cordones-Cook, Juanamaría. 1996. "The Afro-Uruguayan Theater of Andrés Castillo." *Latin American Theatre Review* 29 (2): 31–36.

Goldman, Gustavo. 1997. *¡Salve Baltasar! La fiesta de reyes en el barrio Sur de Montevideo.* Montevideo, Uruguay: Impresora Federal Nuevosur.

Mayo, Carlos A. 1997. "Patricio de Belén: nada menos que un capataz." *Hispanic American Historical Review* 77 (4): 597–617.

Montaño, Oscar D. 1995. "Los afro-orientales. Breve reseña del aporte africano en la formación de la población uruguaya." In *Presencia africana en Sudamérica*, ed. Luz M. Martínez Montiel, 391–441. Mexico City, Mexico: Consejo Nacional Para la Cultura y las Artes.

Montaño, Oscar D. 1997. *Umkhonto: la lanza negra. Historia del aporte negro-africano en la formación del Uruguay.* Montevideo, Uruary: Rosebud Ediciones.

Montaño, Oscar D. 1998. "Ansina: la senda del guerrero." In *La herencia cultural africana en las Américas,* vol. 1, ed. Beatriz Santos, 113–120. Montevideo, Uruguay: EPPAL.

Pacheco, Roberto. 2001. "Invisible but Not Forgotten: The Afro-Argentine and Afro-Uruguayan Experience from the Sixteenth to the Twentieth Centuries." MA thesis, Florida International University.

Pereda Valdés, Ildefonso. 1965. *El negro en el Uruguay: pasado y presente.* Montevideo, Uruguay: Revista del Instituto Histórico y Geográfico del Uruguay.

Rama, Carlos M. 1969. *Los afrouruguayos.* 3rd ed. Montevideo, Uruguay: Editorial "El Siglo Ilustrado."

Restall, Matthew. 2000. "Black Conquistadors: Armed Africans in Early Spanish America." *The Americas* 57 (2): 171–205.

Rout, Leslie B. 1976. *The African Experience in Spanish America, 1502 to the Present Day.* Cambridge, UK: Cambridge University Press.

Scheüss de Studer, Elena F. 1984. *La trata de negros en el Río de la Plata durante el siglo XVII.* 2nd ed. Buenos Aires, Argentina: Libros de Hispanoamérica.

Williams, John H. 1987. "Observations on Blacks and Bondage in Uruguay." *The Americas* 43 (4): 41–428.

V

VanDerZee, James (1886–1983)

James VanDerZee, Harlem's most prolific and well-known photographer, is respected for his portraits of proud, middle-class African Americans in Harlem in its most dynamic era—the 1920s and 1930s—although he continued to work until his death in 1983.

James VanDerZee was born in Lennox, Massachusetts, in 1886 and spent time in Virginia and New Jersey before permanently settling in Harlem, New York. In 1915, VanDerZee opened his first of several photo studios in Harlem. He was an artist of the Harlem Renaissance, an era that saw a proliferation of African American culture and a growing black middle class. He photographed soldiers, children, church and civic groups, graduations, sports teams, and hundreds of weddings, as well as mortuary portraits, which were sometimes the only images family had of their deceased loved ones. Committed to showing his sitter in his or her best light, VanDerZee was a skilled at retouching photographs, and he made his subjects as attractive as possible. He used props to tell stories and sometimes used a technique called photomontage, where multiple negatives are used in printing to give the images depth or enhance narratives. VanDerZee also photographed a number of promi-nent figures, including Adam Clayton Powell, Sr., Marcus Garvey, Joe Louis, Muhammad Ali, and Bill Cosby, among others. He kept and stored his best work, which amounted to 75,000 glass and film negatives.

VanDerZee was discovered by the mainstream art world in 1969, when the Metropolitan Museum of Art exposed many of his images in a controversial show titled "Harlem on My Mind." Life-sized prints were made from his negatives, and VanDerZee earned worldwide acclaim. Many in the black community protested the show because of its anthropologic and ethnographic undertones; the emphasis was more on the documentary versus the aesthetic contributions of Harlem artists. Ironically, VanDerZee's carefully composed, artistic, and embellished photos became useful in documentary research, and contained much more information about what Harlem was like in the 1920s and 1930s than the other documentary photographs produced around the same time. Because VanDerZee was a professional portrait photographer, his images presented the black community in Harlem the way that they themselves wanted to be represented and remembered.

Noelle Theard

See also Photography and the African Diaspora.

FURTHER READING

Haskins, Jim. 1991. *James Van DerZee: The Picture-Takin' Man*. Trenton, NJ: Africa World Press.

Willis-Braithwaite, Deborah, and Rodger C. Birt. 1998. *VanDerZee Photographer 1886–1983*. New York: Harry N. Abrams.

Van Sertima, Ivan (1935–)

Ivan Van Sertima has offered scholarship for over a quarter century in the area of rewriting African history and reconstructing the African's place in world history, particularly in the field of the African presence in ancient America. Indeed, during this turbulent and exciting period, he has been in the vanguard of those scholars fighting to place African history in a new light.

Van Sertima was born in Kitty Village, Guyana, on January 26, 1935. He was educated at the School of Oriental and African Studies at London University, where he graduated with honors. From 1957 to 1959, he served as a press and broadcasting officer in the Guyana Information Services. During the decade of the 1960s, he broadcasted weekly from Britain to both Africa and the Caribbean. He came to the United States in 1970, where he completed his postgraduate studies at Rutgers University in New Jersey. Van Sertima began his teaching career as an instructor at Rutgers in 1972.

Van Sertima is a literary critic, a linguist, and an anthropologist, and he has made a name for himself in all three fields. As a linguist, he compiled the *Swahili Dictionary of Legal Terms* based on his field word in Tanzania in 1967. As a literary critic, he is the author of *Caribbean Writers*, a collection of critical essays on the Caribbean novel. He is also the author of several major literary reviews published in Denmark, India, Britain, and the United States. In recognition for his work in this field, the Nobel Committee of the Swedish Academy asked him to nominate candidates for the Nobel Prize in Literature from 1976 to 1980. However, the cornerstone of Van Sertima's legacy will probably be his authorship of *They Came Before Columbus: The African Presence in Ancient America*—a groundbreaking historical work and a literary hallmark. The ideas and themes presented were not novel, but Van Sertima's book was the first such work of its type written by an African to comprehensively address the subject.

In 1979, after the publication of *They Came Before Columbus*, Van Sertima founded the *Journal of African Civilizations*, an equally momentous achievement. The journal quickly gained a reputation for excellence and uniqueness among historical and anthropological journals and is recognized as a valuable information source for both the layperson and student.

From 1979, the *Journal of African Civilizations* published works by and about many of the world's finest Africanist scholars in a series of magnificent anthologies. These works include *Blacks in Science, Nile Valley Civilizations, African Presence in Early America, Black Women in Antiquity, Egypt Revisited, Egypt: Child of Africa, African Presence in Early Europe, Golden Age of the Moor, African Presence in the Art of the Americas, Great Black Leaders, Great African Thinkers* (coedited with Larry Obadele Williams), and *African Presence in Early Asia* (coedited with Runoko Rashidi). In 1998 Transaction Press produced Van Sertima's last major text—*Early America Revisited*—the closest thing so far to being the definitive statement on the subject of Africans in early America. On July 7, 1987, Van Sertima appeared before a Congressional Committee to challenge the Columbus myth. In November 1991, he defended his thesis in an address to the Smithsonian Institute. In this arena, Ivan Van Sertima has emerged clearly and distinctly as the undefeated champion.

Runoko Rashidi

See also Guyana.

FURTHER READING

Van Sertima, Ivan. 1977. *They Came Before Columbus*. New York: Random House, 1977.

Van Sertima, Ivan, ed. 1992. *Early America Revisited*. New Brunswick, NJ: Transaction Press.

Venezuela: Afro-Venezuelans and the Afro Descendientes Movement

THE ORIGIN OF ENSLAVED AFRICANS IN VENEZUELA

The commercial instrument that Westerners created to implement the capture and relocation of millions of Africans to Venezuelan lands was expressed in the "*Asientos De Negros*," a monopolistic contract between the Spanish crown and the countries dedicated to this commerce. The *Asientos de Negros*, signed by the Spanish crown, was first fulfilled with Portuguese slave trade companies (1576–1640), then French companies (1702–1712), and next the English company (1713–1773), to which was joined the contraband of the Dutch companies, and, finally, the free commerce of blacks after 1782.

To justify the slave trade, those involved in this terrible business (church, political, scientific, and economic powers) turned to biological, religious, and ideological justifications that they established throughout history. Today those justifications are known as racism and racial discrimination (Garcia 2001,113)

From the period that runs from 1576 until the slave trade legally ended in Venezuela in 1810, one can calculate that between a half million enslaved men and women entered Venezuela legally and as contraband (Garcia 2004, 65). The first censuses conducted by the church in the so-called curacies of towns indicated that 80 percent of the inhabitants were of African origin represented by the following ethnicities:

Congo-Loango-Mondongo-Malemba-Sundi (today the Republic of the Congo, and part of the Democratic Republic of the Congo [formerly Zaire])

Angola, Mbuila (Republic of Angola)

Tare, Mina, Arara, Popo (People's Republic of Benin [formerly Dahomey])

Mandinga, Wolof (Gambia, Senegambia, Senegal)

Nago-Yoruba-Lucumi, Carabali (Republic of Nigeria)

The ethnicities that appear in the registry documents show the African civilizations, and therefore the cultural, symbolic contributions, agricultural techniques, and religions that these African men and women brought. This provides an entire intellectual body of material that goes beyond the reductionist concept of the workforce.

THE PROSLAVERY SYSTEM IN VENEZUELA AND THE WORK OF AFRICAN MEN AND WOMEN AND THEIR DESCENDENTS

African men and women were subjugated to forced agricultural work. The principal agricultural production units to which the enslaved men and women were subjugated were the following:

Cocoa haciendas, which constituted the accumulation of wealth for the ancient province of Venezuela, constituted one place of forced labor. Most of the cocoa haciendas were situated on the coasts of Venezuela, and many of the Afro-descendent towns in Venezuela today were ancient enclaves of cocoa exploitation where the enslaved men and women worked. Four thousand cocoa haciendas existed in the subregion of Barlovento. The Africans and their descendents generated wealth from cocoa for landowners and the Spanish crown.

Gold mining was another area of forced labor for Africans and their descendents, as gold represented a symbol of distinction and of capitalist value in Europe. The gold mines of Buria (in the state of Yaracuay) were established at the beginning of the 17th century in Venezuela.

Precious pearl gathering was one of the cruelest production units; the slave was placed in a cage and dropped to the sea floor to look for pearls; many died by immersion when their lungs burst. This practice was carried out on the island of Cubagua, close to the island of Margarita.

Coffee haciendas at the end of the 17th century and beginning of the 19th century were important for capitalist accumulation. Coffee haciendas were typically located in zones of mountainous climates and worked by enslaved people of African origin.

Indigo haciendas also played a dynamic role in the economy as did cattle ranching, which developed in smaller proportions toward the Venezuelan plains.

Sugar cane plantations were another production unit that the colonialists developed. This type of work, in contrast to work on the cocoa and coffee haciendas, was more intensive and exploitative. The great sugar cane plantations were located in El Tocuyo (state of Lara) and San Mateo (state of Aragua).

THE COLONIAL SLAVERY SYSTEM AND THE NAMING OF PEOPLE ACCORDING TO THEIR RACIAL FEATURES

As in the rest of the Americas and the Caribbean, the slavery system was characterized by the following aspects:

Permanent Forced Labor

For the intensive production of agriculture and precious metals it was necessary to organize the work of the enslaved people as a principal tool of the productive process, where not only manual labor but also intellectual work, that is to say the slaves' knowledge of technologies for working the land, knowledge about traditional medicinal practices, and knowledge about constructing houses, among other things, was decisive in building the economies of the so-called New World.

For example *The Regulations of Work for the Chuao Hacienda* in the year 1817 are as follows:

1. The bell will ring, as is the custom in the towns, at five in the morning to call the slaves from 12 to 60 years of age to worship God and give thanks singing out loud.

2. For this, all will come out with their iron tools; the worship concluded, the list with the number that has been assigned to each slave will be passed around so that each will answer his or her name, and next, will march to work in what the foreman has prepared.

3. Later, the foreman will be vigilant toward the precise completion of the respective jobs.

4. Everyday at sundown the bell will ring to call together the slaves, big and small, so that they will gather at the patio; they will be obliged to pray.

5. The prayer and worship of the Lord concluded, the list will be passed to all according to their numbers.

6. At nine o'clock at night, the five bells will ring, which will be the signal to all the slaves to retire to sleep. The foremen will make the rounds where the slaves sleep.

Process of Religious Acculturation

The Catholic Church, in complicity with the administrative military power, instigated a process of compulsive acculturation to eliminate the religious systems of the Afro-descendents, and convert them to Catholicism. This torturous practice of conversion to Catholicism that began at 5 in the morning with learning the rosary was linked to the work schedule to inculcate submission as an attitude toward life. The Church intended to eliminate the original religions; however, many African religious practices have been preserved today throughout the continent.

In Venezuela, there exist two religious creations as products of this process: The first was the Afro-Catholic practices that were the structure of a religious parallelism (not syncretism) between the Catholic religion and the African religious elements expressed through the Africans' reinterpretation of the Catholic images that the Western Europeans attempted to impose as "patron saints." The second was the Afro-Indigenous spiritualism of Maria Lionza that arose as an answer to the Catholic imposition. The term "Afro-indigenous" is used as most of the spiritual references of the essential components of this "spirituality" are indigenous and African.

Process of Depersonalization

One of the strategies for making the Africans and their descendents submit was the psychological reinforcement that they (the enslaved) were not people, did not have an identity, and were subject for life to be "slaves," and that the only way to be a person was to assume obedience toward the master. One of the acts of greatest significance to achieve depersonalization was to eliminate the original names of the Africans and their descendents and to give them a Catholic, apostolic, and Roman name.

In African traditional cultures a person's name contains a symbol, a history, and a destiny; by changing the name the colonialists were erasing the historical memory of the origin civilizations. In Venezuela, very few names and ethnicities of African origin were conserved, in contrast to Colombia, a country that has the greatest number of African ethnicities on the American continent.

Loss of the Original African Languages

Language, an essential instrument that synthesizes identity, culture, and religiosity, was eliminated in most cases. This strategy was fundamental to avoid communication between the enslaved people. In the Americas and the Caribbean, many African languages were diluted with indigenous and European languages, and languages such as Creole, Garifuna, Palenque, and the religious symbolic languages of the Regla de Ocha-Abajua-Arara-Kongo (Cuba) or of Candomblé (Brazil) arose.

In Venezuela, languages of African origin were not conserved, with the exception of a type of Creole spoken in the Eastern part of the country (the states of Sucre and Bolivar) as a result of contacts since the Colonial era with maroons and migrants from the Anglophone and Francophone Caribbean who migrated to these locations in Venezuela.

Rape

The rape of African women by the masters was a permanent fixture in the slavery system. At the same time, the exploitation of a woman's womb to produce new enslaved men and women constituted an economic strategy to construct a new hacienda of enslaved people.

ETHNIC CLASSIFICATION IN THE COLONIAL SYSTEM OF THE HUMAN GROUPS THAT INHABITATED VENEZUELA

The following terms were used to classify people in Colonial Venezuela: Jet-black, brown, mestizo (white and Indian), *Bachaco* (a Venezuelan term for a large red ant used to describe people of dark skin with reddish curly hair), *Bozal* (a term used to refer to African-born black slaves), dark *Zambo* (refers to a person who is half black and half Indian), pale *Zambo* (Indian and white), *Pardo* (literally means "brownish-gray"), mulatto, light mulatto, quadroon (white and mulatto), Quinteron (white and quadroon), and "a step backward" (when the skin color was darker than that of the mother). These names were compiled from the censuses taken by the parish priests during the 17th, 18th, and 19th centuries. This type of naming appears in the newspapers of the colonial and postindependence era, such as the *Gazette of Caracas* and *The Venezuelan*. The dominant sectors also used these connotations to create differences among the enslaved people. At the same time they reflected and continue to reflect the racial condition metamorphosized in these adjectives.

Cimarronaje as an Answer to the Proslavery System

Confronting the cruelty and privation of liberty to which the Africans were subjugated during the proslavery system were acts of uprising and head-on *cimarronaje*. *Cimarronaje* can best be described as the quality of the runaway African, or maroon. The word carries with it a sense of resistance as well as escape. The "legal *cimarronaje*" encompasses the setting up of alternative communities outside of enslavement; "Confrontational *cimarronaje*" includes all forms of violent fights against the proslavery system in all of its expressions.

In this way the uprisings of enslaved men and women emerge during the 16th century with the Negro Miguel (1522), who established an alliance with the indigenous Jiraharas and Gayones in the state of Maracay and with the enslaved Africans to demand their liberty from the intense labor to which they were subjugated in working the gold mines in the town of Buria. This act is considered the first uprising against the colonial exploitation in Venezuela. Some of the most significant uprisings include the following:

- Uprisings of maroon men and women occurred in the 17th century in the valleys of El Tuy and Caracas.
- The Rebellion of Andres Lopez del Rosario (Andresote) in 1732 was the first confrontation against the company Guipuzcoana, which held a monopoly on commerce and had introduced enslaved men and women into Venezuela.
- The building of communities (quilombos) of runaway slaves, or maroons, including Ocoyta. One such community, Cumbe, led by the African Guillermo Rivas between the years 1768 and 1771, represented for three years a liberating reference for the enslaved Africans and their descendents in this region.
- The military uprising of Jose Leonardo Chirinos (1795) in the San Luis sierra (state of Falcon) as a result of the influence of the Haitian rebellion of 1791. This rebellion is known as the first preindependence rebellion. Today, the symbolic remains of Chirinos rest in the National Pantheon.

"Legal *Cimarronaje*" was the legal technicality established by the Law of Indians, through which enslaved men and women could obtain their freedom as is the case of the African Jose del Rosario Blanco, founder of Curiepe (a town of free blacks), a fugitive from Curaçao who received his liberty for having served in the Spanish army. African women also participated in the head-on *cimarronaje*, including Masnu Alagrin (Ocoyta Cumbe in 1791) and Josefina Sanchez (Taguaza Cume in 1794).

Within legal *cimarronaje* were freedoms earned by the testamentaries, that is to say the freedom the landowners gave to some of their enslaved people for reasons of compassion or religion. Another form of buying their respective freedoms was through the work of *haciendillas* (small haciendas). This had to do with a legal system in the Black Code of 1789 (Nation's General Archive, 1789), which held that if the masters could neither feed nor meet the needs of the enslaved people, they would have to give them a small piece of land so that they could cultivate it and sell its fruits, and the enslaved people took advantage of this to sell their fruits and accumulate money to buy their freedoms. Venezuela records many cases of enslaved men and women who bought their freedoms using the system of *haciendillas*.

This Black Code, issued May 31, 1789, consisted of several chapters, such as the one referring to education, reoriented essentially to Catholic conversion through a permanent instruction, followed by baptism, attending mass, and administering the holy sacraments. Another chapter of the Black Code refers to the occupation of the "slaves" where it expressed that "the principal occupation of the slaves should be agriculture and other country work, and not of trades of sedentary life" (idem). This is where they give two hours daily for rest so that they could work on a small piece of land called a hacienda to cultivate minor fruits that the enslaved people could sell. Nevertheless, the masters did not comply with this Black Code of 1789, which was a replica of France's Black Code of Colbert (1695); from there began the enslaved population's permanent pursuit of escapes, uprisings, and clashes.

The enslaved men and women's entire freedom movement in the first years of the Spanish conquest and colonization was the antecedent to the War of Independence that started in Venezuela in the year 1808.

The War of Independence and the Participation of the Enslaved Men and Women

At the beginning of the War of Independence, the General Captaincy of Venezuela had the following population:

Native Spanish: 12,000
Creoles: 200,000
People of color: 406,000

As this statistical distribution of the population shows, most of the population in Venezuela was constituted by what the colonialists called "people of color." Once the War of Independence began, the so-called white *Peninsulares* (Spanish born in Spain) and white Creoles (children of the Spanish, born in Venezuela) who were disputing the power were offering liberty, bread, land, and work to the enslaved African population.

Among the independence supporters (white Creoles) were Manuel Espana, Pedro Gual, General Francisco de Miranda, and Simón Bolívar. The "Royalists," or those who wanted to preserve the colonial power, included Jose Tomas Boves, Monteverde, and Rossete. Both groups left behind testimonies that it would have been impossible to fight without the participation of the enslaved men and women who made up the majority of the Venezuelan population.

Bolívar, after his first failures in initiating the War of Independence, turned to Haiti. The Haitian model, which, after more than a decade of fighting (1791–1804), had achieved with blood and fire its liberty from French and English imperialism, was the first of the African Diaspora to construct a liberating hope different from the European and North American models. This model would serve as a reference for several precursors and leaders of the independence movement, but only as military support and refuge, not as a political model to implement for the future construction of the Republic of Venezuela. Bolívar turned to the Haitian president Alexander Petion on January 2, 1816; there he received support, and Bolívar, to express his sentiments toward Petion upon arriving at Carupano (a city in the eastern part of Venezuela) on June 16, 1816, launched his decree abolishing slavery (Bolívar 1970, 458). This initiative from Bolívar is the result of a commitment that he had made before the Haitian President Alexander Petion, to whom he announced that he would decree the freedom of the "slaves," expressed in a letter that Petion sent to Bolivar. Beforehand in July of this same year, in the town of Ocumare de la Costa, Bolívar launched the second decree of the abolition of slavery on July 6, 1816; this appealed the decree of Carupano, which conceded personal liberty to the slaves who took up arms. Many enslaved men, women, and boys and girls older than 12 joined the army led by Bolívar.

Thanks to the decisive support from the Haitian government, Venezuela achieved not only its independence but also the independence of Colombia, Peru, Bolivia, and Ecuador.

In the pursuit of the enslaved people's freedom, on February 15, 1819, at the famous Congress of Angostura, Bolívar insisted: "I abandon to your decision that reform or the revocation of all of my statutes and decrees, but I implore the confirmation of the absolute liberty of the slaves, as I would implore my life and the life of the Republic" (Bolívar 1970, 589)

During the 13-year War of Independence the Africans and their descendents participated in battalions with arms in hand, the women as lancers and nurses. Their former masters gave them liberty to participate in this war that did not limit itself to Venezuelan territory, but rather these Africans crossed the Andes to free Colombia-Panama, Ecuador, Peru, and Bolivia from the dominating Spanish colonialism. They resisted cold, hunger, and calamities and made up the only army in the history of humankind that helped liberate other countries without invading or subjugating them to new forms of colonialism. Most of the men and women who crossed the Andes were of African origin.

Once the War of Independence ended, the former masters began to claim their previously enslaved men and women who had participated. The masters demanded their rights to the enslaved people unless the state would pay the price they had cost at purchase. This shameful act produced indignation in the African soldiers who had to abandon the army to once again incorporate themselves into the proslavery system. All of Bolívar's decrees were thrown out, and the Republic would be uniquely and exclusively for the white Creoles, reproducing the colonial and proslavery system of the Spanish crown.

THE FIRST LEGAL EXCLUSION OF THE AFRICAN MEN AND WOMEN AND THEIR DESCENDENTS IN THE NEW BOLIVARIAN REPUBLIC

"What to do with the products of enslavement?" was one of the questions proposed by the legislators in the congress of the rising re-public. They began to trace reformist lines to forget about the Bolivarian proposals for abolishing slavery. They invented laws such as the Law of Birth or the Law of Manumission, which held that children who are born of the wombs of slaves will only be given liberty when they have reached 18 years of age, whereupon they will have to compensate their master for their 18 years of maintenance with whatever labor that the master chooses. In short, the enslaved men and women who participated in the War of Independence continued to be subjugated to the proslavery system.

The Law of Manumission was like a first step to advance toward abolition. A few articles are:

> Art. 1— The children born to slaves from the day of the publication of this law in the capitals of the provinces will be free
>
> ...
>
> Art. 2— The owners of female slaves will have the precise obligation to educate, dress and feed the children that are born from the day of the publication of this law, but they, in recompense, will have the duty to indemnify the masters of their mothers for the costs of their nurturing with their labors and services that they will offer until completing 18 years of age (Law of Manumission of 1821, Congress of Cucuta).

Thus, the Law of Manumission was a continuation of slavery through other means. Many times the masters hid a person's birthdate so as not to have to give him or her freedom at 18 years old. In essence, enslaved labor continued as the law said the one to be set free had to pay for his or her maintenance, bed, and housing with labor.

The first Law of Manumission was decreed in the city of Cucuta on July 21, 1821. And in 1830, the Law of Manumission of 1821 was modified; instead of granting liberty when the enslaved person was 18 years old, the enslavement was prolonged three more years, until he or she was 21 years old.

THE ABOLITION OF SLAVERY

The rising republic approved the Constitution of 1830 in which Africans and their descendents were not included as citizens, and slavery as an institution prevailed. According to the official registration, this left 62,000 Africans and Afro-descendents in conditions of enslavement. In addition, the Constitution of 1830 stated that a citizen must "know how to read and write" and "be owners of property." The abolition of slavery was not considered.

This constitution, the first after the War of Independence, bestowed political rights only on the free men and landowners. To elect and be elected, one had to be a free man, owner of a property, with a minimum annual rent of 50 pesos, or in a professional position, office, or industry that earned wages of no less than 100 pesos a year. This was a legal way of excluding women, the enslaved, and most dispossessed sectors.

Slavery continued in practice until 1854 when, for economic, social, and political reasons, the president, Jose Gregorio Monagas, liberated the enslaved African men and women by decree. Taking into account that the War of Independence in Venezuela and the Andean area ended in 1824, the enslaved men and women had to wait 30 years for the state to abolish slavery, so many of those who had fought were older than 60 years and in deplorable physical and mental states.

It's important to note that the government, instead of indemnifying enslaved people, indemnified the slaveholders. To indemnify the masters was the principal condition to abolish slavery. Without indemnification the abolition of slavery would not have taken place. According to the law passed by congress on March 24, 1854, 3 million pesos were allotted to indemnify the owners of some 13,000 enslaved men and women and 27,000 freedmen and freedwomen.

Following are a few articles of the Decree of the Abolition of Slavery:

Art. 1— Slavery in Venezuela is abolished forever.

Art. 2— The legal obligation for the freedmen to lend services ends, leaving them in full possession of their freedom.

Art. 3— The introduction of slaves into the territory of the Republic is prohibited forever, and those who are introduced against this prohibition, under whatever pretext, will through the very act enter immediately into full possession of freedom.

Art. 4— The slave owners will be indemnified for the value that these have according to the rate, or in case of illness according to the physicians' judgment, with the funds directed toward or that will be directed toward this purpose . . .

In many cases, until the state repaid the cost of each enslaved man or women, some masters did not proceed to liberate them.

FEDERAL WAR, THE MODERNIZATION OF THE VENEZUELAN STATE, AND THE EXCLUSION OF THE AFRO-DESCENDENTS

The Federal War (1859–1863), led by Ezequial Zamora, resulted from internal fights between the system of large estates and the monopoly of land on the part of the oligarchy. Hence, the platforms of this war were bread, land, work, and equality. Most of those who joined the Federal army were the enslaved men and women who now found themselves in a situation of semislavery, without land, without food, and without education. Believing the objectives of independence were incomplete, a large contingent of Afro-descendents participated in the Federal War in search of equality and citizenship.

The Venezuelan state had not made itself responsible for the agreements established in the laws that favored equality and social responsibility.

The proponents of miscegenation and racial equality in Venezuela maintain that racial inequality ended with the Federal War, but the reality was something else: inequality continued. The only favorable outcome was a pact made with certain rebel leaders who were given some land and political power.

The population of African origin continued in a situation of semislavery, earning salaries that were paid with tokens with which they could only buy in the establishments of their former masters or hacienda owners, where the prices of the products cost 200 percent more than in the normal market. The laborers did not have access to education or dignified work. Some could not come out from the yoke of their former masters, even more than a decade after slavery was abolished.

In the 20th century, with the beginning of modernization in Latin America states, most of the modernist ideologies (the Marxists as much as the positivists) conceptualized one Latin America of mixed race that should deepen its miscegenation to enter modernity. The 20th century brought the so-called modernization of American societies, state reform, laws, and processes of urban development, among other things.

These ideas, at the continental level, indicate how this current will be converted into a dominant ideological position for what may be called "modernization with ethnoexclusion," not only in Venezuela but also in the entire continent. Proponents of this view include the intellectual Marxist and Peruvian Carlos Mariategui.

It is in this intellectual framework that two principal ideologies of modernity and miscegenation in Venezuela may be examined. The first is Venezuelan economist Alberto Adriana who, in the 1930s and 1940s, put forward a thesis of reducing the black population. According to Adriani, Venezuela had a high population of African origin; therefore, in the immigration plan the government set forth for those years, it was maintained that they could limit the entry of African peoples coming from the Antilles owing to the fact that they could corrupt the incipient democratic institutions.

Then there is Arturo Uslar Pietri, father of Venezuelan miscegenation. With respect to the modernization of the Venezuelan state, Uslar maintained that Indians and Africans and their resulting mixtures were people incapable of positive contribution to modernity. In other words, he believed that if the ethnic composition of Venezuela's population was not greatly modified, it would be almost impossible to change the course of history and make Venezuela a modern state (Garcia 2001, 82). These perspectives would establish the ideological foundations of the second ethnic exclusion of Afro-descendents in the conception of the construction of the modernity discourse and its projection into the legal, administrative structures of the states.

The public policy that was implemented in most republics of Latin America had these great ideological weights that molded the political practices of the institutions, continuing the racist, discriminatory, and exclusive ideas that emerged with the republics of the 19th century.

From the year 1945 the process of populist government was initiated in many parts of Latin America. The process was often preceded by a coup d'état, like the one that occurred in Venezuela on October 18, 1945. The seven-person civic military junta included Dr. Luis Beltran Prieto Figueroa, an Afro-descendent who was not aware of his African ancestry. The 1948 presidential election was won by the writer Romulo Gallegos. In his campaign he had used the figure of the Afro-descendent as an emblem, demonstrating the high electoral percentage that the population of African origin represented. Once Gallegos was installed into power some intellectuals wrote articles in the press complaining that "the blacks were ruling" (Uslar 1948, 4).

In this period the recognition of the Afro-descendent component passed silently. The government of Romulo Gallego, toppled by a militaristic coup, is replaced by a terrible dictatorship that proposes a project of the "national ideal," in which the race would be bettered by bringing in large quantities of migrants from Western Europe. Racism deepens, and large quantities of lands are handed over to the European migrants, putting the Afro-descendents aside with their misery. The dictatorship of Marcos Perez Jimenez (1948–1958) contributed to deepening the theory of miscegenation in the sense that he believed the whiter the population, the better Venezuela would be.

In 1961 a new constitution was ratified that included recognition of the indigenous although Afro-descendents were not mentioned anywhere. Despite the fact that the constitution says, "we are all equal" without discrimination based on race, racial discrimination continues in Venezuelan society. The Afro-descendent sectors did not exist in educational programs, and recognition of their historic and cultural contributions did not exist. Thus, the 1961 constitution brings an end to diversity.

MULTIETHNIC AND MULTICULTURAL STATES: THE PROCESS OF MODERNIZING THE STATES WITH ETHNIC INCLUSION

At the end of the 1980s a process of understanding the ethnic was initiated in Latin America on behalf of some states, such as Nicaragua, which launched the Law of Autonomy in 1987 where communal lands and the Garifuna language were guaranteed.

But it is in the 1990s when Latin America states initiate a second phase of modernization where the ethnic element comes into play. In 1991, Colombia approves a new constitution expressing the country's multiethnic and multicultural character, as in other constitutions that were approved in the Andean countries.

Nevertheless, in 1993, Colombia drew up specific laws to address Afro and indigenous groups. In the case of the Afro-descendents, Law 70, known as the Law of Black Communities, was approved. Ecuador considers nominal inclusion of the Afro-Ecuadorian in its new constitution, and the Law of Afro-Ecuadorian Populations is initiated.

THE CONSTITUTIONAL ABSENCE OF VENEZUELAN AFRO-DESCENDENTS

When Venezuela begins to discuss a new constitution, the Afro-American Foundation and the Union of Black Women propose that the state incorporate the Afro-Venezuelan notion into the multiethnic character and cultural diversity and as a foundational element of the republic. There are demands that the new constitution should include historic, political, and cultural recognition of African men and women and their descendents as well as a reconsideration of the collective property of the lands of the former *cimarrones* and *cimarronas*. Nevertheless, these propositions are ignored. In the preamble the Constitution of the Bolivarian Republic of Venezuela (CRBV) expresses the following: "The Venezuelan people, in exercise of its creative powers and invoking the protection of God, the historic example of our liberator Simon Bolivar and the heroism and sacrifice of our aboriginal forbears . . ." (CRBV 1999, 1), ignoring the role played by African men and women and their descendents from 1552 until the present day in the fights for the independence and dignity of the Venezuelan people.

If other Latin American countries were able to understand the necessity of modernizing their states without ethnic exclusion (Colombia, Ecuador, Brazil, Nicaragua, Peru), why then were Afro-descendent men and women left legally excluded in Venezuela? The preamble to the CBRV does not fulfill the legal reordering that began to be carried out with the organic laws from the year 2000. None of the laws make reference to the Afro-Venezuelan notion as an essential component, despite the suggestions the Network of Afro-Venezuelan Organizations made, although the topic had been attached to the draft of the Law of Culture and the Law of Education.

With changes of ministers and vice ministers and a reconsideration of the same drafts, these articles have been eliminated, arguing that here "we are all the same" and incorporating the Afro variable is introducing a false problem because we are all of mixed blood and, moreover, this category does not appear in the CRBV.

The Afro-Venezuelan dimension does not appear in the constitution, the organic laws that govern the different sectors of the Venezuelan state, or in the nation's strategic programs, plans, and projects. The institutional absence of recognition of the Afro-Venezuelan communities is evident in the planning of the state. In the Venezuelan state no organism attends to the situation of the Afro-descendents as in Colombia, Ecuador, Peru, and Brazil, because the Afro-descendants do not exist in the Constitution or the organic laws. There is no legal mandate to create state organisms for the Afro-descendent communities.

THE ABSENCE OF
VENEZUELA ANTIRACIST LAWS

Despite the fact that antiracist laws do not exist in the constitution, nevertheless, Article 21 appears, expressing:

All people are equal before the Law, consequently:

1. Discriminations founded on race, sex, creed, social condition or those which, in general, have as an objective or a result to annul or diminish recognition, enjoyment or exercise of the conditions of equality, rights, and liberty of all people will not be permitted.

2. The law will guarantee the legal and administrative conditions so that equality before the law will be real and effective; it will adopt positive measures favoring people or groups that may be discriminated against, marginalized or vulnerable; it will especially protect those people who for any of the aforementioned conditions find themselves in a circumstance of manifested weakness and will sanction the abuses or mistreatments that are committed against them.

This article is one of the most advanced in the subject of combating racism. However, to date no media and no racist aggressors have been penalized according to what is established in this article.

Since President Hugo Chavez took office, the government has emitted over a thousand anti- racist messages through various means; owing to the fact that the president is of African origin, some of his ministers are Afro-descendents. Still, in several nightclubs Afro-descendent people are still barred entry. And the police, above all those from the east of the city (where the whites and millionaires live), have been organized with the assumption of racial prejudices, thereby committing excesses toward the Afro-descendent population. This can take place because neither in the penal code nor in any other sphere of the Venezuelan legal apparatus is there any antiracist law that penalizes racism.

CONTEMPORARY AFRO-VENEZUELAN MEN
AND WOMEN: DEMOGRAPHICS

Since colonization began at the end of the 19th century, the ethnic dimension appeared in the censuses by way of terms such as black, mulattos, people of color, *pardo*, *zambo*, and mulatto. But with the imposition of the concept of "racial equality" these same terms disappeared from the population censuses from the end of the 19th century until the 2000 census. Before the 2000 census took place, the network of Afro-Venezuelan organizations communicated to the National Statistic Institute the necessity of incorporating three questions about the Afro-descendent communities: How many are we? Where are we? How are we?

The directorship of the institute rejected the proposal on the grounds that racial differences had been overcome in Venezuela. Still, a few sources, such as a report by the Inter-American Development Bank and the *Organización Afronorteamericana* expressed without foundation that the Afro-descendent population in Venezuela oscillated between 10 and 15 percent. Recently, the Institute of Scientific Investigations, the Department of Anthropology, estimated that Afro-descendents were 14 percent of the population in Venezuela, but this figure does not have statistical backing.

In 2004, the minister of planning, through the National Statistic Institute, conducted the first social survey since 1999. The Network of Afro-Venezuelan Organizations made a proposal to the Ministry of Planning to structure three questions about Afro-descendents in Venezuela. The Ministry of Planning agreed to include the questions on the social survey at the national level, which should produce some statistical indicators about Afro-descendent populations in this modern era. This represents a substantial advance with regard to public policy and recognition for Afro-descendent people and will provide valuable insights into the current situation of Afro-descendants in the workforce, health, and home conditions. Recent studies of poverty conducted by the social investment fund found that most of the municipalities with Afro-descendent populations experience critical and extreme poverty.

PRESENCE OF AFRO-DESCENDENT POPULATIONS

In Venezuela, the Afro-descendent communities are located largely in the ancient enclaves of the enslaved men and women in the central and western coastal zones. The states with the largest Afro-Venezuelan populations, both urban and rural, are the following, in order of highest to lowest population: Vargas, Miranda, Aragua, Sucre, Falcon, Carabobo, Zulia, Yaracuy, Bolivar and the Capital District.

This Afro-descendent population is characterized not only by phenotypical features, but also by rural and urban styles of life, religion, culinary habits, cultural identity, agricultural techniques, solidarity, and collective labor, among other distinct features.

Of the seven strategic areas of sustainable development in Venezuela, four correspond to Afro-descendent communities in the states of Miranda, Aragua, Bolivar, and Zulia. These communities are located in environmental settings important for the country for their water reserves and agricultural potential.

In the media, the lack of racial diversity is clearly seen in the absence of Afro-descendents on soap operas, television news, and advertisements. Ninety percent of the actors, journalists, and reporters are of Caucasian descent. Afro-descendents are assigned the worst roles (crooks, prostitutes, servants, chauffeurs).

PRESENCE OF THE AFRO-DESCENDENTS IN SCHOOL CURRICULUM

In 2003, the Network of Afro-Venezuelan Organizations conducted a study on the Afro-descendent presence in the Venezuelan school system and found that racial discrimination exists in school texts, in both the formative texts used for teacher training and in the classroom texts where children learn about history, identity, culture, and lifestyles.

In history texts, the contributions of African men and women appear in only four instances: first when they arrive as "slaves for their physical strength and as physical labor"; second, when the black woman "gave milk from her breast to Simón Bolívar, the liberator"; and third, when the *zambo* Jose Leonardo Chirinos rose up in 1795 against Spanish colonialism. The fourth is a reference to "the first-rate Negro" when in full battle during the War of Independence a general shouted "Why do you flee, coward?" "I don't flee, my general," the first-rate Negro responds to him, "I come to tell you goodbye because I am dead." This historiographical vision of the coward continues to be repeated in school texts and in official contemporary discourses when the Battle of Carabobo, which sealed the independence of Venezuela, is commemorated. Images of families in textbooks are generally white and Western, which is to say the nuclear family of mother, father, and children. In texts referring to culture, only folkloric reductionism is highlighted in music and dance. This analysis was gathered in the project Prevention of Racism in the School System, which the Afro Network conducted in 2004.

In October 2003, the government issued a presidential decree to eliminate October 12 as the day of discovery, substituting it with the Day of Indigenous Resistance. In this decree the participation of Afros in the processes of cultural resistance is recognized. This has created a space to honor the resistance of the African men and women and their descendents in the fights for independence in the country.

AFRO-DESCENDENT ORGANIZATIONS IN VENEZUELA

In Venezuela, Afro-Venezuelan organizations frequently work in the area of culture reduced to a folkloric conception in the popular imagination. A census was taken of more than 300 organizations in this type of work as well as traditional organizations in the area of Venezuelan Afro-Catholic religious celebrations. But in 2000 the creation of the Network of Afro-Venezuelan Organizations, which unites 23 Afro-Venezuelan organizations in the eight states with the most important African-descended presence, has begun the process of breaking with the folkloric vision of the majority of organizations. The Network of Afro-Venezuelan Organizations articulated an organic process where self-recognition as Afro-Venezuelans and Afro-descendents is important to have the objectives and goals clear to achieve the benefit of the Afro-Venezuelan communities. The fulfillment of the first Afro-Venezuelan National Encounter (May 2001) was of utmost importance, as was the participation in the Pre-conference Against Racism (2001) and later participation in the Third World Conference Against Racism in South Africa in 2001, where Venezuelan representatives met with the official representatives so that they would include the Afro-descended notion in the discourse of the conference.

In two years the group structured a team whose forces have been directed toward recognizing the Afro-descended communities in public policy, in the legal scene (organic laws), and in the sphere of multilateral organizations (United Nations Educational, Scientific, and Cultural Organization, Inter-American Development Bank, World Bank). An important step was to include in the Andean Letter of Human Rights and the Andean Social Letter (pushed by the Andean Parliament), several articles of recognition of Afro-descendent men and women in the subject of social and human rights. In the spheres of public policy the group is working in the following areas with some achievements:

Culture: Cultural infrastructure, funding for associations, recognition in the area of tangible and intangible patrimony, publications.

Education: Incorporation in the discussions in the area of curriculum reform (a demand put before the Ministry of Education).

Agriculture: Common lands (case of Yaracuy).

Technology and communication: Creation of information centers and communal broadcasting in communities.

Health: Fight against the most common illnesses in Afro communities (leukemia, prostate cancer, uterine cancer, HIV).

Tourism: Balance the politics of participation of the African-descended actors in the tourist areas as most of the beaches (which are now the greatest tourist destinations) are located in Afro communities.

Environment: Many of the national parks are located in African-descended communities (Tacarigua de la Laguna, Guatopo, San Esteban, the Sierra of San Luis, among others).

Sustainable development: several of the seven axes of sustainable development designed by the state are located in African-descended communities: Carenero-Tacarigua de la Laguna, Sur del lago de Maracaibo, Sur de Aragua, and the state of Bolivar.

Legal area: Reaffirm the international pacts Venezuela signed; 168 of the OIT; focus on economic, social, and cultural rights; put into practice the Durban Plan of Action, signed by Venezuela but until now not implemented; convene an Interministry Commission; and fight to reconsider in the drafts of the laws of culture and education, the articles referring to Afro contributions.

In March 2002, together with other African-descended organizations in South America, a proposal was made by Afro descendientes organizations to the Organization of American States for a resolution against racial discrimination that will go toward propelling an Inter-American Convention Against Racism, an initiative driven in the past OAS assembly in Santiago, Chile (June 7–8, 2003). The Venezuelan government and the Brazilian government propelled this initiative. On September 24, the Ministry of Foreign Affairs, after pressure from the Network of Afro-Venezuelan Organizations, signed the Convention's optional Protocol 14 for the Elimination of Racism and Discrimination.

THE SIX PRIORITIES OF THE AFRO-DESCENDENT POPULATION

First priority, to carry out an amendment to the National Constitution that recognizes the moral and political contributions of the Afro-descendents in the historic construction of Venezuela.

Second priority, "to count ourselves," to know how many Afro-descendents live in Venezuela as well as where they are and how they are. This has to do with the social survey, which will gather information about exclusion, poverty, health, and so on. These quantitative data should be used to influence public policy.

Third priority, education, to incorporate Afro-descendant communities into the

school system, to elevate the rate of schooling, and to incorporate African contributions in all levels of the curriculum from preschool to university.

Fourth priority, putting into practice the Durban Plan of Action.

Fifth priority, to push the Convention on Cultural Diversity in the United Nations with the aim of promoting the traditional cultures of African origin.

Sixth priority, to promote the creation of a public space to channel the social, economic, cultural, ecological, and communicational demands of the Afro communities.

As a result of the permanent struggles to attain recognition of Afro-descendent men and women, three of these priorities have been achieved. First, the history, culture, and global contributions of Afro-descendents have been incorporated in the new Venezuelan educational curriculum. Second, President Chavez has created a presidential commission to combat and prevent racism. Third, the Durban Plan of Action through the Vice-Minister for Africa has been put into practice.

Jesus Chucho Garcia
Translated by Elizabeth J. Turnbull

See also Argentina: Afro-Argentines; Brazil: Afro-Brazilians; Chile: Afro-Chileans; Colombia: Afro-Colombians; Hip-Hop, Latin American; Uruguay: Afro-Uruguayans.

FURTHER READING

Acosta Saignes, Miguel. 1967. *La vida de los esclavos negros* [The Life of Black Slaves]. Caracas, Venezuela.

Acosta Saignes, Miguel. 1978. *La vida de los esclavos negros en Venezuela* [The Life of Black Slaves in Venezuela]. Havana, Cuba: Casa de las Américas.

Adriani, Alberto. 1987. *Labor venezolanista* [Venezuelanist Labor]. Caracas, Venezuela: Academia Nacional de la Historia.

Alvarado, Lisandro. 1956. *Historia de la Revolución Federal* [History of the Federal Revolution]. T.V. Caracas, Venezuela.

Bolívar, Simón. 1970. *Cartad del libertador* [Letter from the Liberator]. T.VIII. Caracas, Venezuela: Banco de Venezuela.

Bolívar, Simón. 1967. *Obras Completas* [Complete Works]. T.2. Caracas, Venezuela.

Código negro [Black Code]. 1789. Archivo General de la Nación. Sección Real Cedulas.

Constitución de la Republica Bolivariana de Venezuela [Constitution of the Bolivarian Republic of Venezuela]. 1999.

Derechos Colectivos de los pueblos afroecuatorianos [Collective Rights of the Afro-Ecuadorian People]. 2000. Quito, Ecuador.

Fondo de Inversión Social. 2001. *Proyecto País* [Project Country]. Caracas, Venezuela.

García, Jesús. 1986. *Nomenclatura de la trata negrera y la esclavización.* [Nomenclature of the Black Slave Trade and Enslavement]. Mimeo.

Garcia, Jesús. 1989. *Barlovento tiempo de cimarrones* [Barlovento, Time of Maroons]. Barlovento, Venezuela.

Garcia, Jesús. 1990. *África en Venezuela* [Africa in Venezuela]. Caracas, Venezuela: Edit. Lagoven.

Garcia, Jesús. 1995. *La diáspora de Kongos en las Américas y el Caribe* [The Diaspora of Congo in the Americas and the Caribbean]. Caracas, Venezuela: UNESCO-Cona.

Garcia, Jesús. 1998. *Africanas, esclavas y cimarrones* [African Women, Women Slaves, and Maroons]. Caracas, Venezuela: Edit. Fundación Afroamerica.

García, Jesús. 2001. *Descontrucción, transformación y construcción de nuevos escenarios de las prácticas de la Afroamericanidad* [Deconstruction, Transformation and Construction of New Scenarios of the Practices of Afro-Americanism]. Caracas, Venezuela: Clasco-UNESCO.

Garcia, Jesús. 2002. *Comunidades Afroamericanas y transformaciones sociales* [Afro-American Communities and Social Transformations]. Caracas, Venezuela: Clasco-UNESCO.

Garcia, Jesús. 2004. *Aprendamos de la historia y la cultura afrovenezolana.* [Let's Learn About Afro-Venezuelan History and Culture.] *Cartilla para niños.* Caracas, Venezuela: Red Afrovenezolana.

Humboldt, Alejandro. 1956. *Viaje a las regiones equinocciales del nuevo continente* [Trip to the Equatorial Regions of the New Continent]. Caracas, Venezuela: Ministerio de Educación.

Ley 70 de la Comunidades Negras [Law 70 of the Black Communities]. 1993. Congreso de Colombia.

Mosquera, Joaquín. 1825. *Memoria de la reforma a la ley de manumisión* [Memory of the Reform of the Law of Manumission]. Caracas, Venezuela: Congreso de la República.

Rondon Márquez, R.A. 1954. *La Esclavitud en Venezuela.* [Slavery in Venezuela]. Caracas, Venezuela.

Uslar Pietro, Arturo. 1948. "*Los negros mandando*" [The Blacks Ruling]. *Periódico El Nacional.*

Uslar Pietro, Arturo. 1937. "Venezuela Necesita inmigración" ["Venezuela Needs Immigration"]. *Boletín de la Cámara de comercio de Caracas.*

Veracruz

In African Diaspora history, Veracruz is significant because of its international impact and the large concentration of African-descent peoples in the region who contributed their culture and labor to its development. Only a few areas in Mexico have such large concentrations of Afro-Mexicans.

The region was once home to ancient Olmec Indians. Considered the earliest civilization, evidence of their presence remains scattered throughout the state of Veracruz in the form of gigantic carved stone heads with distinct African features. Direct links appear to exist between the Olmec and the Manding of West Africa. The heads, weighing tons, are considered one of the wonders of the world.

Veracuz is one of 31 Mexican states. It covers approximately 45,000 square miles and extends 425 miles along the Gulf. It is a major international location for commerce and trade of sugar cane, coffee, fruits, and tobacco. It is also a significant tourist destination. The population has large concentrations of Afro-Mexicans (African-Spanish genetic mixtures, also known as Creoles), mestizos (Spanish-Indian genetic mixtures), and Indians. Several cities and towns clearly reflect the African influence, for example, Mandinga, a derivative of the West African Mandingo. Its ethnic diversity resulted in the creation of a vibrant, unique and colorful culture.

Veracruz and Yanga are two key cities. Veracruz was the site of the first Spanish expedition in 1519 led by Hernan Cortes. Villa Rica de la Vera Cruz was Mexico's first "European" city. The oldest and grandest port in Mexico and business establishments dating to the 1800s are located there. Veracruz was occupied by Spain, France, and in 1914, the United States. Each time the troops were quartered in the Plaza de Armas.

Yanga is believed to be the first free African town in the Americas. Gaspar Yanga (sometimes spelled Nyanga) was an enslaved African fighting to free the enslaved. He led uprisings against the Spanish and is considered a regional hero. A village of free Africans was founded sometime between 1624 and 1635 as San Lorenzo de Los Negros. The name was changed to Yanga in 1932. The African heritage of the majority population is proudly articulated, manifested in the population's phenotypic characteristics, the city's politics, and its cultural history.

The synthesis of African cultural movements and rhythms with Spanish cultural styles has created unique regional traditional music and dance. The regional dance, *zapateado*, consists of rapid footwork and rhythmic flowing movements. During the 1870s, Cuban refugees fleeing war-torn Cuba brought a dance style known as *danzon*. Popular among the poorer Jarochos (people of Veracruz), it was considered scandalously sensual by the elite. Eventually, however, it became popular throughout the region. An Afro-Veracruz contribution is the well-known song *La Bamba*, popularized worldwide in the 1950s by Ritchie Valens; it derives from the musical style known as *son*, which is a part of traditional culture in Veracruz.

Valerie Smith

See also Maroon and Marronage; Mexico: African Heritage; Yanga and *Cimarronaje* in Mexico.

FURTHER READING

Bennett, Herman L. 2005. *Africans in Colonial Mexico: Absolutism, Christianity, and Afro-Creole Consciousness, 1570–1640.* Blacks in the Diaspora. Bloomington: Indiana University Press.

Hernandez Cuevas, Marco Polo. 2004. *African Mexicans and the Discourse on Modern Nation.* Lanham, MD.: University Press of America.

Restall, Matthew. 2005. *Beyond Black and Red: African-Native Relations in Colonial Latin America.* Albuquerque: University of New Mexico Press.

Vieux-Chauvet, Marie (1916–1973)

Marie Vieux-Chauvet was born in Haiti; her mother originated from Saint Croix (Virgin Islands) and her Haitian father was deeply involved in politics. She married very young to a physician and bore him two children. She started her career as a writer with the tale "*Ti sò la chouette*" (Ti Sò the Owl) and a pantomime *La Légende des fleurs* (The Flowers' Legend, staged in 1946). She divorced and married a Haitian businessman, Pierre Chauvet, and bore him a son. She published her first novel, *Fille d'Haïti* (*Daughter of Haiti* 1955), under the name of Marie Chauvet. This novel earned her a literary award, the France-Haiti Prize. She followed with *La Danse sur le volcan* (1957) and *Fonds des nègres* (1961). Her masterpiece, *Amour, Colère, Folie* (*Love, Anger and Death*), was published in 1968 during the worst years of the François Duvalier dictatorship. The manuscript was accepted for publication by the famous French publishing house, Gallimard. However, the Chauvet family, afraid of potential reprisal by Duvalier, bought all the copies except for the few that had already been sold. They arranged for Chauvet's departure from Haiti and her subsequent divorce. While in exile, Marie Vieux remarried, to an American citizen;

she later died in New York in 1973 from brain hemorrhage caused by a tumor. In 1986, her novel *Les Rapaces* was published posthumously in Port-au-Prince, Haiti, under her maiden name, Marie Vieux. More recently, her second novel, *La danse sur le volcan* (*Dancing on the Volcano*, 1957) has been reprinted in France under the name of Marie Vieux-Chauvet.

Marie-José N'Zengou-Tayo

See also Feminism and Black Women in the African Diaspora; Fanon, Frantz (1925–1961); Haiti; Négritude.

FURTHER READING

Chancy, Myriam. 1997. *Framing Silence: Revolutionary Works by Haitian Women.* New Brunswick, NJ: Rutgers University Press.

Dayan, Joan. 1995. *Haiti, History and the Gods.* Berkeley: University of California Press.

Shelton, Marie-Denise. 1992. "Haitian Women's Fiction." *Callaloo* 15 (3): 770–777.

Virgin Islands

The Virgin Islands (VI), formerly the Danish West Indies (DWI), comprises Saint Thomas, Saint John, Saint Croix, and dozens of adjacent islets. The islands are located in the northeastern Caribbean about 991 miles southeast of Miami, Florida. The islands, once inhabited by Ciboneys, Arawaks, Tainos, and Caribs, were encountered by Christopher Columbus in 1493. Subsequently, after the displacement of the indigenous inhabitants, the Spanish, Dutch, British, French, and Knights of Malta held sway over one or more of the islands in the 16th and 17th centuries. However, other than a British occupation in 1801–1802 and 1807–1815, Denmark was the only European nation to permanently colonize Saint Thomas in 1672, Saint John in 1717, and Saint Croix in 1733 Consequently, a cosmopolitan group of Europeans and mainly Africans would come to dominate the islands' population. Among the Europeans, the Dutch came to dominate the population on Saint Thomas and Saint John while the British would do likewise on Saint Croix. There were also some Danes, French, Germans, Jews, Spaniards, and other Europeans in the islands.

By 1680, people of African descent dominated the population of the Virgin Islands, and unlike many of the Europeans, they would make the islands their home. Among the Africans, there are reports of Congolese, Igbo, Ijaw (Kalabari), Mandingo (Mandingspeaking), Yoruba, and Akan peoples in the DWI. Indeed, sizable numbers of Africans came from the area of the Danes' most intense trading activities on the Gold Coast (present-day Ghana). From the late 1600s to the early 1800s, an estimated 75,000 Africans from West and West Central Africa were forcefully brought to the islands.

In the colonial DWI a political and socio-economic hierarchical system emerged in which the European minorities dominated the slave society. In the political sphere, Denmark, through the charted Danish West India Company (1671–1754) and later under crown rule, controlled the islands with governing officials at varying levels of subordination. Mainly the Danes, a minority among the other European population, controlled the government, serving as civil servants, soldiers, and clergy in all three islands. Aside from 1755 to 1874 when Christiansted, Saint Croix served as the capital, Charlotte Amalie, Saint Thomas was always the seat of the government. In Saint Thomas and Saint John, although sugar cane and cotton were cultivated, the important port of Charlotte Amalie was a principal entrepôt in the West Indies during the 18th and 19th centuries. The Dutch and British were prominent among the elite class of Europeans and were employed as merchants and plantation owners. As in Saint Croix, a small number of freed persons were in the middle to lower status of the society. They labored mainly as craftspeople, tradespeople, and farmers with some made to perform duties in the local freedmen militia. However, for most of the slave era in Saint Thomas, the majority of African descendents were in the lowest rank of the society serving as slaves on plantations and the harbor.

Alternatively, Saint Croix's main economic activity focused on sugar and cotton production. There was a similar hierarchical system in Saint Croix: the British were the most prominent, freed persons were in the middle to lower status, and the largest enslaved population of the three islands was forced into the lowest status. In fact, in 1789, enslaved persons exceeded 88 percent of the population of the DWI. In 1803, the year Denmark became one of the first European powers to end the slave trade, the enslaved African population peaked at about 35,000.

Even with harsh Danish slave laws and punishment, people of African descent resisted enslavement in various forms. Throughout the slave era, petite and grand (maritime) maroonage—activities ranging from temporarily running away into the woods to sailing as far away as North America—was one of the most used forms of resistance. In the 1700s, there are reports of at least one maroon community in Saint Thomas and another one referred to as Maroonberg in Saint Croix. Indeed, in 1789, there are accounts of more than 1,000 enslaved Africans being at large. Earlier, in November 1733, Akans, who were known for their utmost discontent with enslavement, primarily through the Akwamu people of the Gold Coast (under the leadership of Nyamma), revolted and for several months controlled Saint John; they intended to establish an Akan state in the island and two of the other surrounding islands. It took support of troops from Saint Thomas, British, and French islands for the Danes to regain control. Subsequent conspiracies and plots to revolt were reported in 1746,

1759, and 1801. However, it was not until 1848, with island-wide revolts of enslaved Africans led by Moses Gotlieb and others of Saint Croix, that enslaved persons were able to force the Danish authority to abolish slavery.

In the emancipation and postemancipation period, there were slight societal structural changes in DWI. In the new era, a complex color and class stratification very much influenced the political and socioeconomic structure of the colony. In the mid-19th century, a small group of people of French descent from Saint Barthelemy migrated to Saint Thomas and became mainly fishermen and farmers. The individuals of mixed ancestries were basically in the middle and lower echelon of the society. However, through the 1849 Labor Act, ex-enslaved persons were forced to continue to labor on the various estates. However, in 1878, an island-wide labor uprising in Saint Croix, led by Mary Thomas and others (with women well represented in the leadership), helped workers gain greater power to negotiate labor contracts individually. While dealing with natural disasters, including earthquakes, hurricanes, cholera epidemics, and malaria outbreaks, in addition to a declining economy, Virgin Islander workers formed labor unions, and continued to press for improved working conditions well into the 20th century.

In 1917, the United States purchased the DWI, bringing the territory into a new era with changes in the political, economic, and social institutions of the islands. Fundamental services of the islands, including education, health care, and housing, received attention in the early years of American tutelage. After years of delayed political rights, Virgin Islanders were granted American citizenship in 1927. In the 1930s, the Danish-style colonial structure was reorganized more along the lines of a U.S. form of government with greater separation of the executive, judicial, and legislative branches and an expanded franchise. In the 1930s and 1940s, in coordination with the U.S. federal government, Virgin Islanders made some effort to improve the rum production, handicrafts, deep-sea fishing, tourism, and other industries of the failing economy of the islands. Additionally, during the World War II period, there were greater commercial and trade activities, which temporarily produced an upsurge in the economy. In the 1950s, 1960s, and 1970s, there was further development of self-government, and islanders gained the right to elect the governor. In the 1960s and 1970s, although the sugar industry was phased out, various industries developed, and some of the largest businesses in the Caribbean were established, including Hess Oil Refinery and Harvey Aluminum Company. Additionally, there was tremendous growth in the tourism industry, and large numbers of Americans and other Caribbeans migrated to the territory in a continuous stream into the 1990s. With this economic growth, the USVI had one of the highest per capita incomes in the Caribbean, but it was accompanied by some social tensions among groups in the islands.

The modern USVI society, with historical precedence, has a relatively diverse population. The 110,000 residents are scattered throughout the three major islands. The sizable numbers of minority groups could be described as people of European descent (mainly Americans with some local-born Jews and people of French descent who have a small African-descent admixture), Hispanics (mainly local-born Puerto Ricans/Afro-Puerto Ricans and immigrant Dominicans), and people of Asian descent (mainly relatively recent East Indian and Arab immigrants). However, the largest group in the USVI is Afro-Virgin Islanders (about 48 percent) and various Afro-Caribbean migrants (about 27 percent) (U.S. Department of Commerce 1999, 17).

Politically, there are a number of minorities in the government but Afro-Virgin Islanders are found throughout the islands' political structure. The government is modeled after the U.S. governmental system and has separation of the executive branch, a unicameral 15-person leg-islative, judicial branches, and a nonvoting representative to Congress. The status of the Virgin Islands is colonial, an organized but unincorporated territory of the United States.

In the economy, many business owners of European, American, and Asian descent are prominent in the economic sector. However, the economy is saturated with people of African descent in the lower and middle income brackets, though a few have risen into upper middle to upper echelons of the economy. The USVI economy is mainly centered on tourism, manufacturing (including petroleum refining and watch assembly), and business and financial services (U.S. Department of Commerce 1999, 5, 6).

Most Virgin Islanders, although having adapted and shared many European and American cultural practices, have strong connections to the wider African Diaspora (especially with the large numbers of Afro-Caribbean immigrants in the island). Most islanders are of African origin, and African retentions are evident in the culture. In the islands, the English Creole (and the now defunct Dutch Creole) language is influenced by certain African grammatical-syntactical and tone features with a small vocabulary of regularly used African-derived words such as *dun dun* (Yoruba origins), *kunu-munu* (Twi origins), *kallalloo* (Fon origins), and *mumu* (Igbo origins). Additionally, the proverbs and aphorisms of Akan are also evident in Virgin Islander sayings. There are kinship-based societal organization and traditional community arrangements of homes, which are clustered together with the use of traditional utilities (such as the mortar and pestle and the yabba pot) for dietary meals (funji/cornmeal, kallalloo, tamarinds, and yams) and herbal remedies (bead vine bush/*Abrus precatorius*).

Additionally, the traditional social activities influenced by Africans are seen in historic and contemporary dances (bamboula, quelbe, masquerades, and mocko jumbi), songs (caruso), instrument usages (drums and banjo), storytelling (Anansi stories), and game playing (Warri). Indeed, many of these cultural expressions are noticeable throughout the year but some have also been institutionalized in the annual carnivals in Saint Thomas, Saint John, and Saint Croix.

Besides the aforementioned African retentions that Virgin Islanders shared with other African diasporic societies and peoples, Virgin Islanders historically have had among the most intimate interactions with other African diasporic peoples. From its inception to the present day, other Afro-Caribbeans have been migrating in a constant stream to the USVI. And in the earlier years of the transfer, African Americans, and many of their leaders (along with their organizations), had taken an active part in the affairs of these islands: three African Americans served as governor of the islands in the 1940s and 1950s. Moreover, Virgin Islanders have migrated to other places where notable individuals such as Edward Wilmot Blyden (Pan-Africanist leader), Frank Crosswaith (labor leader), Hubbert Harrison (activist), Roy Innis (Congress of Racial Equality leader), and Ashley Totten (of the Brotherhood of Sleeping Car Porters) were influential or organized people of African descent.

Mario Nisbett

See also Blyden, Edward Wilmot (1832–1912); Danish West Indies: Oldendorp's 18th-century Findings; Maroon and Marronage.

FURTHER READING

Creque, Darwin D. 1996. *The U.S. Virgin Islands and the Eastern Caribbean.* Philadelphia: Whitmore Publishing Co.

Dookhan, Isaac. 2000. *History of the Virgin Islands.* Mona, Jamaica: University Press of the West Indies.

Kea, Ray A. 1996. "'When I Die, I Shall Return to My Own Land': An 'Amina' Slave Rebellion in the Danish West Indies, 1733–1734." In *The Cloth of Many Colored Silks: Papers on History and Society, Ghanaian and Islamic in Honor of Ivor Wilks*, ed. John Hunwick and Nancy Lawler, 159–191. Evanston, IL: Northwestern University Press.

Pope, Polly. 1972. "A Maroon Settlement on St. Croix." *Negro History Bulletin* 35 (7): 153–154.

Tyson, George R., and Arnold R. Highfield, eds. 1994. *The Kamina Folk: Slavery and Slave Life in the Danish West Indies.* US Virgin Islands: Virgin Islands Humanities Council.

U.S. Census Bureau. 2003. *2000 Census of Population and Housing, Social, Economic, and Housing Characteristics PHC-4-VI, U.S. Virgin Islands.* Washington, DC: U.S. Census Bureau.

U.S. Department of Commerce. 1999. *Virgin Islands: 1997 Economic Census of Outlying Areas.* Washington, DC: U.S. Department of Commerce.

Warner-Lewis, Maureen. 2003. *Central Africa in the Caribbean: Transcending Time, Transforming Cultures.* Kingston, Jamaica: University of West Indies Press.

Westergaard, Waldemar. 1917. *The Danish West Indies under Company Rule (1671–1754).* New York: The Macmillan Company.

Vodoun

TRUE FACE AND THEOLOGICAL IDENTITY

Belief in supernatural beings constitutes the very essence of all religions. Christianity, for example, has its God, its Christ, its saints, its angels, and its demons. No less than any other religion, Haitian Vodoun has its own credo and pantheon of supernatural beings, *zanj, espri, lwa,* and so on, with their iconographic representations or *vèvè.* It has its rites, its liturgy, its priests or *houngan,* its priestesses or *manbo,* its initiates, its temples or *houmfò,* its ceremonies, and its festive days, the whole paraphernalia one could expect from any religion.

Contrary to the view that Haitian Vodoun is a polytheist religion, the fact is that Haitian Vodoun is a monotheist religion. Highest in its pantheon is a unique and supreme God, the *Bondye* or *Gran Mèt.* The latter delegates some of his powers to the *lwa,* the forces of good, who act in his name and with his permission. Like all religions, Vodoun prescribes the worship and

In a Haitian Vodoun celebration in Miami in 2008, Ingrid Llera leads three other *mambos* (priestesses) in salutations to divinities (*loa* or *lwa*), demonstrating how Vodou has made a second migration, this time with the Haitian Diaspora. (Stefano Giovannini/Stefpix.com)

veneration of the *Gran Mèt* and the other supernatural beings from which adherents expect " . . . remedy for ills, satisfaction for needs, and the hope of survival" (Métraux 1958, 11).

As in the case of Lucifer and other evil spirits, some Vodoun *lwa* betrayed the trust of the *Gran Mèt* and became venal spirits and evildoers: they are called *lwa dyab, movezespri, move lwa*. They represent the forces of evil and are served by bad *houngan* called *bòkò*. These are experts in sacrilegious ceremonies aimed at satisfying the lower instincts of followers who come to take their advice.

From antiquity to modern times people have always expressed their faith in the existence of supernatural beings endowed with the power to affect their lives. Some call it religion; others, superstition; still others label it magic. The choice of the educated must be clear: tolerance and respect.

CONTEMPORARY STRUCTURE

Temples: Houmfò and Sosyete Houmfò

Although Vodoun has somewhat managed to formalize some of its concepts, it is far from reaching the level of organic systemization to be found in most modern religions. Each *houmfò* or Vodoun temple is dedicated to the *lwa* venerated by its faithful and forms an autonomous entity placed under the authority of its own *houngan* and *manbo*, priests and priestesses, also known respectively by the name of *papa lwa* and *manman lwa*. Besides their association to a specific *houmfò*, the adherents also form a kind of confraternity or *sosyete houmfò*. The latter may include several sanctuaries and is headed by a president chosen among the most prestigious and influential members. *Houngan* and *manbo* are attended by a hierarchical personnel composed of *hounsi kanzo* and *hounsi*, or initiates of rank,

konfyans, or apprentice-houngan,

hougenikon, or choir leaders,

laplas, or masters of ceremonies,

ogantye, *boulatye*, and *triyangliye*, or musicians,

rènsilans, or sergeants-at-arms,

bagikan, or servitors of the bagi,

kodrapo, or flag bearers,

bosal, or novices,

pèsavann, former sextons or defrocked sacristans who know by heart the prayers and psalms of the Catholic Church in Latin or French. Though not officially members of the Vodou clergy, they play the Catholic priest's role in rituals that are not within the competence of the *houngan* or *manbo*.

Entrance onto the grounds of the *houmfò* is gained through the *pòtay*, a physical or symbolic gate guarded by *Legba*, master of the homes and the roads. With respect to its appearance, the *houmfò* is an ordinary house not unlike other residences in the neighborhood. As a rule it should have at least two, preferably three, rooms built in a row. It may happen however that the financial situation of the *houngan* or the *sosyete* does not allow for more than one room for the sanctuary.

The room that opens onto the façade of the *houmfò* is called *bagi*. It houses the *pe* or altar. The *pe* is a concrete or stonework platform, varying in size with the dimension of the *bagi* and having lateral openings that are used to place offerings. There can be several *pe* inside one *bagi*, depending on the importance of the *houmfò* and the adherents' financial means. The second room, at the other end of the *houmfò*, is called *sobagi* and is used for storing the sacred objects associated with the *lwa*. The third room, the one in the middle, functions as a corridor of communication between the other two and may serve as *djevò* or initiation chamber at the right moment.

The surface of the *pe* must be large enough to accommodate the numerous ritual objects that are to be placed on top of it. Among them:

- several *govi*, ritual jars consecrated to the *lwa* served by the *houngan* or the *manbo*; they are wrapped in silk or velvet, in the *lwa*'s favorite color;
- an indefinite number of *pòt tèt*, white pottery ritual cups consecrated to the *hounsi-kanzo* of the *houmfò*;
- a Haitian national flag, Vodoun standards, flowers;
- a crucifix and a perpetual lamp like those found in Catholic churches.

In front of the *pe* or sometimes on the *pe* itself, is a small basin, the basin of *Danbala*, the *lwa* of lakes and rivers. In *houmfò* where aquatic *lwa* are honored, it is sometimes big enough for a person to bathe in. Also in front of the *pe*, and fixed to the ground, are metallic supports or *asen* used to carry ritual objects.

Inside the *bagi*, one can find liquor, rum, wine bottles, and other offerings that adherents or visitors brought the *lwa*. Also kept inside the *bagi* are sacred clothes and ornaments, such as the hat of *Bawon Samdi*, *lwa* of the dead; the crutch of *Legba*, master of the roads; the hat of *Zaka*, *lwa* of agriculture, and so on. These items are to be worn by the devotees in a trance.

The interior walls of the *houmfò* are painted white and decorated with *vèvè*, iconographic emblems for the *lwa*, especially those venerated in the *houmfò*. For example, the boat represents *Agwetawoyo*, master of the seas; the heart, *Ezili*, *lwa* of love; the snakes, *Danbala* and *Ayida*, *lwa* of lakes and rivers, and so on. There will also be pictures of Catholic saints such as Saint James the Greater, Saint Peter, and Our Lady of Perpetual Help, representing, respectively, *Ogou*, *Legba*, and *Ezili*. The *non vanyan* or mystic name of the *houngan* or *manbo* in charge of the *houmfò* is also inscribed on the wall, not far from the Haitian national flag, the coat of arms of the republic, the picture of Haiti's president, and other patriotic or governmental motifs. The exterior walls are likewise decorated with religious and national designs.

On the plot of land adjoining the façade of the *houmfò* that opens into the *bagi* lies the *peristil*, an open rectangular shed varying in dimension with the importance of the temple and the size of its congregation. Big temples can have several *peristil*, respectively consecrated to different rites and *lwa*, but there will always be a main one. In the middle of the *peristil* stands the *potomitan*, a pillar decorated with multicolored stripes, at the bottom of which are placed the sacred objects of the *lwa* invoked during ceremonies and offerings. The base of the *potomitan* is a circular concrete or stonework structure that is in fact the *pe* of the *peristil*. The *potomitan* represents the "mystic passageway" of the *lwa*, the road they will take to come down and become incarnated in their devotees at the moment of what is called "theomorphosis," *lwa*'s embodiment or Vodoun religious trance (Férère 1989, 42). Prayers, invocations, ritual dances, and sacrificial offerings to the *lwa* take place around the *potomitan*. The *potomitan* can be considered the most important location in the Vodoun temple.

If the *houngan*'s or *manbo*'s means allow for it, the courtyard of the *houmfò* may include small huts with their small *pe* consecrated to *lwa* of lesser rank. Also in the courtyard stand tall trees, called *repozwa*, under which adherents go to pray. In the vicinity of some *houmfò*, one can sometimes see a structure resembling a tombstone surmounted by a cross and carrying offerings: it is the altar of the *Gede* or spirits of the dead. Finally, on the property of the *houmfò*, there will always be domestic animals and fowl of all kinds—goats, pigs, bulls, turkeys, pigeons—waiting for the day when, after being offered in sacrifice, they will be served as food to the congregation and guests attending the ceremony.

Vodoun ritual sacrifice may well be the most misunderstood and misrepresented aspect of the Haitian religion. Yet it is in perfect harmony with the accepted tradition that existed in many religions, including Judaism and Christianity, and consisted of offering an animal to the gods in order to obtain their favor and appease their anger. At no time in history has Vodoun ever prescribed human sacrifices as some authors, like Spencer St. John and Houston Craig, have sensationalistically and improperly claimed. Some *lwa* prefer sacrifices without blood: offerings such as vegetables, fruit, rum, and various delicacies.

THE PANTHEON OF THE *LWA*

Rites

As a whole, the various Haitian Vodoun liturgies have been classified under several rites, according to their ceremonials and modus operandi. The most popular are the *Rada* rite and the *Petro* rite, followed by other less important rites, such as the *Kongo, Nago, Dantò, Zanda, Kanga, Boumba*, and *Kita* rites. Some rites identified by the names of *fanmi* (family) or *nachon* (nation) evoke their African origins: Ibo, Siniga, Bandara, Awousa, Mondong, Ginen, and so on.

Each rite has its own ceremonials, invocations, chants, rhythms, and instruments. For example, during services of the *Rada* rite—the most elaborate of all—three drums or groups of three drums are used; the biggest one is called *manman penba*. For *Petro* services, drums are paired up: the big one is called *gwo baka*, and the small one, *ti baka*. The two rites also differ in terms of their divinities' characteristics and attributions. *Lwa* themselves are not necessarily different, although they are in some cases. *Lwa Rada* are assumed to be kind and benevolent whereas *Lwa Petro* are harsh and demanding. The latter are mostly invoked for material gains or the satisfaction of personal ambitions. Some of them sometimes require formidable commitments. For example, *Bakoulo Baka* has the reputation of being so ferocious that Vodou adherents will not even dare to utter his name, let alone invoke him.

Besides the rites, it is fitting to mention the ceremonies consecrated to the *Gede* family, *lwa* of cemeteries and spirits of the dead, which must not however be confused with the souls of the dead. They take on great significance in Vodoun theology but do not belong to any particular rite, unless one wants to recognize a *Gede* rite. However, their leader, *Gede Nibo*, is considered a *lwa Rada*. *Gede* have a reputation for vulgarity, immorality, and depravity. They use deception to break into services offered to other *lwa*, in order to eat, drink, play tricks, and say dirty words, and they are chased away by the congregation for misbehaving.

Nomenclature

A complete inventory of Vodoun *lwa* is difficult to establish because of, for example, their ever-rising number, owing to the fact that devotees regularly create new gods through the beatification of the spirits of deceased initiates. The word "*lwa*" is the one most commonly used, but other words, such as *mistè, sen, zanj*, and *espri* also identify Vodoun divinities. Experts have time and again attempted the individual classification of *lwa* under the headings of rites, family, or nation. Such a classification has some advantage, especially for minor divinities, if tracing their African roots is needed. As for major *lwa*, they are found in almost every rite under the same or slightly modified names. For example, for *Ezili Freda Dahome*, goddess of love in the *Rada* rite, there is a corresponding *Ezili Je Wouj Petro*, who is jealous and ready to bring down her rivals. Therefore, it is understood that, at any time, the most significant divinities may in turn belong to the rite in which adherents choose to serve them.

Each divinity has specific attributes and powers. Here are a few examples:

- *Legba*, the most powerful and important of all the deities, is the intermediary between the *Gran Mèt* and the other *lwa*. He opens the mystic passageway to the *mistè*, *espri*, *zanj*, *sen*, and *lwa* who want to appear. He holds the keys to the *pòtay*, the *potomitan*, and all the roads and homes. All services must begin with a salute to him. Vodoun iconography sometimes portrays him as a crippled old man shuffling down the road with the help of crutches or a stick. However, beware of this deceptive appearance: *Legba* possesses extraordinary strength and agility, which he infuses into the devotees he incarnates.
- *Agwetawoyo* or *Agwe*, the Neptune of Haitian Vodoun, is the *lwa* of the ocean and patron of sailors.
- *Ogou Balendjo* is a warrior sea spirit and the captain of *Agwetawoyo*'s boat.
- *Agawou*, spirit of storms, is a member of the same crew. He shares his powers with *Badè*, spirit of the winds, and *Sogbo*, *lwa* of thunder.
- The couple *Ayida* and *Danbala Wedo* are the *lwa* of the rainbow, the rivers, lakes, and springs.
- *Loko Atiso*, *lwa* of medicinal plants, shares his powers with his cousin *Zaka*, the minister of agriculture, as Vodounists call him, who makes plants grow.
- *Ogou Feray*, the blacksmith, is the *lwa* of war and fire.
- *Ezili*, the Venus of Haitian Vodoun, is the beautiful coquette, the sensual *lwa* of love. She demands that her devotees marry her—which is what is meant by *maryaj Ezili*—live with her, and sleep with her in a special bedroom, twice a week, on Thursdays and Tuesdays.

The following list gives an idea of the magnitude of the Pantheon of the *lwa* (Métraux 1958; Rigaud 1953; Benjamin 1976):

Achade Boko, Achade Bosou, Adelayid, Aganman, Agasou, Agawou Tonnè, Agawou Wedo, Agwetawoyo, Amisi Wedo, Anwezo, Atibon Legba, Avadra Bon Wa, Awoyo, Ayizan, Azagon, Azaka Mede, Badè, Bayakou, Belvenis Bosou Twakòn, Boko Legba, Brize Makaya, Brize Penba, Dam Tenayiz, Danbala Flanbo,

Danbala Gran Chimen, Danbala Wedo, Danbala Yawe, Djobolo Bosou, Ezili Boumba, Ezili Dantò, Ezili Freda, Ezili Je Wouj, Ezili Mapyang, Ezili Towo, Grann Alouba, Grann Ayizan, Grann Brijit, Grann Ezili, Grann Simba, Grann Sogbo, Ibo Kikilibo, Ibo Kosi, Ibo Lazil, Ibo Lele, Ibo Petro, Kanga, Klemezin Klèmèy, Labalèn, Lasirèn, Legba Atibon, Legba Ayizan, Legba Evyeso, Lenglensou, Loko Atiso, Makanda, Marasa/Dosou/Dosa, Marinèt Bwachech, Mèt Kafou, Ogou Achade, Ogou Badagri, Ogou Balindjo, Ogou Batala, Ogou Chango, Ogou Donpèd, Ogou Tonnè, Silibo, Sofi Badè, Sogbo, Ti Jan Petro, Ti pyè Dantò, Towo Petro, Twa Simbi, Twafèy Twarasin, Zaka, Zazi Boutonnen, Zenglen Zen.

From the *Gede* family:

Bawon Lakwa, Bawon Sanmdi, Bawon Simityè, Gede Doktè Piki, Gede Fatra, Gede Loray, Gede Mòpyon, Gede Nibo, Gede Pisenandlo, Gede Senk Jou Malere, Gede Soufrans, Gede Tikaka, Gede Tipete, Gede Trase Tonm, Gede Zarenyen, Jeneral Fouye, Kaptenn Zonbi.

ICONOGRAPHY

Because of its syncretic nature, Haitian Vodoun has developed a dual iconography in which one detects simultaneously the European influence and the presence of the African substratum. The representation of a great number of divinities can be found both in the form of pictures of Catholic saints and drawings called *vèvè*.

Vèvè

Vèvè are symbolic drawings that the celebrant, acting as both priest and artist, draws around the *potomitan* at the beginning of ceremonies, while addressing the *lwa* they represent with ritual words. They play an extremely important role during Vodoun ceremonies because they identify the *lwa* being invoked and expected to come down by way of the *potomitan*. Depending on the rites and divinities, the drawing is made with wheat or corn flour, ground coffee, charcoal ashes, or even gunpowder for war divinities and some *lwa Petro*. If many spirits are invoked, several *vèvè* may be linked together around the *potomitan* and cover a large portion of the *peristil* area to form what is called a *milokan*. In addition to being located on the altar of the *peristil*, offerings (animals, food, and beverages) that are intended for the *lwa* are also placed on the *vèvè*. Vodoun adherents believe in the power of the *vèvè* to attract the divinities.

Many authors have researched the history and evolution of the *vèvè* and generally seem to agree on their cosmopolitan origin, though with some divergences. Alfred Métraux emphasizes their Afro-European features (1958, 148). Louis Maximilien goes back to pre-Columbian America while adding the influence of Western magic (1945, 42). Although René Benjamin (1976) does not altogether dismiss Maximilien's pre-Columbian theory, he disagrees with the hypothesis that magical motifs replaced American Indian ones. On the whole he grants vital significance to the symbolism of the *vèvè*.

Pictures

The Vodoun-Catholic symbiosis has been highly misunderstood and has given rise to many controversies, vexations, and calumnies. Although Vodounists see no harm in including Christian beliefs into their African heritage, Christian clergy and their overzealous flocks have demonstrated the most uncompromising sectarianism. Speaking of the syncretism at issue, one can observe, for instance, the devoted practice of the Catholic religion by Vodoun adherents and the parallelism that exists between the dates of the Christian festive calendar and Vodoun celebrations: the Catholic All Saints' Day and the service of *Gede* on November 2nd; Vodoun Christmas, when ritual baths of purification take place to obtain the protection of the *lwa*; the celebrations of Holy Week, and so on. But the most conspicuous feature of the Catholic influence is the assimilation of a great number of *lwa* to the pictures of Catholic saints. Several lists illustrating those correspondences have already been published. However, it is important to acquaint the uninitiated reader with their real religious significance to avoid taking them literally. So what are the origins and meaning of this practice?

The use of Catholic pictures to represent *lwa* is derived from a subterfuge slaves resorted to when, faced with the strict prohibition to practice their own religions, they started pretending to worship Catholic saints, while in reality they served their *lwa*. A Catholic picture, adopted to represent a Vodoun divinity, is not an object of veneration because of the Christian virtues of the saint, but rather because of his or her name or an iconographic detail in the picture. That is how, for example, the chromo of Saint Joseph holding lilies in his hands corresponds to *Loko Atiso*, *lwa* of medicinal plants, and Saint Peter corresponds to *lwa Pyè Dantò* and *Pyè Danbala*. The same type of analogy determined that Saint Patrick and the Immaculate Conception, with serpents at their feet, be associated with the *lwa* couple, *Danbala Wedo* and *Ayida Wedo*, the serpent gods. The same picture sometimes corresponds to several *lwa* as can be observed in the following list (Métraux 1958; Benjamin 1976):

Achade Ogou: Saint James the Greater
Agwetaroyo/Agwe: Saint Ulrick
Ayida Lakansyèl: Our Lady of Mount Carmel
Ayida Wedo: Immaculate Conception, Our Lady of Grace
Ayizan: Saint Lucy
Bawon Sanmdi: Saint Gerard Majella
Bosou Twa Kòn: Saint Vincent de Paul
Danbala Lakansyèl: Saint Moses
Danbala Wedo: Saint Patrick
Ezili: Mater Salvatoris, Our Lady of Perpetual Help
Grann Alouba: Mater Dolorosa
Grann Batala: Saint Anne
Grann Brijit: Saint Brigid

Grann Ezili: Mater Dolorosa
Gede Nibo: Saint Gerard Majella
Jan Batis Trase Tonm: Saint John the Baptist
Kaptenn Zonbi: Saint Francis of Assisi
Klemezin Klèmèy: Saint Clare
La Sirèn: Caridad del Cobre
Legba Atibon: Saint Anthony of Padua
Legba Mèt Potay: Saint Peter
Legba Mèt Kafou: Saint Lazarus
Legba Nago: Saint James the Greater
Lenglensou: Saint Michael
Loko Atiso: Saint Joseph
Marasa: Saints Cosmas and Damian
Ogou Badagri: Saint James the Greater
Ogou Balindjo: Saint James the Greater
Ogou Batala: Saint Philip
Ogou Feray: Saint George
Ogou Chango: Saint George
Pyè Danbala : Saint Peter
Pyè Dantò: Saint Peter
Silvani Mede: Our Lady of Ransom
Simbi Twa Kafou: The Three Kings
Simbi Yandezo: The Three Kings
Simbi Bwa: The Three Kings
Simbi Dlo: Saint Raphael
Ti Jan Dantò: Saint John the Evangelist
Zaka: Saint Isidore

CONCLUSION

In 1953, in *La Tradition Voudou*, Milo Rigaud underscored Vodoun's ability to "forever survive." Around the same time, Alfred Métraux, in *Vaudou haïtien*, stated the opposite: "it will have to disappear." Today, half a century later, it still survives and keeps on providing a considerable service for the mental health of Haitians. In the face of their daily trials, Vodoun worship offers them a source of hope, an illusion maybe, the feeling they have some control over their spiritual and physical environment, thanks to the *lwa*.

Gérard Alphonse Férère
Translated by Pascale Bécel

See also Candomblé; Haiti; Petwo; Rada; Santería.

FURTHER READING

Beauvoir, Max. 1988. Interview with Camille Lownds Benedict. *Voodoo in the 20th Century.* Fama II Productions.

Benjamin, René S. 1976. *Introspection dans l'inconnu.* New York: French Printing Publishing Company.

Davis, Wade. 1985. *The Serpent and the Rainbow.* New York: Simon and Schuster.

Davis, Wade. 1988. *The Ethnobiology of the Haitian Zombi.* Chapel Hill: University of North Carolina Press.

Desmangles, Leslie. 1992. *The Faces of the Gods: Vodou and Catholicism in Haiti.* Chapel Hill: University of North Carolina Press.

Erickson, Carolly. 1976. *The Medieval Vision.* Oxford, UK: Oxford University Press.

Férère, Gérard A. 1976. "Haitian Voodoo: Its True Face." *Caribbean Quarterly* (September–December).

Férère, Gérard A. 1979. *What Is Haitian Voodoo?* Philadelphia: Saint Joseph's University Press.

Férère, Gérard A. 1989. *Le Vodouisme Haïtien / Haitian Vodouism.* Edition bilingue. Philadelphia: Saint Joseph's University Press.

Férère, Nancy T. 2005. *Vèvè: L'Art rituel du Vodou haïtien / Ritual Art of Haitian Vodou / Arte ritual del Vodou haitiano.* Boca Raton, FL: Educavisions.

Laguerre, Michel. 1989. *Voodoo and Politics in Haïti.* New York: Saint Martin Press.

Laroche, M. 1976. "The Myth of Zombi." In *Exile and Tradition.* Halifax, Canada: Longman and Dalhousie University Press.

Maximilien, Louis. 1945. *Le Vodou haïtien.* Port-au-Prince, Haiti: Imprimerie de l'Etat.

Métraux, Alfred. 1958. *Le Vaudou haïtien.* Paris: Gallimard.

Rigaud, Milo. 1953. *La Tradition voudou et le voudou haïtien.* Paris: Niclaus.

Roumain, Jacques. 1942. *A Propos de la campagne anti-superstitieuse.* Port-au-Prince, Haiti: Imprimerie de l'Etat.

Roumain, Jacques. 1943. *Le Sacrifice du tambour assotor.* Port-au-Prince, Haiti: Publications du Bureau d'Ethnologie.

Saint-Gérard, Yves. 1992. *Le Phénomène zombi: la présence en Haïti de sujets en état de non-être.* Toulouse, France: Editions Eres.

Wailer, Bunny (1947–)

Neville O'Riley Livingston—immortalized as Bunny Wailer of "Wailers" fame—was born in Jamaica, West Indies, on April 10, 1947. He is the last living member of the original vocal group once known as the Wailing Wailers, which included Peter Tosh and Bob Marley.

Wailer's relationship with Marley and Tosh stretched back to his childhood, when all three lived under the same roof in Trenchtown, a neighborhood in Kingston, Jamaica, in the late 1950s. His history with Marley goes back further than his history with Tosh, as the two lived in rural Nine Miles, St. Ann, before their families moved to Trenchtown. As teenagers Wailer, Marley, and Tosh spent countless evenings practicing their harmonies under the tutelage of the legendary Joe Higgs.

Wailer, considered by some in the reggae industry to be a recluse, has an etherealness about him that belies his undeniable presence both on and off stage. Still he remains one of the pivotal pillars of a Jamaican recording scene that distinguished itself with ska in the early 1960s, rocksteady in the late 1960s, and reggae in the 1970s.

Wailer, like many struggling black youth in Jamaica, became a target for police harassment and was arrested for marijuana possession in 1967. Despite the fact that the police found no marijuana on his person, he was convicted on officer testimony that he had stashed a bag in a nearby barrel. He ended up serving a year and two months in prison, an experience that undoubtedly inspired the captivating track "Battering Down Sentence" on his seminal (solo) album, *Blackheart Man* (1976), his first album after the Wailers parted ways.

With tracks like "Rastaman," "Reincarnated Souls," "Bide Up," "Fig-Tree," "Armagedeon," "Dreamland," "Battering Down Sentence" and the title track "Black Heart Man," the album is regarded by many as Wailer's masterpiece. His subsequent albums, *Protest* (1977), *Struggle* (1978), and *In I Father's House* (1979) continued in the same rootsy vein as *Black Heart Man*, with varying degrees of success until he made a distinct change in his approach to the reggae recording scene in the 1980s, when he started to incorporate various elements of the dancehall music style that had arrived on the scene. Wailer's master plan apparently was to promote involvement of Rastafari with all the various branches of reggae music that were emerging at that time.

In 1990, Wailer released his historic *Time Will Tell: A Tribute to Bob Marley*, for which he received his first Grammy award in 1991. The second album that he received a Grammy award for was *Crucial: Roots Classics* released on the Shanachie Label in 1994. This album essentially collected the "Roots" reggae singles released during the early 1980s along with tracks from the original Roots album *Struggle*. Wailer's third Grammy award was for *Hall of Fame: A Tribute to Bob Marley* (1995), making Wailer the recipient of the most reggae Grammy awards so far, save for Ziggy Marley, who has also received three Grammys.

A relatively recent album release from Wailer is *Communication* (2000). In it he expresses the view that the absence of communication has led to many of the world's current wars, conflicts, and state of tension (Barnett 2001).

Wailer, a soulful and spiritual Rastaman and an artist is still a major force in the reggae music industry. In early 2005, Wailer released a seven-CD box set entitled *The Wailers: The Legacy*, which not only recaps the early music of the Wailers but also includes a personal testimonial from Wailer on the trials and tribulations that he, Bob Marley, and Peter Tosh encountered on their way to worldwide fame.

Michael Barnett

See also Jamaica; Marley, Robert Nesta (Bob) (1945–1981); Rastafarianism; Reggae; Tosh, Peter (1944–1987).

FURTHER READING
Barnett, Michael. February 2001. Personal interview with Bunny Wailer. Miami, Florida.

Walcott, Derek Alton (1930–)

Born January 23, 1930, on the British-colonized Caribbean island of Saint Lucia, Derek Walcott's creative work draws strongly on his pluralistic background. Raised with the influences of both Caribbean and European society, Walcott's poetry and plays explore identity as it connects to culture, race, history, and myth. An artist who experienced firsthand the conflicting traditions and values of native, colonial, and postcolonial structures, Walcott works with literary and historical traditions to express hybrid identity.

Awarded the Nobel Prize for literature in 1992, Walcott has developed an oeuvre that questions the construction of the past and the effect of such constructions on the present. Walcott's use of language plays a large part in this examination, as when he includes Caribbean patois alongside colonial British English in his epic work *Omeros* (1990), a Homeric tale spanning nations and history in its quest to follow threads of human development across traditionally imposed borders of time, land, and culture. Although most widely known as a Caribbean author, Walcott's work incorporates the conventions of multiple cultures, emphasizing the connections between them.

Walcott's father died in 1931, and his mother, a teacher at a Methodist infant school, supplemented his colonial education. He graduated from St. Mary's College in Castries, Saint Lucia in 1947. He then proceeded in 1950 to the University College of the West Indies in Jamaica on scholarship. After his graduation in 1954, he taught in Saint Lucia and Grenada, and his writing career began to flourish. After winning a fellowship from the Rockefeller Foundation to study American theater in 1957, he returned to the Caribbean and began the Trinidad Theatre Workshop. His awards include a Guinness Award for Poetry, a Royal Society of Literature Award, the Queen's Medal for Poetry, the Cholmondeley Prize, and fellowships with the Eugene O'Neill and MacArthur foundations. In 1971, his play *Dream on Monkey Mountain* received an Obie for the best foreign off-Broadway production. He is an honorary member of the American Academy and Institute of Arts and Letters.

Walcott's poetry collections include *The Prodigal* (2004), *Tiepolo's Hound* (2000), *The*

Bounty (1997), *Omeros* (1990), *The Arkansas Testament* (1987), *Collected Poems: 1948–1984* (1986), *Midsummer* (1986), *The Fortunate Traveller* (1981), *The Star-Apple Kingdom* (1979), *Sea Grapes* (1976), *Another Life* (1973), *The Gulf* (1970), *The Castaway* (1965), and *In a Green Night* (1962).

His plays include *The Odyssey: A Stage Version* (1992), *The Isle Is Full of Noises* (1982), *Remembrance and Pantomime* (1980), *The Joker of Seville and O Babylon!* (1978), *Dream on Monkey Mountain and Other Plays* (1970), and *A Branch of the Blue Nile* (1969).

Amanda Conrad

See also Caribbean Migrations: The Caribbean Diaspora; Creole, Creolity, Creolization; Mulatta; Trinidad and Tobago.

FURTHER READING
Baugh, Edward. 2006. *Derek Walcott*. Cambridge Studies in African and Caribbean Literature 10. Cambridge, UK: Cambridge University Press.
Terada, Rei. 1992. *Derek Walcott's Poetry: American Mimicry*. Boston: Northeastern University Press.
Thieme, John. 1999. *Derek Walcott*. Contemporary World Writers. Manchester, UK: Manchester University Press.

Walker, Alice (1944–)

Alice Walker is a Pulitzer Prize–winning author of such texts as *The Color Purple* (1982), *The Temple of My Familiar* (1989), and *Possessing the Secret of Joy* (1992). In addition to her writing, Walker is also a noted activist and social critic credited with coining the term "womanism." Born February 9, 1944, in Eatonton, Georgia, to sharecropping parents, Walker has received numerous awards for her books and other publications. Walker is an author whose writing is heavily influenced by her own childhood experiences. As a young girl, Walker was shot in the eye with a BB gun causing scar tissue to envelop her eye. She suffered alienation as a result of her deformity before the scar tissue was finally removed. As a young woman Walker attended first Spelman College and then eventually received her bachelor's degree from Sarah Lawrence College in 1965. Upon graduation she worked in the New York Welfare Department before relocating to Mississippi with her husband. In Mississippi, Walker taught black studies at Jackson State University where she released her first book of poetry in 1968. It was also during her tenure at Jackson State that Walker participated in the Civil Rights Movement and helped with voter registration among African Americans. Her first novel, published in 1970, *The Third Life of Grange Copeland*, is said to be based on her experiences within the civil rights struggle in Mississippi.

In 1973, Walker, along with Charlotte D. Hunt, located the unmarked grave of Zora Neale Hurston. The two paid for a tombstone marker for the African American writer and folklorist, and through their efforts Hurston received much deserved attention from the literary world.

As an activist, Walker has not only participated in the Civil Rights struggle but has also spoken out against the U.S. embargo against Cuba in the 1980s. As a feminist scholar, she has challenged traditional definitions of feminism and has developed a framework she has termed "womanism." Within her text *In Search of Our Mothers' Gardens: Womanist Prose*, womanism is introduced to address the particular needs and demands of African American women. Womanism therefore combines the concepts of the Civil Rights Movement with Walker's own brand of black feminism to provide an alternative to African American feminists. Walker has also been an active campaigner against the practice of female circumcision, which appears both in *The Color Purple*, *Possessing the Secret of Joy*, and *Warrior Marks*, a non-fiction book and film she produced on the subject with Pratibha Parmar in 1993. Her concept of "womanism" echoes in the works of other writers across the African diaspora.

Walker has received numerous awards for her writings, including the Pulitzer Prize, the Rosenthal Award, and the Lyndhurst Prize. Despite these accolades and general critical acclaim, Walker has also been criticized for her negative depictions of African American men within her fiction. Additionally, she has received criticism for her books and ironically, her participation in the documentary project *Warrior Marks* was labeled by some African feminist scholars as an ethnocentric work that ignored African women's agency.

Walker, who now lives in California, continues to be a prolific writer and social activist despite these criticisms. In addition to those mentioned, her works include *Once* (1976), *Meridian* (1976), *The Same River Twice: Honoring the Difficult* (1996), *By the Light of My Father's Smile* (1998), *Absolute Truth in the Goodness of the Earth* (2003), and *We Are the Ones We Have Been Waiting For* (2006).

Tiffany Pogue

See also Feminism and Black Women in the African Diaspora.

FURTHER READING
Bloom, Harold, ed. 2002. *Alice Walker*. Broomall, PA: Chelsea House Publishers.
Hendrickson, Roberta M. 1999. "Remembering the Dream: Alice Walker, Meridian and the Civil Rights Movement." *MELUS* 24 (3): 111–128.
White, Evelyn C. 2004. *Alice Walker: A Life*. New York: W.W. Norton & Company.

Walker, David (1785–1830)

David Walker was the first prominent African American human rights activist. His views on armed resistance to oppression as well as African American self-help strategies remain influential to African American social discourse. In Wilmington, North Carolina, on September 28, 1785, he was born free under North Carolina law by virtue of having a free mother and slave father. He early learned to read and write, and he read extensively on the subjects of revolution and resistance to oppression. In 1826, Walker then moved to Boston, Massachusetts, where he became a writer for *Freedom's Journal*, the first African American newspaper, and a leader in the Massachusetts General Colored Association. His Prince Hall Mason membership and his used clothing store helped establish him as a community leader.

During 1828, Walker's speech to the Massachusetts General Colored Association called for African Americans to produce positive change by helping each other, while opposing the inaction of those that allowed racism to flourish. He added to this argument using four published abolitionist articles to make his pamphlet *Appeal to the Coloured Citizens of the World* (1829), thereby making it titularly an African Diaspora text. The *Appeal* articulates Christian philosophy and calls for African Americans to study and attack Thomas Jefferson's *Notes on the States of Virginia* (1785), particularly since Jefferson was himself an owner of slaves. In addition, he expresses the hope that the inhumane treatment of African Americans will end. His message to African Americans was that slavery was inhumane and armed revolt was justified in destroying this system.

In 1829, Walker worked tirelessly to have his pamphlet circulated nationally and internationally by mailing it and hiding it in the clothes he sold to sailors from his store. Copies of the *Appeal* were delivered to a minister in Savannah, Georgia, who informed the police of the *Appeal*. The police then informed the governor of Georgia. This led the Georgia state legislature to enact a law prohibiting the circulation of materials that could cause a slave rebellion and making the violation of this law a criminal offense. The legislature even offered a reward for Walker's capture, $10,000 alive and $1,000 dead.

Even abolitionists disagreed with Walker's message and strategies, including William Lloyd Garrison, who printed parts of the *Appeal* in addition to reviewing it in the *Liberator*. Many abolitionists did, however, support Walker's conclusion that chattel slavery must end immediately.

Walker was warned to settle in Canada, but he refused to leave Boston. On June 28, 1830, he died in Boston under mysterious circumstances leading many to believe foul play was involved. Walker's appeal for African Americans to become instruments of their own liberation has proved vital to their strategies for obtaining full citizenship and human rights.

Aaron Ogletree

See also African Americans and the Constitutional Order.

FURTHER READING

Aptheker, Herbert, ed. 1965. *One Continual Cry: David Walker's Appeal to the Colored Citizens of the World*. New York: Humanities Press.

Bennett, Lerone, Jr. 1968. *Pioneers in Protest*. Chicago: Johnson Publishing Company.

Hinks, Peter P. 1997. *To Awaken My Afflicted Brethren: David Walker and the Problem of Antebellum Slave Resistance*. University Park: Penn State University Press.

Hinks, Peter P. 2000. *David Walker's Appeal to the Coloured Citizens of the World*. U.

Walker, George William (1873–1911)

George William Walker (1873–1911) was a gifted dancer, comedian, and businessman and a leading figure in black musical theater. Born in Lawrence, Kansas, he began his career in entertainment performing in a medicine show. Around 1893, he traveled west to California, where he met Antiguan actor Bert Williams.

The two had a 16-year partnership, working together first in minstrelsy, and later in vaudeville and black musical theater. By the time of his death, Walker had become (with Williams) the first black recording artist, working with Victor Talking Machine Company beginning in 1901. He had also headed an all-black theatrical company, the Williams and Walker Company.

The performers' partnership began as "Walker and Williams," with Walker as the comedian of the duo. Years later, however, Williams one day playfully decided to perform in blackface, using burnt cork to cover his naturally fair skin. He was an overwhelming success; so much so that the two eventually changed their billing to Williams and Walker. Williams continued to perform in blackface, with hits like "Nobody," but Walker never used blackface makeup during his career.

In many ways, the offstage Walker reflected the character he played onstage. Onstage, Walker was a flamboyant, fashionable, citified "dandy." A dynamic person, he used the character type—which had originated as a stereotype in minstrelsy—to his advantage. Outspoken and active, he was "a race man," committed to supporting and defending blacks' rights. He publicly shared his vision to erect an "Ethiopian" theater created for and by Afro-Americans. He fought for—and won—the Williams and Walker Company's placement in first-class theaters, which was unprecedented. He also played a founding role in creating the Frogs, a black theatrical company based in Harlem, New York. In 1899, he married Aida Overton, a talented dancer and outspoken proponent of civil rights for blacks. Walker would play a significant role in the development of her career. Bert Williams died in March 1922, after collapsing while performing "Under a Bamboo Tree."

From 1898 to 1909, Walker and Williams starred in numerous original productions, creating their own company and employing black people as cast and crew. The shows, mounted in New York City, were *Senegambian Carnival* (1898), *A Lucky Coon* (1898), *The Policy Players* (1899), *Sons of Ham* (1900), *In Dahomey* (1902), *Abyssinia* (1906), and *Bandanna Land* (1907). *In Dahomey* brought them their greatest success, however; it had the distinction of being "the first book-length musical written and played by blacks to be performed at a major Broadway house" (Bordman 1978, 190).

While working on *Bandanna Land* years later, Walker fell ill; he was suffering from syphilis, which was at that time an incurable disease. He retired from the stage in 1909, and died on January 6, 1911. He was 38 years old.

Camille F. Forbes

See also Williams, Egbert Austin (1874–1922).

FURTHER READING
Bordman, Gerald. 1978. *American Musical Theatre: A Chronicle*. New York: Oxford University Press.
Charters, Ann. 1970. *Nobody: The Story of Bert Williams*. New York: Macmillan.
Phillips, Caryl. 2005. *Dancing in the Dark, a Novel about Bert Williams*. New York: Knopf.
Rowland, Mabel. 1923. *Bert Williams—Son of Laughter*. New York: English Crafters.
Smith, Eric Ledell. 1992. *Bert Williams: A Biography of the Pioneer Black Comedian*. Jefferson, NC: McFarland.

Walker, Sheila Suzanne (1944–)

Sheila S. Walker is an anthropologist who has done perhaps the most far-reaching African Diaspora connections in the contemporary period, aided by the fact that she has fluency in several languages where African diaspora communities reside. She is president of Afrodiaspora, Inc., a nonprofit organization that is developing video documentaries, a digital archive, and educational materials concerning the African Diaspora. She has been the director of the African Diaspora and the World Program at Spelman College in Atlanta, Georgia. Previously she was the William and Camille Cosby Endowed Professor in the Humanities and Social Sciences at Spelman, and director of the Center for African and African American Studies and Annabel Irion Worsham Centennial Professor of Anthropology at the University of Texas at Austin. She has also held faculty appointments at the University of California at Berkeley and the College of William & Mary and visiting professorships at Smith College, the Schomburg Research Center, and the City University of New York. Walker has also conducted extensive field research and participated in cultural activities throughout Africa and the African Diaspora in the Americas.

Walker's scholarly and popular publications include the edited volume *African Roots/American Cultures: Africa in the Creation of the Americas* (Lanham, MD: Rowman & Littlefield, 2001) and video companion documentary *Scattered Africa: Faces and Voices of the African Diaspora; The Religious Revolution in the Ivory Coast: The Prophet Harris and the Harris Church* (Chapel Hill: University of North Carolina Press, 1983); *African Christianity: Patterns of Religious Continuity*, coedited with George Bond and Walton Johnson (New York: Academic Press, 1979); and *Ceremonial Spirit Possession in Africa and Afro-America* (Leiden, Netherlands: E.J. Brill, 1972).

Walker's scholarship and fluency in Spanish, French, Portuguese, and Italian have informed her consultancies to governments, public history and culture initiatives, museums, archives, repositories, and development agencies. Her memberships in African Diaspora organizations include the steering committee of the Association for the Study of the Worldwide African Diaspora; the advisory council of the Association for the Study of African American Life and History; chairpersonship of the Education and Culture Expert Committee for the National Summit on Africa; a jury member at Festival Panafricain de Cinéma de Ouagadougou in Burkina Faso;

the African Burial Ground Project; the advisory committee for the African Voices Project at the National Museum of Natural History, Smithsonian Institution; the board of directors of the West Africa Research Association; and the advisory committee of the Constituency for Africa in Washington, D.C.

Walker organized a landmark 1996 conference, The African Diaspora and the Modern World, cosponsored by the University of Texas at Austin and the United Nations Educational, Scientific, and Cultural Organization (UNESCO). She also served as an international lecturer at the March 2000 Instituto Superior de Formación Afro, Organizaciones Mundo Afro in Montevideo, Uruguay. Walker has held membership on the UNESCO World Decade of Culture's International Scientific and Technical Committee, La Route de l'Esclave, since its 1994 inception.

Gloria Harper Dickinson

See also African American Women.

FURTHER READING

Rastafari.com. www.rastafari.com. Accessed February 24, 2008.

Walker, Sheila S. ed. 2001. *African Roots/American Cultures: Africa in the Creation of the Americas.* Lanham, MD: Rowman and Littlefield Publishers.

Ward, Frederick (1937–)

The now African-Canadian poet, novelist, screenwriter, playwright, artist, composer, actor, and teacher Frederick E. Ward was born in Kansas City, Missouri, in 1937. Ward was set before a keyboard at once by his tailor father and music-loving mother. As a youth, he studied art on a scholarship at the University of Kansas. Later, returning to music, he imbibed composition at the University of Missouri. This startling and unique genius fuses jazz rhythms, blues surrealism, and rap diction in impeccably musical texts.

Like a rolling stone—or a restless Beat—Ward went to Hollywood to write songs, then pursued jazz piano with Oscar Peterson in Toronto. In the mid-1960s, he traveled to Arizona, where he took up Black Mountain–styled poetry under the gaze of Robert Creeley. Ward's first book, *Poems*, appeared in 1964. His next was an edited anthology, *Six Baha'i Poets* (1966). This work signaled Ward's adherence to the Baha'i faith as well as to the kaleidoscopic, cosmopolitan vision of his brother Baha'i and "Aframerican," Robert Hayden (1913–1980). (Like Hayden, Ward assembles words "raced" by street talk and mama wisdom, Afrocentric "roots" plus rainbow multiculturalism.) After witnessing the Detroit riot of 1968, Ward exchanged its burning tenements for the Gothic and medieval architecture of Ville de Québec, spending two years in the walled city. Just as revolutionary fervor reached a boiling point in Quebec in 1970, Ward booked passage to Denmark to practice piano. However, a dockworker's strike stranded him in Halifax, Nova Scotia. Befriended by refugees from the Africadian (African-Nova Scotian) village of Africville, which Halifax had just bulldozed into rubble, Ward remained in the city throughout the 1970s and early 1980s, teaching and writing the bulk of his oeuvre.

Ward's first—and finest—novel, *Riverlisp*, appeared in 1974. It is a series of sketches of the inhabitants of an Africville-like community, semirural, yet located within a city. Multiple narrators offer fragmented, "musicalized" accounts of mixed-up quests for love and spiritual salvation. It most recalls the African-American fiction masterpiece *Cane* (1923) by Jean Toomer (1894–1967), but it is distinctly more Joycean in method and elliptical in structure. The next two novels, *Nobody Called Me Mine* (1977) and *A Room Full of Balloons* (1981), repeat the strategies of *Riverlisp* but are more African American in locale. Ward's second poetry collection, *The Curing Berry*

(1983), yields again his patented union of sound and sense, perhaps no better articulated than in "Blind Man's Blues," the narrative of an incestuous, dysfunctional love affair.

Since moving to Montreal in the 1980s, Ward has not published any further books. However, his role in the feature film he wrote, *Train of Dreams* (1987), won him Best Actor laurels at the Chicago International Film Festival. Moreover, plays, short stories, and poems—often new—continue to turn up in every significant gathering of African-Canadian literature, as well as those of queer Canadian writers.

George Elliott Clarke

See also Canada and the African Diaspora; Nova Scotia and the African American Diaspora.

FURTHER READING
Ward, Frederick. 1977. *Nobody Called Me Mine: Black Memories.* Plattsburgh: Tundra Books of Northern New York.

Warner-Vieyra, Myriam (1939–)

Myriam Warner-Vieyra is a Guadeloupean author whose novels are powerful renditions of the experiences and psychological traumas of French Antilleans in France and Africa, where they face oppression, isolation, rejection, and disillusionment. Their suffering and hopelessness lead them to the abyss of despair and to mental alienation. At times, Warner-Vieyra inserts incisive sociopolitical commentaries into her stories. In all of her texts, the writer mixes dreams, hallucinations, the Caribbean and African occult, and memory flashbacks within a realistic narrative frame. Her deceptively simple and rather unassuming style sustains haunting images of disenchantment, betrayal, disfiguration, castration, and suicide.

Warner-Vieyra's literary crisscrossing mirrors her biographical trajectory. Born in 1939 in Pointe-à-Pitre, Guadeloupe, at age 12 she joined her mother in France. In 1961, she married the Benin-born filmmaker Paulin Soumanou Vieyra, and they settled in Dakar, Senegal, where she worked for many years as a librarian and still resides. She travels occasionally to Guadeloupe and frequently to Paris, where her three children and four grandchildren live.

Warner-Vieyra's first work, *As the Sorcerer Said...*, narrates the story of Zétou, a talented teenager who leaves the island where she lives happily with her nurturing grandmother to go to France to be with her abusive mother. Zétou's forced abandonment of her sunny Caribbean matrix, the lack of schooling and contact with other adolescents, emotional isolation, and her mother's mistreatment and betrayal, eventually lead the young girl to a Paris psychiatric ward.

Much like Zétou, the eponymous protagonist of Warner-Vieyra's second novel, *Juletane*, is severed from Guadeloupe at age 10. With the death of both parents, Juletane is sent to live in Paris with her godmother, an unmarried middle-aged seamstress. After her godmother's death, she meets and marries Mamadou, an African student with whom she embarks for Africa when he receives his law degree. Aboard the ship bound for her husband's homeland, Juletane discovers that he is also married to an African woman. Immediately after learning of Mamadou's deceit, Juletane envisions her return to Paris, but she stays in Africa. Later, grieving over the miscarriage of a child, which leaves her sterile, and not adjusting to the polygamous situation, especially when the husband takes a third wife, Juletane grows mentally ill, kills the first wife's children, and ends up in an insane asylum, where she dies. Her story is conveyed to readers through her diary. Warner-Vieyra's most recent works include fictional writings in several publications and *Femmes échouées* (*Shipwrecked Women*), a collection of nine short stories set in the Caribbean and France, which have themes similar to those in her novels.

Françoise Pfaff

See also Guadeloupe; Négritude.

FURTHER READING

Fragd, Lulamae. 2002. "Reading Your Self Home: Myriam Warner-Vieyra's *Juletane*." *CLA Journal* 15 (4): 477–496.

Lionnet, Françoise. 1992. "Inscriptions of Exile: The Body's Knowledge and the Myth of Authenticity." *Callaloo* 15 (1): 30–40.

Lionnet, Françoise. 1993. "Geographies of Pain: Captive Bodies and Violent Acts in the Fictions of Myriam Warner-Vieyra, Gayl Jones, and Bessie Head." *Callaloo* 16 (1): 132–152.

Ngate, Jonathan. 1986. "Reading Warner-Vieyra's *Juletane*." *Callaloo* 29 (Autumn): 553–564.

Pfaff, Françoise. 1995. "Conversations with Myriam Warner-Vieyra." *CLA Journal* 39 (1): 26–48.

Warner-Vieyra, Myriam. 1980. *Le Quimboiseur l'avait dit . . ..* Paris: Présence Africaine. Published in English as *As the Sorcerer Said. . . ,* trans. Dorothy S. Blair. London: Longman Drumbeat, 1982.

Warner-Vieyra, Myriam. 1982. *Juletane.* Paris: Présence Africaine. Published in English as *Juletane,* trans. Betty Wilson. London: Heinemann, 1987.

Warner-Vieyra, Myriam. 1988. *Femmes échouées.* Paris: Présence Africaine.

Warner-Vieyra, Myriam. 2000. "La nièce de ma voisine-cousine." In *La nouvelle sénégalaise: Texte et contexte,* ed. James Gaasch, 217–26. Saint-Louis, Senegal: Editions Xamal.

Washington, Booker T. (1856–1915)

See Tuskegee Institute/Tuskegee University.

Water Mama/Mami Wata

"Mami Wata" (Mama Water) is the pidgin English term for a female nature spirit that is widely used along the Atlantic coast of West Africa and the Americas. Many indigenous cosmologies included nature spirits, which were believed to bring material wealth and protect fertility, as long as the required sacrifices were performed. Nature spirits were considered to be present in the rivers and creeks, locations that became important trading sites for the transatlantic slave trade and the palm oil trade. Aspects of the European trade shaped the Mami Wata beliefs; for example, the female figureheads carved on the prows of European trade ships were often perceived to be representations of water spirits.

In Calabar, an important slave port in the Cross River region of southeastern Nigeria, Mami Wata was the generic term used to refer to the indigenous *ndem* nature spirits of the Efik and Ibibio people. The landscape of the city is dominated by the Calabar River and the Qua River. In the local cosmology, the human world (*ererimbot*) was mirrored by an underwater world of spirits (*obio ndem*). Some people were believed to have existed in both worlds, as related in the popular Efik drama, *Asibong Edem.*

In the traditional religion of Calabar, the worship of *ndem* spirits was practiced by women who were initiated into the office of priestess. The *ndem* priestess could identify the presence of *ndem* spirits in people's lives and could specify the necessary sacrifices to make to the spirits. Certain foodstuffs and objects associated with fertility were considered appropriate sacrifices to be left at the shore, such as eggs and red and white cloth. *Ndem* spirits were believed to be capricious and demanding, capable of bringing about both good events, such as wealth and fertility, or bad events, such as madness caused by spirit possession or death by drowning. In Calabar, *ndem* were often represented as mermaid figures, light skinned, with long hair, and carrying a comb and mirror. Other *ndem* were considered to take the form of water snakes and precious jewels, which could sometimes appear as shimmering lights beneath the water.

Mami Wata appears throughout coastal West Africa by different names. Many narratives of sighting Mami Wata exist throughout the Caribbean as represented artistically in the work of the Carriacou artist (Canute Calliste) where she is a major figure in the folklore and oral literary tradition. Representations in Latin America merge her also with Yemaya, the Yoruba orisha of the sea. A number of Mami Wata Festivals are held annually in Africa and the Americas.

Phillipa Hall

See also Candomblé; Grenada; Osun (Oxum/Ochun/Oshun); Santería; Yemoja/Olokun in the Diaspora.

FURTHER READING
Boone, Sylvia Ardyn. 1990. *Radiance from the Waters: Ideals of Feminine Beauty in Mende Art.* New Haven: Yale University Press.
Caliste, Canute. 1989. *The Mermaid Wakes. Paintings of a Caribbean Isle.* (Text by Lora Berg and Margaret Deutsch.) London: Macmillan Education, Ltd.
Edyang, E. A. 1986. *Asibong Edem.* Calabar, Nigeria: Wusen Press.
Hackett, R. 1985. "From Ndem cults to Rosicrucians: A study of religious change, pluralism and interaction in the town of Calabar, southeastern Nigeria." PhD diss. University of Aberdeen.
Kalejaiye, Dipo. 2006. *Mammy-Water and Other Stories.* Frederick, MD.: Publish America.

Wells-Barnett, Ida B. (1862–1931)

Ida B. Wells-Barnett was a journalist, fiercely brave antilynching crusader, racial uplifter, suffragist, and orator. Founder and cofounder of numerous organizations for racial and gender equality, she made it her life's mission to travel internationally to garner support for her crusade against the lynching of black people.

Ida Bell Wells was born during the Civil War on July 16, 1862, in Holly Springs, Mississippi. Wells attended both Shaw and Fisk University, but the 16-year-old quickly returned to assume responsibility for raising and caring for her remaining siblings after her parents died. Wells secured a teaching position 6 miles away after lying about her age.

In 1884, Wells gained notoriety after refusing to give up her first-class train seat to make room for white passengers. She was forcefully tossed off the train by three white men. She sued the railroad and won, but later lost on appeal. This incident caused her to begin writing in a local Baptist church paper, the *Living Way,* reporting on local, statewide and national issues plaguing black people in a racially hostile climate. Her articles were so well received that other newspapers across the country began to print her column. In 1889, Wells bought a one-third interest in the paper *Free Speech* and served as editor as well. She also became secretary of the National Afro-American Press Association, the first woman to be so elected, and she spoke and wrote on lynching, discrimination, and women's right to vote. The vocal Wells was later terminated from her teaching post in 1891 because she criticized the Memphis Board of Education for the poor conditions of black schools. She resolved to work full time as a journalist.

In 1892, three of Wells's friends were lynched; they were businessmen who ran a new store that competed and took away business from another store owned by a white man. Wells began to print editorials against lynching and to research the subject. She urged all black people to leave Memphis and go west. Many heeded to her call, and Memphis businesses suffered. Wells found that most lynchings were not the result of a black man being accused of raping a white woman, as generally reported, and suggested that in one-third of lynching cases in which there was an accusation of rape, most of those incidents were rather relationships of mutuality and that it was rather white women who desired black men. An angry white mob ransacked and burned the office of her newspaper *The Free Speech,* threatening to lynch her on sight. Wells, who was fortunately out of town on engagements in Philadelphia and New York, learned of the incident and was advised not to return.

Wells began writing for a New York newspaper, the *New York Age,* and became part owner. In 1892, she published *Southern Horrors: Lynch Law in All Its Phases.* In 1895, she published *A Red Record,* a work on race lynching in America, and in 1900, *Mob and Rule in New Orleans.* Wells's publications on lynching, in which she recorded actual cases, names, and testimonials, educated America and Europe on the conspiracy against African Americans' lives. Wells traveled to Europe to continue her cause against lynching, meanwhile working with the suffragist movement fighting for equality for women as well as championing the racial cause. She also established the Anti-Lynching Committee in England in 1893.

In June 1895, Wells married Ferdinand Barnett, a respected Chicago lawyer, founder and editor of the *Conservator,* the first black newspaper in Chicago; she had two sons and two daughters with him. Wells did not permit her new life to prevent her activism and even traveled to suffragist and racial uplift meetings while nursing her children. In 1909, Wells became a founding member of the National Association for the Advancement of Colored People, from which she would later resign because it failed to take what it considered her militant stance against lynching. Wells was also an outspoken opponent of Booker T. Washington's racial politics. She was a member of the National American Women's Suffrage Association. A friend of Susan B. Anthony and Jane Addams, she fought alongside them for women's voting rights and to integrate the organization fully. Wells, who was discouraged from marching in the historic 1913 suffrage parade in Washington, D.C., for

fear of offending southern white women, defiantly joined in.

Wells was effectively active as a journalist, an orator, and an organizer of movements and organizations. She established the first black women's civic clubs in Chicago and Boston and was a founding member of the National Association of Colored Women's Clubs in 1896. In 1910, she formed the Negro Fellowship League, an organization that provided housing and transportation for black southerners relocating to the North. Wells founded the Alpha Club, the first black women's suffrage organization in 1913. With Jane Addams, she won the fight against the segregation of Chicago schools. Moreover, Wells served as a probation officer in Chicago from 1913 to 1917, the first black woman to do so. In 1930, although a Republican, she ran unsuccessfully for the state senate as an independent. In 1931, Ida B. Wells died at 69 years old, a celebrated representative of Chicago and the entire country.

Miriam C. Gyimah

See also Feminism and Black Women in the African Diaspora; Jim Crow; National Association for the Advancement of Colored People (NAACP); Till, Emmett (1941–1955).

FURTHER READING
Decosta-Willis, Miriam, ed. 1995. *The Memphis Diary of Ida B. Wells: An Intimate Portrait of the Activist as a Young Woman.* Boston: Beacon.
Duster, Alfreda M., ed. 1970. *Crusade for Justice: The Autobiography of Ida B. Wells.* Chicago: University of Chicago Press.
Giddings, Paula. 1984. *When and Where I Enter.* New York: William Morrow and Co.
Giddings, Paula. 2008. *Ida: A Sword Among Lions: Ida B. Wells and the Campaign Against Lynching.* New York: Harper Collins, Amistad Books.
McKissack, Patricia, and Fredrick McKissack. 1991. *Ida B. Wells-Barnett: A Voice Against Violence.* New York: Enslow Publishers.
Schechter, Patricia A. 2001. *Ida B. Wells-Barnett and American Reform, 1880–1930.* Gender and American Culture Series. Chapel Hill: University of North Carolina Press.
Shelf-Medearis, Angela. 1997. *Princess of the Press: The Story of Ida B. Wells-Barnett.* New York: Lodestar Books.

Sterling, Dorothy. 1988. *Black Foremothers: Three Lives*. New York: The Feminist Press.

West African Students Union (WASU)

The West African Students Union (WASU) was jointly founded in 1925 by Ladipo Solanke and Dr. Bankole Bright for the purpose of organizing African students in London. Solanke had reacted strongly to the representation of Africans as curios at the 1924 Wembley Exhibition and sought the assistance of Casely Hayford and other West Africans in challenging this racial representation without any appreciable success. As early as 1919, the Committee for the Welfare of Africans discussed purchasing a home to house West African students who were studying in London. At a reception held at the Lincolnshire Room, Westminister, on May 22, attended by such colonial luminaries as Sir Hugh Clifford, Lord Henry Cavendish-Bentinick (member of parliament), Sir Sydney Olivier (a Fabian, former govenor of Jamaica, and liberal defender of poor Jamaicans), Sir Victor Buxter, and others, the committee's purpose was to consult Africans about a memorial honoring Africans who had fought in World War I. They already had 2000 pounds in their possession. In 1929 WASU sent Solanke to Nigeria to solicit financial assistance and backing for its building, which would be run as a hostel. Solanke remained until 1932, consequently creating a number of WASU branches along the West African coast in Ghana, Nigeria, Sierra Leone, and Liberia. Casely Hayford became the first patron of WASU in 1927, followed by Prempeh I, the exiled king of the Asante (Ashanti) in 1931, and actor/activist Paul Robeson in 1935. On January 1, 1933, WASU moved into its rented premises in Camden Town, and later purchased its own property in 1938 in the same borough.

From its inception, Solanke saw WASU as a microcosm and precursor of a federated West African state, ultimately leading to a federated African state. This was radical thinking in 1925 and was translated practically in the orientation of WASU's policies; three of its objectives define its political vision: (a) to act as a bureau of information on African history, customs, law, and institutions; (b) to present to the world a true picture of African life and philosophy, thereby making a definitely African contribution toward the progress of civilization; and (c) to foster a spirit of national consciousness and racial pride among its members. These objectives are still as relevant as they were in the mid-1920s, and they provide the basis for African cultural and political organizations today.

In 1934, when the Colonial Office established a hostel known as Aggrey House to rival that of WASU's, many students abandoned WASU. Still, WASU had wide affiliations with groups and organizations of different political persuasions. This was characteristic of all African political organizations in London, whether controlled by West Africans or Caribbeans. The reason, ostensibly, was to circulate WASU's ideas and, more importantly, to solicit support for its decolonization objectives from as wide a spectrum as possible. These organizations included the National Union of Students, British Centre for Colonial Students, and the League of Coloured Peoples. WASU also had close ties with the Fabian Colonial Bureau, the Labour Party, and other left wing organizations.

Although WASU took several stances, its membership was not in agreement about expressing a hard political line. Solanke, the secretary-general, had an unwavering support for Britain over all the other European powers and characterized Britain's past misdeeds as blunders. Some felt that receiving a British education compensated them, despite Britain's violent colonial record. Despite WASU's persistent involvement with the causes and conditions of the African, it fell short of a holistic view of independence.

WASU's political development was empowered by the wide range of political activists who shared its platforms and events, including George Padmore, C. L. R. James, and Kwame Nkrumah. The unexpected invasion of Ethiopia by the Italian fascists under Mussolini was the most politicizing event in WASU's history, although Britain forestalled, along with the League of Nations, on taking a prompt response. Still, this never hindered WASU from proclaiming the leniency of the British colonial system, although expressing its own political agenda. WASU in the end maintained a bipartisan position in relation to Britain and Africa.

Amon Saba Saakana

See also Decolonization; Garvey, Marcus Mosiah (1887–1940); James, Cyril Lionel Robert (1901–1989); Nkrumah, Kwame (1909–1972); Padmore, George (1901–1959); Pan-Africanism.

FURTHER READING
Adi, Hakim. 1998. *West Africans in Britain, 1900–1960: Nationalism, Pan-Africanism and Communism.* London: Lawrence and Wishart.
Fryer, Peter. 1984. *Staying Power: The History of Black People in Britain.* London; Pluto Press.
Geiss, Immanuel. 1974. *The Pan-African Movement,* trans. Ann Keep. London: Methuen and Co.
Olusanya, G. O. 1982. *The West African Students Union and the Politics of Decolonisation, 1925–1958.* Ibadan, Nigeria: Daystar Press.

West India Regiments

West India Regiments were black troops the British army first enlisted in the 1790s. This was a conscious decision to use black troops to fulfill the growing demand for military forces in the Caribbean. The original plan was to recruit black men who had been born in the New World. This proved more difficult than expected as planters resisted this potential threat to their workforce. The government resorted to purchasing slaves from specially commissioned traders. After the slave trade was abolished in 1807, a major source of recruits was Africans rescued from slave ships.

Almost constant warfare between Britain and France from 1793 to 1815 greatly increased the need for troops. Eight black regiments were commissioned in 1795. More were added to incorporate the new Guiana territory in South America and black troops from captured French islands (Dominica, Guadeloupe, and Martinique).

By 1798 there were 12 black regiments of 10 battalions, each with 95 privates. Commissioned officers were all white but noncommissioned officers were often black. With the war's end in 1798, the battle focused on the legal status of these black troops. West Indian parliaments wanted to make them subject to local slave laws. In concession to this opposition, West India Regiments were to form only one third of troops in island garrisons.

Within the military, West India Regiment troops were granted pay and status equal to that of white soldiers of similar ranks, and West India Regiment soldiers were encouraged to believe they enjoyed higher status than the enslaved. In 1802, the Eighth Regiment mutinied in Dominica on rumors from local enslaved Africans that their regiment was to be disbanded and they were to be sold as slaves. Seven were executed, and the regiment was disbanded. Those not implicated in the mutiny were drafted into other West India Regiments, and the rest were redeployed in other military offices or with white regiments in the Caribbean.

The Mutiny Act, outlining terms of service in the British military, was amended in 1807 to state that all blacks in the King's service were free. By 1811, West India Regiments also had posts for teachers to help the many African recruits become literate in English.

West India Regiments were used more extensively inside and outside the Caribbean as white troops were deployed elsewhere. During the War of 1812, West India Regiments participated in the attack on New Orleans. This marked the first time these troops were engaged outside the Caribbean. They were also involved in West African campaigns from the 1830s to the 1880s. By 1815, Caribbean garrisons were defended mainly by West India Regiments, along with foreign white troops.

Individual regiments were periodically disbanded, and only two remained by 1888. In 1927, the entire regiment was disbanded, although it was revived in 1958 under the Federation of the West Indies, an amalgamation of several British colonies. The regiment was disbanded once again in 1962 when the federation disbanded.

Grace Turner

See also Bahamas: Liberated Africans; *Creole* Incident.

FURTHER READING

Buckley, Roger Norman. 1979. *Slaves in Red Coats: The British West India Regiments, 1795–1815.* New Haven, CT: Yale University Press.

Western Hemisphere African Diaspora Network (WHADN)

WHADN is the acronym for the Western Hemisphere African Diaspora Network, the brainchild of the Africa Union Western Hemisphere African Diaspora Forum organized by the Foundation for Democracy in Africa and the African Union, and held in Washington, D.C. between December 17 and 19, 2002. WHADN's mission is to encourage and facilitate the utilization of the collective talents and resources of the African Diaspora in the Americas and the Caribbean to advance the collective interests of Africans on the continent and throughout the Diaspora. This will be accomplished through joint projects by the WHADN and the African Union.

The first objective of WHADN is to encourage and facilitate the enduring cultural, social, and economic ties to Africa within the Western Hemisphere Diaspora communities; second, to develop and identify funding for capacity-building projects by Diaspora civil society organizations in the Western Hemisphere Diaspora and the African Union; and third, to work with the African Union to create mechanisms to represent the views, concerns, and interests of the African Diaspora within the African regional organization. WHADN works on the following programs: democracy, governance and rule of law; health and the environment; peace and security; education; trade and economic development; science, research, and technology; communication; and arts and culture. WHADN represents the following geographical locations: Latin America (including Mexico and Central America), the Caribbean, Brazil, the United States, and Canada.

The programs and activities within WHADN are specific to the needs of the people in the Diaspora and Africa. For example, the Education Working Group's vision is of an Africa that consistently provides quality education for all. Toward this goal, the Working Group's activities focus on providing human and material support for Africa's efforts in education for self-reliance and sustainable development on the continent and extending the efforts to the Diaspora. The Education Working Group achieves this through the following objectives: to increase literacy in African languages, develop curriculum, facilitate technology exchange and capacity building, expand education opportunities, and facilitate interuniversity collaboration and funding.

The Trade and Economic Development Committee proposed a framework for recommendations as prerequisites to effective and meaningful participation in African trade and development by Africans in the Western Hemisphere Diaspora. These recommendations included considering the Africa Diaspora as a business partner with the African Union; promoting the African Growth and Opportunity Act; developing capital markets, commodity markets, and commodity pricing; becoming involved in reparation and labor issues. The WHADN secretariat organizes the participation of its network members at national, regional, and international events and organizes delegations from the Diaspora to participate in the African Union Summit of Heads of State and Government to meet and discuss issues of interest with members of the African Diaspora.

Fred Oladeinde

See also African Union (AU).

FURTHER READING
The Foundation for Democracy in Africa Web site, www.democracy-africa.org.
Western Hemisphere African Diaspora Network Web site, www.whadn.org.

WHADN

See Western Hemisphere African Diaspora Network.

Wheatley, Phillis (ca. 1753–1784)

One of the most outstanding women of the African Diaspora in North America, Phillis Wheatley flourished in Boston, Massachusetts, where—within a brief life span of only 31 years—she established herself as a poet. Wheatley was born around 1753 in the Senegambia area of West Africa, of either the Fulani or Wolof nation. She was abducted at the age of seven by slave raiders and taken across the Atlantic in the slave ship *Phillis* (for which she was named). She seems to have been taken to the coast through the infamous Goree island in Senegal, a fact that has led some biographers to assume that she was of Senegalese origins. Surviving the Middle Passage, she ended up in Boston, Massachusetts, where on July 11, 1761, she was sold to Susannah Wheatley, the wife of a tailor. A woman of kindly disposition and perspicacity, Susannah Wheatley was quick to recognize this intelligent mind and creative genius. She began by personally teaching her reading and writing. And as she hoped, young Phillis proved herself a prodigy. Within two years, she was able to read the Bible and to begin studying Latin. By the age of 13, she was already writing poetry, including "On Being Brought from Africa to America."

Baptized on August 18, 1771, Wheatley was able to purchase her own freedom the following year. By the age of 20, she had composed enough poems to fill a volume, *Poems on Various Subjects, Religious and Moral*, which she published in London in September 1773. Before the publication of the poems, she visited England in the company of her former mistress to prepare her manuscript for the press. During this visit she made her debut as a literary celebrity. She charmed London's literary circles and high society with her wit, youth, circumstances, and achievements. She was visited by, among other celebrities, Granville Sharp, Thomas Gibbons, the Earl of Dartmouth, and Brook Watson. Voltaire, then living in England, described her in a 1774 letter to a friend as a writer of *"très-bon vers anglais"* (very good English verse). On returning to the United States, she visited Benjamin Franklin and was visited by General Washington, to whom she addressed one of her tributary poems.

After the death of Susannah Wheatley in 1774, Phillis Wheatley remained in Susannah's family home supporting herself with her poetry and by working as a seamstress. On April 1, 1776, she married a free black, John Peters, described as "jack-of-all-trades grocery keeper, dandy and advocate for black rights before Massachusetts courts" and moved with him to Wilmington, Massachusetts. Wheatley bore three children, all of whom died before her. She died in poverty on December 5, 1784, aged only 31.

Close reading of Wheatley's poetry reveals that beneath the apparently complacent exterior of her poetry lies strong subversive undertones informed by a strong commitment to black freedom and nostalgia for "Afric's fancy'd happy seat" or the "pleasing Gambia" from which she was snatched as a child.

Chukwuma Azuonye

FURTHER READING

Azuonye, Chukwuma, and Steven Serafin, eds. Forthcoming. *The Columbia Anthology of African Literature*. New York: Columbia University Press.

Busby, Margaret, ed. *Daughters of Africa: Poems by Black Women*. New York: Penguin.

Dathorne, O. R. 1974. *The Black Mind: A History of African Literature*. Minneapolis: University of Minnesota Press.

Gates, Henry Louis, et al., eds. 1997. *The Norton Anthology of African-American Literature*. New York: W. W. Norton and Company.

Gikandi, Simon, ed. 2003. *Encyclopedia of African Literature*. New York: Routledge.

Herdeck, Donald E. 1974. *African Authors: A Companion to Black African Writing, Volume 1: 1300–1973*. Washington, D.C.: Inscape Corporation.

Irele, F. Abiola, and Simon Gikandi, eds. 2004. *The Cambridge History of Africa and Caribbean Literature*. 2 vols. Cambridge, UK: Cambridge University Press.

Jahn, Hanheinz, Ulla Schild, and Almut Nordmann. 1972. *Who's Who in African Literature: Biographies, Works, Commentaries*. Tübingen, Germany: Horst Erdmann Verlag.

Killam, Douglas, and Ruth Rowe, eds. 2000. *The Companion to African Literatures*. Bloomington: Indiana University Press.

Merriam-Websters. *Webster's Dictionary of American Authors*. 1996. New York: Smithmark Publishers.

Williams, Chancellor (1898–1992)

Chancellor Williams was a university professor, and author-historian. Williams rose to prominence with his 1971 work, *The Destruction of Black Civilization: Great Issues of a Race from 4500 B.C. to 2000 A.D.*

Williams was born the youngest of five children in Bennettsville, South Carolina, on December 2, 1898. His father had been a slave, and his mother a cook, nurse, and evangelist. He received his undergraduate degree in education and a master of arts degree in history from Howard University. He studied in England, serving as a visiting research scholar at Oxford University and the University of London. When Williams began his field research in African history in Ghana (University College) in 1956, his primary focus was on African achievements and autonomous civilizations before Asian and European influences. His last study in 1964 was both ambitious and comprehensive, covering an amazing 26 countries and more than 100 language groups. Williams began to assert that African historians have a responsibility to perform independent research and investigations so that the history of African people could be told and understood from their perspective without the relying on the validation of white historians.

In *The Destruction of Black Civilization*, Williams sought to debunk many of the pervasive racial myths that littered historical accounts of Africa, African people, and their cultures and civilizations. He maintained that "by the start of the new millennium, African people would be suffering the same problems that African people of 4500 BCE suffered unless ... we take a step back and give a critical, crucial, and correct analysis of the problems that confront us"(xxi). In an effort to provide this corrective frame, Williams shifted the main focus from the history of Arabs and Europeans in Africa to the Africans themselves. In this way, Williams uncovered valuable paradigms for examining the political and social transitions that have occurred in African societies and how they differ from European modes of thinking, inquiry, and acquisition. He also focused on how the ideologies and value systems of the oppressors unconsciously become those of the oppressed. Not only did the book correctively describe these civilizations, but it also probed the conditions created by slavery, colonialism, and neocolonialism and delved into possible solutions for solving problems those forces created.

As Williams's health began to deteriorate in the 1970s, he enlisted the help of several contemporaries and mentees to help him complete his work. However, Williams remained an avid scholar and researcher who still lectured and wrote. Williams published more than 50 articles, professional books, and lectures, and the lesser-known *The Rebirth of African Civilization* (1961).

In addition to being a historian and professor, Williams was editor of a newsletter, *The New Challenge*, an economist, a high school teacher and principal, and president of a baking company. He died in 1992.

Jason Esters

See also Africa; "African" in African American History.

FURTHER READING
Williams, Chancellor. 1987. *The Destruction of Black Civilization: Great Issues of a Race from 4500 B.C. to 2000 A.D.* Chicago: Third World Press.

Williams, Egbert Austin (1874–1922)

Egbert "Bert" Austin Williams was a black comedian of Afro-Caribbean origin who captivated American audiences with his dynamic stage presence and skill. Williams moved to the United States at a young age and later became the leading comedian of his time, white or black. He was first known as the comic half of Williams and Walker and worked in vaudeville and musical theater with black American George William Walker. Their partnership lasted 16 years, ending when Walker retired from the stage in 1909. Williams continued to perform, and by the end of his life, he had headlined in major vaudeville venues; made more than 60 records for Columbia Records; integrated Broadway's famous *Ziegfeld Follies*; starred in a musical comedy with an otherwise all-white cast; and, upon his death, brought blacks and whites together for the first time at the once whites-only Grand Masonic Temple in New York City.

Williams and Walker met in about 1893 and began performing as Walker and Williams, with Walker as the comedian. Years later, Williams playfully decided to perform in blackface, using burnt cork to cover his naturally fair skin. Ironically, he discovered his gifts as a comic through that very means. The two changed their billing to Williams and Walker, and Williams continued to perform in blackface. Walker played a fashionable citified "dandy," whereas Williams played a dimwitted, slow-moving rural character. Although these character types had begun as stereotypes in minstrelsy, Williams and Walker revised them in their performances.

The two starred in several original productions in New York between 1898 and 1909: *Senegambian Carnival* (1898), *A Lucky Coon* (1898), *The Policy Players* (1899), *Sons of Ham* (1900), *In Dahomey* (1902), *Abyssinia* (1906), and *Bandanna Land* (1907). *In Dahomey* brought them their greatest success and had the distinction of being "the first book-length musical written and played by blacks to be performed at a major Broadway house" (Bordman 1978, 190).

After Walker's retirement, Williams starred in a final black musical theater production, *Mr.*

Lode of Koal. After its financial failure, he surprised both blacks and whites by taking a featured role in Florenz Ziegfeld's *Follies*; he was the first black performer in the annual revue, and he joined the cast amid controversy. He also intermittently headlined as a "single" (solo comedian) in vaudeville and continued recording for Columbia. Later, Williams appeared in film, performing his famous poker pantomime in *A Natural Born Gambler* and expanding one of his comic monologues for *Fish* (both in 1916).

A frustrated dramatic actor, Williams sought opportunities to play characters other than the one that had made him famous. He left Ziegfeld in 1919, hoping to fulfill his ambitions. His final production, *Under the Bamboo Tree*, a "play with music," was a starring role that incorporated both comical and dramatic elements, and he planned to take it to Broadway. While performing in Detroit on February 27, 1922, however, he fell gravely ill, and the show was canceled. On March 4, 1922, Williams died. He was 47 years old.

Camille F. Forbes

See also Walker, George William (1873–1911).

FURTHER READING
Bordman, Gerald. 1978. *American Musical Theatre: A Chronicle.* New York: Oxford University Press.
Charters, Ann. 1970. *Nobody: The Story of Bert Williams.* New York: Macmillan.
Phillips, Caryl. 2005. *Dancing in the Dark.* New York: Knopf.

Williams, Eric Eustace (1911–1981)

Eric Eustace Williams was born on September 25, 1911, in then British colonial Trinidad, the eldest of 12 children. His father was a minor postal clerk and his mother a homemaker. A brilliant student and athlete, Williams was educated in Trinidad, eventually winning the single Island scholarship offered annually in his field, which allowed him to attend England's Oxford University in 1932. In 1938, he received a doctorate of philosophy for his groundbreaking dissertation on British slavery in which he explored its connection to the development of capitalism and dismissed the notion that its abolition had been solely on humanitarian grounds.

In 1939, Williams was offered a faculty position teaching political science at Howard University in Washington, D.C. While there, in addition to writing numerous articles and three books, he published his revised doctoral thesis as *Capitalism and Slavery* (1944). He also accepted a consultancy position with the newly formed Caribbean Commission, which required extensive travel, research, and communication within the wider non-English-speaking Caribbean region. Williams eventually left Howard in 1948 to become head of the commission's research branch in Trinidad.

During this period, Williams's calls for independence and his insistence on self-determination for Caribbean peoples became the stuff of legend. Increasingly alienating his superiors on the commission, by 1955 his contract was effectively terminated. But the charismatic Williams had captured the public's attention and with a firm grasp of the social and political needs of the citizenry, hitherto not experienced in the country, in 1956 he founded Trinidad and Tobago's first modern political party—the People's National Movement (PNM)—which has been the country's leading party since independence. Fielding a slate of candidates throughout the entire country, based on a cohesive national program and on the premise that only a team of committed people held together by a common set of principles could hope to solve the intractable problems besetting it, that same year, the PNM garnered enough popular support to win the general election.

Williams served first as Chief Minister, then Premier of Trinidad and Tobago under Great Britain from 1956 until 1962 when he became the first Prime Minister of newly independent Trinidad and Tobago. He remained in that capacity until his death on March 29, 1981. Throughout his life, Williams never ceased to uphold the fundamental aspirations of the Caribbean nation he inherited, nor did he waver in his faith in its people.

Under Prime Minister Williams's leadership, Trinidad and Tobago prospered—creating disciplined internal government, attracting foreign investment, and developing diplomatic relations between the Caribbean and nations of the First and Third Worlds. Ever the historian, while prime minister, Williams took time to write several books including a much-needed history of the West Indies, *From Columbus to Castro: The History of the Caribbean, 1492–1969* (1970), and his autobiography, *Inward Hunger* (1969)—a record not only of his personal development but also that of an emerging contemporary nation.

In the 1970s, Williams faced down a Black Power uprising that was combined with an army mutiny and persistent industrial unrest. Popular will thwarted his desire to retire from public life in 1973, and in 1976, Prime Minister Williams again led his country through political change as it became a republic.

Throughout the last years of Williams's life, his government, boosted by oil revenues from the 1970s world energy crisis, in a bold and impudent move, took the opportunity, amid much opposition, to lay the very foundations that today make Trinidad and Tobago an economic force to contend with. Several energy-based industries were established, in every case with majority ownership by the government and people of Trinidad and Tobago. Education and training in preparation for the dawning era, as well as appropriate legislation and the development of human resources—always hallmarks of Williams's vision—became even more entrenched as he moved his country toward the "sustainable development" model that would, some 30 years later, become a buzzword of the 21st century. Indeed, there can be no doubt that Williams is largely responsible for leaving a country that, today, possesses one of the highest profiles in the energy-intensive industry—a profile that continues to bear fruit for future generations. With a population of some 1.3 million, Trinidad and Tobago is currently the world's leading exporter of methanol and nitrogenous fertilizers, the principal supplier of natural gas to the United States, and home to the largest liquefied natural gas facility in the Western Hemisphere.

With the genuine respect and affection that his name engenders, Eric Williams justly earned his moniker as "The Father of the Nation" of Trinidad and Tobago.

Christine Cohn
Kenneth Julien

See also Capitalism and Slavery; Trinidad and Tobago; University of Woodford Square.

FURTHER READING
Azeez, Malik A. 1989. "The Legacy of Eric Williams: A Selected Bibliography." *Current Bibliography on African Affairs* 21 (3): 267–273.
Cateau, Heather, and Selwyn H.H. Carrington, eds. 2000. *Capitalism and Slavery: Fifty Years Later: Eric E. Williams—A Reassessment of the Man and His Work*. New York: Peter Lang.
Cudjoe, Selwyn R., ed. 1993. *Eric E. Williams Speaks: Essays on Colonialism and Independence*. Calaloux: University of Massachusetts Press.
Palmer, Colin A. 2006. *Eric Williams and the Making of the Modern Caribbean*. Chapel Hill: University of North Carolina Press.
Solow, Barbara L., and Stanley L. Engerman, eds. 1987. *British Capitalism and Caribbean Slavery: The Legacy of Eric Williams*. New York: Cambridge University Press.

Williams, Henry Sylvester (1869–1911)

Founder of Pan-Africanism, Henry Sylvester Williams was the first person to organize a global movement of persons of African descent.

However, because of his premature death, his place as the progenitor of the movement was largely usurped by longer-lived and better-known contemporaries such as W. E. B. DuBois. Others were able to carry on, if not to finish, the work Williams left behind. Williams was an organizer of the historic 1900 conference in London that attracted delegates from around the Atlantic world and inspired a global consciousness on the part of those of African descent to unite on the basis of shared experience, heritage, and common opposition to European colonization and oppression. Pan-Africanism had a huge impact on 20th century struggles for black liberation and freedom—in Africa and elsewhere—as well as decolonization, the Civil Rights Movement, and the Black Power Movement in the United States.

Williams was born in 1869 at Arouca, Trinidad, in the then British West Indies. He was the eldest of five children born to Bishop and Elizabeth Williams, both of Barbadian descent. Bishop Williams was employed as a shipwright. Williams, a very bright student from a working-class family, attended the common schools and started off working life at age 17 as a teacher. At 18 Williams became head teacher and a founding member of the Trinidad Elementary Teachers Union.

Eager to make something of himself, Williams taught throughout Trinidad before leaving for the United States at the age of 22. Williams's first stop was New York in 1891. He probably worked as a porter for the Pullman Company and made the acquaintance of Sir Henri-Gustave Joly de Lotbinière, an influential French Canadian lawyer-politician. In 1893, Williams arrived in Halifax, Nova Scotia, Canada to study law at Dalhousie College. Williams was only the second black student to attend the university, which was a Presbyterian institution. Dalhousie's president, the Rev. John Forrest, was a strong advocate of educational opportunities for African descendants. However, by Williams's second year, he had abandoned his studies and left for London, having

experienced racism so intense that he was even assaulted by a fellow white student at the library.

In 1897, thanks to his patron Joly de Lotbinière, a member of the English Bar, Williams was admitted to Gray's Inn. There he satisfied the entrance requirements by passing a preliminary examination in Latin, English, and history. During this time Williams made his living giving lectures through the Church of England Temperance Union. He also had the opportunity to travel around Britain and acquaint himself with the black community. Williams became engaged to the secretary of the Temperance society, Miss Powell, a middle-class white woman four years his senior. They married in 1898, despite opposition from the bride's father, and eventually had five children. In 1900, Williams organized the first Pan-African Conference, a three-day gathering that took place on July 23, 24, and 25 and drew delegates from around the African Diaspora. The conference discussed a number of themes and topics relevant to persons of African descent, such as racism and colonialism. After the conference, Williams set about spreading the word. He embarked on lecture tours to set up branches of the Pan African Association in Jamaica, Trinidad, and the United States. In 1901, the Trinidad branch was launched. Unfortunately, the Pan African Association was short-lived, mainly because Williams was not able to devote his full time to organizational work.

In 1902, Williams returned to London to read for the bar at Gray's Inn. His call to the bar qualified him to practice in South Africa, where he stayed for two years. He was frequently called on by South Africans to speak out against white racism and prejudice. Williams was South Africa's first black lawyer. Williams left South Africa in 1905 and returned to London, where he intended to be the first person of African descent to seek and achieve elected political office. In 1906, he was elected to the Marylebone Borough Council. Despite not reaching Parliament, Williams led a gathering of black Britons there and became the first person of African descent to speak before the House of Commons. Over the next few years he defended Africans involved in the campaign against racism in South Africa. He also spent time in Liberia, Guinea, and Sierra Leone. In 1908, his health broken, Williams returned to his native Trinidad, where he tried to establish a law practice. In March 1911, he died of chronic nephritis. He left behind a widow and four children and one yet to be born.

Justin M. Johnston

See also DuBois, William Edward Burghardt (1868–1963); Pan-Africanism; Trinidad and Tobago.

FURTHER READING

Contee, Clarence G. 1973. *Henry Sylvester Williams and Origins of Organizational Pan-Africanism: 1897–1902.* Washington, D.C.: Howard University Press.

Green, Jeffrey. 1998. *Black Edwardians: Black People in Britain, 1901–1914.* London: Frank Cass.

Hooker, J. R. 1975. *Henry Sylvester Williams: Imperial Pan-Africanist.* London: Rex Collings.

Mathurin, Owen Charles. 1976. *Henry Sylvester Williams and the Origins of the Pan-African Movement, 1869–1911.* Westport, CT: Greenwood Press.

Sherwood, Marika. 2004. "Williams, Henry Sylvester." *Oxford Dictionary of National Biography.* Oxford and New York: Oxford University Press.

Wofford, Chloe A.

See Morrison, Toni (1931–)

Wolof

Wolof is the dominant ethnic group and language in Senegal. Historically, the Wolof people formed the core population of the Jolof Empire that covered most of the area of present-day Senegal by the mid-15th century. Wolof people were also an important minority in the Serer kingdoms of Sin and particularly Saloum. They are one of the groups represented in the African Diaspora.

The colonial capital of Saint Louis, the modern capital of Dakar, and the major railroad towns were all in Wolof-speaking areas. As a result, Wolof became spoken in numerous towns throughout Senegal and in other rural areas. Non-Wolof urban migrants tended to adopt the Wolof language and ethnicity within a generation or two. During the colonial period, groundnut was cultivated much more than traditional millet and sorghum in Wolof areas.

Wolof belongs to the northern branch of the West Atlantic subcategory of the Niger Congo language family. Wolof is the lingua franca of Senegal and one of six national languages in the country given official recognition by the government (together with Jola, Manding, Pulaar, Serer, and Soninke). Close to 90 percent of the population of Senegal understand Wolof. Significant populations of Wolof are also found in the Gambia, Mauritania, Ivory Coast, Mali, France, Italy, Spain, and the United States.

Wolof is also the trade language of the majority of non-Wolof people groups in Senegal. This means it is the language of choice when people of different ethnic groups meet, even in government offices and universities. Wolof has increasingly become the first language of many young people from non-Wolof groups in Senegal, especially in cities. Wolof is the official language in Gambia and is also widely spoken in Mauritania.

Wolof culture has had a definite though less chronicled effect on African Diaspora cultures. Historians such as Bridget Bereton have identified the Wolof as an active presence in the shaping of resistance to oppressive conditions, cuisine, and other cultural practices among African peoples in Trinidad.

With westernization or modernity, traditional social, hierarchical structures are being eroded. The major Wolof social distinctions are between urban elite versus rural peasants and other modern class structures introduced by the post-colonial state. The former dominate the government bureaucracy and all modern sectors of the economy, while peasants are the productive backbone of the groundnut basin. Wolof family structure tends to be less traditional in urban areas, and polygamy continues in law and practice. Islamic law is the norm in rural areas, interpreted by clerics in accordance with Wolof custom. Inheritance is generally patrilineal, although matrilineal inheritance was historically equally important for nobility.

Safietou Kane

See also Africa.

FURTHER READING

Colvin, Lucie Gallistel. 1981. *Historical Dictionary of Senegal*. London: The Scarecrow Press.

Diop, Cheikh Anta. 1960. *L'Afrique Noire Precoloniale*. Paris: Presence Africaine.

Diouf, Mamadou. 2001. *Histoire du Senegal*. Paris: Maisonneuve et Larose.

Women and Islam

The study of women and Islam must be linked, on the one hand, to the context of globalization in which we live, and on the other hand, to the topicality of women's situations with respect to the world's religions and, more specifically, the Muslim religion. Further with the spread of Islam in the African Diaspora, the place of women in Islam demands clarification. Many African Diaspora women in places like Trinidad and the United States have embraced Islam.

The Safiya Hussayni case (2001) in which a Nigerian woman was sentenced to be stoned to death for adultery garnered attention. Thanks to the mobilization of human rights organizations, women's associations, and the entire international community, this woman was acquitted and escaped a humiliating death. The question of human rights in Islam has become more crucial than ever before, particularly in the new Pax Americana period. What is Islamic law, and in particular, what are Koran and Sunna, which is law derived from Muhammad's practice?

Since the Iranian revolution in 1979 and the founding of the Iranian Republic, a view of Islam, characterized by oversimplified representations, has been clashing with fundamentalists' positions that are totally hermetic to any emancipative approach to women. World attention has been brought to Islamic women via the U.S. war in Afghanistan, the ongoing Iraq war, and the U.S. war on terrorism.

Given the issue of women and Islam, one can apprehend all the complexity of the politico-religious debate within which women constitute a very important stake. Issues related to Islam and modernity are not new or unique. At the end of the 19th century a reformist movement in Islam came to life in a few Arab countries, such as Egypt, in the aftermath of socioeconomic changes and contacts with European civilization. This movement allowed for the emergence of an elite: thinkers who attempted to adapt the teachings of Islam to the new exigencies of the times. They appealed to the Islam of origin, but questioned whether Islam as it was lived in the seventh century could solve the numerous current challenges facing Muslim societies in a world dominated by an ever more sophisticated technology. Though it is true that a Muslim country such as Pakistan has accepted many scientific challenges, the fact remains that the question of human rights has arisen with acuteness in many countries with a Muslim majority.

As the West has questioned the situation of women within Muslim societies, four points have been neglected:

1. The Koran gave women a legal status superior to the one enjoyed by other women in the world;

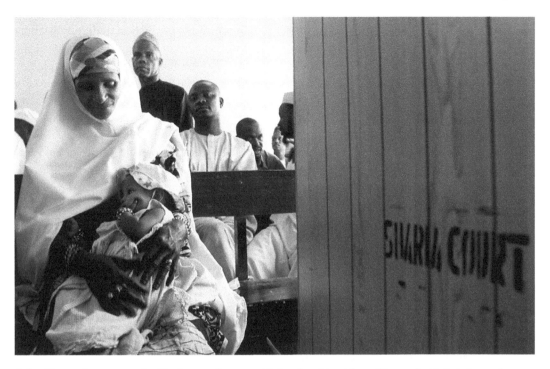

Safiya Hussayni appears at the Sharia appeals court with her daughter Adama Hussayni at Sokoto in northern Nigeria, on March 18, 2002. Hussayni was convicted of adultery in October, 2001, by an Islamic court, and sentenced to death by stoning. (AP Photo/Saurabh Das)

2. Women's fate has varied from country to country;

3. Until the middle of the 20th century the way of life for Muslim woman hardly differed from that of women in the rest of the Mediterranean Basin;

4. In the arduous struggle for emancipation, Muslims have targeted religion less than rigid social and mental structures.

From this neglect arise the following critical perspectives:

1. The political thought of Islam through the debate on democracy and secularism.

2. Islam facing liberalism and the question of individual rights, mainly women's place in Muslim society.

3. Finally, the demand for a new exegesis of religious texts: the updating of Ijtihad (the tools by which one approaches the Koran and Sunnah) or effort of personal

interpretation being able to bring about a "concession" with regard to individual liberties. Under these conditions, women's situation assumes a major stake.

In reality, the will of Muslim women to accede to freedom of expression and increasingly participate in working life opens the reflection onto their living conditions. Breakthroughs have been the development of feminism in Islam and the sudden emergence of Muslim women in the public space, but also the expression of religious needs with an approach, for example to Sufism, that is their own.

Feminist reflection attempts to dissociate in Islam what belongs to the sociological reality of scripture from its manipulation or tendentious interpretations. It is indeed the situation of confusion, which gives meaning to the feminist exegesis,

The wearing of the veil or hijab may be confirmed as a form of deviation between the "letter" of the law, which fundamentalists apply rigorously, and the "spirit" of the law, which does not turn it into a compulsory norm. The veil touches all religions as a sign of humility before God. Originally, the term "hijab" designated anything (cloth, screen, or tree) that prevents seeing, that is to say, marks the boundaries between public and private spaces. According to tradition, the Prophet had a revelation of the veil on the day of his wedding with beautiful Zainab on whom men cast lustful glances. His friend 'Umar, the future caliph, imposed it also on Medina's female residents, a city with a laxer morality than Mecca. The Koran, however, destines it for the Prophet's wives and the new female faithful to differentiate them from women who have not yet been converted.

Why did it become the norm? The Koran asks women "to bring down the veil over their bosom" (from the Arabic word *Jouyoub*, which may also be translated as low neckline) and goes no further. Different cultural interpretations of this have resulted in the white haik (white being a Sunni color) worn by North African women, the black chador worn by Iranian women, and the carapace (burka) that wraps up Afghan or Saudi women's bodies. Nevertheless, the Koran by no means arbitrates modalities of dress that are symbolic and cultural more than strictly religious, although the sanctification of (sexual) modesty is undeniable. For Islam the woman's whole body is *awra*—a word that can be translated as "thing left to be discovered," that is to say, what is hidden, and this refers as much to the (male and female) body's genitalia as to private life. This cardinal notion of *awra* justifies and sanctifies (sexual) modesty. It was codified very early. *Awra* and hijab mark the boundaries between public and private spaces, man and woman. This is a radical sexual separation, which is imposed, normalized, and so internalized by mentalities that it suffices to explain the repulsion Western women's exhibition of their nudity provokes in many Muslim women.

In contrast to the Biblical traditions that burden women with the weight of the original sin, Islam prescribes for her women an astonishingly modern respect as early as the seventh century: God belongs as much to women as to men. Two hundred verses are dedicated to women in the fourth Sura, precisely called "Women." Female faithful are destined for the same eternal Paradise as male faithful, and the same punishment if they are "hypocrites" or "idolaters." God's favorites are the mothers: "Paradise is under mothers' feet," one of the Prophet's famous hadiths says. But wives and children are all "blessings of this world," God's invaluable gifts. "Women are man's other half," a hadith relates; still another says, "The best among you is the best to his wife." Finally, what could be a more beautiful tribute than verse 21 in Sura "Ar-Rum," which states: "Among God's Signs is that He created for you mates from among yourselves, that you may dwell in tranquillity with them."

Repudiation is another much debated question. Particularly used to terminate a marriage, repeating it three times for repudiation to become final was a matter of allowing the man to reflect, go back on his decision, and reunite with his wife even if he uttered the formula three times. Repudiation has sometimes become an expedient method for an irascible husband to decide on his wife's dismissal. How many traditions have been distorted and have become discriminatory in that manner?

The question of women is most revealing of an Islam that attempts to reconcile "law and confession, citizen and believer, piety and good citizenship, public law and high religious principles." But there are parallels of this both in Christianity and Judaism. The law has often perverted the original inspiration and exacerbated the imbalance of the Koranic letter.

The will to modernize in Muslim societies as well as the centrality of women in any undertaking for development and human progress require control of the religious questions because they constitute the basis of collective psyches.

In conclusion, to avoid fixing the woman issue in an antagonism in which all the conservatives want to contain it, one must move beyond a feminist interpretation, which today seems to be delivering all its potential, often also caught in its own state, colonial or imperial agendas. However, Muslim women need new resources and allies for this arduous struggle where gains are constantly called in question, and there is good reason to keep fighting until exhaustion to pull off a small victory (for example in Senegal revising family law to change paternal authority into parental authority or in Mali drawing up of family law launched by the authorities). The exploration of the sphere of human rights in Islam is a way of renewing feminist theories in Islam and broadening the foundation of such a reflection.

Penda M'Bow
Translated by Pascale Becel

See also Feminism and Black Women in the African Diaspora; Nation of Islam (NOI).

FURTHER READING
An-Na'im, A. A. 1990. *Toward an Islamic Reformation: Civil Liberties, Human Rights, and International Law.* Syracuse, NY: Syracuse University Press.
Bessis, S., and S. Belhassen. 1992. *Femmes du Maghreb: l'enjeu.* Paris: Lattès.
Boudhiba, A. 1986. *La sexualité en Islam.* Paris: PUF.
Eposito, J., and J. O. Voll. 1996. *Islam and Democracy.* New York: Oxford University Press.
Ghassan, Ascha. 1987. *Du statut inférieur de la femme en Islam.* Paris: l'Harmattan.
Tabari. 1980. *Mohammed, sceau des prophètes.* Paris: Editions Sindbad.

Woods, David (1959–)

Born in Trinidad in 1959, David Woods is an atypical Africadian (African-Nova Scotian) *and* Afro-Trinidadian-Canadian writer and artist. He is distinct among Africadians because his offshore roots mark him as a "come-from-away" playwright and poet, one who settled in Dartmouth, Nova Scotia, with his family, in 1972, when he was 13. He stands out among other Afro-Trinidadian-Canadian writers—such as Claire Harris (1937–), M. Nourbese Philip (1947–), and Dionne Brand (1953–)—for choosing to highlight "indigenous" African-Canadian culture and history (with its strong African American idiom) as opposed to addressing the Anglophone-Caribbean Diaspora in the metropoles of Toronto, London, and New York.

Woods has found his media, his models, his muses, and his métier, all within Halifax, Nova Scotia's capital (where he studied briefly at Dalhousie University), and in nearby Preston—north and east—the site of Canada's largest all-black community, some several thousand people, whose roots date back to the 1783 black loyalist exile from the fledgling United States. From the early 1980s to the present, Woods has served Preston—and Africadia—as a community organizer and social worker. More importantly, he has chronicled and celebrated his people as a poet, playwright, actor, filmmaker, painter, impresario, and curator.

Woods has staged numerous original plays, but published none. He seldom publishes poetry in "little magazines." He works intensively within African Nova Scotia, caring little for what outsiders may think.

His major literary work is a collection of poetry, *Native Song* (1990), which also includes eight original paintings. Although the title nods to Richard Wright (1908–1960) and his famous novel, *Native Son* (1940), Woods's persona is closer to that of Jean Toomer (1894–1967) and the alienated, intellectual, male speakers of *Cane* (1923).

Much of *Native Song* communicates the same portentous *Weltschmerz*, the same preachy abstractions. Woods's finest lyrics are pithy portraits of archetypal folks and community foibles. See "Signs": "She blamed it on stomach flue / but nine months later—/ Everybody knew!" Try "Love": "I love that girl so much / My hair getting kinkier." The models for these effective poems are both African Americans: Langston Hughes (1902–1967) and Frederick Ward (1937–), himself also an immigrant to Nova Scotia.

Whatever reservations one may harbor about Woods's poetry, his sumptuous, intensely hued, and pride-inspiring paintings merit only acclaim. In 1998, Woods organized a historic showing of Africadian art and fine crafts, In This Place, which toured Nova Scotia and won national attention. One result of this mighty curatorial intervention was Woods's coauthorship of a historic catalogue, *In This Place: Black Art in Nova Scotia*, published in 1998. Woods now runs Halifax's B-Space Gallery, a business retailing Africadian visual art, sculpture, books, and recordings.

George Elliott Clarke

See also Brand, Dionne (1953–); Canada and the African Diaspora; Philip, Marlene Nourbese (1947–); Wright, Richard (1908–1960).

World Congress of Black Writers and Artists

The first World Congress of Black Writers and Artists was an initiative by the publishing house *Présence Africaine,* founded in 1947 by Senegalese intellectual Alioune Diop (1910–1980), who linked his destiny to that of Africa. Throughout his life, Alioune Diop focused on the defense of the values of African civilization. The congress coincided with a flourishing of black literary productions, such as the publication of the *Anthology of Black Poets of French Expression 1900–1945* edited by Leon Damas, the *Anthology of New Black and Malagasy Poetry* edited by Leopold Sédar Senghor in 1946, and *Black Orpheus* by Jean-Paul Sartre. These announced the beginning of a great literary movement of black peoples.

The First Congress of Black Writers and Artists still resonates in the memory of African and African Diaspora generations after the memorable days of September 19 through 22, 1956 at the Descartes amphitheater of the Sorbonne University in Paris. The most distinguished intellectuals from Africa, Europe, the United States, and the Caribbean gathered to discuss "The Crisis of Negro-African Culture." The congress was also memorable because the echo of the racism of the U.S. government was heard through the absence of W. E. B. Dubois and Paul Robeson who were denied visas.

The first congress followed a long line of Pan-Africanist congresses of the beginning of the 20th century in London, New York, Brussels, and Manchester, England. The Second International Congress of Black Writers and Artists was held in Rome from March 26 to April 11, 1959, under the theme "Negro-African Unity of Cultures." The World Festivals of Black Arts of Dakar (1966) and Lagos (FESTAC 1977) also followed the First Congress.

The African Society of Culture (ASC) was created from the first congress with the mission of "establishing linkages of solidarity and friendship among the peoples of culture of the black world." ASC worked for the affirmation, defense, and enrichment of national cultures, ensured the promotion of respect of human rights, and struggled for economic rights of each individual in all communities without distinction of race or religion. In 1958, the United Nations Educational, Scientific, and Cultural Organization (UNESCO) accorded a consultative status category A to the ASC. A 50th anniversary of this event was held at the Sorbonne in Paris, in 2006.

Among the participants to the first congress were G. Sekoto (South Africa); P. Tchibamba (Equatorial Africa); Abbé Mario P. Andrade and M. Lima (Angola); P. Blackman and G. Lamming (Barbados); Tibério (Brazil); Pasteur T. Ekollo, François Sengat Kuo, Benjamin Matip, Nyunaï, and F. Oyono (Cameroon); A. R. Bolamba (Congo); Bernard Dadié (Ivory Coast); W. Carbonel (Cuba); N. Damz, Paulin Joachim, and P. Hazoumé (Dahomey); H. M. Bond, M. Cook, J. A. Davis, W. J. Ivy Fontaine, and Richard Wright (United States); P. Mathieu and Moune de Rivel (Guadeloupe); J. Alexis, R.P. Bisanthe, René Depestre, A. Mangones, E. C. Paul, R. Piquion, J. Price-Mars, and E. Saint-Lot (Haiti); Cédric Dover (India); M. James and J. Holness (Jamaica); Andriantsilaniarivo, Jacques Rabemanjara, and F. Ranaivo (Madagascar); L. Achille, Aimé Césaire, Frantz Fanon, and Edouard Glissant (Martinique); M. Dos Santos (Mozambique); B. Hama (Niger); B. Enwonwu, L.A. Fabunmi, M. Lasebikan, and J. Vaughan (Nigeria); Mamadou Dia, C. A. Diop, David Diop, Diop O. Socé, A. Seck, L. S. Senghor, Bachir Touré, and Abdoulaye Wade (Senegal); D. Nicol (Sierra Leone); H. Bâ and A. Wahal (Sudan), F. Agblemagnon (Togo).

Babacar M'Bow

See also Pan-Africanism; *Présence Africaine.*

FURTHER READING

Congress of Black Writers and Artists. dubois-paris2006.fas.harvard.edu/reflections.html/ (Accessed February 25, 2008).

Fanon, Franz. 1963. "Reciprocal Bases of National Culture and the Fight for Freedom." (Speech at the Congress of Black African Writers, 1959). *The Wretched of the Earth. (Les Damnes de la terre).* New York: Grove.

World Systems Theory

See Cox, Oliver Cromwell (1901–1974).

WPA

See Rodney, Walter (1942–1980).

Wright, Richard (1908–1960)

Richard Wright was the author of six novels, two collections of short stories, seven works of nonfiction, a collection of essays, and a host of unpublished works now housed at the Beinecke Library at Yale University. As a poet, fiction and nonfiction writer, playwright, essayist, journalist, bluesman, and social critic, Wright gave to the world a deluge of words during the 52 years of his short life. Born on September 4, 1908, at a plantation in Roxie, Mississippi, located 15 miles from Natchez. Wright stayed briefly in the backwoods until his parents moved into town with Wright's maternal grandparents where he lived until the age of four. Nathaniel Wright, an illiterate sharecropper, was unable to find work, so he moved his family to Memphis, Tennessee, in an effort to find employment. It was here that Wright's life fragmented and totally deteriorated from 1914 to 1920, starting with Nathaniel Wright's early desertion of his family and Ella Wright's struggles as a single parent earning low wages from domestic work. Because of this, young Wright endured years of transient housing and disruptive moves between Memphis, Elaine, Arkansas, and Jackson, Mississippi, where his maternal grandparents now resided.

Despite the social, political, and religious edicts of the Deep South that supported race codes and insisted on black inferiority and staunch Jim Crow separatism in every aspect of life, young Wright thrived, but his food was knowledge. Literature gave the young self-taught writer reason to live and to hope, which he demonstrated at age 16 through writing and then having published in a Negro newspaper his first short story entitled "The Voodoo of Hell's Half Acre," which garnered the wrath of his zealous grandmother for its sacrilegious language.

Graduating as class valedictorian from ninth grade at age 17 in 1925 with little racial nor economic hope of a better future, Wright cast his eyes North and arrived at age 19 in Chicago, Illinois, in 1927. A coworker took him to a meeting of the John Reed Club of the

Chicago Communist Party at which Wright met the great white intellectuals and leftist writers of *New Masses* and other party organs who changed his philosophies of life and writing into a Marxist perspective. After that meeting Wright, like other Marxists, saw the solution to racial inequities through a class war against capitalism. The young recruit went home and wrote his first poem "I Have Seen Black Hands" reflecting his new proletarian ideology, which replaced the Christianity Wright had rejected earlier. Starting out as a respected poet, Wright plunged enthusiastically into his writing apprenticeship with these party intellectuals.

"Big Boy Leaves Home" earned him the *Story* prize in 1936 along with a contract with Harper and Row for any other stories. Working for pay as a writer for the Federal Writers Project, he openly broke with the communists. Moving to New York in 1937, he earned a Guggenheim Fellowship, which allowed him to complete the first draft of his novel *Native Son,* which was later published in 1940. Its publication garnered Wright national and international acclaim and earned him the mantle of race leader as the foremost black writer in America.

While turning out his novel-turned-short story "Almos' a Man" (1940); his novella *The Man Who Lived Underground* (1941); and the text for the photographic *12 Million Black Voices: A Folk History in the United States* (1941), which still holds its position as a classic in the genre, Wright worked with Paul Green to adapt *Native Son* to the stage and commenced work on his autobiography, *American Hunger,* which Dorothy Canfield Fisher of the Book-of-the Month Club insisted be shortened. As *Black Boy* (1945) that autobiographical work became and still remains a classic as well.

Wright bade farewell to America in 1946 and moved with his Jewish wife, Ellen, and daughter, Julia, to Paris, where he remained until his death in 1960. There, Wright took on

global concerns as a Pan-Africanist humanist affiliated with African nationalist Kwame Nkrumah and Caribbean nationalists C. L. R. James and George Padmore, all leaders at the Manchester Conference of 1946 in England to spearhead initiatives for decolonizing Africa.

Three novels with American settings appear in this period: *The Outsider* (1953), *Savage Holiday* (1954), and *The Long Dream* (1957), which eluded his critics. In addition, he wrote three travel books: *Black Power: Record of a Land of Pathos* (1954), about Nkrumah's reforms in Ghana; *The Color Curtain: Report on the Bandung Conference* (1955), about African and Asian race leaders meeting in Indonesia and voting not to align themselves against the West; and *Pagan Spain: A Report of a Journey into the Past* (1957), about Franco's fascist policies and persecutions of Protestants whom Wright labeled "white Negroes." A collection of essays entitled *White Man, Listen!* (1957) provided Wright's assessment of the criteria required of black literature, similar to what he had done earlier in 1937 with "A Blueprint for Negro Writing." The collection has additional commentary about the political affairs of Africa and Asia, which was not published in his travel books. He was working on a fourth travel book, *French West Africa,* when he met his untimely death of a heart attack in a Paris clinic on November 28, 1960.

See also Black Paris/*Paris Noir*; Pan-Africanism.

FURTHER READING
Chinosole. 2001. "Individual and Collective Selves Portrayed in Wright's *Black Boy*." In *The African Diaspora & Autobiographics: Skeins of Self and Skin,* 15–35. New York: Peter Lang.
Fabre, Michel. 1973. *The Unfinished Quest of Richard Wright.* New York: William Morrow.
Gilroy, Paul. 2002. *Against Race: Imagining Political Culture Beyond the Color Line.* Cambridge, MA: Harvard University Press.
Smith, Virginia Whatley. 2006. *Richard Wright's Travel Writings: New Reflections.* Jackson: University of Mississippi Press.

Y

Yaad Hip-Hop

Yaad/yard hip-hop is the hybrid form of dance-hall (reggae) and hip-hop (rap) music and culture. It bridges the experiences of migrational identities of the past and present through music. It embodies the diasporic memories of Jamaicans who reside in foreign locations. Yaad/yard evokes ties to a certain form of Caribbean identity and place of origin. Yard refers to a backyard urban space and/or one's free space outside the house, that is, one's neighborhood, one's community, or one's land. Yard also functioned as the setting for a variety of Caribbean plays, novels, videos and films. Here it is a significant factor in how Jamaicans and their offspring construct their identity in a foreign location. Chevannes (2001) and Adams (2000) argue that "diasporic memory" is the memory of a particular reference point, a land, with which there are primordial ties of sentiment but to which there may be no real or enduring return. Yard becomes a diasporic memory space. The yaad/yard becomes a vital reference point in the process of self-definition among the African-Caribbean peoples (Chevannes 2001).

Migrations and transnational identity between Jamaica and North America fuse the experiences and contemporary expressions of black music in addressing the movement of people from a variety of locations in the African Diaspora. In examining dancehall (developed in Jamaica) and hip-hop music (a hybrid of the Jamaican sound-system, rhythm and blues, and the New York City urban lifestyles of North America as are 'Jamericans' themselves), the foundation from which the two forms of music emerged is transfigured in urban centers, where the music converged to form a new variation of the previous black music expression of reggae and rap.

Reggae and rap music have allowed for the experiences of African descendants to be deployed into the public forum of Western culture. The two genres of music have successfully created a multilingual expression, which has given voice to the voiceless. The relationship between the spoken and written word has allowed a rich amount of historical narratives to surface. Thus, the popularity of the two genres of music has functioned in exerting the cultural and political voice of the oppressed.

The conceptualization of yaad/yard hip-hop as a new black cultural aesthetic and identity speaks to the migrational and transnational identities that reside in foreign locations. The urban center becomes the space and place where the identities of African diasporans are reconfigured. The poor inner-city communities of North America are locations where marginalized black populations live. The term "ghetto" has been romanticized for the purpose of corporate economic gain. For the individuals and families that migrated to and reside in these centers, the realities of urban life in the United States is a reflection and extension of sentiments of their former identities. Therefore, the formulation of yaad/yard hip-hop as a new cultural identity is a tangible expression and extension of the migrational and transnational experience of a new generation of Afro-Caribbean people in foreign locations. This new identity provides an infinite amount of autonomy and freedom for young women and men in the African Diaspora to refashion the symbols, language, and idioms of their memory of home. Thus they create or invent a new or temporary yaad/yard (home) within the contexts of the oppressive sociopolitical Euro-American context that becomes a tangible expression of their experiences and identity.

La Tasha Brown

See also Caribbean Migrations: The Caribbean Diaspora; Hip-Hop Culture in the African Diaspora.

FURTHER READING
Adams, J. C. 2000. "Contested Space: Psychosocial Themes around the Construction of Caribbean American Identities." *Wadabagei: A Journal of the Caribbean and Its Diaspora* 1: 29–51.
Chevannes, B. 2001. "Jamaican Diasporic Identity: The Metaphor of Home." In *Nation Dance: Religion, Identity, and Cultural Difference in the Caribbean*, ed. P. Taylor, 129–136. Bloomington: Indiana University Press.

Yanga and *Cimarronaje* in Mexico

Mexico's Yanga may be considered the precursor of the maroon tradition in the New World for having led enslaved Africans in an uprising demanding their freedom. Their objective was achieved when the Spanish Viceroy was forced to grant the establishment of a free black settlement in the heart of the Spanish colony in 1631. Originally named San Lorenzo de los Negros and later renamed in honor of its founder, today this town located near the city of Córdoba, Veracruz, boasts of being "the first free *pueblo* of the Américas." Indeed, Yanga existed well before Toussaint L'Ouverture who led an uprising against the French in Haiti and before the North American states had rebelled and freed themselves from English rule.

Yanga landed on the shores of Mexico on a ship from Africa sometime during the second half of the 16th century. The descriptions of his origins found in historical documents suggest that he was from the Bari nation of South Sudan, possibly shipped via Angola. Yanga fled to the mountains of Sierra de Zóngolica, in south-central Mexico, in 1579, shortly after arrival in Mexico and for over thirty years, he organized his group of fugitive *cimarrones* (maroons) into a functioning community that included a military arm headed by an Angolan named Francisco de la Matosa. In the year 1612, rumor spread all over Mexico that a Black uprising was planned and that a king (Yanga) would be crowned on the day of general uprising planned for January 6th, the traditional "Day of Kings."

To settle colonial Spanish society's fears, the contemporary Viceroy, Don Luis de Velasco, ordered the public decapitation in the central Plaza of Mexico City of scores of black men and women who had been jailed for petty crimes. A curfew was imposed on the black population countrywide, and the viceroy immediately dispatched troops to Veracruz to destroy Yanga and his ideals. In charge was Captain González de Herrera, who took with him 100 soldiers, a similar number of adventurers, and 150 Indian bowmen. Another 200 Spanish, mulatto and mestizo mercenaries joined these. Two Jesuit missionaries accompanied the raiders' attempt to break Yanga by religious persuasion, and it was one of these two who kept a diary of the event.

This campaign saw Yanga defeated militarily, but he refused a complete surrender. Instead he accepted a peace treaty, which included the establishment of a town in the designated area, about 20 kilometers southeast of Córdoba,where his people would live as free men and women. In return, Yanga promised not to allow escaped slaves to find refuge in his town, and to respect civil and church authorities. Gradually Yanga faded from national prominence as Afro-Mexicans progressively became integrated into colonial society. As Spanish authority strengthened in the region other towns were built as direct response to the challenge of black self-rule. Yanga's achievement was also diminished as it became relegated to a distant memory of fear in the mainstream (white) society's mind. The event and date of his death are unclear; there is no narrative—oral or written—nor a clearly discernible collective memory in today's area people, presumably Yanga's descendants. One version has it that he was assassinated in front of the church of his own town. Another claims that he was summoned to Mexico City by colonial authorities only to meet his assassins en route.

Chege Githiora

See also Diasporic Marronage; Mexico: African Heritage.

FURTHER READING

Archivo General de Indias. AGI: Seville, Spain.

Archivos Generales de la Nacion. AGN: Mexico City, Mexico.

Archivos Municipales, Cordoba. AMC: Veracruz, Mexico.

Bennett, Herman L. 2005. *Africans in Colonial Mexico: Absolutism, Christianity, And Afro-Creole Consciousness, 1570–1640* (Blacks in the Diaspora). Bloomington: Indiana University Press.

Hernandez Cuevas, Marco Polo. 2004. *African Mexicans and the Discourse on Modern Nation.* University Press of America.

Moreno, Enrique Herrera. 1892. *El Cantón de Córdoba.* Veracruz, Mexico: AMC.

Restall, Matthew. 2005. *Beyond Black and Red: African-Native Relations in Colonial Latin America.* University of New Mexico Press.

Yemoja/Olokun

Originally worshipped in West Africa both as one complementary orisha and as two separate entities, Yemoja and her lover Olokun were sundered in the Middle Passage to reappear in Orisha practices across the Diaspora as the powerful sea goddess. The Yemanja Festival in Salvador, Bahia, Brazil, is a huge annual celebration in Rio Vermellio. Variations exist throughout the Diaspora where Yemanja is one of the most powerful orishas and is seen as the major spirit of the sea where the colors of blue and white, as well as dances that mirror the movements of the ocean, mark her presence.

Zora Neale Hurston's collection *Every Tongue Got to Confess: Negro Folk-Tales from the Gulf States* (2001) contains at least one amazingly exact African American retelling of an Ifa Yoruba West African religious moral tale about Olokun. Hurston's version of the 20th-century American woman's folktale recounts with astonishing exactitude Olokun the merman's counsel to a man who has been on a quest; Olokun tells him to be vigilant, cautious, and wise if he will be safely reunited with his wife and son. In this way Olokun, known in Benin as a woman's god, shows himself to have retained in the family-shattering Diaspora his ability to teach, with love, patience, and restraint, how African Americans may safely gather their loved ones back together.

Literary, musical, and autobiographical voices of the African Diaspora continually describe how, separated in the Middle Passage, the fish king savior and his mermaid bride tirelessly gather their scattered descendants together, reteaching them practices founded on love, gentleness, mutuality, and faith, crucial qualities if this tried but tireless people mean to heal themselves. Grief-maddened women in Tina McElroy Ansa's *Ugly Ways* (1993), Rosa Guy's *The Sun, the Sea, a Touch of the Wind* (1995), Ntozake Shange's *Liliane* (1994), and Bertice Berry's *Redemption Song* (2000) search for healing in the lovers who rise from rivers and seas to offer them and their communities healing. Edwidge Danticat's revolution-crossed lovers in *Krik? Krak!* (1996) find peace only when the hero, despairing of rescue by Agwe, the green-eyed sailor, descends peacefully to the bottom of the sea, to await his lover in the mermaid's kingdom. In Toni Morrison's *Love* (2003), it is only when the spirit of the narrator has died and embraced the powers of the real ocean that she can outgrow girlish fantasies of loving a false merman and return, mermaid-like, to influence the living to put an end to intracommunity persecution.

Alexis Brooks de Vita

See also Osun (Oxum/Ochun/Oshun); Santeria.

FURTHER READING

Cabral, Len, Richard Young, and Judy Dockrey. 1993. *African-American Folktales for Young Readers.* Little Rock, AR: August House Publishers.

Fatunmbi, Awo Fa'lokun. 1993. *Yemoja/Olokun: Ifá and the Spirit of the Ocean.* Plainview, NY: Original Publications.

Fuja, Abayomi. 1962. "The Beautiful Girl and the Fish." In *Fourteen Hundred Cowries.* Ed. Abayomi Fuja. Ibadan: Oxford University Press.

Hurmence, Bernice, ed. 2001. *Before Freedom, When I Just Can Remember: Twenty-seven Oral Histories of Former South Carolina Slaves.* Winston-Salem, NC: John F. Blair.

Hurston, Zora Neale. 2001. *Every Tongue Got to Confess: Negro Folk-Tales from the Gulf States.* New York: William Morrow.

Knappert, Jan. 1995. *African Mythology: An Encyclopedia of Myth and Legend.* London: Diamond Books.

Rhyne, Nancy, ed. 2002. *Slave Ghost Stories: Tales of Hags, Haunts, Ghosts, and Diamondback Rattlers.* Orangeburg, SC: Sandlapper Publishing.

Thompson, Robert Farris. 1984. *Flash of the Spirit: African and Afro-American Art and Philosophy.* New York: Vintage Books.

Wolkstein, Diane. 1980. *The Magic Orange Tree and Other Haitian Folktales.* New York: Schocken Books.

Z

Zami

Audre Lorde's autobiographical narrative *Zami: A New Spelling of My Name* (1982) is the author's deliberate utilization of the submerged Afro-Caribbean term "zami." The integration of ethnic and sexual identities is behind the author's positive appropriation of the Caribbean creole word "zami" for her self-naming: this term is typically a derogatory naming of lesbians, derived from *les amies,* French for "friends."

Early in the book Lorde defines black "dykes" as "powerful women-oriented women—who would rather have died than use that name for themselves" (15). Her definition removes the sexual connotations from this identity, focusing instead on strength in the face of an oppressive mainstream society and creating alliances among women of African descent regardless of their sexual orientation. Lorde simultaneously rejects the popular myth in African diasporic communities that homosexuality is a European import and urges black readers to recognize the full range of subjectivities within their cultures. Correspondingly, throughout *Zami* she portrays the troubling tendency within predominantly white circles (feminist, lesbian, socialist) to deny the rich diversity of their memberships; she describes how, in hopes of generating greater political efficacy or safety, they concentrate on sameness, further ostracizing those within their ranks who might be gay *and* of color, socialist *and* lesbian. The text echoes the powerful themes of Lorde's other prose, especially her concern with challenging the interwoven structures of racial, national, gender, class, and sexual privilege in U.S. society. Lorde's description of the book as a "biomythography" suggests her refusal to be hemmed in by already existing, limiting categories: in the word and in her narrative readers find myths (both celebrated and challenged), her own self-authored story, the collective biographies of influential people in her life, and, although perhaps not as overtly, pointed references to geography/cartography.

As Lorde grew up, her parents' strong longing for Grenada, their island home, left her in a conundrum because the United States, the only place she knew, was not supposed to be able to define her. By the end of the narrative, however, Lorde has created a more permanent and self-determined relationship to the United States and comes to embrace her position as a member of the African Diaspora, recognizing that neither her Caribbeanness, Americanness, nor Africanness should be denied.

Significantly, the text concludes: "[In Carriacou, Grenada's sister-island] it is said that the desire to lie with other women is a drive from the mother's blood" (256). Lorde thus connects her Caribbean heritage, her lesbianism, and her often-fraught relationship with her mother as inseparably entwined and essential to her sense of self.

A number of groups of black women writers (and black lesbians) have begun to use the term "zami" to describe themselves.

Giselle Liza Anatol

See also Grenada; Lorde, Audre (1934–1992).

FURTHER READING

Lorde, Audre. 1982. *Zami: A New Spelling of My Name*. Trumansburg, New York: Crossing Press.

———○———

Zanj (Zinj, Zang)

Zanj is a general geographical and quasi-ethnic Arabic- and Persian-language descriptor usually referring to the locations, peoples, and/or cultures of East Africa during the past three millennia. Zinj, an alternative phrasing, is sometimes attributed to Persian, and African American historian John G. Jackson (1970) argued that in fact the Persian term *Zinj* preceded the Arabic term *Zanj* and was first recorded in the third century BCE. Various early Greek and Talmudic Jewish geographies also refer to Zangay, Zangistan, Cape Zingis, or Zangion in the East African region. On other occasions, Zanj was used to refer to various African people or places ranging from eastern to central or even western African locations, based on the known geographies of the times.

In the African Diaspora, the term *Zanj* is also found within Haitian and other Caribbean spiritual terminologies, often referring to ancestor spirits, angels, or other supernatural forces, much as terms like *mashetani* (spirits) were imported into East African cultures from Islamic influence.

Both Persian and Arab worlds have had intensive bi-directional economic and cultural relations with eastern Africa and the continent beyond for the past three millennia and more. As with most non-Western cultures, discrete delineations between identities and geographies were not common in these cultures, so terms such as *Zanj* functioned as what one scholar has called "mobile classificatory labels" (Moreas-Farias 1985). The term *Zanj*, which reached its widest usage during the medieval period, generally referred to East Africa, East African people, and East Africanity, or East African culture. As such, the term was somewhat slippery and could include different people, places, or things at different times and in different places. At some points during the height of Arab Islam in Southwest Asia, the term seems to have taken on quasiracial connotations of blackness, as it was often used to distinguish "black slaves" from "white slaves," usually referred to as Mamluks. Some have taken Zanj to mean slave, or black slaves, but this would not be accurate, because even during the height of slave economies from East Africa to southern Asia, there were equal or greater numbers of free, nonenslaved Zanj in these regions. These Zanj were either ex-slaves, or had never been enslaved, but were rather traders or otherwise engaged in local cultures and economies.

As a "mobile classificatory label," the term *Zanj* shifted over time and circumstance. For some time, Bilad al-Zanj (the land of Zanj) referred to the area from Mogadishu down to Pemba Island in the south. On the other hand, Zanj was also often a much more generalized term referring to peoples and places throughout the range of eastern Africa and portions beyond, including Ethiopia (which was sometimes, and equally vaguely, called Habash, Habashi, or Habasha, among other terms), Sudan, Congo, and southern regions as well.

Several Arab geographers also identified places south of Nubia and along the Niger River and in Ghana as Zanj. One possibility rarely considered is that, rather than reflecting misunderstandings and generalizations on the part of Arab geographers, this could also indicate the traveling and intermixing of East African peoples in other portions of the continent. Indeed, in several Arab texts, Zanj, or related terms such as Zabaj, are also located in India and even as far as Indonesia.

Probably the most famous reference to Zanj in history is the famous Zanj Rebellion, a major political and spiritual rebellion of enslaved and free Zanj peoples, allied with other supporters and dispossessed peoples during the Abbasid caliphate in Baghdad. The powerful rebellion lasted from 868 to 883 CE (255 to 270 of the Islamic era) and set up an independent state in southern Iraq between Basra and Baghdad. Lasting 15 years, during the height of Abbasid power, the Zanj rebels managed to secure a large expanse of territory, set up their own government and ruling ideology, issue coinage, and threatened to shake Abbasi power to its foundations. Only a major countercampaign, after many failed attempts, finally ended the revolt, but not before social relations and hierarchies in the Abbasid Caliphate were profoundly reshaped, and many of the rebels were promised freedom and upper mobility within the new dispensation.

Slavery in the Arab world was very different from modern chattel slavery in the Atlantic system. Slaves were generally accorded basic human rights and often gained their freedom. Plantation slavery was rare; instead, domestic service, concubinage, and work as soldiers and sailors were the norm. However, in the salt flats of southern Iraq and western Persia an exploitative plantation slavery did emerge, where large contingents of enslaved Zanj were employed in ditch and canal digging, clearing hardpan salt crusts from the low-lying soil surfaces, draining marshlands, and growing sugar and cotton on a large scale. From the seventh century at least, growing numbers of Zanj slaves worked in these exceedingly harsh conditions, and two early rebellions broke out in 689 and 694–695.

The more substantial movement, known as the Zanj Rebellion, broke out in 868, with the arrival of 'Ali ibn Muhammad, a serial rebel of Persian origin. Finally, he found more success by joining forces with disgruntled Zanj slaves and other oppressed peoples of the Abbasid society. As the Abbasid caliphate, a dominant global power of that era, came under internal and external political and economic stress, its leadership compensated by imposing an exorbitant tax on African imports and other goods, disproportionately affecting African importers and traders and the peasants who frequented them. This disruption of an African global trade network stretching into Asia was thus a major impetus for the rebellion, an element overlooked in most previous studies. When the Zanj rebels began their insurrection and started their own military force under the egalitarian Kharijite-inspired leadership of Muhammad, free Zanj traders, impoverished peasants, and others disaffected under Abbasi rule joined in the movement, rapidly giving it greater numbers and power. Zanj slaves numbering in the tens of thousands provided the numerical and military foundation of the movement, but it was in fact a multiethnic association linked by an egalitarian brand of militant Shia (Kharijite) Islam.

Major battles ensued, the Abbasid army was repeatedly defeated, and major cities such as Basra fell into rebel hands. The fortified town of al-Mukhtara (the chosen, or elect city) in the salt flats, became the capital of the putative Zanj state. As their strength grew, enslaved Zanj, free Zanj, and the poor or disaffected generally from throughout South and Southwest Asia flocked to join in the free society in which property rights and power could be had by all. The Zanj ideology was based on full social equality for all true Muslim believers, following the distinct line developed by 'Ali ibn

Muhammad, as distinct from the Abbasid Sunni fold, and prohibiting enslaving anyone of faith. Thus, this new state created a safe zone for Muslim slaves and potential slaves. The Zanj adopted the Kharijite (proto-Shia) slogan "Judgment alone belongs to God," referring to an interpretation that said believers could not be enslaved. 'Ali ibn Muhammad declared himself the Mahdi, or Shiite messiah, and these ideas were imprinted on coins that were minted as a new regional currency. Two major scholars of the time, al-Tabari and al-Masudi, wrote disparagingly of the rebellion and the Zanj, based firmly as they were in Baghdad and the Abbasid society and hierarchy. However, much of what we know comes from a critical reading of their texts.

At its height, the rebellion threatened to capture Baghdad, the most important city in the Islamic world at that time, but the movement was gradually undermined by the full military and naval forces of the Abbasid Empire. Most of the surviving rebels were incorporated into the caliphate armies, having gained their freedom; taxation was reduced; and the transoceanic African-Asian trade surged once again and was restored to its prominent role in the global economy. Although the institution of slavery continued, as did the presence of Zanj slaves among these populations, large-scale plantation slavery was never again resumed at the same level in the Arab world, until outside forces, mainly the British and French, combining with Zanzibaris, Omanis, and other Africans and Arabs, imported Atlantic-style chattel slavery into the Indian Ocean in the 19th century, just as it was being outlawed in the New World. For a thousand years, the reverberations of the Zanj Rebellion altered and dampened the severity of slave and labor relations for Africans as well as for others living within the Arab and Muslim worlds.

In the aftermath of the ninth-century Zanj Rebellion, whose memory conjured powerful images for centuries, the term *Zanj* took on an increasingly negative or threatening connotation in some Asian societies, and scholars have even speculated that non-Zanj African populations became preferred in the regional slave trades of southern Asia as a result. At the same time, Zanj peoples were also thought of as bearing numerous positive qualities throughout the years, being renowned as traders, sailors (sometimes known as Siddis), soldiers, and often attaining positions of leadership and prominence throughout Asian societies in Persia, Arabia, and India.

Malik Ambar was one such example. Born in Ethiopia in the mid-16th century, he was sold into slavery in the Hejaz, Baghdad, and finally Mocha, where he received an education, converted to Islam, and rose to great prominence commanding the armies of local potentates. Deserting, he formed an independent army of indigenous Deccani Arab and African mercenaries, with British artillery and a Siddi navy. Ambar eventually seized the sultancy and declared himself regent minister of the whole region, all the while holding off the surging Mughal Empire to the north.

One further result of the geography of the category Zanj is the naming of Zanzibar Island, off the coast (and an integral part) of modern-day Tanzania, a primary center of trade for many centuries in the latter half of the past millennium. Zanzibar essentially means "Zanj coast" in Arabic and is yet another element in this mobile classificatory label, in this case part of its heartland.

Jesse Benjamin

See also Iraq: The African Presence in Early Iraq.

FURTHER READING
Jackson, John G. 1970. *Introduction to African Civilizations.* New York: University Books.
Moreas Farias, Paulo Fernando de. 1985. "Models of the World and Categorical Models: The 'Enslavable Barbarian' as a Mobile Classificatory Label." In *Slaves and Slavery in Muslim Africa,* ed. John Ralph Willis. Totowa, NJ: Frank Cass.
Muhammad, Akbar. 1985. "The Image of Africans in Arabic Literature: Some Unpublished Man-

uscripts." In *Slaves and Slavery in Muslim Africa*, ed. John Ralph Willis. Totowa, NJ: Frank Cass.

Rashidi, Runoko, ed. 1995. *African Presence in Early Asia*. 10th anniversary ed., 2nd ed. New Brunswick, NJ: Transaction Books.

Segal, Ronald. 2001. *Islam's Black Slaves: The Other Black Diaspora*. New York: Farrar, Straus and Giroux.

Zanzibar and the Southwest Indian Ocean in the African Diaspora

The southwest Indian Ocean is home to a variety of African Diaspora communities of which Mauritius, Seychelles, Zanzibar are prominent members. Zanzibar, for example, is a multiethnic archipelago in the southwest Indian Ocean. It is part of the Swahili coast, which stretches from Mogadishu to Mozambique. The archipelago, situated some 36 kilometers east of the Tanzanian port city of Dar es Salaam, consists of four islands: Pemba and Tumbatu in the north and Unguja and Mafia in the south. The archipelago contains many more islands besides those mentioned above. These include: Bawe, Changuu (or Prison Island), Chumbe and Latham Island (Fungu Kizimkazi). The population on the islands (particularly Pemba and Unguja) are of African, Indian, Arab and European descent. According to the U.S. Department of State Report on Tanzania in 2006 "much of Zanzibar's African population came from the mainland." The "Shirazis trace its origins to the island's early Persian settlers. Non-Africans residing on the mainland and Zanzibar account for 1 percent of the total population. The Asian community, including Hindus, Sikhs, Shi'a and Sunni Muslims, and Goans, has declined by 50 percent in the past decade to 50,000 on the mainland and 4,000 on Zanzibar. An estimated 70,000 Arabs and 10,000 Europeans reside in Tanzania."

The dominant religion on the island is Islam (90 percent) and the remaining population are Hindu, Roman Catholic, Anglican and Buddhist. Several sects exist within Zanzibari Islam and these serve to diversify belief and cultural practice. African beliefs (such as the importance of ancestral veneration) are also important in Zanzibar and these have creolised the dominant religions. The language of Zanzibar is Kiswahili. The islands have a long history of maritime trade and the population relies on the abundant marine life for subsistence, livelihood and culture.

HISTORY

For more than 300 years, Zanzibar islands and communities along the East African coast have cultivated trade links with cities and people of Oman and the Persian Gulf. The more than 800 Arabic manuscripts which contain Arabic literature and rhetoric are indispensable to studies of the history of ideas, diseases, treatments, witchcraft, astronomy, navigation, slavery, poetry and art of eastern Africa. Lodged at the Zanzibar National Archives, they offer proof of a well-established cultural and political connection between Asia and Africa before the arrival of the Europeans in the region. Two hundred years ago Zanzibar was one of the wealthiest islands in the southwest Indian Ocean. Its Indian, Pakistani, Goan, Arab and European communities were at the centre of an influential commercial empire. The basis of this empire was slavery. The slave economy was facilitated by the presence of a monsoon season that allowed for communication between the Asian settlements of Bombay (India), Shiraz (Persia), Muscat, Aden (Oman), Mombasa, Kilwa (East Africa). Traders and sailors from the east encountered the Bantu and Cushitic people living along the African coast.

On the southern tip of Zanzibar, the village of Shangani (Stone Town) a small fishing village in the twelfth century rapidly became a trading centre and *the* commercial empire of the Indian Ocean region. The town first experienced European occupation with the arrival of the Portuguese in 1498. Some 200 years later, Sultan Bin Seif of Oman took over Zanzibar and built the magnificent *Ngome Kongwe* (Old Fort) to defend the island and the wealth of the Omanis from the Portuguese and Mazrui Arabs based in Mombasa. Zanzibar's deep and protected ports (that have coral reefs all around) and (its once) abundant source of timber and mild weather meant that it was ideally suited for trade, settlement and the cultivation of spices. Cloves were first introduced into Zanzibar in 1818 and still constitute up to 70 percent of the island's exports.

Enslaved Africans were the labour force behind the success of Zanzibar. At the height of the slave trade more than 60,000 people were transported annually from the mainland to Zanzibar and from there sent to other markets in Arabia, the Indian Ocean and America. The sultan received a tax on every sale. Tippu Tip, the servant of the sultan and historically a famous slave trader on the East African coast, is said to have owned more than 700 plantations. Today his house is a landmark for those interested in the history of slavery.

The relocation of the Omani sultanate from Muscat to Zanzibar in 1832 provided traders with further impetus to move to the island and settle there. According to Laura Fair, slaves mostly from East Africa transformed the island into a complex, multicultural society and "the most productive clove plantations in the world." In 1890, Zanzibar became a British protectorate. In 1875, slavery was abolished but the practice continued for a while after. In Kelly Askew's work on Tanzania it is revealed that despite abolition, clear distinctions remained between slaves and the free, urbanites and rural dwellers, mainlanders and islanders and Arab and African. The poor treatment of Africans by Arabs, the privileges enjoyed by those of Arab descent and their favourable treatment by the British during colonial rule (1890–1946) cre-

ated much resentment among Africans in Zanzibar. Stone Town was also further divided by the Europeans staying in Zanzibar. Sports clubs, administration offices and hotels were associated with and sometimes reserved for specific European groups — such as the Dutch, English and American. Furthermore and according to Jonathon Glassman, in the "Time of Politics" (1957–1963), processes were already in place that would serve to further divide the population. Political parties emerging at this time reflected the ethnic divide. There was the Zanzibar National Party (ZNP), which was "for" the Arab minority, and the Afro-Shirazi Party (ASP), which was led by Abeid Karume and represented the interests of the Afro-Shirazi and the Africans.

In 1964 pro-liberation activists on the mainland (i.e., in Tanganyika) led a revolution that brought Zanzibar under Tanzanian rule. Popular accounts tell of the exodus of Arabs, the confiscation of Arab and Indian property and the resettlement of Africans in Stone Town. By and large, the revolution was meant to solidify identity, redistribute resources and simplify an otherwise complex and fluid social world into a homogeneous whole. This involved violence that, as David Parkin argues, was a means to "reverse an earlier historical memory of violence against Africans." The Revolution also heralded the re-engineering of Stone Town and Zanzibar society. Shortly after 1964, the first president, Abeid Karume called upon the assistance of engineers, architects and planners from Germany, China and Russia to reconstruct the town's outlying neighbourhoods. The rebuilding included N'gambo or the "other side," which was then, and still is, principally inhabited by those of African descent.

CONTEMPORARY ZANZIBAR

Today, the population of Tanzania stands at 39.5 million. Zanzibar has a population of 1.1 million with some 441,664 people living in the capital of Zanzibar, Stone Town. Zanzibar is also a semi-autonomous state that currently forms a part of the United Republic of Tanzania (URT). The president of Zanzibar is ultimately in control of matters in the islands and is a member of the URT cabinet.

Tanzania remains one of the poorest countries in the world with a debt of 7.5 billion US dollars in 2006, and the government is using 40 percent of its income to service this debt. Agriculture employs 90 percent of the population and produces 57 percent of exports. Industry accounts for 17 percent of the GDP. Zanzibar is more urbanised than the mainland and population density is higher with some 260 people per square kilometre. However, the density is bound to increase as the local tourism industry improves and undocumented migrants come to live and work in Zanzibar in order to benefit from this industry.

Literacy levels remain low in Zanzibar. Along with this poverty there are a high illiteracy rate (60 percent of women are illiterate), malnutrition, low life expectancy (48 years) and a growing HIV AIDS infection rate in Zanzibar. A country analysis report by the Zanzibar Ministry of Finance and Economic Affairs confirms this: "Poverty is both perverse and widespread. Data indicates that 61 percent of Zanzibaris are without basic livelihood needs. Rural areas are hardest hit. In comparison to Unguja, Pemba is hit the most with 64 percent of the residents in that island living in deprivation compared to 59 percent for Unguja."

The Zanzibar Declaration of 1991 heralded the liberalisation of the economy and improved the tourism industry. In 1996, Tanzania received approximately 326,000 tourists. In 2001 Zanzibar received 76,000 tourists. By 2006 this number had grown to 137,111 and generated 1,362,000 US dollars. The Ministry of Tourism, Investment and Trade as well as the Zanzibar Commission for Tourism (ZCT) estimate that the island will receive 5 million US dollars and some 500,000 tourists in 2013. The plan of the ministry, the ZCT, the Zanzibar Association for Tourism Investment (ZATI) and the Zanzibar Investment Promotion Authority

(ZIPA) is to increase facilities and to diversify the tourism industry so as to increase foreign direct investment.

In 2000, UNESCO declared Stone Town a World Heritage Site that symbolises the harmonization of cultures. Since this declaration, government, civic organisations and international donors have been involved in the preservation and management of tangible heritage (buildings, monuments and infrastructure) in Stone Town. To a certain extent, this has encouraged the privileging of Arab/Omani history and architecture and the marginalisation of Africans and the African diaspora's contribution to heritage in the town. Nevertheless, the emerging cultural tourism industry in Zanzibar is encouraging tourists to travel outside Stone Town and to encounter African diaspora heritage, such as that which is to be found in the southernmost village of Makunduchi where the descendants of Shirazi Persians celebrate a harvest festival known as *mwaka kogwa*.

The Afro-Shirazi have also contributed to and creolised Bantu and Arab musical traditions and practices. Many, for example, continue to use various drums in their celebrations or *ngoma*. Celebrations will also include distinctly Islamic elements such as *dhikr* or *vikr*, the throwing of the breath. As noted elsewhere, practices of scent are also a distinct and creole feature of the Afro-Shirazi in Unguja. These involve the use of scent and associated receptacles, fabrics, contexts for religious, curative and political purposes. Thus, the Afro-Shirazi have a rich and as yet not fully documented culture and heritage.

In terms of tourism, Afro-Shirazi do not appear to be benefiting from the emerging tourism industry. Despite the fact that the industry created some 10,436 jobs in 2006, very few Afro-Shirazi seemed to be employed in the industry. Part of the problem according to the 2006 Zanzibar Tourism Policy Statement, is the low level of education and training available to Zanzibaris. At present an undocumented number of

migrants are coming to Zanzibar from mainland Tanzania. This population is generally better educated and obtaining work in the tourism
industry. Such new arrivals are creating some
tensions in the society in the battle over scarce
resources.

Donor agencies such as the Aga Khan Foundation (AKF), Swedish International Development Agency (SIDA), UNESCO, The Danish
International Development Agency (DANIDA),
are working closely with local civic organisations and groups to educate the population of
Afro-Shirazi and prepare them for work in the
emerging economy. The majority of Afro-
Shirazi continue to work on plantations and to
support their families by cultivating land for
subsistence.

Unlike other African diaspora in the southwest Indian Ocean such as the Creoles in Mauritius, the Afro-Shirazi maintain close links
with mainland Africa despite the tendency to
make the distinction between islanders and
mainlanders.

See also Indian Ocean and the African Diaspora;
Mauritius; Seychelles Islands; Swahili; Zanj.

FURTHER READING
Askew, Kelly. 2004. *Performing the Nation: Swahili
Music and Cultural Politics in Tanzania.*
Chicago: University of Chicago Press.
Boswell, Rosabelle. 2006. "Say What You Like:
Dress, Identity and Heritage in Zanzibar." *In-
ternational Journal of Heritage Studies* 12(5):
440–57.
Boswell, Rosabelle. 2008. "Scents of Identity: Fra-
grance as Heritage in Zanzibar." *Journal of
Contemporary African Studies* (May 2008).
Fair, Laura. 2004. *Pastimes and Politics: Culture,
Community and Identity in Post-Abolition
Urban Zanzibar, 1890–1945.* London: James
Currey.
Mussa, I. 2006. "City Tourism: A Case of Dar es
Salaam, Tanzania. Presented at the UNWTO
Workshop for Africa, Tourism Destination
Management — Routes to Success." Addis
Ababa, Ethiopia, 27–29 March 2006.
Parkin, David. 2003. "The Commercialisation of
biomedicine and the politics of flight in Zan-
zibar, Tanzania." In Robin Cohen, ed. *Migra-
tion and Health in Southern Africa.* Pretoria:
Van Schaik.
Sheriff, Abdul. 1987, *Slaves, Spices and Ivory in
Zanzibar.* London: James Currey.

Zeta Phi Beta

On January 16, 1920, five college women on
the campus of Howard University marked a
significant event in the history of African
American women. The five women, also
known as the five pearls, Arizona Cleaver (Ste-
mons), Pearl Ann (Neal), sisters Viola Tyler
(Goings) and Myrtle Tyler (Faithful), and Fannie Pettie (Watts) organized Zeta Phi Beta
Sorority Inc. They adopted the colors royal
blue and white and espoused four fundamental principles for their organization: scholarship, community service, sisterly love, and finer
womanhood. With assistance and support
from Phi Beta Sigma Fraternity Inc.'s founders
A. Langston Taylor and Leonard F. Morse, the
sorority and fraternity became the first constitutionally chartered brother and sister Greek
letter organization. The organization was incorporated on March 30, 1923, in Washington
D.C.

Between 1920 and 1923, Zeta Phi Beta
Sorority expanded to include national chapters
in southern states. As of 2006, the nonprofit organization had more than 125,000 members
nationwide. The organization has eight inter-
continental regions and more than 800 chapters in the United States, Europe, the
Caribbean, Asia and Africa. Zeta Phi Beta has a
membership intake policy that forbids all
forms of hazing. Membership is by invitation
to women with a notable record of community
service who are currently pursuing a baccalaureate degree or in possession of a baccalaureate
degree. The organization has always played a
substantive role in the National Pan-Hellenic
Council and established the National Educa-

tion Foundation, which provides scholarship and grants to students in pursuit of higher education.

Throughout its history, Zeta Phi Beta has achieved a number of historic milestones as the first Greek letter organization to charter a chapter in Africa in December 1948 and the first to form adult and youth auxiliary groups, including the Amicae, the Archonettes, the Amicettes, and the Pearlettes. The sorority was also the first Greek letter organization to centralize its operations in a national headquarters, which is presently located in Washington, D.C. The women of the organization have long been associated with social, political, and economic movements throughout U.S. history, including voting rights, equal opportunity, school desegregation and integration, and social and economic justice.

One of multiple examples of Zeta women is humanitarian, entrepreneur, and philanthropist Eartha Mary Magdalene White (1876–1974) who established the Clara White Mission, which continues to provide supportive services for the homeless and displaced youth. Distinguished alumni of Zeta Phi Beta have represented multiple disciplines, including politics and law, science and engineering, the arts and social sciences, entertainment, education, and sports. The distinguished service of Zeta Phi Beta's members also includes leadership positions in the United States Senate and House of Representatives as well as in federal, state, and local courts.

In 2002, with the leadership of International Grand Basileus Barbara C. Moore, the sorority adopted Z-Hope (Zetas Helping Other People Excel) as a national service initiative to consolidate and enhance its programs targeting health care, education, HIV/AIDS, hurricane relief, prenatal care, literacy, addiction, voting registration, and violence. The organization's Stork's Nest program provides prenatal care, promotes education, and provides support to mothers. The sorority instituted the ZOL Program (Zeta Organizational Leadership Pro-

gram) to train and assist local, regional, and state officers, including advisers to youth affiliates. The organization is affiliated with numerous national organizations and nonprofit organizations. Since 1997, Zeta Phi Beta Sorority's National Educational Foundation partnered with the National Institutes of Health and the U.S. Department of Energy to examine overall developments in genetics research, particularly the Human Genome Project in minority communities. Zeta Phi Beta continues to play major roles throughout many local, national, and international communities.

Rose C. Thevenin

See also Alpha Kappa Alpha; Delta Sigma Theta; Kappa Alpha Psi; Phi Beta Sigma.

FURTHER READING
Brown, Tamara L., Gregory S. Parks, and Claranda M. Phillips, eds. 2005. *African-American Fraternities and Sororities: The Legacy and the Vision.* Lexington: University Press of Kentucky.
Kimbrough, Walter M. 2003. *Black Greek 101: The Culture, Customs and Challenges of Black Fraternities and Sororities.* New York: Fairleigh Dickinson Press.
Ross, Lawrence C., Jr. 2000. *The Divine Nine: The History of African-American Fraternities and Sororities.* New York: Kensington Books.

Zobel, Joseph (1915–2006)

Joseph Zobel, novelist, short story writer, poet, and artist, is best known for his autobiographical novel *La Rue Cases-Nègres* (Black Shack Alley) (1950), which was adapted by Euzhan Palcy into the award-winning film *Rue Cases-Nègres* (Sugar Cane Alley) (1982). Zobel was born in Rivière Salée, Martinique, in 1915; migrated to France in 1946; worked in Senegal from 1957 to 1974 as an educator and producer of cultural programming at Radio Senegal; and retired to rural France where he sculpts, practices the Japanese art of flower arranging, and continues to publish. His works include *Les Mains pleines d'oiseaux* (1978), *Poèmes de moi-même* (1984), *Mas badara* (1983), *Si la mer n'était pas bleue* (1987), *Poèmes d'amour et de silence* (1994), *Le Soleil m'a dit* (2002), and *Gertal et autres nouvelles* (2002), which contains excerpts from his journal.

Zobel's early work is part of a decade of groundbreaking literary developments in the Francophone world. His first novel, *Diab'la*, written in 1942, was deemed so subversive that it was censured by the Vichy regime. It was finally published in 1947, one year after his short story collection *Laghia de la mort*. The first and second editions of *La Rue Cases-Nègres* appeared in 1950 and 1955, coinciding with Aimé Césaire's two editions of *Discours sur le colonialisme*. Other important literary events of that period were the founding of *Présence Africaine* in 1947; the first French editions of Jacques Roumain's *Gouverneurs de la rosée* in 1946 and 1950; Mayotte Capécia's *Je suis Martiniquaise* (1948); Aimé Césaire's collections *Soleil cou coupé* (1948) and *Corps perdu* (1949); Frantz Fanon's *Peau noire, masques blancs* (1952); Camara Laye's *L'Enfant noir* (1953); Jacques Stéphen Alexis's *Compère Général Soleil* (1955); and the convening of the First International Congress of Black Writers and Artists at the Sorbonne (1956).

Inspired by Richard Wright's *Black Boy*, which was translated into French in 1947, *La Rue Cases-Nègres* examines the trajectory of a five-year-old boy born on a sugar cane plantation who, against tremendous odds, graduates from a prestigious urban high school and passes the *baccalauréat*. However, this plot summary, centering on struggle, survival, and triumph, tends to mute other issues that Zobel addresses: race, class, gender, and color; the legacy of slavery, exploitation, and prejudice; the construction of family, masculinity, and identity; education and schooling; and migration to the city. Set in colonial Martinique less than 80 years after the abolition of slavery, *La Rue Cases-Nègres* traces the literal and sym-

bolic journey of José Hassam, who is raised first by his maternal grandmother, Man Tine, and then by his mother, Délia, and mentored by elderly cane cutter Médouze and schoolteacher Stéphen Roc. Ironically, the novel tracks the growth of a future writer during the same historical period in which African diasporic literary movements—*indigénisme*, the Harlem Renaissance, *negrismo*, and Négritude—were being formulated and put into practice. The sequel to *La Rue Cases-Nègres*, *La Fête à Paris* (1953), which opens with the protagonist on a ship bound for France, was reissued under the title *Quand la neige aura fondu* (1979).

Renee Larrier

See also Guadeloupe; Martinique; Négritude.

FURTHER READING
Julien, Eileen. 1987. "La Métamorphose du réel dans *La Rue Cases-Nègres*." *The French Review* 60 (6, May): 781–787.
Warner, Keith Q. 1988. "Emasculation on the Plantation: A Reading of Joseph Zobel's *La Rue Cases-Nègres*." *College Language Association Journal* 32 (1, September): 38–44.

Zong Massacre

See African Americans and the Constitutional Order.

Zouk

Zouk is dance music that was created by black, French Caribbean musicians from Guadeloupe and Martinique in which the lyrics and the name of its leading group, Kassav, are all in Creole and the music makes use of the *gwo ka* drum, peculiar to Guadeloupe and an important retention of the African roots of Antillean people. These factors highlight the place of zouk within the African Diaspora. Originally meaning party, pleasure, or unrestrained festivities, "zouk" has now come to mean—in both Martinique and Guadeloupe—Antillean music in general, swinging music that makes the crowd dance.

The name "Kassav" was selected because it is the name of a folk dish common in the French Caribbean; it is a carefully prepared blend of manioc with other ingredients. Similarly, zouk is a very careful and unique blend of musical influences, including U.S. jazz, soul, and funk; soukous from French Africa; cadence-rampa and compas from Haiti; salsa from Latin America, Cuba, and Puerto Rico; biguine from Guadeloupe and Martinique; merengue from the Dominican Republic; and soca and calypso from Trinidad.

As zouk has evolved, the use of the traditional *gwo ka* drum has been replaced by electronic instruments, such as synthesizers, rhythm box, and samplers, to give it a more "international" flavor; however, that development has not detracted from the unique Antillean flavor of the music produced because of the structure and arrangements of the songs, the French Creole lyrics, and the way in which foreign music is mixed into zouk. The characteristic sound of zouk that would establish Kassav as a leading group and zouk as internationally popular dance music took about five years and many attempts to produce. Those attempts culminated in the 1984 hit, "*Zouk-la sé sèl médikaman nou ni*" ("Zouk is the only medicine we have"), which won Kassav the first gold record—France's Disque d'Or—ever awarded to a French Caribbean group.

A number of developments that coincided with the appearance of this song served to give an additional boost to Kassav's phenomenal success. Zouk was both a political and a cultural phenomenon. From the early 1980s on,

the upsurge of black racial consciousness in Europe and the sweeping social reforms brought about during President Mittérand's regime gave greater freedom to the municipalities of the departments and regions. It is significant that Kassav wanted "to show the world that the Antilles exist" (Guilbault 1993, 170), as well as to have the world recognize that Antillean people are a mixture of different races and cultures. Kassav was followed by a number of other groups, including Zouk Machine, an all-female group; Malavoi, which performs zouk and other Antillean music; and a number of solo artists, such as Martinican Joycelyne Béroard, who became lead singer for Kassav, and Guadeloupean Tanya St Val. After 1988, a number of new zouk styles, new arrangements, and new composition formats came into being.

Jeannette Allsopp

See also Calypso; Guadeloupe; Salsa.

FURTHER READING

Berrian, Brenda F. 2000. *Awakening Spaces: French Caribbean Popular Songs, Music, and Culture.* Chicago: University of Chicago Press.

Guilbault, Joycelynne. 1993. *Zouk: World Music in the West Indies.* Chicago: University of Chicago Press.

Manuel, Peter, Kenneth Bilby, and Michael Largey. 1995. *Caribbean Currents: Caribbean Music from Rumba to Reggae.* Philadelphia: Temple University Press.

Rabess, Gregory. 1983. "Cadence Music." In *Eruptions.* Roseau, Dominica: M.C.A. Publications.

Zumbí of Palmares (1655–1695)

Palmares is the most renowned maroon community in Brazilian history. Situated in the interior of the northeast province of Sergipe, Palmares thrived throughout the 17th century. Beginning as a barely accessible, humble refuge for a few dozen escaped slaves, Palmares grew into a confederation of settlements that at its peak boasted more than 20,000 residents. In addition to escaped slaves, the community attracted poor women, indigenous Indians, free mulattos, and white settlers, many of whom sharecropped on Palmares land. Developing its own subsistence agriculture, artisan production, iron production, and trade links with other settlements, Palmares's economic surplus supported a political class and a military for defense as well as raiding to obtain supplies and future inhabitants. All property belonged to the community, and a shortage of women resulted in matriarchal heads of family; wives had multiple (up to four or five) husbands to do the work. Palmares was a dynamic mix of Portuguese, West African, Amerindian, and especially Angolan practices, which influenced its religion, its political and military structures, and a creole language unintelligible to most Portuguese.

Zumbí was Palmares's most famous leader. He was born in Palmares in 1654 but was kidnapped as a baby during one of many military incursions against the community. He was baptized and raised by a Catholic priest who taught him to read and write Latin and Portuguese. At 15 Zumbí escaped back to Palmares, and within two years he was taking important political positions within the community. His military and leadership skills won him further promotions, and by 1677 Zumbí was the head of the Palmarino military. In an essentially military coup he overthrew the great chief, Ganga Zumba, and became the new leader.

From this point on, Zumbí turned on the Portuguese colonial order, convinced that until it was defeated there would be no peace for Palmares—only future enslavement. For 13 years (1680–1693), Palmares aggressively raided the surrounding settlements, putting the Portuguese on the defensive. The king of Portugal offered Zumbi and his family amnesty and freedom from enslavement if they desisted, but Zumbí refused. After 1690, however, bigger and better-equipped Portuguese armies with artillery were sent against Palmares, and in 1694 the community's defenses were broached. Zumbí escaped, but government troops executed most of the men and attempted to sell the women and children into slavery along the coast. The women were said to have killed their children and starved themselves rather than be sold into slavery. Meanwhile, Zumbí continued the raids, but less than a year later he was betrayed into a Portuguese ambush by a trusted lieutenant. He was castrated and mutilated, and his head was publicly displayed on a pole to prove that he was not immortal.

For contemporary African-Brazilians, Zumbí of Palmares continues to be a very important political and cultural icon for his association with a way of life that offered an alternative to European slavery and as an aggressive and heroic defender of freedom for Africans and their descendents.

Scott Ickes

See also Brazil: Afro-Brazilians; Maroons and Marronage; Yanga and *Cimarronaje* in Mexico.

FURTHER READING
Freitas, Décio. 1996. *Zumbi dos Palmares*. Luanda, Angola: Ministério da Culture.
Funari, Pedro Paulo de Abreu. 1996. "A arqueologia de Palmares." In *Liberdade por um fio: História dos quilombos no Brasil*, ed. João José Reis and Flávio dos Santos Gomes. São Paulo, Brazil: Companhia das Letras.
Karasch, Mary. 2001. "Zumbi of Palmares." In *The Human Tradition in Latin America*, ed. Kenneth Andrien. Wilmington, DE: Scholarly Resources.
Schwartz, Stuart. 1996. "Rethinking Palmares: Slave Resistance in Colonial Brazil." In *Slaves, Peasants, and Rebels*. Urbana: University of Illinois Press.

Index